HINDU NATIONALISM IN THE INDIAN DIASPORA

'A timely and important book adding to our understanding of the complexities of the diasporic experience and its relationship to India.'
—Kavita Puri, Writer and Broadcaster, BBC

'This book is so extraordinary and important that it deserves a very wide readership... An unrivalled perspective of the recent rise of a Hindu nationalism as a global project. It is crucial reading for those interested in Hindu nationalism's global footprint.'
—Joya Chatterji FBA, Professor of South Asian History, Trinity College, University of Cambridge, and author of *Shadows At Noon: The South Asian Twentieth Century*

'A carefully researched, deep dive into the Hindutva in diaspora phenomenon. The focus of Anderson's excellent, historical-political work is Britain, but he tells a story that spans India, its diaspora, and globally networked nationalisms more broadly. This is a book for these times, and for times to come.'
—Nikita Sud, Professor of the Politics of Development, University of Oxford

'[A] careful and illuminating study... A major contribution to our understanding of Hindu nationalism as a global project.'
—Thomas Blom Hansen, Reliance-Dhirubhai Ambani Professor, Stanford University

'Anderson's important study of rightwing Hindu nationalism in multicultural Britain makes a critical intervention... A must-read for all scholars interested in Hindu religious nationalism.'
—Tanika Sarkar, Retired Professor, Modern History, Jawaharlal Nehru University, Delhi

'[A] uniquely rich and highly readable account ... The book is a must read for anyone interested in the global reach of Hindu nationalism and its diasporic forms.'
—William Gould, Professor of Indian History, University of Leeds

'This book offers meticulous documentation of how the expression of Hindu identity in India and abroad became connected...through an organization whose political party now rules India. This is the best account of the process we have, and hence is an important contribution

ind Rajagopal, Professor of Media Studies, New York University

EDWARD T.G. ANDERSON

Hindu Nationalism in the Indian Diaspora

Transnational Politics and British Multiculturalism

OXFORD
UNIVERSITY PRESS

Oxford University Press is a department of the
University of Oxford. It furthers the University's objective
of excellence in research, scholarship, and education
by publishing worldwide.

Oxford New York
Auckland   Cape Town   Dar es Salaam   Hong Kong   Karachi
Kuala Lumpur   Madrid   Melbourne   Mexico City   Nairobi
New Delhi   Shanghai   Taipei   Toronto

With offices in
Argentina   Austria   Brazil   Chile   Czech Republic   France   Greece
Guatemala   Hungary   Italy   Japan   Poland   Portugal   Singapore
South Korea   Switzerland   Thailand   Turkey   Ukraine   Vietnam

Oxford is a registered trade mark of Oxford University Press
in the UK and certain other countries.

Published in the United States of America by
Oxford University Press
198 Madison Avenue, New York, NY 10016

Copyright © Edward T. G. Anderson, 2024

Chapter 3 is adapted from Edward Anderson and Patrick Clibbens, '"Smugglers of Truth": the Indian diaspora, Hindu nationalism, and the Emergency (1975–77)', *Modern Asian Studies*, vol. 52, no. 1 (2018), pp. 1729–73. © Cambridge University Press 2018. Reproduced with permission.

Chapter 6 is adapted from Edward Anderson, '"Neo-Hindutva": the Asia House M. F. Husain campaign and the mainstreaming of Hindu nationalist rhetoric in Britain', *Contemporary South Asia*, vol. 23, no. 1 (2015), pp. 45–66. Reproduced with permission of https://www.tandfonline.com/.

All rights reserved. No part of this publication may be reproduced, stored in a retrieval system, or transmitted, in any form or by any means, without the prior permission in writing of Oxford University Press, or as expressly permitted by law, by license, or under terms agreed with the appropriate reproduction rights organization. Inquiries concerning reproduction outside the scope of the above should be sent to the Rights Department, Oxford University Press, at the address above.

You must not circulate this work in any other form
and you must impose this same condition on any acquirer.
Library of Congress Cataloging-in-Publication Data is available
Edward T. G. Anderson
Hindu Nationalism in the Indian Diaspora: Transnational Politics and British Multiculturalism

ISBN: 9780197746202

Printed in the United Kingdom on acid-free paper

CONTENTS

Acknowledgements   vii

Introduction   1

1. 'From Videsh Vibhag to Vishwa Vibhag and now Vishwa Sangh': Establishing Hindu Nationalism Abroad, from East Africa to Britain   25

2. Training Camps and the Development of a Global *Parivar* (Family)   79

3. Transnational Hindutva Networks: The Indian Emergency (1975–7) and the Evolution of Homeland-Diaspora Relations   125

4. From Milton Keynes to Ayodhya: The Vishwa Hindu Parishad and the Global Campaign for the Ram Temple   163

5. Charity, *Sewa* (Service), and the 'Model Minority'   209

6. 'Neo-Hindutva': Hindu Nationalism Goes Public   263

Conclusion   325

Glossary and Abbreviations   341
Notes   349
Bibliography   443
Index   463

ACKNOWLEDGEMENTS

Research projects are often as laborious and stressful as they are inspiring and fulfilling. That most certainly has been the case for this one, which was a long time in the making. There are numerous people who have supported me in many different ways over a long period of time, culminating in the completion of this book, to whom I am greatly indebted.

I owe my interest, and the understanding I have attempted to develop, to a number of inspirational teachers across various institutions. At Leeds, David Hall-Matthews first sparked a great curiosity in the politics, society, and history of India. William Gould, whom I also first met at Leeds, encouraged me to pursue this interest. Subsequently, my two years at Jawaharlal Nehru University were, for so many reasons, life-changing. I learned an enormous amount under the tuition of Gopal Guru, Valerian Rodrigues, Gurpreet Mahajan, Pralay Kanungo, Kavita Singh, and many others. But I also gained so much more outside of the classrooms: the experiences, friendships, and discussions (often heated and always fortified with chai or Old Monk!), enjoyed in that incredible enclave of New Delhi, will stay with me forever.

My subsequent studies at Cambridge were equally formative, and the Centre of South Asian Studies ended up becoming a home from home for nearly a decade. The Centre's staff throughout my time there—Barbara Roe, Kevin Greenbank, and Rachel Rowe—were unwaveringly friendly and supportive in so many ways. I owe a considerable debt of gratitude to Cambridge's multidisciplinary community of South Asianists, and to many in the History Faculty—especially the inspiring and path-breaking scholars associated with the World History group—for helping me to better understand so many things. Learning from Aishwarj Kumar, Gordon Johnson, Jaideep Prabhu, Julius Lipner, Leigh Denault, Norbert Peabody, Priyamvada Gopal, Shailaja Fennell, Shruti Kapila, Sujit Sivasundaram, Tim Harper, and many others was a great privilege. In particular, two mentors from that time who had an enormous impact on me and my work are very sadly missed: Chris Bayly and David Washbrook. Chris initiated the MPhil on which I was part of the first cohort and was unfailingly generous in sharing his pioneering insights into global histories of South Asia and beyond. He also gave me my first break in teaching, which has, over the years, helped to inform and enrich my research in numerous ways. David served as my doctoral advisor and helped me understand the history of India, and so much more, in new and exciting ways. His ability to be so gregarious and friendly, while unimaginably knowledgeable—providing devastating, incisive critiques of my work and that of others—always floored me and will never be forgotten. As well as my teachers, I must also thank all of those whom I have taught, and who in turn have taught me so much. A special mention must be made to two extraordinary women, Humaira Chowdhury and Malya Bhattacharya.

It is hard to put into words the influence that Joya Chatterji has had on my life. She is the most remarkable teacher, advocate, and friend that anyone could hope for. Joya is a person who will provide counsel and sympathy in difficult times, and make a big fuss of you when there is something to celebrate. Joya took a chance on me early on, but the term 'PhD supervisor' doesn't come close to reflecting the role that she performed. I will never be able to repay the support and inspiration that she has provided me with over the years. Throughout this time, the inimitable Anil Seal has always been at her side; in turn, he has given me a great deal of affection, encouragement, and mirth. I can only hope he realises how much I appreciate him.

Those whom I learned alongside (and often from), and who patiently listened to me moan about everything under the sun,

ACKNOWLEDGEMENTS

were also an important part of my life at Cambridge: Aditya Balasubramanian, Alastair McClure, Ali Khan Mahmudabad, Asiya Islam, Bérénice Guyot-Réchard, Beverly McCann, Chris Moffat, Danika Parikh, Darragh Coffey, Darren Harvey, Devyani Gupta, Elisabeth Leake, Ishaan Mukherjee, James Hadfield, Joe Francombe, Joseph McQuade, Laurence Gautier, Luna Sabastian Mark Condos, Mike Clark, Nick Evans, Partha Pratim Shil, Sundeep Lidher, Tom Maguire, Tripurdaman Singh, Saumya Saxena, Sophie-Jung Kim, Tobias Müller, Teresa Segura-Garcia, and Uttara Shahani. Since joining Cambridge in 2009, Patrick Clibbens and I have led curiously parallel lives: studying, working, quizzing, and conducting research together, and both eventually ending up in the North East. He has been a constant source of sage advice, intelligent conversation, formidable knowledge, and reliable friendship.

On a more formal level, I must recognise two significant sources of funding that enabled me to carry out my research: the Arts and Humanities Research Council, for supporting my doctorate, and the Smuts Memorial Fund for supporting my time as Smuts Research Fellow in Commonwealth Studies. Generosity has been shown over the years by the Cambridge Political Economy Society, the Spalding Trust, the Cambridge Bombay Society, and various others. Thanks to numerous institutions which have invited me to speak on my research (leading to conversations which invariably improve the work itself), and also to those who have hosted me as a visiting academic: the University of Mumbai, the Centre for Development Studies in Kerala, and the South Asia Centre at the London School of Economics. I am also grateful to Darwin College, where I spent four happy years during my PhD, and Trinity College for providing me with a new home as a postdoctoral scholar. Beyond these places, my long-standing involvement with the British Association for South Asian Studies has been enriching in numerous ways.

Academic projects can never be undertaken without the encouragement and intellectual support of others. I have been very fortunate, over the years, to have benefited from conversations— some relatively brief, others extensive and ongoing—with so many exceptional individuals for whom I have the utmost respect and appreciation. I owe so much to those whom I have had interactions with that have ultimately informed my understanding. They include Amogh Dhar Sharma, Andrea Major, Angana Chatterji, Arkotong Longkumer, Arvind Rajagopal, Charles Taylor, Christophe Jaffrelot, Deborah Sutton, Deepa Reddy, Ed Simpson, Eviane Leidig, Harsh Mander, Humayun Ansari, Jacob Copeman, Jean-Thomas Martelli, John Zavos, Justin Jones, Kate Sullivan de Estrada, Katharine Adeney, Katherine Schofield, Kavita Puri, Lalit Vachani, Lisa Mitchell, Lucy Delap, Max Kramer, Mukulika Banerjee, Naresh Fernandes, Nikita Sud, Nilanjan Sarkar, Nitasha Kaul, Ornit Shani, Patricia Jeffrey, Peter van der Veer, Philippa Williams, Polly O'Hanlon, Priya Swamy, Rachel Dwyer, Ram Rawat, Ramachandra Guha, Rohit De, Sahana Udupa, Salil Tripathi, Sanal Mohan, Sanam Arora, Sanjay Kak, Sarah Ansari, Shalini Sharma, Shohini Ghosh, Sidharth Bhatia, Tahir Kamran, Tanika Sarkar, Taru Dalmia, Thomas Blom Hansen, Vasudha Dalmia, Virinder Kalra, Wendy Doniger, and Yasmin Khan.

I must also thank all of the people who spoke to me, in Britain and in India, while conducting the research for this book. I am extremely grateful for all the time and insights given to me by those who were willing to share their experiences and perspectives.

Thank you also to Hurst for their faith in the work. Michael Dwyer, in particular, who has encouraged/badgered me about the book with a great deal of patience, but also has been incredibly supportive and a good friend. I am also very thankful to Lara, Daisy, and others at Hurst, as well as the anonymous peer reviewers, who have helped improve the book in many ways. Another form of help has often come from my dear compadre, William Allen, who can always be relied upon for grammatical wisdom and loyal friendship.

The latter stages of this book's long gestation took place in my current hometown of Newcastle upon Tyne. I'd like to extend my gratitude for the warm welcome that the city, and especially my new colleagues at Northumbria University, have provided me and my family with over the past three years. New friends here, including Peter Mitchell, Sonali Dhanpal, Gareth Fearne,

ACKNOWLEDGEMENTS

Sol Gamsu, Sherene Meir, Gareth Roddy, Matthew Kelly, Daniel Laqua, Katherine Baxter, Peter Hill, Claudine van Hensbergen, Felicia Gottmann, Katarzyna Kosior, Joe Street, and others, have improved our life here immeasurably.

And, finally, completing this book and pursuing my chosen vocation could not have been possible without the encouragement and understanding of my family. My mother, father, and brother instilled in me the intrinsic value of learning, and my in-laws have also always been enormously supportive (an overwrought PhD student would not be most parents' idea of a suitable boy). Above all, it is the love of my wife, and more recently my two children, which has always kept me going and put things into perspective. This book is dedicated to them.

INTRODUCTION

In 1966, the first *shakha* (branch) of the Hindu Swayamsevak Sangh—the overseas wing of the core Indian Hindu nationalist organisation, the Rashtriya Swayamsevak Sangh (RSS)—was established in Britain. Less than fifty years later, in 2014, Narendra Modi led the Bharatiya Janata Party (BJP) to a dramatic election victory in India that would transform the political landscape of the world's largest democracy. This followed a campaign during which the Indian diaspora, and particularly the expatriate Hindu nationalist movement, played an unprecedented and significant role. Although not concerned specifically with diasporic support for the BJP, this book considers the development of Hindu nationalist organisations in Britain and elsewhere in the Indian diaspora in the interceding years. Hindu nationalism is a majoritarian, conservative, and militant political ideology and ethno-religious movement that rejects pluralistic secularism and is ascendent in contemporary India. The central question the book explores is how and why this movement and ideology became popular and influential amongst India's diaspora in the years since independence in 1947.

This then leads to many further questions that the book grapples with. What is the extent of diasporic Hindutva (literally Hinduness, or the dominant ideology of Hindu nationalism) and where is it to be located? Where has overseas support for Hindu nationalism come from, and in what ways has it developed? Why does Hindutva resonate with a diaspora population? What forms does it take? Is it a co-ordinated 'export' of the homeland, or does it represent something distinct and even organic? In what sense might it even be said to have grown into a significant, dynamic, and syncretic expression of British Hindu identity? What should we make of an apparent tension at the heart of diasporic Hindutva: people supporting a chauvinistic, majoritarian ideology applied to one country, whilst negotiating recognition and minority rights in another? Why is it that some of the most outspokenly patriotic Indians are those who have chosen to live outside of their motherland, or may have never lived in India at all? And what are the ramifications of all of this—both for India and for countries that are home to Indian communities around the world?

To frame contemporary, global Hindutva, consider these five scenes that have occurred in the past decade...

In September 2014, just four months after leading the BJP to an extraordinary landslide result in the sixteenth general election since independence, Narendra Modi stood in front of a crowd of nearly 20,000 members of the Indian diaspora in New York's iconic Madison Square Garden. 'No Indian leaders have ever received this kind of reception. I am indebted to you,' Modi told the crowd. 'I will repay this debt. I will fulfil your dreams of India.'[1] The crowd erupted in euphoric applause.

The audience comprised a small portion of the United States' four-million-strong Indian American community, often lauded as a 'model minority' for their striking educational and professional achievements, but less frequently discussed as a political force. Many of this diaspora population—whose disposition towards Hindutva is often talked about in India (although not always well understood)—had played an active role in Modi's 2014 campaign and would go on to push for his re-election in 2019. Along the way, some Modi devotees would even campaign for Donald Trump, whose belligerent, Islamophobic populism resonated with many Indians (despite the fact that Indians in America suffered from both the racism that Trump emboldened, and his capricious approach towards visa and immigration policy). Regardless, the two leaders often referred to their friendly rapport and, after the BJP's re-election, they joined hands in Texas for the 'Howdy Modi' rally in

2019—the largest ever political event held by a foreign leader in the United States—reciprocated not long after with the 'Namaste Trump' extravaganza in Gujarat.

This was political theatre for the digital age, streamed across the world with multiple publics in mind, and made viral through the indefatigable social media campaigning of Hindutva's ubiquitous acolytes. Similar rallies to those seen in the US also took place on the other side of the Atlantic. In 2015, Modi held another spectacle for the diaspora, this time at London's Wembley Stadium. An estimated 60,000 British Indian supporters turned out to hear Modi speak, introduced by British Prime Minister David Cameron, who excitedly told the audience: *'Kem Cho Wembley'* (roughly, 'How are you, Wembley?' in Gujarati). For Cameron, these were prospective voters: an ethnic minority community that has been gradually, and relatively successfully (although perhaps only temporarily), lured away from Labour by the Conservative Party in recent years.

The Wembley *tamasha* (show) was an extraordinary moment. The organisers claimed that Nelson Mandela and Pope John Paul II were the only foreign visitors to have ever been met by bigger crowds in Britain.[2] The stadium welcome was made even more remarkable by the fact that for a decade, following the Gujarat 'riots' of 2002 (seen by many as an anti-Muslim pogrom), Modi was effectively prohibited from visiting Europe and the US. This 'de facto travel ban' was lifted in the UK by the Conservative-led government in 2012, as the Gujarat Chief Minister's rise to power was gathering pace.[3] Britain has also seen overlaps of right-wing political support: during the 2019 General Election, the UK branch of the Overseas Friends of the BJP proclaimed Labour to be 'anti-India', and publicly campaigned for the Conservative Party in dozens of marginal constituencies.[4] Although we should be wary of the actual impact this had, it constituted a rare and bold intervention; it is extremely uncommon for representatives of the ruling party of a country to make such an explicit effort to influence an overseas ally's election.

Not long after this, on 5 August 2020, nearly three decades after a sixteenth-century mosque in the north Indian city of Ayodhya was torn down by Hindu militants, Narendra Modi laid the first brick of a new temple that was to stand in its place. The site has been claimed by many Hindus to be the birthplace of the god Ram and, for several decades, mobilisations around this space have reflected some of Hindutva's core concerns: assertiveness and militancy, a Hindu renaissance and the nationalisation of Hindu culture, a rejection of secularism, and a hostile attitude to Muslims and other minorities. The Indian diaspora have long been involved in activism related to the Ayodhya temple project.

The sympathetic relationship between the Conservative Party and Hindu nationalism witnessed at Wembley Stadium appeared to be manifested in a tweet from 'Boris Johnson' two days after Modi inaugurated the construction of the Ayodhya *mandir* (temple). An image of the British Prime Minister and Home Secretary Priti Patel conducting a Hindu ritual was accompanied by the text: 'I'm a big fan of Indian Culture So I Did "SHRI RAM ABHISHEK" With Our Home minister at my Residence On 5th of August.'[5] At the time of writing, the tweet had garnered 17,500 retweets and nearly 80,000 likes. But all was not as it seemed—the message had been posted from a counterfeit account, set up just one month earlier.

The fake story represented not just a desire for global approbation, but also the centrality of the internet and digital misinformation in the recent rise of Hindu nationalism in India and beyond. This is a feature shared with other twenty-first-century ethnic nationalist and populist movements, but is arguably more prominent in India and its diaspora, with its legions of fanatical 'keyboard warriors', than anywhere else. Boris Johnson may not have said anything about the Ayodhya temple, but the start of its construction, which for some symbolised another nail in the coffin of Indian secularism, was a joyous occasion for many Hindus across the world. Some Indian Americans were so enthused that they paid for digital renderings of the *mandir* to be displayed on an enormous billboard in New York's Times Square, producing striking optics that were received with delight by Hindu nationalists back in India. Others conducted online *pujas* (Hindu ceremonies) to mark the construction of the Ayodhya temple: a necessity brought on partly by the Covid pandemic, but also reflecting a long history of Hindus connecting across borders via the internet.

INTRODUCTION

Digital misinformation was also deemed to have played a role in the unprecedented outbreak of communal tension and violence in Leicester during August and September 2022. The Midlands city, which saw a large influx of Asian migrants in the 1960s and 1970s, is amongst the most diverse in Britain: 43.4% of the city identified as Asian in the 2021 census; 17.9% of Leicester's population are Hindu and 23.5% are Muslim.[6] It is frequently framed as a multicultural 'success story'—a reputation that, while laudable and fitting on various levels, also obfuscates the difficulties and hostility faced, historically and in the present day, by its migrant and diaspora communities. But various residents and analysts have also spoken of long-standing and building animosity between many Hindus and Muslims in the city. Following an India versus Pakistan cricket match, held in Dubai on 28 August, tension spilled over into violence. Videos circulated widely online showed crowds of people on the streets of Leicester chanting *"Pakistan murdabad"* ("death to Pakistan"), as clashes erupted between groups of young Hindu and Muslim men and numerous arrests were made.

Violent flashpoints broke out at various moments in the subsequent weeks, peaking on the weekend of 17–18 September. Hundreds of masked Hindu men marched through an area of the city with a large Muslim community, shouting *"Jai Shri Ram"* (Hail Lord Ram) and other slogans with an intimidating effect. Later, young Muslims descended upon a Hindu neighbourhood and pulled down a saffron flag on a Hindu temple.[7] Rumours spread like wildfire. The Indian High Commission released a statement condemning 'the violence perpetrated against the Indian community'.[8] MP for Leicester East, Claudia Webbe, spoke out about 'fringe elements led and inspired by extremism and rightwing ideology rearing its head in the UK', and the city's Mayor and Police Chief Constable identified online disinformation as a key factor.[9] An investigation by the BBC analysed 200,000 tweets and found that more than half originated in India, many containing the hashtag #HindusUnderAttack and circulating anti-Muslim perspectives, and a range of 'fake news' and misinformation, on the events in Leicester.[10] A more recent article claimed that messages and memes that fanned the flames were circulated in WhatsApp groups of Hindus in Leicester by 'India-based BJP activists'.[11] A number of reports also suggested that many involved in the disturbances were people who had arrived in the UK relatively recently, and a large proportion of people who participated in on-the-ground agitations were not in fact from the city itself. During and in the aftermath of the disturbances, many members and leaders of Hindu and Muslim communities redoubled their efforts to restore, or build, unity and cordial relations. However, the violent scenes in Leicester—for many, shocking and unanticipated—underlined the extent to which the communal politics and enmity of South Asia could be felt tangibly on British streets. Transnational Hindutva was on the radar in the UK perhaps more than it had ever been before.

The final vignette that starts this book relates to the burgeoning, ever-evolving Indian American population. This diverse range of communities is spread across the United States, but with a particularly high concentration in the New York metropolitan area. At almost exactly the same time as the Leicester tensions, in August 2022, during celebrations in Edison, New Jersey, to mark India's seventy-fifth Independence Day, the annual parade included a yellow bulldozer adorned with photos of Narendra Modi and the incendiary Uttar Pradesh Chief Minister, Yogi Adityanath. For many onlookers the significance of the bulldozer would be lost. But for others it was a clear provocation—a sinister reference to the demolition of homes and businesses belonging to Muslims and those who have opposed the Hindu nationalist establishment in recent years. Hindutva has a relatively strong foothold in New Jersey, and in October 2016, Indian Americans in Edison hosted an eye-catching event in support of presidential hopeful Donald Trump, billed the 'Humanity United Against Terror Charity Concert'. However, many have resisted communalism in North America, and there was a strong backlash to both Hindutva-inflected Trump support and the New Jersey bulldozer incident. Many condemned the vehicle's inclusion in the rally, including Muslim groups and the Mayor of Edison. New Jersey's two US senators, Bob Menendez and Cory Brooker, even released a statement that spoke of 'leaders and members of New Jersey's South Asian community who were angered and deeply hurt by the

INTRODUCTION

inclusion of a bulldozer in the India Day Parade', explaining that 'The bulldozer has come to be a symbol of intimidation against Muslims and other religious minorities in India, and its inclusion in this event was wrong.'[12] The parade organisers, New Jersey's Indian Business Association, eventually issued an apology for 'blatant divisive symbols', but, once again, communal tensions and the growing presence of Hindutva in diasporic communities and political spheres beyond the subcontinent had been laid bare.[13]

A short introduction to the Indian diaspora

The Indian diaspora is numerically the largest, and one of the most dispersed, in the world. Recent figures from the Ministry of External Affairs list 208 countries, from Afghanistan to Zimbabwe, in which Indian citizens live.[14] The range of countries that contain citizens who are of Indian origin is equally extensive. Alongside its numerical scale, the history of the Indian diaspora is long and varied too. Migration within and beyond the Indian subcontinent is a constitutive, and in many senses defining, feature of its history, culture, religion, economy, and society in the broadest sense.

The Indian diaspora is endlessly plural and diverse. In fact, to call it 'a diaspora'—much less a homogenous community— is misleading. There were ancient patterns of mobility, over short and long distances, and also myriad forms of movement in precolonial India, no less ordinary than sedentarism. There are those who migrated during the colonial period, and there are the postcolonial flows of people (many of whom were uprooted by the very process of decolonisation and state-building in South Asia). There are around seventeen million Non-Resident Indians (NRIs): citizens of India who include the 'techies' of Silicon Valley and the millions of labourers in the Gulf (as well as a significant number of 'international students'). And there is at least as numerous a diaspora of 'People of Indian Origin': citizens of other countries, who range from the descendants of indentured labourers in Fiji, the Caribbean, and many other former colonies, to a postcolonial 'passenger class' of migrants who moved to Britain, Australia,

Canada, and beyond in the wake of Partition.[15] There is, too, a huge amount of migration within and between the neighbouring nations of South Asia and across the Indian Ocean: a perennial movement of people defined by both fluidity and stuckness, across borders porous and obstructive. There are those who maintain close links and affinity with the homeland, and others for whom the Indian connection goes no further than a box ticked on the ethnicity question of a census. The Indian diaspora might also be delineated along lines of region, language, caste, gender, occupation, and religion—all of which are represented in the same dizzying diversity, albeit in different concentrations, outside South Asia as within.

Given this incredibly multifarious and multitudinous range of peoples, there are of course issues with terminology. But, for pragmatic reasons—and by no means a desire to essentialise—this book will often refer to 'the Indian diaspora', 'the Hindu community', 'Indians overseas', and so on. The term 'South Asian' is occasionally used to refer to communities from across the subcontinent, although it is acknowledged that this can risk generalising, and that many reject these broader markers of identity (see Chapter 5). Another example of terminology that fails to capture nuance, and is problematic on various other levels (but used quite happily by some), are certain 'hyphenated identities': British Indian, East African Asian, Indian American, etc. Again, these are used, rather reluctantly, not as analytical categories, *per se*, but for practical reasons.

Britain's Indian population—although often, inaccurately, referred to as a monolithic 'community' (or subsumed into an even more essentialised 'Asian' grouping)—reflects much of the heterogeneity mentioned above. The presence of South Asians in Britain can be traced back at least 400 years. When the East India Company was making its first forays into the subcontinent, Indians were travelling in the other direction. This 'counterflow to colonialism' comprised businessmen, priests, cooks, artisans, servants, ayahs, traders, diplomats, clerks, sportsmen, physicians, writers, princes and princesses, politicians, soldiers, sailors, and students.[16] Many of these were travellers and sojourners—part of a circulatory pattern of mobility, in which most (but not all) would return to the subcontinent or on to other parts of the world.

The arrival of the HMT *Empire Windrush* into Tilbury Docks from the West Indies on 21 June 1948, while a watershed moment, must not be framed as the start of migration to Britain. Doing so elides Britain's long history of racial and ethnic diversity, and its ever-dynamic and shifting demography. This narrative plays into the hands of an indigenist rhetoric that evokes an invented and imaginary homogeneity and racialist 'purity', and frames migration as a recent 'problem', even a 'crisis'. But from the middle of the twentieth century, migration of a new kind and scale did, quite rapidly, emerge in the UK. The post-war period was a major turning point in Britain's evolving population: large numbers from the Caribbean and other colonies and former imperial territories—including the recently decolonised and partitioned Indian subcontinent—arrived in the UK, partly in response to policies that encouraged immigrants to fill labour shortages in the wake of the Second World War. This was facilitated by the 1948 British Nationality Act, which created a new status of 'Citizen of the United Kingdom and Colonies' and thus gave millions of people from Commonwealth states, and those still under colonial rule, the right to live and work in Britain.

Over the course of the 1950s, 1960s, and 1970s, a substantial Indian diaspora began to take shape, located in especially high concentrations in London and industrial (but increasingly deindustrialised) cities and towns of the Midlands and north of England. A young, predominantly male, and ostensibly transient population began to relinquish the 'myth of return', were joined by family members from the subcontinent, and evolved into close-knit communities of increasingly settled family units.[17] This shift saw a consolidation of Hindu communities, the establishment of associations, institutions, and edifices, and the increasing 'continuation' of religious practices. This was partly supported by an increasingly more conducive (and sometimes financially supportive) multicultural milieu.

Although the post-war period of migration was the major turning point in Britain's evolving ethnic and racial demography, for Indians an equally defining moment was the influx of East African Asians in the 1960s and 1970s. Approximately one-third of Britain's Indian population (and perhaps considerably more of the Hindu community) originated from the former British colonies in East Africa, who became 'twice-migrants' under varying degrees of coercion due to Africanisation policies.[18]

From the late nineteenth century a substantial Asian population moved to and settled in what is today Kenya, Uganda, and Tanzania. Many achieved considerable success, supported in part by certain commercial and administrative opportunities afforded by the colonial state. But these same policies also contributed towards the relatively segregated lives of Asians in East Africa. This became a factor in growing enmity with African populations, leading to the mass emigration of Asians following the independence of various African states (the most notorious example being Idi Amin's brutal expulsion of Uganda's Asians, who were given just ninety days to leave in 1972). The East African Asians' enhanced levels of social, political, and cultural capital (discussed in Chapter 1), as well as their 'mobility capital' and close-knit kinship networks, enabled them to establish or 'transplant' a variety of caste, business, cultural, and religious organisations and networks in their new host societies.[19] It is in this context that the establishment and development of Hindu nationalism in Britain can be understood.

It is also important for the great success of many South Asians in contemporary Britain, America, and elsewhere not to obfuscate the enormous struggles faced by these communities. Many lived, and still live, in deprivation—a reality at odds with the essentialising stereotype of the 'model minority' (explored in Chapter 5). Many Indian migrants to Britain were dislocated and dispossessed of assets and homes, uprooted from their communities, and their attempts to settle elsewhere were often met with great resistance. In Britain this involved a barrage of anti-immigrant violence and rhetoric, and the creation of new laws in the 1960s and 1970s devised to exclude colonial and Commonwealth citizens. As Ian Sanjay Patel has recently written: 'The idea that the Windrush generation was welcomed by governments, and that British traditions of rights and rule of law were gifted to colonial populations who then migrated to Britain as so many pupils gone to meet their teacher, are national superstitions exposed by the hostile environments of past and present.'[20] Even today, the stereotype of the affluent and highly skilled Indian migrant (a reality partly engineered by restrictive immigration policy) erases the lived experience of India's huge number of refugees and undocumented migrants—many of whom come to Britain, the US, and elsewhere—whose circumstances and fate are very different to the image that many people paint of the 'model minority'.

The political identities and affiliations of Indian communities around the world come in many hues and levels of intensity. In the twenty-first century there is an increasingly dominant received wisdom that 'the diaspora' has a tendency to be aligned with the politics of Hindu nationalism. While Hindutva does resonate with many—and some of those who are drawn to Hindu nationalism express their proclivities at a great volume—this received wisdom essentialises a demographically and historically disparate series of communities into a monolithic, single 'diaspora' entity, and elides a deeply layered and multifaceted history of political diversity. The Gadhar Movement's revolutionary anti-imperialism in North America from the 1910s, and the Indian Workers' Association's campaigning in Britain from the 1930s onwards, represent just two significant examples of leftist activism that emerged in the first half of the twentieth century. The 1970s saw the rise of Asian Youth Movements, led primarily by young, second-generation British Asians, who took to the streets to stand up against the violent racism of the National Front and others who sought to oppress Britain's growing Black and Asian population. These groups would form alliances with anti-racist allies and other racial minorities, and often organised under a broad and inclusive identity of 'political blackness'—a shared non-white solidarity that many South Asians began to eschew by the end of the twentieth century.

In more recent decades, a slew of organisations—such as the Southall Black Sisters, the South Asia Solidarity Group, and the International Dalit Solidarity Network—represent various facets of South Asian diasporic struggles against patriarchy, racism, communalism, casteism, and other forms of discrimination. A lot of political activists in the Indian diaspora have specifically been concerned with resisting Hindutva. Other political factions have included Sikhs organising (sometimes militantly) for secession and self-determination in a proposed, separate state of Khalistan, a substantial but often overlooked minority of Indian Muslims fighting against both radicalisation and Islamophobia, and, of course, members of the Indian diaspora whose political activities have occurred in wider movements less defined by ethnicity. These represent just some portions of the remarkably broad spectrum of the Indian diaspora's political identities that go beyond Hindutva. What is more, many overseas Indians—much like any other section of society—take little interest, nor maintain any connection, to the politics of their homeland.

Mainstream political representation for Indians in Britain has been a long and slow process. The UK's first Indian MP was Dadabhai Naoroji—a towering figure, elected as the representative for Finsbury in 1892, who opposed British colonialism and earned himself the sobriquet 'the Grand Old Man of India'. But after the Communist MP Shapurji Saklatvala lost his seat in the 1929 General Election, Britain would have to wait nearly six decades for another MP of Indian origin. While the Labour Party has had considerably more politicians from ethnic minority backgrounds (and continues to today), in June 2021 a rather remarkable situation emerged in which three of the most senior cabinet ministers in the Conservative government, and Labour's London Mayor, were all children of South Asian immigrants (two with Muslim parents from Pakistan, and two having Hindu parents from East Africa).[21] In October 2022, Rishi Sunak became the UK's first Hindu Prime Minister.

The South Asian diaspora has a historical tendency towards the centre-left parties: Indians overseas have overwhelmingly supported the Labour Party in Britain and the Democratic Party in America, for instance. The long affinity with Labour has historic roots—it was under Clement Attlee's government that India was 'granted' independence (something that Churchill would not countenance). Left-wing parties have historically been seen as less aggressively anti-immigrant, and more multiculturalist, than those on the right. There are, however, signs that this allegiance

INTRODUCTION

is shifting, especially in terms of the Indian diaspora's support for the Conservative Party in Britain (discussed in Chapter 6). Much of this mainstream politics has become infused and entwined with the politics of Hindu nationalism.

Hindu Nationalism in the Indian Diaspora—*the book's position and context*

Located within this historical narrative of the Indian diaspora, this book explores the global growth and development of Hindu nationalist ideology and organisations. Hindutva—the majoritarian, conservative, and militant ideology of the Hindu nationalist movement—is increasingly dominant and transformative in India. Historically, Hindutva has often, but not always, manifested in involvement with the Sangh Parivar—the diverse 'family' of organisations, usually led by upper-caste Hindus (although ostensibly seeking cross-caste unity), that emanates from the principal Hindutva institution, the Rashtriya Swaymasevak Sangh (National Volunteers Corps—RSS). The RSS is one of the largest volunteer-based institutions in the world, and often described as 'paramilitary', with perhaps up to six million members (estimates vary considerably and there is no membership data). Through this diverse, interconnected constellation of some of the largest civil society organisations across India (many of which have counterparts overseas), the Hindu nationalist movement advocates a muscular Hindu Renaissance that also challenges—indeed seeks to undo—Gandhian pacifism and Nehruvian secularism, and 'reinstate' the land to an imagined pre-invasion 'purity'. It is, ultimately, preoccupied with the transformation of the consciousness of all Indians, and of Indian society in its entirety.

Although inherently nationalist and geographically rooted, Hindutva involved global and universalist rhetoric from the outset. V.D. Savarkar (1883–1966)—the author of the ideology—famously proclaimed in his seminal 1923 book, *Essentials of Hindutva*, 'the only geographical limits to Hindutva are the limits of our earth!' India as holyland is the very bedrock of Hindutva: Savarkar's often-quoted definition of a Hindu is, 'A person who looks upon the land that extends from the Indus to the sea as his Fatherland and Holyland'.[22] However, it is notable that this leaves plenty of room for diasporic adherents.

While this book's primary focus is on Britain, the approach and lens are transnational in nature: diasporic politics and identity can rarely be effectively understood without thinking about layers of connectivity that transcend national borders. As illustrated in the opening vignettes, Hindu nationalism has evolved into a major movement that has not only transformed the socio-political and cultural landscape of India, but also has spheres of influence across the world thanks in large part to India's substantial diaspora. The Hindutva of the diaspora, however, is not simply a lobbying force, nor a carbon copy of the movement in India. While it is closely linked to Hindu nationalism in the homeland, it is inaccurate to think just in terms of being 'transplanted' (a trope frequently, but often erroneously, used to understand diasporic culture).

Global Hindutva *is* often the product of strategies of expansion and sustained co-ordination from India. Many aspects bear a striking similarity to the movement in India and forms of mimesis are important to maintaining uniformity with the movement as a whole, and also for the diaspora to feel connected to their homeland culture. An RSS-produced pamphlet, *Sarsanghchalak Goes Abroad*—published to document the Supreme Leader's 1995 'international tour'—provides a list of a dozen organisations, in a section titled 'Sangh Work Abroad', that have been established in the UK.[23] Many of these are direct equivalents of groups that exist in India, but a number are distinct, or substantively different, to the traditional institutions of RSS network.

There are significant divergences and idiosyncrasies to Hindu nationalist organisations and praxis abroad. This represents a 'vernacularisation' or 'translation' of Hindutva, in which it evolves and adapts to local contexts and requirements. This has occurred not just internationally, but in India too—a trend that a number of scholars have identified, and that has played an important role in the successful expansion of the movement in various places and times.[24] Many studies of Hindu nationalism focus purely on organisations of the Sangh Parivar—the diverse and interconnected 'family' of organisations that emanates from the RSS. Particular focus is given to the largest and most prominent groups, like the BJP, the VHP (Vishwa Hindu Parishad), and the RSS itself. While these institutions of course demand attention—and much of this book is focused on them—important and influential expressions of Hindutva can be found in much less well-known groups or even organisations that do not explicitly espouse Hindu nationalism.

There exists a significant and growing literature on Hindu nationalism and Hindutva more broadly that this book engages with. Many research projects and publications can be linked to the rise of the Hindu nationalist movement in the 1980s and 1990s (leading up to, and after, the destruction of the Babri Masjid in 1992), and then again around the time of the election of BJP governments (first in 1998/9 and, of course, since 2014). This literature is far too voluminous to discuss or list in depth—and it is referenced throughout the book—but some of particularly significant scholarship has been produced by: Christophe Jaffrelot, Tanika Sarkar, Peter van der Veer, Achin Vanaik, John Zavos, Manjari Katju, Pralay Kanungo, Bruce Graham, William Gould, Ornit Shani, K.N. Panikkar, Jyotirmaya Sharma, Nikita Sud, Meera Nanda, Thomas Blom Hansen, Angana Chatterji, Bipan Chandra, Shubh Mathur, Gyanendra Pandey, Arkotong Longkumer, Chetan Bhatt, A.G. Noorani, and many others.[25]

Beyond these scholarly and critical approaches, there is also a substantial body of writing that serves to promote or eulogise Hindutva, and provide positive perspectives on the ideology, its institutions, and its leaders. A large amount of this is 'in-house', for instance literature produced by the RSS publisher, Suruchi Prakashan, the RSS newspaper, *Organiser*, or myriad online resources (some of which stretch back to the early days of the internet). The existence of this corpus points to Hindu nationalism's deep-rooted distrust of the media and academia, anxiety around leftist and secular influences, and desire to produce an alternative discourse (ultimately as part of a totally reimagined, restructured society). This is seen in groups like the Hindu Vivek Kendra (HVK—Hindu Knowledge Centre)—a Sangh Parivar unit that describes itself as 'a resource center for the promotion of Hindutva ... both in

India and abroad'—and the Hindu Sahitya Kendra (HSK—Hindu Literature Centre), a Leicester-based book distributor and shop, launched in 1984 and described as a 'service project' or 'project arm' of the Sangh in Britain.[26]

The dissemination of literature for Hindus abroad, including books and pamphlets specifically produced for a diasporic readership, has long been considered important by Hindutva leaders, especially as a way to convey certain information and messages to younger generations, and as a palliative for corrupting influences and means to mitigate risk of losing a connection to one's culture. Golwalkar, perhaps optimistically, saw 'open[ing] good libraries containing books in our languages' as a solution to migrants who felt marginalised, bored, and 'lonely' abroad.[27] Historically, the transnational circulation of this literature has been considered significant by some, providing a tangible connection to the homeland; however, in recent decades, this flow of ideas has been superseded almost entirely by digital material of various forms. Hindu nationalist groups were in fact particularly early adopters of new technologies: in 1995, the Supreme Leader of the RSS told an audience in the Sangh's Leicester office: 'It is also a matter of happiness that a computer has been placed here as also a fax machine to facilitate cotacts [sic] with all parts of the world'.[28] The following year, the RSS launched the Global Hindu Electronic Network, through the Hindu Students Council in the US.[29] The web has evolved into a major location for the development of transnational Hindutva, which Rohit Chopra suggests should be viewed as a 'majoritarian right-wing counterpublic', and which 'defines itself as beleaguered or under siege, from a minority group, the state, ideology, or some combination of these'.[30] Various forms of literature have specific significance for diasporic and Hindu nationalist audiences: they can forge common identity and goals, reifying an imagined community, be deeply affective and help with 'crafting social identities', and be part of a 'communications circuit', in which ideas circulate and are engaged with in complex and dynamic ways, beyond hermetically sealed and neatly defined 'local' and 'global' epistemes.[31] This book draws upon and analyses this diverse literature and its impact in depth.

INTRODUCTION

Although diasporic Hindutva has not received anywhere near as much academic attention as the movement in India, there have been a number of important contributions that this book engages with and builds upon. The American context has received somewhat more scholarly attention than Britain: Prema Kurien, Vinay Lal, Arvind Rajagopal, Devesh Kapur, and Martha Nussbaum are among those who have advanced our understanding of Hindutva in the US.[32] Biju Mathew and Vijay Prashad's 'Yankee Hindutva' idiom was also a noteworthy intervention— elucidating the adaptability of overseas Hindu nationalism and its relationship with the public and political life of the Hindu diaspora in the United States (as were two illuminating and popular, but somewhat polemic, books by Prashad).[33] More recently, Sangay Mishra has explored contemporary transnational Hindutva, set against the internal contestations and fissures of a heterogenous diaspora, in his important research on the 'political lives of South Asian Americans'.[34] And Walter Andersen and Shridhar Damle's substantial volume on the RSS (which was criticised for its 'sympathetic' perspective and lack of critical distance), contained a chapter on 'the RSS overseas', informed by Damle's first-hand experience as an office-holder in the American wing of the HSS.[35]

Touching on aspects of the Hindu nationalist movement across various countries, Christophe Jaffrelot (probably the most eminent and prolific scholar of Hindu nationalism) and Ingrid Therwath have shed light on the organisational infrastructure and strategy that enabled the Sangh to spread abroad.[36] In an insightful critique of Benedict Anderson's essay on 'long-distance nationalism', they highlighted a major limitation to Anderson's paradigm: 'Mere nostalgia or even spontaneous mobilisations are invoked to explain this phenomenon, but fail to explain the mechanisms that lie behind it.'[37] Although the rise of ethnic and religious nationalism amongst migrants has been hastily attributed to guilt, frustration, and political irresponsibility, scholarly, historically informed, and sensitive analyses of the phenomenon are not so common.

Among the most detailed accounts of transnational Hindutva are not academic studies, *per se*, but advocacy reports from groups seeking to raise public awareness of the movement and its connections to militancy in India and anti-minority politics (especially Islamophobia and violence against Dalits). These reports, which often feature academics among the authors, include a 2004 report by the activist network AWAAZ—South Asia Watch, entitled 'In Bad Faith? British Charity and Hindu Extremism'.[38] The AWAAZ report was primarily an exposé of Sewa International UK, the British charity with connections to the Sangh, which distributed funds raised in Britain through Sangh Parivar affiliates in India. Similarly detailed reports have focused on the United States: on transnational flows of funding, Hindu nationalism on university campuses, and on the infrastructure and influence of contemporary Hindutva.[39] Recently, various other reports, pieces of investigative journalism, polemics, and works of advocacy intended to 'lift the lid' on transnational Hindutva have emerged, in line with the ascendence of the BJP, the 'saffronisation of the public sphere',[40] and the entrenchment of Hindu supremacy in India, framed by many as fascistic and extremist.

In recent years, however, an important and more nuanced body of work has emerged that relates to the Hindutva of the diaspora (either directly or indirectly), focusing on the internet and other forms of mediatisation.[41] Online spaces have proved extremely important for various political movements, but their significance for radical, populist, and expatriate or 'deterritorialised' politics (and instances where they intersect, such as with diasporic Hindutva) can hardly be overstated. The Indian diaspora have been pioneering innovators in the development and use of online technologies and media, as have Hindu nationalist activists. The internet problematises the 'here' and 'there' binary, allowing the individual and community to transcend space in new ways, which forces us to reconsider and complicate our existing notions of diaspora, citizenship, sovereignty, and even the nation-state itself. These ideas, and the various technologies and online spaces that underpin them, are considered throughout this book.

The book also adds to a relatively small but valuable body of literature on Hindu nationalism in Britain. Some pieces in a little-known edited work—*In Quest of a Secular Symbol*, the outcome of a conference in 1993—were among the first to consider a more

INTRODUCTION

global perspective.[42] It began to redress earlier misunderstandings or oversights of Hindutva in Britain, for instance Kim Knott's reference to the HSS as a 'boy's youth group' in her otherwise valuable study of Hinduism in Britain.[43] Taking a much more critical stance, and pushing against 'academic neutralism' and 'dispassionate sociology' that failed to grasp the 'dense historical, social, economic and political complexities' of Hindu practices in the UK, the work of Chetan Bhatt is particularly important in this small field.[44] Others that have also provided robust critiques of diasporic Hindutva in Britain include the work of Parita Mukta, Gita Sahgal, Pragna Patel, Amrit Wilson, and Kalpana Wilson, who all provided robust and impassioned challenges to the patriarchy of Hindutva.[45]

More recently, various other scholars have made important contributions to the understanding of Hindu nationalism in Britain. Notable among them is John Zavos, who has substantially advanced our understanding of the public representation of Hindu (nationalist) identities and British multiculturalism—themes that this book engages with deeply.[46] The work of Dhooleka Raj and Papiya Ghosh has also provided important points of departure for this book. In many ways, their joint influence is perhaps surprising. Ghosh provided a rare insight into opposition to Hindutva in the diaspora, and framed diasporic identities and politics as 'extending the subcontinent'.[47] Conversely, Raj implored us to 'resist understanding diasporic South Asians by going to South Asia'.[48] But Raj's approach was far from parochial. In a pioneering article on the interplay between multiculturalism, Hindutva, and religious and ethnic identity formation (based on fieldwork in the early 1990s), she argued: 'Instead of a *natural* "product" of ethnic identity, the pro-Hindu agenda must be understood processually as a response to both national multiculturalism and trans-national politics.'[49]

Hindu Nationalism in the Indian Diaspora builds on Raj's critique of research that frames diasporas in terms of 'transplanted culture':

> Ethnographies of Asians in Britain ... continue resolutely to focus on the present-day and produce ethnographies without time ... [E]ven those anthropologists who worked 'at both ends of the

migration chain' assumed two self-contained and present-time societies for comparison existing 'here' and 'there'. [This type of research] tends not to set ... observations in a wider context of the creation of group identity, culture, and community with respect to changing dynamics of power and representation.[50]

This book attempts to tread a more nuanced path—taking in multiple perspectives and using a wide range of material—in order to uncover and understand Hindu nationalism in Britain that is sensitive both to history and contemporary context, as well as global and local influences and cross-fertilisations.

Chapters and structure of the book

The structure of this book combines elements of chronology and theme. Each chapter focuses on key aspects and periods of Hindu nationalism in Britain and beyond. The first chapter considers the initial development of the Sangh Parivar overseas, in East Africa from the mid-1940s, and its early period in Britain from the mid-1960s. This constitutes a crucial formative context from which diasporic Hindu nationalism evolved multivalent, multidirectional relationships with organisations and ideologies both in India and elsewhere in the diaspora. It then considers some of the core elements of the Sangh modus operandi, particularly the *shakha*—the branch meeting format at the heart of the RSS—and certain key office holders within the institutional structures (including 'local' volunteers, as well as full-time Sangh workers sent from India). The chapter explores why Hindutva and the RSS has resonated specifically with diasporic Hindus.

Hindu nationalist training camps and conferences—held both in the diaspora and in India, and also attended by visiting RSS leaders and Hindutva ideologues—are considered in Chapter 2. These camps facilitate a direct link with the homeland, global networks of fellow *swayamsevaks* (volunteer members) and organisers, and the mother organisation. The chapter focuses on two innovative forms of training camp, which act in different ways as key spaces for the development of the organisation and its co-ordination from India.

Both the camps and the regular *shakha* meetings are in many senses alike to the Hindutva of the homeland, but they are also syncretic in many ways. They constitute distinctive, dynamic inflections of Hindutva in local contexts, adapted to the specific requirements of the Indian diaspora. Notably, and in different ways to the Sangh in India, the HSS plays a crucial pedagogical role: it seeks to provide an emotional and cultural bond to the homeland not just for first generations but, perhaps even more importantly, for British-born children of migrants. Coeducation is also a significant HSS innovation.

The Sangh's transnational networks have also enabled a 'reverse' influence of the diaspora on India—a dynamic that is explored especially in chapters 3 and 4. This was particularly pronounced in two watershed episodes for Hindu nationalist politics in the final decades of the twentieth century: the Indian Emergency and the Ayodhya Ram temple dispute. The former was a pivotal moment in the history of postcolonial India, when in 1975 Prime Minister Indira Gandhi suspended elections, banned various organisations, jailed thousands of political opponents (including Hindu nationalists), and imposed other draconian measures. The Emergency has been referred to in the titles of significant new monographs as 'democracy's turning point' and even 'India's first dictatorship'.[51] Until recently, however, this seismic moment in India's postcolonial history was only really thought of as a domestic political event.

Another critical episode that reached a crescendo in the late twentieth century involved the Ram temple dispute mentioned earlier in this introduction. Hindu nationalists mobilised mass (and often militant) support over claims that a small plot of land in a city in the state of Uttar Pradesh, occupied by a sixteenth-century mosque until it was razed in 1992, was the birthplace of the deity Ram and was once the site of a Hindu temple, which should be rebuilt. Both episodes involved a substantial role for the diaspora—in engagement, influence, publicly expressed support, and financial assistance. Through their much-overlooked impact in Britain, these issues require interpretation as global moments, with enduring effects upon the Sangh abroad and the Indian diaspora more broadly.

Chapter 5 explores charity and public service—areas in which Hindu nationalists in the diaspora have engaged actively and with tangible success, although they have also also caused various controversies. *Sewa* (charity or service) has been central to the Hindu nationalist movement in India from its very earliest days. Public service and various forms of charity, often performative in nature, are a means for expansion and building legitimacy, support, visibility, and membership. But *sewa* also functions as a way in which the overarching goals of Hindutva—the substantive and comprehensive transformation of society—can be achieved.

One of the most conventional ways in which Indians abroad are understood to intervene in the life of the homeland is through remittances. Diaspora-to-homeland capital flows are often considered in literature on migration and 'long-distance nationalism' in a wide range of contexts. In the case of India, the media and various activists have focused on the diasporic funding of Sangh Parivar affiliates in India; as mentioned above, some of the most detailed accounts of diasporic Hindutva have been exposés by advocacy groups. While this is discussed in the book, an increased focus is given to more syncretic and nebulous forms of Hindu (nationalist) philanthropy in Britain.

The fifth chapter considers the development of Hindu nationalism outside the 'traditional' boundaries of the Sangh, exploring the imbricated relationship between philanthropy and acts of public service both in the *karmabhoomi* (land of action) and the *matrubhoomi* (motherland).[52] It discusses the controversies related to the global fundraising after the 2001 Gujarat earthquake, during which large sums of money were collected outside India by organisations connected to the RSS. The chapter's primary case study, however, analyses the establishment of Sewa Day— an annual event with a focus on acts of public service in local communities. Although imbued with the rhetoric of community cohesion, interfaith relations, citizenship, and 'Big Society' voluntarism, Sewa Day also reflects the directives of key RSS ideologues. Sewa Day has enabled the promulgation of the notion of Hindus as 'model minority'—a potent trope for (conservative) Hindu identity and the othering of Muslims in Britain. Yet this new initiative—ostensibly distinctive to the diasporic environment—also represents the institutionalisation in Britain of highly visible, performative public service: a motif at the heart of the RSS itself.

The book's final chapter explores the ways in which Hindu nationalism has outgrown the ideological and institutional boundaries of the Sangh Parivar. This builds on the author's previous work on 'neo-Hindutva' to show how this has happened in particularly significant ways in the diasporic context. Studies of Hindutva in the postcolonial period, both in India and the diaspora, have tended to focus on the core organisations of the RSS family. This fails to take due account of the innovative, dynamic forms of Hindu nationalism of organisations outside, or on the periphery, of the Sangh Parivar, which, in turn, have influenced it. 'Soft' neo-Hindutva groups avoid explicit connections with Hindu majoritarian politics, while 'hard' neo-Hindutva is less reticent about these associations. But, for various different reasons, they position themselves outside of the institutional and ideological framework of the Hindu nationalist movement (as it is conventionally understood). Both forms are increasingly prevalent in transnational articulations of Hindu identity, but soft neo-Hindutva, the book argues, has developed in close dialogue with British multiculturalist policy.

Various inflections of Hindutva are to be found within representative and ostensibly 'mainstream' Hindu organisations and umbrella groups. This kind of Hindu(tva) representation—and thereby the mainstreaming of Hindu nationalism—operates within a multiculturalist milieu that permits, and even demands, the construction of a *public* ethnic identity, as opposed to a purely private one.[53] The final chapter explores ways in which British Hindu-ness has become increasingly politicised and conflated with Indian diasporic identity. Hindutva, moreover, has become normalised in the mainstream representation of Hindu identity. Diasporic Hindutva is not simply 'expatriate nationalism'—rather, it serves as an expression of multivalent British Hindu identity. Its rhetoric of assertive Hindu pride is both connected to, and distinct from, Indian politics and nationalism. The dynamic relationship between these markers has undergone significant transformations, with modes and levels of interaction with the homeland continually being developed and renegotiated. The ways in which the diaspora has influenced the homeland, in the context of global Hindu nationalism, is much more profound than simply a one-way flow of nostalgia, funds, and even political support. In fact, the diaspora has emerged as an increasingly important, but also distinctive, facet of the Hindu nationalist movement itself.

1

'FROM VIDESH VIBHAG TO VISHWA VIBHAG AND NOW VISHWA SANGH'[1]

ESTABLISHING HINDU NATIONALISM ABROAD, FROM EAST AFRICA TO BRITAIN

It is part of the accepted doctrine of the Hindu religion that its practice develops in its adherents both a love for Bharat (India) as the Holy Land of the Hindus and the spirit of eternal Hinduism which means love for the whole of humanity regardless of race country nationality religion sect faith caste or creed and furthermore that this spirit enables such adherents to become better and more useful citizens.[2]

These opening words of the Hindu Swayamsevak Sangh's Trust Deed, submitted to the Charity Commission for England and Wales in 1974, encapsulate much of the organisation's spirit. They highlight that, from their early days, the group has sought to reinforce, and in many ways manufacture, connectivity and devotion to India. But simultaneously, the statement reveals an organisation that understands its position, albeit ambivalently, within the multicultural milieu of late twentieth-century Britain. Moreover, the references to universality intimate the multidirectional, global networks of transnational Hindutva that emerged during the second half of the century. Latent in the Trust Deed is also a fundamental, seemingly paradoxical, tension of diasporic Hindutva—support for a chauvinistic, majoritarian ideology applied to one country, whilst negotiating recognition and minority rights in another. Moreover, Hindutva is fundamentally rooted in territory—the holy land of Mother India. How, then, can this be meaningful for 'deterritorialised' Hindus?

However far from being paradoxical, the so-called 'long-distance nationalism' of the Sangh resonates deeply with British Hindus, and represents a syncretic, dynamic, and idiosyncratic expression of British Hindu identity.

This chapter considers the establishment and growth of the Rashtriya Swayamsevak Sangh (RSS) abroad. The overseas development of Hindu nationalism, in the form of the RSS and its diasporic wings—the Bharatiya Swayamsevak Sangh (in Africa) and the Hindu Swayamsevak Sangh (elsewhere)—has followed the same *shakha*, group meeting, format of the movement in India. But while many aspects of the Hindu nationalist modus operandi have been replicated to the letter, there are also many modifications and shifts in traditional format, resulting in a 'vernacularised' form of Hindutva praxis.

The chapter is divided into two main parts. The first sheds light on the early development of the Hindu nationalist movement, which first took root outside India in Kenya. It then shows that the exodus of East African Asian migrants in the late 1960s and early 1970s was a critical juncture for the establishment and proliferation of Hindu nationalism in Britain. The section ends by considering various key actors and co-ordination involved in establishing the HSS, and examining the role of touring RSS leaders, and diaspora-based full-time workers (*pracharaks*) and temporary workers (*vistaraks*).

The second major section of the chapter analyses continuities and co-ordination between the HSS and the RSS. This is considered primarily through the Sangh's fundamental unit—the *shakha*. These hour-long, quasi-military male gatherings constitute a powerful blend of ritual, choreography, physical exercise, and indoctrination. This chapter unpicks their form, content, development, and meaning in the diaspora, paying close attention to degrees of convergence and divergence from their format in India.

Throughout the initial period of overseas growth, elements of both mimesis and co-ordination with the 'mother organisation' in India were crucial. This was partly the result of a diasporic script written into the ideological and institutional framework of the Sangh from early on. However, rather than being simply a carbon copy of the Indian RSS, subtle but important deviations and modifications developed abroad. *Shakhas* in Britain have addressed what senior RSS leader and ideologue H.V. Seshadri referred to as the 'crucial challenge to ... cultural identity faced by the Hindus [abroad]',[3] helping some to negotiate the perceived dilemmas of Westernisation, materialism, permissiveness, marginalisation, and weakening connectivity with the 'Mother-soil'.[4]

While there exists a body of valuable scholarship on the Hindu nationalist movement's foreign forays, much that has been written on diasporic Hindutva—and, indeed, cultural and political organisations of the Indian diaspora more broadly—fails to sufficiently elucidate nebulous and complex relationships with the homeland. Some scholars have either deliberately or naively paid little attention to the Indian context and the thinly veiled connection between Hindu nationalism of the diaspora and that of India. This can reflect a heavily ethnographic, 'community studies' approach, which has not made use of the rich diversity of source material available, and is often problematically unreflexive. While it is important to bear in mind Dhooleka Raj's appeal to 'resist understanding diasporic South Asians by going to South Asia', in the case of Hindutva abroad, an understanding of Indian institutions, and political, social, and historical contexts, illuminates crucial layers of transnationalism.[5] Conversely, other literature on diasporic Hindutva—academic, activist, and a blend of the two—has overemphasised connectivities and facsimile with the Sangh Parivar of India. In seeking to rectify earlier misunderstandings and lay bare the radical nature of the parent institution, this fails to understand or explain the compulsions of diasporic Hindu nationalism.

This book aims to offer a more nuanced and sensitive reading, recognising that Hindu nationalism represents an important intervention in the identities of many members of the Indian diaspora. It is neither disconnected from the homeland, nor is it simply an ideological export from the Sangh offices of Nagpur, New Delhi, and Mumbai. Hindu nationalism abroad, whilst connected to India and numerous nodes of expatriate Hindutva around the world, represents a discursive, fluid, quasi-cosmopolitan, and vernacularised articulation of diasporic Hindu identity.

I—East Africa and the first shakha *overseas*

A legend surrounds the founding of the first RSS branch outside India, which is frequently recounted both orally and in Hindu nationalist literature.[6] The story's central protagonist is Jagdish Chandra Sharda Shastri, who was a teacher at an Arya Samaj school in Amritsar, Punjab, and a committed RSS *swayamsevak*. In 1946, Shastri decided to leave India to undertake a new job at the Arya Samaj Girls' School in Nairobi. The Arya Samaj—a Hindu revivalist movement, founded in Bombay by social reformist Dayananda Saraswati in 1875—was first started in Kenya in 1903. The Arya Samaj's missionary activities beyond the subcontinent—establishing educational facilities and sending gurus to British colonies of Africa, the Pacific, and the Caribbean—was a groundbreaking and highly influential moment in the history of global Hinduism, and in some senses a precursor to transnational Hindutva identities and networks.

One year before independence, and two years before the RSS's ban following Mahatma Gandhi's assassination by a Hindu extremist, Shastri set sail from Bombay to Mombasa to take up his new post. Standing on the deck of the SS *Vasna*, one tempestuous evening in the middle of the Indian Ocean, he had a serendipitous encounter with another passenger—a Gujarati called Manek Lal Rughani. This would prove a turning point in the Sangh's history. The meeting, memorialised by Shastri in his *Memoirs of a Global Hindu*, led to the first *shakha* outside India.[7]

Shastri identified Rughani as a fellow *swayamsevak* by the khaki shorts of the Sangh uniform, then the two young men faced 'towards the Motherland' and spontaneously burst into song, singing the Sangh *prarthana* (prayer) 'Namaste Sada Vatsale Matrubhoomi' (Hail to Thee O Motherland).[8] For the remaining ten days of the voyage, they would 'play games' with other young men and sing nationalist songs. Shastri speaks of fellow passengers becoming *swayamsevaks* on board the ship, highlighting the important proselytising, expansionist dimension to the RSS. He also mentions that they 'exchanged addresses'—laying the foundations for the East African Sangh network—and promised one another 'to start a branch of Sangh in each town'.[9]

But this fabled course of events was not entirely spontaneous. Before leaving, Shastri had spoken to Chamanlal Grover, the first Sangh *pracharak* who co-ordinated overseas activities. From this point on, Chamanlal maintained contact with active *swayamsevaks* abroad from Keshav Nagar, the RSS headquarters in New Delhi.[10] Shastri wrote that Chamanlal and other *karyakartas* (active workers/ organisers) blessed his decision to emigrate: 'I also promised them that wherever I go, Sangh will go with me; and wherever I went, I would organize Sangh work'.[11]

The first official *shakha* of the Bharatiya Swayamsevak Sangh (BSS)—as the RSS was initially called overseas—was founded on 14 January 1947 in Nairobi. Shastri was a critical figure in this early development. In his memoirs, he writes of a deep commitment to spreading the word of Hindutva: 'From 1947 to 1977 my attachment to Sangh work in East Africa was so consistent and so intimate that there was not a single week, let alone a month, when I was not involved in its activities'.[12] Growth, according to Shastri, was rapid, facilitated particularly by the arrival of Laxmanrao Bhide—the first *pracharak* officially deputised to oversee the diasporic growth of the Sangh. During 'missionary' tours of the region, Shastri drew upon and maintained records of *swayamsevaks* who had emigrated from India, which were then used by RSS *pracharaks* to develop the organisation in countries beyond Kenya.

The top-down management of Hindutva networks has been downplayed in Sangh accounts, which emphasise the spontaneity and organic nature of *shakha* activity overseas.[13] An example of this somewhat disingenuous emphasis is Mohan Bhagwat's address in 2008, to the Vishwa Adhyayan Kendra (VAK—Centre for International Studies)—a Mumbai-based, diaspora-oriented Sangh Parivar affiliate, established in 1997. Bhagwat stated that the overseas activities of the RSS 'were not started by some national debate and resolutions but by *swayamsevaks* who went abroad out of the need they personally felt in organizing the Hindu community there'.[14] The same organic spirit is stressed in an interview with Shankarrao Tatwawadi, former head of the RSS's Vishwa Vibhag (Global Division): 'The Vishwa Vibhag is not an outcome of any pre-planning, nor is it a product of any systematic survey or implementation'.[15] Instead, he argues that the 'discipline inculcated by the RSS' is taken by *swayamsevaks*, 'naturally', to wherever they migrate.[16]

Although the initiative and dynamism of diaspora *swayamsevaks* was critical, co-ordination from the movement's hierarchy also played a significant part.[17] For instance, Tatwawadi reports that the Nairobi *shakha* was not set up until senior *pracharaks* in India had been consulted and their consent given. While recognising certain 'needbased changes in the working patterns' of HSS branches overseas, Sangh leader Sharad Kunte acknowledges that 'senior RSS authorities in India often take special interest, discuss, advise and provide guidelines for the smooth functioning of the HSS'.[18] The executive role of the central office was stated more plainly in an RSS pamphlet: after listing 'Sangh activities ... going on in 47 countries', it states that 'all these activities are co-ordinated by the Vishwa Vibhag of Rashtriya Swayamsevak Sangh'.[19] This kind of statement, although somewhat overplaying the real extent of centralisation and capacity for global co-ordination, does reveal a significant degree of symbiosis.

The nature and extent of this relationship requires us to rethink the genealogies of the Sangh's global reach. The major gatherings of Hindu nationalists outside India that surprised observers in the late 1980s and early 1990s—such as those in Washington DC and Milton Keynes (discussed later in the book)—did not emerge out of thin air. They were the outcome of well-entrenched and carefully cultivated networks of Sangh activism. The diasporic support for the BJP from the end of the twentieth century, although the result of a range of different factors (for some, much less ideologically

'VIDESH VIBHAG TO VISHWA VIBHAG AND NOW VISHWA SANGH'

motivated), can also be partly traced to this early development of overseas Hindutva.

Even before the first *shakha* had started, the RSS was in touch with emigrating *swayamsevaks*, communicating via post and telephone, and also meeting those who visited India on return trips. Chamanlal oversaw the first period of overseas activity from India and he 'unofficially' started the Vishwa Vibhag (World Division) in 1950.[20] In Sangh literature, his influence is given a particular significance, underlining not just his personal role, but also the importance with which global activities of the Sangh are increasingly seen. In an interview, Hindu nationalist leader Subramanian Swamy mentioned Chamanlal's contributions, framing him in the 'humble, unsung hero' rubric familiar to the Sangh.[21] His death in 2003 precipitated a vast array of eulogies from numerous senior international Sangh office holders, from Singapore, Australia, and Sri Lanka, to Canada, Thailand, and Britain. Many of the most important Sangh leaders gave tributes; Sushma Swaraj, at the time a minister in the BJP government, called him 'a living idol of saint as described in our Shastras'. L.K. Advani wrote that 'one cannot think of Jhandewala [the location of the RSS's Delhi headquarters] without Chamanlalji'.[22]

While these quotations also reflect the later role of the Vishwa Vibhag in co-ordinating overseas visits for senior Sangh leaders, its original role was to maintain contact with ordinary volunteers and organisers. Chamanlal played a central part in establishing networks of connectivity with India, which proved invaluable for the transnational political mobilisations during the Emergency in the mid-1970s.[23] 'Chamanlal has always tried to see that those who go abroad are not lost there,' one RSS book tells us. 'He has even inspired many such *swayamsevaks* to organise the Indians in their respective countries and to keep the love for the motherland alive in their mind'.[24] Bhide also later used records Chamanlal kept of *swayamsevaks* who had emigrated, while expanding the Sangh and encouraging the growth of *shakhas* in East Africa.[25]

New technologies have changed this process, but the spirit is much the same. In an interview in 2014, Anil Varktak, then head of the Vishwa Vibhag, said: 'Still today we do that [corresponding with *swayamsevaks* overseas] ... even when there is no *shakha*', adding that these days contact is maintained, 'mostly by email'.[26] A senior HSS *karyakarta* in the United States describes another level to the Vishwa Vibhag connectivity: 'Once Jagdish ji [Shastri] insisted that he should get the birthdates of all the Vishwa Sangh *pracharaks*. Now, everyone gets a message on his birthday. There are blessings from him waiting for the concerned person on the day, either through a personal call or email.'[27] This informal, personal communication has particular importance for those in the diaspora; it has maintained, or created, an emotional bond with those dislocated by migration. Young second- and third-generation British *swayamsevaks* have also spoken of being able to have contacts in various parts of India when returning on visits—often providing a link for those who have few or no direct family ties remaining with the homeland.

Another dimension of this diaspora connectivity is in the publication of correspondence from international *swayamsevaks* and *shakhas* in RSS weeklies, *Organiser* and *Panchjanya*. 'People would send us stories by snail mail', I was told by a *pracharak* in Delhi, which would often be published in the periodicals. This has both provided the RSS with information from abroad and given diaspora workers a confidence-boosting sense of global significance, as well as a direct link with the homeland, and a sense of status and validation. More formal examples of reporting on the activities of the diaspora from India can also be found, often making use of reportage from the local press.[28] Since the 1990s the digital revolution and the pioneering use of online spaces by the Indian diaspora have transformed these print media dynamics.

Laxmanrao Bhide and peripatetic Sangh leaders

The development of the Sangh in East Africa was not, therefore, simply the product of a serendipitous meeting of *swayamsevaks*. The establishment and growth of the BSS involved various layers of co-ordination. Senior leaders and pioneering full-time workers played important roles, both in the early period and in later years. Whilst Chamanlal had unofficially launched the international operations of the Sangh in 1950, Laxmanrao Bhide—described by the RSS as the 'architect of international Sangh work'—established the Vishwa Vibhag in a formal sense a decade later.[29]

Bhide became the first Vishwa Vibhag *sanyojak* (convenor) and the first *pracharak* based outside India, moving to Kenya to work full-time for the Bharatiya Swayamsevak Sangh in 1959, and making Nairobi his base.[30] He subsequently travelled 'extensively in Africa, Europe, USA and South East Asia to spread a Sangh influence in these areas amongst Hindus'.[31] Shastri writes that during his extended holidays as a school teacher he would accompany Bhide on missions throughout the Indian Ocean region, to the Seychelles, Madagascar, Mauritius, and elsewhere in East Africa; 'the only purpose of this travel would be to establish new *shakhas* and to keep in touch with the existing ones'.[32]

Bhide's dynamism is perhaps exaggerated in some accounts. The claim that he 'travelled to about 80 countries around the world' is both unfeasibly large and discrepant with other sources.[33] This underlines the need to treat Sangh hagiographies with caution. Nonetheless, the peripatetic nature of Bhide's work was clearly important. In 1983, a newsletter published by Bedford-based Vasudev Godbole, under the grandiosely named Indian Institute for Research into True History, described Bhide as 'a roving ambassador of RSS'.[34] Corroborating his active role, a timeline of the Sangh in Mauritius lists twelve separate visits between 1977 and 1997.[35] As well as overseeing the development of the Sangh in synchronicity with the RSS in India, Bhide and other *pracharaks* facilitated visits to East Africa from a wide range of senior *adhikaris* (officials) and other Hindu nationalist leaders. These international tours—while of great significance both to the Hindu nationalist movement and to our understanding of transnational networks more broadly—have generally been overlooked by scholars.

One of several important dimensions to tours is that they sustain a communication network. This was especially valuable in earlier periods, when technologies for transmitting information and instructions either did not yet exist or were harder to access, and the Sangh had yet to fully exploit the possibilities of its own print media. Andersen and Damle underline the importance of these rather clandestine networks in relation to early Sangh mobilisation within India: 'Reluctant to employ publicity or mass communication, the RSS created an informal communications system based on verbal messages carried by RSS leaders, who were almost continually touring the country'.[36] Like domestic peregrinations, overseas tours, therefore, enabled a crucial face-to-face transmission of practical directives about Sangh organisation as well as more ideological messages. There is also an important 'reconnaissance' function to tours. Rajendra Singh, RSS Sarsanghchalak (Supreme Leader) from 1994 to 2000, stated two objectives of his 1995 European trip: '[to get] acquainted with the workers here ... [and] to understand the problems being faced by the Hindu Community here and to seek solutions for them'.[37] They also fulfilled a more inspirational and ideological purpose—events at which various leaders would speak would help to inculcate a sense of unity, resolve, homeland pride and, overall, Hindutva. Finally, there is also a symbolic power to these tours—literally bringing the homeland, or representatives of it, to diaspora communities.

Numerous senior leaders from the RSS, the Jana Sangh (later the BJP), and other affiliated groups visited Africa from the middle of the twentieth century.[38] Deendayal Upadhyaya, one of the Sangh's most important political leaders and ideologues, visited Nairobi in 1963, and Atal Behari Vajpayee, who went on to become the first Hindu nationalist Prime Minister of India, visited Kenya five times from 1965.[39] However, it is worth noting that the first Sarsanghchalak to visit Kenya was Rajendra Singh, in 1997—no less than fifty years after the founding of the BSS.

Six months after Upadhyaya's death in 1968, Swami Satyamitrand Giri laid the foundation stone for 'Deendayal Bhavan' in Nairobi— the most important hub for Hindutva activity in East Africa.[40] From the moment of its inauguration the building played a key role for sections of Kenya's Hindu community. Its wide range of facilities grew over the years to include an office, playground, reading room, reference library, meeting room, audio and video library, shop for Hindutva literature, kitchen, and a nursery school.[41] It was from Deendayal Bhavan that the African chapter of the Overseas

'VIDESH VIBHAG TO VISHWA VIBHAG AND NOW VISHWA SANGH'

Friends of the BJP was inaugurated by party spokesman Vijay Jolly. An *Organiser* account of the launch highlighted an enduring connectivity between India and East Africa, even after the period of mass emigration from the late 1960s:[42]

> Shri Jolly found great connectivity of senior BJP and RSS leaders especially with Kenya. In a visitor's book located at Deendayal Bhawan in Nairobi, he found ... the autographs of former Indian Prime Minister Shri Atal Bihari Vajpayee, the late Hindutva ideologues K.S. Sudarshan,[43] H.V. Seshadri, and D.B. Thengadi, RSS Sarsanghachalak Shri Mohan Bhagwat, veteran VHP leader Shri Ashok Singhal, and Gujarat Chief Minister Shri Narendra Modi.[44]

In many ways, these Hindu nationalist connections across the Indian Ocean reflect the interaction between East African Asians and Indian cultural and religious figures more broadly.[45] A 1955 report from the Indian High Commission in Nairobi noted that, 'Unlike Indians in countries like West Indies, Fiji and Mauritius, Indians in East Africa are not cut off from India and they have always been making efforts to keep cultural contacts with India and hence several people have been visiting East Africa on the invitation of societies like Arya Samaj, Sanatan Dharma Sabha, Sri Guru Singh Sabha and Theosophical Society, etc.'[46]

This picture of enduring emotional and practical connectivity to India must be understood in the context of high levels of segregation—economic, educational, residential, cultural, and linguistic—developed and maintained by Asians in East Africa. Much of this was the consequence of British ordinance: trading incentives and administrative positions in the colonial bureaucracy exacerbated ghettoisation. The existence of separate lavatories at railway stations—marked Europeans/Asians/Natives— underlines the extent of the 'tripartite'.[47] The impetus for segregation also came from Indian communities, with regional, linguistic, and caste concentrations reinforced by patterns of chain migration, endogamy, and existing business networks.

The significant and disproportionate success of many Indians in a wide range of sectors of the East African economy, and

African experiences of marginalisation and racism from the Asian population, led to considerable African–Asian enmity.[48] This would eventually be a key factor in the 'Africanisation' policies that pushed the Indian populations out of the region in the second half of the twentieth century. The 'social and ritual exclusiveness' of East African Asian communities, and associated tensions, were observed anxiously from India.[49] The Nairobi-based Indian High Commission's 'Annual Report on Uganda for the year 1954' noted that 'the relations between Indians and Africans have not been happy'.[50] Inequitable trade relations, failure to integrate with the African population, and attitudes of superiority expressed by Asians were commonly noted as causes of hostility.

But simplistic accounts of the 'colonial sandwich'—the term used to describe the socio-economic hierarchy, with Indians occupying a middle ground between Europeans and Africans—elides often nebulous layers of solidarity and collaborative anti-colonial activism, illuminated in Sana Aiyer's valuable history of Indians in Kenya.[51] In 1951, the BSS even 'invite[d] Mr. Jomo Kenyatta's team of [Mau Mau] freedom fighters to our annual camp'.[52] A photograph of the occasion shows Kenyatta next to the Indian High Commissioner, Apa Pant, who would later represent India at the Bandung Conference.[53]

Crude stereotypes of tripartite also belie significant levels of internal diversity and socio-economic differentiations, as well as caste segregation and religious sectarianism, *amongst* Asians in East Africa. Between 1890 and 1951, in just three Kenyan cities (Nairobi, Mombasa, and Kisumu), separate schools were established by the Arya Samaj, Shree Sanatan Dharam Sabha, Cutch Gujarati Hindu Union, Gujarati Balmandir, Bohras, Ithnasheris, Ismailis, Memons, Sunnis, Jains, Sikhs, and Goans.[54] The Hindu Council of Kenya, an umbrella group formed by the BSS to try to achieve some degree of ecumenism, was not formed until 1973, by which point most Asians had left East Africa. The Indian Ministry of External Affairs was particularly concerned by divisions between Muslims and Hindus in the wake of partition, monitoring the situation in a series of reports.[55] But rather than seeing communal tension in

East Africa simply as 'an overseas extension, if not a reflection' of problems in India, as suggested by an Indian diplomat in 1952, it must also be understood in light of local circumstances and the production of migrant identity.[56] Hasmita Ramji argued that by way of the East African experiences of British Hindu Gujaratis, 'increased knowledge of the "other" seemed to reinforce an idea of who they were'.[57]

Without extant membership data (as with the RSS in India), it is difficult to quantify accurately the popularity of the BSS. Chetan Bhatt's claim, that 'It would be difficult to find a Hindu schoolboy who grew up in a major city in Kenya or Uganda in the 1950s or 1960s and did not attend a BSS *shakha* or sporting event of some kind', is hard to substantiate and may be treated as an exaggeration.[58] But for certain sections of the East African Hindu population, the Sangh was unquestionably a significant part of their lives.

Dhiraj Shah, a Birmingham pharmacist and senior leader of the HSS (President since 2008), spoke of the East African context in more personal terms in an interview. Born in 1950 in Mombasa, Shah attended *shakha* from the age of six or seven; 'Most of my friends were neighbours or people who I had met through *shakha*, every day we would go to *shakha* for an hour'.[59] Shastri also describes the rapid expansion of the Sangh in East Africa. Within ten years of the establishment of the first *shakha* in 1947, he claims that 'there were *shakhas* in all the major towns of Kenya and in all the major cities of East Africa'.[60] He adds, optimistically, 'Within a period of twenty years Hindu society had turned into a close, well-knit community in these countries'.[61]

This was to transform dramatically. The exodus of Asians from East Africa from the late 1960s was striking in scale and speed. In 1969, there were approximately 363,000 South Asians in East Africa;[62] by 1984, there were just 85,000.[63] The majority of those left during a four-year period, between 1968 and 1972. The newly independent nations pushed out their Asian populations under varying degrees of coercion. In Kenya laws were brought in to exclude Asians from public offices and to introduce considerable obstacles to trade. As well as legislative impediments, Asians increasingly faced more quotidian forms of hostility. In Tanzania, Julius Nyerere's programme of African socialism and *ujamaa* (oneness) also encouraged mass Asian emigration. Dar-es-Salaam, a city once dominated by its Indian population, underwent a striking demographic shift: in 1960, Asians comprised 29% of its population, but by 1969 they were just 11%.[64] The Ugandan process of Africanisation was even more dramatic and notorious. Unsatisfied with measures taken by his predecessor, Milton Obote, President Idi Amin implemented a draconian expulsion, and in August 1972 Uganda's Asian population were given just ninety days to leave the country.

Many East African Asians had UK citizenship as British imperial subjects, and under the British Nationality Act (1948) had a right to enter and reside in the UK. This was restricted by increasingly obstructive and racialist legislation, including the Commonwealth Immigrants Act (1962, 1968), and Immigration Act (1971). Possession of British passports no longer guaranteed a right to settle in the United Kingdom.[65] These legislative developments both reflected and contributed towards growing anti-immigration sentiment, exemplified by Enoch Powell's infamous 1968 'Rivers of Blood' speech. The East African Asians who did manage to secure entry settled in geographical concentrations that reflected their population densities in Africa. This caused considerable concern amongst certain local authorities. In 1972, Leicester City Council—which now celebrates the significant contributions that East African Asians have made to the region—issued a notice in the *Uganda Argus* newspaper attempting to discourage prospective immigrants, warning them that there were no jobs or housing available. The British government also attempted to implement a policy of dispersal from areas that already had high immigrant populations and pressure on employment, housing, schools, and social services. Despite this, East African Asians settled particularly around Leicester, Birmingham, and London (and within those cities, in concentrated areas). Much like the chain migration processes that had taken them or their ancestors to East Africa, the new refugees gravitated towards conurbations in which they already had kinship connections.

While the full context of this exodus is beyond the scope of this book, its consequences fall squarely within it. It is impossible to definitively gauge the proportion of Hindus in East Africa who were involved in Sangh activities. But what is certain is that the genealogy of the Hindu nationalist movement in Britain, to a very large extent, is indelibly East African Asian.

The establishment of the Sangh in Britain

The emigration of tens of thousands of East African Asians to Britain had a significant and enduring impact on the constituency of Britain's Indian population. The exodus was also a defining moment in the history of Hinduism and Hindu nationalism in the West. A substantial proportion of British Hindus are of East African origin.[66] By 1971 there were 44,860 South Asians in Britain with East African origins. Including progeny, their number rose dramatically to 181,321 by 1981; by 1991, this figure had leaped 72.2% to 312,155.[67] The Ugandan exodus alone led to around 29,000 settling in Britain in a matter of weeks, with nearly as many having already emigrated in the preceding three years.[68]

The proportion of British Sangh adherents with roots in East Africa is very significant.[69] Many involved with the Sangh in Britain are of Gujarati origin: Shastri claims that 'Gujarati speaking swayamsevaks form nearly 90% of [HSS] members'.[70] Similarly, a majority of Gujaratis in Britain—perhaps up to 70%—are of East African origin.[71] The proportion of Hindus was also much higher amongst the Asian migrants from East Africa than that of migrants 'directly' from India.[72]

In the 1960s and 1970s, East African emigration was an important catalyst for the establishment of a wide range of South Asian religious and cultural organisations in Britain, of which the Hindu Swayamsevak Sangh (HSS) was only one.[73] In 1961 there was just one registered Hindu temple in Britain. A decade later, only one more had been constructed, but by 1981 there were twenty-five and by 1991, seventy-eight.[74] Today there are more than 180. This growth, as many observers agree, was to a large degree (although by no means exclusively) thanks to the efforts of East African Asian 'twice-migrants'.[75]

Not only were East African Hindus eager to establish (or transplant) these organisations in Britain, they also had the necessary skills and experience. They were distinctive to the earlier, post-independence wave of migrants who came directly from South Asia, in that 'on the whole they were English-speaking, professionalized, and entrepreneurial, had often accumulated capital, and had no intention of returning to India'.[76] East African Asian 'twice-migrants' had in fact been actively discouraged from returning to India and were acutely aware of their insecure status. But having already experienced expulsion and insecurity, they had an extra incentive to remain closely connected— emotionally, culturally, and personally—with the homeland. This was arguably exacerbated by the British government's reluctance, and often resistance, to furnish the Commonwealth subjects with the citizenship and recognition to which they were entitled. The opposition and racism from British residents with which their move was met provided a further impetus for 'sticking together'.

Furthermore, unlike the more piecemeal migrations of those directly from the subcontinent, East African Asians generally migrated as 'complete, multigenerational family units'— something that had a profound impact on the manner and success of their settlement.[77] Despite their convoluted connection to the homeland, East African Asians became key players in the establishment and maintenance of traditional Indian values in Britain, partly a result of 'the presence of elders and an accepted authority structure'.[78] In addition, they had developed deep-rooted kinship networks, both within tight-knit communities and across the world. Their experiences of segregated socialisation and ability to negotiate life as a minority outside India all contributed towards the rapid establishment of various community organisations and spaces.[79] These factors help to explain why East African Hindus in particular were in a strong position to successfully establish branches of the Sangh in Britain.

Patterns of migration and settlement can be understood through the model of 'mobility capital', coined by Joya Chatterji to explain the 'bundles of assets, competences, or dispositions' possessed and developed by migrants.[80] Parminder Bhachu's characterisation of Sikh East Africans as 'experienced settlers with traditionalistic values' can also be applied to East African Hindus, who possessed both the ability and the inclination to establish religious and community organisations.[81] The following sections, against the backdrop of these migratory profiles and experiences, consider the development of certain identities, ideologies, and institutions amongst Hindu communities in Britain.

Although the Indian population in the UK grew in the wake of the Second World War, expanding considerably from the 1950s, the British wing of the RSS—the Hindu Swayamsevak Sangh (HSS)—was not established until the second half of the 1960s.[82] According to the HSS, the organisation was founded in London on 2 July 1966 'on the auspicious day of Vyasa Purnima'—one of six main national *utsavs* (festivals) celebrated by the RSS.[83] The significance of the East African context to the development of the Sangh in Britain can hardly be overestimated. However, there were also significant influences directly from India, and some of the most proactive pioneers of the HSS were young men who had been involved in Hindutva organisations in India before moving to Britain to study or work.

Two other Hindu nationalist groups were started before *shakhas* were conducted in a formal sense. In 1964, the Overseas Bharatiya Jana Sangh was founded, with the intention to connect Indian Hindu nationalist politicians to counterparts in Britain. The following year, Naresh Arora, a young law student who had recently moved to London from India, began the Bharatiya Yuvak Sangh—a group for young Hindu men that would host various get-togethers, celebrate festivals, organise talks and 'variety shows', produce a newsletter, and arrange coach trips to the countryside and seaside towns.[84]

By the summer of 1966 a decision was made to start RSS meetings in Britain. The first 'planned formal meeting of Sangh workers abroad', on 14 August 1966, was chaired by none other than Atal Behari Vajpayee, who happened to be in London. A photograph of the occasion shows around thirty men sitting on the lawn of a suburban garden, at the West London home of Kulwant Chaggar—a *swayamsevak* who had recently moved from Nairobi to London. Vajpayee is seen seated on a chair in front of the men, next to a framed portrait of RSS founder K.B. Hedgewar. An account of the meeting shows the degree to which the organisational hierarchies of the Sangh in Britain were linked to headquarters in India:

> Atalji told me in confidence that he knew Shri Satyanarayanji very well from Bangalore and he was the most suitable person to be karyavaha [secretary] of HSS in U.K. But, we had to wait for approval from Man. Madhavrao Muley, Sarkaryavah [general secretary] of RSS at that time. Within two weeks we got the information through Man. Chamanlalji that Shri. M.C. Satyanarayan would be the karyavaha of U.K. It was unanimously decided to have Shri Ramnathji as mukhya shikshak [chief instructor] of London shakha, Shri Kulwant Chhaggar as shikshak and Shri Raman Khatri as gat nayak [group leader].[85]

Shakhas were initially started in West London and Bradford, then shortly afterward in Coventry, Ilford, Leicester, Bolton, Birmingham, and Rugby. At the very beginning, *shakhas* were held in people's homes or outside in public spaces and parks during warmer months, and special events were sometimes held in church or school halls. The importance of developing relationships in the local community, partly as a means to secure a space for meetings, was clear from early on. Amrit Shah, of the Bradford *shakha*, explained that 'Good contacts and relations were maintained with the council, police, members of parliament, other Indian organisations and other non-Indian organisations. This relationship was useful to obtain various schools for *shakhas*.'[86] This dynamic can be understood through Nicholas Van Hear's notion of 'migratory cultural capital'—varying levels of economic, cultural, and social capital, combined with individual and community migratory biographies, that many Indian migrants, especially those from East Africa, possessed.[87]

The HSS provided a cherished space for socialisation and support for recently arrived migrants. This family-like bond would prove particularly important for those displaced from East Africa. Bhupendra Dave remarked that when *swayamsevaks* came over in the late 1960s and 1970s, 'they were looked after and guided by their fellow brothers and sisters in the UK—the Sangh Parivar'.[88] *Shakhas* around the country would also keep in contact with each other: new branches received support and encouragement from more established ones, and occasionally *shakhas* would join forces for special events, sports days, festivals, the visits of Sangh leaders from outside the UK, or simply to bolster numbers if they were dipping too low. Although women are often missing from early accounts of the HSS (and the female equivalent, the Hindu Sevika Samiti, would not be founded in Britain until 1975), it is important to note the role that women played. Dave, involved in the HSS from the very start, stated that: 'As always, all *swayamsevak*'s families, in particular their wives, played a crucial part in cementing family relationship[s] during *utsavs* and coach trips and general supporting Sangh activities'.[89]

The person chosen to first lead the HSS, M.C. Satyanarayana, had connections with the RSS at the very highest level. Upon his death in 2015, aged ninety-one, his obituary recorded that he was 'requested' by Hedgewar himself to start Sangh work in Britain.[90] Satyanarayana was a *swayamsevak* during his student days in Karnataka, and worked his way up to become Karyavaha (Secretary) of the Bangalore district. Moving to London in 1965 to work as a statistician for the International Coffee Organization (a UN body), he quickly set in motion plans to start a Sangh branch in the UK. But while some of the pioneers of the Hindu nationalist movement in Britain had migrated directly from India, a huge proportion of those involved early on were East African Asians.

In a crucial source for understanding diasporic Hindutva, *Hindus Abroad: Dilemma: Dollar or Dharma?*, RSS leader H.V. Seshadri describes asking a gathering of 'important workers' in Britain where they had got involved in the Sangh. Of the group, only eight had begun their relationship with the RSS in India, whilst eighteen responded that they had joined in the UK. Seshadri continues: '"What about the others, the majority here?" I asked. "Made in Kenya", came the loud chorus and up rose 35 hands'. He added:

'I could not help remarking, "whatever may be your 'make', the 'patent' is of Bharat!".'[91]

The East African experiences of those involved in nascent Hindu nationalist groups in Britain constitute a crucial, formative phase—a 'golden hour ... fundamental to the subsequent formation of the Hindutva movement in the UK'.[92] Hasmukh Shah, a prominent HSS and VHP leader in Britain, spoke of his childhood in Kenya in a video made by his son (also an active *swayamsevak*, who has been President of the National Hindu Students Forum):

> I became aware of my Hindu identity at the tender age of eight years, on the *kabbadi* playing field of a Sangh *shakha* in a small town called Nakuru in Kenya ... Daily *shakha* became a catalytic crucible for many of my friends and I, where we inculcated daily Hindu *samskars* (world-views).[93]

A Sangh biography of Ratilal Shah of Bradford, who was born in Kenya in 1942 and began going to *shakha* at the age of ten, also connects the beginning of the HSS in Britain to the migration of East African Hindus.[94] Ratilal's story is not typical, in that after moving to England for higher education in the early 1960s, he returned to Kenya for many years, before eventually settling in Britain only in 1987. His experiences highlight the important kinship networks and stability that Sangh affiliation can provide for those unsettled by migration: 'Once he arrived back in Kenya his Sangh duties never stopped', and later, 'He returned to the UK, London, at the age of the 47 and moved to Bradford where he immediately went back to *shakha*'.[95] Dhiraj D. Shah, the HSS President from 2008, underscores the importance of the East Africa connection, and alludes to patterns of chain migration that have strongly influenced the Sangh and geographies of Hindutva in Britain; 'We would be together all the time and that link has come over here'.[96] Similarly, Dinesh Mistry, writing of a group of friends who arrived in Britain in 1967, stated: 'we were all going to the same *shakha* in Nairobi so we had decided to start a *shakha* in whichever town we settled'.[97]

These examples provide glimpses into the enormous East African influence on the Sangh's development in Britain (and, subsequently, elsewhere in the West). Boosted by the new arrivals, the Hindu nationalist movement rapidly developed. London and the Midlands became epicentres of HSS activities, where a large proportion of Indians had migrated in both the post-independence wave and, later, from East Africa. The Sangh grew quickly over the late 1960s and early 1970s, and on 29 April 1973 the organisation was legally established as a registered charity.[98] Four of the seven founding trustees were from Kenya, with the remaining three from Karnataka, Punjab, and Nagpur (a city in the state of Maharashtra where the RSS was founded and maintains its base). In 1977, Bhide decided to transfer the overseas headquarters of the RSS from Nairobi to Leicester, ushering in the next phase of the Sangh's diasporic development.[99] An RSS account also highlights London's importance, noting that Jagdish Sood, Karyavaha of Kenya, left East Africa at the request of Madhavrao Muley (RSS General Secretary) to settle in London. The British capital was felt to be the best place to mobilise against Indira Gandhi's Congress government: 'His one-room residence became the centre of Sangh activities'.[100] The role played by Hindu nationalist activists in Britain during the Indian Emergency (1975–7) is the focus of Chapter 3.

The role of RSS leaders, pracharaks *and* vistaraks

RSS luminaries were not only important at the beginning of the Sangh's establishment in Britain. Throughout the history of the diasporic Sangh, the visits of senior leaders have been critical to the movement's development and maintenance of continuity with the ideologies and practices of the homeland. The overseas tour of Rajendra Singh in 1995—the first of its kind by a serving Sarsanghchalak—is of particular note. His experiences are documented in depth in *Sarsanghchalak Goes Abroad*, an RSS publication that serves as a crucial source for understanding the global Sangh. Because the pamphlet chronicles speeches, it serves as an illuminating (partial) itinerary of Rajendra Singh's public appointments. Several speeches had proselytising intentions, others more of a co-ordinating role. Table 1.1, which shows Singh's schedule, demonstrates the diverse range of his interactions, covering many parts of the country and speaking to both 'closed' audiences of the Sangh, as well as in more public settings. This is typical of visits from senior Hindu nationalist leaders—seen also, for instance, in Mohan Bhagwat's 2016 tour—showing their desire to promulgate Hindutva and promote the Sangh in the diaspora, and engage with the widest possible cross-section of the Hindu community. Of course this list is not exhaustive, covering only his speeches; photographs also show Singh at a Swaminarayan temple, and we can only speculate about other, more private, appointments.

Table 1.1—Appointments of Rajendra Singh, RSS Sarsanghchalak, during visit to Britain in 1995.[101]

Date	Event	Location
14/4/1995	Guidance on Workers' Responsibility.	Ilford Hindu Centre, East London.
14/4/1995	'Dr Ambedkar', address on the occasion of Dr B.R. Ambedkar's 104th birth anniversary celebration organised by the Friends of India Society International.	Royal National Hotel, London.
15/4/1995	'Guidance to Campers' at the Hindu Sevika Samiti *shibir* (camp).	Phasels Wood scout camp, Hertfordshire.
15/4/1995	'Re-establishment of Hindu Glory'. Address to delegates at UK branch of Vishwa Hindu Parishad.	Bharatiya Vidya Bhawan, London.
17/4/1995	'Historical responsibility of the *Swayamsevak*'. *Dikshant* (guidance) at European Sangh Shibir. 'Role of the Cultural Ambassador'. Lecture at European Sangh Shibir.	Rotterdam, Netherlands.
19/4/1995	'Press Conference'. Hosted by Friends of India Society International.	Institute of Directors, Pall Mall, London.

'VIDESH VIBHAG TO VISHWA VIBHAG AND NOW VISHWA SANGH'

Date	Event	Location
21/4/1995	'Spirit of a World Dharma'. Address at public function.	Bradford.
22/4/1995	'Keshav Pratishthan'. Address on the occasion of inaugurating the central office of the Hindu Swayamsevak Sangh.	Leicester.
22/4/1995	'Rays of Light Spreading from Bharat'. Address at function organised by HSS.	Leicester.
23/4/1995	'Reminder of the New Year's Day Resolution' address.	Preston Manor High School, Brent, London.
24/4/1995	Code of Guidelines of Workers	Stanmore, North London.
24/4/1995	'A Vibrant Society is Adequately Creative'. Address to *swayamsevaks*.	*Madhav Shakha*, Edgware.
24/4/1995	'Guidance to Young Workers'.	Kenton, London.
24/4/1995	'Hinduism—the Third Alternative' address. Hosted by the National Hindu Students Forum.	School of Oriental and African Studies (SOAS), London.

Rajendra Singh's visit signalled a new era in the importance not just of the HSS in the diaspora, but of the diaspora to the RSS. That his successor, K.S. Sudarshan, visited Britain in August 2000, just a few months after becoming the leader of the RSS, signalled that this dynamic was to endure. During this visit hundreds of *swayamsevaks* and *sevikas* travelled from around the country to hear him speak in London, and later he addressed HSS organisers and the *Karya Kari Mandal* (Central Executive Committee). These appointments, as well as 'a public function held in his honour at the famous Swaminarayana Mandir at Neasden, North London', were reported in a *Sangh Sandesh* article.[102]

The breadth of both Singh and Sudarshan's interactions with other divisions of the Sangh Parivar, and even with Hindu groups outside the Sangh, indicated the increasingly diverse permeation of Hindu nationalism in Britain. This was seen again much more recently, with the September 2014 UK visit of Dattatreya Hosabale, the RSS Sahsarakaryavah (Joint General Secretary), which included more than fourteen separate engagements.[103] One of Hosabale's appointments was an HSS-hosted 'interactive event' including 'leaders from over 40 organisations' held at the Swaminarayan temple in Stanmore, North London.[104] Following Hosabale's tour, Priti Patel MP, then the Prime Minister's 'UK Indian Diaspora Champion', wrote to the HSS to congratulate them on hosting Hosabale, heaping praise on the Sangh and emphasising that 'Shri Hosabale plays a very important role in providing top-level ideological and political guidance'.[105]

When Mohan Bhagwat visited Britain in 2016—reportedly his sixth visit since becoming head of the RSS in 2009—he not only met leaders of Hindutva and Hindu groups, but even held a 'breakfast meeting with top business leaders' and Deputy Mayor of London for Business, Rajesh Agrawal.[106] Reports in the Indian press even suggested that Bhagwat would have audiences with Archbishop of Canterbury, Justin Welby, actor Leonardo DiCaprio, Sir Richard Branson, Sir David Attenborough, 'Cambridge and Oxford dons', and 'address a gathering of 10,000 NRIs' for the fiftieth-anniversary celebrations of the HSS. These rumours—none of which seemed to materialise (the meetings with the big stars did not happen, and the HSS gathering was in fact attended by around 2,000)—appeared in an article by Swati Chaturvedi, author of the *I am a Troll* exposé of online Hindutva activists.[107] The claims were subsequently reported very widely across print and digital media. This underlines the extent to which both Hindutva advocates and critics are engaged in a mutually reinforcing process of publicising the achievements and influence (whether real or imagined) of diasporic Hindu nationalism.[108]

Pracharaks have played a significant part in the development and co-ordination of the Hindu nationalist movement abroad, although their contributions have not yet been properly considered by scholars. All senior Sangh leaders are *pracharaks*—described in the RSS constitution as 'full-time workers selected from amongst those devoted workers of high integrity whose mission is to serve the society through the Sangh and who, of their own free will, dedicate themselves to the Cause'.[109] But only a small proportion of *pracharaks* work their way up to achieve senior, 'All-India' executive positions. The vast majority—who number around 2,500 (representing just 1% of all *karyakartas*)—maintain relatively low-profile, but crucial, roles in the institutional structure. Although ostensibly unassuming, they have been referred to as the 'lifeblood' or 'backbone' of the RSS, and 'committed ideologue[s] with excellent organisational and people-management skills'.[110] They do not simply work for the RSS, but are delegated or 'loaned' to various divisions of the Hindu nationalist network. A very large proportion of BJP leaders, for instance, started out as RSS *pracharaks*, often working their way through the student and youth wings of the Sangh Parivar, before becoming Hindu nationalist politicians. This structure ensures, to some degree, a level of ideological consistency and oversight.

The life of a *pracharak* is in many ways modelled on an ascetic: itinerant (as and when required), abstinent and unmarried, and renouncing of material possessions (receiving no salary, but provided with accommodation and vegetarian diet). They were referred to in a 1951 publication as 'apostles of the new movement', and 'as Swami Vivekananda envisaged it, must be men of iron will and steel character, who will become the living embodiments of the spirit of Vedanta and will spread the ideals from space to space'.[111] But their peripatetic nature is far from the withdrawal from the world that is often associated with asceticism; 'They become one with the local languages, customs, dress and food habits and move about as symbols of national union of hearts'.[112]

Despite their transcendental aura, the *pracharak*, or '*Karma Yogi*', is also usually cosmopolitan in certain ways. They are often from urban, middle-class and upper-caste backgrounds, and frequently are both college-educated and English-speaking.[113] An internal account states that 'in the 1940s most *pracharaks* were highly-educated young men who could have made a success of almost any career'.[114] Furthermore, they are worldly insofar as they often travel widely, although during their excursions remain within quite narrow circles, and even display antipathy towards other groups and cultures (for instance, disdain for the 'loose' morals of the West). Therefore, this is a far cry from the cosmopolitanism predicated on 'mutual respect', such as that theorised by Kwame Anthony Appiah.[115]

In relation to India, Andersen and Damle note that the 'real power in the RSS structure resides with the *pracharaks*, who form a communications network outside the "constitutional" system'.[116] Comparable dynamics are at play in the diaspora, and while it has received little academic attention, the significance of dedicated Sangh workers overseas cannot be underestimated. They perform a crucial role in linking the HSS to the mother organisation, enabling the movement to grow abroad, and providing a bridge between the 'first generation' of diaspora Sangh organisers and the new generations who may not have experienced the Indian RSS first-hand. An RSS brochure published in 2010 tells us that 'presently 10 *pracharaks* are sent from Bharat'.[117] The use of the word 'sent' is worth emphasising. Just fifteen years later, a Mumbai-based co-ordinator for international RSS work stated that twenty-five *pracharaks* 'work towards spreading *shakhas* overseas'.[118] The discrepancy may be due to the latter figure including those working on diaspora-related issues from the homeland. Among those based abroad are currently two *pracharaks* based in Britain (Ram Vaidya and Chandra Kant Sharma), and at least four in the United States. Many more visit parts of the world with Indian communities on a short-term basis.

In Britain, the *pracharaks* are based at the HSS *Kendriya Karyalaya* (central office) in Leicester, which serves as a residence as well as operational headquarters for the HSS.[119] The office itself, named Keshav Pratishthan after the RSS's founder, resulted from co-ordinated efforts between Britain and India. In 1995, Sarsanghchalak Rajendra Singh officially inaugurated the office during his UK visit. He noted the importance of its central location 'in the Hindu bazar', adding that 'our workers had been trying to have this office set up for some years'.[120] Keshav Pratishthan also functions as a communications hub: Singh noted in his visit that it must 'maintain constant link with Bharat' to 'facilitate contacts of Bharat with the outside world'.[121] This highlights the multidirectional nature of the HSS-RSS relationship, with instruction and support from India, as well as 'reporting back' from the diaspora.

Diasporic *pracharaks* in Britain are far from rooted to Leicester. They have much broader territorial responsibilities, spending considerable time travelling around Britain and overseas to co-ordinate the Sangh and propagate Hindutva. This itinerant lifestyle, and the ostensible lack of income or fixed address, is widely spoken about, adding to the *pracharaks*' renunciant, monkish personae. Their magnetism and ability to attract new followers has given them particular currency as the movement has expanded abroad; 'many *pracharaks* ... came to be regarded as *gurus* by the *swayamsevaks* of the *shakhas* which they directed'.[122]

Ram Vaidya is the principal RSS *pracharak* in both Britain and continental Europe. The son of one of the RSS's senior-most leaders, Manmohan Vaidya, he moved to Britain in 1999 from Nagpur, the Maharashtrian nerve-centre of the RSS.[123] The 2006 'HSS Trustees Report' refers to him as a 'full time Sangh Preacher (Pracharak)',[124] and the 2011 report states, 'HSS (UK) wishes to acknowledge and appreciate Dr Ram Vaidya's contribution, for the past ten years, in the promotion of Sangh work in the UK'.[125] AWAAZ reports that he was 'sent' to work for the HSS from the RSS in Nagpur, 'to evaluate the operations and structure of the HSS UK, and to expand HSS work in Europe, including co-ordination of European annual training camps'.[126]

Pracharaks are not simply a means to spread the methods of the Sangh *out* of India, but also provide a conduit for reporting *back* from the diaspora. As was noted in relation to India, the *pracharak* is 'appointed and controlled strictly from the top'.[127] The significance of this 'back to India' flow will be brought out in the chapters that follow. These networks are maintained increasingly with the use of new technologies. *Pracharaks* today, including those at the very top, are adept at exploiting the potential of email, WhatsApp groups, and a wide range of social media.

In spite of the influential role played by *pracharaks* and Sangh leaders, and the respect accorded to them, the movement is ostensibly without hierarchy: 'There is no distinction between a "*swayamsevak*" and a "leader" in Sangh. All of us are *swayamsevaks* and are therefore equal... This is in fact the secret of the remarkable growth of the Sangh.'[128] Hedgewar cautioned that 'no man, including himself, should be honoured as the embodiment of the RSS'—it is the saffron flag, and by extension the nation itself, that must be the focus of devotion.[129] This ethos relates to broader goals of Hindu unity. The RSS constitution states 'All such walls of separation as untouchability, casteism, social discrimination, provincialism, linguism, etc. are automatically washed away by this all powerful current of Hindu unity [in the Sangh]'.[130] This emphasis against hierarchy (and, to an extent, the state), and particularly the lack of dependence on a central leader—in spite of the reverence for Hedgewar ('Doctorji') and Golwalkar ('Guruji')—are core reasons why some have been wary to term Hindutva 'fascist'.[131] Furthermore, as a political force, it has largely operated through electoral democratic structures (leading Jaffrelot to frame contemporary India under the BJP as 'electoral authoritarianism' and an 'ethnic democracy').[132] But many others have argued that it is appropriate to understand contemporary Hindutva through the lens of fascism, even if it is distinctive from European totalitarianisms.[133] Others see parallels with right-wing extremism or even fundamentalism as more apposite.[134] Setting this question to one side, while there is no doubt that certain leaders are revered (and, at the political level, Modi's concentration of power and cult of personality is disquieting for both those outside and many within the Sangh Parivar), there remains an undeniable level of solidarity within the Sangh itself.

In a discussion with Vaidya in 2014, the UK *pracharak* referred to 'family values' and emphasised that 'everyone is equal'. He noted that whilst senior members may have more knowledge and therefore authority, there was no superiority *per se*. Although the rhetoric of egalitarianism must not be taken uncritically, time spent with Hindu nationalist groups does support Vaidya's claims. In London, I was surprised by the informality and relative lack of deference shown by younger *swayamsevaks* towards the esteemed *pracharak*—high-fiving and back-slapping, rather than the feet-touching and *pranaam* that one might have expected. During the *shakha* itself, his role was identical to the most inexperienced of *swayamsevaks*, standing in line for the flag ceremony and sitting on the floor during the *bauddhik* (discussion), which took place in a large circle.

These observations might support the idea that while the *pracharak* is a crucial role for the functioning of the RSS, it is often a position of neither significant power nor glamour.[135] But there may also be a dimension specific to the role in the Indian diaspora. Cultural and generational differences could perhaps inform the distinct dynamic between British-born youths and the Indian-born *pracharak*. One interviewee with considerable experience of organisational aspects of *shakhas* even suggested that the relationship between organisers from India and England is not always smooth: 'The HSS guys and the RSS guys don't often get along'.[136] The *karyakarta* explained that RSS workers and visiting *swayamsevaks* have a different 'majority group' attitude that grates with some British Hindus, and which is often 'more authoritative [and] much more open about how they don't like Muslims... Whereas HSS will be a little bit more subtle about that'.[137] This alludes to certain cultural distinctions and power dynamics, which give the *pracharaks* a position of different, and in certain ways diminished, influence. Whilst these figures play vital and under-considered roles in the HSS, Basu et al.'s assessment of the *pracharak* as 'the real kingpin of the whole organisation' is an exaggeration in the diaspora.[138]

The comments about differences of perspective also raise another issue: the composition and internal dynamics of Hindutva organisations in the diaspora, vis-à-vis settled and second- or third-generation people of Indian origin, versus those who have moved to the UK relatively recently. There are some suggestions that more passionate advocates of Hindutva are newer migrants, who arrive in Britain having been immersed in the majoritarian political milieu of India (and, by extension, lack the multicultural or cosmopolitan perspectives of more 'experienced' diasporic Indians). Many claimed, for instance, that the unrest in Leicester was partly caused by 'recent migrants to the city [who] hold far right Hindu nationalist views'.[139] This position, of course, somewhat elides the much longer history of diasporic Hindutva that is delineated earlier in this chapter and throughout the book. The hate crime expert Chris Allen (whose appointment to lead Leicester City Council's inquiry into the 2022 disturbances led to strident and co-ordinated outcry from Hindutva groups, and ultimately his withdrawal from the role), suggested that 'blaming outsiders and imported ideologies' is perhaps partly an effort to protect Leicester's reputation for multicultural harmony.[140] The narrative certainly requires more nuance. Hindutva is not simply 'imported' as some kind of ideological baggage; recently arrived migrants may also be more susceptible to the socialisation and other functions that overseas Hindutva groups provide, such as on university campuses and during Hindu festivals. But it is certainly the case that Hindutva—and Hindu and Indian identities and politics more generally—are inflected in new ways by recent émigrés, who play a particular role in 'diasporic' Hindu nationalism.

Also important to the development of the Sangh in Britain are *vistaraks*, young men (or women, in the case of the Sevika Samiti) who dedicate a stretch of their life to the expansion and development of the Sangh. This may be days, weeks, months, or up to one year. The role of a *vistarak* bears a similarity to that of the *pracharak*, with the major distinction being that they commit to a finite period of full-time work. Often deputed to various locations, their focus is specifically Sangh proselytisation and growth (*vistar* means 'expansion' in Hindi).[141] In this sense, the position is directly comparable to the *Khuruj* (proselytising tour) of Tabligh Jamaat followers, or even the missionary activities expected of young Mormon men. One *karyakarta* I spoke with referred to the tenure of a *vistarak* as 'a sabbatical', and HSS has translated the role as 'Voluntary Youth Workers' or 'Outreach Workers'.[142] They have also been framed as a kind of work experience or internship—an adaptation to appeal to younger generations. *Vistaraks* are, however, scarcely mentioned in any scholarly literature, whether on India or the diaspora.[143]

Opening new *shakhas*, or strengthening existing ones, is at the heart of the *vistarak* role.[144] The work is essentially evangelical— the HSS *Guidelines for Vistaraks* states that 'the *vistarak* should try his best to meet as many Hindu families as possible. Our objective is to make them understand our mission (Sanghathan) and win their hearts'.[145] Importantly, the position can have a transnational dimension in the diaspora. This reflects the convention in India, where it is deemed 'essential' that *vistaraks* spend time in regions different from their own.[146] This is important to the imagination of a community: the RSS members are able to conceptualise the nation more broadly, but they also bring themselves and their experiences to other parts of the nation. Expanding this transnationally, we can perhaps see both a symbolic, and an actual, reification of a transnational Hindu *samaj* (society) in the sojourning of *vistaraks*.

The first *vistarak* in Britain was Sharad Shah. A young and active *swayamsevak*, Shah initially arrived in Birmingham from Kenya in 1972 to do his A-levels. Frustrated at the lack of regular *shakhas* in the city and following an RSS youth leadership camp in India, he returned to Birmingham from Kenya in January 1978 to become 'the first UK *vistarak*'.[147] There are currently more than 100 *vistaraks* volunteering in the diaspora.[148] Dijesh, a young *swayamsevak* from Northampton, blogged about his experiences as a *vistarak* in 2010–11, volunteering '24 hours a day, 7 days a week', first in the Midlands and then in New Zealand.[149] Performing *vistarak* duties has also connected communities across Europe, with examples of *swayamsevaks* and *sevikas* travelling throughout the continent.[150] There are also instances of members of the diaspora conducting *vistarak yojana* (tours) in India.[151] Manoj Ladwa—who went on to become an important young leader in the Hindu nationalist movement in Britain—conducted a formative tour of India as a *vistarak*, 'meeting various political, social and administrative leaders and connecting with Bharat in an unprecedented way'.[152] According to HSS leader, Arun Kankani:

> This initiative also paved the way for similar visits by young Sangh *karyakarta[s]* to go on exploratory tour[s] in Bharat. This has added a unique dimension in *vistarak yojana* of Sangh and has been instrumental in shaping the expansion and impact of Sangh in society.[153]

The tours, therefore, do not simply allow the participant to spread influence, but also constitute important experiences for the *vistarak* themselves, which then impacts on the communities to which they return.

The final item of the HSS *Guidelines for Vistaraks* underlines the interconnected nature of the various wings of the Sangh in Britain: '*Vistaraks* should have basic knowledge about the sangh parivaar [*sic*], FISI, BJP, NHSF, SEWA, KAT, VHP and Hinduism'.[154] This is particularly relevant as *vistaraks* can be 'deputised' to other sections of the Sangh Parivar, both in India and abroad.[155] In India, large numbers of *vistaraks* are deployed to support political campaigns of the BJP and the Bharatiya Janata Yuva Morcha (Indian People's Youth Front), the BJP's youth wing.[156] In Britain, Bhatt claims that in the National Hindu Students Forum, which he describes as 'a key RSS project', 'about half of its central executive are RSS members or younger RSS officers (*vistaraks*)'.[157]

Some distinctions between RSS and diasporic *vistaraks* should be noted. In particular, the tenure of a *vistarak* in India often serves as a probationary period for a more permanent role as *pracharak*.[158] In the diaspora, the *vistarak* role has a different emphasis, and in my entire research only one source (a newspaper) ever mentioned 'NRI' *pracharaks*.[159] Often, *vistarak* roles appear to be taken by young adults, commonly as a sort of 'gap year' (even though the duration may be only a few weeks). Nonetheless, their emphasis on the expansion of the HSS and establishment of *shakhas*, which is at the very core of the RSS's mission, remains the same globally. Whereas the small number of overseas *pracharaks* provide a direct link to the HSS's 'mother organisation'—vital for both the homeland 'headquarters' and the diasporic wings—the role of *vistaraks* is distinct. Although some proselytical duties are similar, the *vistarak* role has particular significance; as second- or third-generation migrants, they can provide a level of engagement with their diaspora-raised peers that the Indian-born *pracharaks* are unable to achieve.

II—Shakhas in Britain: continuities, co-ordination, and adaptation

Sangh meetings are one of the key vehicles for the development of Hindu nationalism in the diaspora. But how and why is the *shakha* format meaningful and appealing for Indians overseas? What are the international *shakhas'* similarities and differences with their Indian equivalents, and what are their layered functions and meanings? While many underlying elements of the RSS's Hindutva ideology are conveyed through the *shakha* format in Britain, in certain areas the HSS depart from traditional practices.

The *shakha* has been the chief means of growth, organisation, activity, ideological inculcation, and training for the Sangh. With no formal membership process or data, the only measure of the RSS's size is the *shakha*. If you regularly attend one, you are a *swayamsevak*. Underlining the importance of the meetings for the identity of its members, an RSS directive states, 'The Shakha, in fact, is not an end in itself, but just a means to achieve the end, which in brief is social transformation… Thus, through the instrumentality of the Shakha, men are moulded, and they in turn enter varied social fields to ennoble them with Hindu fervour.'[160]

In India, *shakha* is usually a daily activity, either in the early morning or evening, taking place outdoors. All participants are male. Although they vary in age, there is an emphasis on young men. In the diaspora, mixed-age socialisation is striking, although *shakhas* subdivide into different age groups for certain activities. While there are proportionately fewer older *swayamsevaks*, those who remain tend to progress through a byzantine series of ranks and responsibilities. The relatively smaller number of older *swayamsevaks* is due to a high dropout rate—games and peer socialisation elements appeal more to younger members (and their parents, who are usually responsible for getting them to attend in the first place). Time constraints of work and family life, as well as simply 'growing out' of the *shakha* (as with members of the Boy Scouts, and other such groups), means that numbers tail off amongst older demographics.

The programme of each *shakha* is carefully choreographed, routine, and consistent. It begins with the hoisting of the saffron flag, which members salute whilst a Sanskrit *prarthana* (prayer) is recited.[161] The *swayamsevaks* perform the entire ceremony, known as *Achar Paddhati* (correct system), in regimented lines, with certain members performing specific roles. The ritual is repeated at the close of the session.

Shakha is reminiscent of military or cadet corps drill, and this is not a coincidence.[162] There is also a direct influence from the colonial police and, many have argued, fascist youth groups of mid-twentieth-century Europe.[163] Various games and exercises follow the flag ceremony: *lathi* (a bamboo stave) training, *kabaddi* (a contact sport, favoured by the Sangh over other 'non-indigenous' recreations) and other games, yoga, the singing of patriotic songs, and *bauddhik*—a philosophical, moral, historical, economic, and political discussion. Physical games have always been seen by Sangh leaders as a hugely important part of the RSS shakha, creating 'joyous carmaderie [sic] and fervour'.[164] Golwalkar even claimed that 'Kabaddi sums up our whole training'.[165] Each *shakha*, lasting approximately one hour, closes with another flag ceremony and the Sangh *prarthana*, 'Namaste Sada Vatsale Matrubhoomi' (Hail to Thee O Motherland). But this daily hour is not meant to be isolated; 'the RSS work is our duty for the other 23 hours'.[166]

In Britain as in India, *shakhas* have been at the core of the HSS modus operandi since the outset. In certain ways diasporic the overseas meetings are indistinguishable from those in India, but in other ways they are highly distinctive and 'vernacularised'. Just as the RSS prioritised expansion between 1925 and 1948, the HSS 'gave absolute priority to multiplying the number of *shakhas*' in their early years.[167] In their Trust Deed, the HSS lay out five 'programmes ... to advance Hindu religion and to educate the public in the Hindu ideals and way of life'.[168] The first two relate to *shakhas*:

a) Set up branches or units (shakhas) where Hindus of the UK could congregate on the basis of their dharma.
b) Provide facilities for training of mind and body and develop good character.[169]

Trustees' annual reports, submitted to the Charity Commission (along with financial statements), contain substantial data on the HSS. While much of this is hard to corroborate, and therefore needs to be treated with caution, they provide a wide range of revealing information on Hindu nationalism in Britain that warrants scrutiny.

Attendance figures and financial numbers show that while the HSS is by no means a ubiquitous organisation for Britain's Hindu community, it is a popular group with a stable, perhaps growing, membership. In 2021, they claimed that 82 *shakhas* were operating in Britain, with an average weekly attendance of 1,903. Since 2005, the average number of *shakhas* has been 67 and average weekly attendance has been 1,537. Although their reports claim that between 2005 and 2021, the number of towns that the Sangh operates in increased from 33 to 82, this might be down to a different method of enumeration (e.g. urban areas or boroughs rather than separate cities and towns). Between 2009 and 2016, the number of *Bala Gokulams* (groups for young children), grew from 4 to 33, but then went down to 22 in 2020. For comparison, in the United States—which has the most extensive Sangh network outside India—there are 222 *shakhas* in 166 cities across 32 states, with an average weekly attendance of 8,880.[170] In financial terms, the gross annual income for the Hindu Swayamsevak Sangh UK, on average across the years 2007–20, is £338,791.[171]

These figures suggest, until 2014, a mix of moderate growth (in terms of attendance) and stagnation or slight decline (in terms of number of *shakhas*, turnout at camps, and income). Since 2014, the figures provided by the Sangh indicate more noticeable growth. The increased popularity of the HSS may be related to the wider acceptance and attraction of Hindu nationalism both in India and overseas, but also linked to the growing diaspora. The election of Modi, and his wide travels across the world, which are met by enthusiastic crowds of NRIs, has removed certain stigma and increased institutional capabilities. Hindu nationalism today is now essentially 'mainstreamed'.

But in spite of the recent growth, numbers in the past have plateaued (or, at best, grown at the same rate as the Hindu population).[172] Drop-out rates in the HSS (as with the RSS) are a well-established problem for the Sangh leadership. Anecdotal evidence, based on a wide range of informal conversations, suggests that many Hindus and Indians in Britain had not even heard of the organisation—Indian politics has little place in the lives of many diasporic South Asians. Many *shakhas* struggle with numbers:

people have told me that many are attended by fewer than ten *swayamsevaks*. We also need to note that the figures in Table 1.2 are those given by the Sangh, and are not necessarily reliable.

Table 1.2—Hindu Swayamsevak Sangh figures for 2005–21[173]

Year (ending in March)	Number of shakhas	Number of towns	Average total weekly attendance across all branches	Swayam-sevak Annual Training Course (SSV) attendance	Sevika Samiti Annual Training Course (SSV) attendance
2005	62	33	1,090	216	112
2006	62	33	1,100	238	112
2007	64	35	1,100	205	120
2008	60	32	1,100	200	107
2009	63	32	1,150	191	114
2010	59	40	1,200	203	95
2011	61	41	1,350	173	111
2012	59	39	1,325	172	107
2013	56	39	1,400	172	80
2014	52	41	1,325	153	80
2015	74	47	1,700	186	84
2016	78	47	1,850	175	80
2017	78[i]	68	2,050	1,910[iv]	
2018	79	66	2,350	258[v]	
2019	82	82	2,200	208	112
2020	77	85[ii]	2,303	396[v]	
2021	82	82	1,903[iii]	N/A	N/A

[i] From the 2017 report onwards, the number of shakhas is disaggregated between male and female shakhas (with the former being more numerous). From 2017, therefore, the table states the total number.

[ii] The reason why it is possible that there are more towns than *shakhas* is that there are also *balagokulams* (children's play-groups) that are not enumerated in the table above. In 2020, it was stated that there was a total of 26 of these groups.

[iii] The drop in attendance was attributed to *shakhas* being moved to an online format, due to the Covid-19 pandemic. The residential annual training course was also cancelled but 'an alternative online programme' was attended by 'about 250 young children aged between the ages of 12 to 16', and 'some 80 odd senior members'.

[iv] 2016 marked the fiftieth anniversary of the HSS in Britain, and an enormous camp for both male *swayamsevaks* and female *sevikas* was organised—the 'Sanskriti Maha Shibir'—apparently in place of the training camps.

[v] The SSV training camps in 2017 and in 2019 (documented in the subsequent years' reports) were attended by both male and female participants.

Synchronicity and divergence from the Indian model of shakhas

The remainder of this chapter considers the relationship between diaspora Hindu nationalism and the Sangh of the homeland, the reasons for layers of synchronicity and divergence, and why Hindutva appeals to migrant communities. Some scholars, including Chetan Bhatt and Parita Mukta, argue for high levels of coherence and co-ordination between diasporic Hindutva organisations and the Indian Sangh. Similarly, Jaffrelot and Therwath propose that 'In short, the overseas components of the *Sangh Parivar* look for their material and ideological leadership nowhere but in the motherland.'[174] Zavos, in slight contrast, recognises direct inspiration and close ties on some levels, but contends that the HSS 'exist as independent administrative structures [from the RSS]'.[175] While there is truth in both perspectives, a more detailed analysis of the relationship, and the degree of facsimile, is needed.

On a superficial level, the British *shakha* has many similarities to those in India. The flag-raising ceremony, the nomenclature, the organisational hierarchies, many of the games and songs, and various other aspects are all congruous with RSS meetings. A glance at an annual report of the HSS shows identical administrative structures, with the same Sanskritised names for office holders: Karyawaha (Secretary), Bauddhik Pramukh (Director of Educational/Intellectual Activities), Nidhi Pramukh (Treasurer), and so on. Symmetry with Indian Sangh activities reflects the importance placed on mimesis within India as well. BJP leader K.R. Malkani emphasised that 'Doing the same exercises, singing the same songs,

listening to the same *bauddhiks* they came to think and feel alike...
One *swayamsevak* would feel at home in the company of another
swayamsevak even if he did not always understand his language'.[176]
This 'deliberate conditioning' can also be expanded to include
diasporic *swayamsevaks*.[177] But it must be noted that the image of the
Sangh as a well-oiled, entirely synchronised movement has clear
propaganda purposes; in actual fact *shakhas* can be rather more
haphazard and less co-ordinated than often presented. Attendance
can be patchy and discipline not always maintained in ways that
might be expected or desired.

In conversations with *shakha* leaders and *pracharaks*, many of
the same themes and phraseology relating to identity emerge;
they speak of nurturing 'core' and 'traditional' values and
'character building'. One told me that the HSS format is 'pretty
much identical' to that of the RSS. A Canadian HSS document,
in reference to the RSS and HSS, states: 'Same Goal, Vision,
Ideals. Same Prarthana, Same Geet. Same Achaar-Paddhati.
Same "Utsav". Similar Operation. Same Structure One "Guru"
(Bhagwa Dhwaj). Still believe in plurality.'[178] The document—a
PowerPoint slideshow—shows images of *swayamsevaks* from across
the world: from Britain to Canada, Guyana to India. The sense that
other volunteers, miles or even time zones apart, are conducting
an identical activity, has affective potency. Whilst we can only
speculate about the context in which the slideshow was used, it
points to the symbolic power of *shakha*, which forges a connection
with India, an imagined past, and an emergent global Hindu *samaj*.
This is taken to an extreme in the form of the 'cyber-*shakha*' and
'e-*shakha*'—innovative online developments (when first launched
in 1999 and 2008, respectively) through which *swayamsevaks* in
multiple time-zones co-ordinate group meetings through video-
conferencing technology and a file-sharing platform.[179] This kind
of proto-Zoom format was rolled out much more widely during
the Covid-19 pandemic.

Diasporic *shakha* conformity with the Indian modus operandi
is the product of a carefully planned and implemented strategy,
operating on multiple levels, as well as less formal, aleatory
encounters. Residential training camps, the focus of Chapter 2,

form a key medium by which synchronicity is achieved. In addition to the presence of *pracharaks* and more sporadic visits by senior RSS leaders, *shakha pravas* (visits) by regional *karyakartas* also helps to maintain the 'systematic standards'.[180] The circulation of literature is also a crucial method of communicating the Sangh's modus operandi. Since the late 1990s the internet has been a key medium, and space, for both the HSS and the global promulgation of Hindutva more generally.[181]

Various publications, produced in India and increasingly overseas, have supported *shakhas* in numerous ways. The Hindi volume *Aao Khelen Khel* (Come Play Games), for instance, is a pamphlet containing hundreds of *shakha* games and their rules.[182] The HSS in Britain produced a similar volume in PDF format for easy and wide circulation.[183] Many of the games found within are identical: *kabbadi, kho-kho,* and *Ram Raja Raaavan*. Other important PDFs in circulation include a Kenyan *Sangh Geet* book—116 pages of Hindutva songs, transliterated into the Roman alphabet, 'specially for those who cannot read Devanaagari'—and an eight-page document on *Achar Paddhati*, produced by the American HSS, which explains, in precise detail, the terminology, choreography, and methodology of the *shakha* ceremonies.[184] A twenty-minute YouTube video in English, apparently for a diasporic audience, also shows how to conduct the *Achar Paddhati*.[185] It features an introduction by Mohan Baghwat, serving as an interesting parallel to earlier periods during which tours in-person were the only way to have a comparable level of senior co-ordination.

Adaptation of the HSS

Yet despite these methods of producing conformity with the RSS, the parallels have been over-emphasised. This is particularly a consequence of those who have sought to demonstrate dangerous links to the Sangh in India, but it also reflects the Indian Sangh's effort to present the HSS as reflecting their global status. In fact, however, there are many examples of HSS *shakhas* adapting to diasporic environments.[186] In East Africa, Shastri notes that 'BSS was not officially affiliated with RSS, because in Kenya we followed an independent *karya paddhati* (working methodology) which was better suited to the East African situation, legally correct and acceptable in a foreign land'.[187] A similar proviso is sometimes given for the Sangh in Britain.

In addition to innovation and difference, there are also pressures to gloss over the links between various elements of the Sangh family. In Britain, the HSS is frequently distanced from the RSS, and its leaders emphasise a lack of formal linkages.[188] The HSS is often described as 'RSS-inspired', or 'separate but [with the] same core values', which obscures the organisational hierarchies, connected to India, through which the British charity is run.[189] It is rare that references to this separateness elucidate the important and dynamic ways in which the Sangh has developed idiosyncratically in the diaspora, adapting to the circumstances of overseas Hindus. This is also obfuscated by scholarly narratives infused with a common, but problematic, preoccupation with framing diaspora cultural and religious practices in crude terms of 'transplanted' or 'imported' ideologies and organisations.

One example, though, was recently expressed by Arun Kankani, whose experience spans the Indian, British, and American wings of the Sangh. He explicitly emphasised the importance of innovation to diaspora Hindu nationalism:

> One either grows or decays—status quo is not possible in the life of an individual or organization... Innovation is a must for any commercial corporation in changing time. It is true for non-profits too. Carefully encouraging innovation in a safe environment has been in the Sangh DNA which has helped in Sangh growth all over the world. UK can take pride that it has not only kept the tradition but took it to new heights.[190]

Adaptation is not just the product of the HSS's organic trajectory, but is sanctioned from the highest echelons of the RSS. While in Britain in 1995, the RSS's Supreme Leader, Rajendra Singh, told Sangh workers, 'The *shakha* system can be altered according to the requirements of the local situation. But while making such changes, we should not lose sight of our direction and our basic principles.'[191]

Language is a key element of difference between the RSS and the HSS. While the flag ceremony involves the same terminology of the Sangh, and certain songs are sung in Sanskrit or Hindi (often with the help of transliterated 'hymn-sheets'), the lingua franca of most *shakha* activities is English.[192] Similarly, when senior Hindu nationalist leaders visit from India, they usually make efforts to speak in English at public events.[193]

Another notable distinction is the uniform, or comparative lack thereof, found in diaspora *shakhas*. *Swayamsevaks* at regular meetings wear casual clothes—a contrast to the famous, pseudo-military khaki shorts or trousers that are mandated by the Indian RSS (although not in fact always adhered to). At larger, more public meetings—and during certain events and parades—the Indian RSS members must wear the khaki shorts/trousers with a white shirt and black cap, whereas British *swayamsevaks* dress in simple black trousers and white shirts. The bamboo staff (*lathi*) which is frequently carried by RSS members when in full uniform— and forms an important part of their martial training—is rarely seen in the diaspora. Bhatt notes that 'when a *shakha* does take place in uniform ("full *ganvesh*") this is a matter of great pride among organisers'.[194]

There are several other, important contrasts, however. British meetings occur only once a week, in contrast to the more demanding daily *shakhas* in India. In India, *shakhas* are usually held outdoors on open ground and in parks, whereas the HSS hold their meetings inside community centres, sports centres, or schools (for which there are sometimes hire charges). This is one reason why British meetings are held weekly, although more common reasons given point to busier lifestyles in the West and other logistical issues.[195] For instance, Shastri mentions a meeting in August 1966, at which *karykartas* agreed that 'daily *shakhas* in England was not possible because of the long distances and the pace of life there'.[196] But this reasoning is partly to save face. In fact, there is a diminished appetite for *shakhas*, and increased competition with a wide range of other social activities; attendance can drop to single figures, even when only meeting weekly. This is different to the East African situation, where daily *shakhas* used to be held, and India, where, in certain more remote areas, '*shakhas* provide practically the only source of recreation, leisure-time socialisation, and intellectual training'.[197]

Whilst the aforementioned HSS games book in many ways serves to replicate the RSS modus operandi in Britain, a quick glance indicates some significant differences. The emergence of the PDF format is a clear departure from the cheaply published Indian pamphlet, and prominently placed at the front of the document is a page on 'Health and Safety in *Shakha*'. Football is also included—it is one of the most popular games at British *shakhas* and often a major draw for younger *swayamsevaks* (many of whom have limited interest in the ideological or cultural dimension of the Sangh). This is a clear divergence from the RSS in India, where 'indigenous' games are emphasised. Golwalkar once even chastised Nehru, and other Indians, for playing cricket—'[proof] that the English are still dominating our mind and intellect'.[198] The contradiction between the eschewing of 'Western' games but having a daily ceremony and uniform that directly imitates the colonial police and military is palpable.

At a *shakha* I attended, one game involved leaping over a gap marked out on the floor while calling out the name of a different deity each time—a game that combined the pedagogical and cultural element with the physical (and was quite a challenge for many). Another game tasked teams of four to cross the length of the hall without touching the floor, but with the aid of two chairs, a task requiring good communication and co-operation, and reminiscent of corporate 'team-building' exercises.

Perhaps the most significant departure, however, is the heterosociality of the HSS. Coeducational elements to *shakhas* are common in Britain and elsewhere in the Indian diaspora. Unlike their entirely segregated counterparts in India, in Britain the Hindu Swayamsevak Sangh and its female equivalent, the Hindu Sevika Samiti (Hindu Women Volunteers Committee), operate various events with elements of mixed-sex overlap and collaboration.[199]

In India, the Sevika Samiti shares the RSS's philosophy of Hindutva, but it has an important difference in approach, as it promotes substantively different gender roles. The Hindu nationalist movement has an ambivalent position on gender norms. On one hand, the Sevika Samiti fosters *nari shakti* (woman power) and a 'feminization of violence'; on the other hand, the Sangh promotes the patriarchal notion of *matruvat paradareshu*—all women, except one's wife, are to be treated as one's mother.[200] These distinctions between the Hindutva of the Sangh and the Samiti are, to an extent, ironed out in Britain. For the purposes of the Charity Commission, the Sevika Samiti and Swayamsevak Sangh are parts of the same organisation, and share the same Charity Commission registration number. Financially they are administered together, with Sevika Samiti costs accounted for in the HSS's annual financial statements. They also have a small subsection on the main HSS website.

More importantly, many *shakha* meetings, *sewa* activities (see Chapter 5), special events, and even certain residential camps (see Chapter 2) involve coeducational elements. At one meeting I attended in east London, *swayamsevak* boys and *sevika* girls met concurrently in different rooms of the same building. However, they convened together, performing the flag ceremony in parallel rows before separating during the middle of the meeting for physical activities. Girls and boys reconvened for the important *bauddhik*, or intellectual tuition, and performed the closing flag ceremony together.

British *shakhas* are sometimes mixed for practical reasons, particularly due to fewer participants and leaders. They are often forced to share a space (such as a hall) which is divided for certain activities. It is even reported that many *shakhas* have mixed games (except the most physical, like *kabbadi*). Whilst summer camps are usually, but not always, run independently, the *sevikas* and *swayamsevaks* do outreach work together, in particular during the annual Sewa Day activities (see Chapter 5). The mixed-gender *bauddhik*—a powerful space for discussions on society, morality, politics, and identity—is a particularly significant adaption of the traditional rubric.[201] While there is a rich literature on the complex and contradictory roles of women in the Hindu nationalist movement in India, the diasporic angle to this clearly demands further investigation.[202]

'Sangh: A Man-Making Mission'[203]

Coeducation in the British Sangh is somewhat surprising, given Hindutva's preoccupation with manliness. In a section of *Bunch of Thoughts* devoted to 'Moulding Men', Golwalkar writes that 'the one mission to which the RSS is wholly and solely dedicated' is to stimulate 'a self-sacrificing and disciplined and virile national manhood'.[204] Although the dilution of the homosociality is significant, the masculine fraternalism of *shakhas* is not discarded in the diasporic context. At a lecture I attended in Leicester, the speaker—an RSS leader—echoed Golwalkar in emphasising the need to make 'Men with capital M'.[205]

The inculcation of machismo through *shakhas* is critical in India, but overseas it has particular resonance and meaning. In India, the RSS propagate the sense that an assertive Hindu masculinity needs to be reclaimed following 'one thousand years of foreign domination'—a Hindutva mantra.[206] Golwalkar was obsessed by weakness and strength; quoting Vivekananda's famous 'I want men with muscles of iron and nerves of steel', in *Bunch of Thoughts*, and proclaiming that 'we alone are responsible for our downfall and unless we eradicate that fatal weakness from ourselves'.[207] To 'rebuild' a population of strong Hindu male figures, largely to countenance (while simultaneously justifying) the threatening construction of the Muslim Other, qualities of tolerance and Gandhian *ahimsa* (non-violence) were increasingly shelved over the second half of the twentieth century, 'in favour of the self-relying hero and militant *ksatriya* values'.[208] The RSS interpretation of physical fitness, therefore, is a manifestation of 'how the body can be construed as a political object in nationalist projects'.[209]

The role of *shakhas* as a space for physical training and self-defence has slightly different, but still significant, connotations in the diaspora setting. At HSS summer camps in the United States, counsellors told Jessica Falcone that the primary aims of physical activities were '[to] toughen the "soft" Hindu kids', and promote 'authentically Hindu' games, drills and dances.[210] The assertive and militant aspects of *shakhas* may have particular resonance for children of migrants, with both real and perceived threats of violence and discrimination.[211] This sentiment was echoed by Bob Blackman, MP for Harrow East, who, in a speech at an HSS training camp in 2014, framed the need for 'self-defence' within the familiar matrix of the 'model minority':

> Hindus are the most law abiding citizens with 0.005% rate of imprisonment. The smallest sector of any identifiable group. They are more likely to be victims of crime rather than perpetrators. So actually when you see young people learning the art of self-defence that is a big deterrent to being victims of crime and there is nothing wrong with defending yourself from aggressors. So that is something to celebrate.[212]

But there is also clearly a distinction; whilst in India, RSS training might be seen to be 'designed to turn the volunteer into a foot soldier in the service of Hindu ideals', involving preparedness for actual communal conflict, in the diaspora, such training has different emphases.[213] One may also add, but not without inviting criticism from various quarters, that the martial training of the HSS (and, perhaps even to an extent, the RSS) is still largely symbolic. Whilst the violence and physicality of the HSS is primarily confined to the *shakha* and *shibirs*, the group unity that the Sangh engenders, within a safe, familiar environment, provides a sense of 'security'.

In the post-9/11, post-7/7 landscape, the 'War on Terror' discourse has played an important part in the 're-masculinization' of Hindu men.[214] In India, the siege mentality against Muslims has no mathematical basis, and is rooted in politics of fear and fallacious 'saffron demography'.[215] But in Britain, Hindus have an actual minority status—not just in relation to the majority population, but also compared to Muslims (and even Pakistanis). The 2021 Census of England and Wales counted 1,032,775 Hindus and 3,868,133 Muslims, with 1,587,819 British residents classifying themselves as ethnically Pakistani, and 1,864,318 identifying as Indian. Feelings of victimisation evoked by the Hindu right, therefore, resonates with Hindus in the West who experience various forms of marginalisation and discrimination, and also perceive themselves to be under threat from, or simply in conflict with, other minorities.[216] This is seen viscerally in ITV's undercover filming of an HSS training camp, in which a participant openly states: 'I hate Muslims. I live in Bradford. I have to hate Muslims... It's full of Pakis. It's terrible.'[217] Romila Thapar has even suggested that, in India, the 'mentality of the ghetto'—the 'danger of the majority from the minority'—is partly influenced by *actual* minorities in the diaspora, creating 'a minority identity of the Hindu within India'.[218]

While scholars have helped illuminate the 'War on Terror' factors to contextualise Sangh popularity in the United States, in Britain there are other dynamics to consider. Two moments in the late 1980s and early 1990s—the Rushdie Affair and repercussions of the Babri Masjid demolition (discussed in Chapter 4)—have been critical.[219] The strength and violence of the Sangh has a direct relationship with more self-reflexive forms of assertiveness; Seshadri addresses Hindus in the West when he writes that, '"aggressive Hinduism" should become the dominant note of their lives', specifically in reference to, 'the right "Hindu image" ... to be projected'.[220] The promotion of physical training, toughness, and group unity also relates to the perception that individualism and material comforts of the West constitute a danger for Hindus.

Culture, values, and the pedagogy of the HSS

Sangh discourse on the diaspora is preoccupied with the deleterious impact that the host society may have on Hindus outside India. Second-generation Hindus overseas are considered particularly susceptible to picking up bad habits from morally bankrupt host societies, and many have discussed the 'disdain' South Asian migrants have for the lax ethics of the West, its declining parental authority, licentiousness, culture of instant gratification, weakening family units, and so on.[221] The HSS has performed a specific role in this context, providing segregated spaces for socialisation away from 'corrupting influences', in which curative 'Indian' values can be transmitted.

While Britain is acknowledged as the 'Karmabhoomi, a land of our economic sustenance', by certain UK-based Hindu nationalist activists, India remains 'Matrubhoomi, the land where we draw our inspiration from, the land where our unique culture evolved'.[222] This source of spiritual benefits is presented 'as providing a righteous path for combatting the social ills associated with Britain'.[223] Dhiraj Shah elaborated on this in 2007:

> I do see dangers for the coming generations. They are under a lot of pressure influence from the host culture, there is a growing culture of one-parent-families and break up of marriages, there are drugs issues which we fear will harm the community in the later years... Efforts are already going for our children to maintain their essential values which have been the keystone to our community's way of life, respect family and elders, things like that.[224]

Immense pride is taken in promoting the 'discipline' of the HSS, both by sections of the Hindu community in Britain and the RSS in India (who see the HSS as playing an ambassadorial role). Seshadri, for instance, said that at the end of the 1984 Hindu Sangam in Bradford, the city's Chief Inspector of Police told HSS leaders: 'I have come here to offer my compliments for the exemplary discipline and self-restraint displayed by your volunteers'.[225] Seshadri even claims that Sangh's 'spirit of discipline and social harmony' was so impressive to the police authorities that they were 'pleading with the *swayamsevaks* to join the police force'.[226] In a similar vein, in relation to deference to elders, I was told by a *pracharak* in Delhi that the RSS/HSS promotion of 'family values' was gaining currency amongst wider publics in the West, who increasingly looked to Indian communities to emulate their respect for the elderly. Whether these accounts are accurate or exaggerated, the feelings of righteousness and influence that they claim is of significance.

Another core value of the Sangh is the submission of the ego. But in the diaspora, where there is a perceived emphasis on individualism, the promotion of selflessness and communitarianism is felt to have especially high value. Swami Tilak, in a 1990 article on the 'contagious disease' and 'obnoxious trend' of Westernisation, wrote: 'they stop going to temples and dislike to participate in the religious and cultural activities. They live with their own world. Dollar is their God, night-clubs their temples and whisky *amritam—soma!*'[227]

However, the *shakha*'s emphasis on comradeship and community is not simply a cushion against the individualism, materialism, and iniquity of the West. It also reflects a perceived need to maintain a strong and reliable group identity in the face of marginalisation. Tight-knit *shakhas*, inspiring discipline and pride, serve as bulwarks against discrimination and cultural condescension.[228]

The homogenised *achar paddhati* is both a symbolic and affective aspect of HSS unity. The procedure, and its standardisation across India and around the world, represents discipline and serves to 'create the spirit of oneness'.[229] Mohan Bhagwat said in a recent video made for American *shakhas*: 'By making *swayamsevaks* streamlined to the same procedure, it also sublimates their egos into a collective ego of the society'.[230] The invented tradition of the flag ceremony not only provides continuity with a 'past', but also a connectivity with India and even a global Hindu *samaj*.[231] Although other aspects of *shakhas* are adapted overseas,[232] the strict maintenance of the rituals that open and close the meetings is of great emotional and institutional significance.

Pedagogy constitutes one of the most significant aspects of *shakhas* for Hindus living in the Indian diaspora. *Shakha* is an important space for British Hindus to learn about, and celebrate, 'homeland' culture. A major thrust to these cerebral elements is to instil self-confidence. For these reasons, the HSS has an accentuated emphasis on young people, constituting an important departure from the RSS's roles. Whilst education is also at the heart of the Hindu nationalist project, the emphasis, angle, and spaces in which this occurs is different overseas. In India, rather than occurring in the *shakha*, education is principally the focus of different branches of the Parivar.[233] On the diasporic emphasis on education, one Hindu leader explains: 'The American Hindu is perpetually concerned that his children are brought up in the Hindu tradition',[234] and American Hindutva writer David Frawley states that 'overseas Hindu are quick to build temples but slow to start schools, though their main complaint is that their children are losing their culture!'[235]

'VIDESH VIBHAG TO VISHWA VIBHAG AND NOW VISHWA SANGH'

The *shakha* has emerged as a key space for cultural instruction for sections of the Hindu diaspora, particularly second and third generations who may not have direct 'access' to India. The thrust of this pedagogy relates directly to the minority experience of Hindus abroad. Hindutva narratives of unity and belonging resonate powerfully in the face of alienation.[236] Vijay Prashad, in his pioneering scholarship on Hindu nationalism in the United States, argues that an important impetus for 'Yankee Hindutva' is that it provides 'a way for migrants to reconstruct their dignity in a racist society. Through their activities, they try to show that Indians have a great culture, one even superior to US culture.'[237]

When I asked Anil Vartak why the RSS gained popularity abroad, his response was that it was a 'Natural feeling. As he grows, he wants to find out who is he... Hindus abroad want to find out about their ancestors and culture'.[238] This illustrates an existential element to the Sangh's pedagogy: Hindu identity as a process of becoming. Partha Chatterjee sees an egocentric history as fundamental to the Hindutva project; 'Ancient glory, present misery: the subject of this entire narrative is "us". The mighty heroes of ancient Indian were "our" ancestors, and the feeble inhabitants of India today are "ourselves".'[239] In different ways, this narrative of struggle and loss speaks to migrant, minority communities. Others have suggested that the cultural thrust of the HSS is also connected to a mitigation of guilt about leaving 'Mother India'.[240]

But the 'invention of tradition' also has practical purposes, for instance equipping Hindu children born abroad with knowledge of Indian culture for return visits to relatives in the homeland. Many Hindu (nationalist) organisations are especially proactive in providing resources for young British Hindus to explain their culture, history, and religion to non-Hindus. The websites of all major groups, for instance, contain material on how to explain basic tenets and traditions of Hinduism.[241] Sangh enculturation, then, is not just a response to parental desires and anxieties of lost identity, but also more practically responding to a need for young people to be able to explain their culture to outsiders. Martha Nussbaum reports that the American HSS leader, Ved Nanda (a professor at Denver Law School), regards the central values of the *shakhas* as cultural: 'Hindus,' he said, 'need to understand their own past and its major texts.'[242] In particular, the Sangh—along with the VHP and other groups—provides standardised and unapologetic responses to 'misunderstood' aspects of Hinduism, from cow worship and arranged marriages, to vegetarianism and the caste system.[243] The 1992 RSS book *Widening Horizons* emphasises, grandiosely, this cultural diplomacy: 'The most significant service rendered by the *swayamsevaks* living abroad is that they, by their word and deed, are recognised as the *real* cultural ambassadors of Bharat in their respective countries.'[244] While this is certainly an exaggeration on many levels, the intent behind the claim is revealing.

The *bauddhik* is the primary vehicle for the transmission of 'Indian' culture and Hindu values within the *shakha*. Whilst this focuses on Hindu culture and history, there is less emphasis on religious or scriptural aspects of Hinduism. But this discourse is less systematic than has been suggested. According to a volunteer who leads these discussions, the *bauddhik* is 'totally ad hoc and totally independent... It's not as systematic or co-ordinated. They are just a group of people who would like to preserve some kind of identity together.'[245] Disheartened, he reported that most people who run *shakhas* are not properly equipped to convey the culture; 'the two or three people who do know their stuff go around the country trying to deliver these *bauddhiks* as much as possible. But they only reach one place every couple months'.[246] On occasion, teachers are also brought in from abroad, to visit camps and larger gatherings, as well as ordinary *shakhas*. The HSS has even been licenced by the Home Office to sponsor 'religious worker' and 'voluntary worker' migrant visas under Tiers 2 and 5 of the Points-Based visa system, registered as a provider of 'Social work activities without accommodation'.[247]

Various other methods of cultural instruction are employed within *shakhas*, including preparation for performances, such as that of the Ramayana play I witnessed during a Sewa Day event in 2012 (see Chapter 5). The pedagogy of the HSS has seen more innovation in the United States, where the HSS recently launched a

'Dharma Bee' contest, building on the huge popularity and success of spelling bees amongst the Indian American population.[248]

Despite these efforts, the impact of Sangh pedagogy is disputed. The *bauddhik* instructor told me: 'what I can gauge about what the kids know, it's always zero. A lot of times they ... don't know things like Rama and Sita are married or ... we're talking like eleven-, twelve-year-olds, not six-year-olds'.[249] Airing his scepticism about the degree of cultural and spiritual knowledge, he said 'it's almost reduced to just "We are Hindus"', adding '[people] don't know their own philosophy but claim to be guardians of it'.

Conclusion

Understanding the establishment of the Sangh overseas is vital to our comprehension of its later global character. The East African history of the Sangh did not just precipitate its development in Britain, but also influenced its meaning and complexion. The Bharatiya Swayamsevak Sangh in Africa and Hindu Swayamsevak Sangh in Britain have provided spaces for first-generation migrants, and their children and grandchildren, to socialise with their peers in an ostensibly wholesome and positive environment. The promotion of homeland culture and values are ways of 'maintaining tradition', as well as antidotes or palliatives to a materialistic, modern, and alien world. But this, perhaps, is a generational impulse, as much as it is rooted in cultural chauvinism. Furthermore, the marginalisation and racism experienced by migrants can be interpreted as leading to 'reactive ethnicisation', 'whereby home country culture and traditions are reaffirmed and acquire a heightened significance as a self-defence mechanism against discrimination'.[250] It is in this context that the promotion of assertive 'manliness' and group unity is especially resonant to the Hindu diaspora. These forces are at once parochial and transnational. Anderson notes that, 'That same metropole that marginalizes and stigmatizes him simultaneously enables him to play, in a flash, on the other side of the planet, national hero'.[251]

However, Anderson's formulation of 'long-distance nationalism' fails to account for the complexities of diasporic Hindutva. It wrongly implies that this phenomenon can be understood as an expression of devotion and patriotism emanating organically from members of diaspora communities. In doing so, it fails to understand the highly choreographed ways in which 'long-distance nationalism' has been cultivated, co-ordinated, and mobilised from the homeland.[252] The Vishwa Vibhag in Delhi, along with a number of pioneering leaders and *pracharaks*, facilitated this co-ordination (in a manner that requires a reappraisal of the primacy of Nagpur and Maharashtra in the governance of the Hindu nationalist movement). But Anderson also fails to delineate the layers of idiosyncrasy that are found in diasporic inflections of ethnic, cultural, and religious nationalisms. These can only be unpicked through a close, multidisciplinary examination of the movement in both the homeland and the diaspora.

Conditions of the Indian diaspora have created a fertile environment for the development of Hindu nationalism. Various dislocations—personal, cultural, social—caused by migration have strengthened nostalgia for 'home', creating a 'nationalist romanticism'.[253] Hindu nationalist organisations (like religious, caste, and other community groups), also provide prestige and leadership positions, which may compensate for the downward social mobility that many experienced upon migrating.[254] The Sangh has facilitated a psychological, educational, and cultural connection to the homeland, deemed of great importance to migrant communities and their children. This is also important in relation to family and kinship networks many still have in India, where the idea of 'losing touch' with the homeland is often stigmatised. The RSS has also provided more tangible connections, organising overseas tours of gurus and Sangh luminaries, and even facilitating return trips for diasporic *swayamsevaks*.

It is helpful, therefore, to understand the HSS through Deepa Reddy's rubric, which argues that 'Hindu transnationalisms need to be treated equally as (quintessentially ethnic) vernacular forms that negotiate local legal, social, moral, and political environments in ways that variously concentrate or dilute their ideological emphases'.[255] Participation in the HSS is only the preserve of a minority of British Hindus, and only one of many responses to marginalisation, racism, and the desire to maintain (or build) homeland values and connections. Many young people involved in the HSS have limited interest in, or even consciousness of, the ideological context for their physical exertions. But for others, the socio-political influence woven into the activities of *shakhas* is a potent force.

2

TRAINING CAMPS AND THE DEVELOPMENT OF A GLOBAL *PARIVAR* (FAMILY)

Training camps play a crucial role in the RSS and perform specific functions for Hindu nationalist adherents overseas. Regular camps, whether in India, Britain, or other parts of the diaspora, are aimed at enthusiastic young *swayamsevaks*, as well as more senior adult leaders. Part of their function is to provide a more immersive and intensive space for many of the elements of *shakhas* considered in the previous chapter. But an even more crucial aspect is to train promising young recruits and the established *karyakartas* (active workers/organisers) in how to conduct *shakhas* and advance the institutions and ideas of the Sangh. They offer a context for leaders—both Indian and overseas—to travel widely, coming into contact with their counterparts around the world, thereby engendering organisational and ideological coherence, and reifying their imagination of a global Hindu community. Through this, camps provide a powerful link—both institutional and emotional—between the diaspora and the homeland.

This chapter considers various types of camps around the world, but pays close attention to two innovative forms of camps developed specifically for the diaspora. The Sangh Internship Programme (SIP) is a creation of the HSS in Britain that represents a major deviation from the Indian *shibir* (camp) format. It is aimed at young male and female adults and focuses on 'leadership' and 'self-improvement', with only limited resemblance to traditional RSS residential training camps. The other dynamic and striking device is the Vishwa Sangh Shibir (World Sangh Camp)—a spectacular gathering that has taken place in India every five years since 1990, drawing participants from the Sangh across the world.

Just as with the *shakhas*, HSS training camps represent varying levels of Sangh mimesis and connectivity, divergence and idiosyncrasy. Unlike regular *shakhas*, however, different types of camps feature differing levels of personnel overlap: from various parts of the world, groups of the RSS family, and levels of the hierarchy. Camps help to standardise and systematise the pedagogical, ideological, and practical content of regular meetings. Not enough attention, however, has been paid to the way in which training camps provide various services, deepening attachment to the Sangh and particular conceptions of Indian and Hindu culture and identity, as well as reifying 'the Hindu community' for a variety of audiences—in ways that have special resonances for members of the Sangh in the diaspora. Camps serve an important social function. But organisationally, the camps provide a crucial connection—instructional and supervisory, but also discursive—between ordinary grassroots members and senior Sangh leadership.

As with the RSS in India, camps formed a central role in the HSS's operations in Britain from the outset. The HSS Trust Deed, filed with the Charity Commission when it registered as a charity in 1974, asserted that to 'organise courses for more intensive training and conduct camps' was one of the key methods by which they hoped to achieve their stated aims 'to advance Hindu Religion (Dharma) and educate the public in the Hindu ideals and way of life'.[1] Camps in Britain were intended to foster a sense of unity and 'strength in numbers', as well as provide a forum through which members could be instructed. The organisers of *shakhas* and training camps in Britain have often attended the RSS-run training camps in India. Many camps, both in Britain and elsewhere, also provide an important opportunity to showcase the organisation, and its ideology, in various ways. Participants and organisers often invite friends and family, as well as internal and external guests, to a public function, known as a *samarop*, at the end of the camps.

But in most senses these camps are highly clandestine. They provide secluded, affective spaces for bonding and networking, and constitute ephemeral enactments of a Hindu *samaj* (society) for the participants. In contrast to the showcasing of 'model minority' qualities seen in HSS camps' public functions, the diaspora *shibirs* also allow for the expression and promotion of less 'diluted' forms of Sangh ideology and rhetoric.

There are two kinds of training provided in camps (although these elements are often taught alongside each other). On one hand, camps instruct in practical, organisational skills: the running of *shakhas*, training sessions, and other activities. This constitutes a key way in which the modus operandi of the Sangh is communicated, and thereby Hindutva is spread. It is analogous to the training and monitoring of franchisees, with the mother organisation using these meetings to supervise the output and concerns of its global emissaries.

On the other hand, camps involve more abstract, character-based training. To a degree, this represents a more intensive and immersive version of what is inculcated in *shakhas*, with the added advantage of being led by the most senior and proficient Sangh leaders. This aspect is emphasised more publicly; a 2015 HSS statement stressed that camps are 'aimed at building character, based on discipline, respect, knowledge and selfless action'.[2] Also crucial to the *shibirs* is the establishment, maintenance, and development of global kinship and organisational networks.

In an address to British *sevikas* during his 1995 European trip, RSS Sarsanghchalak (Supreme Chief) Rajendra Singh underlined the manifest, tangible purposes of the camps and the influence they have. In his 'guidance to campers' he stated: 'Camps are so planned to inspire the participants to be strong. By working together we develop a sense of unity and we forget about our separate identity'.[3] This desire to challenge individualism has particular resonance for Hindutva groups, and South Asian communities more broadly, in the diaspora. A noteworthy Sangh pamphlet on diaspora Hindutva—*Hindus Abroad: Dilemma: Dollar or Dharma?*—is full of diatribes against the materialism, hedonism, and self-interest that have afflicted Hindus overseas.[4] These concerns are, of course, familiar to migrant communities the world over. Through camps, Hindus can, ostensibly, address these issues and find solutions. Sangh leaders have also often emphasised the importance of camps in attenuating sectarian, linguistic, regional, and caste differences. Golwalkar once referred to Indian *shibirs* as 'practical processes of national integration'.[5] Comparably, the diaspora camps provide consolidation for diaspora Hindu communities, and even integrate their cohort into a homeland culture.

As well as addressing moral and social issues, camp leaders convey various practical skills and knowledge. The camps enable the formation of formal and informal networks and the development of organisational strategy, enabling contact amongst emergent, younger cadres from across the country, and between them and the Sangh leadership. This enables a level of centralised, hierarchical co-ordination, which is superficially not visible in the day-to-day running of local *shakhas*. It also helps to dissolve parochialism, fostering a wider, pan-Indian outlook for the participants. For the diaspora, camps in India provide an opportunity for HSS members to have a direct link with the 'mother' organisation, and facilitate encounters with fellow *swayamsevaks* and organisers from all over the world.

The form of the residential training camp in the broadest sense has a variety of origins, from Presbyterian to military. Many influences from and parallels with these other forms can be identified within Sangh *shibirs*. Although the most common connection is made with the Hitler Youth (often in the context of Golwalkar's much-quoted and quarrelled-over praise of Nazi 'race pride'), the links with Mussolini's Opera Nazionale Balilla and Avanguardisti are much more substantive. Hindu Mahasabha leader B.S. Moonje's visits to the meetings and training camps of Italian fascist youth groups in 1931 provided inspiration for his protégé, Hedgewar, and his nascent RSS.[6] Similarities with Robert Baden-Powell's Scout Movement, from the uniform and flag ceremony, to the shared ethos of discipline and unity, are also striking. Although we lack the evidence to know if this had a direct influence on Hedgewar's organisation, the Scout Movement was brought to India in 1909, growing rapidly around the years of the RSS's formation (with particular popularity in Maharashtra).[7] Other important influences for these training camps are *akharas*—including those adopted by the Hindu Mahasabha, and *gurukuls*—including those in the modified form of the Arya Samaj.[8]

Background to training camps

Training camps have been at the core of the RSS's functioning since shortly after its birth in the 1920s. Their central position reflects their indispensable role in the growth of the organisation. At the core of a range of training camps is the *Sangh Shiksha Varg*, originally known as the Officer Training Camp (the influence of the colonial police/military camp is apparent not only in name), but later given a 'more indigenous' title.[9] It can be roughly translated to Sangh Instructor Training Camps. These intensive summer camps, intended for the most committed, more senior members, feature a more intellectual and strategic focus, and produce *mukhya shikshaks* (chief instructors). Also important are camps for *karyakartas* (officers), which host younger trainees rising through the ranks. There is an expectation that *pracharaks* and office bearers attend these camps, and *swayamsevaks* who display potential to be RSS leaders of the future are chosen through a selection process. There are also various subdivisions of camps, with more advanced levels of training only offered to those who have attended other camps and received commendations from their seniors.

Camps have many crucial functions beyond imparting knowledge and instruction on how to conduct *shakhas*. They are also spaces for the inculcation of *samskars*—'values' or good and virtuous behaviour—and a sense of oneness/camaraderie. 'Fired with the vision and trained in the technique,' Golwalkar preached, 'the Swayamsevaks carry forward the torch of this Rashtra Dharma to every nook and corner of the land.'[10] Training camps inculcate ideology, but also enable expansion of the Sangh, as they produce the individuals who are capable of starting new *shakhas*, and in turn training instructors themselves. In addition, they have profile-raising elements, often involving public displays of marching, various performances (such as martial arts), and speeches. In this sense they are both 'morale-boosters' for the organisation and fora for capturing the attention of wider publics in striking, highly choreographed moments.

Residential camps also provide a brief glimpse of a pseudo-utopian society, underlined by harmony, discipline, and, most importantly, unity. The Sangh's vision for an idealised Hindu *samaj* requires organisational efficiency, which is enacted on a micro-level at these camps. It was in this sense that Hedgewar referred to the RSS as the 'Hindu Rashtra in miniature' in his last ever speech, in 1940.[11] The residential camp's prototypical nature is enhanced by the fact that they are 'isolated from the outside world', often in schools over summer holidays, for instance, and are also 'totally self-sufficient'.[12] In this sense, the *shibir* is a 'heterotopian' space, following Foucault's idiom, marking 'the disintegration of society in the state of exception… [T]he situation in which the division between private and public is suspended'.[13] They are not then utopian, in that they are not 'sites with no real space', but are, 'counter-emplacements… sort of effectively realized utopias'.[14] The notion of *shibirs* as heterotopias is explored in depth at the end of this chapter.

Camps are designed to promote a sense of solidarity, and age groups are sometimes mixed to encourage feelings of inclusivity (although certain activities and camps remain age-segregated). A statement on a 2014 camp in Hertfordshire, UK, recorded: 'For nine days everyone stays as one family developing friendship, working together and learning the importance of sharing and embracing simple life skills'.[15] As with scout and cadet corps camps, the participants lionise adversity. Golwalkar specifically emphasised 'the glory of suffering', and accounts of camps in India and overseas frequently draw attention to cold weather, spartan accommodation, and strict regimes, all contributing to the Sangh's 'character building' project. The camps, therefore, are seen to inject a vital toughness into an urbanised, pampered younger generation.

Sangh camps also involve performance: predominantly marching, displays of martial arts, or music and song. In India, this is often very public, featuring parades through the streets and public functions consisting of speeches and pseudo-military drills. In Britain, the 'public' elements are more isolated. Whilst the marching of *swayamsevaks* in India is often intentionally to provoke and intimidate Muslim communities (with routes often carefully mapped through Muslim neighbourhoods[16]), in Britain there is no evidence of comparable practices.

I—The development of Sangh camps in the diaspora

The first formal HSS camp in Britain, for established Sangh members, occurred over a weekend in the summer of 1970, near Rugby in Warwickshire. One of the organisers, recalling the event, underlined the crucial and developmental role that camps play. Dhiraj Shah stated that the camp was planned at the very first HSS annual general meeting in 1968 in order to achieve centralisation and 'so that all *shakhas* then follow certain systematic standards'.[17] Shah recalled that as many as seventy people participated in the camp, including visiting senior Sangh workers from East Africa: 'It was a memorable event and one of the milestones in Sangh history'. Rules for UK *shakhas* were established, crucially, 'on open ground'. As the first chapter showed, this ritual is at the very core of all Sangh activities. For the diaspora, it has an added importance of being a symbolic and nostalgic link to the homeland. The camps therefore enable the HSS to emulate the original format, and thereby bring the organisation, and its members, as close as possible to India itself.

Other forms of national camps were launched in Britain over the 1970s, with the key Sangh Shiksha Vargs—sometimes referred to as residential youth leadership training courses—starting in 1975. These remain an important annual fixture for the most committed *sevikas* and *swayamsevaks*. They usually last between one week and ten days, and comprise a range of physical activities, practical instruction on the running of *shakhas*, and ideological instruction and discourse. Many sources attest to the inspiration, confidence, and energy provided by camps. One report from a camp held in 2008 described it as 'like a spark, which ignites a charge in each one of us to go back to the *Samaj* (society) and glow to make a positive difference'.[18] HSS members also speak of camps as 'reinforcing... Hindu pride', and cultivating their love and dedication for the organisation and fellow members.[19]

Although much of this occurs in private, HSS organisers in Britain and other parts of the diaspora do invite participants' family members, and various other guests from the Hindu community and beyond, to certain functions. These usually consist of speeches, performances, and various choreographed displays, held in hired halls or outdoor spaces, which occur at the culmination of the training camps. Videos and photographs circulated on social media highlight band demonstrations and uniformed marching displays. One Facebook video from a 2012 camp held near Leicester shows dozens of uniformed *swayamsevaks* performing in a military-style marching band. In a decorated sports hall they approach a life-size triptych of Golwalkar, Hedgewar, and Vivekananda, then turn to a seated audience of approximately 100 people. Through posting online, this and similar videos and photographs reach a domestic and global audience of many more.

In private, and to a greater extent than regular *shakhas*, camps provide opportunities for immersive *bauddhik* sessions— discussions on philosophical, moral, historical, economic, and political topics (see Chapter 1). A report on a camp for young adults held near Birmingham in 2008 lists various provocative subjects debated, ranging from 'Hindus are cowards and lack courage' to 'What can be done about conversion of Hindu girls?'[20] Although there is a benign stated aim 'to mould and inculcate good values and *sanskaars* in our youth', it is clear that a more ideological, antagonistic pedagogy takes place.[21]

In 2015 elements of training camps clearly *not* curated for public consumption were broadcast to the British public on the 'Charities Behaving Badly' episode of the documentary series *ITV Exposure*. Covertly filmed footage of an HSS youth leadership camp in Hertfordshire depicted an HSS instructor, in front of a roomful of teenagers, denigrating Muslims and speaking of an anti-Hindu, Christian 'secret conspiracy'. The HSS were featured as one of three charities, alongside groups providing platforms for Islamists and white supremacists, accused of promoting 'hatred and extremist views'. The exposé led to the British Sangh's second run-in with the Charity Commission in a decade, raising questions about the public awareness and even legality of Hindutva organisations in Britain, which is considered in more depth in Chapter 5.

The age bracket for youth leadership camps—particularly the *tarun* (17–30-year-old) group—is deemed a priority by the HSS. Not only is this a key stage in the process of 'moulding men', but it is the point at which many young members stop attending *shakha*. If persuaded to stay, it is also an age where *swayamsevaks* can step up to a greater level of responsibility within the organisation.

The emphasis on leadership at camps relates to encouraging proactive, emotionally invested, and enduring engagement with the Sangh that bridges the adolescent period. During these years, changing personalities, priorities, and levels of independence all lead to high drop-out rates. Camps are an important interface between older and younger generations: a press release on a 2014 camp stresses the role played by 'fulltime workers and parents who take time out of their work and personal life to support the youth leaders of tomorrow'.[22] There is also a hope that skills gained during these sessions might be transferrable—partly a way of making them more attractive to young people on the cusp of leaving school and university. 'The nine-day training course,' a report on the same 2014 camp claimed, 'created future leaders in the workspace, society and more importantly the Hindu Samaj.'[23]

Sangh sources are effusive about the discipline and spirit of these camps, but they do, of course, serve a promotional purpose. Occasionally, however, we find accounts that buck this trend. Hansen quotes a Sevika Samiti activist in Thane, Maharashtra, who said in 1992: 'Our society has become lethargic and the people do not want any discipline. Our camps are always held on holidays and nobody wants to get up early to attend these camps... Now we have to adjust our timings according to the TV programs'.[24] Similar attitudes can be found in Britain. In an uncharacteristically candid internal report, Dijesh, a young *vistarak*, writes, 'If I'm quite frank and honest, I've heard and observed several criticisms of our Sangh Shiksha Vargs in the past few years. These usually revolve around the lack of discipline together with the lack of general quality surrounding the varg'.[25] Camps, therefore, like *shakhas*, are presented as the epitome of discipline—particularly during public functions—but in reality may be rather less ordered than they appear to outsiders. Moreover, attendance at these camps remains modest when looked at next to the considerable UK Hindu population.

A crucial aspect of HSS training camps is that they facilitate important interactions and exchanges between leaders of the movement and grassroots members. The camps provide an opportunity for senior Sangh leaders—both from Britain and, less frequently, from India—to contribute towards training, 'inspire' the participants, and monitor the condition and development of the organisation. But while the role of Indian organisers deputised from RSS headquarters to training camps in Britain is clearly important, the level of homeland control is difficult to disaggregate. An emphasis on a top-down '*duplication* of the RSS modus operandi',[26] and an underplaying of diasporic agency, also elides the considerable levels of divergence and idiosyncrasy in both *shakhas* and camps.

The British Sangh leadership and most proactive organisers—including the members of the Kendriya Karyakari Mandal (Central Executive Committee)—engage with Sangh groups around the country through the various camps. Visiting leaders from the Sangh hierarchy in India also attend camps overseas. For instance, when Rajendra Singh visited Europe in 1995—the first serving Sarsanghchalak to ever tour overseas countries—several camps were on his itinerary. An RSS biography of Mohan Bhagwat, current head of the RSS and one of many key figures in the movement to adopt a hands-on approach to the global cohort, glowingly states:

> Shri Mohanji has inspired hundreds of youths to dedicate themselves for Sangh and work for the Hindu society selflessly. Shri Mohanji has travelled extensively abroad to UK, S[outh] Africa, Mauritius, Kenya and Netherlands and in India visiting every state at least twice a year. He visited US for the first time on the occasion of birth centenary of Param Poojaniya Shri Guruji Golwalkar.[27]

Leaders of other organisations in the Parivar, especially the VHP, also attend camps around the world. Satyamitranand Giri (1932–2019), founding member of the VHP in India and patron of the VHP-UK, was particularly active in this regard.

Visits by Sangh leaders—whether regional or global—are often presented as junior members receiving 'wisdom' and 'inspiration' from the luminaries. But there is also a fair degree of mutual exchange and leaders' visits viewed as a form of reconnaissance. A guide on 'Roles and Responsibilities of Karyakartas', produced by the Canadian wing of the Sangh, underlines the importance of '*pravas*' (journeys or visits) for both parties. It stresses that 'Pravasi Karyakartas should be more in the listening mode', and 'plans made by the National... teams will percolate down to all the shakhas and input from the shakhas reach upwards'.[28]

Exchanges are not simply bilateral, nor do they follow a homeland–diaspora binary. Camps around the world may be visited not just by leaders from India or the country in which they are being hosted, but also by Sangh *karyakartas* from elsewhere in the world. For instance, the first British camp in 1970 had visitors from East Africa and, more recently, in 2010, Arun Kankani led a major training camp in Leicestershire, attended by 173 *swayamsevaks*.[29] Kankani was the National Secretary of the American wing of the HSS from 2006, and subsequently Director of Sewa USA, and had also been a Sangh *karyakarta* in Britain from 1990 to 1994.[30] Similarly, Sangh leaders from Britain are sometimes present at the camps of other HSS branches around the world, sharing knowledge and experience, and serving as important connectors between overseas wings of the Sangh. This transnationalism of camps underlines both a global outlook on behalf of the Hindu nationalist movement and the multi-directional fluidity of cross-border ties for diaspora populations around the world.

Camps held outside India also attract regular participants from several different countries of the Indian diaspora. In 2008, *Sangh Sandesh* reported that a European *shibir* held in Sweden was attended by 135 *swayamsevaks* from at least seven different countries, including Britain.[31] Ravi Kumar, the New Delhi-based Vishwa Vibhag Sah Samyojak (Joint Co-ordinator of World

Division), attended, reflecting the particular role played by Vishwa Vibhag *pracharaks* in overseas camps. Four years later, a camp at Chinmay Ashram in Trinidad hosted fifty-eight participants from six countries, and 'functionaries' included the UK-based *pracharak*, Ram Vaidya.[32] A British *swayamsevak* who attended this Trinidadian *shibir* told me that the Sangh is 'like being part of a family'. This is also the case with British camps, which can include *swayamsevaks* from India as well as elsewhere in the diaspora. These meetings facilitate an exchange of knowledge within the Sangh network, reinforcing the idea of global Hindu *samaj*, and extending traditional understandings of homeland–diaspora binaries. One participant at the HSS's fiftieth anniversary *Maha Shibir* (Great Camp) in Hertfordshire—which included participants from fifteen countries—commented that: 'This is going to set a new benchmark, a new standard, for various countries, and they may also explore [organising] something like this in the future'.[33] The intra-diaspora influence, and even sense of competition, is clear. This influence is enhanced through publicity and various technologies: a series of press releases, YouTube videos, Facebook pages, and other online content—created especially for the Maha Shibir—ensured that its impact was maximised.

In addition to inviting leaders from within the Sangh Parivar, training camps in Britain also invite other public figures, predominantly, but not always, from 'the Hindu community'. This serves as an opportunity for the HSS to showcase their discipline and training, to bring the organisation into the mainstream, and for the *swayamsevaks* to receive recognition and affirmation. The list of chief guests (see Table 2.1) shows an incredible level of connectivity and networks amongst Hindu leaders in Britain and beyond. Importantly, the presence of guests from other organisations serves to reinforce the Sangh's 'ecumenical' credentials, and provides an opportunity to publicise the Hindutva message, and to reify the rhetoric of unity. The involvement of political figures indicates the Sangh's reach beyond Hindu-oriented representatives. It also shows that whilst these individuals and groups might be reticent about sharing a public stage with the HSS, in private fora they are less concerned.

TRAINING CAMPS AND THE DEVELOPMENT OF A GLOBAL *PARIVAR*

This is reflected in India, where guests at major functions are often from outside the Sangh. The origins of this can be traced to the very beginnings of the RSS. At the second ever training camp in Nagpur in 1927, Hedgewar invited 'leading citizens' to the camp, which 'clicked very well as a method of attracting the sympathy of outsiders for the Sangh'.[34] This not only elicited praise for the disciplined ranks of *swayamsevaks*, it gave the volunteers encouragement and a sense of approbation.

Table 2.1: Chief Guests at HSS (UK) annual residential training camps, 2004–2022

Year	Chief guest	Biographical information
2004	Arjun Vekaria	Founder-President of Hindu Forum of Britain
2005	Ashok Kumar	Labour MP, Middlesbrough South and East Cleveland
2006	Baroness Sandeep Verma	Conservative life peer in House of Lords
2007	Swami Dayatmananda	Head of Ramakrishna Vedanta Centre UK
2008	Ishwarbhai Tailor	Chairman of Hindu Forum of Britain; Chairman of Hindu Gujarat Society, Preston
2009	Rameshbhai Pattni	Trustee of Chinmaya Mission UK
	Satyanarayan Shastry	Former Director of Bharatiya Vidya Bhavan (London)
2010	Philip Carr-Gomm	Head of the Order of Bards, Ovates and Druids
2011	Narendra Kandel	President of Nepalese Business Association, UK
2012	Alpesh Patel	Chairman of UK-India Business Angel Network
2013	Swami Japananda	Chairman of Sri Ramakrishna Sevashrama, Karnataka

Year	Chief guest	Biographical information
2014	Bob Blackman	Conservative MP, Harrow East
2015	Dame Asha Khemka	CEO of West Nottinghamshire College Group
2016	Mohan Bhagwat	This year was the fiftieth-anniversary celebration of the HSS UK, and it involved a three-day 'Sanskriti Maha Shibir' in London. It was inaugurated by RSS chief, Mohan Bhagwat, and was attended by many other dignitaries from Britain and beyond.
2017	Acharya Vidyabhaskar	Head of Sanskrit and Indian Philosophy, Omkarananda Ashram, Switzerland
2018	Swami Sarvasthanandaji	Head of Ramakrishna Mission and Vedanta Centre, UK
2019	Amarjeet Bhamra	Initiator and Lead Secretariat of the All Party Parliamentary Group (APPG) on Indian Traditional Science
2020	N/A	Camp replaced by online programme due to Covid-19 pandemic
2021	N/A	No information provided
2022	Theresa Villiers	Conservative MP, Chipping Barnet

Politicians are occasionally invited to attend camps and *utsavs* (festivals). An undated image, probably taken in the early 1990s, shows Paddy Ashdown on a stage at an outdoor *shibir* function.[36] Bob Blackman, the Conservative Party MP for Harrow East, a strong ally of the Hindu nationalist movement, has attended many Sangh events, including as a chief guest at training camps. In a speech at the end of the annual residential youth training camp in August 2014, Blackman told the audience that his first visit to an HSS camp was in Leicester in 1992. Blackman's speech, as reported on the English-language website of the Sangh 'media centre', Vishwa Samvad Kendra, underlined his commitment to the Sangh:

> Far too many myths have been allowed to develop about what HSS does which needs to be dispelled… Being peaceful is the core value of Hinduism and to maintain peace one needs to be vigilant. One should be ever willing to go to war in order to maintain peace.[37]

Unlike some other external guests of the HSS, Blackman appears to have a good understanding of the Sangh. He claimed, for instance, that the 'HSS brother organisation has presented two great prime ministers to India', adding that, 'We recognise media bias exists out there against HSS and Sangh community in general'.[38] Blackman also ostentatiously celebrated the BJP election victories in 2014 and 2019, and in 2020 was awarded the Padma Shri (a significant civilian honour conferred by the President of India), which he announced with a tweet containing the hashtag '#BharatMataKiJai'.[39]

Other guests are perhaps less knowledgeable about the organisation. Invitations may be accepted in the spirit of naïve multiculturalism, and their understanding of the ideology of Golwalkar and Hedgewar, whose images visitors stand before and even garland, is probably limited. The Mayor of Tameside, for instance, who attended a Sangh camp in 2008, described the HSS as 'a national Charity which seeks to promote universal values amongst Hindu youths in Britain', and offered 'a warm welcome to the Borough' to the visiting *swayamsevaks* from around Britain and overseas.[40] It seems unlikely that he, and many other outsiders, including numerous guests from local and national politics, would be familiar with the nature of the organisation they are endorsing. However, the point here is that the participation of these figures in flagship Sangh events shows that the HSS network is by no means hermetically sealed or insular. We can also identify a circle of non-Sangh Hindu organisations and individuals in the UK that are sympathetic towards Hindutva organisations. These dynamics are discussed, in the context of 'neo-Hindutva'—inflections of Hindu nationalism *outside* the traditional institutional and ideological framework of the Sangh Parivar—in the final chapter of this book.

Deviations from the RSS model—the 'Sangh Internship Programme' (SIP)

Although HSS training camps in Britain undoubtedly emulate the Indian structure (although with certain important deviations), an interesting innovation was introduced in 2009 with the 'Sangh Internship Programme'. This is emblematic of a more adaptive, syncretic streak to diasporic Hindu nationalism that has enabled the movement to provide services for younger generations, for whom the Indian Sangh orthopraxy has only limited relevance. The 'internship' model, with a clear focus on personal development (which, in turn, can benefit a community), illustrates how a simplistic understanding of 'cultural reproduction' is insufficient for understanding the dynamic, vernacularised nature of many diaspora cultural and social movements.

The SIP is a structured programme, held over seven weeks in the summer, 'designed to enable members of HSS UK to apply their time and skills to develop Sangh in the UK, deepen their understanding of its mission and also improve themselves in the process'.[41] The promotional literature goes on to claim: 'Through *abhyas vargs* [practice camps/programmes], real projects and personal learning, *swayamsevaks* and *sevikas* will gain a greater understanding of their capacity to take a project from an idea to implementation'.[42] It was launched with its own slick website and a distinctive logo. There is little mention of the HSS, except for the 'Sangh' in the SIP name.

The tone of the SIP is distinctly modified from RSS norms. In a video from the first camp, a participant speaks in subtly different terms to the traditional language of the RSS. He refers to the SIP as a 'self-improvement' and 'leadership' programme, and mentions sessions on, 'choice, *sewa*, adding value, community, communication, creativity'.[43] Most notable is that SIP is coeducational. A female participant talks of 'things that I might wish to change within Sangh', and mentions that, 'we can all see that something needs to be done, and it's quite refreshing talking to people who are willing to look beyond the confines of what we already have'. Another states that 'SIP is just another way to spread the Sangh, and maybe look inside Sangh to see, are we really using the right methodologies for our vision and mission'. This tone reflects a strikingly less didactic style than that usually found in training camps, with the impetus for the direction of the organisation (ostensibly) coming from the young participants, rather than the Sangh hierarchy.

Photographs from various SIP camps show that they represent something entirely different to the Sangh's traditional modus operandi. Sessions are mixed in gender, they wear no specific uniform, nor is there any sign of marching drills or flag salutes. Instead, pictures from various camps posted to Facebook show young people playing board games, at a 'high-wire treetop trail', performing various *sewa* activities (including cleaning a public park and gardening), doing archery, participating in team-building exercises, and holding group discussions.[44]

'Projects'—various personal and small-group assignments by individual members—form an important element of SIP. Much of this is oriented towards developing online content. Their website explains that 'during the programme the participants are tasked to take an idea towards some tangible outcome and also design in the continuation of the project'. This ranges from publishing a series of stories on HSS elders in *Sangh Sandesh* to producing a promotional video for Kalyan Ashram Trust UK (another UK wing of an Indian Sangh organisation, the controversial 'tribal upliftment' charity, Vanavasi Kalyan Ashram). Another project—a long report entitled 'Think Policy'—considers the involvement of Hindus in the UK political process. The SIP blog also acts as an important space for reflection on spiritual and political issues. Posts from 2011 included 'Bhajans: Boring or bonding?', 'Vasudhaiva Kutumbakam—The whole world is one family', 'Riots in Croydon', and 'Democracy in the spotlight' (which discussed Nitin Gadkari and Smriti Irani's 2011 visit to Westminster).[45] The extent to which the SIP project has attempted to engage people through social media is itself a notable innovation, and chimes with comparable developments in India.

SIP represents a way in which the HSS has tried to address the 'relative collapse in attendance amongst post-secondary school age groups'—a cause of great concern for the Sangh.[46] Although a clear departure from the increasingly outdated modes of traditional Sangh camps, it would be wrong to consider the RSS format as a yardstick bereft of context. Just as RSS *shakhas* borrowed much from European pedagogic modes of inculcating patriotism, the HSS SIP is also an eclectic blend of youth leadership programmes, the culture of internships and gap years, and various New Labour and Conservative citizenship initiatives. Many similarities, for instance, can be made with the model of civic responsibility and social citizenship promoted as an essential component of the national curriculum following the 1998 Crick Report.[47] In other ways, however, SIP reflects traditional concerns of the Sangh— consolidating the organisation and its influence, promoting certain conceptions of Hindu culture and values, and nurturing a young generation of conscientious *swayamsevaks* and *sevikas*.

II—Indian-based camps

To fully understand the Sangh overseas we must also consider the activities of diasporic *swayamsevaks* and *karyakartas* outside the countries in which they live. Although this dynamic plays an important role, scholars have almost entirely ignored it. Camps in India provide HSS members a direct link with the organisation in India. They enable British members to meet fellow *swayamsevaks* and organisers from not only India, but all over the world. It is felt to be important that these camps facilitate the unity and consistency—*achar paddhati* (see Chapter 1)—that has such an important ideological and affective role for the Hindu nationalist movement.

These 'return' visits (sometimes the first time the participant has been 'home') illustrate various core and evolving dimensions to the transnationalism of diaspora communities. They constitute the 'multi-stranded social relations of origin and settlement', and the 'sustained linkages and ongoing exchanges' that are central to understandings of transnationalism.[48] But transcending the 'bifocality' identified by Steven Vertovec,[49] the intra-diaspora interactions amongst communities from various places around the world—and the effect these exchanges have—illustrate the need for a much more fluid approach to understanding migrant kinship networks, global institutional networks, and individual and group identity formation.

While the attendance of diaspora *swayamsevaks* at regular RSS camps in India is relatively infrequent, it is not insignificant. There are also reasons why the HSS does not publicise their participation in Indian camps. That such visits are not mentioned in documents submitted to the Charity Commission may have something to do with the organisation's desire to publicly distance the HSS from the RSS. Nonetheless, there is evidence of diasporic volunteers at Indian camps. In their study based on fieldwork in the 1970s and early 1980s, Andersen and Damle noted such as the presence of East African Asians in RSS Officer Training Camp, '[who] had come to India to take instructional training in the RSS discipline and intended to implement the discipline within their overseas RSS affiliates'.[50] More recently, the RSS have also held intensive courses at their Nagpur headquarters, and in various other places, for the most dedicated and senior Sangh leaders from overseas.

Training camps in India enable organisers and instructors to learn the methodology first-hand, familiarise themselves with ideological and political developments, and meet fellow *swayamsevaks* and leaders of the Sangh in India. These meetings also enable the Indian leadership to keep a tab on their overseas operations, convey instruction, and even learn from their global cohort. Ashok Singhal, former VHP President, wrote that they enable international members to 'work more effectively for the causes of Hindu consolidation'.[51] In 1990, the RSS's Vishwa Vibhag launched a new form of camp—the five-yearly Vishwa Sangh Shibir (World Sangh Camp)—directed specifically at the diasporic Sangh.

The inaugural Vishwa Sangh Shibir was held in Bangalore, in December 1990. This bold and striking new initiative marked a sea-change for the global Hindu nationalist movement. Yashwant Pathak, an HSS (USA) leader and professor of pharmacology in Kentucky, remarked that this constituted a third stage of the Sangh's global presence: 'from Videsh Vibhag to Vishwa Vibhag and now Vishwa Sangh'.[52] The major Vishwa Sangh Shibirs (VSS) are symptomatic of the increasing scale, confidence, and infrastructure of the Hindu nationalist movement around the world.

Crucially, their significance does not just represent the development of the Sangh overseas, but reflects back on the RSS network in India as well. Sharad Kunte, a senior Sangh *pracharak*, referred to the VSS as 'a glorious harbinger of the success of the Sangha activities on the home front of India as well as on the international level'.[53] The Indian side of the movement, therefore, regards the global activities of the Sangh, and their increasingly tangible impact in India, as highly consequential.

In a speech in Mumbai in 2008, Mohan Bhagwat articulated the sense that the VSS ushered in a new era in the development of the Sangh:

> The first phase work was mainly aimed to make overseas Indians know their identity. The second phase was oriented towards organizing them and making them known as a cultured and potential society. The thrust of the third phase is to have RSS of various countries that will transform the whole society as per the ancient call of *vasudhaiva kutumbakam* [whole world is one family] and *krunvanto vishwamaryam* [let us make this world a noble place to live in] for the good of all.[54]

Vishwa Sangh Shibirs have been held every five years since 1990, with most camps in either Gujarat or Maharashtra. These camps grew rapidly in scale, plateaued in 2005 and 2010, and then sharply rose in attendance in 2016 (partly buoyed by Hindu nationalist electoral success).[55] 'Delegates' at VSS camps are not Indian *swayamsevaks* but members of the HSS and other affiliated organisations of the RSS family abroad. The figures listed in Table 2.2 for attendance at Vishwa Sangh Shibirs do not include the Indian volunteers who participate in certain aspects of the camp, such as marching displays at public *tamashas*, which can involve many hundreds or even thousands of local members.

Table 2.2: Locations, participants, and countries represented at Vishwa Sangh Shibirs (1990–2016)[56]

Year	Location	Participants	Countries
1990	Bangalore, Karnataka	200	20
1995	Baroda (Kayavarohan), Gujarat	350	28
2000	Mumbai, Maharashtra	570	32
2005	Gandhinagar, Gujarat	520	38
2010	Pune, Maharashtra	517	35
2016	Indore, Madhya Pradesh	746	43

Another interesting feature of the camps is that they offer a wide range of activities and entertainment, in a clear departure from the traditional modus operandi of RSS camps. There is a strategic element to the camps: 'We deliberate on the present and future of Hindu society living outside Bharat, the future road map of Hindu organisations, and all related matters'.[57] There is also a training component, in which the techniques and methods of the RSS are conveyed to current and future leaders of Sangh branches around the world.

The camps involve a strong ideological component, with Hindutva leaders giving lectures on a wide range of topics: some India-specific, others more global in perspective. Other functions are distinctive from regular RSS camps, tailored specifically to the diasporic clientele. Some of these involve an almost 'touristic' aspect: an acknowledgement that for the foreign participants the camp constitutes a major foreign trip and holiday, at considerable expense. Furthermore, for many participants it is their first experience of the RSS 'mother organisation', and, for some, even their first time in India.

However, the participants are gaining not simply skills and knowledge, but also less tangible forms of inspiration and motivation. This is partly conveyed through the form of the camp—a heterotopic, liminal space, arrived at through a carefully planned and powerful pilgrimage-like journey. The camps, therefore, have both centripetal significance (bringing together people from a wide range of locations) and a centrifugal impact (participants leaving the camp, and returning to their bases across the world, with a variety of new knowledge, experiences, and connections). Yet it is important to recognise that the participants at VSS camps are not just learning from the RSS. They are also exposed to Sangh branches from other countries outside India. The VSS provides a platform for the transfer of knowledge across various global wings of the Sangh, as well as the creation and development of global networks of contacts. Through new technologies, these relationships often begin before they meet in person, and endure long after the camps.

There is a particular focus on younger cadres at Indian camps, which Ram Vaidya, the UK *pracharak*, told me were 'teacher training, so they can take *shakhas*'. This is important as a 'refresher' for established members, but perhaps more so for up-and-coming *swayamsevaks* and would-be organisers. The 2010 VSS brochure identifies 'a file of young and dynamic Sangh *karyakartas*... [who] have a strong attraction and affinity for their roots in India', and states their desire to experience 'the original RSS headquarters and their work here'.[58] This was echoed in a discussion I had with a young *karyakarta* at a Sangh event in Britain in 2014, who told me that, when in India for the 2010 VSS, he had also visited Keshav Kunj, the Delhi RSS headquarters, as well as the Nagpur 'crucible' of the Hindu nationalist movement.

Camps also illuminate other aspects to the overseas Hindu nationalist movement's specific focus on youth. The part played by the Sangh in conveying religious, cultural, and moral values to children is regularly emphasised; the HSS is even sometimes referred to as 'a youth-oriented organisation'.[59] They are explicitly promoted as being better-placed than parents to perform this crucial task: 'Though most of them are well educated and economically well placed,' Seshadri writes, 'they now feel hopelessly ill-equipped to face the cultural and spiritual crisis facing them.'[60] But while most migrant parents are eager to offer their children access to their homeland culture, the version offered by the Sangh is often laden with Hindutva chauvinism. Anil Vartak, the RSS's India-based international co-ordinator, explained that the aim of an India-based camp for overseas *swayamsevaks* was to teach Hindu customs and traditions, as well as Sanskrit and 'ancient Indian science', with the objective of cultivating 'awareness and pride in our culture'.[61] Camps both play a direct pedagogic role for the young participants and train HSS leaders in how to provide this overseas. The youth focus also reflects a desire to 'pass on the torch' to a future generation to ensure continuity and allay fears that the Sangh may die out with the first-generation migrants.

However, while a Sangh-published review of the VSS stated that 'the most notable presence was of the youths', a closer examination suggests that this statement is sometimes based on either a subjective or optimistic interpretation of 'youth'.[62] A breakdown of participants at the 2010 camp shows that in fact relatively few were young; just 68 under the age of 26, compared with 157 between 26 and 45, and 272 over 46.[63] An account of the 2016 camp tells us that just 50 of the 750 participants were 'kids'.[64] Of course part of the point of the camps is to train more senior leaders who can then use their organisational skills and knowledge to 'pass on the torch'. But to some extent, the highlighting of youth at the camps therefore reflects more the *desire* for a new generation of 'torch bearers' in the Sangh abroad, even if the reality does not always match this.

Socialising and building networks

The opportunity to interact with members of the Sangh Parivar from across the world is a particularly significant feature of the *shibirs*. Campers often refer to the 'inspiration' provided by their counterparts elsewhere in the diaspora. In one enthusiastic report from a VSS, a young British *sevika* explained that in her dormitory accommodation:

> I was placed in a lower bunk below an Australian, beside a South African and Sri Lankan on the left, a Thai and Nepali on the right and across a Kenyan and Mauritian girl. We were from around the globe, with diverse upbringings, day-to-day lives and cultures; however we were sharing the same ultimate vision and path and

so where we were from didn't matter. That was probably the most inspiring thing of all.[65]

In the issue of *Sangh Sandesh* published after the 2010 *shibir*, reports from American, Kenyan, and British members all drew attention to these transnational interactions. Bhavin Davdra, leader of a Leicester *shakha* and former National Hindu Students' Forum Vice-President, elucidated this intra-diaspora inspiration somewhat differently. He expresses frustration that the Sangh in Britain is not as successful as its counterparts in other parts of the world, some of which, he states, '[have] become household names across the country and in political circles'. But this seems to motivate him—he ends his short article by asking the reader: 'how much time will YOU give?'[66] In these interactions, the *shibir* provides a stimulating enactment of an 'ethnoscape'—a dynamic landscape of connectivity enabling identities to form across global flows of ideas and international organisational networks.[67] These encounters require us to reconceptualise tidy binaries of 'home versus diaspora' and understand diasporic identity formation in dynamic, multipolar ways.

In addition to encounters with regular *swayamsevaks*, interactions with senior leaders make a great impact upon British volunteers. Accounts of VSS camps highlight the striking range and number of senior Hindutva personalities and ideologues present at the camps. Speeches and instruction sessions by an array of Parivar luminaries feature at the centre of numerous reports, photographs, and videos. Sangh leaders present at the 2010 *shibir* included Ashok Singhal (VHP President), Swami Vigyanand (VHP General Secretary), Sitaram Kedialaya (RSS All-India Sewa Pramukh), Badrinath Murthy (Vishwa Adhyayan Kendra President), Mohan Bhagwat (RSS Sarsanghchalak), and Ram Lal (BJP General Secretary). In the wake of their election victory, the BJP sent even more senior leaders to the 2016 camp: External Affairs Minister Sushma Swaraj, Lok Sabha Speaker Sumitra Mahajan, BJP General Secretary Ram Madhav, and party President Amit Shah.[68]

The presence of these dignitaries is not ceremonial; the RSS periodical, *Organiser*, reported that, in 2010, they 'informed the *swayamsevaks* about the *sewa* activities, VHP activities and BJP's position in Bharatiya polity in details [*sic*]'.[69] Madan Das (RSS Joint General Secretary) spoke of the importance of introducing *shakha* training to children born outside India, and Champat Raj (VHP Associate Joint-Secretary) informed campers about the ongoing efforts to construct a Ram temple in Ayodhya.[70] The Parivar leaders also give the diasporic participants crucial approbation: Sumitra Mahajan told campers in 2016 that they were 'the true ambassadors of Indian culture'.[71]

In addition to the pantheons of Sangh leaders and ideologues at these major *shibirs*, the VSS camps also host other charismatic personalities with Hindutva connections. Notably, they include prominent gurus and leaders of Hindu *sampradayas*, as well as a range of public figures, politicians, business leaders, and even government officials. The involvement of leaders—Sangh and other—is important not only for their lectures, guidance, and strategic input, but also for more quotidian encounters with the *shibir* participants. A Harrow-based delegate recalls the experience of the 1990 camp as the first time overseas *swayamsevaks* were able to meet 'revered *pracharaks* and senior-most *swayamsevaks*'.[72] In 2010, the 'electrifying and inspiring' presence of Jagish Shastri—the overseas Sangh pioneer discussed in Chapter 1—appeared to leave a particularly great impression on campers.[73] These encounters have a profound impact on many participants, while enabling the RSS leaders to provide guidance and exercise oversight.

The affective impact can also be seen in an account by Dijesh, a young *swayamsevak* from Northampton, who recorded his tenure as a *vistarak* in 2010–11, during which he attended the Pune *shibir*. Dijesh tells of a particularly moving moment during a humid morning *shakha* involving the now wheelchair-bound Shastri. Despite his infirmity, the HSS trailblazer struggled to his feet to salute the saffron flag: 'What immense respect, love and understanding he must have for our cause!' Dijesh wrote.[74] These encounters are clearly important not only for the visiting HSS members. A *swayamsevak* in his early twenties told me about a trip he had made to India (not for a VSS camp), in which he underlined the importance of 'face-to-face contact' he had with

Sangh leaders. That this young man, a relatively junior figure in the HSS, was granted time with high-ranking office holders highlights the importance with which they (and by extension, the Sangh leadership), view the visits of young diasporic members.

Camps facilitating multi-directional, polycentric influence

Vishwa Sangh Shibirs must not be understood as having unidirectional influence from the homeland to the diaspora. On the contrary, they facilitate meaningful, multivalent exchanges which flow in various directions. Sangh leaders often remark on their diasporic cadres who have invested time and money into developing Hindutva abroad. This is clearly inspiration for RSS members and leaders in India. Shastri declared that 'exertions of Sangh *swayamsevaks* will definitely make Hindu society abroad, a strong, assertive, united and well-disciplined force to make our dream of "*Vasudhaiv Kutumbakam*" (the whole world is one family) a reality'.[75]

An account of the Pune VSS of 2010 is titled 'An exposure to global, confident Hindutva'.[76] The ambiguity is pointed—these camps expose members of diasporic Sangh branches to the Sangh of the motherland, but similarly, the motherland is emboldened by their global cohort. A crucial aspect of Indian RSS camps is that they allow *swayamsevaks* and office holders from particular localities—often quite isolated in India—to come into contact with groups from across their country. Through doing this, they not only imbue members with the confidence that they are part of something bigger—not just a larger organisation, but a legitimate and righteous movement. They also allow for an imagination of the nation—indeed the Hindu *rashtra*—itself. By the same measure, international camps and conferences provide a glimpse, and even a manifestation, of the global Hindu *samaj*.

In addition to these more abstract levels of inspiration, there is evidence of more concrete examples of influence. Overseas *swayamsevaks* are known to convey their experiences of running *shakhas* overseas, and various diasporic modifications of Sangh orthopraxy, to the homeland organisers. An intriguing report

TRAINING CAMPS AND THE DEVELOPMENT OF A GLOBAL *PARIVAR*

from 1999 mentions a VHP-UK office holder meeting Chamanlal (the Vishwa Vibhag pioneer discussed in Chapter 1) after a visit to RSS projects and *shakhas* in Jammu and Kashmir. Although one might imagine the dynamic would be one of guru and disciple, there appeared to be a more equal exchange. The British *swayamsevak* recalled:

> We discussed various issues. He was mainly concerned that the students and *swayamsevaks* between the ages of 18 to 25 do not come to *shakha* because it is held every morning and they are too busy in their studies and they cannot attend the *shakha*. I told him that they should have a *shakha* once or twice a week in the evening or at the weekend so that *shakha* is in touch with the students and they can come when they are not studying in the evenings. He liked the idea. During my short stay in India I tried to have meetings and exchange views with Sangh *Karyakartas*.[77]

The implication is that the exchange between the British organiser and the senior Indian worker involved the former giving advice to the latter. The *shibirs*, therefore, seem to expose Indian *swayamsevaks*, organisers, and workers to various diasporic practices that may lead to possible reverse influences.

VSS camps are an opportunity not just for the RSS to showcase the mother organisation and communicate ideology and strategy, but also for the HSS (and other diasporic divisions of the Sangh) to publicise the work they are doing. In turn, this has an influence on the Sangh in India. Camps have daily *bauddhiks*, discussions on philosophical, moral, historical, economic, and political topics, which are sometimes lectures given by leaders from abroad. In 2010, a leader of the Finnish HSS gave a demonstration of *e-shakha*—a video-conferencing platform, developed to facilitate transnational *shakhas*, which at the time had registered users from twenty-seven countries across five continents.[78] During the 'live demonstration', the shibir was beamed to the diaspora and vice-versa: *swayamsevaks* participated from Finland, Malaysia, Belgium, the USA, Germany, Norway, the UK, Australia, and the West Indies, as well as some *swayamsevaks* from the VSS camp itself.[79] Later, during the same camp, British Sanghchalak Dhiraj

Shah 'explained the importance of saving the Hindu family in foreign lands', and his American counterpart, Ved Nanda, 'spoke on geo-political situation and stressed that Hindus will have to assert themselves'.[80]

The contributions of the HSS around the world, as conveyed by these overseas leaders, was said to leave 'an indelible impression' on the RSS dignitaries.[81] A report on the camp in the *Organiser* following the camp went even further: 'This rise of the Hindu power on the world scenario was very much visible at every step and at every moment'.[82] Another level to the two-way influence occurred in the 2005 Gujarat *shibir*, through a system by which 'host families' volunteered to accommodate the visiting *swayamsevaks*. An article reveals the impact this had: 'Naturally the cordial bonds that were developed... have been alive far beyond the *Shibir*... The true Hindu culture of such relation was proliferated in a touching and beautiful way'.[83]

The influence that the *shibirs* and the diasporic Hindutva leaders are able to have in India goes beyond the boundaries of the camp, and even of the Sangh. Due to the increased scale of the VSS camps, as well as concerted efforts to publicise them, they attract press attention within India. To give one example of many, the *Times of India* published a preview before the Mumbai camp in 2000, reporting that hundreds of 'NRI Hindus' from thirty-five countries would participate in the camp, and mentioned appearances from L.K. Advani and Murli Manohar Joshi. A senior RSS leader told the *Times of India*, 'Delegates... will discuss issues relating to Hindu identity and its assertion in the face of growing incidents of insult to Hindu deities the world over'.[84] The discourse of the camps, then, is exposed to a much wider public.

While much of what happens at the camps occurs behind closed doors, large finale events, featuring marching, martial arts displays, and speeches are attended by a broader 'laity'. The Vishwa Adhyayan Kendra (VAK), a co-organiser of the 2010 *shibir*, circulated leaflets calling on people to attend the closing 'public programme'.[85] Reports from various camps claim that thousands attend these receptions, which also host VIP guests and speakers, and draw on tropes familiar to political rallies. While figures may well be exaggerated, the presence of large numbers of 'civilians' at *shibir* events is well documented, representing an important feature with various ramifications. Their presence at a camp explicitly oriented towards diasporic audiences suggests the generation of a 'pizza effect' of sorts, resulting in a re-enculturation of Sangh activities, in which the practices of foreign *swayamsevaks* may be 're-imported' to India.[86] The high levels of social and cultural capital wielded by members of the Indian diaspora certainly puts them in a position to influence the local population in ways that invoke Peggy Levitt's notion of social remittances—'ideas, behaviors, identities, and social capital that flow from receiving- to sending-country communities'.[87] The apparent 'popularity' of Hindutva overseas is deployed by the Sangh as approbation of their activities within India. This dynamic is certainly at play when it comes to the BJP drawing upon diasporic support in moments that frequently hinge around the creation of eye-catching media content. These flows enable the diaspora to influence Hindutva *within* India—both in the political sphere and beyond—to a far greater degree than we have hitherto acknowledged.

Displays and symbolism of strength and unity

The public events at various types of Hindutva camps are replete with striking enactments and visual metaphors of discipline, strength in numbers, and unity. Marching displays, rows of geometrically aligned *swayamsevaks*, and other forms of group choreography are the most common examples of this. Foreign *swayamsevaks* visiting these camps witness hundreds of Indian *swayamsevaks* performing martial drills in traditional full uniform (not worn in Britain nor much of the diaspora). In addition, on occasion, the British *swayamsevaks* get the experience of wearing these uniforms, giving them parity with their RSS counterparts.

At one camp, though, foreign participants marched through the streets in their HSS uniforms, in which the khaki shorts and white shirts of the RSS are replaced with black trousers and a white polo shirt.[88] In 2016 the RSS revamped their much-ridiculed '*chaddis*', switching them for full-length trousers: although in the pipeline for some time, it is noticeable that the innovation occurred in the diaspora many years before the mother organisation made the same adaptation. So, while the Indian camps provide foreign participants with a sense of togetherness and experiences that they would not get overseas, such as marching through streets, at the same time the diaspora *swayamsevaks* are able to expose wider publics to their adapted modus operandi.

A video from the camp held in 2010 shows another intriguing, symbolic enactment of unity and group power. On stage, during one of the nightly 'cultural programmes', eight men are shown lifting a boy using only one finger each.[89] Next to them, an animated compère waves a *lathi* in the air whilst shouting '*Bharat Mata ki JAI!*' ('Victory to Mother India!') into a microphone, to which the audience respond with excitement. The spectacle is an old game or trick, also familiar from corporate team-building exercises or motivational speeches. However in the context of the *shibir*, the game is redeployed as both pseudo-miraculous and an exemplification of Hindutva unity and the power of the Sangh's 'strength in numbers'.

Mass camps involve other eye-catching, theatrical occasions, with seas of identically uniformed, perfectly aligned *swayamsevaks*. These spectacles are not only of great symbolic and ritual significance for the participants, but are also powerful moments for outside audiences, and produce compelling images for the media. Metaphorically and literally the individual is subsumed into a monolithic group. While these tropes are also invoked in *shakhas*, the mass spectacles do this in a way that smaller meetings cannot. Arresting pictures have even appeared in mainstream media in Britain and elsewhere around the world. Image searches for the RSS bring up, almost exclusively, pictures from camps: the power of these images is clearly understood by Sangh devotees and detractors alike. Indeed articles about other smaller camps and other topics are often misleadingly illustrated by images from the larger camps.[90]

The instrumentalisation of theatrical mass displays, with spectacular reconfigurations of pre-existing rituals of power, is long-established. But with the advent of social media and boom in online video content, these images can be viewed more widely than ever before. This is evidenced by hundreds of videos of Sangh training camps and festivals (almost entirely of the marching displays and speeches to large crowds), many from the VSS camps, found on YouTube, Facebook, and elsewhere. Many of them accumulate large numbers of views and are shared widely. These videos also encourage discussion—usually in the form of glorification—in the comments beneath them, enabling further transnational exchanges.

The impact of the overseas camps is even felt by those who did not attend them. Attendees relate their experiences and knowledge to wider publics in Britain upon their return. This proselytical priority is underlined in the motto of the first camp in Bangalore—'*Pradeepayem Jagat Sarvam*', translated as, 'it [is] our duty and desire to spread the light of knowledge all over the world'.[91] John Zavos recounts lectures in Manchester in which the speakers reported in detail on their visits to the 2005 VSS in Gujarat.[92] Hindu nationalist groups, and specifically the *shibirs* of the HSS, therefore enable what Dhookleka Raj referred to as: '[the] process of India "becoming a homeland" in the context of "structured social changes that have allowed the possibility of a return to India"'.[93] Developing this idea, the title of an internal account of the VSS in 2000—'NRIs flock to RSS camp to *become* global Hindus'—clearly invokes notions of identities 'in process', matters of becoming.[94] The return to the homeland experienced in camps aimed at the diaspora gives new, layered meanings to the relationship between the 'routes' and 'roots' of migrant communities, as considered by Paul Gilroy.[95]

In Manchester, 'the global Hindu community was performed in this lecture'.[96] This 'reporting back' on foreign camps was also witnessed, in more informal ways, in my interactions with *swayamsevaks* and *karyakartas* in Britain. A global Hindu community performed at the *shibirs* in India is thereby echoed around the world by returning participants. Performance, in this context, both 'contributes to the processes of collective memory that are vital for diasporic experience' and provides 'an aesthetic or sense that dramatises the present condition'.[97] These transnational experiences of returning to the homeland, and also interacting with fellow diaspora communities from across the world, thus lead to the creation and re-negotiating of diasporic consciousness. Often brief returns to the homeland and their afterlife—whether for special events or more quotidian visits—are missing from accounts of the development of migrant identity.

In addition to accounts of overseas camps in *Sangh Sandesh* and other publications, the VSS camps also produce and distribute a substantial, glossy souvenir volume to attendees. A press release in 1995 refers to this as 'a world reference book on Hindutva covering all important aspects of personal, social and national life', noting that 'a copy was presented to every delegate'.[98] The cover of the 2010 publication features a giant, muscular portrait of Ram standing over a model of the proposed Ayodhya temple. Next to him, over a background of the world map, are various symbols of Hindu-ness representing Ayurveda, yoga, classical music, and Hindu texts. More recently, websites, blogs, and social media are increasingly important spaces where stories, photographs, and videos from the *shibirs* are circulated.

Pilgrimage and other 'functions' of the VSS

Attendance at Vishwa Sangh Shibirs goes far beyond 'training' purposes. Anil Vartak explained to me that people use the camp as part of bigger visits to India—'sightseeing and homecoming all merge together'.[99] Often the VSS, or other RSS camps, will be part of a broader itinerary for a visit to India, which can include tourism, family reunions, pilgrimage, and even business appointments. These multiple 'purposes' to *shibirs* invoke familiar themes to pilgrimages and *melas*, resonating, for instance, with Farhat Naz's observation that, '[Swaminarayan] festivals serve [the] dual purpose of producing opportunities for global and social business contacts along with the religious ones'.[100] In this light, it is unsurprising that the majority of VSS camps have so far been either in Gujarat or Maharashtra, where many diaspora Hindus have close connections.

Tourism is increasingly important for the Indian diaspora, especially for parents who are eager to acculturate their children

TRAINING CAMPS AND THE DEVELOPMENT OF A GLOBAL *PARIVAR*

who may never have been to India before. Touristic elements are even built into the experience—a press release ahead of the camp in 1995 described 'delegates' being 'welcomed by the villagers in traditional manner by *kumarikes* (girls) with *kalesh* (copper vessel) and coconut on their heads'.[101] Another account of the same camp noted: 'Those who attended… mention[ed] that in the typical village ambiance of Kayarohan they got a glimpse of the Real India… The NRIs and foreigners also experienced the unique bullock-cart rides for the first time in their lives!'[102]

The Pune camp even involved a performance of 'a typical Gujarati folk dance', and a video from the opening of the camp shows a range of performances: a marching drill from a girls' cadet corps, martial arts displays with swords and other weapons, a small boy dressed as Rama who draws his bow amidst *dhol* (drum) playing whilst onlookers take photographs, a procession of carts drawn by cows decorated with *kumkum* (a red powder).[103] *Shibirs* showcase not only the Sangh, but also India more broadly (as it is understood and presented by Hindutva adherents). There is a sense that India needs to improve for the benefit of its diaspora. Mohan Bhagwat noted in 2008 that 'the PIO community of the whole world would feel a sense of pride and security ONLY when the Hindus of Bharat will get organized'.[104] This is counterintuitive to many understandings of long-distance nationalism, in which the diaspora are expected to prove their worth and loyalty to the homeland, not vice-versa.

Tourism has often been imbricated and blurred with pilgrimage in various contexts around the world. Similarly, features of pilgrimage and visits to holy places are incorporated into trips made for VSS camps. The camps themselves often host religious leaders: for instance, Satyamitranand Giri attended all six camps before his death, and Narayankaka Dehkane Maharaj was present in 2010. Thus, the *shibirs* also provide an opportunity for spiritual encounters within the volunteers' wider itineraries. Kunte writes that the camps enable *swayamsevaks* to 'visit their relatives [sic] ancestral homes here in India, visit holy and historical places and *Tirtha[s]* [and] *kshetras* (places of pilgrimage) and others [sic] tourist attractions'.[105] But the pilgrimage aspect of *shibirs* runs far deeper than manifest religious appointments.

The 'return' to India is momentous for participants at the camps. The sacred geography of Bharat is deeply instilled, and regularly reinforced, for *swayamsevaks*. They extol it in the Sangh prayer, 'Namaste Sada Vatsale Matrubhoomi' (Hail to Thee O Motherland), recited at every *shakha* meeting the world over: 'O great and blessed Holy Land, be laid down in thy cause... We, the children of the Hindu nation, bow to Thee in reverence'.[106] This is the very bedrock of Hindutva: Savarkar's very definition of a Hindu is 'A person who looks upon the land that extends from the Indus to the sea as his Fatherland and Holyland'.[107]

That the camps provide an emotionally charged 'return' to sacred Mother India is critical:

> During those camps I felt as if I had undertaken a pilgrimage—*tirth yatra*. To my mind, *tirth yatra* means not only a visit to a sacred river or holy place, but any place where good people meet with good intentions, for a good cause. Therefore, I call these *shibirs* or camps as *tirth yatras*, or travel to holy places.[108]

Shastri even compared them to 'semi *kumbh melas*'. The importance of holy places can go beyond resemblance: the second VSS, in 1995, was held in Kayarohan, 'a holy place', where 'it is believed that Maharshi Sage Vishwamitra had done long meditations'.[109]

Developing these explicit references, a reading of the *shibirs* as pilgrimage is revealing. The *tirtha*, as a crossing place or pivotal centre, resonates closely with the site of the VSS *tamashas*, as epicentres to which people travel from all over the world. We can therefore understand the camps as places of centripetal convergence. The *tirtha* of the *shibir* even represents a temporary crossing over from HSS to RSS. Moreover the pilgrim, as temporary sacred renouncer, has a fleeting transcendence of the mundane.

Holy sites for pilgrimage are often, particularly in Hindu traditions, in peripheral locations. This inaccessibility adds to the obstacles and challenges that are requisite features of pilgrimage. While travel for pilgrimage is becoming easier, longer and more ambitious journeys are becoming increasingly common. The pilgrimage-like tours are emphasised in the commentary to a video of the 2010 *shibir*: 'After long journeys hundreds of Sangha and

Samiti *karyakartas* from around the world gathered in the divine city of Pune, Maharashtra, along with their families'.[110]

The notion of *shibirs* as pilgrimage is reinforced by the financial burden of attending. The considerable expenses of pilgrimage, and the various hardships and risks involved, constitute 'means of acquiring merit'.[111] Many accounts of Indian camps allude to this. Kunte, for instance, remarked that: 'Swayamsevaks in the HSS section ... often felt honoured and eager to visit the holy lands of Bharat ... in spite of the travel expenses'.[112]

In light of this outlay, it is unsurprising to learn that the Pune *shibir*'s participants included eleven doctors, twenty-six academics, sixty-one businessmen, and eighty-two 'professionals'.[113] Almost ironically, as seen in rows of bunk-bed accommodation, money is spent on austerity. This recalls Colman and Elsner's observation that 'pilgrimage provides the opportunity to experience a form of temporary renunciation'.[114] The act of *dana* (giving), whether in the form of the expense of pilgrimage, a donation to the Sangh, or in volunteer labour, acts as a cleansing and transformative force.[115]

Beyond familiar '*kala pani*' taboos, wider stigma attached to migrating—for instance guilt at 'abandoning' the homeland and, to some extent, negative connotations to the pursuit of capital accumulation in the 'amoral' West—are also significant factors in diasporic donations and pilgrimage-like journeys.[116] Once, when speaking to an Indian American at a Delhi temple many years ago, I was told that religious donations were in some sense atonement for making money in less-than-moral ways. He said he hoped that contributing might 'purify the money', and even deepen attachment: 'giving a dollar is like putting a seed in the ground'. This chimes with Golwalkar's guidance to the diaspora: 'earning and amassing money should not be their sole aim'.[117] We might also consider Coleman and Elsner's argument that an ability to spend lots of money demonstrates a pilgrim's 'sound financial reputation', and thereby 'donations are both expressions of piety and also, in effect, self-advertisements'.[118] The concentration of Banias and other mercantile castes among the Gujarati-dominated Hindutva organisations in the diaspora is well known. For many of these communities, Sanskritisation, social mobility through the emulation of upper castes, has been a significant trend.[119] Elaborate pilgrimages and the donation of income to gurus and for religious edifices has played an important role in these processes.

Another significant dimension, related to the costs of pilgrimage, is voluntary labour. At a *shibir*, various types of *sewa* are performed, and *swayamsevaks* participate in many aspects of running the camp. On Christian pilgrimage, Eade and Sallnow note that at pilgrimage sites, 'lay helpers are enjoined to set an example in self-sacrifice to other pilgrims by giving freely of their time and labour [in the spirit] of the "pure" gift'.[120] Whilst with the *shibirs* this may not have salvationist undertones, a comparable sacrificial and comradely discourse is evident. Not only have the foreign *swayamsevaks* contributed towards the running of the camp, but also local RSS members. This provides another dimension to the bond between the diasporic members and those in India, of which more will follow. In this respect, Pnina Werbner's observation that during pilgrimages 'transformations of personhood and home often require a highly structured and elaborate series of symbolic acts' feels particularly apt for the *shibir*.[121]

Communitas and the equalising effects of shibirs

Pilgrimages are equalising moments, producing 'a relative and temporal obliteration of social cleavages'.[122] This is an important quality that is shared, in certain ways, by the *shibir*, also reflecting a broader philosophy of the Sangh. Victor Turner famously proposed the notion of pilgrimage as 'communitas'—spaces that 'liberate the individual from the obligatory everyday constraints of status and role'.[123] A number of scholars have applied the notion of communitas to India, arguing that Hindu pilgrimages can produce a particularly poignant, albeit temporary, annihilation, or diminution, of caste division, engendering feelings of group belonging.[124] This level of unity, during which 'differences in social status are blurred for a certain, limited time, to make way for solidarity among individuals', has particular resonance with the Hindu nationalist movement, which has reinterpreted and instrumentalised the format of pilgrimage.[125] This is discussed in the context of the Ram temple movement in Chapter 4.

The notion of Sangh *shibirs* as locations of communitas is compelling. Ram Lall Dhooria, author of a revealing memoir of life as a *swayamsevak* in the mid-twentieth century, recalls training camps with affectionate detail:

> While iron discipline prevailed, the atmosphere of sociality and camaraderie that prevailed there was truly remarkable. There was no question of high or low. The question of caste, for instance, was simply conspicuous in its absence. We all played together, sang together, ate together… We were all Hindus and the children of Bharat Mata.[126]

Games at *shakhas* and *shibirs*, which inherently involve a high degree of bodily contact, appear to provide a powerful illustration of the Sangh's desire to remove normative caste boundaries. Similarly, the sharing of food—an act of profound symbolism—further enhances the ostensible blurring of social division at camps.

The VSS meets share this equalising aspect. A report on the 1995 Gujarat *shibir* emphasises that the participants 'experienced the same by daily practice. It was an exercise in community living'.[127] At the camps a wide range of differences—including age, citizenship, country of birth, regional background, and various socio-economic factors—are transcended (if not broken down) for short periods of time. This is achieved by everyone following the same schedules, meals, and even accommodation, as well as dressing in the same uniform for certain drills. The camp, in its most basic form of an act of coming together, shows parallels with Turner's notion of pilgrimage as 'normative communitas'. His identification of a 'need to mobilize and organize resources to keep membership of a group alive and thriving, and the necessity for social control among those members in the pursuance of these and other collective goals', may also be applied to the Sangh.[128] It is in this sense that *shibirs* play a part in re-energising the Hindu nationalist movement.

Yet, while there are various examples of pilgrimage blurring social divisions, and perhaps even providing 'liberating' roles (for instance new opportunities for women in public and political spaces), the applicability of communitas to the Indian setting, either for pilgrimage or *shibirs*, must not be overstated. Christopher Fuller argues that Hinduism can, but does not always, follow levelling trends.[129] This is also true of the Hindu nationalist project, which relentlessly promotes the notion of Hindu 'oneness'. Fuller observes that pilgrimage can either 'dissolve *or sustain*... customary divisions of gender, kinship, caste, or class'.[130] Although pilgrimage may stimulate feelings of cultural, religious, and social unity for some, critiques of communitas go beyond identifying Hindu exceptions to Turner's universalist claims.[131] Peter van der Veer, for instance, was astute in his criticism of Turner's attempt to move away from functionalist arguments about religion in order to objectivise the 'ideological message' that 'everyone is equal before God'.[132]

The degree of communitas present in the Hindu nationalist movement has been overemphasised partly as it presupposes an illusory level of diversity. This means that the notion of communitas should be applied with restraint to the *shibirs*. Arafaat Valiani expresses surprise at the physical contact found in RSS meetings, noting that despite caste differences, 'the branch members were on an equal footing within the boundaries of the *shakha*'.[133] Yet in the same breath, Valiani also records that the members of the *shakha* that he studied in Gujarat were all Patels, Banias, or Brahmins.[134] Jaffrelot's accounts of Hindu nationalist camps have also noted high levels of Bania participants and few, if any, members from scheduled castes.[135] The issue of possible pollution through physical contact at camps is erroneous, as there are high levels of pre-existing caste homogeneity, often obfuscated by the Sangh and overlooked by some scholars. This also belies the movement's ostensible inclusivity. It has often been seen to hold a rather contradictory position of welcoming all into the fold and promoting a unified Hindu society—which for some has felt genuinely progressive—while simultaneously upholding the caste system, and drawing its leadership, overwhelmingly, from the upper castes.

This relative lack of diversity is even more pronounced in the diasporic Hindu nationalist movement, and therefore at the

Vishwa Sangh Shibirs. As shown in Chapter 1, certain regions and castes dominate the Sangh in Britain. Similarly, a huge proportion of those at the *shibirs* are Gujaratis, many with common roots in East Africa. Furthermore, the pool of the most proactive volunteers is narrower still, limited to those who can actually afford the *shibir*. Many of them have been in touch, often even attending other events together previously, and share a dense fabric of social and other kinship network connections. So, all in all, whilst elements of communitas might indeed exist, and while the Sangh try to emphasise the 'unity in diversity' that is enacted at *shibirs*, the actual degree of heterogeneity is in fact rather narrow.

The heterotopia of the Sangh Shibir

The egalitarianism of the *shibir* is reinforced in Sangh literature, reflecting the spirit that is, ostensibly, at the core of Hindutva. This illustrates the way in which the camps are about much more than just training. They are Hindutva ideology as praxis; enactments of an idealised Hindu society. In this sense, they may be understood through the Foucauldian idea of the 'heterotopia'—an 'other space', 'outside of all places, even though it may be possible to indicate their location in reality'.[136] Heterotopias can be compensatory spaces, whose 'role is to create a space that is other, another real space, as perfect, as meticulous, as well arranged as ours is messy, ill constructed, and jumbled'.[137]

Appropriately, one of the heterotopias that Foucault considered was the South American Jesuit colony—highly regulated environments, with strict routines, and numerous duties, imposed on all members. His description of these 'other spaces' chimes with the *shibirs*, but also with the colonial martial influences of the Sangh, seen in their khaki marching uniforms and highly regimented, busy schedules. Dhooria recalls that at camps 'one had to observe the tight schedule of activities with scrupulous care and attention'.[138] An account of a 2001 'NRI' Instructor Training Camp near Bangalore reflects this:

The camp is structured like the ancient *gurukuls*. A typical day at the camp begins at 4:45AM. At 5:30AM it's yoga, 6:00AM it's physical exercise, 8:00AM is breakfast time followed by a three-hour break for washing clothes, bathing. Between 11:15AM and 12:15 PM it's lecture/discussion hour followed by lunch and a break till 3:15PM for a second lecture session. The evenings are for creative pursuits—Indian folk music, poetry writing or singing *bhajans*.[139]

The margins and boundaries of the camp are also significant, defining what is inside and what is outside. Camps, as heterotopias, 'presuppose a system of opening and closing that both isolates them and makes them penetrable'.[140] Policing this boundary, engendering particular behaviours and feelings, is key to heterotopic spaces. Entrance is only granted to those who perform the requisite 'gestures'.[141] An account of an Indian camp from the mid-twentieth century, for which a password was required to enter, provides a clear example of this: 'there were several cases of the "sentries" at the barred or wooden gates spanking even some innocent *swayamsevaks*, taking them to be "enemy agents", should latter fail to remember their "password"'.[142] Even diaspora-oriented camps are also known to have their own 'police force' patrolling the periphery, wearing badges marked *Suraksha Vibhag* (Security Division).[143] This evokes Anne Hardgrove's observation that 'the production of community entails performances of marking the symbolic boundaries of community in order to produce an internal space of community'.[144]

The gated nature of camps is striking. An imposing, specially constructed archway at the end of a long driveway had to be traversed by participants at the Pune *shibir*, both marking the entry into an exclusive space and implanting a subconscious message of securitisation. This was emphasised by a flock of armed police at the opening function of the camp—part of VHP President Ashok Singhal's entourage. The image of armed security also acted as an allusion to the threatening other—a salient reference as, in the *shibir*, alterity is abolished.

The registration process at the VSS sees delegates being welcomed with garlands and *tilaka* (a mark applied to the forehead). The participants then register with camp facilitators at a bank of computers and are issued with badges on lanyards, which the *swayamsevaks* can be seen wearing throughout the period of the camp. This ritual process—of entering into the secure confines of the camp—further enhances the feeling of the *shibir* as a unique, heterotopian space. A fascinating insight from the Gandhinagar *shibir* in 2000 alluded to a particular significance of the closed camp for diasporic participants. Veteran *swayamsevak* M.G. Chitkara revealed that 'Foreign delegates numbering over 500 are not so vocal in expressing their thoughts as their counterparts in India. They rather prefer to discuss issues closed-doors'.[145] This illustrates a reticence about overt expressions of Hindutva that is felt by many Hindus, including *swayamsevaks*, in the diaspora—for both pragmatic and ideological reasons.

The camps inwardly and outwardly showcase the efficiency, harmony, and unity that the Sangh offers to provide. Many sources paint romanticised pictures of *shibirs*. This is important for the participants themselves, as an actualisation of the Hindutva ideology with which they are imbued, as well as for wider audiences. Camps, according to the RSS, are 'acclaimed as models of discipline and cultured behaviour', and spaces where members, 'all stay and play together, eat and chat together, sing and pray together, thereby actually experiencing the concept of "nation as one family"'.[146] In 1960, Venkata Rao wrote that 'Not a whisper of hatred of any one is heard in the camp or routine activities of the volunteers. Only the positive image of the Mother country is made to occupy the entire mind and heart of the *swayamsevak*.'[147]

Parables that exemplify the discipline and good character found at camps are frequently recalled in the Sangh. One story tells of a 1937 camp at Nagpur in which 2,000 *swayamsevaks* bathed in a tank in an orange orchard, and, to the land-owner's 'astonishment', not one orange was taken.[148] Another story recalls a public function with thousands of young *swayamsevaks*, during which 'the spectators were amazed to see not a single child moving from the seat when a paper kite came floating in the air and landed right in front of the children'.[149]

In addition to the participants and their highly disciplined, moral behaviour, the space of the camp itself is eulogised. This is particularly powerful for the diaspora-oriented camps, as showcases for a positive image of India. Chitkara described the 'calm and green environment' of the VSS camp in 2000, as 'a mental revitalizer and motivation':

> Spread over 200 acres of lush green shallow valley with agricultural land, herbal plants and forest wealth, the Keshav Srishti [the temporary camp, named after Hedgewar] provides an ideal place for the Sangh Parivar to deliberate on issues confronting Hindu community across the globe.[150]

These camps, therefore, provide bucolic, idealised versions of what India could and should be—a fantasy India, for the diaspora to tap into when they return 'home' for fleeting visits. Certain elements provide a national microcosm. The parade during the *shibir* in 2010 featured participants in regional dress from across the country— Punjabi *pugris* and Malayali *lungis*, alongside Marathi *sarees*— seemingly drawing on modes familiar to Republic Day parades. An account of the *shibir* in 1995 claims that 'Those who attended ... mention that in the typical village ambiance of Kayarohan they got a glimpse of the *Real India*'.[151] This relates, more broadly, to the importance placed on camps, rallies, and other meetings hosting participants from the geographical breadth of the organisation. This pan-Indian representation provides a sense of national togetherness that is otherwise only imagined.[152] At the Pune VSS, an 'exhibition' of images of sculptures from across India provided a chronological dimension to the geographical presentation of India.

On one level, this sanitised version of India is highly touristic. Ravi Kumar, a *pracharak* of the Vishwa Vibhag, after noting the great expense spent by visiting *swayamsevaks*, wrote that *shibir* participants 'come with their own nostalgic ideas about Bharat'.[153] Members of diasporas often have rose-tinted visions of the homeland that disappoint them when they return. Salman Rushdie wrote that 'physical alienation from India almost inevitably means that we will not be capable of reclaiming precisely the thing that was lost; that we, in short, create fictions... imaginary homelands, Indias of the mind'.[154] Return trips often provide rude awakenings to the realities of India, which occupies an imaginary status most of the time. Even Sangh sources note that 'the external environment too in Bharat shocks them: the dust and din, the dirt and squalor, the rush and scramble—all these make them allergic to Bharat'.[155]

The process of creating an idealised version of India at the VSS camps is dialectic. To borrow Paul Basu's evaluation of the Scottish tourist industry, the HSS and the RSS are 'joint-agents in a complex "imagineering"' of India.[156] So, in spite of an actual return trip, the imagined home remains a mythic place, 'imbued with the desire of the diasporic imagination rather than the real place'.[157] Through the *shibirs*, a sanitised, idyllic version of India can be constructed especially for the diasporic participants. Therefore, somewhat paradoxically, the overseas volunteers are treated simultaneously as part of the fold, but also their special treatment means that they are, in William Safran's terminology, 'strangers within the gates'.[158]

The heterotopian dimension to training camps is hugely enhanced in Vishwa Sangh Shibirs. They represent liminal, ephemeral 'third spaces', often occurring at the margins of urban conglomerations, and partially circumventing the state (ironically perhaps, as manifestations of cultural nationalism).[159] The 2005 VSS took place on an undeveloped plot of land on the outskirts of Mumbai. An account tells us that the wasteland 'was almost magically transformed into the well developed and spik-n-span venue of the VSS by the enthusiastic and devoted RSS volunteers in Mumbai'.[160] The organisation of these camps is also a statement of intent for a Hindu society, a substantiation that the RSS are up to the task of creating a new India.

It is not just the environment of the camp that has affective powers, but the process of construction itself. The acts of voluntarism in organising and putting together camps creates a bond with the diasporic *swayamsevaks* before they have even arrived. Accounts tell of huge numbers of local Sangh volunteers working for many months in advance in order to prepare for the arrival of their overseas comrades, 'ensuring every need of ours was taken care of'.[161] Diana Eck remarked that building a temple 'is simultaneously the process of building a community'.[162]

In the same way, preparing for a camp is a process of building a community—in this case, a global Hindu *samaj*. This is reinforced through various forms of communication in the build-up to the camp. Letters, circulated in an internet group for Hindu-American accountants, show that efforts were made to collect funds in India and abroad to meet the costs of the VSS. A letter template from one of the *shibir* organisers reads: 'All of us are aware of the relevance and significance of VSS. It is indeed an opportunity for each one of us to help the Hindutva cause worldwide. Need is felt that NRIs should continue to remain connected with Matrubhumi and reinforce their roots.'[163] Another letter appeals to potential advertisers for the VSS souvenir publication, to be distributed to 'cultural ambassadors' from around the world.[164]

After the arrival of the participants, the running of the camp also involved many helpers from across the Sangh:

> A team of about 200 volunteers from Pune and other parts was working 24x7 and ensured that the delegates did not face slightest of inconvenience. These volunteers comprising of youth, professionals and IT workers were happy to interact with fellow Hindu brethren from various countries.[165]

Performing these tasks also contributes towards a sense of communitas and is a way of enacting ideology. The services provided at camps—accommodation, medical facilities, canteens—all ostensibly run by *swayamsevaks*, are frequently eulogised. A Kenyan organiser at the Pune VSS glowingly referred to the Indian *karyakartas*, 'working tirelessly in the background to make it a success', and at the Indore camp, an attendee from Hong Kong waxed lyrical about the 'commendable and inspiring discipline, humility and *seva* (service)' of the local volunteers.[166]

Of course, this volunteer-focused narrative is overstated and overlooks paid employees, such as those involved in food preparation, erection of infrastructure, and cleaning. This closely follows the discourse of voluntarism that can be observed in various religious organisations. The construction of temples, for instance, is often primarily attributed to the contributions of devotees—not just financial, but also in terms of labour—underplaying, or even deliberately suppressing, the role of professional labourers. The creation of, and participation in, the camp is predicated on a suspension of the normal routine—a temporary moment for which careers and everyday tasks of the '*karmabhoomi*' are put on hold. The *shibir*, then, is not in fact an enactment of a viable ideal society, but an illusion: not self-sustaining, but inherently ephemeral. The heterotopia 'suspends the everyday and makes room for bathing, rituals, games and cultural contests', and is therefore '"potlatch space"... the space that "consumes", squanders or even destroys the economic logic'.[167]

Conclusion

Training camps form a critical aspect of the development of Hindu nationalism in the Indian diaspora, particularly in relation to accurately following the modus operandi and ideology of the Indian RSS. They facilitate a transfer of knowledge—in both directions—between diasporic actors and those from India, enabling meaningful interactions between the most proactive and dedicated British *swayamsevaks* and their counterparts in India and elsewhere in the world. The development of the Vishwa Sangh Shibirs marks a new dimension, scale, and confidence to the global Hindu nationalist movement.

However, all *shibirs*, and especially the VSS camps, go far beyond imparting just skills, knowledge, and 'training'. They are steeped in symbolism and affect, enactments of unity, strength, and connectivity to the homeland. The 'return' involved for diasporic *swayamsevaks* in the Indian camps is powerful. A report on Pravasi Bharatiya Divas (Indian Diaspora Day)—a Ministry of Overseas Indian Affairs initiative established under the BJP-led government in 2003—noted that 'Once "NRI" meant non-returning Indian'.[168] Now, in the context of these *shibirs*, it means something quite different to some of the diaspora. These camps not only represent a highly significant return, but mark an enduring (albeit carefully cultivated) connectivity with India. Camps in India, therefore, are important not just for the diaspora, but also for the Sangh in the motherland. The visiting diasporic *swayamsevaks* are inspirational and affirmative for the Indian RSS, and other associated publics.

The significance of camps must be understood not simply in terms of the 'growth' of the Sangh overseas. Whilst superficially the emphasis is on maintaining the rigid modus operandi of *shakhas* and other Sangh activities, *shibirs* involving overseas Indians— whether held in the diaspora or in India—are highly innovative, dynamic, and syncretic modes. They represent a blend of continuity and tradition (central values for the Sangh), with adaptation and modernisation, a careful balancing act that has enabled the RSS to remain relevant for the diaspora. Given the substantial deviations from Sangh orthopraxy, and the ways in which the Sangh has been adapted to the various requirements and desires of the British Hindu community, it is increasingly inappropriate to frame diasporic Hindutva simply in terms of 'expatriate nationalism'.[169]

3

TRANSNATIONAL HINDUTVA NETWORKS

THE INDIAN EMERGENCY (1975–7) AND THE EVOLUTION OF HOMELAND-DIASPORA RELATIONS[1]

This chapter and the next illustrate that two of the most politically significant episodes in India's democratic history were not national, but global moments. The Indian Emergency (1975–7) and the *Ramjanmabhoomi* (Ram birthplace) movement (*c.*1980s onwards) were turning points in the relationship between India and its diaspora. Although separate, and in many ways different, the development of transnational networks during the Emergency helped facilitate the diaspora Ayodhya mobilisations a decade later. Hindu nationalist actors and multi-directional transnational networks made Indian politics less parochial and de-territorialised it in new ways.

Diasporic Hindutva is often mistakenly understood as a recent phenomenon, shorn from historical context and disconnected from the Hindu nationalist movement in India. The Sangh in Britain and elsewhere is often framed, and to a large degree frames itself, simply as an expression of cultural nostalgia and religious identity. Yet, as this chapter illustrates, the Hindu nationalist networks that began to interest scholars and journalists at the end of the twentieth century were developed and transformed by political struggles in the 1970s, connecting expatriate communities intrinsically to the political landscape of India. This also precipitated a significant shift in the way the Indian state viewed the political possibilities of its diaspora: both as a potentially subversive threat and as a political and economic resource.

The State of Emergency imposed by Prime Minister Indira Gandhi in June 1975 is one of the most infamous episodes in the history of independent India. During the twenty-one months it was in force, the government postponed elections, censored the press, and imprisoned more than 100,000 people without charge or trial. The period also led to an escalation of the authoritarian social programmes of slum clearances and coercive mass sterilisations. Although it is a crucial and consequential moment in Indian political history, there remains a relative paucity of scholarship on the period.[2] This is particularly pronounced in regard to the Indian diaspora, who played a specific role during the Emergency, which constituted a highly significant juncture in the relationship between Indians overseas and the politics of the homeland that has hitherto been largely ignored.

The fortieth-anniversary commemorations of 2015, accompanied by numerous newspaper and magazine articles, underlined the extent to which the Emergency occupies an important role in the political imagination. Many accounts of the period are partisan eulogies by figures in the Hindu nationalist movement whose organisations were banned and members incarcerated. L.K. Advani, veteran Bharatiya Janata Party (BJP) leader, wrote in his autobiography: 'If the Emergency was the darkest period in India's post-Independence history, the righteous struggle for the restoration of democracy was undoubtedly its brightest.'[3] The Emergency continues to be evoked by politicians today: it serves both to criticise the Congress Party (who were in power during the Emergency) and to extol the ostensibly heroic role of their Hindu nationalist opponents. This retelling has been particularly resonant as several leading figures in the BJP in recent years—including current Prime Minister Narendra Modi and A.B. Vajpayee (Prime Minister in 1996 and 1998–2004)—were themselves young opposition activists and upcoming party leaders during the Emergency.

One of the most significant long-term effects of the Emergency was the transformation of the political fortunes of the Hindu nationalist movement. It can be seen as a turning point in the electoral prospects of Hindu nationalism, allowing the Bharatiya Jana Sangh (Indian People's Organisation)—the principal Hindu nationalist political party at the time and the forerunner to the present-day BJP—to enter mainstream politics through its participation in the anti-Emergency coalition and the subsequent Janata government. Although the cadres of the Sangh Parivar often invoke their 'valiant' role during the Emergency, this has received relatively little scholarly or even journalistic scrutiny.[4] Indeed, this lack of critical analysis has enabled the Sangh to elide the great role played by left-wing Congress opponents, and present itself as central to all opposition to the Emergency in a kind of 'second freedom struggle'.

Historians have almost entirely neglected the role of the diaspora during this period in the political opposition to the Emergency. Existing accounts of the anti-Emergency activities of Indians overseas have been produced primarily by members of the Sangh Parivar and need to be treated with caution.[5] The scholarly literature on the Hindu nationalist movement's engagement with the diaspora concentrates overwhelmingly on the period since the late 1980s and seldom recognises the significance of this earlier phase. Similarly, recent work on the Indian state's policies towards its diaspora asserts that New Delhi disregarded its overseas citizens, and persons of Indian origin, until the 1990s.[6]

The Emergency, in fact, is a key event in the history of state–diaspora relations in India, which needs to be viewed through several lenses. Firstly, it is a significant episode in the history of the global Hindu nationalist movement. The Sangh Parivar had been gradually building its cadres overseas since the 1940s. In response to the Emergency, its leaders mobilised and developed this network (as part of a wider campaign by a variety of political groups). Existing Hindutva organisations—and others established specifically to oppose the Emergency—organised protests, lobbied public figures, and encouraged media coverage overseas in an attempt to stimulate foreign governments to put pressure on Indira Gandhi to end the Emergency. Members and branches of the Sangh overseas also interacted with the homeland in order to transmit information, funds, and moral support from abroad. This experience, and their eulogising of it in the years since, had a lasting effect on the Hindu nationalist movement.

The Sangh used the Emergency to strengthen its overseas networks by engaging its members in new forms of activism in opposition to the Indian government. This taught the members new skills, imbued them with confidence, and encouraged the development of a younger generation of leaders. The diaspora's impact in effecting the end of the Emergency, and the subsequent political shifts in India, however, is harder to precisely determine and disaggregate. Indira Gandhi's government expressed anxiety and anger at the negative international press coverage that the diaspora influenced. But, although the Emergency caused concern amongst politicians in Britain and the United States—for whom India's oft-repeated credentials as 'the world's biggest democracy' was, and remains, an important factor in maintaining good diplomatic connections—it did not, ultimately, lead to any substantive ruptures in bilateral relations.[7]

This chapter shows that this crucial episode in the history of Indian democracy cannot be confined to national boundaries. It had transnational impact and was influenced by an increasingly significant diaspora population. In this sense, we can recognise the Emergency, in certain ways, as a global event. Although superficially a domestic political episode, it had repercussions for, and was affected by, Indians in at least three continents beyond Asia (this chapter focuses mainly on those in Britain and the US). The government and its various opponents competed for the political support of the diaspora. Moving beyond specific influence on and by the diaspora Hindu nationalist movement, an understanding of the Emergency's international impact requires a re-evaluation of the 'transnational citizenship' of India's diaspora—used here to denote cross-border engagements in political processes of the homeland (often irrespective of legal citizenship status in regards to nationality and formal, voting-based democratic participation). Lastly, the Emergency can be seen as a turning point in the relationship between the Indian state and its diaspora. It was a 'critical event' that created new avenues for overseas Indians to involve themselves in the politics of the homeland.[8] But it also transformed the way in which the government and political organisations in India perceived the political significance of the diaspora, and attempted to engage them in various new ways. Studying the Emergency sheds new light on the shifting nature of transnational citizenship, diasporic networks, and long-distance nationalism.

The Emergency and the Sangh Parivar in India

On 4 July 1975, less than ten days after the declaration of Emergency, the Congress government banned the RSS, along with twenty-five other organisations, under the Defence and Internal Security of India Rules (DISIR) and the Maintenance of Internal Security Act (MISA). Many of the RSS's leaders and ordinary members were imprisoned under Emergency legislation, as were members of its sister political party, the Jana Sangh. It is unclear exactly how many members of the Sangh were incarcerated during the Emergency, though the RSS and its affiliates frequently make the implausible claim that the vast majority of all those imprisoned were *swayamsevaks*.[9]

Both at the time and subsequently, Sangh leaders have underlined the significance of the episode for the Hindu nationalist movement. Upon the arrest in Nagpur of M.D. Deoras, RSS *Sarsanghchalak* (Supreme Leader), he reportedly said, 'what could not have been achieved in twenty years will be possible in two years'.[10] RSS member Sanjeev Kelkar even stated that the 'Emergency was one of the few good events in the 60-year-old life of independent India... [It] galvanised the nation'.[11] L.K. Advani expresses a vainglorious position in his autobiography, referring to himself as 'both a victim of Emergency and a soldier in the Army of Democracy that won the battle against it'.[12] Similarly, India's current Prime Minister, Narendra Modi, wrote that the Emergency provided him with 'a wonderful opportunity'.[13] In most political or revolutionary movements, the incarceration of members and leaders serves as a badge of honour. For the RSS, which glorifies self-sacrifice, this was particularly potent. Moreover, framing the Emergency as a 'second freedom struggle'—and Hindu nationalists as 'a new generation of *satyagrahis*'—helped the RSS expiate their less-than-heroic part played during the independence movement.[14]

The Sangh's hubristic invocations of the Emergency are not limited to the domestic front. The Hindutva ideologue M.G. Chitkara emphasised the importance of the Indian diaspora, as well as international recognition of the Sangh's gallant role:

> The Swayamsevaks who were living abroad in 80 and odd countries all over the free world spontaneously responded to the call of Mother Bharat and stirred up the conscience of the world... The world-wide protest, especially of the Indians living abroad, proved to be one of the decisive factors in upsetting the calculations of the dictatorial regime here.... Through this, the RSS crossed the national frontiers and became a household word in the entire free world as the creator of a new tradition in the history of national revolutions.[15]

In accounts like Chitkara's, the diaspora are framed almost as righteous guerrillas in exile: beyond the reach of Indira Gandhi's regime, yet sufficiently attached to India to participate vigorously in anti-Emergency activism. The RSS largely generated this version of events themselves, and thus it must be treated with caution.

The extent and impact of the Hindu nationalist movement in opposing the Emergency within India is not entirely clear. The RSS claim that they overtly protested the Emergency and courted arrest in large numbers, describing this as '*satyagraha*' (Gandhi's term for civil resistance).[16] Without independent evidence on the true extent of their role, historians of the movement have often just repeated the RSS's own figures on *swayamsevaks* arrested while noting that they may be subjective. Arvind Rajagopal, in a short but astute assessment of the Sangh's role in the Emergency, doubts their account.[17] He questions the true extent of the RSS's dynamism within India during this period, noting 'a striking paucity of signs of a movement in conventional terms—large gatherings, collective action, clashes with police, specific advances made, etc.'[18] Evidence from some contemporary observers supports this, such as a diplomatic cable from the United States embassy in New Delhi to Washington DC, reporting only 'a very small number of lightly attended meetings at which the government has been criticized'.[19] Christophe Jaffrelot and Pratinav Anil also cast doubt on the Hindu nationalist role during this period. While acknowledging that the Sangh was sporadically active in protests, they note that only a minority of their overall membership got involved and the circulation of underground literature was 'of far less import than is made out', and argue that 'their fight was not so much for democracy as for having the ban on them lifted'.[20] In fact, a range of leftist factions, who were also persecuted during the Emergency, probably played a larger and more successful role in opposing Indira Gandhi both at home and abroad. But although the Hindu nationalist movement's comparisons with Gandhian *satyagraha*—in both scale and character—might be exaggerated, the significance of this period for the organisation cannot be ignored. While the role of the RSS in the anti-Emergency movement is still not well understood, its legacy generates considerable controversy.

The Emergency and Hindu nationalist activism overseas

Scholars have barely touched upon the role of the Indian diaspora during the Emergency. The diaspora's engagement with Hindu nationalist politics of the homeland is usually assumed to have begun with the Ram temple mobilisations from the late 1980s. More widely, awareness of Hindutva 'long-distance nationalism' only really spread after the 2001 Gujarat earthquake fundraising controversies, the 2002 Gujarat violence, and later around the time of the BJP's 2014 election victory.

The overseas networks of Hindu nationalism—which, as explained in Chapter 1, were first established in East Africa from the 1940s, and then Britain, the US and elsewhere from the 1960s—were mobilised to considerable effect, and thus were substantially developed, during the Emergency. Many members of the Indian diaspora maintained an active interest in Indian politics, and Indira Gandhi's attack on her opponents elicited a particularly animated response. The ban on the RSS in India, and imprisonment of many of its members and leaders, spurred the group to engage its overseas supporters in the anti-Emergency struggle. This diaspora was mobilised in two key ways: through an advocacy role, in which protests, various forms of dialogue, and media coverage overseas were designed to stimulate foreign governments to put pressure on Indira Gandhi to end the Emergency; and by interacting with the homeland in order to transmit information, funds, and moral support from abroad.

Immediately after the declaration of the Emergency on 25 June 1975, and even before the RSS ban on 4 July, the Sangh's global networks were set into motion. On 29 June, a meeting of seventy-five anti-Emergency representatives demonstrated outside the Indian Embassy in Washington DC. The RSS-published *The People versus Emergency: A Saga of Struggle*—by far the most extensive, although inherently partisan, account of the RSS's role in the Emergency—claims that 'the plan to bring them all together was made by RSS workers'.[21] The same document records the Hindu Swayamsevak Sangh in Britain kicking into action just two days after the Sangh's ban in India. By 12 July, activists founded a new organisation, 'The Indian Freedom Front', to co-ordinate anti-Emergency mobilisation.[22] On 3 August, it organised a demonstration and march to the Indian High Commission in London, which was covered in British newspapers, and thus 'greatly boosted the enthusiasm of the people'.[23]

Although Sangh sources frequently claim a leading role, or even sole credit, in opposition to the Emergency, they did not monopolise anti-Emergency activism within India or overseas. A number of other groups launched campaigns beyond India's borders, including left-wing organisations (such as the Indian Workers' Association in Britain, and a range of international communists), supporters of Jayaprakash Narayan (the Gandhian socialist opponent of Indira Gandhi, jailed during the Emergency, popularly known as 'JP'), members of the Indian diaspora who had no party affiliation, and various concerned 'third parties' (such as human rights campaigners and Quakers).

A particularly spirited campaign was launched by socialists across the world in 1976 after the arrest of George Fernandes, the Chairman of India's Socialist Party and President of the All India Railwaymen's Federation (the trade union that had led a major strike in 1974, deemed a key trigger for the imposition of Emergency rule). The efforts to free Fernandes were spearheaded by his comrades in Socialist International, a London-based 'solidarity organisation' and umbrella group of socialist parties across the world. With the support of Leila Kabir, George Fernandes's wife, who had fled India at the start of the Emergency, Socialist International gathered a wide range of high-profile leaders to speak out against Indira Gandhi's authoritarianism, including Austrian Chancellor Bruno Kreisky, Swedish Prime Minister Olof Palme, and German socialist politician and Nobel Peace Prize-winner, Willy Brandt. Groups like Socialist International had connections to powerful networks and allies, which was much less the case for Hindu nationalists, whose efforts, therefore, were primarily limited to grassroots activism and attempts to generate sympathetic press coverage.

Sometimes non-Hindu nationalist campaigns interacted and even collaborated with groups or individuals linked with the RSS and the Jana Sangh. The heterogeneity of transnational anti-Emergency activism is key but is elided in Sangh literature. For a number of reasons, the memorialisation of the role of other groups has been less effective than that of the RSS, with a result that their contribution has been downplayed or ignored altogether. In fact, the non-Sangh elements of transnational anti-Congress activism are likely to have been more dynamic, broad-based, and influential, than that of the Hindu nationalists. While this diversity is discussed briefly towards the end of this chapter, the focus here is the nature and effects of Sangh-related activism and activities *claimed* by the Sangh—including the consequences of this memorialisation.

Diasporic efforts to protest against the Emergency and support dissent in India were, to a great degree, co-ordinated from India. Although the claim that RSS members in more than eighty countries participated in anti-Emergency activism is probably hyperbolic, mobilisations were clearly transnational. Before his incarceration in December 1975, Nanaji Deshmukh, RSS *swayamsevak*, a leader of the Jana Sangh, and General Secretary of the Lok Sangharsh Samiti (People's Struggle Committee), wrote a rallying letter to Indians overseas. In it he provided an 'eight-point programme for Indians abroad', with instructions on forming committees, raising funds, engaging local media, and maintaining contact with people in India.[24]

Most RSS-inspired activism occurred in a porous, intersecting quintilateral nexus, including India, East Africa, Britain, Canada, and the United States. Much of the diaspora's efforts were facilitated by Sangh global networks that were already in place (as discussed elsewhere in this book). One individual, Chamanlal Grover—whose pioneering role in the development of the Sangh overseas from the 1950s is discussed in the first chapter of this book—played a particularly pivotal part, and was described as '[a] co-ordinator, a clearing house of information' and 'an unassuming man who kept track of countless details and liaised with many who were underground'.[25]

Of all the foreign centres of Sangh activism, Britain was arguably the most important. Jagadish Sood, *karyavaha* (secretary) of the Kenyan Sangh, moved to London in December 1975 at the order of the RSS General Secretary to help develop the Friends of India Society International (FISI). An RSS source claims that 'His one-room residence became the centre of Sangh activities'.[26] In addition to this 'intra-diaspora' movement, a number of important figures left India to escape arrest and co-ordinate efforts outside the country. Grover's 'successor', Laxmanrao Bhide—the first RSS *pracharak* officially deputed to oversee the diasporic growth of the Sangh—was sent overseas by RSS leaders, shortly after the deceleration of the Emergency. He was instructed 'to organise a pro-democracy struggle' and was closely involved in the formation of FISI.[27]

Two more public personalities tasked with mobilising the anti-Emergency struggle overseas were the Jana Sangh politicians Makarand Desai and Subramanian Swamy. Swamy and Desai went on to become leading figures in FISI, which is discussed further below. Desai, a member of the Gujarat Legislative Assembly, arrived in London on 17 April 1976, after the Centre dismissed the Janata Morcha government, in which he was a minister.[28] He was 'sent to London... to strengthen [and co-ordinate] the agitation abroad', and became 'head of all activities conducted abroad'.[29] One of Desai's key roles was to launch and edit *Satyavani* (Voice of Truth), a monthly journal based in London that served as the FISI bulletin. This published news on the situation in India, largely clippings from the foreign press that were ostensibly based on information 'smuggled' out of the subcontinent by courageous dissidents. Copies were circulated around the diaspora as well as to India itself, boomeranging the information 'back' to the homeland.

Despite Desai's importance during this time, and his larger reputation at the start of the Emergency, today the most well-known individual to 'escape' India during the Emergency is the charismatic and contrary Jana Sangh (now BJP) politician, Subramanian Swamy. Smuggled out of India on the instructions of a number of senior Sangh leaders, he first arrived in Britain in December 1975.[30] In a contemporary account—an open letter from Swamy 'to the people of India'—he emphasised his importance to the Indian diaspora:

> Our 25 million Indian brothers and sisters overseas were horrified at the slander by the present regime against the opposition, and they pleaded with the opposition that a representative should come abroad to tell them the complete facts about India. I was chosen thus to go.[31]

Once abroad, Chamanlal put Swamy in touch with networks of activists, including the HSS in Britain and Indians for Democracy in America. The Sangh also helped to co-ordinate the movement of Swamy's wife, Roxna, who had been asked by Deshmukh 'to go abroad on an exploratory visit to get in touch with RSS sympathizers in the UK and the USA'.[32] For her deputation overseas, Roxna was even provided with 'a blueprint for a fool-proof communications system between Indian Underground Movement and Indian resisters abroad'.[33]

Swamy is an indefatigable character who was, and still is, always on the move, talking at various functions, meeting prominent figures, and speaking to the media. After arriving in Britain he immediately began raising support for the anti-Emergency cause. One of the most dramatic tales, mythologised in no small part through Swamy's own repeated narration of the incident, involved his audacious re-entry to India after his initial tour abroad. Despite a warrant issued for his arrest, Swamy flew back to India and, according to the tale, with the aid of a false beard and turban, walked into his home past a policeman. On 10 August 1976, Swamy entered the Rajya Sabha. As the speaker read a list of obituaries, he theatrically declared: 'Democracy has also died, kindly include that also in the list'.[34] His subsequent 'escape', which he likens to the Scarlet Pimpernel, was aided by the RSS, who arranged his second flight via Nepal.[35] While self-serving and possibly exaggerated, this story is part of the folklore of the period, which increased morale and excitement during the Emergency, and has helped secure the Sangh's reputation ever since. Furthermore, Swamy's vignette underlined, both to those at home and abroad, the possibilities of long-distance activism and the global networks that could make this sort of audacious resistance possible.

Swamy's centrality in the heroic narrative notwithstanding, the first steps to form FISI took place a few months before he came to Britain. One of its first prominent public meetings, which coincided with Swamy's arrival, took place in a Wembley school on 17 January 1976. This was followed by meetings later that same month in Chalk Farm, Ilford, and Croydon. A flyer for these meetings shows Swamy's picture at the top, with a long biography of his credentials as 'a renowned economist', and the title of his talk: 'Current Situation in India'.[36] The most prominent and widely discussed FISI event was a conference at Alexandra Palace in London on 24–5 April 1976. According to a Sangh report, 700 participants attended from thirteen countries, and the public session at the conference drew a crowd of 2,000.[37]

The event was intended to be both informative and strategic. It relayed 'real news' to journalists and the Indian diaspora, and publicised the Sangh's pre-eminent role in fighting for the restoration of democracy. FISI claimed that fifty-two 'chapters' were operating across the world, and a number of policies and principles were decided at the conference.[38] Swamy and Desai were elected President and Secretary, respectively, and London was declared its headquarters. Various operational outcomes emerged during discussions: seven 'global divisions' were created 'for propaganda purposes', with London as the headquarters. News of the conference quickly reached New Delhi, which was concerned with the reports that 'the conference had doubtless boosted the morale of those conducting these activities, and the RSS was behind all of them'.[39]

But the Alexandra Palace conference also had a more ideological, Hindutva element; the novelist and journalist Shiva Naipaul, younger brother of the more famous V.S. Naipaul, attended the conference and published his report on it in *The Times* of London. Summarising the speeches from the rostrum, Naipaul writes: 'Ageless India. Holy India. Vedic India. What, one was forced to wonder, did any of this have to do with the State of Emergency…?'[40]

FISI continued to operate, although in a limited capacity, after the end of the Emergency (for instance hosting a press conference during the first UK visit by a *Sarsanghchalak* of the RSS, in 1995), and still functions today. While we must be wary of attributing to it the influence, or even recognition, that its activists claim, in certain ways they undeniably served as a precursor to more successful forms of Hindu nationalist lobbying nearer the turn of the twenty-first century.

Swamy, Desai, and their co-agitators saw their chief role as liaising with the foreign press, encouraging newspapers and magazines to publish articles on India's political predicament. The intention was to raise awareness among both the general public and foreign governments, which, in turn, would lead to pressure on Indira Gandhi to end the Emergency. Swamy and Desai's educational background added to their (perceived) ability to interact with the media—Desai, a graduate of the Massachusetts Institute of Technology, and Swamy, a PhD holder and professor at Harvard. (Decades later, Swamy's Harvard connection would become mired in controversy, when in 2011 he was dismissed after pressure from students and faculty.[41])

When interviewed, Swamy said his educational background and 'Harvard stamp' gave him 'instant access' to the press, think tanks, and even politicians. A diplomatic cable from February 1977 shows that he was even in dialogue with the US government.[42] Swamy's personality was deemed key to the movement; a Sangh source writes: 'with his intellectual calibre matched by a high sense of drama, his dauntless nature harnessed to a keen political awareness... During this triumphant tour [of the United States] he addressed 162 public meetings and gave 38 TV and radio interviews.'[43] Swamy himself claimed that he appeared in *The Times*, the *Guardian*, the *Economist*, the *New York Times*, the *Washington Post*, the *Los Angeles Times*, the *Denver Post*, the *Toronto Star*, and diaspora publication, *India Abroad*, as well as TV interviews on the BBC, PBS, and Canadian television.[44] When considering the influence of all of these activities, we must, of course, bear in mind Swamy's outspoken, self-assured, and highly ambitious personality, and, more generally, the glamourised chronicling of this period by those who opposed the Emergency, which continues to this day.[45]

Another form of anti-Emergency activism involved publishing advertisements in national newspapers on both sides of the Atlantic. An advertisement in *The Times* on 15 August 1975 (Indian Independence Day) called for JP's release and pleaded, 'Don't let the light go out on India's democracy'. Portraits of JP and Mahatma Gandhi figured prominently. More than 200 people signed the petition, including sixty-five MPs and other public figures, amongst them the economist E.F. Schumacher, the historian A.J.P. Taylor, and the socialist Fenner Brockway. A similar advertisement, although featuring fewer signatories, was published in the *New York Times* on the same day. These and other public notices alluded to a vibrant anti-Emergency movement that extended beyond the narrow circles of the Sangh and FISI. These advertisements were organised not by Hindu nationalists, but by allies and supporters of JP. Another comparable movement rose around George Fernandes—the leader of the Socialist Party, who was on the run until his arrest in June 1976—which was led by leftist allies from across the world. Socialist International, the umbrella group that Fernandes had a relationship with prior to the Emergency, managed to muster vocal support from leading European politicians, signalling a high-profile campaign that makes FISI's efforts look rather low-key in comparison.

An important goal FISI did regularly achieve was to garner column inches on the excesses of the Emergency in the mainstream press in Britain and North America. Although these pieces provided succour (and sometimes new information) to the campaigners who read the publications, quantifying their impact on the Indian government is difficult. The characteristic Sangh line was that this influence on international opinion was a key factor in Indira Gandhi's decision to announce the March elections in January 1977. Whilst this is probably overstated, it is backed up to a degree by the extent to which the foreign press was monitored from India. Moreover, Swamy's influence in the foreign press clearly riled New Delhi, as evidenced by the recommendations of a Rajya Sabha committee convened specially in September 1976 to investigate Swamy.[46]

Bilateral relations under pressure

While it is difficult to measure the global effects of negative coverage in the international press, the Emergency did not cause any major ruptures in diplomatic relations. Neither the US nor the UK government made any formal statement criticising the Emergency, and neither country drastically changed its approach to India.[47] In fact, when the American president Gerald Ford made an offhand comment to journalists that 'I think that it is really very sad that 600 million people have lost what they have had since the mid-1940s', Secretary of State Henry Kissinger admonished the White House.[48] Ford's comment was reported angrily in the Indian press.[49] Britain sought to emphasise that the Emergency was an internal matter and that 'business as usual' would prevail in their bilateral relations. It was anxious to avoid controversies of the kind engendered by Ford's comments. An internal Foreign and Commonwealth Office (FCO) document from 1976 acknowledged that India's politics 'still exercise public opinion in this country', but asserted that the British government must 'guard against giving offence', adding: 'We must not lose from sight the potential that is India'.[50] The familiar narrative of trade and diplomatic bonhomie trumping human rights abuses was the order of the day, and both the US and UK governments prioritised geopolitical and economic interests above the promotion of democracy.[51] In fact, the Emergency may well have been actively beneficial to foreign business interests, and the maintenance of good relations was certainly a priority for international investors.[52]

Certain individuals in the British government went significantly further than the formal government position in expressing active support for the Emergency, notably Cabinet Minister Michael Foot, who defended Indira Gandhi and in October 1976 visited India.[53] One month before Foot, the Leader of the Opposition, Margaret Thatcher, also went to India, although she stopped short of an overt defence of the Emergency itself.

While most American and British diplomats were eager not to aggravate the Indian government, the press did ensure that the Emergency could not altogether be brushed under the carpet. The US Congress held hearings about civil liberties in India during which negative coverage in the American press was read into the Congressional record, alongside statements by members of the diaspora. Some newspaper articles cited in Congress explicitly drew on information provided by diasporic groups like Indians for Democracy or reported on their activities.[54] We know from Ministry of External Affairs (MEA) files and reports from Indian diplomatic missions in the US that this was a matter of concern for the Indian government.[55] In Britain, MPs asked questions in the House of Commons about human rights abuses in India, and were told that diplomats in Delhi had denounced the expulsion of British journalists.[56] Moreover, even the British government's 'business as usual' policy was—at least in Whitehall's eyes— carefully distinguished from anything like approbation for events in India. On the advice of the government, Prince Charles called off a planned visit in 1976 in order to avoid the potential 'political controversy' of what could be construed as the Crown condoning the Emergency regime.[57] The situation in other parts of Europe was rather different, where a range of politicians spoke out against Indira Gandhi's policies. These were mainly socialists, influenced by supporters of George Fernandes, JP, and even transnational communist networks, rather than a consequence of global Hindutva networks.

The Indian government was clearly vexed about negative foreign press coverage. Indira Gandhi publicly denounced the Western media repeatedly during the Emergency for unfavourable reporting, and her envoys to London and Washington registered their protest with the British and American governments in strident terms. She angrily stated that the 'slanderous and malicious news stories' amounted to 'foreign interference'.[58] Lacking the evidence to reveal the reasons that triggered Indira Gandhi's decision to call elections, we cannot definitively ascertain the influence of diasporic activists, mounting criticism in the foreign press, and international pressure. However, there is no doubt that it was a significant cause for concern for her government.

Although the Emergency may not have caused a substantial rupture in India's multilateral relations, its tangible international impact means that it should be understood as a global event. The effect of the diaspora's efforts in terms of advocacy, and the impact of the press coverage they helped to generate, is hard to measure. But it is clear that Indians overseas (and their allies) who lobbied against the Emergency were seen as a threat by the Indian government. And, crucially, sections of the diaspora saw their role as significant, both at the time and in its subsequent narration. In this sense, we can view the 'global event' of the Emergency as contributing towards the generation of a 'diaspora consciousness'— an 'awareness of multilocality'—among Indians overseas.[59]

Censorship of the press, and the transnational 'smugglers of truth'

The diaspora played their own, distinct role in the transnational production and dissemination of literature. In India, severe restrictions were imposed upon the press, with draconian government 'guidelines' distributed on the first day of the Emergency.[60] The government deployed a range of harassment techniques, and leveraged the newspapers' dependence on revenue provided by state advertisements.[61] There was also, arguably, a degree of complicit reticence; Advani famously said to journalists: 'When you were merely asked to bend, you chose to crawl'.[62] Many of these dynamics—from self-censorship to governmental influence over the press—are an enduring feature of the Indian media, not starting with the Emergency, and certainly not absent today.

While many mainstream newspapers were subject to substantial intimidation and censorship, a number of smaller periodicals, including the Jana Sangh's *The Motherland*, and publications associated with other opposition groups, were forced to shut down entirely. Many foreign journalists were gagged or expelled. Some illicit newspapers were produced and circulated in India, such as *Apatkaleen Sangharsh Bulletin* (Emergency Struggle Bulletin) and *Satya Samachar* (True News). However, the production of pamphlets and newsletters overseas was significant, partly as a way of spreading information and partly as an important form of networking and identity-formation for the diaspora.

A range of publications were circulated in and from the diaspora during this period. In Britain, pre-existing vernacular newspapers, particularly *Amar Deep* and *Gujarat Samachar*, began to include various articles criticising Indira Gandhi. However, after pressure from the Indian High Commission (which also exerted influence through their position as clients for advertising), the papers stopped criticism and began to praise the Indian government.[63] But the Emergency also precipitated the launch of new publications: the HSS launched their periodical, *Sangh Sandesh* (Sangh Message), in 1977, which continues to be published today. According to the founding editor and prominent Sangh leader, Dhiraj Shah:

> Because of the Emergency in India, many swayamsevaks all over the world had come into touch with each other... Everybody felt that they needed to keep in touch with each other, and the idea of a monthly newsletter, which gives news about Sangh and swayamsevak activities around the world, was mooted... So in August 1977, one small eight-page Sangh Sandesh was created.... It has today become particularly a point of contact and news item for swayamsevaks all over the world.[64]

Perhaps the best-known publication, launched especially to combat the Emergency, was *Satyavani* (Voice of Truth). This 'newspaper' was first published in June 1976 by FISI as a result of the Alexandra Palace conference in London two months earlier.[65] It included original content, but primarily reproduced reports on the Emergency from the press outside India.[66] A young Narendra Modi—whose overlooked role in co-ordinating diaspora resistance during the Emergency is discussed in more depth below—was responsible for helping to circulate the publication in India. In his book on his experiences during the Emergency he describes a resourceful routine for gathering the content: children of Indians living in London were tasked with going around libraries, reading all the newspapers, and photocopying any stories that related to India.[67] *Satyavani*, in which these clippings were reproduced, was distributed around the world but with particular focus on taking it 'to different corners of India'.[68] After the Emergency, Makarand Desai published a collection of *Satyavani* articles in a volume titled *Smugglers of Truth*, referred to by Emma Tarlo as 'part of the collective exercise of asserting a dominant interpretation of the recent past'.[69]

Sangh literature frequently suggests that these publications provided a major source of information for underground, anti-Emergency networks in India, emphasising Indira Gandhi's iron grip on information. We should, of course, remain wary of this obviously biased interpretation. However, regardless of how politically influential these publications were, their role in connecting members of the diaspora in homeland-oriented political activism is significant. The furtive publications were a means for like-minded activists to coalesce and organise through a tangible medium. Swamy, in an interview, revealed this more prosaic aspect: '*Satyavani* was basically for giving work to our underground. They had to have something to do'.[70] In addition to providing information, the publications had a 'tremendous' impact, partly because 'they got us recruits for the underground'. The *act* of circulating these publications was crucial; 'the cadre had work to do... the morale grew after a period of deep gloom,' Swamy added.[71] Furthermore, the publications encouraged donations to the cause. The activists *outside* India helped to encourage support and recruits to the anti-Emergency struggle *within* India, and provided the movement with confidence.

But missing from Swamy's narrative is a crucial layer of analysis concerning how this activity fashioned 'diaspora'. The circulation of literature allowed Indians abroad to influence and participate in India's political process. For this reason, many accounts emphasise that only Indian citizens living abroad (not foreign citizens of Indian origin) were activists, and funding from non-Indians would not be accepted.[72] While this seems highly unlikely (by the mid-1970s, the majority of Britain's Indian-origin population were already passport-holders), these statements were 'disclaimers' to mitigate criticisms of 'foreign' intervention in Indian politics. The circulation of literature and foreign funding also provided an important medium for the diaspora to enter into the homeland political imaginary. In this sense, we can see it as an example not only of the print capitalism with which the nation is imagined, but of the tools by which global Hindutva *samaj* (society) was made real.

Hindu nationalist politics: Narendra Modi and other protagonists

The RSS's engagement with, and estimation of, the diaspora was greatly enhanced during this period. This experience had an enduring effect on the Hindu nationalist movement and, more broadly, India's relationship with its diaspora, which is still felt today. Perhaps the most significant figure in this category was an ambitious and confident young RSS worker in Gujarat. In 1975, Narendra Modi was a twenty-four-year-old 'in-charge' for the Gujarat region of the Sangh student wing, the Akhil Bharatiya Vidyarthi Parishad (ABVP). With the declaration of Emergency, he took on a dynamic new role.

The Emergency period enhanced Modi's growing reputation as an enthusiastic, charismatic, but intractable *pracharak*, quite out of keeping with the Sangh's ethos of conformity and composure.[73] He also became increasingly known for his aptitude for efficient and passionate organisation, and was appointed the General Secretary of the Gujarat Lok Sangharsh Samiti. Modi, with the characteristic hubris of many Sangh leaders, later framed himself as 'at the core of the anti-Emergency movement'.[74] His work between 1975 and 1977, during which he interacted with 'a wide spectrum of leaders and organisations', was rewarded by a promotion to RSS *Sambhaag Pracharak* (Regional Organiser) after the Emergency ended.[75] It is in this light that Modi referred to the Emergency as providing him with 'a wonderful opportunity'.[76]

But Modi's influence and interactions during the Emergency were by no means limited to India. One of his key roles was to maintain contact with networks of Sangh activists abroad and arrange for the transmission of information 'back' to India. We know of this from Modi's little-known book on the Emergency, originally published in Gujarati as *Sangharsh ma Gujarat* (Gujarat's Struggle) immediately following the Emergency.[77] Of particular interest are the letters to Modi from Makarand Desai, at this point based in Britain. This communication illuminates the kinship networks and methods of mobilisation that the Sangh were engaged in during this period, which predates most existing understandings of global Hindu nationalist politics.

Modi and Desai's letters indicate a two-way conversation—a *'prachaar sanghatan'* (alliance for the purpose of propagation), in Desai's words. In this relationship, Modi provided Desai with information on the situation in India, which Desai then disseminated through the publication of newsletters, including *Satyavani*. Their correspondence illuminates a dual focus on influencing both the Indian diaspora and wider global publics. One letter mentions the importance of cultivating support amongst Gujaratis (and specifically 'the Patel Patidar community'), and another relays that information provided by Modi was disseminated in Britain and subsequently broadcast by the BBC.[78] The transfer of information out of India was not just made by post, with people travelling overseas providing fresh information on the state of affairs in India. *Satyavani*'s updates on the Emergency and opposition to it were said to be met 'with tremendous excitement'.[79]

Much of Modi's role during this period was to facilitate the covert publication and distribution of Sangh literature across India, which was predicated on building networks of contacts.

In one letter, Desai asks Modi: 'From your end try to send us the maximum addresses to which *Satyavani* newspaper can be posted'.[80] Desai was enthusiastic to think creatively about how to 'recirculate' information in India beyond just the written word, even considering trying to make use of radio broadcasts.[81] Modi was in touch with not only Desai, but others in Britain, the United States, and East Africa.[82]

The Emergency was a moment that saw the Gujarati diaspora, who form a very significant proportion of Indians overseas, particularly actively engaged with the political and social affairs of the homeland. Modi's account of the period paints a picture of a tight-knit transnational network of communication, capital flows, and the movement of people. It is a truism that Modi's perspective was Gujarati-centric, but many other sources also note the heavy concentration of activists from the region. Indeed, the Prime Minister's Office in New Delhi observed their substantial role, believing that the Alexandra Palace FISI conference 'was largely funded by the Gujarati community', and expressing a desire 'to win over the Gujaratis [in the UK] to the PM's side'.[83] To achieve this, Indira Gandhi sent the former Chief Minister of Gujarat to Britain on a propaganda mission in 1976.

In particular, we can see the disproportionate involvement of East African Asians (a very high percentage of whom were Gujarati émigrés) in anti-Emergency activism. Swamy, in an interview, suggested that people already expelled from one country had 'nothing to lose' and therefore less to fear.[84] Whilst this mythologised account must be treated with caution, many factors did predispose East African 'twice-migrants' to maintain strong connections with the homeland. This meant they already had a range of communications and kinship networks in place, in addition to a strong sense of involvement in their homeland communities and, to an extent, Indian political affairs. But, quite contrary to Swamy's belief that they had 'nothing to lose', some members of the Gujarati diaspora were beginning to accumulate considerable resources in Britain and elsewhere, some of which they donated to the cause.

Others, while sympathetic, were less keen to engage actively, perhaps put off by fear for their own security and wellbeing.

Situating this political engagement with the homeland in the lived experiences of migrants in Britain during this period is critical. Desai told Modi that while Indians overseas were eager to support the anti-Emergency campaigns, they were reluctant to do so openly out of fear that their host country governments may react badly.[85] Echoing this, an account by Coomi Kapoor, Swamy's sister-in-law, reports that 'Roxna [Swamy's wife] felt the RSS people she was asked to meet seemed a trifle timid and fearful of upsetting the British authorities'.[86] These anxieties reflected their vulnerable status as migrants and minorities, and, for many, a recent history of expulsion from East Africa. In the 1970s, the National Front was in ascendance in England—reacting fiercely to the influx of East African refugees—and Enoch Powell's infamous 'Rivers of Blood' speech was a recent memory. Exclusion and disenfranchisement were compounded by a lack of political representation: from 1929 to 1987 there was not a single Black or Asian MP in the House of Commons.[87] Engagement with homeland politics was perhaps a more attractive, credible, and germane alternative for the Indian diaspora, although one that came with perceived risks.

We must, however, be sceptical of sources that paint all Indians in Britain as ineludibly involved and invested in the Emergency. The diaspora's experience of the episode needs to be located in a broader context, taking into account other struggles and exigencies of the time. The 1970s was a turbulent period for South Asians in Britain: the ascendance of violent racist groups (tragically underscored in 1976 with the murder of Gurdip Singh Chaggar), the rise of radical Asian Youth Movements (from the mid-1970s), the Grunwick Dispute (1976–8), and a range of social and economic struggles all represented political concerns much closer to home.[88] There is a generational dimension to this: while the first generation migrants may have been more invested in Indian politics, younger generations had more interest in (radical) political issues in Britain.[89] Many Asian people during this period identified in terms of 'political blackness' and were engaged in more broad-based campaigns and axes of solidarity, eschewing narrower ethnic politics or forms of 'long-distance nationalism'. Domestic political concerns are all ignored by

Hindu nationalist accounts that place the Emergency as *the* critical struggle of the time.

In addition, the resettlement from East Africa (and particularly Uganda) was extremely fraught, and those who emigrated to Britain had to negotiate a distressing and discombobulating period. They were met by considerable resistance from various political factions and a large proportion of British society in general, with the government's often inadequate provisions for the refugees adding to their anxiety.[90] This sense of precarity was exacerbated by the restrictions on immigration introduced through the Commonwealth Immigrants Act (1968) and the Immigration Act (1971), and the controversies surrounding the Race Relations Act (1976). In short, Britain's Indian population—which by the end of the 1970s had swelled to over three quarters of a million[91]—had many concerns closer to home. But while for many in the diaspora, the Emergency did not represent a critical struggle, for those involved in the activism it constituted a pivotal political moment.

The anti-Emergency mobilisation had a significant legacy for the Sangh Parivar abroad and, later, for the diasporic sections of the BJP. Figures who were active in opposition to the Emergency overseas have taken a leading role in diasporic Hindutva organisations in recent years. Ved Prakash Nanda had attended RSS *shakhas* in Delhi as a young man before travelling to America to study law in Chicago and at Yale.[92] As a lawyer at the University of Denver, Nanda was one of the most prominent figures criticising the Emergency in America, testifying before a Congressional subcommittee about human rights abuses in India in June 1976, and publishing academic articles as well as journalism attacking Mrs Gandhi's actions.[93] He was a central figure in the Hindu Swayamsevak Sangh (HSS) in America for many years, and in 2002 became the organisation's *Sanghchalak* (President).[94] On the other side of the Atlantic, Hasmukh Shah, who served as founding General Secretary of FISI during the Emergency, explicitly refers to the formative nature of the period: 'Those 19 months were the darkest in the history of India, but also made us what we are today'.[95] Shah would go on to become a core leader in the VHP-UK and was closely involved in organising various campaigns and major events around the Ram temple movement from the 1980s (discussed in depth in the next chapter).

For some people, the experience of the Emergency itself was their route into Hindutva organisations. One activist, Mukund Mody, described the impact that the Emergency had on him. Mody had been living in the US for eight years, working as a doctor, when 'the imposition of emergency by Mrs Indira Gandhi in 1975 gave a u-turn to [his] life' and he joined with 'like-minded Indians', most of whom 'belonged to Vishwa Hindu Parishad and RSS', to oppose the government's actions.[96] Mody did not just participate in anti-Emergency activism but supported it financially. Narendra Modi writes in his Emergency memoir that Mukund Mody, in making a major financial contribution to the cause, 'took on the role of *Bhamashah*'—a reference to a sixteenth-century general and Rajasthani folk hero who donated his wealth to Maharana Pratap in order to raise an army against the Mughals.[97]

Mody's mobilisation was not short-lived; instead, he went on to forge relationships with leading Hindutva politicians in India and to play a significant role in diasporic Hindutva organisations in America. Mody described in an interview how he first came into 'close contact' with A.B. Vajpayee in March 1977—the month the Emergency ended—and they organised an international FISI conference together.[98] This personal relationship was renewed over the years each time Vajpayee visited the US, when he would stay in Mody's Staten Island home.[99] In the 1980s, Mody continued to work as Secretary-General of FISI and to organise Hindu youth camps in America for the VHP.[100] In 1990, he travelled to India to meet 'the hierarchy of the BJP', who wanted to open cells of the party in foreign countries ahead of the 1991 general elections. Mody founded the Overseas Friends of the BJP in March 1991 and Advani visited New York City to launch it the following month.[101]

Another important figure in the American Sangh whose experience during the Emergency was formative was Ramesh Bhutada, who moved to Chicago from India in 1968 for postgraduate study. The imprisonment of his father during the Emergency, for his RSS connections, was pivotal for him: 'Although Bhutada was not a political person, he was deeply shaken by this unravelling of democracy in India. He joined protests against the emergency regime and got closer to RSS for the first time in his life, got to understand it and began organizing shakha in his home.'[102] In the decades that followed, Bhatuda was a key leader in many different Sangh-affiliated organisations in the US, including the HSS, the India Development and Relief Fund, and the OFBJP. He has been a major philanthropist for Hindu- and Hindutva-related causes, including various political donations and a recent $1 million gift to the Hindu University of America in Florida, and was also 'instrumental in the "Howdy Modi" event in Houston in 2019 that attracted some 20,000 people'.[103] The experiences of these individuals during the Emergency—and the roles they went on to play in the Sangh overseas—illustrate the extent to which this period was critical in the global Hindu nationalist movement.

The Indian state and 'transnational citizenship'

The final section of this chapter explores what these events tell us about the Indian state's attitudes to its diaspora. The Indian diaspora changed radically in the first few decades after India gained independence. In 1947, the majority of the four million overseas Indians were located in other developing countries—the result of indenture and other forms of intra-empire mobility—but in subsequent years the diaspora grew rapidly in size, changed in demographic composition, and emigrated increasingly to the Global North. Furthermore, over the second half of the twentieth century, these migrants attained increasingly higher levels of social, economic, and political capital. However, Indian government policy towards this growing, dynamic community during this period has scarcely been studied and forms a major lacuna in the recent literature. Some scholars have dismissed the issue altogether: Latha Varadarajan has written that in 'the first four decades after Independence... diaspora issues were consciously sidelined', and moreover that 'the role of the Indian diaspora in shaping the foreign policy agenda of the Indian state was virtually non-existent'.[104] Mario Rutten and Pravin Patel write that East

African Asian 'twice-migrants', feeling that they were ignored by the Indian government, ironically translated 'NRI' (Non-Resident Indian) as 'Non-Required Indians'.[105]

Archival-based histories of overseas Indians have usually focused on the period before independence, examining labour migration and transnational anti-colonial movements.[106] Many studies of the economic importance of the diaspora have concentrated overwhelmingly on the years since the 1990s,[107] regarding the earlier period only as a 'missed opportunity' for the Indian government.[108] Although some scholarship posited the end of the 1970s as a turning point in India's diaspora policy, this has tended to refer only to attempts to encourage foreign direct investment from non-resident Indians, while neglecting the Emergency and the political significance of the diaspora.[109]

The existing literature is particularly inadequate on the earlier history of what can be termed 'transnational citizenship'. Here, the term is meant in a broad sense for various forms of engagement in the politics of multiple nation-states, rather than the more formal, legalistic type, or that which pertains to external or 'non-citizen/denizen' (voting) rights.[110] After 1947, the Government of India refused formal citizenship to diasporic Indians and Nehru instructed the 'older' Indian diaspora to integrate themselves into their adopted homelands. Studies of Indian citizenship therefore typically ascribe the diaspora little relevance from the time of Independence until the 1990s; the intervening decades are more or less blank. In Niraja Gopal Jayal's history of Indian citizenship, for instance, she discusses Nehru's distancing of the diaspora and argues that 'this attitude began to undergo a change [only] around 1998' under Prime Minister A.B. Vajpayee.[111] Chakravorty, Kapur, and Singh's important recent monograph on Indians in America reinforces this view that 'the Indian government and its diaspora shared mutual apathy' until their relations were 'transformed' from the 1990s.[112] This fails to account for important earlier developments; the diaspora was engaged in processes of transnational citizenship during the Emergency and, consequently, the Indian government tried to influence this.

During the Emergency, the attempts to mobilise the diaspora by the RSS and other groups did not go unchallenged by the Congress Party and the Government of India. Overseas anti-Emergency activism was a matter of concern at the highest level, and the diaspora became a proxy battleground for Indian politics. The Indian Ambassador to the United States, T.N. Kaul, wrote to Indira Gandhi personally to keep her informed about the political activities of Indians in America, and to recommend a severe response. In particular, Kaul related to Mrs Gandhi the activities of Subramanian Swamy and the details of the people he met. He informed her that Swamy 'is going round various towns where there are Indians and Indian students, holding meetings and doing some vicious, false and malicious propaganda'.[113] The intensity of surveillance indicated in correspondence between the US and New Delhi—including the length of time Swamy spent in various meetings, for instance with newspaper editors, and what he said during dinner meetings—is striking. Kaul forwarded the text of Swamy's interview with the diaspora newspaper, *India Abroad*, and informed the prime minister that he had unofficially sent a 'bumptious and aggressive' Indian lawyer to challenge his statements. He also suggested that Indira Gandhi should request that the US State Department prevent Swamy's activities.[114]

Other official correspondence refers to anti-Emergency meetings and articles in the foreign press, including details of individual activists and relevant press clippings. One report from the Information Service of India provides a detailed report on a seminar held at a New York state college.[115] Another letter, from the World Bank to Ambassador Kaul, reveals that the embassy attempted to prevent the bank from recruiting two unnamed candidates on the grounds of their activism, though the bank replied that it 'avoids political considerations'.[116]

Later in 1976, the Rajya Sabha appointed a committee to investigate the conduct and activities of Subramanian Swamy. Their report documented his public statements during his time abroad and concluded that it was 'the first ever case of a Member of Parliament carrying on so blatantly his activities in collusion with anti-India elements abroad to malign our democratic institutions and to provide fuel to the fire of anti-India propaganda by the external enemies of our country'.[117] The committee recommended his expulsion from the Upper House—the first time this had ever happened—in order 'to rid the House of persons who are unfit for membership'.[118]

The radical change in the make-up of the diaspora at this time had a number of consequences. Diasporic Indians were increasingly found in the West, and had different citizenship statuses to the 'old' Indian diaspora. Many of the 'overseas Indians' resident in Britain, and most of the thousands migrating to America at this time, were still officially citizens of independent India. The Indian government sought to exert control over these people through their citizenship status by impounding the passports of several high-profile anti-Emergency activists.

These citizenship policies were improvised by officials in Delhi and in embassies abroad in response to pressure from activists in the diaspora. In August 1975, the Indian Embassy in Washington asked the MEA for legal guidance because Indian citizens in the US were asking whether participating in anti-Emergency protests might lead to the revoking of their passports.[119] The ministry replied that:

> If the activities of an Indian citizen abroad are found prejudicial to the maintenance of internal security in India, he will become liable to be dealt with under the relevant Indian laws… All Indian citizens may be advised to conduct themselves as responsible citizens and not engage in any activity which is likely to harm the interests of the enforcement of emergency regulations in India.[120]

The weapon available to them was to impound passports under the Passport Act, a broadly defined power that could be invoked 'in the interests of the sovereignty and integrity of India, the security of India, friendly relations of India with any foreign country, or in the interests of the general public'.[121] A few months later, Indian embassies abroad were instructed to produce a 'blacklist of undesirable Indians'—those 'who indulge in anti-national and unpatriotic activities'—whose passports could be cancelled.[122] This was a strategy decided at the highest level to prevent anti-Emergency activism spreading in the diaspora. But in certain respects, it was a fairly toothless policy as it required the person in question to voluntarily return to India and surrender their passport, so perhaps it can be better understood as an intimidation tactic (which could also have an impact on their families back in India). Additionally, and maybe more impactfully, a number of students supported by Indian government grants had their funding cut, including members of FISI working in Britain, such as Jagadish Mitra Sood, the secretary of the Kenyan Sangh, and Ratnakar Bharati, who made broadcasts on the BBC during the Emergency.[123]

As well as taking concrete actions against individuals abroad where they could, the Government of India also tried to seize as much underground literature as possible. It used the fact that these underground newsletters originated with activists in the diaspora in order to discredit them, declaring that this was proof of interference by the so-called 'foreign hand'. For example, in January 1976, a printed bulletin entitled 'Indians in USA demand lifting of emergency, support Lok Sangharsha—Letter from America' was seized by the police from RSS workers in Madhya Pradesh. The censored Indian press wrote up the story under the heading 'CIA documents seized', informing the public that the RSS members had been carrying 'confidential documents concerning anti-India propaganda by Americans and CIA agents'.[124]

New Delhi also produced its own propaganda, justifying the Emergency, aimed specifically at the diaspora. After the *New York Times* advertisement on 15 August 1975, denouncing the Emergency and calling for JP's release, the Indian government allegedly 'mailed to 5000 addresses in America packets containing booklets and pamphlets carrying vile abuse of JP and the RSS'.[125] Personnel, including government ministers, arrived in Britain and the United States to challenge 'anti-national' sentiments, both in public fora and in conversation with their foreign counterparts. Indira Gandhi sent leading Congress politicians, including former Gujarat Chief Minister Hitendra Desai and Jaisukhlal Hathi, to tour England (travelling to London, Birmingham, and Leicester— heartlands of Britain's Indian population), funded by the MEA.

B.N. Tandon, Secretary in the Prime Minister's Office, wrote on 9 June that '[the] PM is keen that the Indians in UK should sing her praises and Desai and Hathi are being used for this'.[126] The ministers received support from expatriate Congress supporters whose overseas branches had been established long before the Emergency. These were truly transnational actors: the All India Congress Committee invited representatives of the Overseas Congress in Southall to attend its sessions as observers, and in September 1975, Indira Gandhi welcomed to New Delhi a delegation from the Birmingham Indian Overseas Congress, who had organised demonstrations attacking the British media's 'biased' coverage of the Emergency.[127] The MEA's External Publicity Division also armed those Indians who were travelling abroad with government-produced pamphlets, several of which concentrated on the RSS, including such titles as *Triumph of Good over Evil*.[128]

Anti-Emergency activism also prompted the government to think in more positive terms: how it could make use of its diaspora. Indira Gandhi herself, in a letter of 1975, wrote that 'India should use these people in its publicity drive in the same manner as Israel uses the Jews in [the] USA and elsewhere on their behalf'.[129] She went on: 'The Israelis had a tremendous advantage. The Jews are the richest and most tenacious of the communities in [the] US. But we should make an effort. Thought should be given to organising Indian[s] abroad'.[130]

This response to anti-Emergency activism was therefore also a moment of transition in the Indian imagining of its diaspora. T.N. Kaul wrote to the prime minister to suggest that she call a convention in India (though not in Delhi amidst its 'pseudo-intellectuals and doubting Thomases'), where diasporic Indians from the USA, the UK, and Canada could 'contribute towards the mainstream of Indian life'.[131] Kaul had specifically Indians living in Britain and North America in mind; the presence of Indians who had settled in 'East Africa, Fiji or the Caribbean' could cause 'misinterpretations'. It is clear that he too was thinking about diasporas comparatively—even competitively—telling Mrs Gandhi that, '[t]he Israelis, the Irish, the Greeks, the Italians, and others already do this'.[132]

These ideas were in fact put in action almost immediately following the end of the Emergency by the Janata Party—a coalition, including the Hindu nationalist Jana Sangh, that ousted the Congress government. The new Minister of External Affairs, A.B. Vajpayee, created a 'special cell' for 'persons of Indian origin living abroad', and held conferences in Delhi to discuss the diaspora.[133] At one of these meetings, Vajpayee said, 'Though our sons and daughters have gone abroad to work or to reside there, India will never disown them or fail to appreciate and respect their essential loyalty to the culture and heritage of the mother country.'[134] Now in government, Vajpayee—who had been one of the RSS's more high-profile *pracharaks* jailed during the Emergency—was able to act on the Sangh's well-established relationship with the diaspora. Vajpayee himself had a history of engagement with the diaspora that predates even the 1970s. He visited Kenya in 1965 (the first of at least five trips there), and, as discussed in Chapter 1, was even present in London during 'the first ever planned formal meeting of Sangh workers' in Britain in August 1966.[135]

While India did not extend political rights to the diaspora in the immediate aftermath of the Emergency, it was groups formed to oppose the Emergency that kept the matter under discussion through their campaigns. FISI began demanding dual citizenship for overseas Indians from 1978 because, in the words of Mukund Mody, it would 'psychologically influence NRIs and they shall feel part and parcel of India'.[136] FISI continued to push for voting rights at its meetings and conferences throughout the 1980s.[137] Nonetheless, the main avenues for the engagement of the diaspora by the state following the Emergency were economic: in 1979 the Malhotra Committee, which had been appointed by the Department of Economic Affairs, 'made various recommendations to increase the level of NRI investment', leading to the (re-)establishment of a special cell for NRI investment in 1983.[138] Ever since, the importance of diasporic dollars to the Indian economy has been keenly felt, with the BJP particularly vocal in their desire to attract NRI investors. Today, India is, by some margin, the greatest remittance-receiving country in the world, surpassing $100 billion (nearly 3% of GDP) in 2022.[139]

Hindu nationalist governments have been tangibly more proactive in terms of diaspora-oriented policy. It was under Vajpayee's prime ministership in 1999 that the 'Person of Indian Origin' card scheme was launched; this has since been superseded by the Overseas Citizenship of India (although, despite its name, it does not confer full citizenship or voting rights, and in the wake of the Citizenship (Amendment) Act 2019 is more precarious and easier to revoke). In 2000, the High Level Committee on the Indian Diaspora was appointed by the MEA, eventually leading to the establishment of the Ministry for Overseas Indian Affairs in 2004. A year earlier, Pravasi Bharatiya Divas (Non-Resident Indian Day) was launched—a celebration designed to 'strengthen the engagement of the overseas Indian community with the Government of India and reconnect them with their roots'.[140] These all constitute milestones in the transformation of India-diaspora relations. The long gestation of India's twenty-first-century diaspora policies is acknowledged in the committee's report itself, which begins by quoting Vajpayee's speech from the post-Emergency conference held in November 1977.[141] Schemes recommended by the committee were modelled on other countries' diaspora engagement policies: the Know India Programme for young people from the diaspora to visit India, for instance, imitated the Birthright Israel programme that the committee had studied.[142] More recently, there is a sense of India attempting to emulate the Chinese in terms of a diaspora that is closely monitored, influenced, and instrumentalised for political objectives. It is clear that this kind of comparative thinking about India's diaspora must be traced back at least as far as the Emergency.

As we have seen, the Emergency was a critical moment in the relationship between Hindu nationalist politics and activists in the diaspora. Individuals who had been politicised through FISI would go on to be involved in the HSS or VHP, or found new groups such as the Overseas Friends of the BJP. The institutional legacy of the Sangh's anti-Emergency activism has resulted in its role being commemorated while other groups' contributions have been downplayed or forgotten. The omission of non-Hindutva opposition to the Emergency was also reinforced by Indira

Gandhi's government propaganda at the time, which claimed that the opposition was co-ordinated by 'well-organised fascist groups'.[143] However, as mentioned earlier in the chapter, a wide range of other organisations and individuals also actively opposed the Emergency. The Sangh-affiliated *Satyavani* was just one of a plethora of underground newsletters produced in the diaspora and smuggled into India, for instance: *Swaraj*, *New India Bulletin*, and *CRIPP News* (Campaign for the Release of Indian Political Prisoners) were all equivalents produced by left-wing groups.

This diversity has been neglected partly because many other anti-Emergency groups proved to be short-lived. Campaigns around the release of particular politicians, such as the 'Free JP Campaign', had no reason to perpetuate themselves as institutions. For other groups, such as Socialist International, which campaigned for George Fernandes, the Emergency represented just one issue in an ongoing, globally oriented, series of concerns. Furthermore, fraternal relationships between socialist parties and trade unions within India and their counterparts in Europe and elsewhere diminished as these groups fragmented and declined in importance. Other groups, such as the Alliance Against Fascist Dictatorship in India—a far-left group whose figurehead in Britain was Mary Tyler, a schoolteacher who had served five years in an Indian prison for her association with the Naxalites—had a particularly evanescent existence.[144] Moreover, other agendas became more prominent in the politics of Indian diaspora communities during and after the Emergency, especially amongst the younger generation, such as anti-racist campaigns and conflicts over Sikh separatism. These complex and sometimes competing political movements are beyond the scope of this book. However, it does need to be stressed that the lack of institutional continuity on the part of non-Hindutva anti-Emergency groups, in contrast to FISI and the RSS, has allowed the Hindu nationalist narrative of this period to dominate. It was the Hindu nationalists who publicised their version of events in the aftermath of the Emergency and have continued to do so ever since, while leading figures from those groups continually revisit the Emergency years for contemporary political purposes.

After the Emergency, Indira Gandhi sought to use diaspora Congress supporters' organisations to rebuild her reputation abroad. A number of separate Indian Overseas Congress groups contested the right to host her visit to London in November 1978.[145] In the end, she received cheques from the Southall-based group at a dinner in London, and from the Midlands-based group at a dinner in Birmingham.[146] However, the visit did not go as smoothly as Mrs Gandhi intended. She had been invited to address a meeting at the Dominion cinema in Southall for an hour but the moment she appeared she was greeted by 'a barrage of shouting, stamping and whistling' from sections of the audience. She was able to give only a short speech before being 'ushered out from the back of the platform by police special branch officers'.[147] The protests that dogged her visit were organised by groups sympathetic to the left and the Shiromani Akali Dal, a Sikh party, as well as Hindu nationalist groups. The Congress politician Pranab Mukherjee, who accompanied Indira Gandhi on this visit, attributes what he calls the 'ugly and violent' demonstrations in Southall only to rabble-rousing letters circulated by FISI.[148]

During the 1980s, groups styling themselves the Indian Overseas Congress engaged in fierce contests with pro-Khalistan groups, and a number were assassinated, including one of Indira Gandhi's hosts in 1978, Tarsem Singh Toor.[149] In 2001, in response to this confusion and at a time when the BJP's diasporic links were well organised, Sonia Gandhi founded the Congress Party's overseas wings anew during a visit to the United States.[150] Today, Congress continue to play catch-up on the BJP's considerable lead in cultivating diaspora support. Rahul Gandhi has actively tried to engage overseas audiences, but finds he has a great deal of ground to make up and diasporic devotion to Modi remains a major obstacle. While this book has begun to shed light on these dynamics, the position of the diaspora vis-à-vis electoral politics in India is a topic on which further research is required.

Conclusion

The Emergency's legacy is both substantial and complex; some of its lasting impacts on Indian political life are only now starting to be explored and understood. After Indira Gandhi's still-enigmatic decision to call elections in March 1977, Congress's post-independence hegemony was broken by the victorious Janata Party. The Jana Sangh's participation in the Janata coalition constituted its first forays into government. Two decades later, India had its first Hindu nationalist government in the form of Vajpayee's BJP-led National Democratic Alliance. While many view the Emergency as a watershed moment for Congress's domination of Indian politics, in other ways the episode's impact was less straightforward; although defeated in the 1977 elections, Indira Gandhi was reinstated as prime minister in 1980 and Congress recovered almost all the vote share they had lost. But the Emergency's significance must be viewed beyond just electoral politics. The Emergency constituted a crucial moment for the disarticulation of nationalism from the Congress Party, and even from the state itself. Developing Rajagopal's argument that the state failed to confine politics to designated spaces within India during this period—including in its attempt to exert 'control over communications'—we can also consider a transnational dimension to the resistance to the state's 'monopoly' over politics.[151]

While the mainstreaming of the Sangh's political wing neither began nor ended with the Emergency, Hindu nationalist politics underwent an important transformation during this episode.[152] Sangh networks in India were strengthened through their resistance to the government; by engaging in new forms of activism, its members acquired new skills and the movement developed new leaders. Politically, the movement also enjoyed reputational gains. Advani's reference to the shedding of 'political untouchability' was perhaps best encapsulated in Jayaprakash Narayan's pithy declaration to the Jana Sangh: 'If you are a fascist, then I too am a fascist'.[153] In turn, Hindu nationalist retellings of the Emergency also reflected a new self-confidence and heightened morale, still resonant today.

This chapter has illustrated that some of the most substantive, yet currently overlooked, advances made by the Sangh during the Emergency—in terms of capacity, skills, and networks—relate to the global mobilisation of the Hindu nationalist movement. In many ways, the RSS's estimation of the diaspora and its possibilities was hugely enhanced. This was illustrated by a resolution passed by their Akhil Bharatiya Karyakari Mandal (All-India Executive Committee), immediately following the Emergency in 1977:

> Our brother Indians living abroad have also displayed boundless courage of conviction during this period. Their joining the struggle intensified the voice of liberty raised from our soil into a thundering roar reverberating all over the world. They succeeded in mobilizing world-wide sympathy for the struggle of the Indian people.[154]

It is revealing that many of the Indian Hindu nationalist leaders who witnessed the efforts of the overseas wings of the Sangh during this period—such as H.V. Seshadri, Rajendra Singh, A.B. Vajpayee, Subramanian Swamy, and Narendra Modi—maintained a much closer relationship with the diaspora after the Emergency. We must be cautious of the Sangh's own accounts of their 'crucial' role during the episode, which often obfuscates the dynamic, and in many ways more significant, part played by a broader range of groups, particularly various left-wing actors. However, the importance of the period in terms of the confidence and morale that it brought to the Hindu nationalist movement goes beyond their practical contribution to opposing the Emergency. While the Emergency was not the first point at which the Sangh had engaged with the diaspora, it represents a major milestone for Hindu nationalism abroad. It is therefore necessary to revise the common perception that global Hindutva first made an important impact during the Ayodhya mobilisations of the 1980s and early 1990s. Furthermore, it reinforces the need to understand Hindutva 'long-distance nationalism' not as an organic expression of patriotic nostalgia emanating from the diaspora—as envisaged by Benedict Anderson—but as a political movement organised through dynamic and carefully co-ordinated, multidirectional networks.[155]

This chapter has also revealed that the other important aspect of the Emergency was the nature and extent to which the Indian government engaged in a contest to politicise and mobilise the diaspora. This contrasts with the existing literature, which argues that the government largely ignored 'NRIs' throughout this period. Understanding the Emergency, therefore, is vital to comprehending the origins of the diaspora engagement policies put in place by the Indian state at the end of the twentieth century (and still being actively developed today). The Emergency both represented a newfound interest in the diaspora on the part of the government and precipitated a shift in the understanding of the diaspora—as potential threats and assets. In this sense, the Emergency represents a 'global event'. Following a period after independence in which the state largely disregarded Indians overseas—partly as a matter of policy, and partly due to a lack of vision and capacity—we see, from the 1970s, the transition to a situation more familiar today, in which the diaspora were courted for the political and economic roles they could play. The consequences of the Emergency for global Hindu nationalist networks and for India's evolving conceptions of transnational citizenship reverberate to this day.

4

FROM MILTON KEYNES TO AYODHYA

THE VISHWA HINDU PARISHAD AND THE GLOBAL CAMPAIGN FOR THE RAM TEMPLE

On 6 December 1992, Hindu nationalist *karsevaks* (volunteers) stormed a historic mosque in north India and tore the structure apart with bare hands and metal bars. The widely condemned action was a flashpoint in the surge of Hindu nationalist activism at the end of the twentieth century—the culmination of many years of radicalisation. It was connected to a decades-long *Ram Janmabhoomi* movement, which saw the mosque turned into a site of communal and legal dispute shortly after independence (sparked in part by the surreptitious installation of a Ram idol in 1949). The term *Ram Janmabhoomi* literally means 'Ram birthplace' but is also used as shorthand for the impassioned and sporadically violent movement to build—or, as many would insist, 'rebuild'—a Ram temple on the site of the sixteenth-century Babri Masjid in Ayodhya.

Far from being a provincial issue, the movement to build a Hindu temple in place of a mosque built by the Mughal emperor, Babur, in present-day Uttar Pradesh, had a distinctive appeal for Hindus overseas. Hindu nationalist actors and multi-directional transnational networks, through which funds and other forms of support were transmitted, made Indian politics less parochial and de-territorialised it in new ways. Both the agitations leading to the mosque's eventual destruction and the tension that followed it played out in Britain, the US, and elsewhere. As with the political activism around the Emergency, the engagement with the political landscape of the homeland during the Ram temple movement made use of, and developed, existing networks and institutional structures. Many of the same groups and individuals who had been involved, and politically awakened, in the anti-Emergency activism were engaged in transnational components to the 'saffron wave'[1] of the 1980s and 1990s. There were, of course, certain key differences; the Emergency was a cause that attracted support from across the political spectrum. The crusade to construct the Ram temple, by contrast, was exclusively Hindu nationalist and, initially at least, represented the concerns of a much narrower base of supporters in terms of region and caste.

Whilst Indian diaspora mobilisation against the Emergency had a largely practical pretext (predominantly to resist the ban on certain organisations and press censorship, and to call for the release of political prisoners and the holding of elections), the Ram temple mobilisations engaged overseas Hindus for more emotional and ideological reasons. The movement was centripetal in essence, urging Hindus to focus their attention on the city of Ayodhya in the middle of India's 'Hindi Belt'. The first brick with which Hindu activists hoped to construct the new Ram temple was theatrically put in place on 9 November 1989. At the exact moment of its laying, Hindus across the country were called upon to face Ayodhya, Mecca-like, and make an offering of flowers.[2] As Hindus in the north, south, east, and west of the country turned to Ayodhya, both metaphorically and literally, many living overseas also participated in nationalist rituals. This was of huge existential significance for the diaspora, but also widened the scope, ambition, and confidence of those in India. The expansive geographies of pseudo-*yatra* (procession) mobilisations not only staked a claim to the territories in Bharat, but also incorporated and developed global dimensions of the Hindu nationalist movement.

The growth of Hindutva in India in the final two decades of the twentieth century was therefore also mirrored in the diaspora.

At times these two trajectories were interwoven; the Sangh's growth in India had an impact on the Sangh's growth in Britain, and (although we must be careful not to overstate this) the Indian diaspora positively affected the Hindu nationalist movement in India. Jaffrelot and Therwath correctly challenge Benedict Anderson's 'long-distance nationalism' paradigm for placing an overwhelming emphasis on 'a nearly automatic allegiance binds members of an ethnic diaspora to its homeland'.[3] Support for the Sangh Parivar overseas cannot be framed as 'mere nostalgia or even spontaneous mobilisations'.[4] To understand inflections of Hindu nationalism in the diaspora, we must unpick complex, dynamic, and multidirectional political identities and networks, paying close attention to institutional structures and organisational hierarchies in India, Britain, and elsewhere.

The Vishwa Hindu Parishad

At the heart of the Ayodhya mobilisations, in India and overseas, was the Vishwa Hindu Parishad (World Hindu Council) (VHP). Formed in 1964, the VHP constitutes one of the two primary progeny of the RSS (the other being the BJP). As with other organisations of the Parivar it derives its leadership largely from the Sangh, although disagreements (over approach more than ideology) that the VHP has had with the RSS and BJP have caused tension and even acrimony. Its relationship with the electoral wing of the Sangh is key; to a great degree, the organisational strategies and political mobilisation of the Parishad enabled the BJP to win power in 1998/9. While the RSS broadly maintained a distance from the BJP and electoral politics, the VHP was engaged in much more directly political forms of ethno-religious activism.[5]

The VHP may be seen, in some ways, as 'the religious front of the RSS': an ecumenical body for gurus, sects, and their followers.[6] Through committees, councils, and campaigns, the Parishad mimics the proselytism and co-ordinating mechanisms and capabilities of more centrally organised Semitic religions. According to Manjari Katju, one of the organisation's foremost biographers, it combines 'the asceticism of a sadhu with the dynamism of the modern technological age in its endeavour to revitalise Hinduism'.[7]

One key aim of the Parishad from its inception was to consolidate, and in a sense forge, a proud and assertive Hindu majority in India. All 'indigenous' religions are to be drawn into the Hindu fold, Muslim and Christian influences in India are suppressed and their followers are pressured to 'reconvert', caste must be downplayed, and a vast, diverse range of historical and mythological figures are appropriated into a monolithic Hindu pantheon.[8] A major component of this 'miniaturisation of India'[9] has involved the 'Hinduisation' of India's tribal or *adivasi* (indigenous) population: more than 100 million people spread across the country, with a range of animist, syncretic, and vernacular beliefs. Many *adivasis* have been encouraged towards Christianity (since the colonial period) and Maoism (since the 1960s), and the Parishad has sought to counteract these competitors with its own form of missionary activity. Drawing on a genealogy of nationalist Hindu reformers—in particular Vivekananda—the VHP pursues 'anti-superstition' and 're-conversion' campaigns alongside the promotion of standardised (often Brahmanical) Hindu practices and beliefs. It sees its role as a 'guru' to guide Hindus spiritually, and forge a united Hindu population into a political community.[10] In this way, the VHP, alongside other organisations, has been able to permeate Hindutva across broad and diverse geographies of India. This has partly been facilitated through a vernacularised approach, which in some ways reflects layers of adaptability in diasporic contexts.

Most of the VHP's activities are India-based, but, as its name implies, it has always had a global outlook. This is rooted in its mission to serve as an all-encompassing umbrella for each and every Hindu, wherever they are located. Delegates from Trinidad and Kenya attended its first ever meeting in 1964. Two years later, up to 250 attendees from a wide range of countries attended the VHP's first major *sammelan* (conference), which took place during the Kumbh Mela in Allahabad.[11] These participants came from places witnessing an increasing influx of Indian immigrants, like the UK and the US, as well as countries that already had well-settled Hindu populations, like Fiji, Mauritius, and South Africa.

Within just five years of the VHP's birth, branches were set up in Britain and America; today there are global outposts—many of which co-ordinate numerous regional chapters—in around 20–25 countries. These overseas operations are discussed in the final section of this chapter.

The Parishad's international perspective on one level reflects the Hindu nationalist movement's neo-Vedantist universalism, but more specifically a desire to bring together *all* Hindus, irrespective of where they live. The VHP understands that in being able to mobilise the support of Hindus outside India it can maximise its political influence and economic clout. It sees this worldwide approach as a key feature of its overarching, self-claimed mission to organise, consolidate, serve, and protect Hindu society and *dharma*. The global outreach of its founding gurus is another important factor: their founding president, Chinmayananda Saraswati, cultivated a huge global following and the year after the VHP's formation went on a tour of thirty-nine cities in eighteen countries. The hyper-mobility of many gurus owes a lot to the VHP itself, which plays an important co-ordinating and promotional role in the transnational peregrinations of Hindutva-sympathetic religious leaders.

In spite of these important global dimensions—and the activities of the VHP's diasporic branches, which are discussed in depth in the final section of this chapter—the Parishad's principal focus has been on campaigns within India: resisting conversion, opposing cow slaughter, stimulating assertive Hindu pride, forging Hindu unity and orthodoxy, and mobilising against Christians and Muslims. The organisation, and its various subsidiaries, became increasingly political in 1980s when it entered a phase of militant mass activism, buttressing the rise of the BJP as it focused its efforts on *Ram Janmabhoomi*.

The political movement to build a Ram temple on the site of a sixteenth-century mosque in Ayodhya was, in many ways, the defining political struggle of late twentieth-century India. It was both a practical nucleus for Hindutva mobilisation and a metonym for a much wider cause. India, according to the Hindu nationalist historian Sitaram, was 'the land of Ayodhya'.[12] The struggle to replace the *masjid* with the *mandir* was also metaphoric, and even cathartic. India's former glory was to be recovered and razing the 'invader's' edifice was central to this. But *Ram Janmabhoomi* was not just about righting past wrongs: the movement also symbolised the rejection of 'pandering to minorities', and the combative assertion of the majority's primacy. Furthermore, beneath the manifest, tangible aspect of the campaign was an attempt to define what this ostensibly monolithic majority 'community' was, and to assert the Sangh Parivar's right to speak for it. Ram represented a restoration of glory; BJP election slogans from the 1980s to the era of Yogi Adityanath have promised to make *Ram Rajya* (the Rule of Ram) a reality. After two terms of BJP rule in India—and with the Ayodhya mandir construction underway amidst widespread 'saffronisation' across India—this pledge seems finally to be coming to fruition.

Spearheaded by Hindutva leaders such as the BJP President L.K. Advani, and the VHP's Sadhvi Rithambara and Ashok Singhal, the campaign created a history of Ayodhya that reaches back to an imagined, ancient, halcyon era. Although a blend of the historical and the mythical, this was presented as indisputable, objective fact. Islam represents the rupture to this narrative, which, thus, 'becomes precise in numbers and dates when it comes to the repeated destructions and re-erections of the temple and to the multitude of saintly *bhakta* heroes who have died... sacrificing their lives while defending the holy site'.[13] The subjective antiquity of nationalism has a special resonance for Hindutva, which, almost paradoxically, draws on an Orientalist understanding of India that emerged from a Western modernity.[14] This subjectivity was highlighted by the controversial BJP-appointed Chair of the Indian Council of Historical Research, Y. Sudershan Rao, who in 2015 said, 'I went to Ayodhya. Just walk through the streets—you will get a feeling of living in Ramayana times... I had this feeling. You can't call it a myth, that's my experience... What more proof do you want if you are convinced in your heart, your mind?'[15] This position was also reflected in the 2010 Allahabad High Court verdict over how to apportion the land where the mosque had stood, which privileged 'faith and belief' over historical objectivity and expertise. It reinforces Peter van der Veer's argument that to insist on a positivist 'sharp boundary between "religious fiction" and "material facts" in the representation of the past' is 'fallacious'.[16]

This was underlined by the Supreme Court of India's long-awaited and most conclusive judicial ruling, in November 2019, which ordered that the disputed land be handed over to a government-created trust in order to build a Hindu temple where the Babri Masjid had once stood. The Sunni Waqf Board, which had sought possession of the site, was instead offered five acres of land outside Ayodhya, around 20–25km from where they had wished to rebuild a mosque. The verdict came six months after the BJP's second consecutive general election triumph and was broadly viewed as a victory for Hindutva (and, by extension, India's Hindu majority), although the court also ruled that the desecration and destruction of the masjid in 1992 was an illegal act. But in spite of being divisive, the ruling did not result in major civil unrest, as some had feared. Nonetheless, while many hailed the success of 'due process'—and the outcome was celebrated by many Hindus in India and beyond—the verdict also attracted considerable criticism. Zoya Hasan referred to it as 'the endorsement of majoritarian politics by the Supreme Court', while Christophe Jaffrelot raised concerns about 'judicial majoritarianism—or even judicial populism' and the idea 'that religious sentiments prevail over the provisions of the Constitution according to which all citizens are equal, irrespective of their religion'.[17] More broadly, the verdict has been seen to have opened the door, or be linked up, to more challenges to Islamic heritage and litigation around contested monuments as sites for political mobilisation.[18]

From the early 1990s, the VHP ran an office, bookshop, and showroom on a piece of land adjoining the Babri Masjid. Next to a large model of the proposed Ram *mandir* were pamphlets on the dispute, including one entitled *Ramjanmabhoomi ka rakt-ranjit itihas* (The blood-stained history of the birthplace of Ram).[19] The destruction of the Babri Masjid in 1992, the culmination of Advani's electioneering and identity-moulding Rath Yatra (Chariot Pilgrimage), was therefore placed in, and legitimised by, this ancient trajectory, redressing the notions of 'Hindu hurt' and 'majority under siege'. Ayodhya is a metaphor for multiple levels of Hindu identity: it represents the assertion of downtrodden, insulted, and humiliated Hindus over the Muslim occupiers, it serves to place the modern, nationalist Hindu identity in a long and glorious trajectory, and it provides Hindus across the nation a physical focus for their discontents.

There was another highly gendered angle to the Ram temple mobilisations: the mosque was equated to a Muslim domination over female India—Bharat Mata (Mother India). The iconography of Bharat Mata is crucial for Hindu nationalists and is often prominently displayed in many spaces of the Sangh Parivar (although the trope of the nation as mother, which featured in various anti-colonial nationalisms, goes well beyond the Hindu right).[20] In the Hindutva context, Bharat Mata is usually depicted as superimposed onto a map of Akhand Bharat (Greater or Undivided India), and represents both a protector and one who must be protected. This gives rise to a 'dual masculinity'—a brave, muscular, and inherently benign Hindu male ideal, counterposed with an aggressive and threatening Muslim male stereotype, which represents something villainous and potentially defiling (both to individual women and the motherland itself).[21]

Entwined in the discourse surrounding disputes over displaced temples and imposed mosques was a subtext that *mandirs* represent a form of femininity, while the *masjid* is a masculine space, associated with the male body.[22] The demolition of the temple served not just as vengeance, but as a cleansing act: just as Partition was a mutilation of Bharat Mata, the *masjid*—and by extension, Muslims—represented a violation of her sacred territory.[23] Numerous speeches and campaigns simultaneously promoted the notion of Muslim men as lascivious and threatening, and Hindu women as pure and in need of protection. By connecting this with the Babri Masjid issue, which alluded to the mythology of the Ramayana itself, female honour and national honour were conflated in an emotive crescendo. Linked to this was the sexual violence perpetrated in the wake of the demolition—a hallmark of so many ethnic conflicts.

The mobilisations also emphasised an important set of roles for women, not least at the ballot box. The VHP and other groups promoted the notion of *nari shakti* (woman power) but, like many other ethnic nationalisms, highly moderated by the reproductive duty that women were expected to perform in the creation of a Hindu *rashtra* (nation). An important backdrop to the Ram temple mobilisations was the cultivation of a sense of existential threat to Hindu India by way of a demographic timebomb: a fallacious fearmongering that Muslim birth rates exceeding those of Hindus will eventually lead to Hindus becoming a minority.[24] The anxiety is exacerbated by a paranoia of Muslim men wooing and converting Hindu women, by way of what is claimed to be a carefully devised strategy known as 'Love Jihad'. This conspiracy has led to vigilantes, courts of law, and even government 'anti-Romeo squads' intervening in interfaith relationships. These themes are discussed, in the context of Hindu–Muslim relations in Britain, in the final chapter of this book.

The Sangh Parivar's focus on the birthplace of Ram was no accident; Ram was transformed into 'a metaphor of the essential Hinduness of Indian culture'.[25] Over the second half of the twentieth century, the status of Ram—the seventh *avatar* (incarnation) of Vishnu—was metamorphosed into a pre-eminent deity and the personification of a new, militant identity for Hindu men.[26] The Hindu nationalist preoccupation with redressing the persona of Hindu men as effeminate and pacifistic (largely legacies of Orientalism and Gandhism), was reflected in a shifting iconography of Ram as muscular and gladiatorial. Central to this was the creation of a single narrative of Indian history, and Indian mythology, with the VHP and its network of institutions and ideologues as its arbiter.[27]

Three mobilisations defined the rise of the Hindu nationalist movement in the post-Emergency period. All of these engaged with the trope of pilgrimage: the Ekamata Yatra (Pilgrimage for Unity), launched by the VHP in 1983, the Ram Shila Puja (Ram Brick Prayer Ritual) of 1989, and the Advani-led Ram Rath Yatra (Ram Chariot Pilgrimage) in 1990. The Ekamata Yatra was pioneering in its combination of 'traditional' elements of pilgrimage with nationwide mass demonstrations, but the notorious Rath Yatra, which was followed by unprecedented electoral success for the

BJP in the 1991 general elections, was the best known and most iconic of these initiatives.

The strategy of marching along a carefully choreographed route, spreading exhilaration and intimidation along the way, is a time-honoured strategy of the RSS, but the scale and impact of the Rath Yatra was something entirely different. Advani set off from Somnath temple in Gujarat in an air-conditioned Toyota van decorated to resemble Arjun's chariot in the Mahabharata—a fitting metaphor for the BJP's blend of capitalist modernity and Hindu symbolism. The Yatra covered almost 6,000 miles across eight states of northern India and was planned to culminate in Ayodhya itself. In its theatrics and controversy it generated considerable media coverage: this served to amplify the dissemination of Hindutva rhetoric and not only nationalised the issue, but also allowed it to reach a global audience. The campaign was even promoted internationally in advance: Advani addressed followers in London three months before the Yatra began, telling his audience, 'Secularism has come to be equated with allergy to Hinduism'.[28] The Yatra very explicitly represented a departure from secular politics: militant slogans, and music from the popular Mahabharata and Ramayana television series, blared out of the chariot's loudspeakers throughout the route. Advani and his considerable entourage stopped periodically in numerous villages and towns, all the while attracting curiosity, excitement, and new acolytes to the Hindutva cause, and leaving communal tension and violent rioting in its wake.

Advani never made it to Ayodhya. He was arrested, along with VHP President, Ashok Singhal, a week before he was due to reach his destination. But the Yatra's aims had been far exceeded. It had achieved huge publicity, the Ram temple had become the key national political issue of its time, and support for the BJP continued to swell. The Yatra led to widespread outbreaks of violence; communal fervour had been stoked to the extent that just two years later the Babri Masjid would be torn apart by radicalised *karsevaks*, many of whom had participated in the various Ayodhya mobilisations.

Ram Shila Pujas and diasporic donations

While the Rath Yatra is perhaps the best-known of the Ayodhya mobilisations, the Ram Shila Puja (RSP), which began a year before the Yatra, was a crucial precursor. It constituted a turning point for the Hindu nationalist movement and was of particular significance from a global perspective. The RSP made tangible steps towards the construction of a Ram temple (and the destruction of the extant mosque), and was the first, and in certain ways only, of its kind systematically to incorporate the diaspora.

The scheme involved a 'nationwide procession of consecrated bricks', ostensibly for the construction of a Ram temple in Ayodhya. Through this performative 'invented tradition', the VHP ambitiously planned to co-ordinate *pujas* 'at every temple of the country'.[29] In total, according to one set of VHP figures, 275,000 consecrated bricks were sent to Ayodhya and sixty million 'participants' were involved in the RSPs.[30] But beyond the numbers actively involved, the campaign produced powerful images of piles of bricks—loaded with meaning, on various levels, and ostensibly awaiting their destiny—that endured for many years after. Ultimately, and rather ironically, the bricks would not end up being used in the temple, which began construction in 2020, although a leader of the trust involved in the construction of the temple stated in 2021 that '[bricks] donated by devotees during the Ram Mandir movement are of immense importance for us', and that they would be 'preserved and displayed'.[31]

Scale and inclusivity was key to the late 1980s mobilisation—the VHP asserted that 'these religious feelings and fervour of millions of people, rich and poor, with different regional, lingual, caste and class-distinctions is a supreme example of unity of religious feelings amongst Hindus'.[32] Blom Hansen notes that whilst difficult to establish a causal relationship between the widely witnessed spectacles and BJP political success, the campaign allowed the Sangh 'to disseminate its discourse of Ram as a national hero and Ayodhya as the symbolic center of the Hindu nation to very large, and rural, audiences'.[33]

This mobilisation was intended to involve and recruit every Hindu in the crusade of forming a Hindu *rashtra* and spreading messages about Muslim wrongdoings by employing 'a channel through which the slumbering pride of being a Hindu could be invoked'.[34] Ayodhya thus took on a dual meaning: a symbol of Hindu identity, history, pride, and assertiveness, and also a symbol of Muslim barbarism. An unstated, but most certainly intended, consequence of the RSP was the stoking of communal tensions. Both the RSP and the Rath Yatra, which shared a number of ontological and practical parallels with the *shila pujas*, saw outbreaks of rioting in their wake, and eventually the razing of the mosque.[35]

It is less well known that the VHP established *Ramjanmabhoomi muktiyagna samita* (action committees) not only across India, but also throughout the diaspora, to supervise the *pujas* and dissemination of propaganda.[36] Bricks carrying the inscription '*Jai Shri Ram*' (Hail Lord Ram) were transported across the globe and, after sanctification, returned by airmail to their eventual resting place in Ayodhya.[37] The global aspect to the RSPs has rarely been considered in depth, but constitutes a major and potent form of long-distance nationalism.

Overseas RSP efforts were organised through a special division of the VHP. Hari Babu Kansal, VHP Central Joint Secretary (Foreign Co-ordination), claimed that bricks were received from Canada, the USA, Suriname, the UK, Norway, Denmark, Netherlands, West Germany, Belgium, Israel, Zambia, Botswana, South Africa, Nepal, Malaysia, Sri Lanka, Bangladesh, Thailand, Hong Kong, Singapore, Australia, Seychelles, China, Spain, Portugal, Sweden, and elsewhere.[38] In the United States alone, *pujas* took place in thirty-one cities, indicating an impressive mobilisational reach of the North American VHP, which exceeded its British counterpart.[39]

The global reach of the RSP, and the movement for the construction of a Ram temple in Ayodhya more broadly, was a source of great pride and sustenance for the Hindu nationalist movement in India. Widely circulated VHP videos paid special attention to the bricks that had arrived from overseas.[40] Some of these videos were also circulated outside India, giving the diaspora a sense of their place in, and value to, the movement. Anand

Patwardhan's 1992 documentary, *Ram ke Naam*, also contained shots showing foreign bricks.

The RSP also involved the transfer of funds, much of which was raised as explicit contributions for the construction of a Ram temple and some of which came from overseas. Almost all writing on diasporic Hindu nationalism mentions capital flows from the West to India (primarily in the form of charitable donations through organisations of the Sangh Parivar), but evidence is usually anecdotal or lacking altogether. Remittances are inherently difficult to assess. First, there are legal motives for obscuring capital flows; the Charity Commission in Britain prohibits the funding of political activities, as is the case for tax-exempt charities in the US, while India's Foreign Contribution (Regulation) Act strictly controls the extent to which organisations in India can receive overseas funds. In recent years this law has been used to clamp down on so-called 'anti-national' NGOs, including Greenpeace and the Christian humanitarian aid charity Compassion International.[41]

While the transnational funding of the *Ram Janmabhoomi* movement is largely opaque, there is various evidence to suggest it played an important role. Jaffrelot and Therwath claim that Indians in America contributed $350,000 for this purpose in 1993, the year after the *masjid*'s demolition.[42] In Britain, a representative of the Indian Muslim Federation stated that 'two [Hindu] businessmen ... each sent 100,000 pounds to the Sangh Parivar for temple construction'.[43] VHP-UK accounts from 1993 to 2002 refer to an 'Ayodhya Temple Fund', although the total during this period was only £3,800.[44] This does not quite match the 'huge [diasporic] donations intended to build the *mandir*' that Jaffrelot has claimed.[45] However, it is unlikely that this reflects the real level of monies sent to India (also note that pre-1993 figures are not available).

Shortly before the Babri Masjid demolition, Vishwa Bandhu Gupta, an Income Tax Department deputy commissioner in Uttar Pradesh, endeavoured to examine the finances of the VHP. Gupta investigated foreign funding and found that the VHP had applied for Reserve Bank of India (RBI) permission to bring in money from overseas. He stated that the 'RBI refused, as it doesn't grant such permits to groups that indulge in violence or are political in nature', adding that he was sure money still had come from overseas, but requisite documentation had not been submitted to the Income Tax Department.[46]

Because of these sorts of obstacles, a substantial proportion of philanthropic donations for charities and NGOs in India are not sent through official channels, but conveyed via kinship networks—known as *hawala* transactions—rendering them nearly impossible to trace.[47] An investigative journalist, posing as 'a prospective London-based donor for the Ram temple at Ayodhya' in 1999, was told by VHP-UK representatives of the various obstacles to sending funds overseas, but was provided with options for 're-routing' donations through other bodies.[48] The amount that was conveyed in this manner may have been very significant indeed. Another report, also from 1999, claimed that an Income Tax Department investigation of 'Rs. 300 crore [3 billion] coming from NRIs allegedly received by VHP' had been 'mysteriously suppressed'.[49] Another account that also suggested a significant level of diaspora funding to the Hindu nationalist movement around the time of *Ram Janmabhoomi* states that 'Congress (I) General Secretary Kedarnath Singh alleged, in 1990, that the VHP had acquired Rs. 7 billion rupees for the Ram Janmabhumi temple, of which Rs. 2 billion had come from the U.S.'[50] Others have downplayed the level of donations: a VHP-UK leader also told the undercover journalist: 'They do not need our money. An amount of Rs. 15 crore is needed for the temple, that's not such a big amount that it can't be raised in Bharat'.[51] There are, of course, reasons why they might want to obfuscate this legally dubious flow of funds.

Regardless of the extent of overseas funding, an important point is often lost on the more sensationalist exposés of overseas Hindutva: the significance of the diaspora to the Hindu nationalist movement in India is, to a large degree, symbolic, rather than being a crucial source of cash flows.[52] In this sense, diaspora donors to the Ayodhya temple campaign were giving as much for themselves as for the actual cause—an affective display of loyalty to the homeland and their faith.[53] It is also worth remembering that the sending of donations from abroad for the construction of religious edifices has a long history. As many scholars have shown, the conveying of remittances for temples in India (particularly from mercantile communities) is a deeply engrained tradition—even an expectation—with a wide range of reputational, social, business, and spiritual returns at stake.[54]

Indian political groups have also received substantial funds from overseas, although historically this has been strictly regulated. While data on this is very murky, the BJP are thought to receive the lion's share of transnational political donations. In 2018, the Lok Sabha amended the law, without debate, to exempt political parties from scrutiny of international funding they have received, both historic and going forward. But when compared to corporate contributions (of which the BJP receive around 90% of the total gifted to parties in recent years)—as well as the huge number of wealthy prospective donors in India itself, many of whom have become very close to the BJP—the actual impact of diasporic gifts is likely to be relatively modest.[55]

In terms of the less than indispensable international financial support, Hindutva is perhaps more significant to (some) Hindus in the diaspora than the diaspora is significant to the Hindu nationalist movement in India. But although the expatriate impact on Indian politics is often difficult to quantify, and to a large extent intangible or based more on lobbying power, the affirmation provided both by and to the diaspora has an important role in recent 'reinventions' of India.

The Virat Hindu Sammelan

Over a late August weekend in 1989, the birth centenary year of RSS founder K.B. Hedgewar, more than 100,000 people gathered in an open-air amphitheatre in the Berkshire town of Milton Keynes. This extraordinary occasion constitutes one of the most iconic and spectacular moments in the history of the Hindu nationalist movement overseas (although it is far less well-known than, say, the post-2014 international Modi rallies). The Virat Hindu Sammelan (Great Hindu Assembly) has even been cited as the largest individual gathering of Hindus ever outside

India.[56] The 'mini-Kumbha Mela', as it was referred to, involved the support of 'over 300' Hindu organisations and hosted more than fifty gurus and leaders of various *sampradayas* (religious fellowships) from India and elsewhere.[57] It was organised by a substantial, specially assembled committee, with representatives of the VHP-UK and HSS at the helm. The event, which also produced one of the most comprehensive documents of British Hindutva, in the form of a 250-page 'souvenir' publication, was infused with the iconography, ideology, and leadership of the Hindu nationalist movement.

As well as tying in with the anniversary of Hedgewar's birth, the Ram temple movement, which was now approaching fever pitch in India, constituted a crucial context for the Sammelan. Photos of the event depict a rarely seen example of a diaspora Ram *shila* ceremony—consecrated bricks, painted with 'Shri Ram Shila: Virat Hindu Sammelan UK', in both Hindi and English, are seen laid out on a crisp white table cloth beside a garland of bright orange marigolds. Another picture shows various gurus, event organisers, and external guests—including the Mayor of Milton Keynes—anointing the bricks on a specially constructed stage. Performing this ritual connected the participants at the Sammelan to a transnational movement of assertive Hindu chauvinism that culminated, just three years later, in the violent razing of a mosque 4,500 miles away; a pivotal and heinous moment in the history of Indian democracy.

The Milton Keynes gathering has been briefly discussed by some scholars, but on many levels it remains enigmatic.[58] What drove Hindus to congregate in such massive numbers for this festival? How was such an impressive panoply of Hindu and Hindutva leaders assembled on one stage in the Midlands? And why was the event so singular? One response to these questions is prosaic: because a group of people took it upon themselves to organise something of great ambition and scale, which at the time had not, and has not since, been attempted. There are many more specific factors as well: the year it was held was not just the birth centenary of Hedgewar, but also the twenty-fifth anniversary of the VHP's formation.

The Virat Hindu Sammelan (VHS) was also intrinsically related to the *Ram Janmabhoomi* politics of India and the rising confidence and strength of the Hindu nationalist movement. More specifically, it also reflected the growing assurance, clout, and organisational capability of the Hindu nationalist movement in Britain. In turn, the VHS seemingly acknowledged the importance of the diaspora for Hindutva leaders of India. Although many accounts of Hindu nationalism isolate the Sammelan without context, it did not come out of thin air. As we have seen over previous chapters, the Hindu nationalist movement in Britain, and broader transnational networks, had developed in the previous five decades. In particular, the institutional structures, personnel, and kinship networks that facilitated the Sammelan—like those that drove anti-Emergency action—can be traced to East Africa. Rather than being a dramatic birth of British Hindutva, it represented its maturation.

A direct and significant precursor to the Sammelan was the Hindu Sangam—another substantial *tamasha*, held in Bradford in 1984. Like the VHS, the Sangam was for the Hindu community itself, but also to provide a platform for showcasing their commitment, organisational skills, and other positive attributes to a wider public. One of the chief organisers, Hasmukh Shah, who was also a central figure in the Sammelan five years later, explained that the Sangam was inspired by a huge RSS camp held in Pune in 1983.[59] Eager to replicate a similar level of dynamism that followed in the wake of the Pune event, a group of British *swayamsevaks* set about organising a jamboree in the rather different environs of West Yorkshire. Shah recalled that 'an extra burst of inspirational and extraordinary activity had to be injected ... [to promote] *shakha* ideas of Hindu-ness ... widely to the Hindu Samaj'.[60]

The Sangam shared a lot in common with the camps discussed in Chapter 2, but as a one-off event it gathered significantly larger numbers. Approximately 1,200 *swayamsevaks* were said to have attended—at the time probably the biggest Sangh meeting to have occurred outside India—joined on the final day by a wider audience comprising the Hindu community and wider publics (numbering, it is claimed, 10,000).[61] Outsiders were invited to 'witness the discipline, dedication, and humanity of our *swayamsevaks*'.[62] Echoing the rhetoric of Hindutva leaders in India, Shah added euphorically, 'Hindu Sangam was people's dream of Ram Rajya [reign of Ram] coming to life'.[63] At Milton Keynes, the rhetorical and aesthetic stamp of Ram would be further amplified.

The Sammelan was an enactment of the ecumenical raison d'être of the VHP, serving also as a metonym for desired Hindu unity and organisational competency on a national scale. According to Dhiraj D. Shah, a member of the organising team and later the Sanghchalak (President) of the HSS, the idea 'inspiration and guidance' for the event came directly from Swami Satyamitranand Giri, whilst the guru was in Britain in 1987.[64]

Satyamitranand Giri—famous for his nationalistic Bharat Mata temple in Haridwar—was just one of a pantheon of Hindu gurus who attended and gave addresses at the Sammelan. Their presence was facilitated by the Indian VHP. The leaders assembled together on a 'Unity Platform' in front of the crowds, in what a contemporary account called a 'visual demonstration of Hindu solidarity'.[65] With Giri (founder of Samanvaya Parivar and the VHP) were Swami Chinmayananda (founder of Chinmaya Mission and the VHP), Rameshbhai Oza, Pujya Doctor Swami (a senior sadhu of the Bochasanwasi Shree Akshar Purushottam Swaminarayan Sanstha (BAPS) sect), K.S. Sudarshan (Sar Karyawaha of the RSS), and dozens of other gurus and Sangh leaders. Morari Bapu, a Gujarati guru with a substantial following in Britain, was also a guest at the Sammelan, and spoke specifically on constructing a Ram temple in Ayodhya.[66]

The presence of these gurus cannot be understood simply in the immediate context of late 1980s *Ram Janmabhoomi* mobilisation. Rather, it reflected a much longer, deeper relationship that they had nurtured with the Indian diaspora over many decades, much of which can be traced to East Africa. Giri, for instance, was one of the first *shankaracharyas* (monastery heads) to flout orthodox Brahmanical conventions by travelling overseas regularly from the 1960s onwards. He established the iconic and controversial Bharat Mata temple in Haridwar, was instrumental in the establishment of the VHP in India, and later became a patron of the VHP-UK. Such was his stature amongst British Hindus that in 1987 he was honoured by the Bradford Metropolitan Council, to whom he gave an address on 'World Peace and Hindutva'.[67] His influence endured into the twenty-first century. In 2009, his organisation funded a public statue of Gandhi in Leicester, unveiled by Giri alongside Home Secretary Alan Johnson, and various other politicians and public figures.

Pramukh Swami (1921-2016) and the Swaminarayan *sampradaya* have also had a deep, enduring relationship with the Gujarati diaspora. Pramukh Swami's first experience of travelling around the Gujarati diaspora was accompanying his predecessor, Yogi Maharaj, on tours of East Africa and the UK in 1960 and 1970.[68] He subsequently presided over the evolution of BAPS into one of the most prominent, fast-growing, and influential expressions of Hinduism outside India. Many have suggested that BAPS, which emerged in Gujarat in the early nineteenth century, has a close and long-lasting relationship with Hindu nationalism in India and in the diaspora.[69] However BAPS has often refuted these links and insisted that it is entirely apolitical; connections may often be viewed as circumstantial or by association, particularly given its deep roots in Gujarati communities in India and around the world. Its Neasden temple—an iconic and pioneering edifice that is of great pride to many British Hindus, and invariably used by the media and politicians as visual shorthand for the UK's Hindu community—was opened in 1995 by L.K. Advani.[70] It has also often been noted that Swaminarayan temples have been loci for touring Sangh Parivar personalities, and in turn, figures from the Swaminarayan movement have participated in a range of events hosted by the Sangh Parivar in the diaspora and in India itself.[71] But the relationship is not quite as clear-cut as some more polemic analyses suggest, and although an ally to diasporic Hindutva groups in certain ways (although proximity does not necessarily equate to ideological affinity), BAPS is also a competitor, of sorts, by way of its prominent and successful efforts to be a 'public face' of Hinduism.[72]

The Swaminarayan involvement in the Sammelan can be identified as just one moment in this complex and multi-faceted relationship. In addition to the addresses given from the stage, many gurus, Sangh leaders, and Hindutva ideologues (some of whom were not able to attend in person) provided messages and articles for the souvenir brochure. Pramukh Swami wrote: 'It is important today to revive the glory of Hindutva and Hindu *dharma* because it is only the truth which lies within Hindu *dharma* which can resolve the global problems of today.... The glory of Hindutva will be reawakened by *sammelans* such as these'.[73] Madhukar Dattatraya Deoras, RSS Sarsanghchalak, provided a two-fold directive: to promote 'all-round development of the national life in their respective countries' and 'uphold the cause of Hindutva impressively and rightly'.[74] Other dedications came from the President of the Ramjanmabhoomi Trust in Ayodhya, two Ayodhya-based gurus, the Hindu Council of Kenya, the Bharatiya Swayamsevak Sangh in Nairobi, and Acharya Sushil Kumar, a guru based in New Jersey. Representatives of British Hindu groups, including the Brent Hindu Council, the National Congress of Gujarati Associations, and the Kutch Lewa Patel Community in Britain, also presented messages underlining the catholic intentions of the Sammelan. The ecumenical role of the VHP-UK was also asserted through messages of support from leaders of other religious groups and interfaith bodies, tacitly acknowledging the representative credentials of the Sammelan's organisers. These included Robert Runcie (Archbishop of Canterbury), Sher Azam (President, Council for Mosques UK), Hayim Pinner (Board of Deputies of British Jews), and the Director of the Inter Faith Network UK.

Messages of support also came from various political leaders and public figures. Following large images of a muscular Ram and the RSS founder, Hedgewar, on the brochure's opening pages is a full-page portrait and message from Queen Elizabeth II. This is followed by a note from Prime Minister Margaret Thatcher, wishing the VHP-UK 'every success in its work'. Just five months later, Thatcher would visit a *shakha* in her Finchley constituency, where she met British Sangh leaders, received a set of books on Hindutva, watched a display of physical exercises, and even garlanded a bust of Hedgewar.[75] Thatcher, who in spite of her anti-immigration politics had attempted to win over Asian voters since the 1970s, delivered a speech in which she praised 'the self-discipline and training... [and] physical prowess' of the assembled *swayamsevaks*. She also spoke of their 'great culture', expressing gratitude for them 'keep[ing] it alive', and was loudly applauded when she declaimed: 'I have been to India, and I love India'.[76]

The Sammelan's brochure included messages from other political leaders: Neil Kinnock (leader of the Labour Party), Paddy Ashdown (leader of the Social and Liberal Democrats), Bernard Weatherill (Speaker of the House of Commons), and many others. At the Sammelan, British Army Gurkha soldiers marched and 'gave military salute to the Bhagwa Dhwaj [saffron flag] and British flag', which were raised simultaneously by Acharya Sushil Kumar and the Mayor of Milton Keynes, in a poignant, symbolic adaptation of the RSS flag ceremony, as detailed in the first chapter of this book.[77]

What are we to make of these seemingly successful efforts to gain the attention and approbation of figures within the British establishment? It is, to a degree, a strategy by which Hindu nationalists have sought acknowledgement as legitimate representatives of a Hindu community. This can be located in a multicultural landscape in which competition for recognition comes from not just other would-be Hindu representatives, but different ethnic and religious minorities (discussed in depth in Chapter 6). For the politicians who attended or provided messages of support, the Sammelan represented, in Mukta's words, a 'simple assertion of religious faith by minorities whose votes needed wooing'.[78] The lack of consternation by public figures reflected both a level of concealment of Hindutva's most aggressive features, and a general lack of awareness of the political and ideological context.[79] Mukta's identification of the Sammelan as evidence of a 'prominent space carved out by Hindutva forces within British politics', however, is an overstatement.[80] Messages of support from public figures are more likely to indicate a well-meaning but naïve multiculturalism, alongside a cynical but unremarkable attempt to receive the political support of a growing community, rather than any real inroads that Hindutva made in British politics. The involvement of public figures in these events might appear to reify the Hindu nationalists' desired vision of a unified and monolithic community, but in a limited and fleeting way. The same case is less easy to make in the twenty-first century, with a number of politicians strategically and even ideologically siding with their Hindutva-sympathetic constituents.

Although ideological elements to the Sammelan were crucial, and the organisers did indeed incorporate the guests in the Hindutva rituals, there were more straightforward motivations behind inviting local dignitaries. The confidence and sense of achievement provided by putting on an event of such scale was enhanced by recognition from the 'establishment', and this was of significance for those involved. It represented a successful attempt to promote Hindu achievement to wider publics, as well as within 'the community' itself. Dhiraj Shah said, 'one thing that came out was how Hindus can work together', while an attendee, Prem Sagar, stated that 'this Sammelan helps in the whole culture of the Hindus and the whole awakening of Hinduism. It points out what Hinduism means and what it can do'.[81] In this sense, the event was about both instilling a sense of Hindu pride amongst the community and promoting a reputation of Hindus as a 'model minority' (discussed in depth in Chapter 5) to a wider public.

Of course, the Sammelan was still closely linked to Hindu majoritarian ideology and political mobilisation of the homeland. Much of the 'pride' spilled over into the familiar ideology and chauvinism and Hindutva. Morari Bapu told 'a spell-bound audience... that Hindu culture is the "mother of world civilisation because it has taught the world how to eat, how to drink and, in fact, how to live"'.[82] The souvenir publication was replete with unwavering Hindutva pronouncements, including a four-page tribute to the 'Architect of Hindu Unity', Hedgewar. Elsewhere, a lengthy exposition on the Ram temple pronounced: 'For centuries the Hindus have been subjected to humiliation. The construction of the temple at shri Ram Janmabhumi has been one of their cherished dreams and in its fulfilment they see the restoration of their national glory and honour'.[83]

Can the Milton Keynes gathering be understood purely as a mammoth tribute to long-distance religious nationalism? Bhatt emphasises the *'entirely* Sangh Hindutva orientation' of the

Sammelan, also calling it 'the most successful Hindutva project in the UK'.[84] But a more dispassionate analysis is required. Does the enormous attendance at the Sammalen reflect a groundswell of support for Hindutva? Or were attendees more interested in a glimpse of Lata Mangeshkar, renowned Bollywood playback singer, who performed the 'theme song' of the event, *'Hindu Jage Vishwa Jage'* (If the Hindu rises, the world rises)? Another important draw of the Sammelan was the presence of Gujarati *kathakaars* (preachers) Rameshbhai Oza and Morari Bapu. They both enjoy huge popular appeal in Gujarat and the Gujarati diaspora for their readings, singing, and discourses on the Ramayana, which extend beyond their Hindutva proclivities.[85] We might, therefore, apply Blom Hansen's observation that it was often more the spectacle of the Ram Shila Puja and Rath Yatra that drew crowds, as much as any commitment to Hindutva.[86] This position reinforces Zavos's suggestion that the scale of the Sammelan has led to an overemphasis of the VHP-UK's significance.[87]

Outside the specific context of the Sammelan, while for a small minority of British Hindus *Ram Janmabhoomi* was significant, the parochial specificity of it meant that it was not a topic of overwhelming appeal overseas. Rajagopal, for instance, found that second-generation Indian Americans were 'overwhelmed' by the 'alienness' of the Ayodhya mobilisations.[88] Similar observations can be made in Britain. A young Hindu woman in Bradford, for instance, told Burlet and Reid that it did not affect her relationships with her Muslim school friends: 'we didn't feel it was relevant to us because it was over there'.[89] Other informants told them: 'Community leaders are not representative of the whole community', and 'Things from India are dragged over here. Why bring these things here, we are British, it is not right'.[90]

Whereas organisers of the Sammelan saw the event through their own Hindutva lenses, the attendees' experiences were likely to have been much more diverse. One visitor said: 'Coming to this sammelan neither contributed anything to my knowledge of Hinduism nor for my faith. I have my doubts if the best of Hinduism can be affirmed in an unruly crowd situation like this'.[91] Another complained that 'this sammelan [was] completely disorganized', and a child said: 'I did not like going there. It was dirty and I did not meet other kids with whom I could play. There were no good pictures to look at, the crowd was too much and it was easy to be lost'.[92] These banal appraisals temper the organisers' euphoric assessments of the impact and legacy of the event. That three decades on the identity of an authoritative and representative voice of 'the Hindu community' remains contested (as discussed in Chapter 6), and no other Sammelan-like event has occurred since, requires us to reconsider the influence of not just the VHP, but Hindu nationalist organisations more broadly.[93]

The Sammelan was critical in terms of raising the confidence of the organisers, many of whom remain key figures of various Hindu and Hindutva groups to this day. We may therefore locate its importance in terms of a longer 'process of ideology formation with all British Hindus as its target' (even though these bold ambitions may not have been realised), and in a history of the honing of organisational and public relations skills amongst committed diaspora leaders.[94]

While the scale of this pantheon of Hindu leaders was unprecedented in the diaspora, their presence in England was not, with many nurturing diasporic followings for many decades. Some, such as Giri, are so mobile that it seems inappropriate to refer to their presence outside India through a homeland–diaspora, inside–outside, binary. Other gurus have even transcended national borders altogether—almost repudiating the territorialised logic of nationalism—giving sermons and hosting entire residential 'pilgrimages' aboard specially commissioned cruise-liners and airplanes. In 1994 an aircraft took Morari Bapu and 250 followers on a round-the-world flight, stopping at locations with substantial diaspora communities: California, Fiji, Singapore, Kenya, Britain, and Canada, as well as India itself.[95] Rithambara has also provided innovative experiences for her overseas devotees, organising lavish cruise-ship package holidays. In 2011, a seven-day '*Swaroop Bodh Ki Yatra*' (Journey of Self-Discovery), from Los Angeles to Vancouver, featured 'religious and spiritual discourses' and optional stop-offs at the Alaskan glaciers and Disneyland; another cruise, to the Caribbean in 2016, also involved preaching and pleasure, and raised nearly half a million dollars for her NGO.[96]

Rithambara has been an infamous figure in the Hindu nationalist movement since the mid-1980s, one of a small cohort of female firebrands on the Hindu right, including Sadhvi Prachi, Uma Bharti, and Pragya Singh Thakur, who have received considerable media attention. But in spite of the visibility of women in Hindu nationalist campaigns (in the form of a handful of individual leaders, as well as wider participation in grassroots cadres), and instances of women's Hindutva activism providing certain forms of empowerment, various people have argued that it is far from emancipatory. As is the case in so many right-wing and nationalist movements, the participation of women has in fact often served to reinforce gender norms, social (and caste) hierarchies, and patriarchy itself.[97]

Rithambara was part of the Margdarshak Mandal (Circle of Guides, or senior advisory committee) of the VHP, and founder of the Durga Vahini (Army of Durga)—a militant, armed female wing of the VHP that is essentially the women's equivalent of the Bajrang Dal. She is well known for her central role in the agitations around Ayodhya, where she notoriously raised the slogan, '*Ek Dhakka aur do, Babri Masjid tod do*' ('give it one more push, break down the Babri mosque').[98] Rithambara was not present at the Milton Kenyes Sammelan, but over the years she has nurtured an important diaspora following, regularly visiting her adherents and donors in Britain, the US, and other countries.

Her profile has incorporated a discombobulating (although by no means disconnected) admixture of provocative and violent anti-Muslim rhetoric, combined with substantial charitable activities. Most prominent in her philanthropic portfolio is Vatsalya Gram—an enormous residential and educational complex in Uttar Pradesh catering to female orphans and elderly and widowed women. She has three affiliated organisations in Britain that support this work, all registered with the Charity Commission: the Maa Charity Trust UK, based out of Hendon, the Leicester-based Bhaarat Welfare Trust, and the Param Shakti Peeth. Rithambara's 2010 visit to the UK went ahead despite calls from the Council of Indian

Muslims (UK) to Home Secretary Theresa May not to grant her permission to enter Britain.[99] In September 2015, she returned and gave a speech in the House of Commons at an event hosted by Bob Blackman and Stephen Pound, MPs for Harrow East and Ealing North, respectively.[100] More recently, in September 2022, a multi-city tour of the UK—to be held just one month after the serious communal disturbances in Leicester—was cancelled following outcry and protests. Sam Tarry, the MP for Ilford South, in which the VHP Hindu Centre where Rithambara was due to speak is located, made a direct plea to the Home Secretary, stating: 'I am deeply worried about the potential stoking of communal tensions, should her visit be allowed to progress.'[101] While this book cannot discuss Rithambara or her organisations in depth, her role in promoting (Ayodhya-focused) Hindutva ideology in Britain is noteworthy.

Even before the spread of the internet, Rithambara's global presence was not limited to her overseas tours. In the *Ram Janmabhoomi* movement from the late 1980s, audio cassettes circulated both in India and overseas, one featuring a Rithambara speech in which she likened the Muslim presence in India to lemon in milk.[102] In another recording, circulated on a VHP tape, Rithambara proclaims: 'The blood of the foreigners, of traitors who do not pay tribute to their ancestors, will flow'.[103]

In the early 1990s, the Hindu Sahitya Kendra (see Chapter 1) distributed a video produced by J.K. Jain Studios in India and reproduced by a video company in Brent.[104] Rithambara was one of many Hindutva ideologues and gurus featured in this film, which, according to Bhatt, was circulated around Hindu temples, cultural organisations, shops, and even homes on a 'door-to-door' basis, sometimes for free.[105] The ninety-minute film, called 'The Story of Ramjanmabhoomi—Past, Present and Future', was a version of the well-known '*Bhaye Prakat Kripala*' videos produced by the VHP specifically for the Ayodhya agitations.[106] One source claims that 50,000 copies were circulated overseas.[107] In the film, parallels were drawn between historical 'subjugation' under Muslims and contemporary contexts, exemplified by the crusade to 'reinstate' a Ram temple on the site of the Mughal mosque. According to

Bhatt's interpretation of the video, Muslims are portrayed as 'threatening, amorphous, violent and especially dehumanized'.[108] The video also explicitly emphasises an international angle to the 'struggle for *Ramjanmabhoomi*', the defence of Hinduism, and the significance of 'recreating' India as a Hindu *rashtra*.[109]

The 'Story of Ramjanmabhoomi' film's medium itself is important, employing new technologies of computer-generated imagery, and by depicting scenes from the early life of Ram (the watching of which was an act of *darshan* and *bhakti* for many), it followed the runaway success of the Ramayana and Mahabharata television series on India's Doordarshan state network in the late 1980s. This gave authenticity and a tangible, albeit tenuous, connection between the mythological, historical, and present-day.[110] Rajagopal illuminates the massive implications of Doordarshan's broadcasts in *Politics after Television*, showing the central role played by national media in the rise of Hindu nationalism at the end of the twentieth century.[111] The maker of the Ramayana series, Ramanand Sagar, even attended the Milton Keynes Sammelan as a VIP guest. Such was the success and affect of the programmes that when Sagar arrived at the event people 'bowed down to him, touched his feet, kissed his hands'.[112] Sagar took to the stage and called on the crowd to say: 'Jai Shri Ram', which his son recalled 'ignited power in people. The whole Milton Keynes Bowl echoed with Jai Shri Ram chanting. It went up to the clouds.'[113]

The Ramayana has particular significance in the diaspora. The popularity of *Ramakathas* (Ramayana recitals and discourses), *Ramleelas* (performances of scenes), the circulation of texts, and the enthusiasm for on-screen versions (especially the 1987–8 Sagar series), all reflect the diasporic resonance of the Ramayana.[114] In the late twentieth century, the epic enjoyed a surge in popularity and the story, which historically had diverse renderings, became increasingly homogenised. In particular, the protagonist was increasingly re-imagined as an assertive and warrior-like ruler.[115] However, we might also note a particular poignancy of the Ramayana for Hindus overseas. Valmiki's epic tale, with its themes of exile, hardship, struggle, fidelity, and eventual return, speaks to certain experiences and sentiments of Hindu migrants, dislocated from their homeland.[116] Bhikhu Parekh has even argued that the Ramayana 'has come closest to becoming the central text of overseas Hinduism'.[117] The diaspora was therefore simultaneously a proxy for the *Ram Janmabhoomi* mobilisations as well as a site for its deparochialisation, where it was infused with a range of new and significant meanings for the Indian diaspora.

Post-Babri Masjid demolition violence

The destruction of the Babri Masjid on 6 December 1992—including culpability, the state's response, and a longer-term resolution—has been widely debated and contested. The final weeks of 1992 and start of 1993, in the immediate aftermath of the demolition, witnessed the worst outbreaks of Hindu-Muslim bloodshed since Partition. At least 1,250 people died (and perhaps many more) in an 'orgy of violence' across Uttar Pradesh, Gujarat, and Maharashtra.[118] Widespread destruction of property accompanied the carnage.[119]

But post-demolition tensions were not limited to India. 'Retaliatory' attacks on Hindus and Hindu edifices took place in Pakistan and Bangladesh, and the governments of various Middle Eastern countries issued condemnatory statements.[120] A variety of British Muslim groups and other concerned parties also condemned the incident. In both the lead-up to, and the wake of, the razing, the UK-based Indian Muslim Federation raised concerns both in Britain and with Indian politicians.[121] Much of the rhetoric echoed frustration in India that inadequate steps had been taken to prevent the attack on the mosque—an act that many saw as a predetermined strategy rather than a spontaneous crime of passion.

The violence in India 'sent a shock wave through Britain'.[122] Ayodhya both stoked existing tensions and raised them where they previously had not existed. It was followed by a 'wave of arson attacks', which included fires in Hindu temples in Leeds, petrol bombs thrown into a Sheffield *mandir*, and other incidents, including 'a minor blaze' at the Jamia mosque in Derby.[123] A range of evidence also suggests that within Britain, the Ayodhya context was manipulated by opportunistic anti-minority, right-wing groups.[124]

Some reports focused on communal antagonism between Hindus and Muslims.[125] Others emphasised groups and individuals promoting peace and conciliation.[126] The VHP-UK claimed that there were arson attacks on twenty-four Hindu temples and twelve Hindu businesses, but they 'managed to restrain Hindu youths from expressing their anger'.[127] The tension concerned the government enough for the Home Secretary to meet Hindu and Muslim leaders to discuss the violence and acrimony that had spilled over from India to England.[128] The religious politics of the subcontinent was being performed not only on British streets, but in homes as well; Pragna Patel recalled that the Babri Masjid demolition, as well as the Gujarat violence of 2002, 'created schisms not only between the Hindu and Muslim communities in Britain but also within families'.[129]

On certain levels, and for certain people, the *Ram Janmabhoomi* movement also had particular resonance in Britain. Hasmukh Shah of the VHP-UK suggested that 'Those Hindus who live outside India are more sentimental about Ayodhya and other issues because they have the economic comfort zone'.[130] But these expressions of British Hindutva were not just sentimental. The movement spoke to British Hindus on multiple levels. As well as providing an opportunity for assertive and aggressive engagement with homeland politics and political identities, *Ram Janmabhoomi* also influenced intra-minority politics in late twentieth-century Britain. Muslim politicisation after the Rushdie Affair, multicultural competition, and struggles for recognition were all key factors. The Babri Masjid demolition therefore spurred Hindutva identity-formation in Britain, creating and fomenting animosity between Hindus and Muslims in Britain.

Although the focus here is on the relevance of Ayodhya to British Hindu nationalism, it must be remembered that it was also significant for British Muslims. Soon after the Babri Masjid demolition, one young Muslim Bradfordian said: '[Ayodhya] increased the political and religious awareness of Muslims in the same way as the Iran-Iraq war and the Rushdie affair'.[131] The 'Hindu interests' that Patel suggests were articulated for the first time in the context of *Ram Janmabhoomi*, were therefore discursively constituted.[132] In spite of these particular diasporic conditions, and substantial distance—both generational and geographical—from India, certain homeland dynamics pervaded and were reproduced in the wake of the mosque's destruction.

The centripetal ethos of the Ram Shila Puja provided a level of inclusivity, both conceptually and practically, for Hindus overseas. They were able to build on pre-existing networks and institutions, many of which can be traced back to East Africa. In addition, the organisational capacity of Indian, and particularly Hindu nationalist, groups in Britain was substantially enhanced during the Emergency, as discussed in the previous chapter. Not only were groups more competent and skilled as a result of anti-Emergency activism, but the perceived role and purview of the diaspora vis-à-vis the homeland was also emboldened and transformed. This confidence and morale, whether based on real achievements or just those claimed, still resonates to this day.[133]

We can also trace certain individuals who played important roles in Emergency mobilisations and then subsequently Ayodhya-related activities. Hasmukh Shah was, at the age of just twenty-six, the founding General Secretary of FISI in 1975, a key player in running *Satyavani*, and was mentioned in Narendra Modi's book about the period as one of the key overseas activists.[134] Hasmukh Shah went on be leader in the VHP-UK, playing a major role in both the Hindu Sangam and the Virat Hindu Sammelan. Just two days after the Babri Masjid demolition he 'called for moderation' while reiterating his conviction that 'a temple dedicated to Lord Sri Ram on his very birthplace should be built'.[135] Dhiraj Shah—a core leader in the HSS mentioned in several places throughout this book—was amongst the delegates at the FISI conference at Alexandra Palace in April 1976.[136] Thirteen years later, he was a key organiser behind the Sammelan.[137] While we must be careful not to make inferences between these two periods, separated by over a decade, without sufficient evidence, clear connections and continuities can be identified. Further investigation might elucidate both individual and broader organisational developments linking various events and periods in the chronology of Hindu nationalism in the diaspora.

A corollary of the Ayodhya conflict in Britain was the resulting formal establishment of anti-communal activist networks. One group, the Alliance Against Communalism and for Democracy in South Asia, formed in February 1993 from a variety of left, feminist, and human- and civil-rights networks. This later morphed into AWAAZ, a network which in the early 2000s (and also much more recently), prominently criticised Hindutva in India and its support in Britain. In North America, similar groups, such as Non-Resident Indians for Secularism and Democracy, also formed in the wake of Ayodhya.[138] In many ways, these campaigners were fighting against the tide. Rather than censure, many Hindu nationalist organisations and events received approbation from naïve and well-meaning establishment figures, and even public funding.

Limits, absences, and failures from this period are also worth noting. For much of the Indian diaspora, *Ram Janmabhoomi* was a distant and esoteric political struggle that had limited appeal. Many were hardly aware of it. This perhaps represents the experience of the majority of Hindus in Britain (notwithstanding a vocal and influential minority). Similarly, in India, the diaspora's importance to the movement was limited. Whilst the contribution of overseas Hindus was appreciated by the Sangh in their rise towards the end of the twentieth century, it was neither indispensable nor transformative. Furthermore, once the mosque was demolished, the traction of the *Ram Janmabhoomi* movement faded in some senses (although it has been reinvigorated at certain points, particularly since Modi became Prime Minister).

While the tensions in the immediate aftermath of 6 December 1992 were highly unusual, Ayodhya and the demolition of the Babri Masjid continue to have an impact. In 2010, the HSS issued a 'press statement', published in *Sangh Sandesh*, welcoming the Allahabad High Court verdict—seen by many as favourable to Hindu nationalist demands—and expressing 'new hopes of the reconciliation and harmony between Hindus and Muslims in India'.[139] Although this first paragraph seemed positive, the statement then slipped into familiar rhetoric. Beneath a picture of the model for the Ram *mandir*—a highly contentious image in its own right—the statement asserts that 'HSS(UK) fervently hopes and prays' for the constructing of 'a magnificent Ram temple at Ayodhya'. The statement also adds: 'Muslims have no significance for Ayodhya except that the Mughal invader, Babur, erected a structure after destroying a magnificent temple at the site considered the birthplace of Lord Ram'.[140] In 2015, a young *swayamsevak* vented frustration at an HSS camp: 'These people [Muslims] think they have the right to build a mosque anywhere they want. We can't build a temple anywhere we want. But it's just these Pakis they can build... They could literally demolish this [school] and turn it into a mosque, if they wanted to'.[141] While not specifically referencing Ayodhya, the language is certainly familiar. The diaspora has continued to engage in the discourse around the Ram temple, with some fairly conspicuous celebrations of the progress that has been made to build the *mandir* in recent years. This was perhaps most notable around the time of the ground-breaking ceremony for the new Ayodhya temple, following the Supreme Court's 2019 verdict, which led a small group of Indian Americans to pay for images of the temple to be beamed onto billboards in New York's Times Square, resulting in protests from some American Muslims and media content that would be seen the world over.

More recently still, in August 2022, during the shocking scenes of communal conflict between Hindus and Muslims in Leicester, one of the flare-ups involved around 200 Hindu men marching through parts of the city that were home to many Muslims, shouting the slogan 'Jai Shri Ram' (Hail Lord Ram). This phrase, while purely devotional for many, has for a long time been synonymous with the Ram temple movement and Hindu militancy more generally. It was, of course, these same words that appeared on the bricks used in *Ram Janmabhoomi* ceremonies the world over, discussed earlier in the chapter. Snigdha Poonam, in an article titled 'the three most polarizing words in India', wrote that 'while this seemingly harmless phrase originated as a pious declaration of devotion in India, it is today increasingly deployed not only as a Hindu chauvinist slogan but also as a threat to anyone who dares to challenge Hindu supremacy'.[142]

Finally, the Home Office denied a Freedom of Information request submitted in the research for this book that sought to clarify the repercussions of Ayodhya on Britain and uncover information on Hindu–Muslim tensions in the 1990s. The request was rejected under Sections 23(5) (information supplied by or relating to bodies dealing with security matters), 24(2) (national security), and 31(3) (law enforcement) of the Freedom of Information Act, which 'absolves us [the Home Office] from the requirement to say whether or not we hold the requested information'.[143] As we know that meetings between Hindu and Muslim leaders were facilitated by the Home Secretary in the wake of the attacks, we can infer that the Home Office remains concerned about the sensitivity of Hindu–Muslim relations in Britain. This remains an enduring legacy of the Hindu diasporic politics of the late 1980s and 1990.

The VHP abroad

The final section of the chapter considers the wider role played by the VHP within the global Hindu nationalist movement, specifically in Britain and the US. The VHP-UK and the American branch of the VHP (known as the VHP-A) were closely involved throughout the Ram temple mobilisations. But they were also active long before, and after, this period, and have engaged in a wide range of activities beyond those relating to Ayodhya.

The VHP-UK was one of the first officially registered Hindu groups in Britain, forming in 1969 and registering as a charity in 1972. Its constitution specified that 'it will be affiliated to Vishwa Hindu Parishad' in India; as with the RSS, there are very clear lines of communication between the diaspora branches and the Indian 'HQ'.[144] The American branch of the VHP was also founded in the years immediately following the establishment of its parent organisation: a small group of Sangh members based in New York City set up the VHP-A in 1970, and it was formally incorporated in 1974.

The VHP-A operates approximately 20–25 chapters across the country, with varying numbers of 'personnel' and levels of dynamism. In Britain, the VHP-UK run twelve branches, two temples, and a community centre in Croydon. Overall, the VHP claim to operate chapters in at least twenty-four countries, although this number fluctuates and some sources have suggested they have a 'presence' in as many as eighty (which seems unfeasible).[145] The scale of these operations varies dramatically and, in many cases, constitutes just a handful of proactive organisers. Very often the leadership of VHP branches are current or former leaders of various other diasporic Hindu nationalist organisations, especially the HSS. In an interview, Anil Vartak, international co-ordinator for the RSS, stated that the RSS and VHP in Britain have a 'shared goal' and 'similar relationship', as in India.

Through the VHP's web presence, and the influence of their co-ordinating leaders and connected organisations (Sangh-related and beyond), the VHP's footprint might be considered somewhat bigger than their number of branches implies. This is reflected, to some extent, in their budgets. Data submitted to the Charity Commission shows an average annual income of £322,445 per year from 2007–20—a figure only 5% less than the HSS income for the same period.[146] In addition, by running a substantial annual surplus, as well as collecting separate restricted donations, the VHP-UK has accumulated net assets of £3,548,515, as of March 2020.[147] According to slightly older figures, the VHP-A is similarly solvent (although covering a much wider area and population). IRS tax returns indicate that they allocated an average of $330,904 per year to 'programme services' between 2001 and 2012 (although this figure probably does not reflect their total income).[148]

In addition to tax breaks, and sometimes the free use of public facilities such as community centres, the financial position of Hindu nationalist groups is helped by various state grants. Freedom of Information requests reveal that in 2008/9 the NHS gave the VHP-UK £23,000 to run a 'lunch club', Newham Borough Council provided £1,500 for 'language classes' in 2001/2, Croydon Borough Council offered £73,934 for a range of 'social services' between 1998 and 2002, and in 2014, Northampton Borough Council gifted a modest sum of £250 for the VHP-UK to run 'Bollywood dance classes'.

Their publications, online presence, and other information relating to events and advocacy, as well as paperwork submitted to the authorities to comply with the requirements of being tax-exempt non-profit organisations, give some idea of their work. But much of the VHP's networking and co-ordinating activities happen behind the scenes, and there is discrepancy regarding the extent of their influence. Therwath referred to them as 'the backbone of foreign Hindutva', and the VHP-A is visibly quite dynamic, but the RSS's Anil Vartak stated that the 'VHP in UK is not very active'.[149]

In some ways the diaspora branches have an entirely different objective to that of the main VHP. In India they are engaged in root-and-branch societal change and the 'Hinduisation of public life'—clearly not appropriate nor feasible for foreign countries. Overseas, rather than forging a majority culture, bound by nation, they are engaged in the consolidation of a Hindu minority and maintaining a strong sense of Hindu(tva) identity amongst emigrants. In order to achieve this, in both Britain and America, the VHP's first priorities were to establish new branches, coalesce the growing Hindu population, nurture an engaged and conscious community, and serve as a representative, ecumenical body. The VHP achieve this through organising their own activities, as well as co-ordinating other branches of the Hindutva family and supporting their initiatives. In this sense, their influence stretches beyond what it may superficially appear to be.

The ecumenism at the core of the VHP's mission has a special resonance in the diaspora. Forging connections amongst a diverse and disparate minority population is desirable for many emigrants and their organisations, both on a social level as well as creating a sense of security in numbers. Moreover, while in India the Hindu nationalist movement has had to operate in a milieu of highly embedded traditions and networks—idiosyncratic and diverse in practice, language, and locale—in the diaspora they are presented with a more 'manageable' community that is, in certain ways, more receptive to a 'fresh start'. Bidisha Biswas suggests that we might understand the relative success of Hindutva in the diaspora through the lens of 'brokerage': 'mechanisms to build and forge links between groups that had earlier not seen themselves as part of a cohesive group'.[150] This kind of 'brokerage' is explicitly reflected in the Parishad's strategy: in 1984, the VHP-A passed a resolution during a New York conference that 'urge[d] all the Hindus of the world—back home and abroad—to act in a broad and nationalistic manner rising above their personal beliefs and creeds, parochial languages, and provincial and sectarian considerations'.[151]

The diasporic VHP's ethos often bears a strong resemblance to that of its parent institution, but in terms of strategy and programmes there are some departures. The stated aims of the VHP-UK range from being indistinguishable from its Indian counterpart—strong support for Kashmir as 'an integral part of India' and belief in the 'tremendous sentimental and religious value' of Ayodhya—to issues which are more diaspora-focused—advocating a British Hindu identity over the 'Asian' marker and promoting the teaching of Indian languages and Hindu culture to young British Hindus.[152] On some issues of importance to the Indian VHP, overseas branches clearly digress from the homeland organisation; on the question of economic liberalisation, for instance, the VHP outside India has not adopted the vocal opposition of the homeland organisation, in order not to alienate its entrepreneurial NRI support base. Overall, though, the VHP and its international branches are very close, both ideologically and organisationally.

One area in which the VHP and RSS overlap in the diaspora—and diverge quite considerably from their Indian counterparts—is through their cultural and educational activities. The VHP's role both in India and abroad is to promote certain notions of what it is to be Hindu. But for migrants, who might be conscious of losing their connection to the homeland (especially those with children), this has particular connotations. It can also provide them with tools and a vocabulary with which to explain their culture to outsiders. Overseas branches of the VHP organise events on Hindu festivals, bringing together leaders and devotees from a wide range of sects, host lectures by visiting gurus and ideologues, and put on classes to teach languages (mainly Hindi, Gujarati, and Sanskrit), yoga, and various other aspects of Hindu culture. Efforts to prevent émigré Hindus becoming 'estranged' have also involved the circulation of literature as well as the creation of online content. Hari Babu Kansal, Central Joint Secretary (Foreign Co-ordination) of the VHP, expressed this missionary element in a 1989 essay: 'If we can mobilise resources and arrange dissemination of information about Hindu religion extensively in a systematic manner, many more people may feel attracted towards Hinduism'.[153] Also departing from what is provided by the VHP in India, the VHP-UK offers a matrimonial service. This underlines the importance of endogamy—and fear of exogamy, conversion, and cultural 'dilution'—that many migrant communities feel, and also has a particular significance for Hindutva's 'saffron demography'.[154]

Unlike the RSS *shibirs*, which concentrate on discipline and physical training as much as ideological inculcation, camps organised by the VHP focus principally on encouraging Hindu togetherness and disseminating a Hindutva-inspired pedagogy. Another important strand to the VHP's global mission is the organisation of major, international conferences, which aim to keep a wide array of organisations close-knit, and mitigate against, in the VHP's words, the problem of 'Hindus living in the foreign countries... getting alienated from their original land and Dharma'.[155] These have been held around the world, from Denmark and Nepal, to the Netherlands and Singapore, each one hosting a transnational group of delegates from Sangh Parivar and other Hindu organisations.

In 2014, the VHP launched the World Hindu Congress: a far glitzier and more ambitious 'global platform for Hindus to connect, share ideas, inspire one another, and impact the common good'.[156] The first meeting, held in New Delhi's five-star Ashoka Hotel, hosted more than 1,500 delegates from over fifty countries, with sub-conferences on economic issues, education, media, politics, women, and youth. François Gautier, the Pune-based French Hindutva activist and writer, reflected: 'many of us sitting there felt that Hindu power had finally returned, after too many centuries of subjugation and humiliation'.[157] The VHP plan on holding a World Hindu Congress every four years, and the second instalment was held in Chicago in September 2018, on the 125th anniversary of Vivekananda's address to the World Parliament of

Religions. The scale and high-profile nature of these events clearly reflects the Modi-era enthusiasm, capacity, and confidence of the Hindu nationalist movement.

A quarter of a century earlier, on the centenary of Vivekananda's iconic speech, the VHP-A organised another major conference: 'Global Vision 2000'. This one-off meeting, held in Washington DC in August 1993, was perhaps the most significant Hindu nationalist event ever to have occurred in the United States. The conference claimed that 15,000 delegates—predominantly Indian Americans but also a substantial contingent of visitors from around the world—convened in the nation's capital for the event. It was held just nine months after the Babri Masjid demolition, at a time when the VHP-A's parent organisation was still banned in India.[158] This did not cause the speakers to tone down their rhetoric. Uma Bharti referred to the razing of the mosque as 'a great and memorable day', denounced secular Indians, and exhorted the audience: '*Kaho garv se, hum Hindu hain*' (Say it with pride, we are Hindu).[159] BJP President, Murli Manohar Joshi, also in attendance, referred to 'a new phase of Indian history' ushered in by the Babri Masjid demolition.[160] Buoyed with confidence and looking to the future, VHP General Secretary Ashok Singhal called for a 'strengthening' of the Hindu Students Council—an offshoot organisation of the VHP-A that has evolved into a major and much-contested group in the global Hindu nationalist movement.[161]

The event caught the imagination of an increasingly Hindutva-sympathetic Indian diaspora, as well as Sangh Parivar leaders from India. But it also was a watershed moment for those diametrically opposed to Hindu nationalism and concerned with its recent proliferation. Shashi Tharoor, then a young writer and fast-rising United Nations official, wrote an article in the *Washington Post* 'on the peculiarly vicious fanaticism of Indian expatriates', in which he claimed the diaspora 'are no longer an organic part of the culture, but severed digits that, in their yearning for the hand, can only twist themselves into a clenched fist'.[162] While Tharoor was correct in identifying a diasporic disposition to Hindutva, his metaphor of 'severed digits' was perhaps not altogether appropriate. The diaspora is geographically, culturally, and spiritually disconnected from the homeland in certain ways, but Global Vision 2000, the Virat Hindu Sammelan, and the numerous other avenues by which the Hindu nationalist movement brings a certain version of the homeland to the diaspora, represents a transnational connectivity that has enabled Hindutva to flourish overseas.

These eye-catching events constitute an important way in which the VHP has sought to forge unity, confidence, and cultural conformity overseas, aimed mainly at a diasporic audience. But the Parishad has also invested in strategies to promote and regulate a Hindutva version of Hindu culture amongst wider publics in international settings, specifically through education, interfaith relations, and advocacy. The overseas VHP has participated in a range of interfaith forums and served as a quasi-official representative of Hindus in various multicultural settings, positioning itself as the pre-eminent voice of a unified Hindu community in an effort to enhance the visibility, recognition, and political clout of Hindus. The VHP also sees this in terms of Hindus integrating into host societies and being viewed as 'good immigrants' (often quite explicitly in opposition to other minorities). One leader stated that '[the] VHP does not keep itself aloof from people belonging to other faiths', and another claimed the VHP 'inculcate values of Good Citizenship, as desired by the Political and Social leaders of this country to make Britain a beautiful mosaic of multi-faiths and multi-cultures'.[163] The VHP-UK is a member of the Inter Faith Network, a well-established body and frequent interlocutor with various levels of government, which was once chaired by long-standing VHP-UK leader, Girdhari Lal Bhan. Through this, Bhan also sat on the Faith Communities Consultative Council, a non-statutory body set up by Tony Blair's government in 2006 to consult 'faith groups' on policy, reflecting the growing salience of religion in community relations and the politics of multiculturalism.

But in spite of the Parishad's ambitions, its success as *the* Hindu representative in a multicultural setting has been rather limited. This is partly a consequence of apathy, competition, or more active opposition from the hugely diverse overseas Hindu population that the VHP seek to represent. In Britain it also reflects the government's reluctance to engage with the VHP-UK, based on apprehension about attitudes towards other minorities in Britain, as well as their counterpart's reputation in India. A senior official of the Faith and Participation Team at the Department for Communities and Local Government told me in an interview that even though the VHP-UK are involved in the Inter Faith Network, he 'wouldn't recommend a Minister meets with them'.[164] Various other groups' claims to speak for the Hindu community, including those not nominally part of the Sangh Parivar network, have often had greater impact, and are analysed in depth in Chapter 6.

One area in which the VHP has had somewhat more success in impacting the public representation of Hinduism is in its efforts to influence school religious education curricula. Its leaders have served as representatives of the Hindu community on a number of Standing Advisory Councils on Religious Education—independent bodies under the jurisdiction of UK local authorities with a wide range of statutory powers relating to the provision of compulsory religious education. In 1996, the VHP-UK made an ambitious new foray into propagating their version of Hinduism to wider publics with the publication of *Explaining Hindu Dharma—A Guide for Teachers*.[165] It is difficult to quantify the exact impact it made and there are no figures available on how many copies were actually used in schools, although it was claimed that 'the book had sold out primarily due to purchases by the VHP themselves'.[166] The publication has been not only circulated around educationalists, but bestowed upon various visitors and dignitaries. While its influence is hard to gauge, the book gives a picture of what the VHP-UK were hoping to achieve. In producing the text, they were staking a claim as *the* voice of a monolithic, albeit internally diverse, Hindu population, stepping into a space afforded to community representatives—often without much scrutiny—in the multicultural, inter-faith environment of late twentieth-century Britain.

Explaining Hindu Dharma follows a familiar matrix of seeking to regulate and codify Hindu culture and beliefs, presenting a customary set of conservative (often Brahmanical) dogma. It promotes the notion that Jainism, Buddhism, and Sikhism 'should be treated as branches of Hinduism', denounces the theory of Indo-Aryan migration, refers to Moghuls as 'invaders' who destroyed temples (including that of Ram in Ayodhya), endorses the work of the HSS and various other Hindu organisations, states that 'marriage and the rearing of children are the principal roles of women', underlines the importance of vegetarianism, and decries homosexuality as 'against nature'. Most problematic for many was *Explaining Hindu Dharma*'s treatment of caste: 'Today it has become fashionable to call the caste system a curse and a crime, a blot on Hindu society. Without looking to the noble origin and evolution of the system some are abusing their Hindu forefathers and cursing future generations.'[167] The book's position on caste is consistent with the VHP-UK's persistent efforts to lobby against the introduction of anti-caste discrimination legislation.

On the other side of the Atlantic, the VHP-A has been involved in much more high-profile and controversial efforts to impact school curricula. A conflict erupted in California in 2005, and was re-kindled again in 2016, around an effort to change sections of school textbooks pertaining to Hinduism and ancient Indian history. The two main protagonists, the Vedic Foundation and the Hindu Education Foundation, are groups that emerged in America in the early 2000s and whose connections to the Sangh Parivar are somewhat obfuscated. They purported to represent the views of concerned Hindu parents in America rather than institutionalised Hindu nationalism. In this sense they might be considered 'neo-Hindutva' organisations—a term that describes the nebulous and often mainstreamed avatars of contemporary Hindu nationalism, and is discussed in depth in Chapter 6.

Both the Vedic Foundation and the Hindu Education Foundation, however, are closely connected, both ideologically and organisationally, to the HSS and VHP-A. In turn, their parent organisations, the RSS and VHP, were also heavily involved in efforts to remould syllabi in India, through the National Council for Education and Research Training, following the election of the BJP-led governments in the late 1990s and again from 2014. Therefore, while the diaspora's attempts to edit school books must be understood in the local context of multiculturalism and the politics of minority representation, it is also crucial to locate the narrative in a wider context that can be traced, directly, to the Hindu nationalist movement's tenacious historical revisionism. So, following Ernest Renan's famous identification of the centrality of 'getting history wrong' to the project of nation-building, the same might be said of diaspora-building.[168]

The complainants in California contended that the textbooks were biased against Hinduism and proposed 160 edits, including passages relating to caste, the position of women in society, and the Aryan migration theory. Although there was broad consensus to change some patently inaccurate excerpts, many of the proposals were met by vociferous challenges from activists and leading academic experts.[169] They claimed the proposed edits were tantamount to a whitewashing of caste and Dalit lives, denial of pluralism and vernacular Hindu beliefs, and obscuring of the lived realities of women in a patriarchal society. The tense episode—which led to lawsuits, and numerous press articles in the US and India—revealed 'deep ideological fissures' over aspects of Hindu culture and history, and the right to speak for a community.[170]

Battle lines were drawn between Hindutva-sympathetic Indian Americans and more secular-minded members of the diaspora. Through deploying the language of civil rights, and voicing anger over the 'demonisation' of an ethnic minority, American Hindu nationalists were able to 'win a sympathetic hearing from well-meaning North American liberals'.[171] The Hindutva lobby was attempting not just to bend objective, historical truth, but to leverage the politics of representation in order to present a version of Hindu culture that regulates diversity and minorities within their own community. For many, including those in the diaspora, this was a wake-up call to the existence of proactive Hindutva networks overseas, and a realisation that these organisations were seeking, and even achieving, recognition as the role of 'official' community representative.

The California textbook controversy represents just the tip of the iceberg in efforts made by the VHP and connected organisations to lobby and regulate the representation of Hinduism in the diaspora. The VHP-UK has been actively involved, alongside other Hindutva groups, on a number of issues considered elsewhere in this book: charity and fundraising activities, lobbying over caste and other issues, and the public representation of Hinduism. These 'struggles for recognition' can be understood in terms of creating Hindu consciousness, asserting the right of certain groups to speak for 'the community', creating an assertive and conservative individual and group consciousness, and 'visibilising' Hindus overseas. As with the textbook dispute, 'voicy' expressions of Hindu nationalist identity often use the framework of rights and the language of multiculturalist self-representation.[172] This has served as an opportunity to come together with other Hindu groups in shared moments of collective outrage. The VHP-UK lent their support to ISCKON's campaign to save Bhaktivedanta Manor—'the UK home of the Hare Krishna Movement', donated by George Harrison in 1973, but subject to a prolonged planning dispute with the local authorities from the 1980s.[173] Similarly, in 2007, the VHP-UK joined hands with numerous other Hindu and Hindutva groups to take on the Department for Environment, Food and Rural Affairs, which had ordered the euthanisation of a temple bull in Wales that had tested positive for bovine tuberculosis.[174] The connection to the historic cow protection movement and rhetoric of the Indian VHP and its ideological forefathers were not hard to identify.

In other campaigns, the VHP-UK has taken the lead. In 2009, the organisation made a formal complaint after the BBC aired an episode of the long-running spy drama, *Spooks*, in which the secret service thwart an attack by Hindu extremists on Muslims in Britain. The VHP-UK's letter to the BBC claimed that the storyline 'maligned' Hindus, giving two pages of evidence to illustrate the exemplary role played by the VHP and the Hindu community in British society, and even claimed that they were 'seeking legal advice as to the damage to [the] VHP's good name'.[175] The National Hindu Students' Forum also lobbied the BBC, encouraging its members to send in a templated letter endorsing the role of the VHP.[176] The *Spooks* controversy demonstrates not just Hindu nationalist 'expert[ise] in the art of being outraged', but a desire to express a united and assertive Hindu voice in the multicultural setting that very clearly shares a lingua franca with the 'identitarian political claims' of other ethnic and religious minority communities.[177] Indeed the very same programme, six years earlier, had been the focus of a deluge of complaints from the Muslim Council of Britain and hundreds of British Muslims, after a programme depicted the radicalisation of Muslim boys.[178]

While the overseas VHP has remained somewhat active in its efforts to police the representation of Hinduism, in recent years a wide range of other organisations—many much more nebulously 'Hindutva'—have emerged in Britain, the US, and elsewhere. In America, these include groups such as American Hindu Anti-Defamation Coalition (based on the Jewish Anti-Defamation League), the American Hindu Coalition, and the Hindu American Foundation; in Britain, the National Council of Hindu Temples, the City Hindus Network, and the Hindu Forum of Britain. This represents a mainstreaming and a vernacularisation of Hindutva, and a radiation of Hindu nationalist ideology and institutionalisation beyond the peripheries of the Sangh Parivar, as it is traditionally understood. This dynamic but often nebulous new development may be understood as 'neo-Hindutva'. The contested role played by these organisations in speaking for 'the Hindu community', and in particular policing the representation of Hinduism, is discussed in depth in the final chapter of this book.

Conclusion

This chapter and the one preceding it have shown that two of the most politically significant and divisive episodes in India's democratic history were not just national, but global moments. The Indian Emergency and the *Ram Janmabhoomi* movement were both turning points as well as 'critical events' in the relationship between India and its diaspora.[179] Although separate, and in many ways different, the transnational networks and individuals developed during the Emergency activism played an important role in diasporic Ayodhya mobilisations a decade later. The Hindu nationalist boom in India during the 1980s and 1990s made an impact overseas and, to a small extent, the diaspora supported the growth of India's 'saffron wave'.

One of the major players in Hindutva's late twentieth-century ascendency was the VHP—a globally oriented, core institution of the Sangh Parivar performing an 'ecclesiastical' role and, through its mass activism, closely involved in the BJP's rise to power. Through branches set up in numerous countries overseas, the VHP has also served as a conduit for globe-trotting gurus, Hindutva ideology, and funds to move between India and the diaspora.

But the VHP's foreign outposts have participated in much more than simply mimicking the modus operandi of its mother organisation. Although many campaigns, such as that around Ayodhya, were specifically focused on the homeland, in more recent years—as the diaspora has become more established and settled—they have turned increasingly to 'domestic' issues: policing the representation of Hinduism in a multicultural milieu, influencing educational curricula, and attempting to forge a united community voice.

Most of the time, the interlocutors of the VHP as community representatives are unaware of the political connotations of Hindu nationalist groups in the diaspora. This naivety may be in part the reason behind the VHP-UK receiving not just tax breaks and the use of Council-owned property, but also grants from local authorities. The same can be said of many Hindu immigrants; Aminah Mohammad-Arif argues that most are not aware of the 'extremist drifts' of the VHP, which constitutes 'one of the major achievements of the VHP'.[180] To many Indians overseas, these groups claiming to represent their interests are seen as benign.

A major element of the VHP's praxis, both at home and overseas, has been to promote a broad-based, catholic Hindu community and to preside over an ecumenism that is inclusive, but also prescriptive of a certain form of conservative Hindu revivalism. This process of disciplining Hinduism's fuzzy edges and rendering real the 'imagined religious community' is closely imbricated with the emergence of Hinduism as a 'metaphysical construct' in the colonial era, based upon 'a single conceptual grammar of civilisational order and hierarchy'.[181] In a certain sense we can observe a comparable dynamic in diasporic environments, in which multiculturalism does not just permit, but often explicitly demands the construction of a neatly packaged, public ethnic identity. In this context, the VHP has drawn on mythologised, pseudo-historical narratives, central to Hindu nationalism, to construct a monolithic community identity rooted in a largely fictionalised antiquity. Ecumenical conferences, educational advocacy, Ayodhya mobilisations, and other battles over history and representation have all engaged with these processes of 'constructing a monocultural homeland in order to be part of a multicultural society'.[182] Avtar Brah's paradigm of 'diaspora space'—in which 'tradition is itself continually invented even as it may be hailed as originating from the mists of time'—is particularly apposite in making sense of the VHP's mission abroad.[183] The VHP's activities abroad, therefore, represent not just an export of Indian Hindutva, but also a further layer to the vernacularisation of Hindu nationalism overseas, which has particular resonance for expatriate Hindus and serves as a transnational linkage between the diaspora and the homeland.

5

CHARITY, *SEWA* (SERVICE), AND THE 'MODEL MINORITY'

This chapter considers the development of the Hindu nationalist movement, primarily in Britain in the early twenty-first century, through the prism of philanthropy and *sewa* (service). These are both important, interconnected values and forms of mobilisation for Hindus in Britain. Charity and *sewa* are central to Hindu nationalism in its broadest sense, but the Sangh in Britain also have specific instructions relating to these themes. An amendment to the Hindu Swayamsevak Sangh (HSS) Trust Deed, resolved at the *Pratinidhi Sabha* (Central Board) meeting in Birmingham on 20 November 1983, declared that a key aim of the organisation should be to:

> Encourage amongst Hindus a spirit of service and self-sacrifice and a determination to alleviate ignorance, poverty and injustice, and render financial assistance from the funds of the Sangh to the aged, sick, poor and distressed Hindu individuals and Hindu organizations with similar objects.[1]

Charity and *sewa* reveal a great deal about the recent history of diasporic Hindutva. Various Hindu nationalist groups and individuals have raised and sent funds to India since the mid-twentieth century, with peaks in the flow at certain points in the movement's history. Chapters 3 and 4 showed that both the Indian Emergency and the *Ramjanmabhoomi* movement involved the collection, transfer, and distribution of capital. The diasporic Sangh have also been involved in charitable activities for as long as they have operated overseas. However, the major turning point was the Gujarat earthquake of January 2001. This had a significant impact on Britain's large Gujarati diaspora, many of whom had family and other close ties to the region. These communities raised large sums of money for aid relief efforts in India, some of which provoked scrutiny and allegations of impropriety.

The chapter begins with this important episode, but its main focus is the British Sangh's relationship with *sewa* in the context of the recently conceived 'Sewa Day' and the earlier 'Hindu Marathon'. Sewa Day was launched as an annual, multi-location, multi-event day of voluntary projects. To a great extent, it constitutes a new trajectory for British Hindu and Hindutva organisations. It has played a rehabilitative role and provided a new public face for Hindu nationalist groups in Britain in the wake of censure after a Charity Commission inquiry into the British Sangh and related scrutiny following the Gujarat violence of 2002. Sewa Day also represents a diversifying of Hindu nationalism beyond the 'traditional' spaces of the Sangh Parivar network, a blurring of its edges, and an adaptation to local conditions and stimuli that provides a platform for the diasporic vernacularisation of the Sangh. In this sense, it constitutes a form of 'neo-Hindutva', explored in more depth in the final chapter.

Sewa Day is carefully framed to resonate with contemporary conceptions of British citizenship and interfaith relations. It is closely, often explicitly, aligned with ideas of civic conservatism and a neoliberal political vision of proactive civil society enterprises in place of government provisions. This can feel especially apposite in an era of austerity. But it also demonstrates commitment to traditional Hindutva values and forms of mobilisation. Sewa Day reifies the Sangh's ecumenical credentials, facilitating and enacting layers of interconnected organisations and individuals. Through performative public displays of *sewa*, the Hindu nationalist movement in Britain has nurtured and projected the notion of Hindus as the 'model minority'—a core trope of diasporic Hindutva.

To understand *sewa* and the Sangh in Britain, we must first consider Hindu nationalist philanthropy. Charitable acts and *dana* (giving) are, like with many religions, a central feature of Hinduism. They are considered key components of the devotee's *dharma* (religious duty), bringing the giver closer to their guru, to God, and, ultimately, to salvation or *moksha* (liberation). They are also at the very heart of the Hindu nationalism. Hedgewar prescribed donations to the RSS from the outset, framing contributions as 'selfless devotion' in order to build a strong, organised society. He reinterpreted the tradition of *guru dakshina* (offering to the guru), with RSS members paying homage and monetary offerings to the saffron flag of the movement. Jaffrelot and Therwath, in their critique of Anderson's 'long-distance nationalism' model, underline the importance of the diaspora for the homeland by emphasising the Sangh's eagerness to engage the affluent Hindu diaspora as a source of funding.[2] But philanthropy is not merely a product of the Indian Sangh's outreach to the diaspora; there are many diasporic impetuses. Sending money to India also serves as 'a means of assuaging the conscience' of those who have become successful and wealthy abroad—another dimension to the 'therapeutic enactments of belonging' that are constituted by diasporic Hindutva.[3] However, it is important, in seeking to understand various layers of meaning, not to disavow a fundamental motivation for many people's charitable donations and acts, such as those seen during Sewa Day—a simple, altruistic desire to 'do good'.

Almost all discussions on diasporic Hindu nationalism—from informal conversations to scholarly publications—mention capital flows from the West to India, primarily via charitable donations through the Sangh Parivar's various organisations. Data on this can be relatively scant, although groups that are registered charities in the UK and US are obligated to declare their financial records. However, philanthropic donations of various types—for schools, religious institutions, or civil society organisations—are often untraceably routed through family and kinship networks via regular remittances. It is also extremely difficult to get a clear picture of political funding. Although now somewhat relaxed by a 2018 amendment to the Foreign Contribution (Regulation) Act (2010), Indian law has strictly regulated overseas financing of political parties. But as smaller campaign contributions (under 20,000 rupees) do not need to be declared, and there remains significant flows of 'black money' funnelled from abroad and moved throughout the country, the true scale and impact of these transnational flows is yet to be fully elucidated. The BJP, however, undoubtedly leads the way in terms of campaigning for, and almost certainly receiving, donations and other forms of support from NRIs.

So while Therwath bluntly writes, 'the fact that the Sangh Parivar draws its funds from foreign sources is a well-known fact', capital flows are actually opaque and under-examined.[4] The most thorough investigations of transnational capital flows to Hindu nationalist organisations are impassioned advocacy-oriented reports produced by anti-Hindutva activists.[5] Although these reports are anxious about the ramifications of diasporic Hindutva, Devesh Kapur, who has probably written in greater depth than any other on the overseas funding of the Hindu nationalist movement, is much more cautious in ascribing significance to it.[6]

What is known for certain is that philanthropic remittances are significant. India's Ministry of External Affairs estimated that foreign contributions to the voluntary sector between 1991 and 2000 totalled at least US$835 million; in the same report it listed numerous Hindutva-connected donors and recipients.[7] According to a recent report, 'seven Sangh-affiliated charitable groups [in the US] spent at least US$158.9 million' between 2001 and 2019, with much of this sum sent for projects in India.[8] The connection between transnational charity and the Sangh has long roots— RSS members in the United States, for example, were involved in fundraising to support relief work after the 1977 cyclone in Andhra Pradesh.[9] Sewa International was started by the HSS(UK) in the early 1990s, initially as a response to a major earthquake in Maharashtra, and subsequently grew to become a multinational charity, underlining the global influence that the British Sangh has had.

A wide range of organisations with connections to Hindu nationalist networks and ideologies, which are either specifically charity-oriented or include *sewa* as part of a broader remit, operate overseas. Some of these focus on activities in their 'host society', but most of them direct their resources towards projects and affiliated groups in India. They include the Param Shakti Peeth, Bhaarat Welfare Trust, and Maa Charity Trust (all connected to Hindutva preacher Sadhvi Rithambara, discussed in Chapter 4 in relation to her role in Ayodhya mobilisations), the Kalyan Ashram Trust (which focuses on 'tribal upliftment'), the Samanvaya Parivar (of Swami Satyamitranand Giri), and Ekal Vidyalaya (which has established tens of thousands of Hindutva-promoting schools in rural India). Many charities based in the diaspora follow a model of fundraising overseas and then distributing donations to various Indian-based NGOs. The Sangh's 'eShakha' site lists no fewer than 215 separate projects and organisations supported by the Indian Development and Relief Fund, noting: 'All these projects may not by maintained by Sangh but most of them are by Sangh or associated'.[10]

Sewa International and the Gujarat earthquake fundraising controversy

On 26 January 2001—India's fifty-first Republic Day—a devastating earthquake hit the Kutch district of Gujarat, killing around 20,000 people and destroying 400,000 homes. The earthquake was so violent that it was felt across 70% of India, and it displaced up to 1.8 million of the population.[11] A major international relief operation was put in place with foreign governments, aid agencies, and NGOs joined by various civil society and grassroots efforts from the Indian diaspora, a great number of whom were personally affected by the disaster.

One strand of this philanthropy precipitated the Sangh's most controversial period outside India, and several groups faced very public allegations about disingenuous fundraising.[12] Critics levelled impassioned condemnations that funds sent to Sangh affiliates in India were connected, directly or indirectly, to the communal violence that spread throughout Gujarat in 2002. This resulted in a formal investigation of the HSS by the Charity Commission for England and Wales, the governmental regulatory body that oversees all registered charities. On the other side of the Atlantic, the US Justice Department launched an investigation into the International Development and Relief Fund, accused of giving the majority of their tax-deductible donations to a range of Hindutva groups that facilitate 'reconversion', 'Hinduisation', and other communal activities.[13]

In Britain, the HSS—through the charity Sewa International UK (SIUK), which they described as a 'service project'—raised £4.3 million in 2001.[14] This was largely a consequence of an extensive campaign for earthquake relief, which sprang into action as soon as the news of the disaster spread around the world. In Britain, this began with an 'emergency public meeting' held at Brent Town Hall in West London, involving a range of Hindu community leaders, politicians, and organisers of the British Sangh Parivar. Narendra Modi, then Gujarat Chief Minister, gave an 'emotional message in Gujarati [that] was telecast live to the gathering'.[15]

The controversy that arose out of the earthquake-related philanthropy focused on two angles. First, that money was disingenuously raised under the name 'Sewa International', which was not a registered charity in Britain and people were unaware that it was actually going to the HSS. Second, that once funds were sent to India, they were not used in a purely nonpartisan humanitarian effort, but also helped to expand the Sangh Parivar network and, by extension, the ideology of Hindutva.

Numerous press articles from Britain, India, and elsewhere, as well as the AWAAZ advocacy report and a high-profile investigative news feature for Channel 4 in 2002, all generated significant scrutiny on the diaspora's support for the Sangh in both Britain and India. Public denouncements of Hindu nationalism came from a range of sources, from left-wing, secular academics and journalists to South Asian Muslim groups and human rights campaigners. The scandal was revealing for many members of the Hindu community—including those affiliated with diaspora Sangh groups—opening their eyes to a type of Hindutva they were not altogether familiar with, nor had necessarily realised they were directly connected to.

Channel 4's incendiary documentary—the culmination of a long period of investigative research—was aired on 12 December 2002, and featured a wide range of interviews and on-location footage in India and Britain. The programme focused on the Kalyan Ashram projects, whose work on 'tribal conversion' and 'upliftment' was linked to violence against Muslims and Christians and the destruction of mosques and churches. It was followed, two years later, with comparable but more detailed revelations in the excoriating report, 'In Bad Faith? British Charity and Hindu Extremism', produced by the advocacy group AWAAZ.[16] Lord (Adam) Patel, one of four House of Lords peers who were Sewa International patrons, expressed anger at being 'cheated' by SIUK, for, he stated, 'raising funds in the name of charity and giving them to extremist organisations that preach hatred against Muslims and Christians'.[17] Conversely, Lord (Navnit) Dholakia, then President of the Liberal Democrats, alongside others involved in the charity, vociferously defended SIUK's reputation and rectitude, denying links with the Sangh.[18]

In October 2002, shortly before the documentary aired, the Charity Commission launched an inquiry, conducted under Section 8 of the Charities Act (1993). But the report, published two years and five months later, was cursory, anodyne, and equivocal.[19] It uncritically cited assertions of innocence given by the HSS, explaining: 'The Commission did not feel the need to explore further the extent of the ideological commonality between the charity and the RSS. This was because the trustees had given their assurance that they acted autonomously.'[20] The inquiry was also scuppered by the Indian government's refusal to issue visas to the commission's investigators.[21] A journalist who had closely investigated the episode (and wished to remain anonymous), suggested to me that the commission thought it may be 'easier to leave this [report] at a slightly inconclusive level'. They were in conversation with the Foreign and Commonwealth Office in London, and conscious of the political ramifications of publishing a damning report (not least because the BJP were in power throughout the period of the alleged transgressions and subsequent investigations). The seemingly tepid outcome of the commission's inquiry, therefore, seems unlikely to have resulted from naivety or incompetence.

Ultimately, the inquiry was touted as a vindication of HSS and SIUK's innocence.[22] SIUK's press release following the inquiry's publication referred to a two-year 'systematic campaign of calumny, innuendoes and disinformation', adding that 'the conclusion of the Inquiry is a strong rebuttal to these malicious campaigns'.[23] SIUK and HSS mobilised the support of key actors in 'the Hindu community', publishing a raft of letters of support and press releases. Between April and September 2003, SIUK listed thirteen 'testimonial letters' on their website, including those from local government councillors, a member of parliament, a business leader, and even the Prince of Wales (now King Charles III).

The Sewa International Charity Commission controversy was a critical juncture for the Sangh in Britain. It revealed core processes and networks that connected India and the diaspora. The episode also highlighted challenges and contradictions in the British government's relationship with Hindu nationalism, as well as some major limitations to the Charity Commission's understanding and management of charities with global reach. Furthermore, it illustrated the complexities of differentiating between a registered charity's religious/cultural activities (allowed by the commission) and political activities (not allowed). This requirement came to the fore less ambiguously during the 2015 and 2017 General Elections, when the National Council of Hindu Temples UK (also a registered charity), 'was rebuked by the Charity Commission for advocating for the Conservatives'.[24]

On certain levels, the fundraising itself was a key process for diasporic Hindu nationalism. Zavos accurately described the Gujarat earthquake as an 'opportunity for Hindu nationalist organisations to develop their profile in Britain'.[25] But the inverse of this was also true: providing humanitarian aid enabled British Indians to develop their profile in India. In this sense, Judith Brown's reference to diasporic philanthropy as 'charitable and religious *investments*' is apposite.[26] Donated money is not charity without return or context, but provides the diaspora with a means to 'intervene in the public life of South Asia'.[27]

These processes could not occur in hermetically sealed spaces. The overseas Sangh fundraising scandals also impacted India. They increased attention on the overseas activities of the Hindu nationalist movement from both the Sangh Parivar and, through press coverage, a broader public. Whilst this was not new—as seen in the diaspora's role during the Emergency and *Ramjanmabhoomi* movement—the level of public awareness concerning foreign backing of the Sangh increased significantly during this period. The RSS even made public statements in India condemning anti-Sangh 'propaganda' and 'wild and false allegations of misuse of funds received from abroad'.[28]

The SIUK episode, and the 2002 Gujarat violence, also made the British Sangh more wary and better adept at distancing themselves from their Indian counterparts—in rhetoric and publicity as well as practice. The experiences appear to have encouraged the Sangh to focus, at least publicly, on outwardly visible charitable activities in Britain that avoided overt Hindu(tva) overtones. Although this trajectory was not entirely new, it was pursued more vigorously and creatively from the second half of the 2000s. Ved Nanda, head of the HSS in the United States since 2005, explicitly connected the India Development and Relief Fund scandal with the need to focus more efforts domestically.[29] British organisers similarly focused on PR-conscious, domestic charitable concerns. In recent years this has been most obvious with 'Sewa Day', the initial years of which form the primary focus of the remainder of this chapter.

Sewa Day

Sewa Day is a significant recent enterprise of the Sangh in Britain—an annual, multi-location, multi-event day that seeks 'the promotion of good citizenship by encouraging and facilitating volunteering in furtherance of charitable purposes for the benefit of the public'.[30] Whilst remittances associated with the Sangh are relatively frequently mentioned, much less is written on their charitable activities outside India.[31] Sewa Day is full of connections to the philanthropy and public service of the Hindu nationalist movement, but it also reveals much more about the nature of diaspora charity and even multiculturalism more broadly. It has close connections with twenty-first-century, multicultural social action, but also owes much of its character to Hindu nationalism and its culture of social service from which it emerged. Sewa Day provides an important case study for understanding the connection between Hindutva and the notion of Hindus as a 'model minority'—the focus of the final section of this chapter.

The HSS and Sewa UK—the name with which SIUK rebranded themselves in 2010—launched Sewa Day in November 2010. In many ways it signalled a rebirth of the Sangh's British charity activities after the SIUK scandal. At the instruction of the Charity Commission, SIUK was eventually established as an independent company and registered charity on 1 April 2010. It was entirely bankrolled by the HSS until the end of the 2010–11 financial year, at which point the HSS transferred £868,539 to SIUK.[32]

Sewa Day is umbilically linked to Hindu nationalism in Britain, although this remains obfuscated for many of those involved in Sewa Day activities, and outside observers. A number of key organisers of Sewa Day are active members of other Sangh offshoots, and there are particularly close connections to the National Hindu Students Forum.[33] Dhiraj D. Shah, the long-term head of the HSS, was also a director of Sewa UK when Sewa Day was established and remains a trustee. Dhiraj M. Shah, the National Chairman of Sewa UK, is also a trustee of the HSS. An Instagram story from the HSS account in 2018 includes a montage of logos belonging to 'Our extended Parivar [family]', which includes the Sewa Day emblem.[34]

Sewa UK also remains closely connected, describing Sewa Day as 'Our social initiative action' and donating funds, although since 2012 it has been a separate charity.[35] The organisational connectivities and personnel overlap—which indicate a high degree of ecumenism and political coherence, but also the relatively small base of Sangh organisers in Britain—are considered in depth in this chapter. But although Sewa Day has these very close connections to Hindutva on a variety of levels, in some senses it has grown beyond the Sangh Parivar. Many of those participating in their activities (either as contributors or beneficiaries of the *sewa*) may be unaware of the origins or context of the initiative, and there is a deliberate effort made to include a diverse range of participants and publics.

Since registering as an autonomous charity in 2012, Sewa Day has been superficially, and in theory administratively, independent from the HSS and Sewa UK. Sewa Day's organisers are eager to promote it as a non-denominational series of events that are not necessarily 'desi' nor Hindu in terms of participants, beneficiaries, or tone. Although they speak of the Sanskritic etymology of the word '*sewa*' and the 'Dharmic traditions of ancient India', they frame it as 'a universal concept', emphasise inclusivity, and rarely mention Hinduism in their online material.[36] Connections with the Sangh are also deliberately downplayed and obfuscated in a variety of ways, in much the same way that the transnational Sangh connections were denied in the SIUK episode.[37] Sewa Day reports, for instance, tend not to contain any direct mention of the HSS, in spite of mentioning many other organisations by name. Aesthetically and semantically there is also often little to hint at Hindu connections, let alone Hindu nationalism.

Despite this, Sewa Day is inherently a Hindu, even Hindutva, initiative. But it is nebulous in many ways, displaying both mimesis and idiosyncrasy vis-à-vis the Sangh's ideology and modus operandi. On certain levels, Sewa Day feels like a product of the era of Community Cohesion and David Cameron's 'Big Society' vision of voluntarism, replete with the rhetoric and imagery of civic virtue and interfaith relations.[38] However it is also intrinsically connected to several cornerstones of Sangh ideology and praxis: public service, sacrifice, and performative, ecumenical displays of discipline and unity.

Visiting Sewa Day events in the third year it took place, in 2012, came about after I made contact with the organiser of an event in East London, who was also *pramukh* (leader) of a London *shakha*. Most of the event volunteers were *swayamsevaks* or *sevikas*; the occasion was held at the same location as their weekly *shakhas*. The programme consisted of a vegetarian Gujarati meal prepared and served to elderly members of the local community, almost all first-generation Indian or East African Hindu migrants. Following the meal was a *Raas Garba* (traditional Gujarati dance), in which I was exhorted to participate, and a *Ramleela* (performance of Ramayana scenes) by the younger *Bala Gokulum* children (both girls and boys). I was made to feel extremely welcome, and my host insisted I share the delicious food. The organiser did not allow me to leave without taking home a portion of chana masala. The children and young adults involved in the event were dedicated, disciplined, and enthusiastic, and appeared keen to make a positive contribution to their local community.

Sewa Day is presented as a decentralised grassroots initiative. Its online registration process, with a range of 'How to…' guides and 'brand guidelines', implies a strong 'crowd-sourced' ethos, in which people volunteer themselves for acts of civic altruism.[39] These 'franchised' processes, modelled for optimum 'organic' growth and minimal administration, suggest a more inclusive approach, in which ostensibly *anyone* can be an active organiser and participant. A press release ahead of the 2012 event invited people to 'set up a project that meets our aims': '(a) to help relieve hardship & poverty, (b) to help the environment, and (c) to bring a little joy to others'.[40] However, in practice, this is just one aspect of Sewa Day's organisational strategy, beneath which are more top-down approaches. Ram Vaidya, the RSS *pracharak* in Britain, told me that the Sewa Day organisation 'invites' different groups to put on events—suggestive of a centralised, executive structure that seems at odds with the notion of a more grassroots, spontaneous, devolved ethos.[41]

Despite the demonstrably positive impact and conscientious intentions of the participants at this, and other Sewa Day events, a critical approach is necessary to best understand Sewa Day and its relationship with Hindu nationalism in Britain. While innovative, and rooted in contemporary cultures of multicultural civil society, Sewa Day simultaneously continues and expands existing traditions of Hindu nationalist social service. Sewa Day represents a maturation of the Sangh, as well as a response to dilemmas faced in the early twenty-first-century SIUK scandal. This has formed an important location for the articulation of the 'model minority' narrative—a trope with specific resonance for diasporic Hindutva.

Cultivating and disseminating a strong public image formed an important element of Sewa Day from the outset. Before the first event had even happened, the Prime Minister's Office released a statement from Cameron expressing his 'very best wishes for National Sewa Day', and noting, 'when I talk about building a Big Society... some people say it will never happen... National Sewa Day shows how cynical that is'.[42] Connections to the Conservative rhetoric and neoliberal strategy of community volunteering in the context of a diminished role of the state as welfare provider—characterised in Britain for several years by David Cameron's 'Big Society' project—run throughout Sewa Day's publicity.[43]

This neoliberal context and a corporate streak to the initiative is underlined in the 'Sewa Day Annual Report 2012', in which the Economic Policy Group, an independent economic and strategy consulting practice, published its findings. Through various graphs and charts, it argued that the 'Social Return on Investment (SROI) meant a net benefit of £4.7 million for Britain'.[44] The report went on to claim that 'We found the projects with the highest social impact were in the category "Bring a little joy to others", which generated an SROI of £12.50 for every £1 invested'.[45] This costing can be seen as a form of accountability, but also of quantifying the value of the Hindu community's contribution in irrefutable, monetised terms, in turn with the mood, perhaps, of austerity.

Deeper ideological resonances between Big Society and Hindu nationalism also exist. Public acts of civic voluntarism provide platforms for (self-selecting) community representatives, thereby speaking to Hindutva's desire to be the political voice of a monolithic 'Hindu community'. In 2010, Sayeeda Warsi, then Minister of State for Faith and Communities, announced: 'in a stronger and bigger society the scope for people of faith to take their places as equals at the public table should become easier not just on so-called "stake-holding" bodies, but as the vanguard of an increasingly decentralised civic society'.[46] The government's relationship with Sewa Day—with annual statements of support and more—also represents, as Zavos has identified, 'the state's concerns to embrace "faith" while simultaneously working to defuse the subversive power of "religion"'.[47] However, the branding of Sewa Day as 'Big Society' remains in tension with the underlying devotional and spiritual dimension to *sewa*, which is of central importance to many of the participants.

On a superficial level Sewa Day appears distant from the Sangh; it claims to be secular and non-denominational, speaks in the language of 'cohesive communities' and 'citizenship', and employs slick corporate costings of volunteer contributions to the community, couched in terms of 'monetised net benefit'.[48] It is also steeped in the idiom of multi- and inter-faith relations (with many projects involving diverse religious community representatives), seemingly a far cry from the cultural chauvinism of Hindutva. Much Sewa Day publicity is even explicitly secular. The T-shirt I was given when attending Sewa Day in 2012—identical to those worn by Sewa Day volunteers in Britain and across the world, connecting them and creating a sense of unity—featured the anodyne slogan 'changing lives around us', alongside the names of Mahatma Gandhi, Queen Elizabeth II, Nelson Mandela, and Martin Luther King Jr. Notably, Sewa Day's website and annual reports tend to focus less on projects that are explicitly related to Hindu communities. Examples of prominently featured projects include cleaning up a public park in Leicester, volunteering at a hospice in Luton, helping a homeless charity in Southall, tidying a canal in West London, singing at a residential-care home in Wembley, and collecting for a foodbank in Wembley.[49]

In spite of this, Sewa Day has been inextricably linked to Hindu communities, even the Hindu nationalist movement, in Britain. The 2012 'Social Impact Analysis' report showed that of almost ninety 'charity, community organisations' (which includes religious groups) involved in Sewa Day, fewer than twenty were listed as 'non-Hindu affiliated organisations'.[50] The NHSF are particularly active: in 2019, they stated that thirty-seven NHSF chapters and 850 members participated, with many (but by no means all) activities taking places in Hindu temples.[51] Sewa Day projects, unsurprisingly, often tend to occur in areas with large Hindu populations (especially London and the Midlands, and internationally in areas with Hindu diaspora populations, including Gulf states, the US, and Hong Kong).

This is largely due to Sewa Day's HSS/SIUK/NHSF lineage. On my visit to Sewa Day, I was told by an organiser that it had sought independence from SIUK on the advice of the Charity Commission. However, a close level of organisational connectivity remains. Many people involved in Sewa Day are also connected to the Sangh, and Zavos argues that 'no organisations have been as heavily represented as those associated with the Hindu nationalist Sangh Parivar'.[52] This is a balance that the organisers appear to have tried to redress. Their branding clearly attempts to present the initiative as cutting across ethnic and religious demographics (which it clearly does, in certain ways), and one of the main recommendations of the 2012 'Social Impact Analysis' report was 'to encourage more organisations to take part that were not affiliated to the Hindu or Indian communities'.[53]

However, a great number of Sewa Day projects are explicitly for a Hindu audience: the *garba* and *Ramleela* that I attended, helping at the Bhakti Shyama care centre run by the Brahmbandhu (UK) Trust, the NHSF in Manchester doing odd jobs at two local *mandirs*, helping in the farm at the Hare Krishna temple in Watford, and even 'participating in blissful Bhajans' in Luton.[54] In spite of this, many events do not easily fit into the mould that might be expected: a project in Abu Dhabi in 2013 collected supplies for the Red Crescent Society, in 2016 a school were given a 'Sewa Pioneers Award' for a book donation drive for a French refugee camp, and an event in 2012 organised with the Leicester-based St Philip's Centre—a Christian organisation focusing on multi-faith community relations.[55] The St Philip's Centre's Deputy Director, Riaz Ravat, even served on the Sewa Day Leicester planning group.[56] These dimensions of inter-faith activity seem to contrast with the antagonism towards Christianity and Islam which Hindu nationalism often engages in.

However, the inclusion of non-Hindu volunteers, beneficiaries, and supporters does not necessarily point to a lack of Hindutva ethos. Publicly, the Sangh does not exclude minorities; in India, and perhaps more emphatically in the diaspora, they underline that they welcome all comers, including Muslims. Although contested, there is also ample evidence that Sangh charitable activities target minorities (which is sometimes linked to a missionary-like objective). In the case of Sewa Day this is hard to prove, but it is clear that the events provide an opportunity to showcase the ostensible universalism of Hindu traditions of charity, whilst promoting the notion that *sewa* is 'embedded in the Dharmic traditions of ancient India'.[57]

Consonance with the Sangh

Sewa Day displays close ideological consonance with the Sangh on a number of levels. Although seemingly counter-intuitive, Sewa Day's projected multifaith inclusivity connects to Hindutva's ecumenical paternalism. The presence of Sikh, Buddhist, and Jain participants and volunteers was underlined in an Early Day Motion tabled by Barry Gardiner MP, which congratulated the launch of the 'cross-community, multi-faith initiative'.[58] Superficially, this might seem a far cry from the Hindu chauvinism of the Sangh. However, it could be interpreted as even more emblematic of its Hindutva lineage, according to which all 'indigenous' religions of India may be incorporated into the Hindu fold (albeit as lesser subdivisions).[59]

This ecumenism—often disputed by Sikhs, Jains, and others—is also pursued by the Sangh Parivar in Britain, but with rather different emphases. A speaker at an NHSF event on Hindu identity in the mid-1990s noted, 'There are many different modes of worship beneath the broad umbrella of Hindu Dharma... When I use the term Hindu I also include Jains, Buddhists and even Sikhs'.[60] More recently, in secretly filmed footage of a 2015 HSS leadership camp, a teacher instructs a class of *swayamsevaks* that Buddhism is 'nothing but part of Hinduism'.[61] I also encountered this rhetoric in my own fieldwork: Ram Vaidya told me that Jainism, Buddhism, and Sikhism are 'not really different to Hinduism' and, as much optimistically as disingenuously, 'India is culturally one'.

Although certain factions take a much stricter position, many in the Hindu nationalist movement advocate that even Muslims and Christians may be accommodated in a Hindu *rashtra*, provided they respect the 'national culture' and cease to expect 'preferential' treatment as minorities. In India, service plays an important role in this narrative, which is also predicated on the notion that Muslims and Christians have Hindu roots and are converts, or descendants of neophytes, who might be 're-converted' through *Ghar Wapsi* (returning home) programmes. Beckerlegge argues that 'Service to "our people" thus becomes a means by which not only to address the needs of the poor and oppressed in the interests of social justice but, no less importantly, to rebuild and unify a fragmented society'.[62]

The inclusive ethos found in Sewa Day and in various other sections of the Sangh Parivar in the diaspora mirrors this aspect of Hindutva ecumenism. Golwalkar gave orders for inclusive charitable efforts, partly based in an emulation of missionary activities: 'We have to work for everybody and anybody, a Christian, a Muslim or a Hindu because calamity does not discriminate'.[63] He even spoke to the British-specific context. Answering the question, 'Some Muslims in UK would like to join us... Should we encourage them to do so?', he responded in the affirmative, but only, rather unrealistically, 'provided they are prepared to own the Hindu culture as their own'.[64]

Sewa Day serves as an opportunity for the Sangh to nurture networks within the Hindu community in Britain and enact elements of ecumenism. Hindu unity is reified publicly by the volunteers, but in turn involves various beneficiaries and others who are often witness to these acts of civic virtue. The unity is both practical (in the performing of the *sewa*) and affective (inculcating various qualities and emotions). While many of the events in the programme occur in secular spaces—schools, outdoor public spaces, community centres—a substantial number occur inside, or in the vicinity of, temples. Bochasanwasi Shree Akshar Purushottam Swaminarayan Sanstha (BAPS) Swaminarayan, ISCKON, Vishwa Hindu Mandir, the Satya Sai Service, and the City Hindus Network have all played prominent roles. The National Hindu Students Forum has been a core partner since the initiative's launch, for which they have been recognised in the 'Sewa Pioneers Awards'. In addition, many programmes involve an explicit or latent element of Hindu culture and religion.

The nature of the activities themselves inculcate togetherness and a sense of community. The charged, enthusiastic atmosphere at Sewa Day events suggests a kind of Durkheimian 'collective effervescence', in which group unity is built around highly energised moments.[65] Photos and videos circulated widely online, show excited volunteers in matching T-shirts, which are supplied with a different design each year, further enhancing the 'team spirit'.

The unity and intra-Hindu connectivities developed through Sewa Day also have international dimensions. It was launched as National Sewa Day in 2010, but the 'national' was dropped in the second year. Sewa Day, being 'embedded in the existing networks and initiatives' of global Hindu and Hindu nationalist organisations, can be seen as part of an effort to nurture and develop these global connections.[66] In documents submitted to the Charity Commission, Sewa Day explicitly state their international outreach.[67] This is a key focus for development. Over the first few years, Sewa Day expanded rapidly to more and more parts of the world: according to the organisers, 2013 involved the participation of 76,000 volunteers across 323 projects in twenty-five countries (an increase of five more countries than the previous year).[68] In 2011, 113 out of 132 projects (85.6%) were in Britain, 2012 saw 107 out of 237 (45.1%) in Britain, and by 2013 just 139 out of 323 (43.1%) were British-based.[69] Expansion in the United States has been particularly strong; in 2016 Sewa Day boasted of a 60% increase in events across America, with projects in thirty-two different locations. While a thorough analysis of the international elements to Sewa Day is beyond the scope of this chapter, the increasingly dynamic centrifugal growth of the initiative, in which India barely features, shows an ambition and drive for global Hindu praxis that looks to India only for (partial) inspiration, not logistics.

Although sceptical about the true reach of Sewa Day activities, Zavos considers this franchised model in terms of 'A network of activism... developing in an apparently rhizomatic fashion'.[70] But his insights concerning social action as a 'site of interconnection', providing ways in which Hindutva groups can impact British Hindu identity more broadly, might be expanded. Through its transnationalism, Sewa Day is actually able to influence a *global* Hindu (nationalist) identity.[71] It may, therefore, be seen as simultaneously parochial and universal: small, hyper-local community projects, which are connected to a global network of like-minded events and organisations, underlined by an ostensibly universal (but ultimately culturally specific) concept of *sewa*. This requires us to complicate existing notions of diaspora communities and their relationship with cosmopolitanism and inclusive citizenship.

Sangh prescription for social work

In spite of various layers of vernacularisation and innovation, the underlying ethos of Sewa Day is not fundamentally new or specific to the diaspora. A similar kind of volunteering and community service is also at the core of the Sangh Parivar's philosophy and praxis.[72] In order to make sense of the charitable activities of Hindu (nationalist) groups in the diaspora, and the ways in which they converge and diverge from their Indian counterparts, we must understand their lineage.

Hedgewar framed the Sangh from its outset in terms of highly visible acts of 'public good'. The very first of these, in 1926, involved the supervision and 'protection' of Ram Navami celebrations in Nagpur, dressed in their now-synonymous, pseudo-police uniforms. The following decade, Hedgewar, in an address in Pune in 1938, spoke of service to the nation as 'a sacred duty to be performed by us'.[73] The notion of 'service' is inextricable from the RSS: the word features ninety-eight times in Golwalkar's *Bunch of Thoughts*, and in the introduction to a later edition, M.A. Venkata Rao wrote that 'Readiness for service and even sacrifice is the chief motif of the movement'.[74]

In India, the Sangh frames its work as selfless service to 'the nation', and in its literature frequently places itself as central in various humanitarian efforts, from protection of Hindu migrants during Partition, to infrastructural support during the 1962 and

1965 wars with China and Pakistan, Bhopal relief work, and aid work in the wake of natural disasters (including the 2001 Gujarat earthquake relief). The Sangh book, *Widening Horizons*, claims that upon witnessing the altruism of *swayamsevaks* after the devastating 1977 cyclone in Andhra Pradesh, a Gandhian leader proposed 'that "RSS" stood for 'Ready for Selfless Service'.[75] RSS workers often refer to themselves as 'social workers' and are eager to be perceived as men of action in times of crisis, publicising their efforts in recent years through vigorous social media campaigns. The Sangh, therefore, is not just keen to *do* social work, but also to promote it as widely as possible.

Social action plays a similarly important role in other organisations of the Sangh family, with dozens of Sangh organisations and affiliates oriented in one way or another to *sewa*, charity, and welfare provision. The most notable is Sewa Bharati—a beneficiary of the HSS and Sewa International fundraising for the Gujarat earthquake philanthropy, discussed earlier in this chapter—but there are numerous other charitable organisations within the Parivar. Their purpose is not just to perform good deeds and inculcate unity amongst the volunteers, but to create a more 'harmonious' society. It is through these acts of service that national unity can be created. The VHP frame their *sewa* projects as:

> New schemes ... to bring the socially backward segments into the main stream of social current on the basis of equality, affinity and unity, by keeping constant contacts with these segments; efforts were made to bring back those Hindus, who were converted to alien faiths, into their original Dharma.[76]

We can see, in this sense, that *sewa* in the Hindu nationalist context is inherently related to perceived threats of charitable work, and associated fears of conversion, by Muslims and Christians.

In India, charitable activities, and the wide publicity of them, have played an important role in enhancing the Sangh's visibility, reach, and reputation. This became a particular focus after Gandhi's assassination and the subsequent, post-independence ban and toxic stigma. From the late twentieth century—which saw both a boom of Hindutva and the liberalisation of India's economy—Hindu nationalist charity initiatives expanded rapidly. In twelve years between 1997 and 2009, the number of Sangh welfare projects in India nearly quadrupled, from 15,063 to 59,076.[77]

Hindu nationalist welfare projects have been linked to efforts to build mass appeal and organisational support (with varying degrees of success), as shown in Soundarya Chidambaram's study of the Sangh Parivar's 'capture of civil society space' in south India, and in many instances since.[78] The breadth of their activities is so great that, in K.N. Pannikar's words, 'there is hardly any area of social and cultural life in which the Sangh Parivar has not made its presence felt'.[79] It is sometimes national, and nationalising, in ambition: one of the BJP's first flagship policies under Modi was '*Swachh Bharat*' (Clean India)—a theatrically conspicuous and often symbolic programme of voluntarism, largely mediated through the media and online spaces. More recently, the 'PM CARES Fund' (Prime Minister's Citizen Assistance and Relief in Emergency Situations Fund) was launched in 2020 to support Covid-19 relief efforts, raising enormous sums of money, while generating considerable controversy and criticism. The RSS, through welfare projects, have also been able to increase their presence in southern India and the Northeast, challenging received wisdom about the inability of the RSS and BJP to 'vernacularise' Hindutva.[80]

Whilst there are substantial contextual differences, the *sewa* projects of the Hindu nationalist movement in the diaspora may also perform a comparative rehabilitative, vernacularising role. The negative publicity generated in the early 2000s—and enduring reticence about the public role of Hindu nationalist groups—is perhaps closely connected to the very visible acts of civic virtue performed during Sewa Day. Furthermore, Sewa Day's language of citizenship, Big Society, and community cohesion is a way of vernacularising Hindutva overseas.

The process of diasporic vernacularisation has required flexibility. For the *swayamsevak*, Hindu society itself is '"Janata Janardana"—god incarnate'; serving the nation is therefore serving God, or '"Samaja-rooppee Parameshwar!" (the god in the form of society)'.[81] *Sewa* directed at India, therefore, has spiritual connotations. However, service within 'adopted' homelands must not be seen in purely desacralised terms. A publication for the Hindu Marathon in 1997 contained an article titled 'Indian, British or Both?'[82] In this article, the author frames Britain as '*Karmabhoomi*'—the land of economic sustenance, in contrast to India, '"*Matrubhoomi*" [Motherland], the land where we draw our inspiration from, the land where our unique culture evolved'.[83] In this sense, we can understand an interplay, in which the culture of *sewa* is part of a strategy that is rooted in 'a righteous path for combatting the social ills associated with Britain'.[84] Ironically, the suggestion that 'you must owe your first allegiance to the country in which you reap your benefits from', is closely in line with Nehru's instruction, following independence, that the diaspora should integrate themselves into their adopted homelands.[85]

The British-based Sangh's commitment to social action, according to Zavos, may be considered in 'primarily two ways': first, by preserving Hindu identity in diaspora environments through cultural, religious, and language instruction, and second, through philanthropy supporting work in India. He argues that Sewa Day constitutes 'a shift of direction, because it is geared towards a social action agenda not in Hindu India, but rather in Britain itself'.[86] But although Sewa Day is qualitatively distinctive in terms of branding and form, it actually follows a long-established prescription for community social action *outside* of Hindu communities.

Public social action specifically relating to the diaspora has been endorsed by Hindutva ideologues and leaders in India since the mid-twentieth century. Golwalkar, in *Bunch of Thoughts*—recommended and made available by Hindu nationalist groups in Britain and across the diaspora—paid close attention to the ethos at the heart of Sewa Day:

> The first thing that our brothers abroad have to bear in mind is, that while carrying on a profession or an employment there, earning and amassing money should not be their sole aim. They should understand and appreciate the problems of the local people and sympathise with their aspirations. Some portion of their earnings should be kept apart for promoting their welfare and enlightening them on the great principles and values of Hinduism. At the same time, they should, by their personal

example and living, demonstrate that they are coming from the land of a great and hoary culture and thus set a personal example to others. If these essential point[s] of conduct are ignored it might very well cause disrepute and often misery and hardship to themselves. Probably, this is one of the main reason[s] why our Hindus in East African countries are put to a lot of trouble these days. In the past our people there, for the most part, did not actively sympathise with the aspirations of the native African people while they were struggling against the White colonialists. They also did not spend out of their earnings for promoting the welfare of the local population, for their education or for enlightening them in the tenets of Hinduism.[87]

This passage highlights another dimension to the formative experiences of East Africa that were discussed in Chapter 1. Golwalkar's reference to antipathy from Africans is self-reflexively attributed to the Indian population's lack of interaction with, and respect for, the local population. Whilst East Africa provided many British Hindus with lessons in how successfully to develop a variety of insular community organisations, it also highlighted the pitfalls of not engaging with wider publics. In this sense, Sewa Day represents a form of pragmatic integration, without ceding cultural distinctiveness, first developed in the East African context, but that shifted easily to Britain. This well-established ethos was apparent when talking to RSS leader Anil Vartak, who emphasised to me that *swayamsevaks* have 'duty as citizen of UK, but religion as Hindu', and that whilst Hindus would remain 'patriotic for India from a cultural viewpoint', this is 'not contradiction with being patriotic for UK'.[88] Vartak also made specific reference to public service, saying that devoting time for society is part of the *swayamsevak* 'attitude', and that this was the same whether 'helping the nation' in India, or working 'for wider society' in the diaspora.

Golwalkar also expressed an anxiety that the failure of Hindus in East Africa to interact with communities outside their own provided other groups with opportunities:

The religious vacuum prevalent there was filled in by the Christian and Islamic missionaries. The upshot of all these lapses on our part was that when the Africans became free, they were dominated by Christian and Islamic propaganda which soon made them lose sympathy for Hinduism or for Hindus in general. They therefore set about to displace the Hindus form their positions of strength and resources. The Hindus have had to leave those countries in large numbers and suffer the loss of their properties and lifelong earnings. This experience should therefore serve as an eye-opener to all Hindus living abroad.[89]

In this sense, *sewa* provides a platform for entering a 'public relations' battleground with other faiths and communities. While Golwalkar's historical analysis might be contested, the idea of different religious groups competing for visibility and approval, as well as respect and rights, has proved important in multicultural environments. Sikh and Muslim groups in Britain, for instance, have been very active in a wide range of charitable endeavours and social action. This dynamic is discussed in depth in this book's final chapter, which considers the public representation of 'the Hindu community' and ways in which it can be discursively constituted—vis-à-vis other religious groups—in a competitive, often highly emotive, faith-relations 'industry'. So although Sewa Day is ostensibly inclusive, the underlying Hindu ethos (and organisational structures), and the way in which it seeks to draw attention to exemplary elements of Hindu culture and communities, mean that we can also understand it as a form of asserting Hinduism in a multifaith 'market place'.

Golwalkar was not the only Sangh leader to promote *sewa* as a form of engagement between Hindus and wider society. In 1989, Golwalkar's successor, M.D. Deoras, exhorted Hindus outside India to 'carry on constructive and social welfare activities with greater zeal with harmonious cooperation of the local people so as to make universal brotherhood a reality'.[90] Hari Babu Kansal, the VHP's Central Joint Secretary in charge of 'Foreign Co-ordination', reported that a VHP Board of Trustees meeting in Milton Keynes discussed proposals for projects 'in the countries of their residence or adoption', including blood donation drives, education for the poor, establishing old age homes, and, more vaguely, 'solving local problems…[and] publishing articles on Hinduism in local papers… etc.'.[91] In a similar vein, Rajendra Singh, the fourth RSS

Sarsanghchalak, gave a 'code of guidelines to workers' in London in 1995, in which he emphasised that 'While Sewa International must continue to be concerned with service work being done in Bharat, it should also pay attention to all such work being done locally'.[92] We can often find the role of diasporic *swayamsevaks* framed in terms of 'public relations'. Also in 1995, Singh told a Sangh camp in Rotterdam, Netherlands, that 'Hindus living in foreign lands have [a] still more important role to play. Because, in a way, these Hindus are ambassadors of Bharatiya culture'.[93]

Following Golwalkar's decree, Sangh *sewa*-related projects with a focus *outside* the Hindu diaspora community emerged in East Africa. Jagdish Shastri's memoirs record that whilst the Bharatiya Swayamsevak Sangh attended first to Hindu concerns, 'it has also worked for and served the needs of indigenous poor and illiterate Africans by organizing medical aid camps, food camps, and blood banks for them'.[94] The year 1989—the birth centenary of RSS founder K.B. Hedgewar—saw a particularly energetic push for co-ordinated *sewa* projects overseas. Two years later, Sewa International was launched. While the diaspora has been active in its support for Sewa International and their work in India, there were also local dimensions, including humanitarian and educational projects directed towards non-Hindus across Kenya. In Canada, Shastri counted his teaching of Indian language and culture as a way by which 'to serve the community and the multicultural society of Canada', and in the United States, the HSS, VHP of America, and Hindu Students Council have all promoted efforts where they have, in the words of the US Sangh chief, 'served the local community, not just Hindus, through seva projects'.[95]

This dual thrust has also been prescribed by the Sangh's senior-most *pracharak* for *sewa*-related activities. In 1997, K. Suryanarayana Rao, RSS Akhil Bharatiya Seva Pramukh (All-India Head of Service), decreed: 'Sewa International will look after the interests of *sewa* related issues not only in the respective countries where they have chapters but also take up global level care of *sewa* work carried out under the Sangh ideology'.[96] Rao himself made it a priority to visit numerous foreign countries during his tenure as Seva Pramukh, underlining the extent to which charity was deemed a key focus for the global advancement of Hindu nationalism.[97]

The Hindu Marathon

The Hindu Marathon—an annual long-distance running event started by the HSS in 1984 and held for seventeen consecutive years until 2000—was a significant enterprise in the recent history of the Hindu diaspora in Britain. It serves as a revealing example of Hindu nationalist organisations mobilising sections of Britain's Hindu community to engage with wider publics in charity-related activities. Organisers claim it grew to become the third largest running event in Britain and played a part in 'establishing "Hindu identity" in place of "Asian identity"'.[98] But even more importantly, from their perspective, 'the Hindu Marathon achieved something that no other program could have achieved—the Sangh brand became public—with a very positive image'.[99]

The first Hindu Marathon took place in Bradford, co-ordinated with the Hindu Sangam—the first major, and in certain ways public-facing, mass gathering of Sangh Parivar organisations and volunteers in Britain. Subsequent marathons occurred in different locations across the country—from Brent to Manchester—introducing the event, and the organisations involved, to numerous audiences. With the HSS at the helm, the Hindu Marathon Committee also involved other key Hindu and Indian stakeholders, including the Swaminarayan Hindu Mission, Arya Samaj, ISKCON, and various Sikh, Jain, and Buddhist groups. Senior Sangh figures also travelled from India to attend the marathon and participate in accompanying functions.

The Hindu Marathon, by also aiming to engage with non-Hindu communities, was precocious in its multiculturalism. The stated aims, for instance, included: 'To promote health, peace and unity amongst all cultures of the United Kingdom (and world) through the spiritual knowledge as expressed in the sacred Hindu scriptures'.[100] One participant later commented that 'This concept of bringing communities together was way ahead of its time—now called Community Cohesion by government and other agencies'.[101] Perhaps on account of this multiculturalist rhetoric, the marathon benefited from local government grants.[102] In its successful organisation and impressive scale, it served both as a self-affirming project for the Hindu participants—generating engagement and interest in the Sangh—and an advertisement to outsiders, promoting Hinduism and 'the Hindu community' at once.

A series of videos produced by the Sangh, both at the time and in retrospect, constitute some of the most illuminating sources on the Hindu Marathon. One of these videos, made by Yajur Shah, the NHSF President and son of senior Hindu nationalist leader Hasmukh Shah, is narrated by Bradfordian Rajnikant Parmar, National Secretary of the Hindu Marathon Committee and a senior HSS *karyakarta*.[103] His commentary reveals a methodology adapted from the Sangh in India for the British context:

> The whole idea was how do we make a mark, an impact, into the community? For example in India when they do all Sangh camps they go out and march in public. The whole idea was to adapt something in this country so that it's acceptable, it's respectable, and at the same time it makes an impact out into the community... It was organised with the aim so that we touch upon all of the communities and involve them and participate them. For example, the Sikh gurudwaras, the Hindu temples, and other organisations who [are] in the city of Bradford. Through them, through their networks, and through their communities we were involving people outside our circles.[104]

The Marathon was seen as an opportunity to showcase various qualities of 'the Hindu community': organisational competence, discipline, healthy lifestyle, piety, and an inclination for 'integration with host community'.[105] While the majority of participants were of South Asian origin, a sizeable minority were white Brits, as well as a smaller number of more serious, international athletes from Africa and elsewhere. In the film of the 1993 marathon a number of non-Hindu participants were featured commenting on the friendliness of the organisers. One middle-aged white man said, 'It's not just for Hindus, it's for everybody. I mean obviously they're the sponsors but ideally we want everybody in the community to run in it. It's a friendship thing'. A younger white runner remarked, 'Well, at the beginning you're always a bit nervous, but there's all this kind of coconut-breaking ceremony and all this chanting and it just takes your mind off your nerves for a little bit so that just makes it a little bit different'. The marathon organisers provided free vegetarian meals for spectators and participants, which they referred to as '*prasadam*, which is offering to God'.[106] Another dimension to this outreach was through sponsorship: a poster of the 1997 marathon shows the logos of the Royal Air Force, the local newspaper *Telegraph and Argus*, Yorkshire Water, and Bradford City Council, amongst others.

But in spite of the 'community cohesion' overtones, the ethos of the marathon was subtly, but acutely, Hindutva. '*Om*' symbols and saffron dominated the aesthetic of the event; a photograph from 1997 shows a uniformed Air Force officer standing at the finish line holding a saffron flag.[107] Many important guests highlighted the Sangh backbone to the enterprise. Various Indian politicians, diplomats, and religious leaders were guests over the years; Mohan Bhagwat's attendance in 1998 is notable, as a decade later he would become the topmost leader of the RSS in India. Shankarrao Tatwawadi, Vishwa Vibhag Samyojak (World Division Convenor) of the RSS, was present at several marathons. In 1993, he said, '[The Hindu Marathon is] very important… because we are inspiring the youth, the Hindu youth, to take part in the games, to take part in Marathon and they should excel in all the physical activities as such. This is one of the events when all the Hindus of the UK they come together'.[108] Chief guests at the 1997 marathon were Indian VHP co-founder Swami Satyamitranand Giri, and BJP Lok Sabha member Ananth Kumar. These Indian guests mixed with various English civic dignitaries; images show the senior Sangh figures interacting with the Mayor of Bradford, Labour MP Gerry Sutcliffe, local councillor Barry Thorn, high-ranking military officers, and others. At the 1993 and 1994 marathons, public figures included Glynn Ford MEP, Sir Bob Scott (Chairman of Manchester's 2002 Commonwealth Games bid), Geoff Thompson (karate champion), and Chief Inspector John Hambleton (Brent Metropolitan Police). Barry Gardiner was a guest at the 2000 race, and Bob Blackman attended the event in 1993—both politicians would go on to develop close relationships with many involved in the Hindu nationalist movement in Britain and beyond. It is important, though, to understand the presence of these dignitaries at the marathons, Sewa Day events, or for that matter other Sangh activities, from various angles: they are invited to witness and celebrate the impressive feats of the organisers, but equally they are eager to attend in order to develop relationships with—and, for the politicians, hopefully win the support of—a community that might otherwise be hard to reach.

Several other elements at Hindu Marathons have alluded to the event's Sangh lineage. Images from the 1986 Hindu Marathon in London show fundraising for Kalyan Ashram and a prominent 'Hindu Swayamsevak Sangh' sign. The video of the 1993 marathon pans across a large banner of Vivekananda, featuring the words: 'Arise! Awake! Stop not till the goal is reached!' Beneath this is written 'World Vision 2000'—the major VHP conference held in 1993 in Washington DC. Vivekananda was also engraved into the glass trophy given to the race's winner. Finishers' medals for other races have included images of Chhatrapati Shivaji Maharaj and Hedgewar. At the 1994 marathon, a man dressed up as Lord Rama, surrounded by men carrying saffron flags, paraded amidst spectators—arguably a provocative act in a city with many Muslims, little over a year after the Babri Masjid demolition.[109]

The marathon also served as an opportunity to assert ecumenical aspects of the Sangh. In 1997, the marathon's chief guest was Sardar Charnjiv Singh, President of the Rashtriya Sikh Sangat (the Sikh division of the Parivar), who reported on his visit to the *Organiser*.[110] Marathon publicity also highlighted participation by British Sikhs (much like the Sewa Day literature and online content).

As well as giving Hindu organisations a platform to increase their influence in British society, the Hindu Marathon played an important role in developing skills among its organisers. Parmar states in his interview, recorded in 2012, that putting on the event 'created very good teams of organisers and *karyakartas*', adding that 'even today, in Hindu Swayamsevak Sangh... the person who is the *kāryavaha* [secretary] was part of the Hindu Marathon team'.[111] On closer inspection, the genealogy of the marathon illustrates not only its role in cultivating present and future cadres, but also the deeply intertwined and overlapping nature of Hindu nationalist networks in the diaspora. The founding Chairman of the Hindu Marathon Committee, Dhiraj M. Shah, was also instrumental in the formation of the Overseas Friends of BJP and NHSF, and would later become the National Chairman of Sewa International UK.[112] Shah also held a number of key offices in the HSS over the past two decades, and his brother, Dhiraj D. Shah, remains a trustee of both the HSS and of SIUK.[113] In addition, one of Sewa Day's trustees, Anand Vyas, is also a trustee of the Kalyan Ashram Trust, the UK branch of the Vanvasi Kalyan Ashram.[114] Hasmukh Shah, an HSS *swayamsevak* who was closely involved in the organisation of the Milton Keynes Sammelan (Chapter 2) was Chairman of the Hindu Marathon committee in 1994, and subsequently held various high offices in the VHP-UK, as a trustee and spokesperson, as well as an advisor to the NHSF.[115]

Manoj Ladwa, a founding trustee of Sewa Day, is another figure who has been central to the diasporic Sangh Parivar and was also involved in the Hindu Marathon. A generation younger than those mentioned above, Ladwa was co-founder and inaugural President of the NHSF while at the London School of Economics in 1991, and a prominent member in the HSS (previously as spokesperson).[116] Since then, he co-founded Saffron Chase, a 'government relations' and 'communications consultancy' firm that in the 2010s worked to rehabilitate the reputation of Narendra Modi and the BJP in Britain. Ladwa 'served as Communications Director for Prime Minister Narendara Modi's 2014 election campaign', and helped to organise the momentous, post-election Madison Square Garden and Wembley Stadium events in New York and London.[117] Subsequently, he has flown the flag for the BJP in various ways— much of this is relatively 'behind the scenes', although he wrote a prominent paean to Modi in *Time* magazine in 2019 (in response to sustained criticism from the international media in the run-up to his re-election), and supported the BJP's communications strategy in the general election that year.[118] He was also vocally critical of Labour under Jeremy Corbyn, and after the party passed a resolution at its conference supporting 'the Kashmiri people's right to self-determination', Ladwa accused it of 'institutional bias against India and Indians', and claimed it had been 'hijacked' by 'hard-left extremists' and 'Jihadi sympathisers'.[119] Not long after this, and following protest from dozens of Indian organisations, Labour shifted its policy on Kashmir. Ladwa's India Global Forum platform, which brings together corporate and political leaders to explore (and perhaps guide) bilateral relations, and the UK-India Awards initiative—coupled with photographs on his Twitter feed with Tony Blair, Barry Gardiner, Rishi Sunak, Jaishankar (India's External Affairs Minister), the powerful gurus Sri Sri Ravi Shankar and Sadhguru, and Modi himself—further underline his influence.

As well as serving as a springboard for individual Sangh leaders, the Hindu Marathon also helped launch organisations themselves, including Sewa International. But perhaps most importantly, the National Hindu Students Forum was first established as a stall at the marathon in 1991. This went on to become one of the most active and largest of the Sangh Parivar affiliates in Britain. It is the main Hindu student body across British universities, currently claiming around 4,000 members across forty-five branches, and has close links to various organisations of the Sangh Parivar, and to Hindutva ideologies and politics. The NHSF engages in many charitable activities—both individually and with other groups (including Sewa Day, which presented them a 'Sewa Pioneers Award' in 2015). Although it does not quite translate, in Jaffrelot and Therwath's analysis, as 'the official correspondent for the ABVP' (in the same way the HSS mirrors the RSS), we can still place them firmly within the British Sangh 'family'.[120] These connections are, however, often obfuscated and nebulous, and many of the NHSF's activities cannot easily be pigeonholed 'Hindutva'. Like with the Hindu Students Council in the US, many members and attendees of their events would not be fully aware of the forum's connections to the Hindu nationalist movement, and the leadership often explicitly denies it.[121] Students might occasionally participate in programmes put on by the NHSF, particularly those arranged to celebrate Hindu festivals, for a variety of cultural, social, spiritual, or even nostalgic reasons, without a sense of who the organisers even are. But there is a multitude of evidence illustrating clear links, both institutional and ideological, to Hindutva and the Sangh Parivar.

Until at least 2004, the NHSF website's 'About Us' page plainly stated: 'NHSF enjoys a close working relationship with HSS UK and benefits from the active involvement of the "karyakartas" (volunteers) within HSS. The spread of this organisation throughout towns and cities in the United Kingdom means that branches of HSS form an integral part of the support network for NHSF UK.'[122] Although their website now describes themselves in different terms, and the explicit connection to the Hindu nationalist movement is often hard to identify, they continue to collaborate with *shakhas* and HSS leaders through events and other initiatives. The 2018 HSS Instagram story, mentioned earlier in the chapter, also includes the NHSF in the montage of 'Our extended Parivar [family]'.[123]

Many NHSF campaigns also echo those of both diasporic and Indian Hindutva. The NHSF has fought against anti-caste discrimination legislation and branded the campaign for its introduction 'propaganda against Hindus'.[124] They have campaigned against the 'sexual grooming' of Hindu girls, deploying the anti-Muslim 'love jihad' trope, such as at the 'Hindu Security Conference' in 2007 (co-organised with the Hindu Forum of Britain and discussed in depth in Chapter 6). In 2009, they organised a campaign against the BBC after an episode of the crime drama *Spooks* was aired that they perceived slighted the VHP (discussed in Chapter 4), and in 2015 the NHSF were also active in welcoming Modi to Britain—'an inspiration', according to NHSF President, Yajur Shah.[125]

Personnel overlap is considerable; Sangh leaders often attend Forum events and vice-versa, and the HSS have even been known to deploy *vistaraks* (temporary, but full-time 'sabbatical' positions—see Chapter 1) to the NHSF. Removing any ambiguity at all, Sanjiv Oza, the first RSS *pracharak* to be based in Britain, wrote in the *Sangh Sandesh* special issue commemorating the fiftieth anniversary of the HSS: 'The rapid growth of NHSF in UK created a breakthrough for enrolling new energetic youths into the Sangh ideological fold'.[126]

One of the most important priorities of the Hindu Marathon was to provide a concrete moment of unity for Hindus in Britain. The national committee included representatives from the geographical breadth of Britain's Hindu communities, reflecting the importance of the marathon as a point of convergence for Hindus across the country.[127] A list of 'sympathisers' and donors at the end of a video of the 1994 marathon underlines this unity in ecumenical terms, featuring not only various core Sangh groups, but many others, including the Brahma Samaj, the Bharatiya Mandir and Prajapati Samaj in Ashton-under-Lyme, the Baladia Leva Patel society in Oldham, the Bolton Indian Cricket Club, the Sikh Association Manchester, the Hindu Sahitya Kendra, the Indian Senior Citizens Centre, the Shree Swaminarayan Temple, Oldham, the Lord Ram Krishna Temple, Warrington, and the Kashmiri Pandit Association of Europe.[128]

A further layer to this Hindu collectivity was evident in marathon sponsorship; although some large corporations were involved (such as Lucozade and Morrisons supermarkets), the vast majority were small, Hindu-run businesses: Sharma Hosiery Co. Limited, Khurana Chemist, K.B. Import and Export, Amee Supermarket, and others. Therefore, the community cohesion we can observe in the Hindu Marathon is less of the sort proposed by the Cantle Report and more a form of *Hindu* community cohesion. Through hosting public, highly visible events, the Sangh organisations, and organisers, asserted their position as the legitimate, authoritative, and virtuous voice of an ostensibly unified community within a larger citizenry.

Of course, on certain levels, Sewa Day and the Hindu Marathon are very different. Whereas public service is the foremost raison d'être of Sewa Day, the Hindu Marathon was not philanthropic per se, but served as a platform for charitable fundraising, which was the prerogative of the participants. However, underlying both events are two broad similarities. Sewa Day and the Hindu Marathon were key moments for cultivating, creating, and enacting a unified Hindu community, and they have provided opportunities to engage with various sections of the British public and establishment, and to showcase an outward-facing, positive image of Hindu values and the Hindu community.

The model minority

Sewa Day and the Hindu Marathon are best understood through the important and increasingly reified narrative of the 'model minority'. The idea of a model minority has been deployed in relation to a number of minority ethnic and immigrant communities across various periods of time and in different parts of the world, but particularly in the United States. It is used to identify minorities who have been 'successful' according to certain socio-economic indicators (primarily income and educational attainment). Although the idea of identifying a particular demographic for their achievements might, at least ostensibly, be celebratory, it is often divisive and controversial, with a range of implications and repercussions for both the 'community' in question, and for those who are not conferred with the same accolade.

Here, the model minority trope is analysed in terms of how attention has been drawn to the high achievements of Hindus in a variety of spheres, and thereby how an essentialised Hindu community is projected, and widely seen, as a 'good' ethnic minority. Some elements of this are quantifiable—high educational achievements, high income levels, low crime rates. Other aspects are more nebulous: civic virtue, loosely defined 'integration', patriotism to the host country (and, increasingly, a space in the 'Britishness' discourse), piety and 'faith' without religious extremism, and broad statements about values that are harmonious with those of the 'host' society.

The corollary is an implied, or explicitly stated, 'Other' that embodies the negative opposite of these attributes. This othering is central to Hindutva ideology, particularly in relation to the stereotyped 'bad' Muslim, and has particular resonance in the diasporic context, especially post-9/11. Notably, the trope is neither consistently deployed nor interpreted; sometimes Indians are presented as the model minority, at other times

CHARITY, *SEWA* (SERVICE), AND THE 'MODEL MINORITY'

Hindus, and even East African Asians. However, this conflation—at times deliberate, for instance the idea of India as 'land of the Hindus'—does not detract from the importance of its relevance to British Hindutva.

The model minority is implicitly related to economic and educational success, and other indexes of social mobility. Indians are less likely to claim welfare benefits than any other ethnic minority (and also less than white British, who are the most likely of all ethnic groups to receive state support),[129] Indians are also the least likely of all ethnic minorities to live in deprived neighbourhoods,[130] most likely to live in a 'food secure' household,[131] most likely to own property,[132] more likely than other South Asian communities to speak English,[133] more likely to achieve at school,[134] are second only to British Chinese people in terms of higher education qualifications (with whom they are joint-highest for holding professional jobs), have lower unemployment rates,[135] enjoy much higher incomes,[136] and fare considerably better than Bangladeshis and Pakistanis in terms of health inequalities.[137] East African Asians fare particularly well: *The Daily Telegraph* 2006 'Asian Rich List' had six East Africans in the top ten (although the current list paints a slightly different picture).[138] Much more recently, political success has added a further dimension to the idea of Indians (and especially East African Asians) as a model minority, exemplified by Prime Minister Rishi Sunak and two successive Home Secretaries, Priti Patel and Suella Braverman. In the United States we see similar trends, heightened, even, due to the highly selective immigration system. In 2022, an astonishing 73% of all H-1B visas, reserved for high-skilled workers in 'specialty occupations', were awarded to Indians, and nearly 80% of the India-born adult population in the US have an undergraduate degree (compared to 30% for the total US population).[139]

Alongside the aforementioned metrics, another phenomenon, frequently and breathlessly affirmed, is the fast-growing trend for some of the world's biggest corporations to appoint people of Indian origin as CEOs, from Microsoft and Google, to PepsiCo and Starbucks. In spite of all this evidence, many have argued against the accuracy and helpfulness of the concept of the model minority.

The notion of a monolithic 'community' possessing a certain status and collective behaviour elides the struggles of many Indian migrants. It emphasises difference and creates divides between communities (undermining collective struggles and solidarity), whilst erasing difference *within* communities. It quantifies success and value to society on the basis of narrow and problematic criteria, and promotes pernicious stereotypes. Therwath simply brands it 'a conservative myth'.[140]

Although many of the demographic indicators are hard to refute (at least on face value), abstract notions of tolerance or integration that are associated with the model minority demand closer scrutiny. There is much in Sewa Day that relates specifically to the model minority. Zavos argues that 'Sewa embeds, or even naturalizes, civic virtue and exemplary citizenship in South Asian diasporic identities'.[141] In both the Hindu Marathon and Sewa Day, this is heavily promoted, and can be located in much broader model minority narratives that the Sangh in Britain have advanced. This is achieved both indirectly, by the benign, peaceable, and competently organised events, as well as more explicitly. BJP MP Ananth Kumar, at the 1993 Hindu Marathon in Bradford, told a reporter: 'Wherever Hindus, Indians have gone throughout the world… they have been like sugar in the milk.'[142] This appropriation of a Parsi aphorism, which implies not just integration but improvement of the whole, stands in contrast to the way in which Muslims in India were characterised by Sadhvi Rithambara, as mentioned in Chapter 3, as lemon in milk.

What is really meant by 'integration'—and its closely related but distinctive bedfellow, 'assimilation'—is rarely very clear at all. Various models of multiculturalism have attempted to reconcile two conflicting demands of plural societies: cultivating a sense of unity and belonging amongst citizens, whilst resisting the suppression of diversity.[143] But in many senses there is an inherent, seemingly irreconcilable tension: if the immigrant has to display and prove the adoption of the majority culture without the reverse being the case, then the idea of integration will always be predicated on upholding unequal power dynamics. Parekh argues that '"We" cannot integrate "them" so long as "we" remain "we"', while Radhakrishnan asks, 'If the Asian is to be Americanized, will the American submit to Asianization?'[144]

When considering the model minority, traditional stereotypes of integration, particularly in relation to anti-Muslim narratives, need to be probed. This essentialised rhetoric has permeated the mainstream and become increasingly reified by 'outsiders'. Even the far-right and those staunchly opposed to immigration indulge in the notion of non-Muslim Indians as 'good immigrants'. Tommy Robinson, then leader of the English Defence League, said in 2013: 'When David Cameron says that multiculturalism has failed. Sikhism, Hinduism, Jews, they haven't failed to integrate into society. Islam has failed.'[145] Robinson, and others on the far-right, have on various occasions supported and even formed alliances with Hindu nationalists.

The nebulous notion of 'integration' is a key reason the model minority resonates with a wider public: a 2018 survey found that 38% of Brits thought Indian immigrants 'make a positive contribution to life in Britain' compared to just 13% perceiving the impact as negative; for Pakistanis the numbers were 23%/27% positive/negative, and for Bangladeshis, 22%/25% positive/negative.[146] Of course the environment of Islamophobia, spread widely by sections of the media and political class, is a key factor here.

Whilst Hindu exceptionalism holds water on certain levels, equating socio-economic and educational achievements with the nebulous concept of 'integration' is problematic. The 2011 census national identity question, along with the religious questions, allows for some interesting comparative findings. Bangladeshis and Pakistanis are *more* likely to report *only* a British identity than Indians (72%, 63%, 58%, respectively).[147] Moreover, Muslims are much less likely to report 'other [non-British/English] identity only', in response to the census question on national identity, than Hindus.

These figures require us to question the notion that economic success and successful public relations clearly translate into 'integration'. Ceri Peach has shown that 'economic success is decoupled from social assimilation and sub-urbanisation is decoupled from residential diffusion'.[148] Although poorer Bangladeshis and Pakistanis are more concentrated in inner-city areas, and Indians wealthier and more suburbanised, all groups remain segregated. A 2013 study corroborated these findings: Indians, Pakistanis, and Bangladeshis were not significantly more ghettoised than each other until at least the 1990s, and until 2011 Hindus were actually more geographically concentrated in Britain than Muslims (with Jews—the model 'model minority' in certain respects—being the least geographically dispersed of all).[149] More recent analysis, though, has suggested that Bangladeshis and Pakistanis are more likely to be residentially segregated than Indians, reflecting socio-economic inequalities.[150] However, 2011 census data showed that the constituency with the highest population of a single ethnic minority group—i.e. most 'ghettoised'—was Leicester East, in which Indians comprised 48.6% of the local population.[151] Census data also indicates that Indian Hindu communities are just as likely to marry within their own communities as Bangladeshi or Pakistani Muslims—a measure, perhaps, that points to no more significant levels of integration (at least in terms of exogamy). Comparable discrepancies can be observed in the United States: Indians are by far the least likely of all Asian American communities to marry non-Asians.[152] A study by Jacob Vigdor in 2006 suggested that whilst Indian Americans were economically 'integrated', on indices of cultural and civic integration they scored poorly compared to other ethnic minorities.[153] This goes against traditional understandings of economic success and sub-urbanisation in America leading to residential dispersal and exogamy. In short, it is a complex picture, and simplistic claims of 'integration', especially when framed in a comparative or even competitive manner, need to be treated with caution. As, of course, does the idea of 'integration' itself.

The Hindu-ness of Hindu success

The connection between Hindu success and Hindu culture is key to the model minority trope. Hinduism is often credited or linked to the high-tech accomplishments of India and its emigrants. Kurien argues that Hindu American leaders use the model minority label to link the diaspora's success to their Hindu religious and cultural heritage, which, they claim, 'gives them a special aptitude for mathematics and science and also makes them adaptable, hard-working, and family oriented'.[154] It often seems to be a subtext to discussions around the striking twenty-first-century trend of major multinational corporations appointing Indian-origin CEOs. A recent *Economist* article that asked 'Why Brahmins lead Western firms...' suggested 'a tradition of bookishness', alongside various socio-economic factors (whilst also noting that in India, merchant castes rather than Brahmins dominate business.)[155] The Orientalist connotations of this thinking—in which certain clearly categorised 'communities' possess particular behavioural attributes—can be clearly identified.

A similar logic can be found in accounts of 'karma capitalism'—a corporate buzzword, in which entrepreneurial tendencies and commercial success are directly connected to Hindu qualities and culture.[156] This reasoning is pervasive. To give just two out of innumerable examples: Pavan Varma wrote in his popular book, *Being India*, 'Like Hindu ritual, IT involves coded language', and Daniel Lak has argued, 'The Hindu seems to have a congenital inclination to differentiate the database around him'.[157] Hindutva champions have been especially enthusiastic to attribute scientific success to a 'rediscovery' of Vedic knowledge (and by extension, a pre-invasion glory to be resurrected). In recent years this has produced controversy and ridicule: a paper delivered at the 102nd Indian Science Congress in 2015 reported findings of 7,000-year-old spacecraft, and Narendra Modi himself has cited the elephant-headed god, Ganesh, as an example of ancient plastic surgery.[158]

All this might seem paradoxical. How could an educated group of migrants—many of whom are scientists, doctors, and engineers—countenance assertions widely denounced as irrational and unsubstantiated? Rajagopal astutely considers these trends in terms of an 'eminently pragmatic' spirituality: '"Hindu" spiritualism is seen as providing a necessary counterweight to the ills of a materialist society and at the same time, as redeemable by the standards of that society itself'.[159] The conflation of Hindu culture with scientific achievement is in fact pushed *especially* strongly by the Sangh to appeal to the highly educated diaspora. At the Pune Vishwa Sangh Shibir in 2010 (see Chapter 2), the stage was bedecked with an enormous banner featuring a familiar montage of figures involved in, and appropriated by, the Hindu nationalist movement. Flanked by portraits of Hedgewar and Golwalkar were the figures of Vivekananda, Shivaji, and Krishna. But also clustered on the banner were portraits of various scientists: Aryabhata, Jagadish Chandra Bose, Homi J. Bhabha, Abdul Kalam, and, most aptly, Indian American astronaut Kalpana Chawla, all beside an image of an Indian space rocket.[160]

The model minority trope has particular salience for East African Asians and their widely proclaimed business acumen, work ethic, and adaptability. In many ways this draws more on regional and caste-based stereotypes and migratory experience than on spirituality. Maya Parmar has written that 'the experiences of numerous displacements, alongside a keen commercial nature, have created the Gujarati as an expert in successful resettlement and relocation'.[161] The East African model minority narrative was quick to be established in Britain, as indicated by a 1972 newspaper headline: 'East African Asians Finding British Success'.[162] The reputation has endured and grown. In December 2012, during a House of Lords debate marking forty years of the Ugandan Asian exodus and their contribution to Britain—on a motion moved by Ugandan Gujarati peer Lord Popat—Lord Janner of Braunstone told the House: 'The Ugandan Asian community has brought so much to this country. It helped to save Leicester's economy'.[163] A decade later saw significant celebrations across Britain—in fact, the first major engagement for King Charles III following the period of mourning after the death of Elizabeth II was a ceremony at Buckingham Palace to commemorate five decades since the resettlement of Ugandan Asians. The event's host, broadcaster Jon Snow, told the assembled guests: 'Today we bask in what Uganda was deprived of, an innovative and dedicated population of motivated people who've done so much to boost our own economy and our own well-being... Uganda's loss has proved Britain's incomparable gain.'[164]

Whilst economic achievements are often trumpeted, in certain ways this success story of Hindus in Britain (which is, of course, a generalisation) obfuscates various issues.[165] Focusing purely on accomplishments can silence the traumatic impact of dislocation, exclude the lives of Indians who suffer from economic hardship, and elide everyday experiences of marginalisation and discrimination.[166] It can simply obfuscate the lived reality of many members of a diverse 'community' (or, perhaps more accurately, population made up of various communities). The same is the case in the US context: while a very substantial proportion of Indian migrants are highly qualified and enter lucrative employment, there is also a much less widely discussed, but significant, number of 'unauthorised' migrants. In the fiscal year from October 2021, 16,290 Indian citizens were taken into US custody trying to cross the Mexico border, many of whom were minorities fleeing 'a climate of discrimination in India', and the US has also received a significant number of asylum seekers—more than 22,000 between 2014 and 2019.[167]

The promotion of the model minority trope is, in many senses, a response to racism, an effort to dispel host society prejudice and negative stereotypes of South Asian migrants. Seshadri, in *Hindus Abroad*, suggested that '[although] Hindus normally do not create trouble… there is a feeling of covert discrimination and lack of opportunities'.[168] This was greatly exacerbated by a popular anxiety in Britain about the rise of Muslim radicalism, first with the Rushdie Affair of 1988–9, then much more pronounced following 9/11 in 2001, and 7/7 in 2005.

This context, along with other factors, led to an explicit distancing of Hindus from Muslims in Britain. Gayatri Spivak's (later renounced) notion of 'strategic essentialism' speaks to the idea of the model minority: through this lens, difference is (superficially) diffused in a struggle for recognition in the face of curiosity, ignorance, or competition.[169] However, the use of essentialism by Hindu nationalist groups would not accurately constitute what Spivak considered 'strategic', in that otherness is operationalised in a dangerously uncritical manner. Conversely, 'strategic hybridity' may be a more helpful way of understanding the deployment of the model minority, in which a fluid conception of overlapping ethnicity and religion is negotiated pragmatically, tactically, and for specific goals.[170] In this sense, the model minority is both an acceptance of difference (and in certain sense, superiority), combined with an effort to emulate and assimilate with a particular, idealised conception of Britishness (particularly, a 'Protestant' work ethic). In the United States, the 'model minority' referred to East Asians before also encompassing Indians, and fits very closely with the idea of the American Dream.

Blackness, Muslims, and the 'Asian' marker

Although in recent years the model minority narrative has been discursively constituted in relation to Muslims, in the past Britain's Afro-Caribbean population formed the negatively framed Other. This emerged from a very different discourse, in which many South Asians in Britain identified, and were categorised, as Black.[171] In spite of shared narratives of alterity and subalternity—manifested in frequent expressions of cross-racial solidarity—the promotion of the model minority trope in relation to a negatively framed Black British population is found in a variety of Hindu nationalist sources. Seshadri's *Hindus Abroad* is replete with examples of Hindus as the model minority, containing several examples of othering relating not just to Muslims, but to Black Britons. This sharply recalls the East African context, with which Seshadri himself was familiar. He writes that 'most of the Blacks [in London] never care to go out for work. Their sustenance is ensured by governmental doles. Day long they eat, drink, sleep, gamble and end up in gang wars in the evenings. They do not care about sending their wards to school.'[172] A section reprinted from an *Organiser* interview even more explicitly juxtaposes the *adarsh* (ideal) Hindus with others, stating that 'the Hindu Sangam afforded a striking contrast to the Caribbean Festival, also held during the same period in UK, which became notorious for vulgarity, drinking, brawl, etc., where the police had a tough time in controlling its participants'.[173]

The model minority is much less frequently framed as a counterpoint to the 'problem minority' of Black Britons (or Americans), but now focuses almost singularly on Muslims as a yardstick. Vijay Prashad noted that the post-9/11 'terror factor' enabled Indian Americans to put themselves forward, alongside Jewish Americans, as 'the vanguard of the new, anti-terrorist Battleship America'.[174] In this sense, Anandi Ramamurthy's framing of Muslims, in the post-9/11 era of institutionalised anti-Islamicism, as 'the new black' is apposite.[175]

Expressions of the model minority are partly driven by a desire to disassociate with Muslims, and particularly distance Hindus from negative stereotypes of Muslims. Partition consciousness, post-Windrush competition, and the Rushdie Affair all advanced the desire by diasporic Hindus to separate themselves from Muslims. The protests around Salman Rushdie's 1988 novel, *The Satanic Verses*, in particular, was a powerful influence. Widely reported protests and even book burnings from a vocal minority of Muslims led to entire communities being characterised as fanatical and 'un-British'; 'moderate' Muslims were pressurised to publicly condemn Ayatollah Khomeini's *fatwa* and reaffirm their commitment to integration. Non-Muslim Asians, throughout and after this episode, were increasingly eager to emphasise their separateness, Balkanising a pan-Asian identity. But, on another level, many perhaps privately admired and even aspired to the assertiveness, togetherness, and political voice that Muslims achieved in the furore. The Rushdie Affair is considered in more depth in the final chapter of this book.

In the American context, Hindu disassociation from Muslims has been explored by a number of academics and other writers.[176] Prashad notes: 'As the "Muslim" increasingly bears the mark of Cain, it opens up immense opportunities for middle-class people of colour to demonstrate their patriotism in anti-Islamic terms.'[177] Whilst Hindu expressions of anti-Muslim sentiment are often quotidian and banal, a related rhetoric is also found in Indian American lobbies, which join forces with Jewish counterparts, and share 'a tendency to identify Islam as the irredeemable Other'.[178] In America, Britain, and elsewhere, racism and Islamophobic abuse levelled against Sikhs, Hindus, and other religious and ethnic minorities has also meant that the 'War on Terror' is by no means only an issue for Muslims. Efforts to address this by retreating into religious identities and emphasising separateness from Muslims has only had limited 'success' in mitigating discrimination. Broader anti-immigrant sentiments and the rise of white nationalism means that far from being 'honorary whites', the South Asian model minority is also a 'perpetual outsider'.[179] In addition to 'traditional' causes for desiring identity separation (as discussed above), the Gujarat violence of 2002 and more recent eruptions of communal politics have played a role in creating and fomenting division amongst British Muslims and Hindus.

There is also a 'competitive' element to expressing difference. Hundal argues that 'The desire for identity separation at national level is closely linked to a grab for government funding and political influence. This in turn has sparked competition between faith-based organisations for attention.'[180] Hindu pronouncements on Muslims as less hardworking, more troublesome, and reluctant to integrate, but recipients of 'handouts' from the state, are almost identical to Hindutva narratives in India (for instance, on Hajj subsidy). Burlet notes that in *shakhas*, 'discussions to encourage youths to have pride in their Hindu identity and be good British citizens often depend on stereotypical references to Muslims'.[181] According to her interviewees, negative portrayals of Muslims and their weak socio-economic position were 'the net result of a lack of dedication to their studies and to hard work, and their limited respect for their elders and other people's values'.[182] Similar stereotypes were revealed in a covertly filmed HSS camp in 2015—a young *swayamsevak* asked the instructor, 'Do you think Muslims are the biggest problem in Britain?', to which the adult responded, 'Yes, for everybody, for everybody'.[183]

A more subtle way in which the model minority trope is forwarded is through the public rejection of 'Asian' identity.[184] On one level, the desire to end the use of the catch-all, pseudo-racial grouping is rooted in a growing saliency of religious identification over ethnicity and geographic origin.[185] In writing on the decline of Asian Youth Movements and the consolidation of distinct South Asian religious and ethnic groups, Philip Lewis argues, 'An imagined unitary "Asian" community was not sufficiently alert to specific issues that troubled different communities'.[186] Moreover, class consciousness has taken an increasing toll on broad-branch migrant solidarity.

But the trend against the Asian marker, implicitly or explicitly, involves a disassociation with not just Pakistanis or Bangladeshis, but actually Muslims themselves; the term 'Hindu', as well as 'Indian' (often in the form of various hyphenated identities), is specifically preferred.[187] The desire to eschew, or at least de-emphasise, Asian-ness is not limited to Hindu nationalist groups, but those of the Sangh Parivar have been a driving force in pushing this demand forward. An NHSF report from November 1995 stated, for instance: 'Emphasis for the current academic year has been placed on the issue of Hindu identity. Students are being educated through lectures and leaflets to identify themselves as Hindu as opposed to Asian'.[188]

Calls by Hindus to cease being called 'Asian' are often sparked by negative news stories in which the perpetrators are Muslim but are referred to as Asian; the Rushdie protests, the 2001 Bradford and Oldham riots, and various 'grooming' or sexual abuse cases are all important examples.[189] The post-2001 'War on Terror' environment solidified and accelerated this trend to disassociate from the Asian marker. Hindus are not the only protagonists in this desire for disassociation. Sikh organisations joined Hindus in petitioning the media to stop using the 'Asian' term, others set up a 'Not all Asians are Muslim' Facebook group, and after the 7/7 terrorist attacks people widely circulated the popular but contested 'Don't freak, I'm a Sikh' slogan over social media and had it emblazoned on T-shirts.[190] There is often a transnational dimension to anti-terrorist rhetoric, which seeks to disassociate Hindus from Muslims. Ballard states that the VHP's line is 'We Hindus are entirely different from Muslims. We've been victims of terrorism by Muslims and we stand shoulder to shoulder with the Brits.'[191] This rhetoric has played into the hands of the far right in Europe and America, which increasingly frames itself as discerningly 'anti-Islamic' (but Islamophobia has also given rise to new articulations of solidarity with Muslims from Hindus, Sikhs, and others).

In 2002, Sunrise Radio, which still describes itself as 'the greatest Asian radio station in the world', made a decision to 'ban' the use of the word 'Asian'. The decision must be understood in light of campaigns from a variety of groups, including Hindu nationalists, to 'dissociate themselves from Muslims'.[192] Avtar Lit, the station's chief executive, said, 'In the wake of September 11 and also following the race riots last year we have had a lot of calls from Sikhs and Hindus worried that in many people's eyes the word Asian links them to events involving Muslims'.[193] An article on the NHSF website articulates the desire not to be lumped with unsuccessful Muslim South Asians very explicitly, citing statistics on employment and income gaps, as well as crime rate differentials.[194] In relation to crime, the low Hindu prison population is often cited as indicative of Hindu respectability and a tacit insinuation of Muslim delinquency. Many Hindu nationalists I spoke to reiterated these statistics, but it is not a new theme. A publication produced for the 1997 Bradford Centenary Hindu Marathon cites Home Office figures, noting that 'Among all the prisoners in the United Kingdom, Hindus account for the least number of criminals proportional to their total number'.[195]

The anti-Muslim stereotyping involved in the disassociation of the Asian marker is more complex than simply the promotion of a negative Muslim (or Pakistani/Bangladeshi) image. As is often the case in othering, the projection of a negative Muslim figure is a process of self-definition. Raj considered these trends manifested in a lecture given by a Hindu youth leader at various university campuses in 1994 and 1995, aptly titled 'Who the hell do you think you are?'[196] The speaker made the point that whilst 'Asian' might have resonance for first-generation immigrants—simply in terms of denoting their geographical origin—for British-born Hindus, this was less appropriate. The speaker went on to disassociate Hindus from the 'Asians' that the media associated with anti-Rushdie protests, anti-white violence, and support for Saddam Hussein. These activities, the speaker emphasised, were 'clearly Muslim'.[197]

The strategy of disassociation with other ethnic minorities has been successful on some levels and not on others. Although occasionally lauding Indians and Hindus as model minorities, the media continue to use 'Asian' as a catch-all, in spite of sustained efforts by Hindu groups to resist this categorisation. Moreover, racist attacks on Asians rarely discern between Hindus and other non-Hindu Asians (even though some organisations, such as the English Defence League and the British Nationalist Party, have tried to forge connections with Hindus and Sikhs on the basis of shared Islamophobia). Violent attacks against turban-wearing Sikhs and on Hindu temples, in addition to mosques and Muslims, occur frequently—growing in the highly polarised, anti-immigrant environments of post-Trump USA, Brexit Britain, and other nativist populisms. Statistics indicate that South Asians are more likely to be victims of hate crimes than any other ethnic group.[198] Following the 7/7 terrorist attacks in London, it was even suggested that levels of hate crime against Hindus and Sikhs were higher than for Muslims; Metropolitan Police Commissioner Ian Blair, acknowledged that Islamophobic racism can affect wider communities: 'The kind of idiot that attacks a turban attacks a hijab or a yamulca for that matter. I am afraid the education of racists is probably not very high.'[199] At the time, the Hindu Forum of Britain expressed unhappiness that, in light of these attacks, the police were more closely engaged with Muslims than with Hindus.[200]

Others, though, have claimed that the 'misdirection' of Islamophobic hate crimes became less common in the late 2000s: 'gangs and individuals had by the end of the decade become reasonably competent in identifying their intended Muslim targets'.[201] More recent figures suggest that Muslims are more likely to be victims of racially motivated hate crime than Hindus and other religious groups, and specifically religious hate crimes against Muslims are more than six times as frequent as those against Hindus (with anti-Semitic hate crimes hugely more frequent still).[202]

The reification of the 'model minority'

The model minority label has become reified and entered the public consciousness in Britain through repetition by the media, politicians, and the general public. Despite aggressive responses to the influx of East African Asians, including Leicester Council's infamous advertisement in the *Ugandan Argus*, on 15 September 1972, discouraging settlement in the city, attitudes changed over the latter period of the twentieth century. Whilst discrimination persists, the role of Indians in the regeneration of certain decaying inner-city areas is often praised. Politicians of all hues have been eager to fete the achievements and qualities of British Indians (not least in an effort to garner their support in elections).

Many Hindutva accounts of dignitaries and other outsiders observing Sangh events are keen to emphasise praise that the hosts, and by extension all Hindus, have received. One account of Margaret Thatcher's visit to the Finchley *shakha* in 1990 noted that she 'spoke highly about the Hindu Family system and said that "we Christians also have similar family bondage"'.[203] Conservative MP Bob Blackman, a long-term supporter of Hindu and Hindu nationalist groups (see chapters 1 and 6), has also contributed to the model minority narrative. In 2014, while addressing an HSS training camp, he said, 'Standing on your own two feet, loyalty to country, family, rule of law are great British values. These are also great Hindu values. Remember the Hindu contribution to the country. The power of our economy is driven by Hindu contribution.'[204]

An important moment for the reification of the Hindu model minority was seen in a remarkable mobilisation to defend the reputation of the Neasden Swaminarayan temple after it was associated with the VHP in 2004 (see Chapter 6). Dozens of testimonials were collected and submitted to the Home Affairs Committee, including a statement from Ken Livingstone, the Mayor of London, in which he stated, 'The Hindu community is a peaceful law abiding community, which has a track record that needs commending and supporting'.[205] More recently, in September 2014, Priti Patel MP, then the government's 'Indian Diaspora Champion', wrote a glowing letter of congratulations to the HSS following a visit by Dattatreya Hosabale, RSS Sahsarkaryavaha (Joint General Secretary). In the letter, Patel commended the HSS and its members 'for bringing the Hindu community together to promote the ideals and values that underpins our way of life, particularly in demonstrating good citizenship, charity and social responsibility to benefit our community and country'.[206] Several other MPs—particularly those from constituencies with substantial Hindu populations—have also attended Sangh events and heaped praise on Hindu nationalist organisations at different points of time, as mentioned at various points throughout this book.

These exemplary pictures of Hindu nationalist groups in Britain obfuscate various tensions and inconsistencies in the deployment of the model minority in the context of Hindutva. Although the tolerance of Hindus is often lauded, on occasion this is seen to be overly lenient. Madhava Turumella of the Hindu Forum of Britain, in an interview on CNN in the wake of the Wendy Doniger furore (in which Penguin India withdrew the eminent Indologist's book, *The Hindus*, in 2014 after protests and lawsuits from radical Hindutva activists), stated, 'We Hindus have been extremely liberal. As a result, we Hindus have been taken for a task… We have tolerated enough'.[207] Similarly, Gandhian *ahimsa* (non-violence), frequently invoked to assert a superior temperament to belligerent Muslims, sits uneasily with certain Hindutva advocates who promote more pugnacious forms of 'self-defence'. These disputes are found within Hindutva in India as well. Van der Veer, for instance, highlighted the tension of Hindu nationalists adopting the Orientalist interpretations of Hinduism as tolerant and peaceful, on one hand, yet, on the other hand, wanting to dispel this notion of Hindus as weak and even effeminate, in favour of a more muscular Hindutva.[208]

Conclusion

Charity and public service are central elements of Hindu nationalism, and outside India this resonates in distinctive and important ways for the diaspora. We can understand the Sangh's public service in terms of four-fold dividends:

1. The manifest and inherent positive impact of work itself (e.g. cleaning a park, collecting for a food bank, or singing *bhajans* in a retirement home);

2. The enhancement of reputation and other rewards earned by those engaged in these visible, performative displays of nation- or community-building;
3. The dividends it provides for the *swayamsevsaks* and the Hindu communities themselves (e.g. exercise in character-building, development of 'good values', and the establishment of group unity and ecumenism);
4. The spiritual, soteriological, karmic benefits, as per the oft-quoted Vivekananda aphorism, 'service to humanity is service to God'.

Overlapping forms of Hindu charity and *sewa* in Britain reflect, in different ways, important connectivities with India—cultural, emotional, political, and fiscal. Sewa Day, to a certain extent, represents a new departure for the Sangh. It may be understood, partly, as a rehabilitative effort following controversies that emerged in the wake of Sewa International earthquake funding and the Gujarat violence of 2002. Sewa Day feels novel for its apparent progressiveness, framed as a form of twenty-first-century multicultural civic pride and shorn of many features commonly associated with Hindutva. However, it is neither entirely new—as seen through the Hindu Marathon initiative—nor is it devoid of subtle (or more explicit) inflections of Hindu nationalism. Local acts of integration and public service, *sewa* directed towards 'host' communities, and even interfaith co-operation have all been prescribed to the diaspora by the Sangh's leading ideologues. To make sense of the Sangh in Britain through charity and *sewa*, we need to understand the historical and transnational context, as well as the local milieu.

This chapter shows the need to understand Hindus in Britain with an eye on the Indian context—historical and contemporary—as well as a nuanced understanding of British South Asians as not simply embodying a 'transplanted culture'.[209] The relationship between the homeland and the diaspora—in this case, India and Britain—is in fact dynamic, imbricated, and symbiotic. Social welfare projects form a core element of the Sangh Parivar and have developed over time. Philanthropic narratives of the Sangh in Britain—from Sewa

International to Sewa Day—are to be understood as an important part of this trajectory, not only influencing, or influenced by, Hindu nationalism of the subcontinent.

Whilst administrative structures are often separate, shared contexts, which are superficially not always easy to identify, produce correlative trajectories. In India, the Sangh has penetrated Indian society through weaknesses and failures of the state in relation to welfare provision and government's increasing reliance, as the economy is further liberalised, on voluntary organisations for welfare delivery. Since 2014, the context for this welfare delivery has obviously been different, but the role played by Hindutva 'service' organisations is more significant than ever.

In Britain, we can also identify charities operating in areas that previously might have seen the state providing for citizens in need. Austerity, recession, and the failure of government to provide for those in need has opened spaces for organisations that are willing to step in. It is notable, for instance, that a large number of Sewa Day activities have involved collecting and distributing essential groceries for foodbanks, and efforts were also mobilised in various ways during the Covid-19 pandemic. In spite of needing to unpick and critically read the meanings of different forms of philanthropy, one must not lose sight of the fact that Sewa Day activities unquestionably have a positive impact and are undertaken by people seeking to help others and improve life for people in the communities in which they live.

It is important to note that the HSS has received consistent (but fairly modest) government funding for running *shakhas* and associated activities. A Freedom of Information request to the National Health Service (NHS) even indicated a grant of £10,500 paid to the HSS for a 'Madhav Kendra' 'Social Day Care/Drop In' scheme in 2008/9.[210] Much more substantial have been the government grants that Sewa Day has received in recent years. Financial statements submitted to the Charity Commission detail that in the financial year to March 2021, Sewa Day was given £101,178 in government grants—40% of their total income of £252,273. The following year, Sewa Day received a government grant income of £42,209 out of a total of £63,392 (67% of overall funds).[211] The financial statements do not detail the nature or purpose of these grants, but the state's support for Sewa Day is clearly very significant indeed. In some ways, this negotiation of British multiculturalism, and the access to resources this can involve, represents a 'vernacularisation' of the Sangh's role in the diaspora, but it also indicates the extent to which Hindutva-connected groups have established and embedded themselves in contemporary Britain. This has partly been supported by efforts to cultivate backing from those with influence. It can manifest in terms of local politicians and other dignitaries invited to witness or join in charitable activities, such as Sewa Day, but it can also take the form of lobbying. In 2016, Bob Blackman MP was flown to India to visit Sewa International projects, with the cost, totalling £2,344, covered by Sewa UK. The purpose of the visit, according to the Register of Members' Interests, was 'To support Sewa International India and Sewa UK projects, including a residential school for children with disabilities, and meet with trustees, volunteers and political figures.'[212] In Parliament, the week he returned, Blackman heaped praise on the charitable work he had witnessed as a result of diasporic donations, and asked the House: 'May we have a debate in Government time to celebrate the contributions of various diaspora [sic] in this country to making life better for people in their countries of origin?'[213] This led Alessandra Barrow to argue that Sewa UK and Sewa International 'have become a Hindutva-diplomatic tool'.[214]

Sewa Day's sanction by Cameron and others as paradigmatic of Big Society civic virtue bolsters Hindu, and Hindu nationalist, claims as the model minority in Britain. One might also see Sewa Day as a form of Indian 'soft power'. The 2012 Social Impact Analysis report expresses Sewa Day's aim of 'institutionalising the concept of "sewa" into British society'.[215] However, the partial concealment of 'Hindu-ness' in Sewa Day feels like a compromise, or a concession to multiculturalist pragmatism. This is rather different to Seshadri's ideas of 'the "Right Hindu Image" to be projected', which he emphasised should be diffident, 'aggressive', and unapologetic.[216] Similarly, Golwalkar repudiated the notion that overt use of the word 'Hindu' should be avoided; 'it is only defeatism or inferiority complex to think so'.[217] In this sense, Sewa Day, and the diverse and dynamic British Sangh Parivar from which it emerged, is reflective of certain core Hindutva values, but also indicative of a syncretic, vernacularised, and nebulous form of Hindu mobilisation in Britain.

6

'NEO-HINDUTVA'

HINDU NATIONALISM GOES PUBLIC[1]

On 25 October 2003, during Diwali celebrations, two men entered the Sanatan Dharma Hindu temple on Ealing Road in West London. After declaiming that people should convert to Christianity, they desecrated a *murti* (image) of Ram, breaking the statue on the floor. The incident caused great anxiety amongst the local Hindu community. Many were dismayed and angered when the perpetrators received what were seen to be light sentences.[2]

Two months later, on 14 December 2003, a 'Hindu Security Conference' was held in London in response. The RSS newspaper, *Organiser*, reported that the conference brought together 'more than 500 representatives from over 150 Hindu organisations'.[3] C.B. Patel, the prominent East African Gujarati publisher of the newspapers *Asian Voice* and *Gujarat Samachar*, spearheaded the gathering. At the time, many felt that existing Hindu representative organisations, notably the Hindu Council UK, were ineffective in the face of anti-Hindu hostility. Patel, who went on to become the Chairman of the HFB Patrons' Council, told the BBC: 'I believe people know up until now Hindus are the easy targets'. He exhorted the Hindu community to emulate Jewish groups in developing 'national co-ordination' and learning 'how to defend ourselves'.[4] A link to anti-Semitism was also raised in different terms by Ramesh Kallidai, who in 2004 told the Home Affairs Select Committee that 'the media has not been very sympathetic in reporting antihindic [sic] incidents... Attacks on, say, Jewish cemeteries get very sympathetic reporting in the national media ... but we also wish that they are sympathetic when Hindu temples get attacked. They are not.'[5] The relationship between Hindu and Jewish organisations, anti-Semitism and 'Hinduphobia', Hindutva and Zionism, is explored later in this chapter.

The Ealing temple attack and subsequent conference was a formative moment for Hindu representation in Britain. The Hindu Forum of Britain was established in the wake, in 2004, and Ramesh Kallidai, a dynamic and sometimes controversial community leader, appointed its first Secretary General. The umbrella group, which claimed to speak on behalf of all British Hindus, almost immediately established itself as the country's preeminent Hindu representative organisation. Although, ostensibly, entirely separate from the Sangh Parivar and the Hindu nationalist movement, it became, in certain ways, a source of new and often coded expressions of diasporic Hindutva.

The attack also led to a meeting between the newly established Hindu Forum and the Crown Prosecution Service's Director of Public Prosecutions, on 18 December 2004, facilitated by Keith Vaz MP. In an early press release, the Forum reported that the Crown Prosecution Service had agreed to hold biannual consultation meetings with the Hindu community, and to appoint Kallidai as an independent advisor to the London Criminal Justice Board.[6] The press release also mentioned 'regular incidents from 1993 where Hindu temples and festivals had been vandalised or students and individuals attacked'. Kallidai also raised these attacks with the Home Affairs Select Committee, albeit shorn of their post-Ayodhya context.[7]

The circumstances of the Hindu Forum's establishment reflect a number of core themes that indicate a resonance with Hindutva and the Sangh Parivar. Their push for ecumenical representation of a purportedly 'united Hindu community' recalls the raison d'être of the Vishwa Hindu Parishad. Their desire for a more assertive

Hindu identity, in response to perceived weakness, is also resonant of a key concern of Hindutva and proto-Hindu nationalist leaders, from Tilak and Vivekananda to Savarkar and Hedgewar. The sense that the Hindu community was under siege by an aggressive 'Other' (in this case Christian, but perhaps more frequently Muslim), is a central trope of Sangh rhetoric. Moreover, the focus on hurt Hindu feelings, offended and outraged by denigration and insult, which must be responded to with temerity not tolerance, are all core precepts around which supporters of the Sangh Parivar are mobilised. Indeed, as Neeti Nair has shown, the weaponisation of hurt religious sentiments has constituted a central tool for challenging secularism, and a means by which majoritarianism has been advanced, in India (and elsewhere across South Asia) since independence.[8] But in the Western multicultural setting this manifests very differently: rather than hurt sentiments being used to marginalise minority communities, in the diasporic context they are instrumentalised in various 'struggles for recognition'.

This book's final chapter examines the complex nexus of Hindu representation, multiculturalism, and Hindutva. It explores how ecumenical Hindu organisations—which assert a right or even mandate to represent the views and concerns of the Hindu diaspora—have played a role in the mainstreaming of Hindu nationalism, both within Hindu communities and in society at large. This normalisation has been, in part, forged and facilitated by the multicultural milieu in which the Forum and other groups operate, and has seen Hindu nationalist ideology permeate into wider political spheres. The articulation of these ideologies and identities related closely to the increased public salience of religion in 'multi-faith' Britain of the twenty-first century.

Representative organisations, notably the Hindu Forum of Britain and the National Council of Hindu Temples, require us to re-evaluate certain core understandings of diasporic Hindu nationalism. Their relationship with multiculturalism, often mediated through performative tropes of outrage and offence, play a central role in this narrative. A prime example of this, considered in depth, involves the forum's objection to an exhibition of paintings by the artist M.F. Husain in 2006. Amongst other activities of the

Hindu Forum, it illustrates how highly public, Hindu articulations of 'blasphemy' have helped to normalise Hindutva in Britain and make it mainstream. Whilst elements of this narrative are distinctly domestic (i.e. British), the transnational context links it, discursively and practically, to India and to other parts of the Indian diaspora.

Hindu nationalism, especially manifested in representative organisations and advocacy groups, has also emerged into a new political role in recent years. Groups and individuals have not just made efforts to lobby on specific issues (such as caste legislation), but have increasingly tried to push Hindu voters away from traditional electoral tendencies and towards an anti-Labour, pro-Conservative voting bloc.

I argue that a reconceptualisation of Hindutva is required. Hindu nationalism, particularly in the diaspora, has outgrown the institutional and ideological boundaries of the Sangh Parivar. The 'traditional' network remains important, but it has been joined by a diverse and growing array of new players in the Hindutva ecosphere. These idiosyncratic inflections of transnational Hindutva can be understood as 'neo-Hindutva'—a term that helps identify and understand the vernacularisation of Hindu nationalism, which, drawing on Deepa Reddy's identification of Hindutva's 'diffuse logic', is both nebulous and in process, and can become 'a mediating discourse in its own right'.[9] I first proposed neo-Hindutva in a 2015 article, and suggested it might be split between two broad 'categories': 'hard' neo-Hindutva—not reticent about being connected with Hindu nationalism, but, for various reasons, often departing from the positioning and praxis of the Sangh; and 'soft' neo-Hindutva—often more concealed and prone to avoid explicit linkages with Hindu majoritarian politics. The categories are not watertight but have fuzzy edges—individual organisations might contain elements of both, and groups representing one or the other may be linked. Hard and soft neo-Hindutva can be found in the diaspora, although in the context of the representative organisations we most frequently find the latter category: avoiding overt associations with the Hindutva network for diplomatic and pragmatic reasons, out of principle, and to be, ostensibly, more inclusive.

Neo-Hindutva can be seen as a start-point for thinking about the dynamic and vernacular ways in which Hindu nationalism has evolved over recent years, often into increasingly mainstream and normalised (but also obfuscated) forms of rhetoric and mobilisation. These trends can be simultaneously global and local, are increasingly expressed and negotiated in online spaces, and frequently are manifested through the language of blasphemy and offence, 'Hinduphobia', the 'art of being outraged', and the 'politics of grievance'.[10] Although nebulous, these new inflections of Hindutva, which have grown into new forms and spaces in recent years, constitute a powerful and often misunderstood facet of diasporic identity and praxis that demands our attention.[11]

A short chronology of multiculturalism and diaspora Hinduism

It is important to locate the Hindu Forum, and other representative organisations, within the evolution of British multiculturalism and diasporic Hinduism. Over the 1980s and 1990s, Hinduism developed in Britain in several key ways: crucially there was a shift from primarily domestic worship to the construction of temples. In addition to this congregationalisation of Hinduism, growing numbers of Hindu organisations also point to evolving institutionalisation. Both of these processes relate to a broader 'Semitising' of Hinduism that had occurred since the colonial period.

Towards the end of the twentieth century, Britain's increasingly settled Hindu population, with greater social, political, and economic capital—coupled with a planning system less resistant to diverse religious edifices—led to more, and increasingly impressive, *mandirs*. In 1971 Britain was home to approximately 138,000 Hindus but just two temples; a decade later, there were 278,000 Hindus and 25 temples. By 1991 this had grown to 379,000 Hindus and 78 temples; in 2001 there were 560,000 Hindus and 109 temples; in 2011 the numbers had risen to 833,000 Hindus with around 150 temples; and by 2021 this had risen to 1,032,775 Hindus and 187 temples.[12] Hindu nationalism also grew over this period—in both India and Britain—intensifying around the turn of the millennium and reaching a new zenith with Modi's election.

The evolution of Hinduism in Britain towards ecumenism, and the wider rise of what Peter van der Veer and Steven Vertovec have termed Hindu 'cosmopolitanism', also coincide with important developments in multiculturalism and multi-faith Britain.[13] During this period, the relationship between the state and religious organisations changed in several key ways, and minorities were increasingly engaged with on the basis of their religious rather than ethnic identities.

The Rushdie Affair—in which Muslims across the world reacted with distress and fury to the publication of British-Indian author Salman Rushdie's 1988 novel *The Satanic Verses*—was a key moment in this shift. It was pivotal for multiculturalism and associated debates around free speech, secularism, and integration, but also, as Talal Asad argued, might be understood as 'a symptom of British, postimperial identity in crisis'.[14] It also led to the construction of more assertive British Muslim identities and increasingly globalised Muslim politics.[15] This was set against a wider backdrop of emergent forms of fundamentalism and Islamism, across the world, that had a dialectic relationship with the concomitant growth of Hindutva. Nair, for instance, observes that the banning of *The Satanic Verses* in India in 1988 led to 'a surge in cases alleging "hurt" Hindu sentiments in courts across India'.[16]

The identity politics around the Rushdie Affair in Britain were part of a process of departure from 'more general Asian and Black identities that prioritised struggles against racism'.[17] This 'rise and rise of ethnicity', as Sivanandan powerfully argued, had begun quite some time earlier, particularly in the 1980s under Thatcher and in the wake of the Scarman Report, which followed the Brixton Uprising: 'The ensuing scramble for government favours and government grants (channelled through local authorities) on the basis of specific ethnic needs and problems served, on the one hand, to deepen ethnic differences and foster ethnic rivalry and, on the other, to widen the definition of ethnicity to include a variety of national and religious groups.'[18]

'NEO-HINDUTVA'

The Rushdie Affair led to new forms of national Muslim co-ordination, and in 1997 the Muslim Council of Britain was formed, bringing together more than 300 affiliated groups from across the country.[19] The *Satanic Verses* protests provided visibility and recognition for Muslims, in part, through the arresting images of rallies and book-burnings on national news.[20] But the Rushdie Affair did not just impact upon Muslim identities; it also galvanised a desire for more unified and politically powerful Hindu voices in Britain. In particular, as will be seen, the episode influenced performative displays of outrage from various communities. Another important, and related, development—exacerbated by terrorist attacks in the West and military invasions of Muslim countries in the early 2000s—was the endemic spread of Islamophobia. In many ways this has encouraged, and provided a basis for, articulations of Hindu identity as differentiated from an othered, negative portrayal of Muslims.

In spite of New Labour spin doctor Alastair Campbell's famous declaration, 'We don't do God', from the 1990s, religious identity, especially that of minority communities, became increasingly embedded in British political discourse.[21] In March 2004, one month before the HFB was launched, Prime Minister Tony Blair announced: 'A large majority of people in this country have some religious faith and we wanted to make sure that the needs and perspectives of the faith communities are taken into account as we develop our policies'.[22] Blair committed himself to work closely with the Hindu Forum from its inception.[23] However, this process of 'multiculturalism to multifaithism', and religion superseding ethnicity or race as a core facet of individual and group identity, had begun well before New Labour. In 1991, Stuart Hall wrote of religion as 'a new process of identification, the emergence into visibility of a new subject'.[24]

In part, this was due to government's pressure on religious organisations to perform as 'service deliverers', especially for the regeneration of urban areas.[25] The establishment of the Inner Cities Religious Council (ICRC) in 1992—'a "text book" product of multiculturalist, inter-faith relations policy'—serves both as an example of the important role of religion in the workings of the state and a counterfactual to secularisation theories.[26] A 1998 government review of the ICRC stated that 'the Home Office recognises that there is an increasing tendency for members of ethnic minority communities to identify themselves in the first instance by their religious beliefs rather than by nationality'.[27]

The significance of religion to government was not limited to pragmatic service delivery. In a speech to the Christian Socialist Movement in 2001, Blair said, 'our major faith traditions—all of them more historic and deeply rooted than any political party or ideology—play a fundamental role in supporting and propagating values which bind us together as a nation'.[28] Theresa May was even more explicit about the centrality of faith, in guiding her own politics as well as in society more broadly. This foregrounding of religious identities created (often unintended) spaces for essentialised public articulations of outrage and offence by community representatives.

The position of the British state towards Hindutva, however, is far from naïve. A multicultural society, and an atmosphere sympathetic to expressions of Islamophobia, provides a fertile environment for impassioned articulations of essentialised ethnic and religious identities. Various campaigns and lobbying efforts, sometimes highly performative, have visibilised Hinduism and become a significant aspect of Hindu public representation in twenty-first-century Britain.[29] These range from resistance to legislation outlawing caste discrimination, to outcry over the state's slaughter of infected temple cows, to uproar about misrepresentation in the media, to objections over various uses (or misuses) of Hindu iconography. They can be thought of as forms of Hindutva political praxis, and more specifically a 'mediating discourse' in the diaspora.[30] Moreover, they serve as moments at which a community can coalesce and (perhaps only fleetingly) display unity and resolve. In this light, John Zavos has argued that, 'performance and spectacle have a vital role to play, as they provide the most effective way to produce representations in this ever-shifting arena—they become "generative political moments par excellence"'.[31] However, whilst the tropes of defamation, blasphemy, and outrage have particular resonance for Hindus in the West, this trend is unique neither to the diaspora nor even to Hinduism.

Zavos has written most extensively and persuasively on Hindu umbrella organisations and Hindu nationalism in the UK, arguing that Hindutva groups have not been 'the most dominant voices in the articulation of a British Hindu identity in national contexts'.[32] Instead, he suggests, *sampradayas* (religious fellowships, such as the International Society for Krishna Consciousness (ISKCON) and the Bochasanwasi Shri Akshar Purushottam Swaminarayan Sanstha (BAPS)), and more recently umbrella groups (such as the Hindu Council UK and the Hindu Forum of Britain), have been more important in terms of the public voice of Hinduism. Zavos argues that whilst such organisations appear not to have direct association or personnel overlap with Hindutva groups, one can still identify a 'presence of a latent Hindu nationalism'.[33] However, he stresses that 'it is important not to over-emphasise this connection'.[34] But this reference to 'latent Hindu nationalism' does not go far enough. Whilst Zavos is right not to oversimplify or essentialise the nature of Hindutva within umbrella groups—which clearly perform a range of functions—there is sufficient evidence to suggest that Hindu nationalism has become a core element of mainstream, representative Hindu organisations.

The Hindu Forum of Britain

After its formation in 2004, the Hindu Forum rapidly asserted itself as the chief interlocutor for the government and other institutions as the voice of Hindus in Britain. Within the first year of its existence, HFB representatives participated in seven major government consultations.[35] In 2006, the publication of *Connecting British Hindus: An Inquiry into the Identity and Public Engagement of Hindus in Britain*, an HFB report sponsored by the Cohesion and Faiths Unit of the Department for Communities and Local Government (DCLG), consolidated the forum's status. Upon its launch, Ruth Kelly, Secretary of State for Communities and Local Government, remarked that this was the first piece of government-sponsored research into Hindu communities in

Britain.[36] The HFB's status was further strengthened as the only Hindu organisation represented on the panel of thirteen 'Faith Advisors' appointed by John Denham in January 2010. Kallidai and other Forum representatives have also advised the London Criminal Justice Board, the Race Hate Crime Forum, the Metropolitan Police Diversity Forum, the Faith Communities Consultative Council, the London 2012 Forum, and the Religious Education Council, amongst other bodies.[37] From the outset, an effective Forum 'tool' for engagement with politicians has been the annual 'Diwali at Westminster' event.

The Hindu Forum's enduring status as a 'go-to' voice for British Hindus is underlined by a long list of official bodies that 'representatives of HFB are appointed to advise', currently displayed on their website, although the true extent of this advisory role is unclear and perhaps much more limited than is implied. HFB President, Trupti Patel, even attended Queen Elizabeth II's state funeral, ostensibly 'representing the Hindu community' (but the presence also of Rajnish Kashyap, General Secretary of the Hindu Council UK, in a more official capacity as part of the 'Procession of Religious Representatives', points to the ongoing 'competition' for representation).[38]

There are many reasons for the forum's early and rapid rise to being recognised as one of the principal representative voices of Hindus. Multifaith policies require official engagement with representatives of various religious communities, but this has encountered particular challenges with British Hindus. Securing a representative of 'the Hindu community' poses difficulties when faced with the great diversity of Hinduism and its much-discussed differences to Abrahamic religions (whose central, organisational hierarchies are more established, albeit still contested). The format of interfaith forums and government consultations inherently privileges organisations that present standardised, essentialist, ecumenical versions of religious communities. Hindu groups have been affected in particular ways by this 'levelling' impulse, increasingly situating their beliefs within the 'World Religions' paradigm.[39] In various ways, therefore, Hinduism's heterogeneity and lack of central authority lends itself to the umbrella organisation format.

Umbrella groups are especially useful for a 'box-ticking', 'take-me-to-your-leader' approach to representation—expressions used by an anonymous DCLG official when talking to me about Hindu umbrella originations.[40] In another interview, Ian Bradshaw, Deputy Head of Integration and Faith in the Tackling Extremism and Hate Crime Division at DCLG, explained to me that the government can get 'nervous' about approaching individual groups, particularly given the internal diversity of Hinduism. From the government's perspective, umbrella groups not only represent a range of views but also 'understand how government works'.[41] The Forum has displayed an ability 'to articulate such ideas in a sophisticated multicultural key'.[42] But they are also well-versed in corporate language, which is increasingly commonplace in the NGO and public sectors. A recent 'Social Impact Analysis for Activities in 2011' report, for instance, framed the forum's 'strategy' in terms of 'delivery and service to the Hindu community and the wider society in the context of developing good interfaith relations with other faith communities to build a cohesive and inclusive Britain'.[43]

The 'nervousness' expressed by Bradshaw reflects a quiet apprehension felt by the UK government about Hindu nationalism in Britain. Whilst domestically it is considered inconsequential in comparison to concerns over radical Islam, the government's position is not as naïve as some suggest. Whitehall officials, especially those at the Foreign and Commonwealth Office, were familiar with the Sangh in India long before Modi's rise to power. Many in the civil service, particularly in the Home Office, are aware of RSS-connected organisations operating in Britain. In the past, the British government has deliberately, although not entirely, avoided public interactions with these organisations. Whitehall concerns over Hindutva have been stimulated by the Gujarat violence of 2002, and by reports of substantial capital flows to the Sangh from the diaspora (see Chapter 5).[44] There are also more general fears that Hindutva is at odds with multicultural cohesion, particularly vis-à-vis British Muslims, and concern over proximity to or the condoning of Hindutva (witnessed, for instance, in the response to extremist Hindutva leader Tapan Ghosh's controversial appearance in Parliament in 2018—see below). But BJP hegemony in India, combined with politicians eager to garner the votes of British Hindus, mean that the likelihood of any government censure of Hindu nationalism in the UK is very slim indeed.

Nonetheless, state wariness of British Hindutva has made the Forum cautious over open connections with the Sangh. In an interview, its then-Secretary General, Swaminathan, told me that, 'With the VHP, HSS... the mainstream government doesn't want to be working with them, like they would work with us. So we also honour their sentiments, that's it.'[45] In spite of this, it appears that the umbrella group retains both ideological and institutional connections to various forms of Hindu nationalism. The British government, for its part, seems less aware that Hindutva ideologies might be perpetuated through umbrella groups.

Behind the government's engagement with the Forum is a belief in their mandate, which they claimed from the outset.[46] The Forum's ambitions are clear:

> We want to be the representatives of Hindus in this country. Not only to the government but to other religious bodies, and to the public fora, like the BBC and community media, all these people want someone to speak on behalf of Hindus. So that's what our role is. The Hindu Forum represents the Hindu fears, Hindu concerns, and Hindu views to the wider community.[47]

From its early days, the Forum claimed to speak for hundreds of British Hindu organisations. This involved an impressive gazetteering of the Hindu landscape in the UK, which bestowed a certain level of credence in itself. But the lists of organisations claimed within the HFB's fold are rarely consistent. Discrepancies in these figures corroborate accusations of their 'cut and paste' approach to representation. Figures given in various documents for member organisations vary wildly. In 2019, the HFB's homepage and 'About Us' page gave totally different numbers: 320 and 420 (although at the time of writing both state 'more then [sic] 300').[48] Numbers in other documents include 240, 274, 284, and 350.[49] But the number of actively participating, fee-paying members may be fewer than twenty.

The (consistently) inconsistent figures might be explained, in part, by the challenges of maintaining an up-to-date website with limited resources. The disparities perhaps also reveal the nature by which Hindu groups seem to be appropriated into the fold of the HFB. Representative and umbrella organisations feel under pressure to claim they speak for a large proportion—if not all—of a particular ethnic or religious community. But while on the surface the Forum's representative claims might appear to be simply an effect of the multiculturalist imperative and the desire to secure government patronage, it is necessary to situate the tendency within the broader context of Hindutva. The majoritarian logic of Hindu nationalism requires hegemony, homogeneity (on certain levels), and unity—what Amartya Sen referred to as a 'miniaturization of India'.[50] Arjun Appadurai speaks of a 'fear of small numbers': this fear perhaps plays a part in the Forum's desire to represent *all* Hindus.[51] The Forum is also competing in a 'market' of sorts—many have referred to the faith-relations 'industry', in reference to the remunerative, vocational, and reputational benefits available in Britain's multifaith milieu. This dynamic may be understood to have colonial roots, in which competition for political and economic resources led to increasingly 'fixed' and exclusive religious categories and, ultimately, animosity and even violence towards the 'other'.[52] In the contemporary setting, for representative organisations to have any kind of competitive advantage over rivals (such as the Hindu Council UK, which the Forum superseded in certain ways), they need to emerge as commanding the greatest 'share' of the Hindu community.

Also important is the Forum's definition of Hinduism itself. In recent years 'dharmic faiths' has emerged as a popular term amongst Hindu and Hindutva groups. Swaminathan explained that 'All the religious, spiritual, cultural ideologies that are born in the land of *Bharatavarsha* or India, can be called [Hindu]. So if you can link it geographically, the land of India … [everything] indigenous to the land of India can be called Hinduism'.[53] This clearly follows the ultra-inclusive, ethno-geographic, 'indigenous' approach, often associated with Hindutva. Despite this, no non-Hindu organisations are listed as members.

Challenges to the Hindu Forum of Britain

The legitimacy of community spokespersons is often queried and contested. The fact that many people have not even heard of them is sufficient, for some, to dismiss their claims to speak for an entire community. Critics of the Forum, specifically, have suggested that they have a limited mandate and are self-appointed representatives. Commenting on a *New Statesman* interview with Bharti Tailor, the Forum's second Secretary General, 'CJ', writes:

> As for... this being the views of the majority of the Hindu Community in the UK—that is total rubbish. The Hindu Forum is about 30 people strong and have no mandate whatsoever of representing the Hindus in the UK... Cutting and pasting a lot of names and addresses of temples from the phone book and sticking them on a website does not make a community org[anisation]. But hey if the rest of you want to be hoodwinked into thinking they are—then please do as long as my taxes ain't paying for their hotair [sic].[54]

Vijay Prashad has also provided a caustic critique of representative advocacy groups:

> It takes little to set up a political shop: the name of an organization, a patron among one or the other party or lobby group, fancy-looking letterhead, a fairly dynamic leader, and preferably a photograph or two of this leader with an important politician from one of the two major parties and/or an important politician from the homeland.[55]

British journalist Sunny Hundal, who referred to Kallidai in 2007 as 'the one-man band that is the Hindu Forum of Britain', is equally dismissive: 'Politicians, the media and other groups interested in race relations continue to court these groups, which are given funding, asked for their opinions and constantly quoted in the press. In this way, a "group" may be only two people in a dingy office, but they are afforded instant clout'.[56]

Challenges to the sort of multicultural political environment in which the Hindu Forum operate go beyond just disputing the mandate of representatives. In 2006 the New Generation

Network published a manifesto critiquing the race and faith relations discourse, and 'self-appointed "community leaders"' in Britain: 'We need an approach that discards the older politics of representation through government sanctioned gate-keepers'.[57] According to the authors, this sort of state multiculturalism had led to 'increasing separation'. The self-selecting bias of spokespersons privileges groups, such as the Hindu Forum, that present disingenuous and ring-fenced versions of a monolithic, homogenised 'Hindu community'.

From its early days, people criticised the Forum's ideological orientation and institutional connections with the Sangh Parivar. British Muslims for Secular Democracy—a group established in 2006 by Nasreen Rehman and Yasmin Alibhai-Brown—issued a statement in 2007 expressing concern at the appointment of Ramesh Kallidai to the government's Commission on Integration and Cohesion (CIC), citing his 'strong links with Hindu fundamentalist and extremist organisations'.[58] This followed one of the more public and fierce media 'exposés' of British Hindutva—a full-page *Evening Standard* article by Andrew Gilligan.[59] Above a smiling family portrait of Kallidai ran the headline: 'Revealed: the Rise and Rise of the Fundamentalist Father'. Gilligan claimed that the Forum's Secretary General had 'clear links to violent Hindu fundamentalists accused of "direct responsibility" for the slaughter of thousands of Muslims'.[60] The article referred to HFB collaborations with the VHP on joint press releases and events, including two meetings with the CIC and the launch of the 'Hindu Charter' in Parliament.[61]

For some, Kallidai's appointment to the CIC did not represent naivety or ignorance, but was consistent with broader post-9/11, Islamophobic, and post-Cold War 'Clash of Civilisations' narratives.[62] The CIC's brief was to 'produce a vision of society where people are committed to what we have in common rather than obsessing with those things that make us different'.[63] Therefore, Kallidai's role, rather than being a misguided irony, as Gilligan's article implied, was actually highly consonant with the emergent timbre of multiculturalist politics. The Hindutva discourse in which Muslims are 'the primary threat to the nation and made to represent symbolically a series of interlinked tropes including terrorism, fanaticism, allegiance to forces external and hostile to the nation', was especially resonant in the post-7/7 multiculturalist milieu.[64] Going a step further, for Anandi Ramamurthy, Kallidai's appointment was explicitly an example of 'the policy objective in criminalising and isolating Muslims as the "problem faith"'.[65]

Although there is, of course, an epistemological overlap between aspects of Hindutva and Islamophobic Western politics, the rise of the Forum was perhaps in spite of its latent Islamophobia rather than because of it. We must not overestimate how carefully DCLG would have scrutinised Kallidai's personal beliefs before the appointment. In interviews, DCLG officials described these appointments to me as 'box-ticking exercises'. It is, of course, ironic that government engagement with an individual described as communalist was the result of 'Cohesion' policies fostered in consequence of the 'race' riots of 2001, and the Home Office Cantle Report, *Community Cohesion*.[66]

Nevertheless, the *Evening Standard* exposé can be seen as a milestone in the trajectory of Hindutva in Britain. Not only was domestic Hindu nationalism featured in the mainstream British press (in a way that is not unheard of today, but was very rare then)—Hindu nationalism outside the traditional Sangh network was laid bare in an extremely public manner. Furthermore, the proximity of Hindutva and government was illuminated more clearly than ever.

The Hindu Forum of Britain, the Hindu nationalist movement, and 'neo-Hindutva'

The Hindu Forum represents a form of Hindutva in many complex ways. Some of these are latent, others more explicit. It also reflects a growing diffusion and normalisation of Hindutva identities in the mainstream representation of Hinduism in Britain, and the increasingly interconnected and overlapping global network of Hindu and Hindu nationalist groups.

Some of the Forum's Hindu nationalist connections are concrete. Hindu Aid—a charity established by Kallidai and HFB in 2003 and funded almost entirely through government grants—carried out projects in India almost entirely through Sewa Bharati, the principal charity of the Sangh Parivar.[67] The *Organiser* details how Hindu Aid won a grant of £137,532 from the Department for International Development (DFID) to work within Hindu communities to raise awareness about global poverty, Millennium Development Goals, and 'increasing global interdependence'.[68] Hindu Aid reports on relief work done by Sewa Bharati were entirely consistent with tasks attributed directly to the RSS in the *Organiser*.[69]

HFB connections with the Sangh have not been limited to overseas activities. On 12 April 2007, Kallidai attended an HSS event at the Advait Cultural Centre in Wembley, celebrating the life of M.S. Golwalkar. The *Organiser* reported Kallidai praising Golwalkar and the expansion of the 'exemplary' RSS, and quoted Kallidai saying that to pay homage to 'Guruji' 'was like holding a candle to the Sun'.[70] The final speech of the ceremony was delivered by RSS Sahsarkaryavaha (Joint General Secretary), Suresh Soni, a veteran Sangh Parivar leader visiting from India. After press coverage in Britain and India, the Forum were forced to release a statement claiming the quotations were out of context: 'our presence at these events does not mean that we agree with the ideology of the host organisation or consider them an appropriate model'.[71]

Kallidai's statements at the House of Commons Home Affairs Select Committee were less ambiguous. On 14 December 2004, Kallidai gave evidence to the Select Committee on Terrorism and Community Relations in the light of controversial allegations made by Jagdeesh Singh of the Sikh Community Action Network (Slough). Singh had previously appeared in front of the committee on 16 November to discuss the wide impact of Islamophobia and anti-terrorism policies, during which he claimed that the Vishwa Hindu Parishad were 'well-known for promoting sectarian violence in India', and, 'continue to function from North London from a prominent location—i.e. the Neasden [BAPS Swaminarayan] Hindu Temple'.[72]

Jagdeesh Singh's statement was met with a vociferous response. The trustees of the Neasden temple mobilised with astonishing vigour, and the Select Committee received a wide range of submissions supporting BAPS. A joint memorandum submitted by eight MPs stated, 'No organisation has its headquarters or any such office or operation in Neasden. We are very concerned that this entirely false accusation goes unchallenged.'[73] Separately, Andrew Dismore MP tabled an Early Day Motion, signed by seventy-two MPs from across the political spectrum, expressing 'deep regret' at Jagdeesh Singh's comments, stating that 'this allegation has caused profound offence to the wider Hindu community in the UK and is damaging to good community relations'.[74] The Mayor of London, Ken Livingstone, also wrote to the committee adding his support, and stating that the Metropolitan Police had not found anything untoward.

Even the Home Secretary, Charles Clarke, submitted a memorandum to the committee, emphasising the positive presence of the Swaminarayan temple and its close relationship with government, detailing a number of official visits and their position on the Inter Faith Network. Clarke also wrote that:

> The VHP is an international Hindu Nationalist organization, most prominent in India but also involved in various activities with British Hindus through the VHP (UK), which is a registered charity. The VHP is not proscribed in the UK, although the Police keep the activities of any organizations accused of extremist activity under close scrutiny and any evidence of illegality under the Terrorism Act 2000 is always thoroughly investigated.[75]

BAPS's own submission included several statements specifically clearing their name, including from councillors and a police superintendent. It was accompanied by an almost bewildering range of generic testimonials, from the Duke of Edinburgh and Bill Clinton to Tony Blair and Richard Branson.[76]

Kallidai gave evidence in person before the committee on 14 December 2004. But rather than just backing BAPS, Kallidai provided unequivocal support to the VHP. After marginalising Singh, stating that 'this person did not represent anyone in the community', he 'vehemently' repudiated David Winnick MP's suggestion that the VHP was 'an organisation of Hindu extremists':[77]

The VHP is an organisation that works with social and moral upliftment of Hindus and the VHP UK is a totally autonomous body from the VHP India ... the VHP has never had in any court of law any evidence proved or provided to link them to a terrorist organisation. So, on the basis of media reports, we should not quickly judge and label an organisation... Most of the Hindu community in the UK and the world consider the VHP to be a peaceful organisation.[78]

The HFB's submission to the committee also referred to attacks on Hindus by Muslims in Britain, which Kallidai followed with a reference to twenty-one incidents of Hindu temples being burnt in the 1990s.[79] These were obliquely attributed to a 'reaction to certain events in India about a mosque' (see Chapter 3 for a detailed discussion of the Babri Masjid demolition, the Ram temple movement, and the VHP).

So why was there such an extraordinary response to comments made in a parliamentary committee meeting by an obscure Sikh activist? The allegations were two-fold: one, that the VHP was engaged in militancy and, two, that it operated in Britain out of the BAPS temple in Neasden. The response was also binary: to absolve the VHP from perceived slurs, and to repudiate the connection with the Swaminarayan *mandir*. The strength of the reaction underlined the political and social capital of the *sampradaya*. In various ways, BAPS has become one of the central representatives, and representations, of Hinduism globally. The organisation, and many of the Gujarati community who form their core following, have accumulated considerable levels of cultural, political, and economic capital around the world. This was very clearly demonstrated in the support they gathered following Jagdeesh Singh's accusations.

But why, then, if attempts were also made to prevent the VHP's name from being tarnished, was such a vociferous effort made to disassociate BAPS from the Hindu nationalist organisation? Since its establishment in 1995, the iconic Neasden temple has built up a considerable reputation as a symbol of the positive role played by Hindus in Britain; the accusation that this place of worship was connected to militancy was deeply upsetting to its devotees. But the connections between the *sampradaya* and Hindu nationalist politics and politicians, from Gujarat to New Jersey, have been widely discussed by scholars, journalists, activists, and others. It is worth noting that their temples—especially outside India, and perhaps none more so than the Neasden *mandir*—are extremely public spaces, and BAPS enthusiastically welcome a diverse range of public figures for widely promoted visits. It has become the go-to place for politicians seeking a photo opportunity to promote their multiculturalist credentials. Various academics draw parallels between Hindutva and the way in which BAPS seek to represent Hinduism; Parita Mukta considers: 'the embroilment of the north London temple with the investiture, practices and insignia of the VHP and the BJP', while Jaffrelot and Therwath argue, 'the Sangh Parivar finds in the Swaminarayan movement a most valuable ally in Great Britain'.[80] Despite evidence suggesting numerous layers of connectivity with Hindu nationalism—both institutional and ideological—BAPS has a history of refuting, and often strongly objecting to, such claims.[81]

While a full discussion of the position of BAPS vis-à-vis transnational Hindutva is beyond the scope of this chapter, the Select Committee episode was revealing of certain significant aspects of Hindu representation and Hindu nationalism in the diaspora, and the ways in which Hindutva is interwoven into the fabric of diasporic Hinduism. The Hindu Forum of Britain's General Secretary did not just rally around BAPS, but also sought to protect the reputation of the VHP: both Indian and UK branches.

The Forum's alignment with the Sangh Parivar was not only in evidence under Kallidai's leadership. In the summer of 2008, Ishwarbhai Tailor, Chairman of Hindu Forum of Britain, was chief guest at the Hindu Swayamsevak Sangh (HSS) Sangh Shiksha Varg (Sangh Instructor Training Camp—see Chapter 2).[82] In 2010, Bharti Tailor, Kallidai's successor as Secretary General, was chief guest, alongside HFB President Arjun Vekaria, at the HSS's Vijaya Dashmi Utsav in Woolwich, South London—a celebration of the day on which the Indian RSS was founded in 1925. An image on the cover of HSS publication *Sangh Sandesh* shows Tailor performing puja in front of a garlanded image of RSS founder K.B.

Hedgewar.[83] The *Sangh Sandesh* article on the event, attended by the UK Sangh leadership and 400 participants and guests, stated: 'Overall the *utsav* [festival] was a wonderful experience for all. Everyone present recognised the hard work of *Swayamsevaks* and *Sevikas* in spreading the message of Hindutva'.[84]

In 2017, another key figure in the Hindu Forum made his proximity to the Sangh known. C.B. Patel—the media proprietor who was instrumental in launching the Forum, and who has remained a patron ever since—hosted an event bringing together leading businessmen with a visiting 'Chief Guest' from India, Dattatreya Hosabale (Joint General Secretary of the RSS). In an article on the event in his own newspaper, Patel stated:

> I have known and followed the RSS for many years and I am very proud of the work they have done in building leaders and characters who work selflessly for the betterment of society. Despite this, they have too often received negative press or even worse been targeted and labelled by those with their own agenda. My own experience of RSS and those working with similar methodology, in UK and otherwise, is that they have been a uniting force for the good for both Hindus and Indians as well as the wider society.[85]

Publicly, though, the Forum has often been cautious, even taciturn, about its associations with the Sangh and Hindutva. Following the *Evening Standard* article 'scandal', its ambivalence about collaborating and associating with Parivar organisations is perhaps unsurprising. In an interview, Swaminathan stated: 'living in this country, a foreign country, if the government feels they [Hindu nationalist organisations] are not to be associated with, then we will always be law-abiding people, so we will not'. He then made an interesting comparison with the British Nationalist Party:

> Mainstream politicians are not very happy to, they won't share a stage with them [the BNP]... So same sort of thing. With the VHP, HSS, they are not illegal or anything unconstitutional in this country, they are happy, they can do whatever they want to, they can run their association, but the mainstream government

doesn't want to be working with them, like they would work with us. So we also honour their sentiments, that's it.[86]

Later, Swaminathan told me: 'We personally don't feel they [the RSS and VHP] are any sort of people that we should be disassociating [with]. We only need to give respect to the wider community and the government'. Discussing the Sangh Parivar generally, and the RSS in particular, Swaminathan told me that 'most of the people, including me, look at it as a patriotic and good organisation'. On the members of the HSS and VHP-UK, Swaminathan said:

> I would say they are well-organised people, harmless people, they are doing their job and the community services. And we work closely with those volunteers, they come to our events, help us, as volunteers, they are the best people when it comes to being organised, disciplined people, I have seen. So why should I be negative about them?

Swaminathan, surprisingly, then segued this topic into talking about the far-right anti-Muslim protest group, the English Defence League (EDL). Out of the blue, he asked: 'What is your opinion on the EDL? The fact is, you know I'm not a supporter of EDL, but the fact is the points that they raise are not wrong'. This appeared to be a statement of sympathy, an acknowledgement that the EDL's criticism of Muslims in Britain was justified. The HFB is not the only 'mainstream', representative organisation that is drawn to the Islamophobic far-right. In February 2016, the National Council of Hindu Temples UK (NCHT—discussed in more depth at the end of this chapter), invited EDL founder Tommy Robinson to speak at their annual conference in a Southall temple. The event was grudgingly cancelled after outrage from anti-racism activists and members of the Hindu community.[87] But the fact that the NCHT was eager to host one of Britain's most notorious white nationalists revealed much about the sort of surprising, often hidden, layers of solidarity and even collaboration between diverse right-wing, anti-Muslim factions that have emerged, globally, in the twenty-first century.

The Forum, and other Hindu representative bodies, maintain and have even developed their Hindutva connections. In fact, in the Modi-era ascendance of Hindutva, it seems as though the lines between 'mainstream' Hindu groups and the Hindu right are becoming increasingly blurred. The Forum has even extended invitations to stridently anti-Muslim political figures from India. In October 2017 a furore erupted after Tapan Ghosh, founder of the Kolkata-based Hindu Samhati, was a guest at the annual Diwali event at the House of Commons. Ghosh is a notorious Hindutva leader from West Bengal whose militant rhetoric on what he views as Muslim efforts to 'Islamise' the state, and India more widely, has earned him several stints in jail and a reputation as one of India's most divisive and radical Hindu nationalist firebrands. The event was hosted in Parliament by Bob Blackman—the Conservative MP for Harrow East, a suburban area with 32.1% Indian residents (the third highest proportion of any UK constituency).[88] Blackman is Vice Chair of the Conservative Friends of India, founding Chairman of the All-Party Parliamentary Group for British Hindus, and for many years has served as a close and vocal ally of Hindu nationalists in Britain and beyond. In January 2020, the BJP government rewarded Blackman and Barry Gardiner MP with Padma Shri awards—India's fourth highest civilian honour.[89]

Several cabinet ministers, including Damian Green, Amber Rudd, Sajid Javid, and Priti Patel, were also guests at the event with Tapan Ghosh. After wide press coverage highlighting his fanaticism, Rudd was compelled to release a statement: 'The home secretary fundamentally disagrees with Mr Ghosh's views on Islam. The home secretary accepted an invitation from the Hindu Forum of Britain to attend an event in parliament last week to celebrate Diwali. She did not speak to Mr Ghosh and was not present when he spoke.'[90] In addition to the HFB event, Ghosh spent time during his UK visit with EDL co-founder Tommy Robinson, recording a video of 'a good discussion on demography and global resistance to Islam', in which they shared their mutual admiration for one another.[91] Ghosh also gave a speech in the House of Commons at an event organised by the NCHT. In spite of the uproar created by Ghosh's invitations to Parliament, Hindu representative organisations appeared unfazed: on 16 May 2019 the HFB and NCHT co-hosted an event in Edinburgh, 'Dharma

Rising', at which the guest of honour and main speaker was the Hindutva provocateur and BJP politician Subramanian Swamy.

Hindu Security Conference

While these examples indicate some concrete connections between the Hindu Forum and the Hindu nationalist movement, it is perhaps more revealing to consider more latent levels of the HFB's Hindutva orientations. The second half of this chapter examines examples of this nebulous 'neo-Hindutva': first, a 'Hindu Security Conference' in 2007, then, in detail, protests against an exhibition of M.F. Husain paintings in 2006. The chapter ends with a discussion of the more explicit and increasingly political role played by diasporic Hindu representative organisations.

These strands of the Forum's activities indicate a consonance with Hindutva that exists both outside of, and intersecting with, the 'traditional' organisations and spaces of Hindu nationalist activism and ideology. It must be noted that these examples are not cited with a view to presenting a comprehensive picture of all the work that the Hindu Forum engages with, but more to identify certain levels on which we can identify Hindu nationalism. By analysing these strands, which can be understood as a form of 'neo-Hindutva', we can identify an increasing tendency towards a normalisation of Hindu nationalism in Britain.

On 21 February 2007, the Forum hosted a second 'Hindu Security Conference' at the London School of Economics. This event generated rhetoric closely associated to the siege-mentality Hindutva of the Sangh Parivar, particularly in relation to Muslims. At the conference Ramesh Kallidai made controversial and widely publicised claims that Muslims were forcibly converting vulnerable female Hindu students on university campuses in Britain.[92] These potent and contentious tropes of Hindu female vulnerability in the face of Muslim male aggression bore striking resemblance to the anti-Muslim 'love jihad' rhetoric commonly deployed in India. Kallidai made these allegations at a session on 'Campus Security', chaired by an officer from the Metropolitan Police's Diversity Directorate.[93] The conference poster contained emotive, alarming motifs: blood-red finger prints, bright yellow 'Do Not Cross' police tape, and a large photograph of a screaming male figure. The topics listed for discussion were 'Faith and Identity', 'Radicalisation and "Violent" Extremism', and 'Safety in Street Crime'.

The Hindu Security Conference provided a bridge between the Forum, other Hindu groups, and various representatives of the state. It was co-organised with the National Hindu Students Forum (NHSF—the British student body, closely linked to the Sangh Parivar, discussed in Chapter 5), and the Metropolitan Police Hindu Association (with the Metropolitan Police's main logo featured prominently on the poster).[94] The conference featured Sir Ian Blair, Metropolitan Police Chief Constable, as keynote speaker; and also hosted Tony McNulty, Home Office Minister for Policing and Security; Richard Barnes, Conservative Party councillor; Alfred Hitchcock, Head of Diversity for the Metropolitan Police Service; and Chief Superintendent Steve Jordan, Security Lead, Commission of Integration and Cohesion, in a Q&A session, chaired by Ramona Mehta of the HFB 'Legal Advisory Committee'.[95]

The conference was covered in the British media, with *Metro* publishing a story the day after the event under the headline: 'Hindu Girls Targeted by Extremists'. According to the report, Kallidai told the audience that 'extremist Muslims make life miserable for Hindu girls', and 'estimated hundreds of girls had been targeted' with 'recruiters... paid £5,000 for each success'.[96] The article went on to state, 'Scotland Yard is to set up a Hindu Safety Forum with "aggressive conversion" as its top priority'. The *Manchester Evening News* quoted Kallidai at greater length:

> The police and other agencies have no idea about the high levels of resentment building up in the Hindu and Sikh communities over aggressive conversion techniques and intimidation by radical Islamic groups on campuses. Families are being broken down, while some of our girls have even been beaten up and had to leave university. We need to look at positive action rather than just speaking about these issues.[97]

Whilst the media broadly avoided questioning the veracity of Kallidai's claims, and many online commenters from across the world voiced support for the Forum's position, there was also a small but vociferous pushback. AWAAZ, the anti-Hindutva group, issued a critical statement on the conference, asking: 'Why are the Metropolitan Police Commissioner and a government minister giving credence to dubious Hindu fundamentalist claims?' AWAAZ's statement went on to argue that the anti-conversion rhetoric and strategy of involving the police and criminal justice system, regardless of whether coercion has been involved, 'has been imported directly from Hindu supremacist groups in India, such as the violent Vishwa Hindu Parishad, an organisation that the Hindu Forum of Britain has defended'.[98]

Although there are strong resemblances to aspects of the VHP's ideology and modus operandi, it is over-simplistic to brand the Forum's rhetoric as a 'direct import'. The narrative of radical Islamism and conversion, including on university campuses, has been prevalent for many years. This was exacerbated by the 7/7 attacks: two of the four bombers were university graduates and one was a Muslim convert. Much of the broader British discourse on Islamist terrorism, including the government's Prevent guidance, focuses on those who are converts.

It is important to recognise the Forum's talk of the 'targeting' of Hindu girls for conversion to Islam not simply in terms of an imported narrative from India, but as a more complex and dynamic, hybrid rhetoric of Hindutva in the post-9/11, post-7/7 British multicultural landscape. Yasir Suleiman's report on female converts to Islam considers the particular challenges of an environment of Islamophobia: 'Islam is not viewed as a valid extension of the values that many British converts have grown up with'.[99] Diasporic Hindutva 'love jihad' rhetoric can be understood in terms of the 'Islamophobia industry', which sustains and condones layers of anti-Muslim attitudes in the public sphere, as much as within Hindutva discourse of the subcontinent.[100] Katy Sian shows that there is also a particular and virulent strand to this amongst British Sikhs, which she links to the legacy of Partition as much as to contemporary Islamophobia.[101] Some in Britain, in recent years, have attempted to bring the Hindutva love jihad trope into dialogue with a wider narrative, a racialised myth prominent in the press and promulgated by politicians and activists on the right and far-right, around Muslim 'grooming gangs'. This has been seen in the establishment of a group named National Hindu Welfare Support, which has close links to the Sangh Parivar and conducts 'community outreach' through the provision of awareness-raising seminars and a telephone helpline, warning of the risk of grooming and exploitation faced by Hindu girls.

The British Islamophobic environment and narrative of Muslim conversion, seduction, or harassment of Hindus is also not just a twenty-first-century phenomenon. During RSS Sarsanghchalak Rajendra Singh's 1995 visit to Britain, the NHSF asked for advice on how to respond to 'Hindu girls [who] are intimidated in universities by Muslims'.[102] Similarly, Dhooleka Raj reported that in the early 1990s, the NHSF sponsored research and lectures to 'raise awareness' of 'a threat of conversion'.[103]

We might connect the fears of Hindu female conversion, as articulated at the conference, to Hindutva demographic propaganda promoting the notion of the Hindu majority under threat by Muslim fertility. In India, birth rate figures are often propagated to instil a fear of the Other and perpetuate the image of lascivious Muslim men.[104] VHP propaganda from 1990 claimed that whilst Hindus adhere to the government's family planning slogan of *'ham do, hamare do'* ('we two, our two'), polygamous Muslims boast, *'ham panch, hamare pachis'* ('we five, our twenty-five').[105] The ultimate fear for the 'Saffron Demographers' is that the proportion of 'Indian religionists' (Hindus, Sikhs, and Jains), will fall below 50% before the end of the twenty-first century.[106] Fears of miscegenation and majority community 'extinction' are not, of course, unique to the Hindutva variety of ethnic nationalism. In Europe and North America the 'Great Replacement' theory, spread by various right-wing, white conspiracists (notably Renaud Camus), has gained considerable traction in recent years, and even become somewhat mainstream through being expressed in varying degrees of bluntness by right-wing political office-holders.[107]

Similar demographic anxieties are articulated in the pamphlet *India Heading Towards an Islamic State: A Warning!*, in which K.V. Paliwal forewarns, 'Another strategic policy to Islamise India is through the explosion of Muslim population by all possible means as conversion of Hindus, abduction of Hindu girls and "*Love Jihad*" etc.'.[108] The concept of 'love jihad'—ostensibly Muslims targeting Hindu girls for conversion by 'feigning' love, but in practice often used to refer to any romantic relationship between a Muslim boy/man and a Hindu girl/woman—has been a common and recurring cause for various Hindu nationalist groups, including the VHP, which in 2009 set up a 'Help Line' to deal with the 'problem'.[109] Since 2014, 'love jihad' has become an increasingly central mobilising issue for Hindutva supporters—it is often a topic of dangerous (digital) misinformation, and through vigilante militants it is the pretext for harassment and violence against young Muslim men (and often Hindu women too). Under the BJP, 'love jihad' has also crept into policy, seen through official inquiries into interfaith marriages, state-sanctioned 'anti-Romeo' squads, and even newly devised anti-conversion laws.

We can clearly identify the love jihad trope in Kallidai's warning to the Hindu Security Conference. The preoccupation with demographic issues, and the notion of Hindus as 'under siege', is central to the Hindu nationalist movement in India. But in the diaspora this discourse has a more potent resonance, where the sense of being outnumbered and threatened, both by Muslims and by the wider population, arguably is felt more acutely. Indeed, the feeling of being 'a community that is under siege' was mentioned explicitly in the wake of the 2022 Leicester communal unrest, in a statement about 'hatred towards the Hindu community' organised by the recently launched Hindutva campaign group, Insight UK.[110] Insight UK, which describes itself as 'an organisation that aims to address the concerns of the British Hindu and British Indian communities', has close Sangh Parivar links and, alongside various campaigns and events, recently produced a report on 'Hinduism in Religious Education in UK Schools' (with support from HFB, HSS, HCUK, NCHT, and VHP) that was circulated to local government Standing Advisory Councils on Religious Education.[111] The open letter to Prime Minister Liz Truss, apparently signed by 181 Hindu organisations, claimed that 'a small, but highly organised band of radical Islamists took full advantage of the community tensions that existed between this marginalised Hindu community and their Muslim neighbours, which had previously lived in peace'.[112]

The M.F. Husain Asia House affair[113]

A year before the Hindu Security Conference, another episode saw the Hindu Forum engaged in a campaign associated with the playbook of Hindutva, but in a different and more public setting. In May 2006, they vigorously mobilised against an exhibition of paintings by the celebrated Indian modernist Maqbool Fida Husain (1915–2011). The exhibition was due to open in Asia House, an independent cultural organisation and gallery in central London. Opposition to it culminated in an act of iconoclasm described in the *Daily Telegraph* as 'the first act of Hindu extremism in Britain'.[114]

The expression of outrage at the art of M.F. Husain in Britain was consonant with an important strand of Hindutva mobilisation in India, but in the diasporic context it had a distinctive meaning. The role of outrage, offence, and performativity in the modus operandi of the Hindu Forum of Britain, and in ethnic identity formation and the public representation of religious groups in the UK more broadly, requires a reconceptualisation of diasporic Hindu and Hindutva identity. While still connected to India on a number of levels, Hindu nationalism in Britain has spread beyond the institutional and ideological boundaries of the Sangh Parivar in a new way. These distinctive inflections of transnational Hindutva might be termed 'neo-Hindutva'. The M.F. Husain protests, and subsequent activities of the Hindu Forum, indicate that expressions of Hindutva have become mainstream and 'normal' in the UK. Whilst elements of this discourse are distinctly domestic, its transnational context links it intrinsically, discursively, and practically to India.

From the mid-1990s to his death in 2011, the work of M.F. Husain, and indeed the artist himself, were targets of Hindutva militancy in India. Even posthumously, his exhibitions have been picketed and vandalised. The disputed works—just a tiny fraction of his prolific oeuvre—represent female Hindu goddesses, sometimes in the nude, painted in the artist's stylised, Cubist-influenced manner. Mobilisations started abruptly in 1996 after an article about Husain, titled '*Yeh Chitrakar hai ya Kasai?*' ('Is this an artist or a butcher?'), was published in a Hindi magazine.[115] Although most of the disputed artworks were created in the 1970s and 1980s, it was only years later that they became a flashpoint around which Hindutva activists rallied.

The fact that Husain was a Muslim was central to the campaigns. When his Mumbai home was ransacked in 1998, Bal Thackeray, leader of the Shiv Sena, justified it in stridently communal terms: 'If Husain can step into Hindustan, what is wrong if we enter his house?'[116] As the issue became a cause célèbre in Indian politics, some secularists rallied round the artist. In 2004, Tapati Guha-Takurta wrote, 'the anti-Husain campaign provides a vivid instance of the kind of terror, censorship, and punitive action that sustains the cultural politics of the Hindu right, sparing neither average citizens nor their celebrity counterparts'.[117]

Ranged against them were activists of the largest Hindu nationalist groups, including the VHP, BJP, RSS, Shiv Sena, and Bajrang Dal (Army of Hanuman). However, there were also several fringe Hindutva organisations, such as the Hindu Janajagruti Samiti (HJS—Society for Hindu Awakening)—a driving force behind Husain's persecution. HJS operates at the side-lines of the Sangh Parivar and is primarily engaged in protests and expressions of outrage at perceived defamation. It is based in Maharashtra but also commands a strong online presence, giving it global reach and perspective.[118]

Anti-Husain activists are fixated on eroticised readings of Husain's works of nude goddesses; paintings that have been interpreted very differently by art historians, critics, and the artist himself.[119] A frequent line of attack, perpetuated by HJS, has been to highlight Husain's 'hypocrisy' and 'hatred for Hindus' by painting Hindu deities in the nude, yet not treating his Muslim subjects in the same way. In many ways, this rhetoric epitomises the communal hatred for Husain, a highly successful, secular

Muslim, lauded by a liberal, cosmopolitan elite. HJS interpret his depictions of female goddesses as a disrespectful, insolent sullying of Hindu feminine purity and the Hindu religion itself, thus creating the basis for an aggressive, performative articulation of protective, hyper-masculine pride.

Husain's most controversial painting was an anthropomorphic depiction of the subcontinent as an unclothed, blood-red female. The work, known as *Bharat Mata* (Mother India), although this title was not given by the artist, was created in response to violence and communal tension in India. It is perhaps a rejoinder to Hindu nationalist *Bharat Mata* iconography (see Chapter 4), but in Husain's version Mother India is prostrated in anguish.

Husain's opponents deployed the law against him systematically, accusing him of obscenity and 'wounding religious feelings'. HJS boasted of having co-ordinated more than a thousand formal police complaints. Cases were filed against him under the Indian Penal Code's section 153A, 'promoting enmity between different groups on grounds of religion and doing acts prejudicial to maintenance of harmony', and section 295A, 'deliberate and malicious acts intended to outrage religious feelings of any class by insulting its religion or religious beliefs'. Justice Sanjay Kishan Kaul of the Delhi High Court, who dismissed one of these cases, stressed that, 'in a free and democratic society, tolerance is vital... It is most unfortunate that India's new "puritanism" is being carried out in the name of cultural purity and a host of ignorant people are vandalizing art and pushing us towards a pre-renaissance era'.[120] In 2008, the Supreme Court dismissed five more cases against Husain, although this did not end his legal struggles, which he once estimated comprised 3,000 separate cases.[121]

With hundreds of cases simultaneously filed in several courts for 'hurting the religious sentiments, displaying obscenity in public places, defaming *Bharat Mata*, and conspiring to cause communal unrest and disunity in the country', Husain offered a pragmatic apology.[122] However, amid the turmoil that the new painting produced, he was forced out of India, spending the last years of his life between London and the Gulf. Hindutva extremists celebrated his exile and eventual acceptance of Qatari nationality as a 'win for Hindutva forces'.[123] Yet a great number of secular Indians (many Hindus among them) bemoaned his forced emigration as symbolising the failure of India's postcolonial, plural cosmopolitanism. M.F. Husain died in London in 2011 at the age of ninety-five and was buried at the Brookwood Cemetery, Surrey.

In opposing the 2006 exhibition *M.F. Husain: Early Masterpieces 1950–70s*, the Hindu Forum asserted its credentials as representative of British Hindus. It argued that the Asia House exhibition 'is already causing considerable offence to many of the UK's 700,000 based [sic] Hindus'. The Forum also urged 'Hindus in Britain to join the protest organised by Hindu Human Rights'—an enigmatic UK-based group.[124] In contrast to the anti-Husain crusade in India, which was a cause célèbre only really for advocates of Hindutva, the campaign made an appeal to all Hindus in Britain. The National Hindu Students Forum also supported the campaign against the London show, alluding to the group's frequently obfuscated Sangh connections.[125] Performances of outrage were planned outside Asia House, directly comparable to protests held across India. However, even more dramatically, on the eve of the demonstrations, an unidentified male entered the gallery and defaced two paintings. The 'youth' sprayed two goddess portraits with saffron paint. Asia House's lack of security was exposed, the insurer withdrew cover for the exhibition, and the owner of the works swiftly cancelled the show for fear of further reprisals.[126] The Hindu Forum of Britain and Hindu Human Rights (HHR) both disassociated themselves from the vandalism, and the perpetrator was never apprehended. The exhibition was abandoned, with Asia House stating 'security concerns' and reports of anonymous threats.

The politics of the campaign was also relevant. One source of anger was that the exhibition was opened by Indian High Commissioner Kamalesh Sharma. This, Ramesh Kallidai told the *Times of India*, reflected 'India's double standards in the treatment of Hindus and other religions'.[127] Arguably, it also highlighted the inextricability of the campaign from homeland politics. Even the Japanese company Hitachi came under fire as a sponsor of the exhibition, with HHR's press release bemoaning their complicity in the 'abuse [of] Hindus and Hinduism'.[128] Although aspects of this protest were distinctive to the British context, and the outraged protagonists were UK-based, the rhetoric and tactics of the HFB and HHR's campaign resembled aspects of Hindutva cultural policing in India. It is important, therefore, to tease out the overlaps from the new features of the British campaign. In doing so, we can elucidate this emergent form of 'neo-Hindutva'.

Hindu Human Rights was founded in London in 2000, 'to highlight cases of persecution and defamation of Hindus and Hinduism around the globe', and is run by SOAS graduate Ranbir Singh.[129] HHR has a primarily web- and protest-based presence, and a diaspora-oriented, assertive Hindutva tone. Online content skips between neo-Vedanta, Hindutva ideology and Hindu (nationalist) politics. Lengthy articles cover topics such as 'Are you an apologetic Hindu?', and 'Caste politics in UK and India'.

HHR protests are replete with Sangh imagery, from the saffron flag and *trishul* (trident), to muscular images of Ram. HHR has been particularly active in cases of image-based 'blasphemy'. In one demonstration it picketed the French embassy in London over French designer Minelli's use of Hindu iconography on a line of shoes in 2005. A photograph shows a diverse group of agitators, one holding a banner bearing the slogan 'Victory to the Prince of Ayodhya', another 'Victory to Lord Ram'. The HFB was also involved in this mobilisation.

Despite being UK-based, the organisation is best understood as quasi-transnational. Its website traffic and social media engagement comes from India as well as other parts of the world, including North America, Australia, and Europe. Its Facebook presence is substantial, with over 132,000 followers from around the world at the time of writing. Its transnational reach was in evidence when, in 2005, the issue of the blasphemous footwear was raised in the Lok Sabha, India's lower house.[130]

Although one can identify sporadic support for the Sangh, it is important to note HHR's self-defined position as an 'alternative to the traditional activism of the RSS and the rest of the Sangh Parivar family'.[131] This is seen in HHR's close relationship with Koenraad Elst, the prominent Belgian Hindutva writer, who has authored many articles for HHR's website, and is often critical of the Sangh.

HHR (and to a certain extent the Hindu Janajagruti Samiti) is an emergent form of 'hard' neo-Hindutva that possesses limited and nebulous formal allegiance to the Sangh, yet are fervent, dynamic, innovative, and often militant in their commitment to more universalist perspectives of Hindutva. Given the Forum's ostensibly mainstream, 'representative' credentials, its alliance with HHR, which has an unequivocally hard-line Hindutva approach, might seem unusual. Both, however, are engaged in similar discourses of outrage, defamation, and 'disciplining' the use of Hindu imagery. In this sense, we might see the Forum as embodying a different, *but related*, form of 'soft' neo-Hindutva, which tends to avoid any public association with Hindu nationalism, but shares ideological overlaps.

The M.F. Husain campaign precipitated a small but anxious backlash. This jeopardised the Forum's claims to represent all British Hindus and challenged their self-projection as the authoritative voice of Hindus in Britain. Several decried the HFB's alliance with HHR. AWAAZ remonstrated that HHR 'are not democratically-elected representatives of Hindu populations or opinion in the UK and represent little beyond their limited and chauvinistic political agendas'.[132] Others expressed consternation that the organisation was quoted by the media as being a legitimate 'voice' of the Hindu community.[133] Labour peer Lord Meghnad Desai condemned the 'outrageous attack on artistic freedom', and wrote to the *Guardian* expressing dismay at the British media's lack of coverage of the attack: 'Would the media have ignored such an event had the protesters been Muslims and not Hindus?'[134]

The extent to which the public, or even the government, possess an understanding of the political ramifications and nuances of conservative Hindu mobilisation (particularly when located beyond the Sangh) remains moot. Arguably, the successful promulgation of Hindus as a 'model minority', which the Forum has consistently projected, has helped to obscure these nuances. Also relevant is the overwhelming focus on Islamic fundamentalism in Britain, with other religions rarely entering the lexicon of religious extremism (for instance in the government's Prevent Strategy).

The M.F. Husain controversy and other cases of Hindu 'defamation' can be tied, somewhat ironically, into the broader development of 'minority religious outrage' that first exploded with the Rushdie Affair, but has become increasingly significant for many groups in the post-9/11, post-7/7, multicultural landscape of Britain. By campaigning against perceived defamation, the Forum has claimed legitimacy and representative credentials in the 'expression and creation' of a Hindu community.[135] This process therefore is partly linked to government funding and other opportunities given to such organisations, which some have suggested has 'sparked competition', incentivising groups to 'build controversies where they can thrust themselves into the media limelight as representatives of a community under attack'.[136] The language and strategy of such claims are linked to the impact of not just Muslim politicisation, but also Jewish communities, in particular through the vocabulary of defamation and blasphemy.

Defamation and Hindu–Jewish connections

This dynamic is especially pronounced in the US, where groups like American Hindus Against Defamation (AHAD) represent what Sangay Mishra refers to as the Indian American 'fascination with the Jewish lobby'.[137] AHAD was formed in 1997 by members of VHP America. Vowing to defend Hinduism against defamation, commercialisation, and misuse, they explicitly copied the tactics and language of Jewish groups (specifically the Anti-Defamation League).[138] They have campaigned on numerous issues of cultural appropriation, ranging from an 'Om'-branded perfume to a caricature of Ganesh in a *Simpsons* cartoon.[139] Wider advocacy efforts have similar inspiration: the US India Political Action Committee, for instance, founded in 2002, models itself on the influential pro-Israel lobbyists, the American Israel Public Affairs Committee (AIPAC).[140] This was preceded by the Indian American Centre for Political Action, formed in 1993 and partly spearheaded by Democratic US Representative Gary Ackerman, who asserted at a fundraiser that 'strong India-Israel relations is very critical to ensuring peace and stability in a part of the world that is characterized by instability, fundamentalist religious bigotry, hatred toward the West and its values and murder and mayhem spawned by acts of cross-border terrorism'.[141]

There are various other even more concrete connections. The Federation of Hindu Associations and the Hindu American Foundation (the Washington DC-based organisation, linked by many to the Sangh, that played a leading role in the California textbook controversy—see Chapter 4), both have close ties with Jewish groups, particularly the American Jewish Committee.[142] Azad Essa, whose book *Hostile Homelands* sheds light on the multi-layered, ethno-nationalist alliance between Israel and India, claims that 'since the abrogation of Article 370 and the CAA [Citizenship Amendment Act], Zionist and Islamophobic groups in the U.S. have been operating in concert with each other to vilify critics of Hindutva'.[143] Indeed the aggressive strategies that Hindutva activists have used 'to stifle critics of Hindu supremacy'— including, but not limited to, the intimidation of academics, claims of victimhood, invocation of progressive values, vilification of critics, and use of soft power—follow 'the same methodology adopted by Zionist organisations in the US'.[144]

In Britain as well, many Hindu organisations imitate Jewish groups in both rhetoric and ambition, and also have direct links. The Hindu Forum publicised their 'warm working relationship with the Jewish community through the Board of Deputies... and the... Community Security Trust'.[145] It described 'close relationships on university campuses', between the National Hindu Students Forum and the Union of Jewish Students, 'where students from both communities have faced similar threats from religious fundamentalists'.

This allusion to 'religious fundamentalists' clearly invokes a 'clash of civilisations' narrative. Certain diasporic Hindu groups have felt drawn to this idea, perceiving an existential threat in their countries of residence, whilst also feeling deeply invested in an alleged threat posed to Hindus in India. This can be compared to the way in which many Jews around the world feel they have a stake in the politics of Israel. These porous and intersecting forms of ethnic politics are even manifested in Hindu and Jewish supporters and divisions of far-right, anti-Muslim political movements, including the English Defence League. Eviane Cheng Leidig's research has also argued a connection between diasporic Hindu nationalists, anti-Muslim sentiment, and online support for Brexit.[146]

Right-wing Islamophobes in the US, too, have found support amongst Hindu nationalists. Donald Trump's 2016 election campaign was helped by various factions: in New Delhi, the attention-seeking Hindu Sena held a number of public *pujas* for Trump, extolling him as the 'saviour of humanity',[147] while in New Jersey the Republican Hindu Coalition (a group led by Chicago-based Modi supporter Shalabh Kumar), held a pro-Trump rally titled 'Humanity United Against Terror' in the lead-up to the 2016 election. As well as speeches—in which Trump proclaimed, 'I'm a big fan of Hindu [*sic*] and I'm a big fan of India'—the *tamasha* also involved much singing and dancing. One routine was interrupted by performers dressed as pantomime terrorists, who were then defeated by men in Navy SEAL costumes. The vignette ended with a rendition of 'The Star-Spangled Banner', followed by a dance to Bruce Springsteen's 'Born in the USA'.

In America, there have even been surprising instances of *quid pro quo* collaborations between radical Hindu groups and extremist Zionist organisations. In 2001, HinduUnity.org—the 'official site' of the Bajrang Dal, which was run from the United States by Rohit Vyasmaan, leader of the Bajrang Dal's US branch—was shut down by its US host server following complaints about hate speech towards Muslims and its blacklist of 'enemies' of Hinduism. It was subsequently 'rescued' by Zionist extremist Rabbi Meir Kahane's group. This led to reciprocal support, with Hindus marching in the annual 'Salute to Israel' parade in New York City in 2001, and one month later Jews joined a protest outside the United Nations against the treatment of Hindus in Afghanistan.[148] Vyasmaan once explicitly articulated their common interests: 'We are fighting the same war… Whether you call them Palestinians, Afghans or Pakistanis, the root of the problem for Hindus and Jews is Islam.'[149] Certain Indians abroad, especially those with a proclivity towards Hindutva, have a great admiration for the Jewish diaspora: its strong maintenance of cultural and community identity, high status as a successful 'model minority', and enduring and influential role in the life of the homeland are seen as features to be emulated.

Jewish and Hindu groups and leaders have also met regularly, sometimes in Israel and sometimes in India. Those representing Zionist and Hindutva organisations have been prominent in the bilateral exchanges.[150] There has also been a transnational, diasporic angle: Essa states that in the 'War on Terror' era 'it became routine for AIPAC representatives to travel to New Delhi or to bring Indian delegations to Israel and D.C. for dialogue'.[151] Vijay Prashad connects this Hindutva-Zionist dynamic to burgeoning diplomacy and strategic ties between India and Israel, particularly under the first BJP-led government from 1999.[152] Since 2014, relations with Israel—which for much of India's independent history were at best lukewarm (and occasionally hostile)—have been transformed dramatically.

In 2017, Modi became the first Indian Prime Minister to visit Israel, and he has regularly spoken of his friendship with Benjamin Netanyahu. This desire to seek alliances with Jewish, in particular Zionist, factions might be viewed through a strategic lens, with a basis in geopolitical and economic (or simply corporate) interests. But it is also underpinned by ideology, arguably drawing upon the ideas behind Savarkar's proclamation that the 'Enemy of our enemy is our best friend', coupled with his call to 'Militarise Hindudom... So long as the whole world is aggressive, we must be aggressive'.[153] A gendered dimension to the relationship between Hindutva and Zionist movements has been elucidated by Akanksha Mehta in her work on 'right-wing sisterhood'.[154] But more than just solidarity, it is noteworthy that under Modi, India appears to be following the route of Israel towards becoming an 'ethnic democracy', with certain democratic features existing alongside two-tiered citizenship, in which the majority enjoy more rights than minorities.[155] Needless to say, there is a considerable irony to the Hindutva/Jewish entente given Golwalkar's admiration of the Nazi treatment of Jews, which he infamously referred to as 'race pride at its highest'.[156] This is conveniently ignored, much like Israel's other relationships with right-wing movements that accommodate varying levels of anti-Semitism.

Hindu-Jewish collaboration in the diaspora is not new; Raj mentions the NHSF working with the Union of Jewish Students to ban Hizb ut-Tahrir from SOAS in the mid-1990s.[157] At the Hindu Security Conference in 2007, 'a representative of the Union of Jewish Students (UJS) spoke about how Jewish and Hindu students had much in common, because India faced the same problem in Kashmir as Israel did in Palestine'.[158] Prashad has recently written about these perspectives in the American setting, which closely ties into the aforementioned model minority trope, reflecting on 'how the Hindus became Jews'.[159] The Hindu Forum of Britain certainly can be viewed from this perspective. On the eve of the umbrella group's creation, C.B. Patel, Chairman of the Patrons Council of the HFB, proclaimed the need to learn 'how to defend ourselves, how to learn from the Jewish community, how to have national co-ordination'.[160]

Multiculturalism, outrage, and 'struggles for recognition'

The British multicultural environment has provided a space for, and even encouraged, emergent forms of political representation and ethnic identity formation. These are often articulated in a shrill timbre of outrage and offence. In the case of the representation of 'the Hindu community', this often draws on Hindutva rhetoric familiar from India. But it is also vernacular, adapting in tone to both the British milieu and to multiculturalism. Policies intended to encourage dialogue and integration have been counterproductive. Responding to this has proved challenging for authorities.

Developing Charles Taylor and Nancy Fraser's seminal contributions to understanding new forms of 'struggles for recognition', Prema Kurien identifies that 'an ironic and unintended consequence of multiculturalist policies is that they could promote the development of religio-ethnic nationalism'.[161] Often this 'unintended consequence' goes unnoticed by a general public and government unversed in non-Western political and cultural movements, and unaware of contentious essentialisms. This need for 'ethnic spokespersons' has 'led to the legitimization of many extremist Hindutva activists': Narain Kataria, an RSS worker and leader of the militant Hindu Unity group, for instance, was awarded a 'Declaration of Honor' from the President of the Borough of Queens, New York, in 2003.[162] This is just one of numerous such examples.

It is especially appropriate to understand public expressions of neo-Hindutva, constituting dynamic forms of political representation and ethnic identity formation, through the lens of 'struggles for recognition'. A nexus of assertive Hindutva and multiculturalist rhetoric has helped forge an institutionalised diasporic Hindu identity. This identity is driven by a 'politically "voicy" Hindu-*tva* concerned with regulating and disciplining public representations of Hinduism'.[163] Policing the representation of Hinduism, amidst vocalised feelings of victimhood and a 'siege mentality'—crucial tropes for Hindutva *within* India—has particular resonance *outside* of India for marginalised, minority communities.[164] This contributes towards highly emotive forms of rhetoric and action, where 'instigating, staging and managing this "righteous anger" is a crucial dimension in mobilising "outraged communities"'.[165]

Hindu public outrage and offence has a discursive relationship with claims of hurt from a variety of other communities. In the case of the Hindu Forum, it was evident when Ramesh Kallidai told the *Times of India* that, 'When it came to Prophet's cartoons, Prime Minister Manmohan Singh personally condemned them. India was one of the first to ban Rushdie's book, *The Satanic Verses*. Why should artistic freedom only be enjoyed by those who hurt and insult Hindus?'[166] Public displays of hurt can be linked to fundamentalism, orthodoxy, authoritarianism, and essentialist notions of religion, with 'leaders in all religions… vying for control over the representation of their communities'.[167] Whilst Muslim protagonists have often been the focus of discussion in recent decades, we must not limit this narrative to any particular group, nor even just minorities. The violent response from Sikhs in Birmingham to Gurpreet Bhatti's play *Behtzi* in 2005 and the high-profile evangelical Christian campaigns and protests against *Jerry Springer: The Opera* in the same year indicated a wider trend in Britain.

The (re)emergence of the category of 'blasphemy' is increasingly noticeable and significant. Kallidai in his *Asian Voice* column wrote, in response to the Om symbol on a pair of sandals, 'yet another blasphemy—will it ever end?'[168] It is worth reflecting on the distinction between blasphemy and insult or offence. The use of blasphemy and defamation often implies a legal element. Ayatollah Khomeini issued Rushdie with a *fatwa* (an Islamic legal ruling). M.F. Husain was prosecuted under Section 153(A) of the Indian Penal Code, which criminalises 'Promoting enmity between different groups on grounds of religion'. Some years later, in 2014, Penguin India were filed with a lawsuit over Professor Wendy Doniger's academic study of Hinduism (discussed later in this chapter), charged under Section 295(A), which concerns insulting religion. This represents another dimension by which the performative and instrumental expressions of outrage are borrowed or influenced from other groups or religious traditions. It is worth considering here the wording of the Indian Penal Code (the origins of which are, of course, colonial and replete with Orientalist perspectives). Section 295(A), which Husain was also accused of transgressing, refers not to personal distress, but to 'outraging the religious feelings of any *class* of citizens of India'.[169] This enabled anti-Husain activists to construct a collective feeling of hurt, reifying a trans-subjective public.

During the Asia House campaign, the Hindu Forum, as the country's pre-eminent umbrella group, was able to exert its influence and voice to present an ostensibly monolithic Hindu community, which used both rhetoric and methods borrowed from other diaspora communities in Britain and abroad. Highlighting the contest for resources and recognition that the multiculturalist state might provide, one online comment from 2006 bemoaned 'rival fundamentalists egging each other on in a politics of competitive grievance'.[170] In India, calls to maim or kill Husain grimly paralleled other instances of protest, in particular those of the aforementioned Rushdie Affair and the Danish cartoon controversy (in which deliberately provocative images of the Prophet Muhammad were published in *Jyllands-Posten* in 2005, resulting in global outrage and violence). In 2006, Shiv Sena leader

Bhagwan Goel 'publicly declared that he would pay a half-million rupee reward for anyone who cut off one of Husain's arms', and the obscure but official-sounding Hindu Personal Law Board allegedly announced a 510 million rupee bounty for his murder.[171] Another discursive relationship with Muslim protest is seen in a strange letter from the Hindu Janajagruti Samiti to Christie's in New York, demanding the withdrawal of Husain paintings from a sale of Indian art, arguing, 'There has been news that infamous Denmark cartoonist is looking for someone to arrange auction of infamous cartoons. Your expression and love for artistic freedom can only be justified if you arrange this auction too.'[172]

The Asia House M.F. Husain incident suggests the increasingly global character of a variety of political struggles that on first inspection might seem parochial. Aided by online spaces—in particular blogs, messaging apps, and social media—Hindutva mobilisation has been able to transcend national borders and coalesce through the trope of outrage, with multi-directional, transnational influences. Outside India, this is perhaps most pronounced in the United States, with several protests against Husain organised by the HJS and an affiliated fringe Hindutva group, Indian-American Intellectuals Forum. Protesters have railed against auction houses selling his paintings, and in 2008 picketed Christie's, New York, before an auction featuring works by Husain. In 2011, an exhibition of Indian modern art was displayed in the San Jose Museum of Art to great indignation from a small minority of Hindus.[173] More recently, a curator at the Boston Museum of Fine Arts reported that they framed M.F. Husain works under glass because of the risk of vandalism.[174] In Britain, Conor Macklin, owner of London's Grosvenor Gallery, spoke of 'pretty gross' violent threats being sent to him, from both India and the UK, in relation to Husain, although the threats were never followed up. Major auction houses in Britain were circumspect just talking to me about their experiences. In 2014, the Victoria and Albert Museum's exhibition of Husain's final paintings was challenged by the Forum for Hindu Awakening (another organisation that we can best understand through the paradigm of neo-Hindutva). The strict bag checks and heightened security measures at the entrance of the exhibition indicated that, even after the artist's death, and outside India, displaying his works remains fraught with risk.

The transnationalism of diasporic struggles for recognition is not global in a unidirectional sense. In the Asia House affair, not only was Hindu nationalist rhetoric and strategy spread beyond India's borders, but the British incident was also widely reported in the homeland. This can be identified in the mainstream press as well as from the Sangh's own publications. The *Organiser* published HHR's press release and an article quoting Ramesh Kallidai, as well as a rambling editorial piece mentioning the London M.F. Husain outrage as a segue to a more general polemic on Christian insults to Hinduism and India.[175] At the other end of the political spectrum, *Tehelka* published an article looking back on the case the following year headlined 'Equal Opportunity Fundamentalism', highlighting the irony of an uncontested exhibition of sensual, nude Chola bronzes exhibiting concurrently at the Royal Academy, and referred to 'London's neo-hypersensitive Hindu community'.[176] Indeed the Hindutva of the Indian diaspora is a source of constant fascination, and often derision, among many people in India. In the recent case relating to the censoring of Wendy Doniger's scholarship, this diasporic influence on India became even more pronounced.

The anti-Husain campaign is an important example of how outrage can be deployed for specific gains. For the Forum, it presented an opportunity to 'speak for the community', to reify their representative credentials, and to articulate an assertive public image of Hindus. This instrumentalisation of outrage can helpfully be compared with India. Writing of the Ram Sethu campaigns (which the Hindu Forum also supported),[177] Jaffrelot has discussed Hindutva and 'the art of being outraged'; he considers the instrumentalisation of indignation, especially during electorally significant moments, and the way in which, 'any disrespect can be portrayed as blasphemy and lay itself to popular mobilizations—which may translate into votes'.[178] The discourse of victimisation, which is core to Hindutva, must be understood in psychological, as well as instrumental, terms. Of course, the material and psychological returns that can emanate from moments of outrage are inextricable. Demonstrations of outrage in themselves challenge notions of Hindu weakness. These concerns have preoccupied Hindu revivalists and Hindutva ideologues for over a century, from Dayananda Saraswati and Lokmanya Tilak to Savarkar and Golwalkar.

The significance of outrage in fomenting political consciousness can hardly be overestimated. As Daniel Cefaï noted, 'there is no collective action without perceiving, communicating, dramatizing and legitimizing an experience of indignation'.[179] The mobilisation of outrage can also be interpreted in terms of Durkheimian 'collective effervescence', in which a community coalesces and establishes group unity in a stimulated, emotionally charged moment.[180] However, as seen throughout Hindu nationalist campaigns, what is framed as a 'spontaneous' outpouring of emotion and anger is in fact carefully orchestrated. The muddle of spontaneity/choreography explains the anachronism of Husain's paintings only being objected to many years after their creation (also contingent on the chronology of Hindutva's late twentieth-century resurgence). We can further understand the arbitrary chronology of expressions of outrage by differentiating between 'pre-emptive' and 'reactive' anti-defamation discourses.[181] Sometimes claims of hurt are even voiced before the offensive material has been encountered. Perhaps the source of the affront is not even important. Social media have played a particular role in incubating collective outrage in ways that are inherently borderless: Richard Seymour argues, 'It no longer matters, beyond a certain point, whether the individual participants are "really" outraged. The accusation is outraged on their behalf.'[182]

The Forum's participation in anti-Husain activism represents an instrumentalisation of 'offence', in which latent demands for recognition are writ large behind the more specific demands to suppress the offending works of art. Naturally, the point of linking campaigns that revolve around offence to new forms of Hindutva is not to devalue them. Hindu culture is, of course, subject to egregious discrimination and insensitivity. It is hard to disagree with US Hindu nationalist leader Ved P. Nanda when he argues, 'If devout Hindus feel hurt and take affront at what they consider to be misrepresentation of symbols of their devotion, these are voices of dissent and should not be dismissed as voices of fanaticism.'[183] However, it is important to understand the context and inspiration for many of these campaigns, which, rather than being spontaneous expressions of upset, are in fact echoes of Hindutva rhetoric that cultivate and instrumentalise outrage and deploy language of cultural appropriation with various layers of subtext and in an inherently political way.

The Asia House controversy was a critical moment in the recent history of diasporic Hindutva. It was a British expression of a key trope of Hindutva mobilisation by a mainstream representative Hindu umbrella group. Some observers may have seen this as anomalous, while others may not have understood the subtext of the Forum's position, but sympathy with Hindutva and alignment with Hindu nationalist organisations was in fact consistent with much of the organisation's positioning throughout its existence. Although it would be disingenuous to pigeonhole it as merely a thinly disguised unit of the Hindu nationalist movement, as Zavos has warned (and there are indeed instances of the Forum taking moderate or even progressive positions on various issues), there also exists a clear link to both the ideology and the organisations of the RSS family.

The M.F. Husain campaign, the 'othering' of Muslims at the Hindu Security Conference, and the sympathy with the EDL are not isolated moments of consonance with Hindu nationalism. The Forum was also involved in cow-protection mobilisations, aligning themselves with the VHP-UK and HSS, and also campaigned to distance themselves from Muslims by rejecting the 'Asian' marker.[184] Moreover, in 2014, the Forum took a number of public positions that unequivocally reflected a stance consistent with right-wing Hindu conservatism: it denounced Wendy Doniger's book *The Hindus*, it strongly resisted efforts to outlaw caste discrimination, and it became increasingly involved in a number of overtly political issues.

Wendy Doniger and the global assault on academic freedom

A long-running campaign against Doniger took a dramatic turn in February 2014, when Penguin, the Indian publishers of *The Hindus*, agreed to withdraw and pulp the book following legal action. Doniger is an eminent American Indologist and Sanskritist, based at the University of Chicago, who has published extensively on Hindu culture and mythology since the 1960s. Since the very beginning of the twenty-first century she has been at the centre of a sustained barrage of attacks on scholars who work on India, and especially on topics relating to Hindu culture, mythology, and history. The campaign against Doniger fits into a long trajectory of attacks against academics and academic freedom that from the mid-2010s appeared to become more widespread, bellicose, and systematic than ever before.

In the case of Doniger, one striking feature was that the crusade was chiefly led from outside India. A lead role was taken by Rajiv Malhotra—an influential American former corporate executive and self-styled public intellectual, who describes himself on his website as 'a best-selling author and pioneer in the research on civilizations and their engagement with technology and media from a historical, social sciences and mind sciences perspective'.[185] Through his 'Infinity Foundation', a dozen published books, and countless public appearances, Malhotra has spent more than two decades seeking to challenge what he considers to be not just Eurocentric misrepresentation, but concerted efforts—neo-colonial and missionary in spirit—to 'undermine Indian culture' or even 'break India' (for instance, through cultivating caste and regional divisions).[186] This has also included attacking a host of scholars of Hinduism, notably Sheldon Pollock, Paul Courtright, Jeffrey Kripal, and Doniger (but also many Indian academics), for their 'insulting' interpretations of Hindu texts and practices, in particular targeting the perceived 'eroticisation of Hinduism'.[187] He has a substantial, global online following and videos of his lectures and vlogs garner not just millions of views, but also transnational exchanges (both in terms of his international interlocutors, but also in comments beneath his videos and social media posts), which constitute significant, multidirectional layers of influence.

Malhotra's standing both globally and in India, and the influence of his narrative on 'Hinduphobia' in the academy and beyond, have risen considerably in the post-2014 period of Hindutva ascendance. In 2018, he was appointed as an honorary visiting professor at New Delhi's Jawaharlal Nehru University—a Congress-initiated bastion of leftist scholarship, and one of the country's leading academic institutions, which has long been an ideological battleground for the Hindu right. The same year, in Britain, he also gave a lecture on 'India and post-Brexit Britain' at the Houses of Parliament at an event organised by the Hindu Forum of Britain and hosted by Bob Blackman MP.

The Doniger ruling in India in 2014 was the result of a lawsuit filed by Dinanath Batra, Sangh-loyalist and convenor of Hindutva group Shiksha Bachao Andolan Samiti. It stated: 'YOU NOTICEE has hurt the religious feelings of millions of Hindus by declaring that Ramayana is a fiction'.[188] Batra has a long track record of agitating against 'Hinduphobic' and 'anti-national' texts, especially those on school curricula. But interestingly, it appears that in his Doniger struggle, Batra was heavily influenced by American Hindutva activists. Basant Tariyal—a VHP America office bearer from Atlanta and overseas leader of the Parivar's vast 'rural education' organisation, Ekal Vidyalaya—was one of several key diasporic players to inform, direct, and fund Batra's campaign.[189] In an interview, Batra also stated that the American wing of the Hindu Janajagruti Samiti encouraged him 'to campaign to stop the book in India'.[190] Also noteworthy in the interwoven, transnational history of 'outrage' was the Sangh's backseat role. Prakash Sharma, spokesperson of the VHP, said that 'in the case of Wendy Doniger, the VHP is following as Batraji leads. Anybody who insults our tradition and culture will not be tolerated.'[191]

The Hindu Forum of Britain then weighed in, supporting Batra's stance. Madhava Turumella, HFB Vice President, declared,

> In the name of alternate thinking people like Wendy cast their evil and idiotic theories. Your freedom of speech should NOT

be our Insult. We are becoming forced victims for this so called intellectuals who take the meaning of free speech to an absurd level.[192]

Turumella also said in an interview on CNN: 'We Hindus have been extremely liberal. As a result, we Hindus have been taken for a task... We have tolerated enough.'[193] This notion of Hindus as submissive and open to exploitation underpinned Hindutva's creation, the Sangh Parivar's rise from the late 1980s, and also is reflected clearly in certain HFB campaigns.

During and after the 2014 Indian General Election, the Forum's proximity to the politics of Hindu nationalism became clearer than ever. Its response to advocacy and the BJP's detractors was particularly striking. In the wake of the British government's 'lifting' of Modi's *de facto* European travel ban, Barry Gardiner—long-time Modi supporter, Chairman of Labour Friends of India, and MP for Brent North—invited the divisive then-Gujarat Chief Minister to visit Britain. But many of Gardiner's colleagues took a very different line: John McDonnell MP hosted a meeting at Parliament in February 2014 in which anti-Hindutva activists called on the British government not to engage with Modi and to push for justice for the 2002 Gujarat violence (in which three British citizens were killed). The Hindu Forum loudly denounced this meeting and, with other Hindu organisations, issued a press release branding the Modi critics 'extremists who abused the privilege and desecrated the sentiments of a peaceful and harmonious British Hindu community'.[194] At the time, this was perhaps the furthest the Forum had gone in 'normalising' Hindutva, in the sense that those who deigned to *criticise* the Sangh Parivar were ostracised and branded fanatics. As in the Asia House incident, these recent examples indicate that the Forum represents a form of neo-Hindutva, adapted to the environment of British multiculturalism.

Caste legislation and the politics of Hindu representation

The Hindu Forum and other representative organisations have also been active in promulgating a Hindutva-infused discourse in

British politics. Perhaps most notably, since the mid-2000s a range of groups have clashed over the issue of caste legislation. During the 2005–10 Labour government, Dalit organisations and various allies made inroads towards the inclusion of caste as an aspect of the 'protected characteristic' of race in the Equality Act 2010. This was based upon a considerable body of evidence that showed the entrenchment of caste discrimination in Britain (although it manifests in significantly different, less violent, ways than in India).[195] It would, in effect, have made it illegal for employers and providers of public services to discriminate against people on the basis of their caste, much in the same way that victimising people for their religion, ethnicity, sexuality, gender, age, or disability is also unlawful. In 2013, Parliament passed an amendment to the Equality Act 2010, which imposed a duty to introduce specific protection against caste discrimination. Yet, under successive Conservative-led governments, these changes were never fully implemented and, following a divisive (and in many ways flawed) public consultation launched in 2017, the plan to outlaw caste discrimination was finally shelved in 2018.

This decision was reached after vociferous and co-ordinated resistance from a number of Hindu organisations. Among the opponents were familiar Sangh-related factions, various Hindu and caste associations, and a number of umbrella groups. Actors in India took a keen interest and played indirect roles. The Forum's part in opposing caste legislation can be traced back to its inception: their 2008 *Caste in the UK* report even quoted the Hindutva ideologue Ram Swarup, praising the system that 'combined security with freedom... [and] provided social space as well as closer identity'.[196] The Forum often joined forces with explicitly Hindutva groups in lobbying against the new laws: in 2011 it attended a lobby group meeting at the House of Commons, and presented its case against caste legislation to Lynne Featherstone MP (the Parliamentary Under-Secretary for Equalities), alongside the NHSF, VHP, HSS, and others.[197]

Anti-legislation advocacy has vacillated between various arguments: one claim is that there is insufficient, credible evidence for caste discrimination being a problem in Britain. Another central position is that legislation 'will introduce, reinscribe or entrench caste identities and boundaries and inter-group tensions amid claims that caste is meaningless, irrelevant, declining or non-existent'.[198] This notion is closely related to what might be viewed as a postcolonial turn in Hindutva discourse: in this instance, drawing on the idea that caste divisions were manipulated, or even fabricated, by Orientalist and divisive colonial forces.[199] Caste organisations and Hindu(tva) groups have also claimed that efforts to highlight and tackle caste discrimination are rooted in 'Hinduphobia', or could have the effect of generating or reinforcing racism. This has also fused with a more communal angle, in which the Christian beliefs of many Dalits and their allies who have mobilised in favour of caste legislation has been highlighted as evidence of a missionary conspiracy to convert Hindus or even 'break' India.[200] Others (sometimes even the same people, rather confusingly), posit that caste is a fundamentally benign institution, mirroring the contradictory nature of the related discourse in India. This position is partly related to anxieties that caste associations—a plethora of kinship institutions that cater to their communities in numerous ways and that have great salience for many diasporic Indians—might be threatened by legislation. (Although leading experts maintained that the proposed caste laws would 'not affect associational activities or religious rituals'.[201]) More broadly, opposition to legislation has often hinged on a 'flattening' of Hinduism's internal diversity in pursuit of a unified community—a position that is connected to a wider narrative within Hindu nationalism, as well as a core mission of umbrella organisations.

The debate on caste was a deeply political issue that generated considerable division, factionalism, and opportunism. This led to Labour (under which there was movement towards legislation) being increasingly framed as 'anti-Hindu', and the Conservatives (under which the new laws were stymied) painted as more amenable to the Hindu community.

One protagonist at the heart of this politicisation was the National Council of Hindu Temples UK (NCHT)—an organisation that has existed in Britain since 1978, but which became openly aligned to Hindutva rhetoric in the 2010s. Under the leadership of Satish Sharma, the NCHT took a strident position on caste legislation and a number of other politically charged issues. Their case against legislation focused particularly on the role played by clergy in the House of Lords, and others who supported the new laws, condemning their 'religious colonialism' as a 'hate crime' against 'Dharmic communities'.[202] The NCHT and HFB explicitly pitted Labour against the Conservatives in the caste debate, which coincided with the 2015 and 2017 elections, encouraging a shift from the overwhelming allegiance that South Asian voters have tended to show for Labour. In a letter to *Asian Voice* in May 2015, just two days before polling, HFB President Trupti Patel mentioned caste legislation and then urged Hindu voters: 'We must also be mindful that we do not unwittingly allow a political party to form a government that will be detrimental to our dharma... Don't vote blindly or because of family tradition.'[203]

In 2015, the NCHT organised a conference called 'Dharma Rising', held in the capacious hall of the Dhamecha Lohana Centre—a Gujarati caste association—in the West London suburb of Harrow. The line-up brought together a diverse range of Hindutva personalities, although interestingly only one— 'headliner' Subramanian Swamy, with whom the NCHT has a particularly close relationship—had a direct or explicit connection to a Sangh Parivar organisation. Rajiv Malhotra gave a rousing address via Skype, with other speeches from the LSE's Gautam Sen, the Belgian Hindutva ideologue Koenraad Elst, the HFB President Trupti Patel, and columnist and businessman Kapil Dudakia. Most speeches included pleas to resist the prospective caste legislation with an undertone related to the General Election, held just one month after the event.

The Harrow conference also saw the launch of 'The British Hindu Manifesto'—a ten-point list of key concerns, co-authored by HFB and NCHT, which led with the caste issue and encompassed concerns ranging from faith schools to the repatriation of Hindu artefacts. But at its core, the manifesto was fundamentally infused with a political slant, much of it closely connected to Hindu nationalism: a demand for the British government to not interfere with Kashmir, explicit and oblique references to Islamic extremism and 'grooming', and a condemnation of human rights violations and acts of terrorism with reference with Bangladesh and Pakistan. Going even further in the organisation's political advocacy, NCHT General Secretary Satish Sharma wrote an open letter just days before the May 2015 General Election imploring Hindus to vote Conservative. 'The Tories are the only party which will not make caste discrimination a punishable offence,' Sharma wrote, pitting Labour and the Liberal Democrats as pro-legislation parties to be opposed, and even branding Labour responsible for 'acts of religious persecution of British Hindus'.[204] This overt political endorsement appeared to contravene rules by which registered charities are obliged to abide, and the Charity Commission announced they would be investigating the NCHT. But their censure seemed to fall on deaf ears: just two years later, at the 2017 General Election, the NCHT again made explicit overtures for British Hindus to vote Conservative. The June issue of their publication, *Shubh Sandesh*, was an effusive advertorial for Theresa May, with numerous quotations and photographs of her visit to the Neasden Swaminarayan temple. The gushing panegyric also fiercely castigated her opponent, Jeremy Corbyn:

> Whether British Hindu voters vote for PM Theresa May who performed Abhishek [a method of worship] with Britain's Hindus and whose party has elevated Indian Origin Parliamentarians to cabinet and Ministerial positions, or whether they vote for Rt Hon Jeremy Corbyn who snubbed PM Modiji's Parliamentary address and whose grandees are determined to foist Caste labels upon British Hindus, it is critical that British Hindus do vote.[205]

Again, the Charity Commission registered its disapproval, reiterating the ordinance that 'charities must not encourage support for a particular political party or candidate', but ultimately the Commission appeared toothless, or unwilling, to actually penalise the NCHT.[206]

While it is impossible to quantify the influence of the caste issue on election results, or the impact of Hindu groups' political campaigning more broadly, there appears to have been an increase in support for the Conservative Party from Indian voters over the past decade. In 2010, just 30% of British Indians voted Conservative, but by 2017 this had risen to 40%.[207] Interestingly, according to one survey, Hindu voters' support for the Conservatives actually exceeded that for Labour in 2015: 49% compared to 41%.[208] This seems like a stark departure when considering that overall South Asian voting patterns are still skewed considerably towards Labour. However, polling data on ethnic minority voting patterns are notoriously inaccurate—with small sample sizes and large margins of error—and any shift to the Conservatives over the 2010s perhaps simply reflected the party's broader success with the electorate as a whole. It may also have little to do with the influence of Hindutva politics: 'The fact is that the economic status of many British Indians resembles a typical Tory voter: in terms of home ownership, household wealth and education, it makes sense that there's a movement of British Indian voters from the left to the right.'[209]

Efforts to draw ethnic minority voters away from Labour is not a new trend: the Anglo Asian Conservative Society was launched in 1976 and in the same year Margaret Thatcher even considered wearing a sari on television in an effort to appeal to immigrant voters.[210] At the other end of her tenure as Conservative Party leader she visited an HSS *shakha* in Finchley, garlanding a bust of RSS founder K.B. Hedgewar, and praising the 'the Hindu contribution to the world' and 'the Hindu family system'.[211] However, these sorts of gestures were fairly token when compared to the Margaret Thatcher who, notoriously, expressed sympathy with those fearful of Britain becoming 'swamped by people with a different culture'.[212] The following year, at the 1979 General Election—in which Thatcher's Tories won a forty-three seat majority and 43.9% of the popular vote (compared to Labour's 36.9%)—an exit poll suggested that 86% of the South Asian electorate had voted Labour.[213]

Evidence shows that a shift in support from Indian voters only gathered pace in the twenty-first century. There are various reasons why this change might have occurred: while Labour are traditionally considered more pro-immigrant and less racist than the Conservatives, boundaries became more blurred with Labour's efforts to appease anti-immigration rhetoric, and the conspicuous presence of senior British South Asians in the Conservative Party. A pro-immigration stance also appears to be a less important issue for many Indian voters, evidenced by support for Brexit. British Indians, it has been claimed, were 'between 1.6 and 2 times more likely to support Leave when compared to other minority groups' (although a sizeable majority of 59% are still said to have voted Remain).[214] For a growing number of British South Asians, the Conservatives—with their reputation as the party of family values, law and order, social conservatism, business, lower taxation, and entrepreneurship—are seen as more closely aligned with their core concerns.

Larger global political issues may also be at play; in recent years some Hindu campaigners have expressed indignation over Labour's stance on India. Jeremy Corbyn, Labour leader from 2015 to 2020, has a track record of criticising Modi. In 2002, he signed a parliamentary Early Day Motion (EDM) calling for an investigation into the failures of the state to protect Muslims during the Gujarat riots.[215] He was also a signatory on a 2013 EDM demanding 'to reinstitute the ban on Gujarat's Chief Minister, Narendra Modi, from entering the UK, given his role in the communal violence in 2002 that claimed the lives of hundreds if not thousands of Muslims'.[216] Corbyn has also attracted the ire of some for his long-standing advocacy for Dalit rights and campaigns against caste discrimination, partly in his capacity as a trustee and honorary chair of the Dalit Solidarity Network UK.

The strength of opposition to Corbyn from some Indians escalated considerably in 2019, in the wake of the Indian government's abrogation of Article 370, which effectively revoked Kashmir's long-held, constitutionally mandated political autonomy. Corbyn vocalised concern over human rights abuses in Kashmir, and the Labour Party conference passed an emergency motion calling for Kashmiri self-determination.[217] This was a major factor in campaigns against Corbyn from Hindus in Britain and beyond, with Labour accused of being 'anti-Indian', 'anti-Hindu', and even 'hijacked by... jihadi sympathisers'.[218] Trupti Patel and

Satish Sharma of the HFB and NCHT co-authored an excoriating open letter to Corbyn that referred to Labour as 'the de-facto mouthpiece for Pakistan', claimed the party was promoting a 'pro-terrorist narrative' and 'the vile prejudice of anti-Indian sentiment', and announced Hindu organisations were disinviting Labour politicians from their events, including the HFB's annual 'Diwali at Parliament'.[219]

Around the same time, the Overseas Friends of the BJP UK announced that they were actively campaigning for Tories in forty-eight marginal seats—a move that led Labour MP Tanmanjeet Singh Dhesi to voice concern over 'foreign external interference in elections'.[220] In contrast to Labour's more strident and human rights-focused stance—a position partly enabled by their status as the Opposition—the Conservative Party under David Cameron, Theresa May, Boris Johnson, and Rishi Sunak have been much more sympathetic to the BJP. Cameron's government reached out to Modi in 2013, before he became prime minister, and the relatively cordial relationship under recent Conservative leaders has been lauded by some Hindu voters. Cameron and Modi embracing one another on stage at Wembley Stadium in 2015 was perhaps first and foremost choreographed to boost the Indian Prime Minister's image, but it also seemed to enhance his British counterpart's electability amongst some Indian voters in the UK. (It is worth noting here that there are at least a third of a million Indian citizens residing in the UK who, as Commonwealth citizens, are eligible to vote in both Indian and British elections.[221])

The creep of communalism into British politics was clearly manifested the next year in the 2016 London mayoral elections. Standing against the Labour frontrunner, Sadiq Khan, Conservative candidate Zac Goldsmith conducted an ultimately unsuccessful campaign that was widely condemned for Islamophobia. Goldsmith explicitly attempted to appeal to Hindu voters in leaflets depicting his visits to temples and stoking fears that Khan would introduce a tax on family jewellery. During one excruciating interview with the British Asian press he declared his 'love' for Bollywood only to be flummoxed when he failed to be able to name a single actor or film.[222] Goldsmith's campaign flyers also showed him shaking hands with Modi and compared his welcoming of the Indian PM to London in 2015 with Khan's no-show at the Wembley rally and Corbyn's efforts to ban Modi from Britain.[223]

A 'shift' in Indian voters from Labour to Conservative, however, may not be as consequential as some have suggested, and connections to the politics of the subcontinent are tenuous. In the 2019 General Election—at which Hindu nationalists called on Indian voters to abandon Labour over their criticism of India's Kashmir policy—Labour won eighteen of the twenty seats with the highest number of Indian voters. More significantly, in spite of some confident and even outlandish claims from Indian campaigners to have swung the 2019 result to the Conservatives, aggregate-level analysis of constituencies with high Indian populations indicates no evidence for this type of influence.[224] Even in Leicester East, the constituency with the highest Asian population in the UK (58.1%), Labour managed to hold the seat and won more than half the votes cast (albeit with diminished majority). Indian voters, therefore, remain diverse in their political leanings and many are still loyal Labour voters. And while the past decade has seen more Indians vote for the Conservatives, there is little hard evidence to back up claims by Hindutva activists that this is a consequence of their efforts. Political analyst Sunder Katwala dismissed claims by the HFB and other lobbyists that they are able to command a 'Hindu voting bloc' of any consequence, and Omar Khan, Director of the Runnymede Trust, admonished 'foreign interventions' and exhorted people not to 'just repeat BJP propaganda designed to divide communities'.[225] In sum, whilst an interesting and significant new dynamic on some levels—and the topic of excited speculation in both Britain and India—any kind of Hindu (nationalist) vote bank politics seems unlikely to (yet) make an impact on electoral outcomes. Perhaps a more likely impact, though, is to sow division and polarisation within communities and even families. But none of this is to say that Hindutva lobbying has been politically ineffectual. Labour leader Keir Starmer, for example, has appeared eager to distance himself from Corbyn's India-related policies and rhetoric. This may be the consequence of the kinds of advocacy discussed here, and may also prove to be a factor in stemming the shift of some Indian voters' support to the Conservatives.

The Labour Party has itself been entangled in Hindu nationalist politics. An insider account of left politics in Brent, West London, during the 1980s, reveals tension arising from the increasing involvement of Indian activists in the Labour Party.[226] In his memoir, Ken Livingstone—the leader of the Greater London Council in the 1980s—even mentions, in passing, 'the infiltration of a Hindu fascist group into the Brent Labour parties'.[227] The entry into Labour of Indians affiliated to the Sangh caused consternation amongst some socialists, leading to an appeal to the National Executive Committee in 1980 to intervene over new members 'from an organisation which nurtures avowedly fascist ideas of killing non-Hindus'.[228]

Other times have seen Labour members explicitly embrace Hindu nationalists. Barry Gardiner, MP for Brent North since 1997, has cultivated an especially close and active relationship with not just the HSS and VHP in the UK, but also the BJP and its affiliates in India. Long before Modi's election to prime minister, Gardiner eagerly promoted his reputation in Britain, facilitated in part by Manoj Ladwa—the influential diaspora Hindutva activist, Modi strategist/lobbyist, and, for many years, Labour Party member.[229] In 2013, Gardiner invited Modi to visit the House of Commons, telling the *Times of India*: 'I rank him on the pinnacle of all political leaders I have known'.[230] Compliments have gone in both directions: the West London MP's personal website used to be topped by a portrait of the Gujarat Chief Minister and a quote that read: 'Gujarat has no greater friend in Britain than Barry Gardiner'. This, too, during a period when Modi was *de facto* banned from visiting the UK.

American politics has also become infused with Hindu nationalist discourse in recent years. Further to the support extended to Trump by the Republican Hindu Coalition, discussed earlier in the chapter, US Congresswoman Tulsi Gabbard is one American politician with deep ties to the Hindu nationalist movement. She has, according to Pieter Friedrich, 'played a significant part' in 'rehabilitating Modi's tainted reputation in the United States', and her 2020 presidential campaign received substantial funding from members of several US Sangh Parivar affiliate organisations.[231] Ram Madhav, one of India's senior-most Hindu nationalist leaders, even attended Gabbard's wedding in 2015 and personally delivered gifts on behalf of Modi—a striking indication of the importance that the BJP see of having a Hindutva-sympathetic political ally in the US.[232] Madhav has spoken of 'diaspora diplomacy', arguing that Indians abroad 'can be India's voice even while being loyal citizens in those countries'.[233] Friedrich is an outspoken and vilified campaigner against Hindutva, and has catalogued a wide range of people with Hindu nationalist links who have entered US politics, or influenced it in different ways (such as through substantial donations), including at the very highest level. The level of Hindutva lobbying is considerably greater, and more advanced, in the US than the UK. A 2022 report indicated that this went well beyond donations (which themselves were substantial and extensive), and in 2018–19, 'HSS members took part in a program to visit the offices of more than 100 Congressmembers, co-ordinated by the Hindu American Foundation.'[234] The report also stated that the Hindu American Foundation 'visited the office of every Congressional signatory of House Resolution 417'—a resolution signed by fifty-one representatives (split evenly between Republicans and Democrats), which asserted that 'strands of the Hindu nationalist movement have advanced a divisive and violent agenda that has harmed the social fabric of India', and 'commend[ed] the United States Government for exercising its authority in 2005 under the International Religious Freedom Act of 1998 to deny a United States visa to Narendra Modi on the grounds of religious freedom violations'.[235]

While there has been a substantial acceleration of the confidence and scale of the Hindu nationalist lobby in the US since the 'Modi wave'—illustrated by the remarkable rallies held in New York's Madison Square Garden in 2014 and Houston's NRG Stadium in 2019—the enmeshing of American politics and transnational Hindutva is not a new phenomenon. Since the late twentieth century a range of groups have acted as public representatives for Hindu/Indian Americans, some promoting 'synecdoche of

Hinduness for Indianness',[236] and cultivating acceptance or even solidarity with Hindu nationalist concerns (both in India and of the diaspora). The Federation of Hindu Associations in Southern California, for instance, has sponsored visits of Hindu leaders and Indian politicians to the US, where meetings have been arranged with public officials. The Hindu American Foundation (HAF) is another group to have a bridging relationship between the cultural and political representation of diasporic Hindus. It has, for instance, campaigned to 'take yoga back' from cultural appropriation and secularisation, and was active in the California textbook controversy (see Chapter 4).[237] It has also played a more explicitly political role. In 2013, HAF published a report titled 'A Nexus of Hinduphobia Unveiled', which sought to discredit and refute claims made by the Coalition Against Genocide—a group of scholars, activists, and organisations who lobbied against Modi visiting the US and in support of justice and accountability over the 2002 Gujarat violence.[238] While Modi was, in effect, banned from travelling to the US for nearly a decade, there have been concerted efforts to protect his reputation: in the immediate aftermath of 2002, 'the Indian American community effectively blocked ... a congressional resolution expressing concern about the violence against Muslims in Gujarat', with groups 'inundating' Senate offices with emails and phone calls.[239]

Hindutva leaders in India see the diaspora as a vital asset to enhance the reputation of Hindu nationalism—globally but also within India—and to refute or offset the frequent criticism that the movement and ideology receives. While the RSS and its affiliates do play a role in this—for instance in organising public events to which they invite public figures and politicians—some of the most dynamic and perhaps most effective Hindutva advocacy abroad involves 'mainstream' Hindu representative organisations and individuals, operating through the framework of multiculturalism. It is important to note, however, that there are myriad advocacy groups representing the political interests of Indian Americans, most of which have no connection with—or are even openly hostile to—Hindu nationalist politics. While a detailed discussion of the location and role of Hindu nationalism in political processes outside India is beyond the scope of this chapter, it is clearly becoming a significant dynamic that demands further scrutiny.

Conclusion

Hindu nationalism has had an indelible impact on the political and social landscapes of Britain and other countries of the Indian diaspora that stretches well beyond the reach and influence of the Sangh Parivar. Whilst the 2006 mobilisation against M.F. Husain in London was significant for the rare *act* of Hindutva militancy outside India, much of the discourse surrounding this controversy was consonant with quotidian expressions of conservative political Hindu identity. Reddy is correct in arguing that diasporic Sangh Parivar bodies provide 'easily translatable arguments and the conceptual infrastructure—a culturally grounded lingua franca—for the assertion of Hindu rights in the diaspora'.[240] But it appears that the rhetoric of Hindutva has outgrown the institutional margins of the RSS, and this is seen especially clearly in the diaspora.

The concept of neo-Hindutva can help us understand and categorise these new forms of Hindu identity, rhetoric, and organisation. Neo-Hindutva undoubtedly has strong family resemblance to more 'orthodox' Hindu nationalism. Yet it is important to identify the existence of Sangh-related ideology *outside*, or on the periphery, of the institutional (and sometimes ideological) boundaries of the RSS fold. This highlights the nebulous nature of Sangh influence. Neo-Hindutva is also a product of the digital revolution. Organisations use new technologies to develop and propagate dynamic identities and ideologies, with some groups even *exclusively* located online.

In its 'soft' form, neo-Hindutva can be understood as an inflection of Hindu nationalist rhetoric that is usually keen to avoid or blur explicit connections with Hindu majoritarian politics. 'Hard' neo-Hindutva, on the other hand, is less reticent about being associated with Hindu nationalism, yet, for various reasons, often departs from the positioning and praxis of the Sangh. The lines have blurred somewhat in recent years, however, with the mainstreaming and increased confidence of Hindu nationalism, meaning that those who tend towards soft neo-Hindutva are often less cagey than before. Because neo-Hindutva operates outside the Sangh Parivar (albeit sometimes overlapping with it), and represents a more nebulous and concealed expression of Hindu nationalism, it is especially well-placed to perform an advocacy role in multicultural and multifaith contexts. This is evident from the way in which the Hindu Forum of Britain has been able to claim that conservative and sometimes puritanical expressions of Hindu identity are mainstream.

In HHR and HJS's far-reaching web-presence and substantial Facebook following, we can observe a truly transnational community, capable of global reach and engagement, and unrestricted by the remit, hierarchy, or doctrine of more traditional institutions. The HFB and NCHT operate in a different, but overlapping space, shaped in important ways by Britain's twenty-first-century landscape of multicultural inter-faith relations. In both instances the influence of the Sangh Parivar—direct or indirect, domestic or international—is not always easy to establish. In moments when Hindutva can be identified, the presence of the Sangh might be obfuscated. In many ways we can also observe a distinctive dynamic, influenced by the compulsions and policies of multicultural Britain, which generates a new, organic, and nuanced inflection of Hindutva. Furthermore, whilst it is important to understand these vernacular expressions of Hindu nationalism in their diasporic context, we must also recognise the intrinsic discursive and strategic links to the homeland, as evidenced in the M.F. Husain case.

Legitimacy is conferred to umbrella groups through interactions with central government and their profile in the press and public sphere, which is often a product of the 'voicy' nature of Hindutva-inflected Hindu representation. But the mandate of these groups, and their messages, are contested by many. In the case of caste legislation, for instance, the fact that many British Hindus had such diametrically opposed views to those of the umbrella groups that loudly denounced those seeking legislation is indicative of the disputed nature of the claims to speak for an entire 'Hindu community'. The same is also the case in North America, where several institutions, cities, and states have taken significant steps to ban caste discrimination in recent years. Nonetheless, in Britain, the move from multicultural to multifaith/cohesion-based policies has further helped create space for ecumenical expressions of Hindu nationalism (perhaps ironic, given Hindutva's traditional insistence on being apolitical and areligious). Despite the government's worries about Hindutva, influenced to a degree by a passionate, secularist, anti-Hindutva lobby, it appears that its understanding of this often does not go beyond the institutions of the Sangh Parivar.

The conservative ecumenism of the Hindu Forum, and other equivalent groups in the US and elsewhere, both contributes towards and reflects an increasingly homogenised and censorious strand of Hinduism. This is intrinsically linked, through a borderless, multidirectional network of transnational Hindutva activism, to both the Hindu nationalist politics and ideology of the subcontinent and that of other parts of the Indian diaspora. In this way, what quite recently might have been considered radical, unconventional expressions of Hindu identity have now become the mainstream, even dominant, discourse in Britain's multicultural landscape (whether or not this represents the majority of British Hindus). This has also leached into the wider political landscape of the UK, US, and other countries: Hindu nationalist leaders in India are increasingly aware of the 'diplomacy' that their overseas allies can conduct, and this has led to new forms of advocacy involving politicians from across the spectrum. Lobby groups and activists may overstate their influence on elections, and politics more broadly, but the visibility they have gained in their political efforts—and the way in which they have inserted certain elements of Hindutva into public and political discourse—is still noteworthy. These various trends require us to reimagine Hindu nationalism itself, in particular by rethinking the role of the Hindu diaspora.

CONCLUSION

Hindu nationalism's global footprint is greater, and more widely acknowledged, than ever before. This is underlined most conspicuously through the frequent international trips that Prime Minister Narendra Modi undertakes, during which he is met by crowds of enraptured devotees in a puzzling blend of choreography and undeniable fervour. Although for some, his global allure may be simply as India's leader, the adoration of Modi is inextricable from his politics. To the delight of many, but consternation of others (including within the Hindu nationalist movement), his autocratic pre-eminence makes him virtually a synecdoche for Hindutva. As this conclusion is being written, the Indian Prime Minister—still, as he approaches the end of his second term in office, hugely popular with a large section of the electorate and diaspora—has just completed two notable tours: the first, in May 2023, to Australia, and then one month later, a formal state visit to the United States.

Australia's Indian population has long roots but numbers have mushroomed in recent years, partly due to an enormous influx of students and the availability of various professional opportunities. After Australia and Britain, India is now the third most common place of birth for people resident in Australia.[1] Many of these people provided Modi with a 'rock-star reception in Sydney', according to the *Guardian*, during which 'thousands of members of Australia's Indian community' gave Modi and Australian Prime Minister Anthony Albanese 'a rapturous stadium welcome'.[2] Just as Cameron and Trump had done in previous years, Albanese lavished praise on his guest in front of the audience of prospective voters: 'The last time I saw someone on the stage here was Bruce Springsteen, and he didn't get the welcome that Prime Minister Modi has got... Prime Minister Modi is the boss!'[3]

The event, held at Australia's biggest indoor arena (which, in fact, was not nearly full), drew excited supporters from across the country, who travelled on specially chartered flights and coaches, dubbed 'Modi Airways' and 'Modi Express'. The rally, labelled a 'community reception', was organised by a newly instated group, the Indian Australian Diaspora Foundation. This claimed to comprise 367 registered 'Welcome Partners' from across Australia, covering a bewildering range of professional, caste, regional, religious, cultural, and local groups.[4] Amongst these were a few more familiar names—including the Hindu Swayamsevak Sangh, the Overseas Friends of the BJP, the Vishwa Hindu Parishad, and Sewa International—groups that, as we have seen throughout this book, have played a significant role in propagating Hindutva over many decades, and in this instance were active in mustering support for the Indian Prime Minister.

The US trip was an even more high-profile affair—a state visit with all the bells and whistles: ceremonial White House welcome, twenty-one-gun salute, state dinner for 400 guests, and an address to a joint session of Congress. The trip also featured a highly televised and photographed yoga session outside the United Nations headquarters in New York for International Yoga Day, an 'awareness day' that has been championed by Modi since its inception in 2015. Yoga has increasingly been drawn upon as a soft power tool in recent years—something that Sheena Sood argues should be viewed as 'Omwashing': 'using yogic culture as a colonial and ethnonationalist tool that diverts the public gaze from their supremacist agendas'.[5] But it is presented and interpreted by most in much more benign terms.

With the US seeing India as a crucial ally, economically but also geo-strategically, due in large part to the 'new cold war' with China, human rights issues were diplomatically skirted— such as awkward truths like the United States Commission on

International Religious Freedom, an independent government body, exhorting Biden's administration to 'acknowledge the Indian government's perpetration and toleration of particularly severe violations of religious freedom against its own population'.[6] Or the fact that Modi was unable to visit the US for nearly a decade and was denied a visa in 2005 under a law that, in the words of the US Ambassador to India, 'makes any foreign government official who "was responsible for or directly carried out, at any time, particularly severe violations of religious freedom" ineligible for a visa to the United States'.[7]

But in the 2023 visit, the terms of this relationship seemed to have been reset. Modi drew from his populist playbook, recalling, in a speech alongside Biden outside the White House, that he had been there three decades before, 'as a common man'.[8] Photographs of this much earlier trip occasionally circulate online, as do various other pictures showing his extensive travels long before he became prime minister or even Chief Minister of Gujarat—indicative of the global perspective of the Hindu nationalist movement, and networks of connections and infrastructure that have been developed through the years. The diaspora was acknowledged by political leaders on numerous occasions: at his arrival ceremony, Modi stated that 'The people of the Indian community are enhancing India's glory in the US'—words echoed by Biden and others.[9] The soft power of India's diaspora is often linked to its status as a 'model minority'—a fact that the Hindu nationalist movement are keenly aware of, and have attempted to leverage in various ways.

Dissent and response

But if the visit was partly about improving the image of India's Hindu nationalist regime, this was not entirely successful. At Modi's address to Congress (which around half a dozen Democrats vocally boycotted), the prime minister raised eyebrows when he stated that 1947 marked freedom 'after a thousand years of foreign rule in one form or another'.[10] This alluded to a key Hindutva trope that, from the movement's earliest days, has been preoccupied with the idea of a millennium-long 'foreign' subjugation. Just a few months earlier, the head of the RSS had told *Organiser*, 'Hindu society has been at war for over 1,000 years—this fight has been going on against foreign aggressions, foreign influence and foreign conspiracies.'[11] The subtext to the '1,000 years' adage, which is frequently coupled with the notion that a muscular Hindu renaissance is required (to return Bharat to its pure, 'pre-invasion' glory), is that Muslim rule in India has always been inherently untenable and may in some ways be equated with British colonisation. And, by extension, Islam and Muslims remain—all these centuries on—external influences that have caused suffering to India's 'indigenous' Hindu culture and society. But the true audience for Modi's statement to Congress was unlikely to be his hosts, many of whom may not have even understood the reference. Rather this was yet another example of international trips, and interactions with diasporic devotees, for which the primary audience is back in India, where the optics of an elite diaspora population fawning over the BJP leader, and India's increasingly assertive global diplomacy, are breathlessly reported on by a sympathetic, compliant media.

Less compliant are the US media—in an extraordinarily rare press conference with Modi (he has *never* held a press conference in India as prime minister), the *Wall Street Journal* reporter Sabrina Siddiqui asked him about 'steps his government would take to uphold free speech and to improve the rights of Muslims and other minorities in India'.[12] The question led to an onslaught of abuse on social media, including 'threats, slurs and baseless accusations'.[13] The White House Correspondents' Association issued a statement expressing their alarm that Siddiqui 'has been subjected to intense online harassment, including from people with ties to the prime minister's political party, questioning her motives, her religion and her heritage'.[14] Strong and public denunciation also came from the US National Security Council spokesman, John Kirby, and the White House Press Secretary, Karine Jean-Pierre, who stated that 'We certainly condemn any efforts of intimidation or harassment of a journalist or any journalist that is just trying to do their job.'[15]

The episode highlighted the extent to which online 'activism' and the 'management of dissent'—for many, indistinguishable from trolling—is an important expression of dedication to Hindu nationalist politics for a considerable number of adherents the world over. This is echoed in the huge investment and innovative work that the BJP have put into digital campaigning, in its numerous forms, particularly since the 2014 election and under the 'IT cell' leadership of Amit Malviya. Another key figure behind the scenes in that campaign was Rajesh Jain, an IT professional who had recently returned from the United States, who presided over a team of '5,000 officers scrutinizing the attitude of the people in 155 key urban constituencies identified as "digital seats," as they had above-average internet penetration and greater social media use'.[16] Through harnessing the power of hundreds of thousands of volunteers, all across the world—and being able to rely on unprecedented levels of political funding—the digital campaign transformed India's electoral landscape.

Digital activism is one way in which the diaspora is included, or can intervene, in the life of the homeland. This goes well beyond just party politics: online Hindutva can be traced back many years and covers an incredibly wide range of perspectives and groups, constituting a global 'ecosphere' of ideology and campaigning that involves a range of co-operating and competing interests. It has not always been controlled (both by design as well as due to limitations of influence), by those at the top of the political hierarchy. A rich body of literature has emerged in recent years (building on prescient early reflections, such as those by Vinay Lal and Arjun Appadurai) that has shed light on the internet and 'long-distance nationalism', online Hindutva, deterritorialised political identities, the spread of disinformation, and transnational activism. This has shown the extent of the internet's influence on Hindutva's recent rise, and the imbrication of the diaspora in this dynamic. Although 'cyber-Hindutva' (a term used in an important 2012 study on the phenomenon by Ingrid Therwath) has not been explored in a dedicated chapter, this book has throughout considered the significance of online spaces in the spread and articulation of global, transnational Hindutva.[17]

One element of this is that Indians overseas are considered as an important means by which India's increasingly negative human rights reputation, globally, might be improved. In spite of hawkish rhetoric about 'self-appointed custodians of the world', behind closed doors, India *is* said to be concerned about the reputational damage and other repercussions of sliding down the ranks of democratic indices, such as Freedom House, the Cato Human Freedom Index, the Democracy Index, the Pew Research Centre (religious freedom), and the World Press Freedom Index.[18] The diaspora are encouraged by Indian politicians to serve as ambassadors for the country, and, more specifically, by Hindu nationalist leaders to promote and normalise Hindutva, and to undermine dissent. The creation of the Overseas Friends of the BJP (OFBJP) in the US in 1991, the launch of which was presided over by L.K. Advani in New York, was from the outset about much more than just the diaspora supporting political campaigns in India. Launched in the midst of the *Ram Janmabhoomi* movement and the negative press that this 'saffron wave' generated, it was intended '[to] educate American lawmakers, the American people, and the Indian American community about the true principles of the BJP'.[19] But the engagement of the diaspora, and the adulation the BJP receives abroad, is also seen to have an impact 'back home': Indian politicians of all hues, but none more so than those of the BJP, are acutely aware that the reception they receive overseas has an audience in India itself.

Rather than simply focusing on the impact this may have on high politics, it is also important to reflect upon the extent to which this political role of the diaspora has an impact on overseas Indians. It provides them with a means by which they can intervene, potentially quite influentially, in the political life of the homeland. This resonates deeply with diaspora communities, who may feel politically marginalised in their countries of residence, but also have various emotions—of detachment, longing, guilt, nostalgia—that provide an impetus for their desire to remain connected. Party politics is only one dimension of this, and by no means a major focus of this book. However, the broader evolution of Hindu nationalism in the diaspora, even if ostensibly 'apolitical', has clearly also influenced the popularity of the BJP overseas, and provided much of the apparatus that has enabled some of the most conspicuous expressions of support for Hindutva politics.

The extent to which the BJP have mustered their global ranks in recent years is noteworthy: one article claimed that ahead of Modi's 2014 General Election victory, 'more than 8,000 overseas Indians from Britain and America flew to India to join his campaign'.[20] In a conversation with an OFBJP activist in the UK at the same time, I was told that 5,000 would be travelling from Britain to campaign in India. These numbers could of course be overstated. And many, if not most, of these people would have been ineligible to vote— India does not permit dual nationality, nor does it grant any kind of voting rights to those with 'Overseas Indian Citizenship'. Since 2014, an Indian citizen living overseas has been able to register as an 'NRI voter', although this still requires the individual to travel to India and cast their ballot in their home constituency; therefore uptake is very low. But there is a sense, disputed by some, that the diaspora might be able to influence the voting behaviour of people 'back home' in other ways. Recent elections have seen the OFBJP co-ordinate telephone campaigns from people's homes across the world, with volunteers provided with spreadsheets of people to contact, targets for the number of calls to make, and instructions on how to effectively canvas and promote the party line. One volunteer, an IT consultant based in the US state of Maryland, said in 2018: 'They are shocked to be getting a call from the United States... We call some rural people too. They look at us as very successful people, so that's the good thing for us to convince them. They think that we speak the truth.'[21] After the 2019 election victory was announced, the President of the OFBJP-USA claimed that at least one million phone calls had been made by more than 1,000 volunteers.[22]

In addition to phone calls, Indians abroad were incorporated into BJP campaigns using digital tools. In 2019, they were encouraged to sign up to an online platform, called 'NRI4NaMo', and in 2014 the *'Chai pe Charcha'* (chat over tea) campaign—a masterstroke of populist politics, in which the leader would speak 'directly' to ordinary citizens across India using video technology—was extended to countries around the world with Indian communities.

Indians overseas have also been urged to participate in election campaigns by making online donations, 'joining WhatsApp groups, submitting suggestions for the party's manifesto, writing blogs and articles "about the development schemes of PM Modi" and organising bike rallies with flags and banners of BJP-Modi and sharing their photos online'.[23] The true extent of this influence is moot, especially given India's vast electorate who are influenced by numerous other factors. Some suggest the effect is very small indeed: 'It's a drop in the bucket,' argues Devesh Kapur. 'We should not mistake organization and vociferousness for actual influence on the ground in India. These are two very different things.'[24] But the fact that this provides the diaspora with a sense of *feeling* involved and engaged in the homeland is significant in and of itself. Much more work is needed on the transnational politics of India, and specifically on relationships between the Indian diaspora and electoral politics in India, and how this connects with polities elsewhere around the world. There is little in-depth research that has been conducted on the OFBJP (from its origins in the early 1990s), the ways in which the diaspora have supported Modi in recent years, and, crucially, the reasons why. Too often, commentators resort to simplistic speculation and unnuanced conclusions—the increasingly important phenomenon demands more research and deeper analysis.

Rejecting communalism

A reflection of this crude narrative can be found in the received wisdom that Indians abroad are invariably pro-BJP, Hindutva-sympathetic, and involved in the promotion and activism of Hindu nationalism. Indeed, these three things are all rather different in themselves. In fact, many Indian citizens and people of Indian origin outside the subcontinent are actively engaged in campaigning against communalism and the Sangh Parivar. There is a long and rich history of radicalism, leftism, secularism, and subaltern and progressive politics in the Indian diaspora. This dissenting tradition is witnessed during the international visits described earlier in this conclusion, and elsewhere in the book, during which many people have taken the opportunity to protest against the BJP government and raise a range of grievances and concerns with India's recent direction of travel. At virtually all substantial public events outside India connected to Hindu nationalism—whether in Texas, New York, Sydney, London, Milton Keynes, or elsewhere—members of the Indian diaspora have turned up with placards and megaphones to express their rejection of Hindutva.

Social movements and protests in India are often echoed and amplified in the diaspora. From the Shaheen Bagh sit-ins against the Citizenship (Amendment) Act, to outrage at the death of Ambedkarite student Rohit Vemula, to the Indian farmers' protests, Indians overseas have publicly expressed their solidarity in various ways. There is a certain degree of overlap between groups that have challenged Hindu majoritarianism and the Indian state more generally. One example is the Khalistan movement, a separatist struggle for Sikh self-determination in Punjab, which in the diaspora has manifested in highly conspicuous and provocative protests, pugnacious rhetoric, violent tensions between different South Asian communities, and 'long-distance' support for militant secessionists. Diplomatic missions, such as the Indian High Commission in London, have been focal points for many of these protests—as well as for those who have campaigned for Kashmiri rights and autonomy—and this has led to considerable concern and anger from the Indian state. Another, very different, instance of globalised South Asian political struggle is found within the Dalit movement and anti-caste activism, which has been active and vocal overseas for many years. Groups like the Dalit Solidarity Network, the Anti-Caste Discrimination Alliance, and Equality Labs are amongst numerous organisations campaigning against casteist oppression in South Asia, working to raise awareness about casteism overseas, and lobbying to ban or criminalise caste discrimination in the US, the UK, and other parts of the South Asian diaspora.

While some of these groups view Hindu nationalism as simply a part of their wider struggles, many organisations have been launched overseas that see resisting Hindutva as a primary aim. Particularly dynamic periods in the creation and activity of these groups have been seen during spikes in Hindu nationalist mobilisation, particularly in the early 1990s, early 2000s, and post-2014. Organisations active in this sense include the South Asia Solidarity Group, South Asia Citizens Web, the Coalition Against Fascism in India, the Feminist Critical Hindu Studies Collective, the Coalition Against Genocide, Non-Resident Indians for a Secular and Harmonious India, AWAAZ South Asia Watch, the Monitoring Group, Women Against Fundamentalism, Students Against Hindutva, the South Asia Scholar Activist Collective, the Campaign to Stop Funding Hate, and Desis Rising Up and Moving. It is noteworthy that some of this resistance has involved a resurgence in broad-based solidarities, cutting across religion, ethnicity, and other narrower forms of identification, that in certain ways evoke the inter-community solidarity, and even political blackness, of the Asian Youth Movement era. To some degree this is a generational difference, although, as we have seen, communal politics has also proved attractive to some young diasporic South Asians. However, Hindutva should not be viewed as a dominant form of political identity for Indians overseas, and is often the preserve of a relatively small minority. The diversity of dissent is beyond the scope of this book, but is an important and consequential feature of diasporic politics and demands further academic scrutiny.

However, one cannot mention this dissent without also talking about the way in which these challenges to Hindutva are received and counteracted. The response to criticism is often vociferous, co-ordinated, and systematic, deploying a range of methods and language that have been informed by various other groups and political factions. Particular energy and vitriol are devoted to academics and their institutions that have deigned to produce critical perspectives on Hindu nationalism or associated topics, with Jasa Macher stating that 'large scale hate mail campaigns, death and rape threats, and smear campaigns against academics by pro-Hindutva online accounts and activists have been ongoing at least since the early 2000s'.[25] Azad Essa argues that there is a particularly clear connection to Zionist efforts to stifle criticism, but equally we can see a number of parallels with the approaches taken by right-wing populists and authoritarian conservatives the world over (with whom alliances have even been struck).[26] Hindutva's detractors are frequently labelled seditious and anti-national, although this is obviously less impactful outside India (except to call into question the loyalty of diasporic Indians, and sometimes instil anxiety due to the vulnerability of OCI status, for instance). One might see some irony in Hindu nationalists, including those representing the Indian government, denouncing 'foreign interference' from abroad: Hindu nationalists repeatedly extol their role in resisting the Emergency in the 1970s from overseas (often alongside foreign allies), during which Indira Gandhi's government referred to them as 'anti-national' and 'unpatriotic'. Much more recently, countries such as Canada and the UK have expressed concerns about efforts to influence domestic politics (for example the OFBJP's campaigns to prevent Labour politicians from winning elections in forty-eight seats during the 2019 UK General Election).

Another line of attack has evolved that draws upon the language of postcolonialism, and the idea that those who critique India in any way deemed unacceptable are driven by prejudice and are part of a conspiracy to 'break' India. This often invokes tropes like Orientalism, 'cultural Marxism', and Eurocentrism, as well as social media-inflected neologisms like libtard, sickular, *tukde tukde* gang, urban Naxal and the Lutyens/Khan Market gang. One especially prevalent line of criticism in recent years has pivoted around the notion of 'Hinduphobia'. This is a highly contested category, which for some represents the articulation of a sense of victimhood, of a kind of anti-India racism that may be equated to Islamophobia, and of lived realities of victimhood and prejudice. But for others it is a term born of a desire to undermine criticism and critical discourse, such as around caste discrimination or the persecution of religious minorities. Raju Rajugopal, a co-founder of Hindus for Human Rights, claims that '"Hinduphobia" is only the latest concept in their lexicon, weaponized both here [in the US] and in India to delegitimize critics.'[27] In Britain, Amrit Wilson calls it a 'fabrication': 'Unlike antisemitism, Islamophobia or anti-black racism, it has no historical or material basis. In the UK, racism against Indians has always been directed at us as "Asians"—and, since the 1990s, in the form of Islamophobia (if we are Muslims)—

but never as Hindus.'[28] These issues are clearly fraught, complex, and impacted by numerous factors and actors. While this book has attempted, primarily, to explore the recent history of transnational and diasporic Hindutva, much more work is clearly required to make sense of the ever-evolving contemporary situation.

Concluding thoughts

This book has sought to illuminate the long and complex history of Hindu nationalism in the Indian diaspora leading up to the current environment we have just considered. The formative period in East Africa set in place transnational networks, institutional structures, organisational hierarchies, and ideologies that would develop and grow into the beginnings of the Sangh in Britain. But despite considerable structural consonance and layers of co-ordination, the Hindu Swayamsevak Sangh was not simply the product of an exported and transplanted ideology. Instead it has developed, adapted, and vernacularised to various local conditions and the particular needs and desires of the Hindu diaspora. The Sangh family has also developed and grown—some wings being closely linked to their Indian counterparts (VHP, Hindu Sevika Samiti, Hindu Sahitya Kendra, and various charitable groups), while others have emerged as quite distinct and tailored to their different context (NHSF, FISI, Indian National Student Association, Sewa Day, Vichaar Manthan). All these groups are connected, on varying levels, to the HSS and its network of past and present members.

Certain aspects of Hindutva and the Sangh's *shakha* format have specific appeal and resonance for Indians abroad. They provide segregated spaces for 'safe' and familiar socialisation and the transmission of (a certain conception of) Hindu values and culture. The diaspora emphasise this distinct pedagogical element, which is particularly valued by first-generation migrants eager to expose their children to this enculturation. This dimension of the HSS, also pursued by the VHP, NHSF, and certain other groups, is partly a palliative to perceived threats of materialism, and the inadequate values and undesirable morality of the host society. It also serves as a response to marginalisation, racism, and downward social

CONCLUSION

mobility experienced upon emigration. In this context, Hindutva's emphases on assertive cultural pride (often chauvinistic in nature), discipline, and physical training strikes a chord amongst some Hindus in Britain. But, contrary to established ideas about the Sangh in India, diasporic Hindutva contains various nuances and idiosyncrasies, both contextual and conceptual.

Charitable activities have provided another significant channel for the vernacularisation of diasporic Hindu nationalism. Flows of funding from the diaspora to the homeland have clearly been an important feature of Hindutva organising, but also a dynamic that is hard to trace and has caused various problems. Following outcry from anti-Hindutva campaigners, scrutiny from the Charity Commission, and enduring circumspection of central government, Hindu groups increasingly focused their philanthropic attentions on concerns closer to home. Accompanying PR campaigns have formed an important conduit for the promulgation of the 'model minority' trope. In many ways, these developments have occurred in liminal spaces, at the borders of what has previously been understood as 'Hindu nationalism'.

Increasingly, Hindu nationalism is no longer as limited to the institutional and ideological boundaries of the Sangh Parivar as they are conventionally understood. Indeed, sometimes these boundaries are rather blurred—often through deliberate obfuscation—but at other times groups that express different forms of Hindutva are both practically and ideologically distinct from the orbit of the RSS. At other times, there may be individuals who are involved in Sangh-related groups, or have direct connections to those who are, but the linkage is concealed. The significant phenomenon that we can identify—on which much more work is required— is the extent to which ideas of the Hindu right have permeated through society, become conflated for broader representations of Hindu-ness and Indian-ness, and emerged as a normalised or even mainstream version of diasporic identity.

This can be found through a range of organisations that operate in an environment of 'competitive' multiculturalism. Since 2004, the Hindu Forum of Britain has positioned itself as an ecumenical representative of 'the Hindu community', and interaction with sections of government has frequently reified their legitimacy. In this way, organisations that represent essentialised visions of Hinduism, and Hindutva itself, are 'in conversation' with British multiculturalism and multiculturalist policy. In fact, multiculturalism, increasingly in the form of 'community cohesion' and 'interfaith relations', has often provided spaces, resources, and other impetuses for the articulation of monolithic versions of Hinduism. However, a range of groups exist, with new ones sporadically emerging, which represent varying levels of Hindutva discourse and serve to function as community representatives (although they are not necessarily in competition with one another, and are often allies).

Although ostensibly mainstream, the Hindu Forum, amongst a range of other Hindu organisations, advance key tropes of Hindutva, particularly through performative, public displays of outrage and offence. Also promoting the notion of Hindus as a 'model minority', these mobilisations have often involved a discursive relationship with the Muslim 'other'. These dynamic and syncretic inflections of transnational Hindutva can be understood as 'neo-Hindutva'. This can be 'soft' (obfuscating or denying connections with the Sangh and Hindutva ideology) or 'hard' (representing more explicit expressions of Hindu nationalism, but sometimes overtly articulating differences with the Sangh). Neo-Hindutva has made particular use of the internet, a key resource of the Sangh as well, enabling borderless and highly accessible online spaces for identity formation and articulation.

There is a substantial and sometimes disorienting range of neo-Hindutva groups that have emerged in the diaspora in recent years, and this book has only managed to touch briefly on some. They include the Dharmic Ideas and Policy Foundation, Sewa Purva Paksha, the Global Hindu Federation, Insight UK, the Hindu American Foundation, the National Council of Hindu Temples, the Hindu Council UK, Hindu ACTion, Operation Dharmic Vote, Advocacy for British Hindus and Indians, the Forum for Hindu Awakening, Infinity Foundation, Hindu Human Rights, the Global Hindu Federation, and many more. We might understand these as neo-Hindutva in that they represent something distinct

CONCLUSION

from more 'traditional' institutions of the Sangh Parivar, and they constitute a significantly vernacularised and nebulous form of Hindu nationalism (although not all these groups can be understood purely through the prism of Hindutva). And this also is not to suggest that there are not myriad connections, influences, and overlaps with the Hindu nationalist movement of the Sangh Parivar. Much more work is needed on neo-Hindutva and the panoply of groups that seem to grow year on year.

Alongside these new dynamics, diasporic Hindu nationalism has been heavily influenced by deputised Indian Sangh workers, co-ordinated from New Delhi, as well as touring senior Hindutva leaders and gurus. These individuals have worked on basic grassroots organisation and instruction, helped to recruit and train members and leaders, provided inspiration and ideological direction, and conducted reconnaissance for the 'parent' organisations in India. But they do not signify a one-way, centrifugal flow of people and ideas from India. Members of the HSS and associated groups have returned to India for special events, training camps, and as part of multi-purpose trips. These spaces are both products of, and stimuli for, transnational Hindu nationalist networks. Camps have enabled important transfers of knowledge and meaningful interactions between diasporic actors and Indian Sangh leaders, but they also represent highly affective enactments of unity, strength, and connectivity to the homeland. Furthermore, these return trips constitute multidirectional, dialectical layers of influence, in which we can observe forms of 'social remittances'—flows of ideas, not just capital, to the homeland—as well as intra-diaspora relationships. Therefore, while on one level training camps in India help with the continuity of the Sangh's ideology and praxis, they also highlight the diaspora's influence on dynamic layers of adaptation and modernisation.

Despite these levels of deviation and independence, the Sangh has provided important impetuses and channels for engagement with the politics of the homeland. Two crucial moments in the second half of the twentieth century—the Emergency and the Ramjanmabhoomi movement—were turning points in this relationship. Although separate, and in many ways different, the development of transnational networks during the Emergency were important to the kinds of political mobilisations seen in subsequent decades. These political episodes were global moments and critical events in the relationship between India and its diaspora, with substantial and multivalent repercussions.

In spite of frequent obfuscation (often due to fulfilling requirements and expectations of registered charities and civil society organisations, as well as upholding the reputation of the 'model minority', although this reticence has diminished in recent years), Hindu nationalist organisations in the diaspora have often maintained umbilical connections to the homeland. Crucially, this relationship has had an impact not just on members of the Indian diaspora and the societies in which they live, but also on the Hindu nationalist movement in India and, by extension, Indian political and social life. These connections are multidirectional—Hindu nationalist groups and political organisations have increasingly attempted to influence the body politic of various places outside the subcontinent, with concerted efforts to lobby on various issues, police dissent, influence and gain approbation from certain politicians, forge alliances with like-minded partners, and improve Hindutva's image. The desire and ability to impact electoral politics in Britain, the US, and elsewhere is a significant development that deserves more attention and analysis, and better understanding of where the influence stems from—be it local, international, or transnational—and what effect it has had.

To make sense of diasporic Hindu nationalism, we must carefully unpick nebulous layers of direct and indirect influence. This requires a sensitive understanding of homeland and diaspora that transcends binaries of 'here' and 'there', and appreciates seemingly contradictory levels of interconnected interdependence, autonomy, and syncretism. Doing this has the potential to shift our understanding of Indian communities around the world, historically and in the present day, but also to alter how we view diasporic identity and politics in the broadest sense.

GLOSSARY AND ABBREVIATIONS

Note: This is a short glossary containing a small number of the words and terms in Indic languages used throughout the text. The book uses italicised roman script, without diacritical marks, for words and short phrases, which are translated in brackets in the first instance. Certain quotations from texts in Hindi and Sanskrit have been transliterated from the Devanagari script for ease of reading. Proper names, including the names of organisations, named training camps, committees, and titles of senior Sangh offices, have not been italicised. Quotations have been left unamended, and hence include variations in spellings, capitalisations, and italicisations (for instance *sewa* and *Seva*).

Hindi/Gujarati/Sanskrit	English
Achar paddhati	Correct system
Adhikari	Official
Akhara	Traditional Indian gymnasium for wrestling, physical training, instruction, and worship
Akhil Bharatiya Karyakari Mandal	All-India Executive Committee
Akhil Bharatiya Vidyarthi Parishad	All-India Student's Council
Ahimsa	Non-violence
Arya Samaj	'Noble Society', Hindu reform movement founded by Dayananda Saraswati in 1875

GLOSSARY AND ABBREVIATIONS

Avatar	Incarnation
Bajrang Dal	'Army of Monkeys' (or 'Hanuman Brigade'), the militant youth wing of the VHP
Balagokulam	HSS young children's group
Bauddhik	Discussion or instruction on a range of philosophical, moral, historical, economic, and political topics
Bauddhik Pramukh	Director of Educational Activities
Bauddhik Yojana	Educational Programme
Bhagwa Dhwaj	Saffron flag
Bhagwan	God
Bhajan	Devotional Hindu song
Bhakti	Devotional worship
Bharat	India
Bharat Mata	Mother India
Bharatiya Jana Sangh	'Indian People's Organisation', a Hindu nationalist political party affiliated with the RSS that existed from 1951 to 1977, the forerunner of the BJP
Bharatiya Janata Party	Indian People's Party
Bharatiya Janata Yuva Morcha	Indian People's Youth Front
Bharatiya Sanskriti	Indian Culture
Bharatiya Swayamsevak Sangh	Indian Volunteer Organisation
Bharatiya Vichara Kendra	Indian Centre of Enquiry
Bharatiya Vidya Bhavan	Indian House of Knowledge
Dalit	Term used for those formerly known as untouchable, today officially 'Scheduled Caste', literally meaning 'broken' (or oppressed)
Dana	Giving
Darshan	Divine sight (of guru, idol, etc.)
Dharmic	According to duty or law

GLOSSARY AND ABBREVIATIONS

Durga Vahini	'Army of Durga', a militant, armed, female wing of the Bajrang Dal
e-shakha	A video-conferencing, file-sharing platform, developed to facilitate transnational shakhas
Ganvesh	Uniform
Ghar Wapsi	'Returning home', a Hindutva programme of 'reconverting' (or 'unconverting') Muslims and Christians
Guru	Teacher
Gurukul	Residential school
Hindu jage vishwa jage	'If Hindus awaken, the world awakens'
Hindu Janajagruti Samiti	Society for Hindu Awakening
Hindu Ottrumai Mayaim	Centre for Hindu Unity
Hindu Rashtra	Hindu Nation
Hindu Sahitya Kendra	Hindu Literature Centre
Hindu Sevika Samiti	Hindu Women Volunteers Committee
Hindu Swayamsevak Sangh	Hindu Volunteer Organisation
Hindu Vidya Mandir	Hindu Temple of Learning
Hindu Vivek Kendra	Hindu Knowledge Centre
Hindutva	'Hindu-ness', the ideology of Hindu nationalism
Jai Shri Ram	Victory to Ram
Janata Party	People's Party
Karsevak	Volunteer worker
Karyakarta	Active worker/organiser/officer
Karyavaha	Secretary
Kathakaar	Preacher
Kendriya Karyakari Mandal	Central Executive Committee (of the HSS)
Khel	Games

GLOSSARY AND ABBREVIATIONS

Lathi	A bamboo staff
Lok Sangharsh Samiti	People's Struggle Committee (during the Emergency)
Mahabharata	One of the two major Sanskrit epics of ancient India (the other being the Ramayana)
Mandir	Hindu temple
Margdarshak Mandal	'Circle of Guides' (core Sangh leadership group)
Masjid	Mosque
Mela	Fair or gathering
Mukhya shikshak	Chief Instructor
Murti	Image
Namaste Sada Vatsale Matrubhoomi	'Hail to Thee O Motherland', the principal song of the RSS, sung at *shakhas* and other gatherings
Nari shakti	Woman power
Nidhi Pramukh	Treasurer
Parivar	Family
Patel/Patidar	Gujarati caste
Prachaar sanghatan	Alliance for the purpose of propagation
Pracharak	Full-time worker
Pranaam	Prayer/greeting
Prathana	Prayer
Pravasi Bharatiya	Overseas Indian
Ram Shila Puja	Ram Brick Prayer Ritual
Ramayana	One of the two major Sanskrit epics of ancient India (the other being the Mahabharata)
Ramjanmabhoomi	Ram's birthplace
Rashtra	Nation
Rashtriya Sevika Samiti	National Women Volunteer Committee

GLOSSARY AND ABBREVIATIONS

Rashtriya Sewa Samvardhan Samiti	National Service Development Committee
Rashtriya Swayamsevak Sangh	National Volunteer Organisation
Rath Yatra	Chariot Pilgrimage/Procession
Sah Samyojak	Joint Co-ordinator
Saha Karyvaha	Joint Secretary
Sahasampark Pramukh	Head of Media and Publicity
Sahsarakaryavaha	Joint General Secretary
Samachar	News
Samaj	Society
Samarop	Public function at the end of Sangh camps
Sambhaag Pracharak	Regional Organiser
Sammelan	Assembly
Sampradaya	Religious fellowship
Samskar	World-view/good and virtuous behaviour
Samyojak	Convenor
Sangh Parivar	Family of Organisations
Sangh Sandesh	Sangh Message
Sangh Shiksha Varg	Sangh Instructor Training Camp
Sanghasthan	Outdoor ground where *shakhas* take place
Sant	Saint
Sarkaryavah	General Secretary
Sarsanghchalak	Supreme Leader
Satyagrahi	'Pursuer of truth', Gandhian activist
Sevika	Female volunteer
Sewa	(Charitable) service
Shakha	Branch
Shankaracharya	Monastery Head
Shastra	Rules

GLOSSARY AND ABBREVIATIONS

Shibir	Camp
Shikshak	Instructor
Shiv Sena	'Shiva's Army', a regional Hindu nationalist political party from Maharashtra
Swayamsevak	Volunteer, RSS member
Tarun	17–25-year-old age group in RSS/HSS
Tirth yatra	Pilgrimage
Utsav	Festival
Vanvasi Kalyan Ashram	RSS-affiliated organisation working with India's indigenous 'tribal' communities
Varishta adhikaris	Senior officials
Vasudhaiva kutumbakam	'The whole world is one family'
Vijaya Dashmi Utsav	A Hindu festival also called Dussherra, one of the main annual *utsavs* celebrated by the Sangh, held on the day the RSS was founded
Virat Hindu Sammelan	Great Hindu Assembly
Vishwa Adhyayan Kendra	Centre for International Studies
Vishwa Hindu Parishad	World Hindu Council
Vishwa Samvad Kendra	World Media Centre
Vishwa Sangh	World Organisation
Vishwa Sangh Shibir	World Sangh Camp
Vishwa Vibhag	World Division (of the RSS)
Vishwa Vibhag Karyalaya	World Division Head Office
Vishwa Vibhag Samyojak	World Division Convenor
Vistar	Expansion
Vistarak	Temporary full-time worker/voluntary youth worker
Yatra	Procession

GLOSSARY AND ABBREVIATIONS

List of abbreviations

ABVP	Akhil Bharatiya Vidyarthi Parishad
BAPS	Bochasanwasi Shri Akshar Purushottam Swaminarayan Sanstha
BJP	Bharatiya Janata Party
BSS	Bharatiya Swayamsevak Sangh
CM	Chief Minister
DCLG	Department for Communities and Local Government
DFID	Department for International Development
DISIR	Defence and Internal Security of India Rule
EDL	English Defence League
EDM	Early Day Motion
FISI	Friends of India Society International
HCK	Hindu Council of Kenya
HFB	Hindu Forum of Britain
HHR	Hindu Human Rights
HJS	Hindu Janajagruti Samiti
HSK	Hindu Sahitya Kendra
HSS	Hindu Swayamsevak Sangh
HVK	Hindu Vivek Kendra
ISKCON	International Society for Krishna Consciousness
LSS	Lok Sangharsh Samiti
MEA	Ministry of External Affairs
MISA	Maintenance of Internal Security Act
MLA	Member of Legislative Assembly
MP	Member of Parliament
NHSF	National Hindu Students Forum
NRI	Non-Resident Indian
OTC	Officer Training Camp
PIO	Person of Indian Origin
PM	Prime Minister
PR	Public Relations

GLOSSARY AND ABBREVIATIONS

RSP	Ram Shila Puja
RSS	Rashtriya Swayamsevak Sangh
SIP	Sangh Internship Programme
SIUK	Sewa International UK
SSV	Sangh Shiksha Varg
VAK	Vishwa Adhyayan Kendra
VHP	Vishwa Hindu Parishad
VHS	Virat Hindu Sammelan
VSS	Vishwa Sangh Shibir

NOTES

INTRODUCTION

1. 'PM Narendra Modi speech at Madison Square Garden', *Financial Express*, 29 September 2014. https://www.financialexpress.com/archive/pm-narendra-modi-speech-at-madison-square-garden-pio-cardholders-to-get-lifetime-indian-visa/1293830/. Accessed on 3 January 2022.
2. Andrew Whitehead, 'Why Indians Abroad Succumb to 'Modimania', BBC News, 10 November 2015: https://www.bbc.co.uk/news/world-asia-34709354. Accessed on 3 January 2022.
3. Jason Burke, 'UK Government Ends Boycott of Narendra Modi', *The Guardian*, 22 October 2012: https://www.theguardian.com/world/2012/oct/22/uk-ends-boycott-narendra-modi. Accessed on 3 January 2022.
4. Haroon Siddique, 'British Indians Warn Hindu Nationalist Party not to Meddle in UK Elections', *The Guardian*, 11 November 2019: https://www.theguardian.com/politics/2019/nov/11/british-indians-warn-hindu-party-not-to-meddle-in-uk-elections. Accessed on 3 January 2022.
5. 'Boris Johnson', 7 August 2020, 'I'm a big fan of Indian Culture So I Did "SHRI RAM ABHISHEK" With Our Home minister at my Residence On 5th of August.' https://twitter.com/BorisUKJohnson/status/1291704936950935554. Accessed on 20 August 2020. The fake account has since been suspended.
6. 'How life has changed in Leicester: Census 2021', Office for National Statistics, 19 January 2023: https://www.ons.gov.uk/visualisations/censusareachanges/E06000016/. Accessed on 4 July 2023.
7. Max Daly, Sahar Habib Ghazi, and Pallavi Pundir, 'How Far-Right Hindu Supremacy Went Global', Vice News, 26 October 2022: https://www.vice.com/en/article/n7z947/how-far-right-hindu-supremacy-went-global. Accessed on 4 July 2023.
8. 'India in the UK', 19 September 2022, 'Press Release: High Commission of India, London condemns the violence in Leicester. @MIB_India.'

https://twitter.com/HCI_London/status/1571805409060462593. Accessed on 18 May 2023.
9. Rajeev Syal, Jessica Murray and Aina J. Khan, 'Leicester violence could spread beyond city, warns local MP Claudia Webbe', *The Guardian*, 20 September 2022: https://www.theguardian.com/uk-news/2022/sep/20/leicester-violence-could-spread-beyond-city-says-mp-claudia-webbe; Reha Kansara and Abdirahim Saeed, 'Did misinformation fan the flames in Leicester?', BBC News, 25 September 2022: https://www.bbc.co.uk/news/blogs-trending-63009009. Accessed on 4 July 2023.
10. Reha Kansara and Abdirahim Saeed, 'Did misinformation fan the flames in Leicester?', BBC News, 25 September 2022: https://www.bbc.co.uk/news/blogs-trending-63009009. Accessed on 4 July 2023.
11. Abul Taher and Nicholas Pyke, 'Violent ethnic clashes in Leicester last year "were stoked by Indian Prime Minister Narendra Modi's Hindu nationalist party", sources claim', MailOnline, 14 May 2023: https://www.dailymail.co.uk/news/article-12081129/Violent-ethnic-clashes-Leicester-year-stoked-Modis-Hindu-nationalist-party.html. Accessed on 18 May 2023.
12. PTI, 'US senators condemn bulldozer display at India Day Parade in New Jersey', *Indian Express*, 3 September 2022: https://indianexpress.com/article/world/us-senators-condemn-bulldozer-display-india-day-parade-new-jersey-8128139/. Accessed on 18 May 2023.
13. Public letter from Chandrakant Patel, President of the Indian Business Association, to Sam Joshi, Mayor of Edison, and John McCormac, Mayor of Woodbridge, 30 August 2022.
14. Ministry of External Affairs, Annexure to Lok Sabha Question no.549, 5 February 2020: https://mea.gov.in/lok-sabha.htm?dtl/32357/QUEATION+NO549+INDIANS+SETTLED+ABROAD. Accessed on 3 January 2022.
15. United Nations, Department of Economic and Social Affairs Population Division, 'International Migrant Stock 2019': https://www.un.org/en/development/desa/population/migration/data/estimates2/estimates19.asp. Accessed on 3 January 2022.
16. Michael Fisher, *Counterflows to Colonialism: Indian Travellers and Settlers in Britain, 1600–1857* (New Delhi: Permanent Black, 2004).
17. Muhammad Anwar, *The Myth of Return: Pakistanis in Britain* (London: Heinemann Educational Books, 1979).
18. T Modood, et al., *Ethnic Minorities in Britain: Diversity and Disadvantage* (London: Policy Studies Institute, 1997), pp.113–14; Roger Ballard, 'The Current Demographic Characteristics of the South Asian Presence in Britain: An Analysis of the Results of the 2001 Census', Centre for Applied South Asian Studies, University of Manchester (2002): http://www.casas.org.uk/papers/pdfpapers/sasians2001.pdf. Accessed on 27 September 2014.

19. Gijsbert Oonk, *Settled Strangers: Asian Business Elites in East Africa (1800–2000)* (Los Angeles: Sage, 2013); Hasmita Ramji, 'Journeys of Difference: The Use of Migratory Narratives Among British Hindu Gujaratis', *Ethnic and Racial Studies*, vol.29, no.4 (2006), pp.702–24; Nicholas Van Hear, *New Diasporas: The Mass Exodus, Dispersal and Regrouping of Migrant Communities* (London: University College London Press, 1998); Joya Chatterji, 'Dispositions and Destinations: Refugee Agency and "Mobility Capital" in the Bengal Diaspora, 1947–2007', *Comparative Studies in Society and History*, vol.55, no.2 (2013), pp.273–304.
20. Ian Sanjay Patel, *We're Here Because You Were There: Immigration and the End of Empire* (London: Verso, 2021), p.281.
21. In June 2021, Sadiq Khan was London Mayor, Rishi Sunak was Chancellor of the Exchequer, Priti Patel was Home Secretary, and Sajid Javid was Secretary of State for Health and Social Care.
22. V.D. Savarkar, quoted in Prema Kurien, *A Place at the Multicultural Table: The Development of an American Hinduism* (New Bunswick, NJ: Rutgers University Press, 2007), p.127.
23. Shankar Tattwawadi (ed.), *Sarsanghchalak Goes Abroad* (New Delhi: Suruchi Prakashan, 1995), p.78.
24. Thomas Blom Hansen, 'The Vernacularisation of Hindutva: The BJP and Shiv Sena in Rural Maharashtra', *Contributions to Indian Sociology*, vol.30, no.2 (1996), pp.177–214; Edward Anderson and Arkotong Longkumer (eds.), *Neo-Hindutva: Evolving Forms, Spaces, and Expressions of Hindu Nationalism* (Abingdon: Routledge, 2021).
25. References to all of these may be found in the bibliography. This list of authors (in no particular order) is by no means exhaustive and there are many important contributions by people who are not mentioned here.
26. 'About Us—Hindu Vivek Kendra', n.d: http://www.hvk.org/about.html. Accessed on 12 September 2015.
27. M.S. Golwalkar, *Bunch of Thoughts* (Bangalore: Jagarana Prakashana, 1966/96), pp.349–50.
28. Tattwawadi (ed.), *Sarsanghchalak Goes Abroad* (1995), p.36.
29. Ingrid Therwath, 'Cyber-Hindutva: Hindu Nationalism, the diaspora and the Web', *e-Diasporas Atlas* (Paris: Fondation Maison des Sciences de l'Homme; 2012), p.7.
30. Rohit Chopra, 'Online Hindutva as a global right-wing counterpublic', *The Immanent Frame*, 12 October 2022: https://tif.ssrc.org/2022/10/12/online-hindutva-as-a-global-right-wing-counterpublic/. Accessed on 1 May 2023.
31. Robert Darnton, 'What is the History of Books?', *Daedalus* (Summer, 1982), pp.65–83; Anindita Ghosh, *Power in Print: Popular Publishing and the Politics of Language and Culture in a Colonial Society* (New Delhi: Oxford University Press, 2006), p.3. See also Francesca Orsini, *Hindi Public Sphere*,

1920–40: Language and Literature in the Age of Nationalism (New Delhi: Oxford University Press, 2002).

32. Prema Kurien, *A Place at the Multicultural Table: The Development of an American Hinduism* (New Brunswick, NJ: Rutgers University Press, 2007); Vinay Lal, 'The Politics of History on the Internet: Cyber-Diasporic Hinduism and the North American Hindu Diaspora', *Diaspora*, vol.8 (1999) pp.137–72; Arvind Rajagopal, 'Hindu Nationalism in the US: Changing Configurations of Political Practice', *Ethnic and Racial Studies*, vol.23, no.3 (2000), pp.463–77; Devesh Kapur, *Diaspora, Development, and Democracy: The Domestic Impact of International Migration from India* (Princeton, NJ: Princeton University Press, 2010); Martha Nussbaum, *The Clash Within: Democracy, Religious Violence, and India's Future* (London: Harvard University Press, 2007), pp.302–37.
33. Biju Mathew and Vijay Prashad, 'The Protean Forms of Yankee Hindutva', *Ethnic and Racial Studies*, vol.23, no.3 (2000), pp.516–34; Vijay Prashad, *The Karma of Brown Folk* (Minneapolis, MN: University of Minnesota Press, 2001); Vijay Prashad, *Uncle Swami: South Asians in America Today* (Noida: Harper Collins, 2013).
34. Sangay K. Mishra, *Desis Divided: The Political Lives of South Asian Americans* (Minneapolis, MN: University of Minnesota Press, 2016); Sangay K. Mishra, 'Hindu nationalism and Indian Ameican diasporic mobilizations', in Ruben Gowricharn (ed.), *New Perspectives on the Indian Diaspora* (Abingdon: Routledge, 2022), pp.59–77.
35. Walter K. Andersen and Shridhar D. Damle, *The RSS: A View to the Inside* (Gurgaon: Penguin Random House, 2018); Dhirendra K. Jha, 'Instead of Offering Objective Analysis, Andersen-Damle Book Helps RSS Perpetuate Convenient Myths', *Scroll.in*, 20 August 2018: https://scroll.in/article/890987/instead-of-offering-objective-analysis-andersen-damle-book-helps-rss-perpetuate-convenient-myths. Accessed on 3 January 2022.
36. Christophe Jaffrelot and Ingrid Therwath, 'Hindu Nationalism in the United Kingdom and North America', in Deana Heath and Chandana Mathur (eds.), *Communalism and Globalization in South Asia and its Diaspora* (Abingdon: Routledge, 2011), pp.44–57.
37. Christophe Jaffrelot and Ingrid Therwath, 'The Sangh Parivar and the Hindu Diaspora in the West: What Kind of "Long Distance Nationalism"?', *International Political Sociology*, vol.1 (2007), p.278.
38. AWAAZ—South Asia Watch Limited, 'In Bad Faith? British Charity and Hindu Extremism' (London: AWAAZ—South Asia Watch Limited, 2004). In the lead-up to the 2014 election in India, AWAAZ and the Monitoring Group also published 'Narendra Modi Exposed: Challenging the Myths Surrounding the BJP's Prime Ministerial Candidate', edited by Gautam Appa and Anish Vanaik.
39. Sabrang Communications and The South Asia Citizens Web, 'The Foreign Exchange of Hate—IDRF and the American Funding of Hindutva' (2002);

The Campaign to Stop Funding Hate, 'Unmistakably Sangh: The National HSC and its Hindutva Agenda' (South Asia Citizens Web, 2008); Jasa Macher, *Hindu Nationalist Influence in the United States, 2014–2021* (released via sacw.net, 2022). The organisation behind the first two reports, Sabrang Communications (run by Javed Anand and Teesta Setalvad), has produced a regular magazine, *Communalism Combat*, since 1993, which features various pieces on transnational Hindutva.

40. Edward Anderson and Christophe Jaffrelot, 'Hindu Nationalism and the "Saffronisation of the Public Sphere": an Interview with Christophe Jaffrelot', *Contemporary South Asia*, vol.26, no.4, pp.468–82.

41. Rohit Chopra, *The Virtual Hindu Rashtra: Saffron Nationalism and New Media* (Noida: Harper Collins, 2019); Arvind Rajagopal, *Politics after Television: Hindu Nationalism and the Reshaping of the Public in India* (Cambridge: Cambridge University Press, 2001); Ingrid Therwath, 'Cyber-Hindutva: Hindu Nationalism, the diaspora and the Web' (2012); Eviane Leidig, 'Immigrant, Nationalist and Proud: A Twitter Analysis of Indian Diaspora Supporters for Brexit and Trump', *Media and Communication*, vol.7, no.1 (2019), pp.77–89; Juli L. Gittinger, *Hinduism and Hindu Nationalism Online* (Abingdon: Routledge, 2019).

42. Rajeshwari Ghose (ed.), *In Quest of a Secular Symbol: Ayodhya and After* (Perth, Australia: Indian Ocean Centre & South Asian Research Unit, Curtin University of Technology Press, 1996). The diaspora-focused papers in this volume were: Arvind Rajagopal, 'Expatriate Nationalism: Disjunctive Discourses', pp.109–39; Gita Sahgal, 'Diaspora Politics in Britain: Hindu Identity in the Making', pp.140–56; Gautam Appa, Ann Rossiter and Gita Sahgal, 'Communal and Anti-Communal Forces in Britain: Continuities and Discontinuities', pp.157–66; and Siddartha Prakash, 'South Asian Student Politics in London', pp.167–80.

43. Kim Knott, *Hinduism in Leeds: a Study of Religious Practice in the Indian Hindu Community and in Hindu-related Groups* (Leeds: Department of Theology and Religious Studies, University of Leeds, 1986), p.50.

44. Chetan Bhatt, '*Dharmo Rakshati Rakshitah*: Hindutva Movements in the UK', *Ethnic and Racial Studies*, vol.23, no.3 (2000), p.561. See also Chetan Bhatt and Parita Mukta, 'Hindutva in the West: Mapping the Antinomies of Diaspora Nationalism', *Ethnic and Racial Studies*, vol.23, no.3 (2002), pp.407–41.

45. Parita Mukta, 'The Public face of Hindu Nationalism', *Ethnic and Racial Studies*, vol.23, no.3 (2000), pp.442–66; Sahgal, 'Diaspora Politics in Britain', in Ghose (ed.), *In Quest of a Secular Symbol* (1996), pp.140–56; Gita Sahgal, 'Secular Spaces: The Experiences of Asian Women Organising', in Gita Sahgal and Nira Yuval-Davis (eds.), *Refusing Holy Orders: Women and Fundamentalism in Britain* (London: Virago, 1992), pp.163–97; Pragna Patel, 'Rama or Rambo? The Rise of Hindu Fundamentalism', in Rahila Gupta (ed.), *From Homebreakers to Jailbreakers: Southall Black Sisters* (London:

Zed Books, 2003), pp.212–33; Amrit Wilson, *Dreams, Questions, Struggles: South Asian Women in Britain* (London: Pluto Press, 2006); Kalpana Wilson, *Race, Racism and Development: Interrogating History, Discourse and Practice* (London: Zed Books, 2012).

46. John Zavos, 'Stamp It Out: Disciplining the Image of Hinduism in a Multicultural Milieu', *Contemporary South Asia*, vol.16, no.3 (2008), pp.323–37; John Zavos, 'Negotiating Multiculturalism: Religion and the Organisation of Hindu Identity in Contemporary Britain', *Journal of Ethnic and Migration Studies*, vol. 35, no.6 (2009), pp.881–900; John Zavos, 'Diaspora Consciousness, Nationalism, and "Religion": The Case of Hindu Nationalism', in Allon Gal, Athena Leoussi, and Anthony Smith (eds.), *The Call of the Homeland: Diaspora Nationalisms, Past and Present* (2010), pp.323–43; John Zavos, 'Small Acts, Big Society: Sewa and Hindu (Nationalist) Identity in Britain', *Ethnic and Racial Studies*, vol.38, no.2 (2015), pp.243–58; John Zavos, 'Digital Media and Networks of Hindu Activism', *Culture and Religion*, vol.16, no.1 (2015), pp.17–34; John Zavos, Pralay Kanungo, Deepa Reddy, Maya Warrier and Raymond Brady Williams (eds.), *Public Hinduisms* (New Delhi: Sage, 2012).
47. Papiya Ghosh, *Partition and the South Asian Diaspora: Extending the Subcontinent* (Abingdon: Routledge, 2007).
48. Dhooleka Raj, 'Shifting Culture in the Global Terrain: Cultural Identity Constructions Amongst British Punjabi Hindus' (unpublished PhD thesis, University of Cambridge, 1997), p.25.
49. Dhooleka Raj, '"Who the hell do you think you are?" Promoting Religious Identity among Young Hindus in Britain', *Ethnic and Racial Studies*, vol.23, no.3 (2000), p.535. Another valuable piece on British Hindutva that engages with some similar themes is Nitasha Kaul and Annapurna Menon's recent chapter 'Hindutva in Western Societies: Entanglements and Paradoxes', in Ruben Gowricharn (ed.), *New Perspectives on the Indian Diaspora* (Abingdon: Routledge, 2022), pp.160–84.
50. Dhooleka Raj, *Where are you from? Middle Class Migrants in the Modern World* (Berkeley, CA: University of California Press, 2003), p.49.
51. Gyan Prakash, *Emergency Chronicles: Indira Gandhi and Democracy's Turning Point* (Princeton, NJ: Princeton University Press, 2019); Christophe Jaffrelot and Pratinav Anil, *India's First Dictatorship: The Emergency, 1975–77* (London: Hurst, 2020).
52. The *karmabhoomi / matrubhoomi* distinction has been made by a number of Hindu nationalist sources, including: M. Shah, 'Indian, British or Both?', in *Bradford Centenary Hindu Marathon* (Bradford: Hindu Marathon National Committee, 1997), p 103. Quoted in Stacy Burlet, 'Re-awakenings? Hindu Nationalism Goes Global', in Roy Starrs (ed.), *Asian Nationalism in an Age of Globalisation* (Richmond: Curzon Press, 2001), p.14.

53. Charles Taylor, 'The Politics of Recognition', in Amy Gutmann (ed.), *Multiculturalism and the Politics of Recognition* (Princeton, NJ: Princeton University Press, 1992).

1. 'FROM VIDESH VIBHAG TO VISHWA VIBHAG AND NOW VISHWA SANGH'

1. Dr Yashwant Pathak, Joint Co-ordinator, Hindu Swayamsevak Sangh (US), in Jagdish Chandra Sharda Shastri, compiled and edited by Ratan Sharda, *Memoirs of a Global Hindu* (Mumbai: Vishwa Adhyayan Kendra, 2008), p.86. Translation: 'from foreign division, to world division and now world Sangh'.
2. Trustees of the Hindu Swayamsevak Sangh, 'Hindu Swayamsevak Sangh (UK) Trust Deed', 1974.
3. H.V. Seshadri, *Hindus Abroad: Dilemma: Dollar or Dharma?* (New Delhi: Suruchi Prakashan, 1990), p.7.
4. Seshadri, *Dollar or Dharma?* (1990), p.23.
5. Dhooleka Raj, 'Shifting Culture in the Global Terrain: Cultural Identity Constructions Amongst British Punjabi Hindus' (unpublished PhD thesis, University of Cambridge, 1997), p.25.
6. Including (but not limited to) H.V. Seshadri, *RSS—A Vision in Action* (Bangalore: Sahitya Sindhu Prakashana, 2001); Shankarrao Tatwawadi, 'Vishwa Vibhag—A Leap Beyond the Shores', in Sharad Kunte (ed.), *Vishwa Sangh Shibir 2010 Souvenir* (Pune: Vishwa Adhyayan Kendra, 2010), pp.201–3; Rashtriya Swayamsevak Sangh, *Widening Horizons* (New Delhi: Suruchi Prakashan, 1992); Jai Prakash, 'The Sangh Fraternity Bringing the World Within its Fold', *Organiser*, 7 May 1995, pp.51–2.
7. Shastri, *Memoirs of a Global Hindu* (2008). Another source on the same incident names the second protagonist as 'Manikbhai Gugani'—indicative of the fallibility of these sources. Tatwawadi, 'Vishwa Vibhag', in Kunte (ed.), *Vishwa Sangh Shibir* (2010), pp.201–3.
8. Rashtriya Swayamsevak Sangh, *Widening Horizons* (1992), p.1. The myth of the story is further entrenched in Shankar Tattwawadi (ed.), *Sarsanghchalak Goes Abroad: A Collection of Lectures Delivered by Prof. Rajendra Singh on Foreign Land* (New Delhi: Suruchi Prakashan, 1995), p.74.
9. Shastri, *Memoirs of a Global Hindu* (2008), p.28. This story is also recorded in the *Samvad* blog, in which the author recalls a conversation with Shastrji from Vishwa Sangh Shibir in Pune, 2010. 'Vishwa Sangha Shibir–2010', n.d: http://shrivishwaniketan.blogspot.co.uk/2011/01/this-issue-of-samvad-exclusively.html. Accessed on 22 August 2015.
10. Shastri, *Memoirs of a Global Hindu* (2008), p.44.
11. Shastri, *Memoirs of a Global Hindu* (2008), p.24. Note that Chamanlal Grover, like many in the Sangh, is referred to in almost all literature by his first name alone. Hence, in this book, he is also 'Chamanlal'.

12. Shastri, *Memoirs of a Global Hindu* (2008), p.34.
13. The emphasis on spontaneity is largely motivated by, firstly, a desire to underline an organic, natural inspiration, and, more recently, a need to distance the Sangh in the diaspora from the Indian parent-organisations, especially in the light of communal violence following the Babri Masjid demolition (1992/3) and in Gujarat (2002), which was condemned by governments around the world. Nonetheless, we must not entirely dismiss the agency of grassroots organisers, who are also crucial to the Sangh's growth and operation.
14. Vishwa Adhyayan Kendra, 'Annual Report 2007–2008', 2008: http://www.vakmumbai.org/presentation/report-2007-2008.pdf. Accessed on 1 January 2015.
15. Tatwawadi, 'Vishwa Vibhag, in Kunte (ed.), *Vishwa Sangh Shibir* (2010), p.201.
16. Tatwawadi, 'Vishwa Vibhag, in Kunte (ed.), *Vishwa Sangh Shibir* (2010), p.201.
17. Christophe Jaffrelot and Ingrid Therwath, 'The Global Sangh Parivar: A Study of Contemporary International Hinduism', in Abigail Green and Vincent Viaene (eds.), *Religious Internationals in the Modern World* (London: Palgrave Macmillan, 2012), pp.346–51.
18. Sharad Kunte, 'Vishwa Sangha Shibir: An Overview', in Kunte (ed.), *Vishwa Sangh Shibir* (2010), p.5.
19. Suresh Chandra Bajpai, *RSS at a Glance* (New Delhi: Suruchi Prakashan, 2011), pp.38–9.
20. Author's interview with Anil Vartak (New Delhi, 3 May 2014).
21. Author's interview with Subramanian Swamy (London, 3 April 2015). See also Rakesh Sinha, 'A tribute to Ma. Chamanlaji: State-Centric life and nation-builders', in Kunte (ed.), *Vishwa Sangh Shibir* (2010), pp.199–200.
22. 'Tributes to Chamanlal Ji', n.d: http://www.vakmumbai.org/chamanlalji.php. Accessed on 22 August 2015.
23. P.G. Sahasrabuddhe and Manik Chandra Vajpayee, *The People versus Emergency: A Saga of Struggle*, trans. Sudhakar Raje (New Delhi: Suruchi Prakashan, 1991), pp.511–43.
24. Sahasrabuddhe and Vajpayee, *The People versus Emergency* (1991), p.516.
25. Shastri, *Memoirs of a Global Hindu* (2008), p.44.
26. Author's interview with Anil Vartak (New Delhi, 3 May 2014).
27. Pathak, in Shastri, *Memoirs of a Global Hindu* (2008), p.87.
28. For instance, a 1971 *Organiser* article notes the opening of Deendayal Bhavan by Swami Satyamitranand Giri, and is accompanied by a photograph captioned, 'Hundreds of Hindus of Nairobi gathered...' 'Swami Satyamitranand Giri at Pandit Deen Dayal Bhawan, Nairobi', *Organiser*, 22 May 1971.
29. 'Tributes to Chamanlal Ji', n.d.; Sharad Kunte, 'Shri Laxmanrao Bhide—Architect of International Sangh work', in Kunte (ed.), *Vishwa Sangh Shibir* (2010), p.198.

30. Shastri, *Memoirs of a Global Hindu* (2008), p.118.
31. Kunte, 'Shri Laxmanrao Bhide', in Kunte (ed.), *Vishwa Sangh Shibir* (2010), p.198. This discrepancy—along with the almost unfeasibly large number of countries and the hagiographical nature of the sources themselves—call for some hesitancy. John Zavos, 'Diaspora Consciousness, Nationalism, and "Religion": The Case of Hindu Nationalism', in Allon Gal, Athena Leoussi, and Anthony Smith (eds.), *The Call of the Homeland: Diaspora Nationalisms, Past and Present* (Boston, MA: Brill, 2010), p.329.
32. Shastri, *Memoirs of a Global Hindu* (2008), p.81.
33. Vishwa Sangh Shibir, *Vishwa Sangh Shibir 2005 Souvenir* (Karnavati: Antar Rashtriya Sahayog Pratishthan, 2005), p.11. Quoted in Zavos, 'Diaspora Consciousness, Nationalism, and "Religion"', in Gal, Leoussi and Smith (eds.), *The Call of the Homeland* (2010), p.329. Kunte, 'Shri Laxmanrao Bhide', in Kunte (ed.), *Vishwa Sangh Shibir* (2010), p.198, states that Bhide 'traveled [sic] in more than 60 countries'. Various other senior *pracharaks* (including Bhaurao Deoras, older brother of Madhukar Dattatraya Deoras, the third Sarsanghchalak of the RSS), spent long periods of time outside of India to help develop the organisation. M.D. Deoras also sent colleagues abroad to seek support during the Emergency when Indira banned the RSS in India (see Chapter 3).
34. Vasudev Godbole, 'Indian Institute for Research into True History Newsletter', no.11, 16 October 1983: http://satyashodh.com/nl11.htm. Accessed on 1 January 2015.
35. 'History of Sangh in Mautitius', n.d.
36. Walter Andersen and Shridhar Damle, *The Brotherhood in Saffron: the Rashtriya Swayamsevak Sangh and Hindu Revivalism* (New Delhi: Vistaar, 1987), p.114.
37. Tattwawadi (ed.), *Sarsanghchalak Goes Abroad* (1995), p.7.
38. The 'earlier visitors of Kenya' listed by Shastri include Sarvashri Bhau Rao Deoras, Dattopant Thengadi, Moropant Pingale, Kedarnath Sahani, Uttamrao Patil, and Jagannath Rao Joshi. Shastri, *Memoirs of a Global Hindu* (2008), p.118.
39. Shastri, *Memoirs of a Global Hindu* (2008), p.118.
40. Shastri, *Memoirs of a Global Hindu* (2008), p.115. Satyamitranand Giri is one of the first Hindutva-sympathetic gurus to gain a large following in the Indian diaspora, particularly amongst Gujaratis. He first travelled overseas in 1962, to Kenya, and purportedly visited over fifty countries in total. 'Swami Satyamitranand Tours United Kingdom', *Hinduism Today*, March 1998: http://www.hinduismtoday.com/modules/smartsection/item.php?itemid=4723. Accessed on 10 January 2013. See also Lise McKean, *Divine Enterprise: Gurus and the Hindu Nationalist Movement* (London: University of Chicago Press, 1996), pp.132–9. As an example of the building's enduring importance, we can observe a Gala Dinner with 200 guests being held on 23 May 2014 to celebrate the BJP's election victory.

This was followed by a special meeting of the Hindu Swayasemvak Sangh, with 120 swayamsevaks: Kul Bhushan, 'Kenya Celebrates Modi Win', *The Indian Diaspora*, 6 June 2014: http://theindiandiaspora.com/news-details/Spotlight/subprimary_news/nairobi-congratulating-modi-with-cakes.htm. Accessed on 5 September 2014.

41. Shastri, *Memoirs of a Global Hindu* (2008), p.115.
42. Even towards the end of the century, after large-scale emigration of Hindus from East Africa, the BSS appeared well entrenched in Kenya. A speech given by RSS Sarsanghchalak Rajendra Singh during his 1997 tour to inaugurate the celebrations of the BSS's fiftieth anniversary also highlights, although less emphatically, their enduring reach. Singh stated that, 'There are 30,000 Hindus in Nairobi, in about 6,000 families. We have in our contact about 4,000 *swayamsevaks* ... probably from 400 families'. Liladhar Bharandia, 'RSS leader celebrates 50 years of service in Kenya', *Hinduism Today*, July 1997: http://www.hinduismtoday.com/archives/1997/7/1997-7-14.shtml. Accessed on 3 March 2013.
43. Sudarshan visited in Kenya in January 2007 and gave a speech to Nairobi University which was published in K.S. Sudarshan, *Hindutva in Modern Perspective* (Nagpur: Shri Bharati Prakashan, 2007), pp.24–39. See also 'K S Sudarshan in Kenya: Hindus for Peace, Noble Ideals', *Organiser*, 4 February 2007.
44. 'OFBJP unit in Africa launched', *Organiser*, 27 October 2013.
45. The Arya Samaj connection with East Africa was particularly pioneering and noteworthy; its Nairobi branch was founded in 1903, less than thirty years after Dayananda Saraswati started the movement in India in 1875. See: Pandit Nardev Vedalankar and Manohar Somera, *Arya Samaj and Indians Abroad* (New Delhi Sarvadeshik Arya Pratinidhi Sabha, 1975); Bhai Parmanand, *The Story of My Life* (Delhi: S. Chand, 1982).
46. Indian High Commission, Nairobi, *Education Report for the two years 1953 and 1954 for East and Central Africa*. National Archives of India [henceforth NAI], Ministry of External Affairs Papers [henceforth MEA], Africa Branch, F.AII/53/6491/31(s).
47. Waruhiu Itote, *'Mau Mau' General* (Nairobi: East African Publishing House, 1967) p.20, quoted in Marshall S. Clough, *Mau Mau Memoirs: History, Memory, and Politics* (London: Lynne Rienner Publishers, 1998) p.72.
48. Frank Furedi, 'The Development of Anti-Asian Opinion Among Africans in Nakuru District, Kenya', *African Affairs*, vol.73, no.292 (1974), pp.347–58; Dent Ocaya-Lakidi, 'Black Attitudes to the Brown and White Colonizers of East Africa', in Twaddle (ed.), *Expulsion of a Minority* (1975), pp.81–97; Michael Twaddle, 'East African Asians Through a Hundred Years', in Colin Clarke, Ceri Peach, and Steven Vertovec, *South Asians Overseas* (Cambridge: Cambridge University Press, 1990), pp.149–63.
49. Indian High Commission, Nairobi, 'Annual Report on Uganda for the Year 1954', NAI, MEA, Africa Branch. F.AII/53/6491/31(s); Michael

Twaddle, 'The Development of Communalism among East African Asians', in Crispin Bates (ed.), *Community, Empire and Migration: South Asians in Diaspora* (Basingstoke: Palgrave, 2001), pp.109–22.
50. Indian High Commission, Nairobi, 'Annual Report on Uganda for the Year 1954', NAI, MEA, Africa Branch, F.AII/53/6491/31(s).
51. Sana Aiyar, *Indians in Kenya: The Politics of Diaspora* (Cambridge, MA: Harvard University Press, 2015).
52. Shastri, *Memoirs of a Global Hindu* (2008), p.37.
53. Hindu Swayamsevak Sangh (Kenya), *Amar Bharati*, August 2016, p.22.
54. Robert Gregory, *The Rise and Fall of Philanthropy in East Africa: The Asian Contribution* (New Brunswick, NJ: Transaction Publishers, 1991), p.111; Elsa Abreu, *Role of Self-Help in the Development of Education in Kenya 1900–73* (Nairobi: Kenya Literature Bureau, 1982).
55. Ministry of External Affairs, 'Annual Report on Tanganyika for the Year 1954'; Indian Commission Nairobi, 'Annual Report on Kenya for the Year 1954', NAI, MEA, Africa Branch, F.AII/53/6491/31(s). Aiyar, *Indians in Kenya* (2015), passim.
56. B.F.H.B. Tyabji, 'On Relations between Muslims and Hindus in the British East African Territories', 23 August 1952, NAI, MEA, Africa Branch, AII/53/6491/31/Secret.
57. Ramji, Hasmita, 'Journeys of Difference: The Use of Migratory Narratives Among British Hindu Gujaratis', *Ethnic and Racial Studies*, vol.29, no.4 (July 2006), p.718.
58. Chetan Bhatt, '*Dharmo Rakshati Rakshitah*: Hindutva Movements in the UK', *Ethnic and Racial Studies*, vol.23, no.3 (2000), p.576.
59. Dhiraj Shah, 'Oral History Project' interview by Dipvandana Shah, Hindu Council of Birmingham, 24 June 2007: http://www.hcb.org.uk/documents/uploaded/ohp/DhirajShah.pdf. Accessed on 3 June 2014.
60. Shastri, *Memoirs of a Global Hindu* (2008), p.40.
61. Shastri, *Memoirs of a Global Hindu* (2008), p.40.
62. Kenya—182,000, Tanzania—105,000, Uganda—76,000. See Hugh Tinker, 'Indians Abroad: Emigration, Restriction and Rejection', in Twaddle (ed.), *Expulsion of a Minority* (1975), p.15.
63. Sanjukta Banerji Bhattacharya, 'India-East Africa Ties: Future Trajectories', *Africa Quarterly, Indian Journal of African Affairs*, vol.49, no.1 (2009), p.18.
64. Judith Brown, *Global South Asians: Introducing the Modern Diaspora* (Cambridge: Cambridge University Press, 2006), p.47.
65. Randell Hansen, *Citizenship and Immigration in Post-War Britain* (Oxford: Oxford University Press, 2000), pp.153–4; Ian Sanjay Patel, *We're Here Because You Were There: Immigration and the End of Empire* (London: Verso, 2021).
66. Due to the limitations of census data, which only since 1991 have contained a question on ethnicity, it is difficult to accurately quantify the exact proportion. See: K. Sillitoe and P.H. White, 'Ethnic Group and the

British Census: The Search for a Question', *Journal of the Royal Statistical Society*, Series A (Statistics in Society), vol.155, no.1 (1992), pp.141–63.
67. Roger Ballard, 'The Current Demographic Characteristics of the South Asian Presence in Britain: an analysis of the results of the 2001 Census', Centre for Applied South Asian Studies, University of Manchester (2002), p.1. In the same ten-year period, the percentage of those from India rose just 2.8%. See David Owen, 'Ethnic Minorities in Britain: Patterns of population change, 1981–91', 1991 Census Statistical Paper No.10, Centre for Research in Ethnic Relations, University of Warwick (1995), p.8.
68. Judith Brown (2006, pp.47–8) estimates that between 1969 and 1971 'almost 24,000' Asians left Uganda, most destined for Britain. At the end of the ninety-day deadline, just 2,000 Asians remained in Uganda. See also Michael Twaddle (ed.), *Expulsion of a Minority: Essays on Ugandan Asians* (London: Athlone Press, 1975).
69. Seshadri, *Dollar or Dharma?* (1990), p.67.
70. Shastri, *Memoirs of a Global Hindu* (2008), p.111.
71. Sheena Shah, 'Identity and Belonging: The Case of the Gujarati Diaspora Community in the United Kingdom, Singapore and South Africa', in Sharmina Mawani and Anjoom Mukadam (eds.), *Globalisation, Diaspora and Belonging: Exploring Transnationalism and Gujarati Identity* (Jaipur: Rawat Publications, 2014), p.147. Despite the introduction of more precise ethnicity categories since the 2001 Census, it is not possible to use this data to quantify how many people in Britain (including second and third generations) have East African roots, as most of those self-define with their Asian/Asian British ethnic groups (Indian, Pakistani, Other, etc.).
72. The numbers being 58% Hindu, 19% Sikh, and 15% Muslim (from East Africa), in contrast to 32% Hindu, 50% Sikh, and 6% Muslim (from India). See Tariq Modood, 'Culture and Identity', in T. Modood and R. Berthoud (eds.), *Ethnic Minorities in Britain: Diversity and Disadvantage* (London: Policy Studies Institute, 1997), p.298.
73. Knott, 'The Gujarati Mochis in Leeds', in Ballard (ed.), *Desh Pardesh* (1994), pp.213–30.
74. Data transcribed from manuscript records of the General Register Office Register of Places of Worship and from the Marriage, Divorce and Adoption Statistics, Series FM2 (London: Office for National Statistics, various dates); cited in Ceri Peach and Richard Gale, 'Muslims, Hindus and Sikhs in the New Religious Landscape of England', *Geographical Review*, vol.93, no.4 (October 2003), p.479.
75. Kim Knott, 'Hinduism in Britain', in H. Coward, J. Hinnells, and R.B. Williams (eds.), *The South Asian Religious Diaspora in Britain, Canada, and the United States* (Albany, NY: State University of NewYork Press, 2000), p.92. We must, though, be careful not to overemphasise the East African Asian factor, or mistake correlation for causation. Although many organisations,

including the HSS, were started mainly by East African Asians, institutions established in Britain from the late 1960s onwards also reflected the settlement and accretion of resources by other Asian communities who had earlier migrated to Britain, as well as the relative economic strength of many South Asian migrants who arrived in Britain from the late twentieth century onwards.

76. Peach and Gale, 'Muslims, Hindus and Sikhs' (2003), p.474. On sojourning, see Mohammed Anwar, *The Myth of Return: Pakistanis in Britain* (London: Heinemann Educational Books, 1979). Judith Brown notes that 77% of men and 57% of women moving to Britain from East Africa were 'fluent or fairly fluent' in English. See Judith Brown, *Global South Asians: Introducing the Modern Diaspora* (Cambridge: Cambridge University Press, 2006), p.49. See also, V. Robinson, 'Marching into the Middle Classes? The Long-Term Resettlement of East African Asians in the UK', *Journal of Refugee Studies*, vol.6, no.3 (1993), pp.230–47.

77. Steven Vertovec, *The Hindu Diaspora: Comparative Patterns* (London: Routledge, 2000), p.90. However whilst stereotypes of business acumen and industriousness may account for the successes of British Gujaratis in recent years, they often obfuscate the challenging early days of settlement and painful experiences of relocation, particularly for those expelled from Uganda by Idi Amin in 1972.

78. M. Michaelson, 'Caste, Kinship and Marriage: A Study of Two Gujarati Trading Castes in England' (unpublished PhD thesis, School of Oriental and African Studies, University of London, 1983); cited in Vertovec, *The Hindu Diaspora* (2000), p.90.

79. Vertovec, *The Hindu Diaspora* (2000), pp.87–107; Bowen, 'The Evolution of Gujarati Hindu Organisations in Bradford', in Burghart (ed.), *Hinduism in Great Britain:* (1987), pp.15–31; Peach and Gale, 'Muslims, Hindus and Sikhs' (2003), pp.469–90.

80. Joya Chatterji, 'Dispositions and Destinations: Refugee Agency and "Mobility Capital" in the Bengal Diaspora, 1947–2007', *Comparative Studies in Society and History*, vol.55, no.2 (2013), pp.273–304.

81. Parminder Bhachu, 'East African Sikhs in Britain: Experienced Settlers with Traditionalistic Values', *Immigrants & Minorities: Historical Studies in Ethnicity, Migration and Diaspora*, vol.3, no.3 (1984), pp.276–96. See also Parminder Bhachu, 'Twice and Direct Migrant Sikhs: Caste, Class, and Identity in Pre- and Post-1984 Britain', in Ivan Hubert Light and Parminder Bhachu (eds.), *Immigration and Entrepreneurship: Culture, Capital, and Ethnic Networks* (New Brunswick, NJ: Transaction Publishers, 2004), pp.163–84.

82. Home Office/Office for National Statistics, 'Immigration Patterns of Non-UK Born Populations in England and Wales in 2011' (2013), p.6: http://www.ons.gov.uk/ons/dcp171776_346219.pdf.

83. Trustees of the Hindu Swayamsevak Sangh, *Hindu Swayamsevak Sangh (UK) Financial Statements* and *Trustees Annual Report* (2012), p.2. The same

preamble is contained in all currently held reports (2007–12). Vyasa Purnima is a festival celebrating spiritual and academic teachers, in particular the Vedic sage Vyasa.
84. *Sangh Sandesh*, Fiftieth Anniversary of HSS Special Edition (2016), p.26.
85. Shastri, *Memoirs of a Global Hindu* (2008), p.47.
86. Amrit Shah in *Sangh Sandesh*, Fiftieth Anniversary of HSS Special Edition (2016), p.36.
87. Nicholas Van Hear, *New Diasporas. The Mass Exodus, Dispersal and Regrouping of Migrant Communities* (London: University College London Press, 1998).
88. Bhupendra Dave, *Sangh Sandesh*, Fiftieth Anniversary of HSS Special Edition (2016), p.31. Emphasis added.
89. Bhupendra Dave, *Sangh Sandesh*, Fiftieth Anniversary of HSS Special Edition (2016), p.31
90. Dhiraj Shah, 'A Saintly Person Departs for Heavenly Abode': http://hssuk.org/a-saintly-person-departs-for-heavenly-abode/. Accessed on 6 December 2017.
91. Seshadri, *Dollar or Dharma?* (1990), p.67.
92. Bhatt, '*Dharmo Rakshati Rakshitah*' (2000), p.577.
93. Hasmukh Shah in Yajur Shah, 'Hindu Sangam', 14 January 2013: http://vimeo.com/57388215. Accessed on 24 July 2014. Hasmukh Shah was a senior HSS leader and key organiser of the 1989 Virat Hindu Sammelan, considered in Chapter 3. See also Shyam Bhatia, 'Communal Tension Grows in Bradford', *Rediff*.com, 13 June, 2001): http://www.rediff.com/us/2001/jun/13uk.htm. Accessed on 22 August 2015.
94. 'HSS UK Stories: Biography—Shri Ratilal ji Shah, Bradford', n.d: https://hssstories.wordpress.com/biographies/. Accessed on 22 August 2015.
95. 'HSS UK Stories: Biography—Shri Ratilal ji Shah, Bradford', n.d.
96. Dhiraj Shah, 'Oral History Project' (2007). Shah moved to Birmingham to study in 1969, and did not return, emphasising his parent's anxieties that Idi Amin's expulsion of Asians in Uganda, 'could spread to Kenya'.
97. Dinesh Mistry, *Sangh Sandesh*, Fiftieth Anniversary of HSS Special Edition (2016), p.35.
98. Trustees of the Hindu Swayamsevak Sangh, 'Hindu Swayamsevak Sangh (UK) Trust Deed', 4 March 1974.
99. Jaffrelot and Therwath, 'The Global Sangh Parivar' in Green and Viaene (eds.), *Religious Internationals* (2012), p.346.
100. Sahasrabuddhe and Vajpayee, *The People versus Emergency* (1991), p.513.
101. Tattwawadi (ed.), *Sarsanghchalak Goes Abroad* (1995), passim.
102. *Sangh Sandesh*, September—October 2000, vol.XI, no.5, p.10. See also Trustees of the Hindu Swayamsevak Sangh, *Hindu Swayamsevak Sangh (UK) Trustees Reports* and *Annual Accounts* (2001), p.3. Cited in AWAAZ—South Asia Watch, 'In Bad Faith?' (2004), pp.47–8.

103. Discussion with a *karykarta* before lecture by Dattareya Hosabale, 'RSS: Shaping a Saffron Future?' (organised by Vichaar Manthan) at De Montfort University, Leicester, 14 September 2014.
104. Hindu Swayamsevak Sangh (UK), 'Interaction with Hindu Organisations', n.d: http://hssuk.org/interaction-with-hindu-organisations/. Accessed on 14 September 2015.
105. Priti Patel, 'Message from Priti Patel MP, the Prime Minister's UK Indian Diaspora Champion, for the event "RSS: A Vision in Action—A New Dawn" hosted by the Hindu Swayamsevak Sangh UK', Letter to Hindu Swayamsevak Sangh (UK), 21 September, 2014: http://hssuk.org/priti-patel-congratulates-hss-uk. Accessed on 12 September 2015.
106. Samvada, 'RSS inspired Hindu Swayamsevak Sangh's 3-day Sanskriti Maha Shibir–2016 begins in London', http://samvada.org/?p=29840.
107. Swati Chaturvedi, 'Mohan Bhagwat Wants to do a Modi in UK, RSS Party with DiCaprio and Branson', *DailyO*, 22 June 2016: https://www.dailyo.in/politics/mohan-bhagwat-modi-in-uk-rss-dicaprio-and-branson-sangh-shakha-vhp/story/1/11329.html. Accessed on 4 January 2022.
108. Two weeks after the widely reported stories, the HSS finally dismissed reports about the possibility of the Hollywood star attending their fiftieth-anniversary camp. Although, as is often the case, the denial was much less widely reported than the initial rumours. Ashutosh Bhardwaj, 'No Film Stars Invited for Sangh's UK Event, Says RSS', *The Indian Express*, 7 July 2016: http://indianexpress.com/article/india/india-news-india/rss-mohan-bhagwat-uk-event-rashtriya-swayamsewak-sangh-2898169/. Accessed on 4 January 2022.
109. Constitution of the Rashtriya Swayamsevak Sangh. Translated and reproduced in D.R. Goyal, *Rashtriya Swayamsevak Sangh* (New Delhi: Radakrishna Prakashan, 2000), p.263.
110. V.M. Sirsikar, 'My Years in the RSS', in Eleanor Zelliot and Maxine Berntsen (eds.), *The Experience of Hinduism: Essays on Religion in Maharashtra* (Albany, NY: State University of New York Press, 1988), p.196; Ravish Tiwari, 'Rise of the Pracharak', *India Today*, vol.39, no.49 (2014), p.22.
111. Anthony Elenjimittam, *Philosophy and Action of the RSS for the Hind Swaraj* (Bombay: Laxmi Publications, 1951), pp.124–5. Another 'internal' account translates '*pracharak*' as 'missionary'. See Sirsikar, 'My Years in the RSS', in Zelliot and Berntsen (eds.), *The Experience of Hinduism* (1988), p.196.
112. Seshadri, *RSS—A Vision in Action* (2001), p.5.
113. Andersen and Damle, *The Brotherhood in Saffron* (1987), p.88. Whilst these observations were based on fieldwork in the 1970s and 1980s, similar trends have been observed in research for this book. Whilst the *pracharak* is a crucial role for the functioning of the RSS—organising at a grassroots level, spreading the Sangh, and forming a 'communications network'—it is a position of neither significant power nor glamour.

114. Sirsikar, 'My Years in the RSS', in Zelliot and Berntsen (eds.), *The Experience of Hinduism* (1988), p.196.
115. Kwame Anthony Appiah, *Cosmopolitanism: Ethics in a World of Strangers* (London: Allen Lane, 2006).
116. Andersen and Damle, *The Brotherhood in Saffron* (1987), p.87.
117. Tatwawadi, 'Vishwa Vibhag', in Kunte (ed.), *Vishwa Sangh Shibir* (2010), p.203. *Sarsanghchalak Goes Abroad* (1995, p.77) stated that there were twelve overseas *pracharaks*, and Anil Vartak, in an interview (3 May 2014), told me that there were twelve *pracharaks* in 2014. This suggests that the number of diaspora-based *pracharaks* has been fairly stable over the past twenty years.
118. Anahita Mukherji, 'Rashtriya Swayamsevak Sangh "shakha" spreads its wings to 39 countries', *Times of India*, 21 December 2015.
119. 'Swayamsevak', 'A History of the Hindu Swayamsevak Sangh', n.d.
120. Tattwawadi (ed.), *Sarsanghchalak Goes Abroad* (1995), p.36.
121. Tattwawadi (ed.), *Sarsanghchalak Goes Abroad* (1995), p.37.
122. Christophe Jaffrelot, *The Hindu Nationalist Movement and Indian Politics* (London: Hurst and Company, 1996), pp.42–3.
123. Ram Vaidya's father is the senior RSS leader and Indian spokesman M.G. Vaidya. Edward Luce and Demetri Sevastapulo, 'Blood and Money', *Financial Times*, 20 February 2003.
124. Trustees of the Hindu Swayamsevak Sangh, 'Hindu Swayamsevak Sangh (UK) Financial Statements 2006' (2006), p.4.
125. Trustees of the Hindu Swayamsevak Sangh, 'Hindu Swayamsevak Sangh (UK) Trustees Annual Report 2011' (2011), p.2.
126. AWAAZ—South Asia Watch, 'In Bad Faith?' (2004), p.48. See also Tatwawadi, 'Vishwa Vibhag', in Kunte (ed.), *Vishwa Sangh Shibir* (2010), pp.202–3.
127. T. Basu, P. Datta, S. Sarkar, T. Sarkar, and S. Sen, *Khaki Shorts and Saffron Flags* (New Delhi: Orient Longman, 1993), p.40.
128. M.G. Chitkara, *Rashtriya Swayamsevak Sangh: National Upsurge* (New Delhi: S B Nangia, 2004), p.367.
129. Andersen and Damle, *The Brotherhood in Saffron* (1987), p.82. The flag is also a 'metonymic mnemonic for the nation'—see Raminder Kaur, 'Spectacles of Nationalism in the Ganapati Utsav of Maharashtra', in Richard Davis (ed.), *Picturing the Nation: Iconographies of Modern India* (Hyderabad: Orient Longman, 2007), p.236.
130. The Constitution of the Rashtriya Swayamsevak Sangh (as adopted on 1 August 1948 and amended up to 11 March 2000), reproduced in Chitkara, *Rashtriya Swayamsevak Sangh* (2004), p.310.
131. Jaffrelot, *The Hindu Nationalist Movement and Indian Politics* (1996), pp.63–4. Subsequent leaders of the RSS have been significantly less autocratic; Madhukar Dattatraya Deoras (Sarsanghchalak from 1973 to 1993) was a technocratic leader of the Sangh—a man of action, whose political

achievements did not earn him the same devotion as his predecessors. Similarly, the leadership of Rajendra Singh (1993–2000), who, revealingly, was referred to as 'Rajju Bhaiya', went a long way to ensuring the status of Sarsanghchalak subdued from the veneration of Guruji and Doctorji.

132. Christophe Jaffrelot, *Modi's India: Hindu Nationalism and the Rise of Ethnic Democracy* (Princeton, NJ: Princeton University Press, 2021).
133. Jairus Banerjee (ed.), *Fascism: Essays on Europe and India* (New Delhi: Three Essays Collective, 2016); Prabhat Patnaik, 'The Fascism of Our Times', *Social Scientist*, vol. 21, no. 3/4 (1993), pp.69–77.
134. Eviane Leidig, 'Hindutva as a variant of right-wing extremism', *Patterns of Prejudice*, vol.54, no.3 (2020), pp.215–37; Julius Lipner, 'Hindu Fundamentalism', in James D.G. Dunn (ed.), *Fundamentalisms: Threats and Ideologies in the Modern World* (London: I.B. Tauris, 2016), pp.93–118.
135. Andersen and Damle, *The Brotherhood in Saffron* (1987), pp.87–8
136. Author's interview with anonymous *karyakarta* (19 March 2015).
137. Author's interview with anonymous *karyakarta* (19 March 2015). Others have noted quite open antipathy towards Muslims by HSS members. This was seen in 'Exposure: Charities Behaving Badly', ITV, first aired 18 February 2015.
138. Basu, Datta, Sarkar, Sarkar and Sen, *Khaki Shorts and Saffron Flags* (1993), p.40.
139. Adam Moss, 'What led to the ugly scenes of violence and disorder in Leicester?', *Leicester Mercury*, 19 September 2022: https://www.leicestermercury.co.uk/news/news-opinion/what-led-ugly-scenes-violence-7603138. Accessed on 26 May 2023.
140. Chris Allen, 'Leicester's unrest is a problem for the whole city, not just Hindu and Muslim communities', *The Conversation*, 28 September 2022: https://theconversation.com/leicesters-unrest-is-a-problem-for-the-whole-city-not-just-hindu-and-muslim-communities-191363. Accessed on 26 May 2023.
141. Interestingly, the HSS translate *vistarak* as 'voluntary youth worker'. See Trustees of the Hindu Swayamsevak Sangh, 'Hindu Swayamsevak Sangh (UK) Trustees Annual Report 2013' (2013), p.5.
142. Discussion with an HSS *karykarta* at Dattareya Hosabale lecture, 'RSS: Shaping a Saffron Future?', Leicester, 14 September 2014; Trustees of the Hindu Swayamsevak Sangh, *Hindu Swayamsevak Sangh (UK) Annual Report* (2011), p.4.
143. Jaffrelot briefly mentions that Vajpayee was sent to Uttar Pradesh as a *vistarak* in 1946: Jaffrelot, *Hindu Nationalism: A Reader* (2007), p.314.
144. Trustees of the Hindu Swayamsevak Sangh (UK), *Guidelines for Vistaraks (Vistarak Yojna)*, n.d. Cited in AWAAZ—South Asia Watch, 'In Bad Faith?' (2004), pp.42–3.
145. Trustees of the Hindu Swayamsevak Sangh (UK), *Guidelines for Vistaraks (Vistarak Yojna)*, n.d.

146. Mathur, *The Everyday Life of Hindu Nationalism* (2008), p.144.
147. 'HSS UK Stories: Story 3- The first UK Vistaarak', n.d: http://hssstories.wordpress.com/2011/08/18/story-3/. Accessed on 22 August 2015.
148. Anahita Mukherji, 'Rashtriya Swayamsevak Sangh 'shakha' spreads its wings to 39 countries', *Times of India*, 21 December 2015.
149. Dijesh, 'About me', n.d: https://www.blogger.com/profile/14603002303555945258. Accessed on 22 August 2015.
150. Trustees of the Hindu Swayamsevak Sangh, 'Hindu Swayamsevak Sangh (UK) Trustees Annual Report 2012' (2012), p.4.
151. n.b. Vistarak Yojana is also a strategy used for election campaigning by the BJP.
152. Arun Kankani, 'Leading through innovation in Sangh work', in *Sangh Sandesh*, Fiftieth Anniversary of HSS Special Edition (2016), p.97.
153. Arun Kankani, 'Leading through innovation in Sangh work', in *Sangh Sandesh*, Fiftieth Anniversary of HSS Special Edition (2016), p.97.
154. Trustees of the Hindu Swayamsevak Sangh (UK), *Guidelines for Vistaraks* (Vistarak Yojna), n.d.
155. This is much the same as the deployment of *pracharaks* around the Sangh Parivar from the RSS. See Basu, Datta, Sarkar, Sarkar and Sen, *Khaki Shorts and Saffron Flags* (1993), p.70.
156. 'Narendra Modi Addressed BJYM Vistaraks (video)', 31 October 2012: http://deshgujarat.com/2012/10/31/recommendednarendra-modi-addresses-bjym-vistaraks/. Accessed on 2 February 2015.
157. Bhatt, '*Dharmo Rakshati Rakshitah*' (2000), p.583.
158. Andersen and Damle, *The Brotherhood in Saffron* (1987), p.87.
159. 'NRIs from 35 countries will take part in RSS meet', *Times of India*, 23 November 2000.
160. Rashtriya Swayamsevak Sangh, *Widening Horizons* (1992), ch.9.
161. The concept of the saffron flag as guru is explored by Jaffrelot in 'The Political Guru: The Guru as Eminence Grise', in Copeman and Ikegame (eds.), *The Guru in South Asia* (2012), pp.80–96.
162. The direct relationship with Italian fascism, and Hindu Mahasabha leader B.S. Moonje's encounters with Benito Mussolini and *Balilla* fascist youth groups, is explored in Marzia Casolari, 'Hindutva's Foreign Tie-Up in the 1930s: Archival Evidence', *Economic and Political Weekly*, vol.35, no.4 (2000), pp.218, 224.
163. Sirsikar, 'My Years in the RSS', in Zelliot and Berntsen (eds.), *The Experience of Hinduism* (1988), pp.190–203; Dhirendra K. Jha, 'Guruji's Lie: The RSS and M.S. Golwalkar's Undeniable Links to Nazism', *Caravan Magazine*, 31 July 2021.
164. Rashtriya Swayamsevak Sangh, *Keshav Baliram Hedgewar: The Master Man-Maker* (1986) pp.12–23; cited in Mathur, *The Everyday Life of Hindu Nationalism* (2008), p.100.
165. M.S. Golwalkar, *Bunch of Thoughts* (Bangalore: Sahitya Sindhu Prakashana, 2000), p.418.

166. A translation of the Marathi notes of a *swayamsevak* attending a 1971 Maharashtra Officers' Training Camp, quoted in Andersen and Damle, *The Brotherhood in Saffron* (1987), p.97.
167. Christophe Jaffrelot, *Religion, Caste, and Politics in India* (New Delhi: Primus Books, 2010), pp.698–9.
168. The emphasis on public outreach is clearly distinctive from the organisation of the homeland. The use of 'religion' in framing the HSS is also noteworthy; in India, the RSS avoids this classification, framing itself as 'a socio-cultural organisation', and locating Hindutva in relation to *dharma*, not 'Hinduism' *per se*. Bajpai, *RSS at a Glance* (2011), p.4; *Constitution of the RSS*, as translated from the original in Hindi and reproduced in Goyal, *Rashtriya Swayamsevak Sangh* (2000), p.257.
169. Trustees of the Hindu Swayamsevak Sangh, 'Hindu Swayamsevak Sangh (UK) Trustees Annual Report 2012' (2012), p.2.
170. *Hindu Swayamsevak Sangh USA: Annual Report 2019–2020*, cited in Jasa Macher, *Hindu Nationalist Influence in the United States, 2014–21* (2022): http://www.sacw.net/article14915.html. Accessed on 12 June 2023.
171. Trustees of the Hindu Swayamsevak Sangh, 'Statements of Financial Activities' (2007–20).
172. Going further back, Bhatt reported in 2000 that there were sixty regular *shakhas*, and RSS figures for 1995 report fifty-three *shakhas*. Bhatt, '*Dharmo Rakshati Rakshitah*' (2000), p.559; Tattwawadi (ed.), *Sarsanghchalak Goes Abroad* (1995), p.74.
173. All data is from HSS annual reports and financial statements (2005–21). Data is destroyed by the Charity Commission after five years, hence data prior to 2005 not available.
174. Christophe Jaffrelot and Ingrid Therwath, 'Hindu Nationalism in the United Kingdom and North America', in Deana Heath and Chandana Mathur (eds.), *Communalism and Globalization in South Asia and its Diaspora* (Abingdon: Routledge, 2011), p.51.
175. Zavos, 'Diaspora Consciousness, Nationalism, and "Religion"' in Gal, Leoussi and Smith (eds.), *The Call of the Homeland* (2010), p.329.
176. K.R. Malkani, *The RSS Story* (New Delhi: Impex India, 1980), p.35; cited in Jaffrelot, *The Hindu Nationalist Movement and Indian Politics* (1996), pp.64–5.
177. Jaffrelot, *The Hindu Nationalist Movement and Indian Politics* (1996), p.64.
178. Hindu Swayamsevak Sangh Canada, 'Hindu Swayamsevak Sangh: A Journey. Global Presence, Growth and Origins': www.hsscanada.org/downloads/presentations/rss_history_short.ppt. Accessed on 26 February 2015.
179. 'e-Shakha': http://eshakha.pbworks.com/w/page/7794045/Shakha. Accessed on 26 February. 2015. See also Ingrid Therwath, 'Cyber-Hindutva: Hindu Nationalism, the Diaspora and the Web', *e-Diasporas Atlas* (Paris: Fondation Maison des Sciences de l'Homme, 2012).
180. Interview with Dhiraj Shah, n.d. Audio transcribed from 'Swayamsevak', 'A History of the Hindu Swayamsevak Sangh', n.d.

181. Ingrid Therwath, 'Cyber-Hindutva: Hindu Nationalism, the Diaspora and the Web', *e-Diasporas Atlas* (Paris: Fondation Maison des Sciences de l'Homme, 2012) n.p.; Vinay Lal, 'The Politics of History on the Internet: Cyber-Diasporic Hinduism and the North American Hindu Diaspora', *Diaspora*, vol.8 (1999) pp.137–72; Sahana Udupa, 'Internet Hindus: Right-Wingers as New India's Ideological Warriors', in Peter van der Veer (ed.), *Handbook of Religion and the Asian City* (Berkeley, CA: University of California Press, 2015), pp.432–50.

182. Vijay Kumar, *Aao Khelen Khel* (Lucknow: Lokhit Prakashan, 2010).

183. No author, *Khel Book* (Hindu Swayamsevak Sangh (UK), n.d.

184. Hindu Swayamsevak Sangh (USA), 'Achar Paddhati', n.d: http://www.hssus.org/content/view/220/70. Accessed on 14 September 2015; *Sangh Geet: A Grand Collection* (Nairobi: Bharatiya Swayamsevak Sangh, 2006).

185. HSSUS, 'Shakha Achar Paddhati Video', 24 August 2013: http://youtu.be/vTQxx1Z0MMc. Accessed on 14 September 2015.

186. This is briefly acknowledged by Bhatt, but insufficient detail or analysis is provided. He wrote: 'The RSS abroad has tended to follow the idea of *desh kal parishthiti* (the circumstances of time and place)'. See: Bhatt, '*Dharmo Rakshati Rakshitah*' (2000), p.577.

187. Shastri, *Memoirs of a Global Hindu* (2008), p.40.

188. Amardeep Bassey, 'Peer Quits Charity Linked to Race Riot Militants', *Sunday Mercury*, 11 August 2002.

189. Press Trust of India, 'RSS-inspired Charity, Hindu Swayamsevak Sangh, Under Probe in UK over "Extremist" Views', *The Indian Express*, 20 February 2015: http://indianexpress.com/article/world/europe/rss-inspired-charity-hindu-swayamsevak-sangh-under-probe-in-uk-over-extremist-views/. Accessed on 22 August 2015. The RSS's official line is also that the VHP, BJP, and the whole plethora of Sangh organisations are 'inspired' by the RSS, but that 'RSS has no wings [or] branches'. Dattatreya Hosabale, 'RSS: Shaping a Saffron Future?' lecture (organised by Vichaar Manthan) at De Montfort University, Leicester, 14 September 2014.

190. Arun Kankani, 'Leading through innovation in Sangh work', in Bhupendra Dave, *Sangh Sandesh*, Fiftieth Anniversary of HSS Special Edition (2016), p.97.

191. Tattwawadi (ed.), *Sarsanghchalak Goes Abroad* (1995), p.9. A more recent North American HSS document also sanctions adaptation 'to suit the local needs'. Hindu Swayamsevak Sangh USA, 'Roles and Responsibilities of Karyakartas', 15 March 2005.

192. Note that there are also specific language elements, which are usually separate sessions to *shakhas*, often organised by the VHP-UK.

193. At a Leicester *shakha* in 1995, Rajendra Singh spoke in English, acknowledging: 'I am mindful of the fact that I am speaking among friends who are used to English' (Tattwawadi (ed.), *Sarsanghchalak Goes Abroad* (1995), p.74.) This was also the case when I heard RSS leader Dattatreya

Hosabale speak in Leicester in 2015. Dattareya Hosabale, 'RSS: Shaping a Saffron Future?' lecture, 14 September 2014.
194. Bhatt, '*Dharmo Rakshati Rakshitah*' (2000), p.583.
195. Shastri reports that 'Kenya is the only country abroad which follows the method of daily shakhas even up to now'. Shastri, *Memoirs of a Global Hindu* (2008), p.41.
196. Shastri, *Memoirs of a Global Hindu* (2008), p.46.
197. Basu, Datta, Sarkar, Sarkar and Sen, *Khaki Shorts and Saffron Flags* (1993), p.36.
198. Golwalkar, *Bunch of Thoughts* (2000), p.445.
199. In India, the Rashtriya Sevika Samiti (National Women Volunteers Committee) was the first 'offspring' of Hedgewar's organisation, founded by Laxmibai Kelkar eleven years after the RSS, in 1936. In Britain, the Hindu Sevika Samiti was founded in 1975, and by 1987 they had ten *shakhas* in the same number of towns. See: 'Swayamsevak', 'A History of the Hindu Swayamsevak Sangh', n.d.
200. Chetan Bhatt and Parita Mukta (eds.), 'Hindutva in the West', *Ethnic and Racial Studies*, vol.23, no.3 (2002), pp.430–1.
201. For instance, see Sikata Bannerjee, *Make me a Man! Masculinity, Hinduism, and Nationalism in India* (Albany, NY: State University of New York Press, 2005), pp.125–8.
202. On the diaspora, see: Gita Sahgal and Nira Yuval-Davis (eds.), *Refusing Holy Orders: Women and Fundamentalism in Britain* (London: Virago Press, 1992); Amrit Wilson, *Dreams, Questions, Struggles: South Asian Women in Britain* (London: Pluto Press, 2006); Pragna Patel, 'Faith in the State? Asian Women's Struggles for Human Rights in the UK', *Feminist Legal Studies*, vol.16 (2008), pp.9–36. On India, see: Tanika Sarkar and Urvashi Butalia (eds.), *Women and the Hindu Right: A Collection of Essays* (Delhi: Kali for Women, 1995); Paola Bacchetta and Margaret Power (eds.), *Right Wing Women: From Conservatives to Extremists Around the World* (London: Routledge, 2002), pp.259–72; Paula Bacchetta, 'Hindu Nationalist Women as Ideologues: The "Sangh" and "Samiti" and their Differential Concepts of Hindu Nation', in Jaffrelot (ed.), *The Sangh Parivar: A Reader* (2005), pp.108–47; Patricia Jeffrey and Roger Jeffrey, *Confronting Saffron Demography: Religion, Fertility, and Women's Status in India* (New Delhi: Three Essays Collective, 2006); Atreyee Sen, *Shiv Sena Women: Violence and Communalism in a Bombay Slum* (New Delhi: Zubaan, 2008); Kalyani Devaki Menon, *Everyday Nationalism: Women of the Hindu Right in India* (Philadelphia, PA: University of Pennsylvania Press, 2010); Dibyesh Anand, *Hindu Nationalism in India and the Politics of Fear* (New York: Palgrave Macmillan, 2011), pp.103–11; Tanika Sarkar, 'Violent and Violated Women in Hindu Extremist Politics', in Wendy Doniger and Martha Nussbaum (eds.), *Pluralism and Democracy in India: Debating the Hindu Right* (New York: Oxford University Press, 2014), pp.280–95; Tanika Sarkar and

Amrita Basu (eds.) *Women, Gender and Religious Nationalism* (Cambridge: Cambridge University Press, 2022).
203. A subheading in an RSS pamphlet—*RSS: Spearheading National Renaissance* (Bangalore: Prakashan Vibhag, 1985), p.42.
204. Golwalkar, *Bunch of Thoughts* (2000), p.343.
205. Dattareya Hosabale, 'RSS: Shaping a Saffron Future?' lecture (organised by Vichaar Manthan) at De Montfort University, Leicester, 14 September 2014.
206. Golwalkar, *Bunch of Thoughts* (2000), p.209. Elsewhere in *Bunch of Thoughts*, Golwalkar writes of 'the past one thousand years when our nation fell before foreign onslaughts', and 'the past thousand-year-long corroding influence of foreigners'—pp.98, 109.
207. Golwalkar, *Bunch of Thoughts* (2000), pp.49, 213.
208. Vasudha Dalmia and Heinrich Stietencron (eds.), *Reconstructing Hinduism: The Construction of Religious Traditions and National Identity* (London: Sage, 1995), p.27. See also Chandrima Chakraborty, *Masculinity, Asceticism, Hinduism: Past and Present Imaginings of India* (New Delhi: Permanent Black, 2011), p.185.
209. Joseph Alter, 'Celibacy, Sexuality, and the Transformation of Gender into Nationalism in North India', *The Journal of Asian Studies*, vol.53, no.1 (1994), p.45. See also: Joseph Alter, 'Somatic Nationalism: Indian Wrestling and Militant Hinduism', *Modern Asian Studies*, vol.28, no.3 (1994), pp.557–88. See also Jaffrelot, *The Hindu Nationalist Movement and Indian Politics* (1996), pp.35–40, and Chakraborty, *Masculinity, Asceticism, Hinduism* (2011).
210. Jessica Marie Falcone, 'Putting the "Fun" in Fundamentalism: Religious Nationalism and the Split Self at Hindutva Summer Camps in the United States', *ETHOS—Journal for the Society for Psychological Anthropology*, vol.40, no.2 (2012), p.171.
211. Devesh Kapur, *Diaspora, Development, and Democracy* (2010), pp.8–9; Falcone, 'Putting the "Fun" in Fundamentalism' (2012), p.165.
212. 'Bob Blackman MP Praises HSS Activities', n.d: http://vskkerala.com/bob-blackman-mp-praises-hss-activities/nggallery/page/1. Accessed on 22 August 2015. See Chapter 4 for a detailed discussion of diasporic Hindutva and the 'model minority' trope.
213. Alter, 'Somatic Nationalism' (1994), p.568.
214. Wilson, *Dreams, Questions, Struggles* (2006), pp.68–71.
215. Jeffrey and Jeffrey, *Confronting Saffron Demography* (2006). Hindu nationalism also cultivates broader anxieties of attack on all sides, from communists, secularists, Christian missionaries, militant Dalits, feminists, foreign corporate interests, neighbouring countries, and others, invoking powerful feelings of victimisation.
216. Catarina Kinnvall, *Globalization and Religious Nationalism in India* (London: Routledge, 2006), p.153. See also: Prema Kurien, 'Multiculturalism and

"American" Religion: The Case of Hindu Indian Americans', *Social Forces*, vol.85, no.2 (2006), pp.725–6.
217. 'Exposure: Charities Behaving Badly', ITV, first aired 18 February 2015.
218. Romila Thapar, 'On Historical Scholarship and the Uses of the Past (interview with Parita Mukta)', *Ethnic and Racial Studies*, vol.23, no.3 (2000), pp.607–8.
219. Patel, 'Rama or Rambo?' in Gupta (ed.), *From Homebreakers to Jailbreakers* (2003), pp.212–33.
220. Seshadri, *Dollar or Dharma?* (1990), pp.38–9.
221. Ballard (ed.) *Desh Pardesh* (1994), p.15.
222. Seshadri, *Dollar or Dharma?* (1990), *passim*; M. Shah, 'Indian, British or Both?', in *Bradford Centenary Hindu Marathon* (Bradford: Hindu Marathon National Committee, 1997), p.103. Quoted in Stacy Burlet, 'Re-awakenings? Hindu Nationalism Goes Global', in Roy Starrs (ed.), *Asian Nationalism in an Age of Globalisation* (Richmond: Curzon Press, 2001), p.14.
223. Burlet, 'Re-awakenings?', in Starrs (ed.), *Asian Nationalism* (2001), p.14.
224. Dhiraj Shah, 'Oral History Project' (2007).
225. Seshadri, *RSS: A Vision in Action* (2001), p.387.
226. Seshadri, *RSS: A Vision in Action* (2001), p.387.
227. Swami Tilak, 'Future Trends in the Lives of Hindus Around the World', in Seshadri, *Dollar or Dharma?* (1990), pp.15–16. See also: Roger Friedland, 'Money, Sex, and God: The Erotic Logic of Religious Nationalism', *Sociological Theory*, vol.20, no.3 (2002), pp.417–20.
228. Falcone, on the HSS in America, suggests that 'the cultural categorization of Hindu immigrants into a "lesser-than-whites" minority has only served to fuel the growth of Hindu supremacist groups in the United States'. Falcone, 'Putting the "Fun" in Fundamentalism' (2012), p.164. See also Gita Ramaswamy, 'Yankee Hindutva Strikes', *Outlook*, 23 May 2011.
229. Mohan Bhagwat, 'Shakha Achar Paddhati Video' (HSS USA video), 24 August 2013: http://www.hssus.org/content/view/220/70. Accessed on 5 August 2015.
230. Mohan Bhagwat, 'Shakha Achar Paddhati Video' (HSS USA video), 24 August 2013.
231. Eric Hobsbawm, 'Introduction: Inventing Traditions', in Eric Hobsbawm and Terence Ranger (eds.), *The Invention of Tradition* (Cambridge: Cambridge University Press, 1983), p.1.
232. A document on 'Roles and Responsibilities of Karyakartas' notes that 'With the consensus of the Karyakarta team, roles and responsibilities can be adapted to suit the local needs'. See Hindu Swayamsevak Sangh USA, 'Roles and Responsibilities of Karyakartas', 15 March 2005: http://www.hsscanada.org/downloads/Roles_n_Responsibilities.pdf. Accessed on 18 September 2015.
233. In particular *Vidya Bharati* (who run by far the largest network of non-government schools in India) and *Ekal Vidyalaya* (whose focus is on schools

in rural and tribal areas). For more on the Indian Hindu nationalist movement and pedagogy, see: Tanika Sarkar, 'Educating the Children of the Hindu Rashtra: Notes on RSS schools', in P. Bidwai, H. Mukhia and A. Vaniak (eds.), *Religion, Religiosity and Communalism* (New Delhi: Manohar, 1996), pp.237–47; Peggy Froerer, 'Disciplining the Saffron Way: Moral Education and the Hindu Rashtra', *Modern Asian Studies*, vol.41, no.5 (2007), pp.1033–71.

234. *Organiser*, 'Republic Day Special', 28 January 1996, p.40; cited in Jaffrelot and Therwath, 'The Sangh Parivar and the Hindu Diaspora in the West', *International Political Sociology* (2007), p.286.
235. David Frawley, *Hinduism and the Clash of Civilizations* (New Delhi: Voice of India, 2009), p.169.
236. Falcone, 'Putting the "Fun" in Fundamentalism' (2012), p.169.
237. Vijay Prashad, *The Karma of Brown Folk* (Minneapolis, MN: University of Minnesota Press, 2001), p.147.
238. Author's interview with Anil Vartak (New Delhi, 3 May 2014). It is perhaps telling that the person the RSS entrusted to co-ordinate the HSS in Britain for almost two decades has a scholarly background (a PhD in Sanskrit from Nagpur).
239. Partha Chatterjee, 'History and the Nationalization of Hinduism', *Social Research*, vol.59, no.1 (1992), p.134. See also Tapati Guha-Thakurta, *Monuments, Objects, Histories: Institutions of Art in Colonial and Postcolonial India* (New Delhi: Permanent Black, 2004), p.xx; Romila Thapar, 'Imagined Religious Communities?', *Modern Asian Studies* (1989), p.210; Romila Thapar, *The Past as Present: Forging Contemporary Identities Through History* (New Delhi: Aleph, 2014).
240. Falcone, 'Putting the "Fun" in Fundamentalism' (2012), p.169.
241. The HSS website has a 'Knowledgebase' section, and the NHSF website contains a section titled 'Why do we?'. Rajendra Singh told young British *swayamsevaks* in 1995: 'Hindus—especially those who live in foreign lands—must possess knowledge about their philosophy. They may have to answer so many questions. They should be able to give proper answers to these questions'; Shankar Tattwawadi (ed.), *Sarsanghchalak Goes Abroad: A Collection of Lectures Delivered by Prof. Rajendra Singh on Foreign Land* (New Delhi: Suruchi Prakashan, 1995), p.13.
242. Martha Nussbaum, *The Clash Within: Democracy, Religious Violence, and India's Future* (London: Harvard University Press, 2007), p.318.
243. Jaffrelot and Therwath, 'Hindu Nationalism in the United Kingdom and North America', in Heath and Mathur (eds.), *Communalism and Globalization in South Asia and its Diaspora* (2011), p.53.
244. Rashtriya Swayamsevak Sangh, *Widening Horizons* (1992), n.p. Emphasis added.
245. Author's interview with anonymous *karyakarta* (19 March 2015).
246. Author's interview with anonymous *karyakarta* (19 March 2015).

247. Home Office, 'Register of Sponsors Licensed Under the Points-based System' (23 March 2015), p.743.
248. 'Welcome to Dharma Bee', n.d: http://www.dharmabee.org/. Accessed on 14 September 2015.
249. Author's interview with anonymous *karyakarta* (19 March 2015).
250. Kurien, *A Place at the Multiculturalist Table* (2007), p.143. See also: Linda Basch, Nina Glick Schiller, and Christina Szanton Blanc, *Nations Unbound: Transnational Projects, Postcolonial Predicaments and Deterritorialized Nation-States* (Basel, Switzerland: Gordon and Breach, 2002); Alejandro Portes, 'Conclusion: Towards a New World: The Origins and the Effects of Transnational Activities', *Ethnic and Racial Studies*, vol.22, no.2 (1999), pp.465–66; Arvind Rajagopal, 'Hindu Nationalism in the US: Changing Configurations of Political Practice', *Ethnic and Racial Studies*, vol.23 (2000), pp.463–70.
251. Benedict Anderson, *The Spectre of Comparison: Nationalisms, Southeast Asia, and the World* (London: Verso, 1998), p.74.
252. Jaffrelot and Therwath, 'The Sangh Parivar and the Hindu Diaspora in the West', *International Political Sociology* (2007), pp.292–3.
253. Prema Kurien, 'Multiculturalism, Immigrant Religion, and Diasporic Nationalism: The Development of an American Hinduism', *Social Problems*, vol.51, no.3 (2004), pp.362–85.
254. Helen Rose Ebaugh and Janet Saltzman Chafetz, *Religion and the New Immigrants: Continuities and Adaptations in Immigrant Congregations* (Walnut Creek, CA: Altamira Press, 2000).
255. Deepa Reddy, 'Hindu Transnationalisms: Organisations, Ideologies, Network', in John Zavos, Pralay Kanungo, Deepa Reddy, Maya Warrier, and Raymond Brady Williams (eds.), *Public Hinduisms* (2012), p.320.

2. TRAINING CAMPS AND THE DEVELOPMENT OF A GLOBAL *PARIVAR* (FAMILY)

1. Trustees of the Hindu Swayamsevak Sangh, 'Trust Deed of the Hindu Swayamsevak Sangh', 1974.
2. 'HSS-UK Denies Allegations Made by ITV Documentary', *Asian Voice*, 28 February 2015: http://www.asian-voice.com/Volumes/2015/28-February-2015/HSS-UK-denies-allegations-made-by-ITV-documentary. Accessed on 17 September 2015.
3. Shankar Tattwawadi (ed.), *Sarsanghchalak Goes Abroad: A Collection of Lectures Delivered by Prof. Rajendra Singh on Foreign Land* (New Delhi: Suruchi Prakashan, 1995), p.13.
4. H.V. Seshadri, *Hindus Abroad: Dilemma: Dollar or Dharma?* (New Delhi: Suruchi Prakashan, 1990).
5. M.S. Golwalkar, *Bunch of Thoughts* (Bangalore: Sahitya Sindhu Prakashana, 2000), p.417.

6. Marzia Casolari, 'Hindutva's Foreign Tie-Up in the 1930s: Archival Evidence', *Economic and Political Weekly*, vol.35, no.4 (2000), pp.218–28.
7. In 1926, the year after the RSS was formed, there were 80,887 Scouts in India. By 1935, this had grown to 272,853. Carey Watt, 'The Promise of "Character" and the Spectre of Sedition: The Boy Scout Movement and Colonial Consternation in India, 1908–1921', *South Asia: Journal of South Asian Studies*, vol.22, no.2 (1999), pp.37–62.
8. Joseph Alter, *The Wrestler's Body: Identity and Ideology in North India* (Berkeley, CA: University of California Press, 1992); Prabhu Bapu, *Hindu Mahasabha in Colonial North India, 1915–1930: Constructing Nation and History* (Abingdon: Routledge, 2013).
9. Virag Pachpore, 'RSS Sangh Shiksha Varg: Moulding Men with Capital "M" for a Mission', *Samvada*, 4 June 2015: http://samvada.org/2015/news/rss-sangh-shiksha-varg/. Accessed on 3 January 2022.
10. M.S. Golwalkar, *Bunch of Thoughts* (Bangalore: Sahitya Sindhu Prakashana, 2000), p.417.
11. B.V. Deshpande and S.R. Ramaswamy, *Dr Hedgewar the Epoch-Maker* (Bangalore: Sahitya Sindhu, 1981), pp.185–6.
12. Kanungo, *RSS's Tryst with Politics* (2003), p.83.
13. Michiel Dehaene and Lieven De Cauter, 'Heterotopia in a Postcivil Society', in Michiel Dehaene and Lieven De Cauter (eds.), *Heterotopia and the City: Public Space in a Postcivil Society* (Abingdon: Routeledge, 2008), p.5.
14. Michel Foucault, 'Of Other Spaces', trans. Lieven De Cauter and Michiel Dehaene, in Dehaene and De Cauter (eds.) *Heterotopia and the City* (2008), p.17.
15. 'Sangh and Samiti Shiksha Varg 2014—HSS', *City Hindus Network*: http://www.cityhindusnetwork.org.uk/events/sangh-samiti-shiksha-varg-2014-hss/. Accessed on 21 August 2015.
16. Christophe Jaffrelot, 'The Hindu Nationalist Reinterpretation of Pilgrimage in India: the Limits of *Yatra* Politics', *Nations and Nationalism*, vol.15, no.1 (2009), pp.1–19.
17. 'Swayamsevak', 'A History of the Hindu Swayamsevak Sangh', n.d.: http://timerime.com/en/event/385719/Hindu+Sangam/. Accessed on 24 July 2014.
18. *Sangh Sandesh*, April–June 2008, p.7.
19. T.A. Johnson, 'NRIs Flock to RSS Camp to Become Global Hindus', 11 August 2001: http://hindunet.org/hvk/articles/0801/66.html. Accessed on 10 January 2013.
20. *Sangh Sandesh*, April–June 2008, p.7.
21. 'SSV—Men from Boys', n.d: http://vistaar-dijesh.blogspot.co.uk/2010_08_01_archive.html. Accessed on 21 August 2015.
22. 'Sangh and Samiti Shiksha Varg 2014—HSS', n.d.

23. Jeel Shah, 'Bob Blackman Praises HSS Activities', n.d: http://hssuk. org/wp-content/uploads/2015/02/Bob-Blackman-attends-HSS-UK-Leadership-Training-Course2.pdf. Accessed on 21 August 2015.
24. Hansen, *The Saffron Wave* (1999), pp.99–100.
25. 'SSV—Men from Boys', n.d.
26. Jaffrelot and Therwath, 'Hindu Nationalism in the United Kingdom and North America', in Heath and Mathur (eds.), *Communalism and Globalization in South Asia and its Diaspora* (2011), p.49. Emphasis added.
27. 'About Mohan Bhagwat Ji', 27 December 2011: http://rssap.blogspot.co.uk/2011/12/about-mohan-bhagwat-ji.html. Accessed on 21 August 2015.
28. Hindu Swayamsevak Sangh Canada, 'Roles and Responsibilities of Karyakartas', 2005: http://www.hsscanada.org/downloads/Roles_n_Responsibilities.pdf. Accessed on 14 September 2015.
29. Trustees of the Hindu Swayamsevak Sangh, 'Hindu Swayamsevak Sangh Trustees Annual Report 2011' (2011). See also: 'Swayamsevak', 'A History of the Hindu Swayamsevak Sangh', n.d.
30. 'Tributes to the Noble Soul', *HSS* UK, n.d: http://hssuk.org/tributes-to-the-noble-soul/. Accessed on 21 August 2015.
31. *Sangh Sandesh*, April–June 2008, p.6.
32. The countries mentioned were the USA, the UK, Kenya, Suriname, Guyana, and Trinidad. 'Vishwa Sangh Shiksha Varg- 2012 at Trinidad', 30 July 2012.
33. HSS, 'Samarop Sanskriti MahaShibir Video', 3 August 2016: https://www.youtube.com/watch?v=TIRE_a53Z5k. Accessed on 2 December 2017.
34. D.R. Goyal, *Rashtriya Swayamsevak Sangh* (New Delhi: Radhakrishna Prakashan, 2000), p.76.
35. Trustees of the Hindu Swayamsevak Sangh, Hindu Swayamsevak Sangh annual reports, 2005–22.
36. 'Mananeeya Satyanarayanji Is No More', n.d.
37. 'Bob Blackman MP praises HSS Activities, n.d.: http://vskkerala.com/bob-blackman-mp-praises-hss-activities/nggallery/page/1. Accessed on 17 September 2015.
38. Jeel Shah, 'Bob Blackman Praises HSS Activities', n.d. In 2014 Blackman celebrated Narendra Modi's election victory (after lending his support to the BJP campaign), and in September 2015, Blackman hosted Sadhvi Rithambara at the House of Commons (see Chapter 4). See also Chapter 6 for more discussion of the relationship between Hindutva and democratic politics.
39. Bob Blackman, Twitter, 25 January 2020: https://twitter.com/BobBlackman/status/1221163933941153792?s=20. Accessed on 31 May 2023.
40. 'Mayoral Blog 2008/09 Councillor Jack Davis', n.d.: http://www.tameside.gov.uk/mayor/blog/july08. Accessed on 16 September 2015.

41. 'SIP is a project of Hindu Swayamsevak Sangh UK', *HSS UK*, n.d: http://hssuk-sip.blogspot.co.uk/p/about-sip.html. Accessed on 17 September 2015.
42. 'Project Overview', *HSS UK*, n.d: http://hssuk.org/project/sip/. Accessed on 17 September 2015.
43. 'Sangh Internship Programme', 'Videos', 7 December 2010: https://www.facebook.com/hssuk.sip/videos/vb.169228753102004/10150357268770160/. Accessed on 17 September 2015.
44. Sangh Internship Programme, photostream, n.d.: https://www.facebook.com/hssuk.sip/photos_stream. Accessed on 17 September 2015.
45. 'Project Outcomes', *HSS UK*, n.d: http://hssuk-sip.blogspot.co.uk/p/sip-project-outcomes.html. Accessed on 17 September 2015.
46. Bhatt, '*Dharmo Rakshati Rakshitah*' (2000), pp.569–93. See also: *Sangh Sandesh*, May–June 1999, pp.4–5; cited in AWAAZ—South Asia Watch Limited, 'In Bad Faith? British Charity and Hindu Extremism' (2004), p.5.
47. Qualifications and Curriculum Authority, *Education for Citizenship and the Teaching of Democracy in Schools (Crick Report)* (London: QCA, 1998); Chris Wilkins, 'Citizenship Education', in Richard Bailey (ed.), *Teaching Values and Citizenship Across the Curriculum: Educating Children for the World* (London: Routledge Falmer, 2000), pp.19–20; Ben Summerskill, 'Pupils to Learn Blairite Values', *The Guardian*, 10 December 2000: http://www.theguardian.com/uk/2000/dec/10/education.schools. Accessed on 17 September 2015.
48. N. Glick Schiller, L. Basch, and C. S. Blanc, 'From Immigrant to Transmigrant: Theorizing Transnational Migration', *Anthropological Quarterly*, vol.68, no.1 (1995), p.48.
49. Steven Vertovec, 'Migrant Transnationalism and Modes of Transformation', *International Migration Review*, vol.38, no.3 (2004), p. 971; Vertovec, *Transnationalism* (London: Routledge, 2009).
50. Andersen and Damle, *The Brotherhood in Saffron* (1987), p.95.
51. Ashok Singhal, in *Vishwa Sangh Shibir 2005 Souvenir* (Karnavati: Antar Rashtriya Sahayog Pratishthan, 2005); cited in John Zavos, 'Situating Hindu Nationalism in the UK: Vishwa Hindu Parishad and the Development of British Hindu Identity', *Commonwealth and Comparative Politics*, vol.48, no.1 (2010), p.13.
52. Dr Yashwant Pathak, Joint co-ordinator, Hindu Swayamsevak Sangh (US), in Jagdish Chandra Sharda Shastri (compiled and edited by Ratan Sharda), *Memoirs of a Global Hindu* (Mumbai: Vishwa Adhyayan Kendra, 2008), p.86. Translation: 'from foreign division, to world division and now world Sangh'.
53. Sharad Kunte, 'Vishwa Sangha Shibir: An Overview', in Sharad Kunte (ed.), *Vishwa Sangh Shibir 2010 Souvenir* (Pune: Vishwa Adhyayan Kendra, 2010), p.6.

54. Mohan Bhagwat quoted in Vishwa Adhyayan Kendra, 'Annual Report 2007–08', 2008, pp.6–8: http://www.vakmumbai.org/presentation/report-2007-2008.pdf. Accessed on 10 January 2015.
55. Final attendance figures for the 2010 *shibir* were only around half of the number projected in communications appealing for donations in the build-up to the camp. See: Ranjeet Natu, 'Donations for Vishwa Sangh Shibir', 23 September 2010: https://groups.google.com/d/topic/social-ca-community/QAGkWXmc1oM/discussion. Accessed on 27 September 2015.
56. Pachpore, 'Vishwa Sangh Shibir 2010: An Exposure to Global, Confident Hindutva', 17 January 2011: http://samvada.org/2011/news/vishwa-sangh-shibir-2010-an-exposure-to-global-confident-hindutva/. Accessed on 8 April 2015; Kunte, 'Vishwa Sangha Shibir: An Overview', in Kunte (ed.), *Vishwa Sangh Shibir* (2010), pp.6–7; Ashutosh Bhardwaj, 'Simply Put: Overseas Swayamsevaks, their Hindutva Project', *The Indian Express*, 11 January 2016: http://indianexpress.com/article/explained/simply-put-overseas-swayamsevaks-their-hindutva-project/. Accessed on 4 January 2022.
57. Shastri, *Memoirs of a Global Hindu* (2008), p.39.
58. Kunte, 'Vishwa Sangha Shibir: An Overview', in Kunte (ed.), *Vishwa Sangh Shibir* (2010), p.5. Sharad Kunte—a former state-level executive president of the VHP and research fellow at the Institute of Research and Development in Oriental Studies (IRDOS) in Pune—was implicated in terrorist activities in 2008 as 'one of those who had organised a bomb-making camp ... near Pune, in 2003'. See: Satyajit Joshi, 'RSS Man Linked to Bomb-Making Camp Again', *Hindustan Times*, 24 December 2008: http://www.hindustantimes.com/india-news/rss-man-linked-to-bomb-making-camp-again/article1-360208.aspx. Accessed on 28 September 2015; Krishna Kumar, 'Hindu Rashtra: Saffron Terror's Hall of Shame', *India Today*, 18 July 2010: http://indiatoday.intoday.in/story/hindu-rashtra-saffron-terrors-hall-of-shame/3/105809.html. Accessed on 28 September 2015.
59. Author's interview with Hemant Padhya, former Bauddhik Pramukh for the East of England (Milton Keynes, 18 December 2013).
60. Seshadri, *Dollar or Dharma?* (1990), p.57.
61. 'NRIs Learn About Indian Culture, Heritage During 17-Day-Long Orientation Programme', *The Times of India*, 6 August 2017: https://timesofindia.indiatimes.com/videos/city/mumbai/nris-learn-about-indian-culture-heritage-during-17-day-long-orientation-programme/videoshow/59939091.cms. Accessed on 4 January 2022.
62. Pachpore, 'Vishwa Sangh Shibir 2010', *Organiser*, 2010. The Sangh Parivar has elevated 'younger' people to the highest offices in recent years, but this has tended to mean people in their forties and fifties. The appointment of Mohan Bhagwat as *Sarsanghchalak* at the age of fifty-nine was considered

to be a 'generational change' in the RSS, and ushered in a period of focus on the RSS youth.
63. 'Samvad—Shri Vishwa Niketan', n.d: http://shrivishwaniketan.blogspot.co.uk/2011/01/this-issue-of-samvad-exclusively.html. Accessed on 18 September 2015.
64. Ami Ganatra, 'Vishva Sangh Shibir (My Tryst with RSS)': https://dharmorakshtirakshitah.wordpress.com/2016/01/31/vishva-sangh-shibir-my-tryst-with-rss/. Accessed on 4 January 2022.
65. *Sangh Sandesh*, January–March 2011, p.20.
66. *Sangh Sandesh*, January–March 2011, pp.16–20.
67. Arjun Appadurai, 'Global Ethnoscapes: Notes and Queries for a Transnational Anthropology', in Richard Fox (ed.), *Recapturing Anthropology* (Santa Fe, NM: School of American Research Press, 1991), pp.191–2.
68. Ashutosh Bhardwaj, 'Simply Put: Overseas Swayamsevaks, their Hindutva Project', *The Indian Express*, 11 January 2016: http://indianexpress.com/article/explained/simply-put-overseas-swayamsevaks-their-hindutva-project/. Accessed on 4 January 2022.
69. Virag Pachpore, 'Summit of Global Hindus: Fifth Vishwa Sangh Shibir', *India Herald*, 19 January 2011: http://india-herald.com/summit-of-global-hindus-fifth-vishwa-sangh-shibir-p2495-1.htm. Accessed on 17 September 2015.
70. 'Vishwa Sangh Shibir 2010', *HSS Mauritius*, 5 February 2011: http://www.hssmru.org/2011/02/vishwa-sangh-shibir-2010/. Accessed on 15 September 2015.
71. Vishwa Samvada Kendra, 'RSS Inspired 5-day Conference Vishwa Sangh Shibir—2015 Begins in Indore': http://samvada.org/2015/news/vishwa-sangh-shibir-indore/. Accessed on 4 January 2022.
72. Rashtriya Swayamsevak Sangh, *Vishwa Sangh Shibir-'90 Souvenir* (Antara Rashtriya Sahayoga Parishad, Bangalore Chapter, 1991), p.99.
73. Pachpore, 'Vishwa Sangh Shibir 2010', *Organiser*, 2010. A senior HSS (US) *karyakarta* commented before the 2010 VSS that, 'I am sure that the presence of Jagdish ji at the VSS will be very inspiring to all of us and the many new swayamsevaks who have heard the romantic story of first shakha aboard a ship and will be blessed by his presence'—Dr Yashwant Pathak, Joint co-ordinator, Hindu Swayamsevak Sangh (US), in Shastri, *Memoirs of a Global Hindu* (2008), p.87.
74. 'Understanding What We Do', 6 January 2011: http://vistaar-dijesh.blogspot.co.uk/2011/01/understanding-what-we-do.html. Accessed on 21 March 2014.
75. Shastri, *Memoirs of a Global Hindu* (2008), p.66.
76. Pachpore, 'Vishwa Sangh Shibir 2010', *Organiser*, 2010.
77. *Sangh Sandesh*, May–June 1999, pp.4–5; cited in AWAAZ—South Asia Watch Limited, 'In Bad Faith? British Charity and Hindu Extremism' (2004), p.5.

78. 'Vishwa Sangh Shibir 2010', 5 February 2011.
79. 'Samvad—Shri Vishwa Niketan', n.d.
80. Pachpore, 'Vishwa Sangh Shibir 2010: An Exposure to Global, Confident Hindutva', 17 January 2011.
81. Kunte, 'Vishwa Sangha Shibir: An Overview', in Kunte (ed.), *Vishwa Sangh Shibir* (2010), p.5.
82. Pachpore, 'Vishwa Sangh Shibir 2010: An Exposure to Global, Confident Hindutva', 17 January 2011.
83. Pachpore, 'Vishwa Sangh Shibir 2010', *Organiser* (2010), p.8.
84. 'NRIs from 35 countries will take part in RSS meet', *The Times of India*, 23 November 2000.
85. RSS Pune, Vishwa Sangh Shibir—Open Program Invitation': http://punerss.blogspot.co.uk/2010/12/vishwa-sangh-shibir-open-program.html. Accessed 16 June 2015.
86. The term originates from a culinary phenomenon of the twentieth century, in which the unassuming, rustic pizza became a feted, even national, dish within Italy as a result of North American Italian immigrants and global popularity. Agehananda Bharati, 'Indian Expatriates in North America and Neo-Hindu Movements', in J.S. Yadava and Vinayshil Gautam (eds.), *The Communication of Ideas* (New Delhi: Concept Publishing Company, 1980), pp.245–56.
87. Peggy Levitt, 'Social Remittances: Migration Driven Local Level Forms of Cultural Diffusion', *International Migration Review*, vol.32, no.4 (1998), pp.926–48; Peggy Levitt, *The Transnational Villagers* (London: University of California Press, 2001).
88. 'NRIs Learn About Indian Culture, Heritage During 17-Day-Long Orientation Programme', *The Times of India*, 6 August 2017: https://timesofindia.indiatimes.com/videos/city/mumbai/nris-learn-about-indian-culture-heritage-during-17-day-long-orientation-programme/videoshow/59939091.cms. Accessed on 4 January 2022.
89. Rashtriya Yodha, 'Vishwa Sangh Shibir—Full Coverage', 14 January 2011: https://www.youtube.com/watch?v=gcKJ2MQ9ZHk. Accessed on 18 September 2015.
90. A Google image search indicates that a picture from the Sangh Shiksha Varg in Karnataka, 2011 (http://www.archivesofrss.org/2011-year-in-pictures.aspx. Accessed on 15 August 2015), has been used in several dozen other articles.
91. Kunte, 'Vishwa Sangha Shibir: An Overview', in Kunte (ed.), *Vishwa Sangh Shibir* (2010), p.6.
92. Zavos, 'Situating Hindu Nationalism in the UK' (2010), pp.13–14.
93. Dhooleka Sardari Raj, *Where are you from? Middle Class Migrants in the Modern World* (Berkeley, CA: University of California Press, 2003), p.182.
94. T.A. Johnson, 'NRIs Flock to RSS Camp to Become Global Hindus', 11 August 2001. Emphasis added; Stuart Hall, 'Cultural Identity and

Diaspora', in Jonathan Rutherford (ed.), *Identity, Community, Culture, Difference* (London: Lawrence and Wishart, 1990), pp.222–37. See also: Stuart Hall, 'Introduction: Who Needs Identity?', in Stuart Hall and Paul du Gay (eds.), *Questions of Cultural Identity* (London: Sage, 1996), pp.1–17; Prema Kurien, 'Multiculturalism, Immigrant Religion, and Diasporic Nationalism: The Development of an American Hinduism', *Social Problems*, vol.51, no.3 (2004), p.365.

95. Paul Gilroy, *The Black Atlantic: Modernity and Double Consciousness* (London: Verso, 1994). See also: Hasmita Ramji, 'Journeys of Difference: The Use of Migratory Narratives Among British Hindu Gujaratis', *Ethnic and Racial Studies*, vol.29, no.4 (2006), pp.702–24.
96. Zavos, 'Situating Hindu Nationalism in the UK' (2010), p.14.
97. Lizzie Richardson, 'Theatrical Translations: The Performative Production of Diaspora', in Anastasia Christou and Elizabeth Mavroudi (eds.), *Dismantling Diasporas: Rethinking the Geographies of Diasporic Identity, Connection and Development* (Abingdon: Routledge, 2016), p.16.
98. 'Vishwa Sangh Shibir 1995 Press Release', 1996.
99. Author's interview with Anil Vartak (New Delhi, 3 May 2014).
100. Farhat Naz, 'Swaminarayan Movement and Gujarati Diasporic Identity', *Man in India*, vol.87 nos.1–2 (2007), p.135. The imbrications of pilgrimage and business are also considered in Christopher Bayly, 'Patrons and Politics in Northern India', *Modern Asian Studies*, vol.7, no.3 (1973), pp.349–88. See also Lise McKean, *Divine Enterprise: Gurus and the Hindu Nationalist Movement* (London: University of Chicago Press, 1996), pp.17–20.
101. 'Vishwa Sangh Shibir 1995 Press Release', 1996.
102. Kunte, 'Vishwa Sangha Shibir: An Overview', in Kunte (ed.), *Vishwa Sangh Shibir* (2010), p.8.
103. Kunte, 'Vishwa Sangha Shibir: An Overview', in Kunte (ed.), *Vishwa Sangh Shibir* (2010), p.7; Similar scenes can be observed in a video of highlights from the 2010 *shibir* near Pune: Rashtriya Yodha, 'Vishwa Sangh Shibir—Full Coverage', 14 January 2011.
104. Vishwa Adhyayan Kendra, 'Annual Report 2007–08', 2008, p.8.
105. Kunte, 'Vishwa Sangha Shibir: An Overview', in Kunte (ed.), *Vishwa Sangh Shibir* (2010), pp.5–6.
106. Aanand Aadeesh, *Shree Gurujee and his RSS* (New Delhi: M.D. Publications, 2007), p.365. Other translations include the lines: 'I bow before you forever O beloved Motherland… O great sacred land I worship'.
107. V.D. Savarkar, quoted in Prema Kurien, *A Place at the Multicultural Table: The Development of an American Hinduism* (New Bunswick, NJ: Rutgers University Press, 2007), p.127.
108. Shastri, *Memoirs of a Global Hindu* (2008), p.39.
109. Kunte, 'Vishwa Sangha Shibir: An Overview', in Kunte (ed.), *Vishwa Sangh Shibir* (2010), p.7.
110. Rashtriya Yodha, 'Vishwa Sangh Shibir—Full Coverage', 14 January 2011.

111. Linda Davidson and David Gitlitz, *Pilgrimage: From the Ganges to Graceland: an Encyclopaedia* (Santa Barbara, CA: ABC CLIO, 2002), p.22.
112. Kunte, 'Vishwa Sangha Shibir: An Overview', in Kunte (ed.), Vishwa Sangh Shibir 2010 Souvenir (2010), p.5.
113. 'Samvad—Shri Vishwa Niketan', n.d.
114. Coleman and Elsner, *Pilgrimage: Past and Present* (1995), p.150.
115. Jacob Copeman, *Veins of Devotion: Blood Donation and Religious Experience in North India* (New Brunswick, NJ: Rutgers University Press, 2009), p.26. For more on pilgrimage and purification, see Knut Jacobsen, *Pilgrimage in the Hindu Tradition: Salvific Space* (Abingdon: Routledge, 2013), p.82. This discourse of *dana* and *sewa* (service) is explored in depth in Chapter 5.
116. The 'polluting' effect of crossing the *kala pani* (black waters) around India, suffered by those leaving India, is a well-known, but still under-researched (and now largely historical) phenomenon. Whilst these Brahmanical taboos dissipated considerably in the twentieth century, certain levels of opposition and stigma attached to emigrating have remained (albeit, paradoxically, alongside upward social mobility associated with emigration). There is an important, yet ambivalent, relationship between these taboos and the purifying qualities of pilgrimage, spiritual remittances, and return. See: Sumita Mukherjee, *Nationalism, Education and Migrant Identities: The England-returned* (Abingdon: Routledge, 2009), pp.30–43; Judith Brown, 'Crossing the Seas: Problems and Possibilities for Queen Victoria's Indian Subjects', in Miles Taylor (ed.), *The Victorian Empire and Britain's Maritime World, 1837–1901* (London: Palgrave Macmillan, 2013), p.115; Douglas Haynes, *Rhetoric and Ritual in Colonial India: The Shaping of a Public Culture in Surat City, 1852–1928* (Berkeley, CA: University of California Press, 1991), p.66.
117. Seshadri, *RSS: A Vision in Action* (2001), p.14.
118. Coleman and Elsner, *Pilgrimage: Past and Present* (1995), p.157.
119. M.N. Srinivas, *Social Change in Modern India* (London: Cambridge University Press, 1966).
120. John Eade and Michael Sallnow, 'Introduction', in John Eade and Michael Sallnow (eds.), *Contesting the Sacred: The Anthropology of Christian Pilgrimage* (London: Routledge, 1991), p.25.
121. Werbner, *Pilgrims of Love* (2003), p.102.
122. Jaffrelot, 'The Hindu Nationalist Reinterpretation of Pilgrimage in India' (2009), p.1. See also Fuller, *The Camphor Flame* (1992), pp.216–17. Note that the 'equality of pilgrims is not always complete … and egalitarianism does not last after returning home'. See also L. Kjaerholm, 'Myth, Pilgrimage and Fascination in the Aiyappa Cult', in A. Parpola and B.S. Hansen (eds.), *South Asian Religion and Society* (London: Curzon, 1986), pp.132–3; cited in Fuller.
123. Victor Turner, 'Pilgrimages as Social Processes', in Victor Turner (ed.), *Dramas, Fields, and Metaphors: Symbolic Action in Human Society* (London: Cornell University Press, 1975), p.207.

124. Jaffrelot, 'The Hindu Nationalist Reinterpretation of Pilgrimage in India' (2009), p.1; Sandria B. Freitag, 'Sacred Symbol as Mobilizing Ideology: The North Indian Search for a "Hindu" community', *Comparative Studies in Society and History*, vol.22, no.4 (1980), pp.597–625.
125. Jaffrelot, 'The Hindu Nationalist Reinterpretation of Pilgrimage in India' (2009), pp.14, 17.
126. Ram Lall Dhooria, *I Was a Swayamsevak (An Inside View of the RSS)* (New Delhi: Sampradayikta Virodhi Committee, 1969), pp.39–40.
127. 'Vishwa Sangh Shibir 1995 Press Release', 1996.
128. Turner, *Dramas, Fields, and Metaphors* (1975), p.169.
129. Fuller, *The Camphor Flame* (2004), p.222.
130. Fuller, *The Camphor Flame* (2004), p.222. Emphasis added.
131. Fuller, *The Camphor Flame* (2004), p.222.
132. Veer, *Gods on Earth* (1988), p.60.
133. Arafaat A. Valiani, *Militant Publics in India: Physical Culture and Violence in the Making of a Modern Polity* (New York: Palgrave MacMillan, 2011), p.151.
134. Valiani, *Militant Publics in India* (2011), p.151.
135. Jaffrelot states: 'Among the ten *swayamsevaks* from the *shakhas* of Vikram Mandal in Delhi who had attended an Instructors Training Camp, only one was a member of the Scheduled Castes while the majority were Banyas'. Christophe Jaffrelot, *The Hindu Nationalist Movement and Indian Politics* (London: Hurst, 1996), p.49.
136. Michel Foucault, 'Des Espaces Autres. Hétérotopies [Of Other Spaces, Heterotopias]', *Architecture, Mouvement, Continuité*, vol.5 (1984), pp.46–9. Translated and reproduced: http://foucault.info/documents/heterotopia/foucault.heterotopia.en.html, n.p.
137. Foucault, 'Des Espaces Autres. Hétérotopies' (1984), n.p.
138. Dhooria, *I Was a Swayamsevak* (1969), pp.40–1.
139. T.A. Johnson, 'NRIs Flock to RSS Camp to Become Global Hindus', 11 August 2001.
140. Michel Foucault 'Of Other Spaces', trans. Lieven De Cauter and Michiel Dehaene, in Michiel Dehaene and Lieven De Cauter (eds.), *Heterotopia and the City: Public Space in a Postcivil Society* (Abingdon: Routledge, 2008), p.21
141. Foucault, 'Of Other Spaces', in Dehaene and De Cauter (eds.) *Heterotopia and the City* (2008), p.21.
142. Dhooria, *I Was a Swayamsevak* (1969), p.41.
143. Ashutosh Bhardwaj, 'At Gates of RSS Meet, an 8-year-old Stands Guard', *The Indian Express*, 2 January 2022: http://indianexpress.com/article/india/india-news-india/at-gates-of-rss-meet-an-8-year-old-stands-guard/. Accessed on 4 January 2022.
144. Anne Hardgrove, *Community and Public Culture: The Marwaris in Calcutta 1897–1997* (New York: Columbia University Press, 2004), ch.2; cited in Deepa Reddy and John Zavos, 'Temple Publics: Religious Institutions and

the Construction of Contemporary Hindu Communities', *International Journal of Hindu Studies*, vol.13, no.3 (2009), p.253.
145. M.G. Chitkara, *Rashtriya Swayamsevak Sangh: National Upsurge* (New Delhi: S.B. Nangia, 2004), p.302.
146. Seshadri, *RSS: A Vision in Action* (2001), pp.182–5.
147. M.A. Venkata Rao, 'Introduction', in M.S. Golwalkar, *Bunch of Thoughts* (2000), p.xix.
148. Seshadri, *RSS: A Vision in Action* (2001), p.179.
149. Seshadri, *RSS: A Vision in Action* (2001), pp.182–3.
150. Chitkara, *Rashtriya Swayamsevak Sangh* (2004), pp.302–3.
151. Kunte, 'Vishwa Sangha Shibir: An Overview', in Kunte (ed.), *Vishwa Sangh Shibir* (2010), p.7. Emphasis added.
152. A camp in Nagpur in 1940, when the organisation was still in its infancy, boasted participants from the United Provinces, Bihar, Bengal, Madras Presidency, Bombay Presidency, the North-West Frontier Province, Sindh, and Punjab. J.A. Curran, *Militant Hinduism in Indian Politics—A Study of the RSS* (Institute of Pacific Relations, 1951), p.14; B.V. Deshpande and S.R. Ramaswamy, *Dr Hedgewar, the Epoch-Maker* (1981), pp.165, 170, 179. Both cited in Jaffrelot, *The Hindu Nationalist Movement and Indian Politics* (1996), p.68.
153. Ravi Kumar, 'Hindu Resurgence Around the World', 29 January 2010.
154. Salman Rushdie, *Imaginary Homelands* (London: Granta Books, 1991), p.10.
155. Seshadri, *Dollar or Dharma?* (1990), p.48.
156. Paul Basu, *Highland Homecomings: Genealogy and Heritage Tourism in the Scottish Diaspora* (Abingdon: Routledge, 2007), p.67.
157. Avtar Brah, *Cartographies of Diaspora: Contesting Identities* (London: Routledge, 1996), p.192, p.4. See also Ozlem Galip, *Imagining Kurdistan: Identity, Culture and Society* (London: I.B. Tauris, 2015).
158. Safran, 'Diasporas in Modern Societies' (1991), p.92.
159. Homi Bhabha, *The Location of Culture* (London: Routledge, 1994); Edward Soja, *ThirdSpace: Journeys to Los Angeles and Other Real-and-Imagined Places* (Oxford: Blackwell, 1996).
160. Kunte, 'Vishwa Sangha Shibir: An Overview', in Kunte (ed.), *Vishwa Sangh Shibir* (2010), p.7
161. Ami Ganatra, 'Vishva Sangh Shibir (My Tryst with RSS)': https://dharmorakshtirakshitah.wordpress.com/2016/01/31/vishva-sangh-shibir-my-tryst-with-rss/. Accessed on 4 January 2022.
162. Diana Eck, 'Negotiating Hindu Identities in America', in H. Coward, J. Hinnells and R.B. Williams (eds.), *The South Asian Religious Diaspora in Britain, Canada, and the United States* (Albany, NY: State University of New York Press, 2000), p.221.
163. Letter from Atul Nagras, VAK Secretary, to 'professional colleague', 1 October 2010. Template uploaded: https://googlegroups.com/group/

social-ca-community/attach/8ee195ec22c655dd/letter%20to%20 CA%20,%20Cs%20etc.pdf?part=4. Accessed on 10 August 2014.
164. Letter from Badrinath Murthy, VAK President, to 'respected sir', 15 October 2010. Template uploaded: https://groups.google.com/d/topic/social-ca-community/0_xtjlX0iXA/discussion. Accessed on 28 September 2015.
165. 'Samvad—ShriVishwa Niketan', n.d.
166. Anita Patel, *Sangh Sandesh* (January–March 2011), p.19; https://dharmorakshtirakshitah.wordpress.com/2016/01/31/vishva-sangh-shibir-my-tryst-with-rss/.
167. Michiel Dehaene and Lieven De Cauter, 'The Space of Play', in Dehaene and De Cauter (eds.), *Heterotopia and the City: Public Space in a Postcivil Society* (2008), p.98.
168. 'NRI Conference Connects India to its Diaspora', Diplomatic cable from the Embassy of the United States of America, New Delhi, to the Central Intelligence Agency et al., 18 January 2008: https://wikileaks.org/plusd/cables/08NEWDELHI193_a.html.
169. Arvind Rajagopal, 'Expatriate Nationalism: Disjunctive Discourses', in R. Ghose (ed.), *In Quest of a Secular Symbol: Ayodhya and After* (Perth, Australia: Indian Ocean Centre & South Asian Research Unit, Curtin University of Technology Press, 1996), pp.109–39.

3. TRANSNATIONAL HINDUTVA NETWORKS

1. This chapter is adapted from an article co-authored with Patrick Clibbens: '"Smugglers of Truth": the Indian diaspora, Hindu nationalism, and the Emergency (1975–77)', *Modern Asian Studies*, vol.52, no.1 (2018), pp.1729–73.
2. Two significant monographs have addressed this lacuna in recent years: Christophe Jaffrelot and Pratinav Anil, *India's First Dictatorship: The Emergency, 1975–77* (London: Hurst, 2020); Gyan Prakash, *Emergency Chronicles: Indira Gandhi and Democracy's Turning Point* (Gurgaon: Penguin, 2018). Noteworthy contributions have also been made by Francine Frankel, Arvind Rajagopal, Ramachandra Guha, Bipan Chandra, Emma Tarlo, and Patrick Clibbens.
3. L.K. Advani, *My Country My Life* (New Delhi: Rupa, 2008), p.202. Advani has written prolifically on his experiences during the Emergency. Immediately following the Emergency, his diary from jail was published as *A Prisoner's Scrapbook* (New Delhi: Arnold-Heinemann, 1978), and then *The People Betrayed* (New Delhi: Vision Books, 1979).
4. A chapter in Christophe Jaffrelot's seminal book on the Hindu nationalist movement discusses the Emergency period in the wider context of the relationship with the JP Movement. Christophe Jaffrelot, *The Hindu Nationalist Movement and Indian Politics* (London: Hurst, 1996), pp.255–81.

See also Arvind Rajagopal, 'Sangh's Role in the Emergency', *Economic and Political Weekly*, vol.38, no.27 (2003), pp.2797–8.

5. Extensive but partisan accounts of the Emergency by those within the Sangh can be found in P.G. Sahasrabuddhe and Manik Chandra Vajpayee, *The People versus Emergency: A Saga of Struggle*, trans. Sudhakar Raje (New Delhi: Suruchi Prakashan, 1991); Advani, *My Country My Life* (2008); Sanjeev Kelkar, *Lost Years of the RSS* (New Delhi: Sage, 2011). A contemporary account published by the Gandhian journalist M.C. Subrahmanyam was based on the recollections of a member of the RSS resident in California, Dr Manohar Shinde; Subrahmanyam, 'Overseas Indians' (1977), pp.60–5.

6. Daniel Naujoks, *Migration, Citizenship and Development: Diasporic Membership Policies and Overseas Indians in the United States* (New Delhi: Oxford University Press, 2013), p.44; Constantino Xavier, 'Innovative Incorporation: Diasporic Representation and Political Rights in India', in Md Mizanur Rahman and Tan Tai Yong (eds.), *International Migration and Development in South Asia* (Abingdon: Routledge, 2015), pp.22–43.

7. Rudra Chaudhuri, 'Re-reading the Indian Emergency: Britain, the United States and India's Constitutional Autocracy, 1975–1977', *Diplomacy & Statecraft*, vol.29, no.3 (2018), pp.477–98.

8. Veena Das, *Critical Events: An Anthropological Perspective on Contemporary India* (New Delhi: Oxford University Press, 1995).

9. This is highlighted by inconsistencies between numbers given by the RSS, and those from the Shah Commission (appointed by the Government of India in 1978 to inquire into the Emergency). The RSS claim that more than 100,000 of its members went to jail. The Shah Commission put the total number jailed during the Emergency at 109,527 (some of whom were probably counted twice). The Sangh numbers implausibly imply that a huge majority of those detained were *swayamsevaks*. Of the 36,039 people arrested under MISA, 2,794 were explicitly recorded as RSS members, and 1,358 were recorded as Jana Sangh members. It is far from clear that a great majority of the remainder should also be attributed to the Sangh Parivar, as RSS sources claim. Furthermore, Jaffrelot has argued that only a minority of the *pracharaks* were imprisoned—only 186 out of a total of 1,356. The picture is further complicated by letters from the imprisoned RSS leader, Deoras, to Indira Gandhi, which take a conciliatory tone. Letters reproduced in Sahasrabuddhe and Vajpayee, *The People versus Emergency* (1991), pp.592–3, and P. Brahm Dutt, *Five Headed Monster—A Factual Narrative of the Genesis of Janata Party* (New Delhi: Surge Publications, 1978), pp.138–48; Seshadri, *RSS—A Vision in Action* (2001), p.368; Jaffrelot, *The Hindu Nationalist Movement* (1996), p.274; Shah Commission of Inquiry, *Interim Report I, Interim Report II, Third and Final Report* (New Delhi: Government of India Press, 1978); Kelkar, *Lost Years of the RSS* (2011), p.136.

10. Kelkar, *Lost Years of the RSS* (2011), p.133.

11. Kelkar, *Lost Years of the RSS* (2011), p.131.
12. Advani, *My Country My Life* (2008), p.202.
13. Narendra Modi, 'Remembering Emergency 1975—The Victory of People's Power!', 26 June 2013: http://blogs.timesofindia.indiatimes.com/narendra-modis-blog/remembering-emergency-1975-the-victory-of-people-s-power/. Accessed on 21 May 2017. Also see the profile on his website, 'Dedicated Life', 14 May 2014, http://www.narendramodi.in/the-activist/. Accessed on 28 August 2015.
14. Subrahmanyam, 'Overseas Indians' (1977), pp.60–5; Advani, *A Prisoner's Scrapbook* (1978), n.p. *Satyagrahi* may be translated literally as 'pursuer of truth'. Coined by Gandhi, the term is usually used in reference to activists and followers of Gandhi during the Indian independence movement.
15. M.G. Chitkara, *Rashtriya Swayamsevak Sangh: National Upsurge* (New Delhi: S.B. Nangia, 2004), p.285.
16. *RSS: In the Forefront of the Second Freedom Struggle* (Bangalore: Jagarana Prakashana, 1979), p.5. These claims continue to be made today; for example, Virag Pachpore writes that 80,000 RSS *swayamsevaks* 'offered satyagraha' and 44,965 were arrested, including '2,424 ladies'. Virag Pachpore, 'The RSS and Emergency', *Swarajya*, 26 June 2015: https://swarajyamag.com/politics/the-rss-and-emergency. Accessed on 10 March 2017.
17. Rajagopal, 'Sangh's Role in the Emergency' (2003), pp.2797–8.
18. Rajagopal, 'Sangh's Role in the Emergency' (2003), p.2798.
19. Embassy of the United States, New Delhi, diplomatic cable to the Department of State, Washington DC (27 September 1975): https://www.wikileaks.org/plusd/cables/1975NEWDE13020_b.html. Accessed on 1 July 2016.
20. Jaffrelot and Anil, *India's First Dictatorship* (2020), pp.367–401.
21. Sahasrabuddhe and Vajpayee, *The People versus Emergency* (1991), pp.510–11.
22. Sahasrabuddhe and Vajpayee, *The People versus Emergency* (1991), p.512.
23. Sahasrabuddhe and Vajpayee, *The People versus Emergency* (1991), p.518.
24. No author, *The Pen in Revolt: Underground Literature Published During the Emergency* (New Delhi: Press Institute of India, 1978), p.12. The Lok Sangharsh Samiti (People's Struggle Committee) was an activist group founded in 1975 by Morarji Desai to demand Indira Gandhi's resignation.
25. Coomi Kapoor, *The Emergency: A Personal History* (New Delhi: Penguin, 2015), pp.130, 137.
26. Jagdish Chandra Sharda Shastri, *Memoirs of a Global Hindu*, compiled and ed. by Ratan Sharda (Mumbai: Vishwa Adhyayan Kendra, 2008), p.116; Sahasrabuddhe and Vajpayee, *The People versus Emergency* (1991), p.513.
27. Sharad Kunte (ed.), *Vishwa Sangh Shibir 2010 Souvenir* (Pune: Vishwa Adhyayan Kendra, 2010), pp.198, 202; 'Profile of Shri Lakshmanrao Bhide', n.d: http://www.vakmumbai.org/llb-02.php. Accessed on 25 August 2015.

28. Sahasrabuddhe and Vajpayee, *The People versus Emergency* (1991), p.531.
29. Sahasrabuddhe and Vajpayee, *The People versus Emergency* (1991), p.531.
30. Author's interview with Subramanian Swamy (London, 3 April 2015).
31. Subramanian Swamy, letter 'to the people of India' (16 November 1976), in Nehru Memorial Museum and Library, New Delhi (henceforth NMML), Jayaprakash Narayan Papers, 3rd Instalment, Subject File 337.
32. Kapoor, *The Emergency: A Personal History* (2015), p.134.
33. Subrahmanyam, 'Overseas Indians' (1977), pp.60–5.
34. *Parliamentary Debates. Rajya Sabha. Official Report*, vol. 97, no. 17 (2 September 1976), col. 8ff. See also 'RainmakerIndia', 'Subramanian Swamy's Underground Life During the Emergency': https://www.youtube.com/watch?v=GiNstP82UrA. Accessed on 16 September 2015.
35. Author's interview with Subramanian Swamy (London, 3 April 2015).
36. Friends of India Society International flyer advertising Subramanian Swamy talks on 'Current Situation in India' (January 1976), Trades Union Congress Papers MSS.292d/954/2, Modern Records Centre, University of Warwick.
37. Sahasrabuddhe and Vajpayee, *The People versus Emergency* (1991), p.532. Countries represented included: India, Britain, Singapore, Kenya, Tanzania, Mauritius, Zambia, West Germany, Denmark, Canada, the USA, and Trinidad.
38. Sahasrabuddhe and Vajpayee, *The People versus Emergency* (1991), pp.531–2. There is no indication what a 'chapter' constituted—perhaps just a handful of people or a proactive individual—and so scepticism on this claim is required.
39. Sahasrabuddhe and Vajpayee, *The People versus Emergency* (1991), p.532.
40. Shiva Naipaul, 'A Philosophical Threat to Mrs Gandhi's Political Power', *The Times*, 9 June 1976, p.8.
41. Swamy first became assistant professor in economics at Harvard in July 1966, where he remained until 1969. Later in his career he taught on Harvard's summer school programme, but was dismissed in 2011 following a student petition and criticism from Harvard faculty members Diana Eck and Sugata Bose. This was related to Swamy's call to demolish mosques in India and remove voting rights from Muslims who did not 'acknowledge that their ancestors were Hindus'. 'Harvard drops Indian MP Subramanian Swamy's courses', BBC News, 8 December 2011: http://www.bbc.co.uk/news/world-asia-india-16081751. Accessed on 25 August 2015.
42. 'Subramanian Swamy suggested to department officer ten days ago that he heard Mrs Gandhi was prompted to set the March election date'. United States Department of State, 'Prime Minister's Health', electronic telegram from US Department of State to New Delhi Embassy, 3 February 1977: https://wikileaks.org/plusd/cables/1977STATE024965_c.html. Accessed on 25 August 2015.

43. Subrahmanyam, 'Overseas Indians' (1977), pp.60–5.
44. 'Report of Committee appointed to investigate the conduct and activities of Shri Subramanian Swamy, Member of the Rajya Sabha' (12 November 1976), NMML, Jayaprakash Narayan Papers, 3rd Instalment, Subject File 318A.
45. Swamy's organisation, the Virat Hindustan Sangam, held a talk in New Delhi on 7 August 2016 titled 'Lessons to be learnt from the Emergency', 'to commemorate the 40th anniversary of Dr Subramanian Swamy's dramatic appearance in the Rajya Sabha during the Emergency in 1976': https://vhsindia.org/7aug/. Accessed on 25 September 2016. This narrative is also drawn upon for and by his considerable overseas following, as he continues to conduct extensive and regular international speaking tours.
46. *Parliamentary Debates. Rajya Sabha. Official Report*, vol. 97, no. 17 (2 September 1976), col. 8ff.
47. Rudra Chaudhuri, 'Re-reading the Indian Emergency: Britain, the United States and India's Constitutional Autocracy, 1975–1977', *Diplomacy & Statecraft*, vol.29, no.3 (2018), pp.477–98.
48. William Borders, 'India Assails Ford for Crisis Remarks', *New York Times*, 19 September 1975; Memorandum of Conversation, Washington DC (4 October 1975), *Foreign Relations of the United States, 1969–1976*, vol.E-8, *Documents on South Asia, 1973–1976*, https://history.state.gov/historicaldocuments/frus1969-76ve08/d211. Accessed on 14 March 2017.
49. In one article in the *Times of India*, M.V. Kamath juxtaposed it with Ford's overriding of the will of Congress and the CIA's involvement in coups. M.V. Kamath, 'India Visit Off, Ford Confirms', *Times of India*, 18 September 1975.
50. P.J.E. Male, 'One Year of Emergency' (1 October 1976), in the National Archives of the UK (TNA), FCO 37/1719 (1976).
51. A UK FCO memorandum titled 'One of Year of Emergency' underlines that 'the prime determinant (which applies to policies towards and relations with the majority of states and regimes in the world) is the pursuit of British interests... With Indian economic power will come increasing regional and world influence based on foundations other than dogma and envy.' Male, 'One Year of Emergency' (1 October 1976), TNA, FCO 37/1719 (1976).
52. Jaffrelot and Anil, *India's First Dictatorship* (2020), pp.410–15.
53. Michael White, 'Foot Rides to Ghandi's [sic] Side', *The Guardian*, 7 January 1977.
54. *Human Rights in India. Hearings before the Subcommittee on International Organizations of the Committee on International Relations, House of Representatives, Ninety-Fourth Congress, Second Session (23, 28, 29 June, 16, 23 September 1976)* (Washington DC: US Government Printing Office, 1976). For articles, see e.g. Kathleen Teltsch, 'Rights League Tells the U.N. India Tramples on Freedoms', *New York Times*, 2 June 1976, read into the record by

Congressman Ed Koch of New York, *Congressional Record—House* (2 June 1976), pp.16255–6.

55. K.V. Rajan, First Secretary (Political), Embassy of India, Washington DC, to Joint Secretary (AMS), Ministry of External Affairs, New Delhi (13 October 1976) National Archives of India, New Delhi (henceforth NAI), Ministry of External Affairs Papers (henceforth MEA), AMS Division, WII/307/1/76.
56. Alastair Goodlad, *Hansard*, HC Deb, vol.895 col.1475 (16 July 1975); Robin Corbett, *Hansard*, HC Deb, vol.914, cols.1346–7 (7 July 1976); David Ennals, *Hansard*, HC Deb, vol.896, cols.491-2W (30 July 1975).
57. 'Minutes of the High Commissioner's meeting with Foreign Secretary Callaghan on 9 September, 1975', NMML, B.K. Nehru Papers, S.No.34.
58. Indira Gandhi, quoted in 'One-Party Rule Not Aim, Asserts PM', *Times of India*, 14 August 1975.
59. Steven Vertovec, 'Three Meanings of "Diaspora" Exemplified among South Asian Religions', *Diaspora*, vol.6, no.3 (1997), pp.277–99.
60. 'Guidelines for the Press in the Present Emergency', Press Information Bureau, Government of India (26 June 1975), quoted in David Selbourne, *An Eye to India: The Unmasking of a Tyranny* (Harmondsworth: Penguin, 1977), pp.374–5, 391. See also Soli Sorabjee, *The Emergency, Censorship and the Press in India, 1975–77* (London: Writers & Scholars Educational Trust, 1977); Kuldip Nayar, *The Judgment: Inside Story of the Emergency in India* (New Delhi: Vikas, 1977).
61. Government of India, *White Paper on Misuse of Mass Media During the Internal Emergency* (New Delhi: Controller of Publications, Government of India Press, 1977), p.3. See also Marcus F. Franda, 'Curbing the Indian Press', *American University Fieldstaff Reports*, South Asia Series, vol.20, nos.12–14 (1976); and Indu B. Singh, 'The Indian Mass Media System: Before, During and After the National Emergency', *Canadian Journal of Communication*, vol.7, no.2 (1980), pp.39–49. Singh argues that other tools of government manipulation of the press included: the merger of privately owned press agencies; the threat of cutting off government-run teleprinter services; and various 'fear-arousal techniques on the newspaper publishers, editors, reporters, and shareholders' (p.41).
62. William Borders, 'India's Press Gains Verve, but There Are Some Qualms', *New York Times*, 11 May 1977, p.3.
63. Sahasrabuddhe and Vajpayee, *The People versus Emergency* (1991), p.512.
64. 'Swayamsevak', 'A History of the Hindu Swayamsevak Sangh', n.d.: http://timerime.com/en/timeline/384686/The+History+of+Hindu+Swayamsevak+Sangh/. Accessed on 3 September 2015.
65. Makarand Desai, 'Introduction', in Desai (ed.), *Smugglers of Truth* (1978), p.7.
66. Amiya Rao and B.G. Rao (eds.), *The Press She Could Not Whip: Emergency in India as Reported by the Foreign Press* (Bombay: Popular Prakashan, 1977).

67. Modi, *Apatkal main Gujarat* (2001), ch. 20.
68. Author's interview with Subramaniam Swamy (London, 3 April 2015).
69. Desai (ed.), *The Smugglers of Truth* (1978); Tarlo, *Unsettling Memories* (2003), p. 33.
70. Author's interview with Subramaniam Swamy (London, 3 April 2015).
71. Author's interview with Subramaniam Swamy (London, 3 April 2015).
72. Sahasrabuddhe and Vajpayee, *The People versus Emergency* (1991), p. 517.
73. Vinod K. Jose, 'The Emperor Uncrowned: The Rise of Narendra Modi', *The Caravan*, 1 March 2012.
74. 'Dedicated Life', 14 May 2014: http://www.narendramodi.in/the-activist/. Accessed on 25 August 2015.
75. 'Dedicated Life', 14 May 2014.
76. 'Dedicated Life', 14 May 2014.
77. It was translated into Hindi in 2001 as *Apatkal main Gujarat* (Gujarat in the Emergency).
78. Undated letter from Makarand Desai to Narendra Modi, in Modi, *Apatkal main Gujarat* (2001), p. 162; Letter from Makarand Desai to Narendra Modi (16 July 1976), in Modi, *Apatkal main Gujarat* (2001), p. 163.
79. Letter from Makarand Desai to Narendra Modi (16 July 1976), in Modi, *Apatkal main Gujarat* (2001).
80. Undated letter from Desai to Modi, in Modi, *Apatkal main Gujarat* (2001), p. 162.
81. Undated letter from Desai to Modi, in Modi, *Apatkal main Gujarat* (2001), p. 164.
82. Modi, *Apatkal main Gujarat* (2001), passim.
83. B. N. Tandon, *PMO Diary II—The Emergency* (Delhi: Konark, 2006), pp. 347, 362.
84. Author's interview with Subramanian Swamy (London, 3 April 2015).
85. Letter from Desai to Modi, n.d., in Modi, *Apatkal main Gujarat* (2001), p. 165.
86. Kapoor, *The Emergency: A Personal History* (2015), p. 134.
87. Jonathan Sayeed (Conservative MP for Bristol East, 1983–92) was half-Indian, but explicitly did not identify as an 'ethnic minority'. Hence, the election of four ethnic minority MPs in 1987—Diane Abbott, Paul Boateng, Keith Vaz, and Bernie Grant—is considered the significant, watershed moment in ethnic minority political representation.
88. Anandi Ramamurthy, *Black Star: Britain Asian Youth Movements* (London: Pluto Press, 2013).
89. This is not, however, to push a spurious, assimilationist-type argument: there is, of course, compelling evidence that the religion, culture, and politics of the homeland are sought in new and energetic ways by younger generations (often even exceeding their parents' connection to the homeland).
90. Mike Bristow, 'Britain's Response to the Uganda Asian Crisis: Government Myths Versus Political and Resettlement Realities', *New Community*, vol. 5,

no.3 (1976), pp.265–79; John Mattausch, 'From Subjects to Citizens: British "East African Asians"', *Journal of Ethnic and Migration Studies*, vol.24, no.1 (1998), pp.121–41.

91. Pre-1990s ethnic population numbers are based on estimates (often using the Labour Force Survey), as the 1991 UK census was the first to include a question on ethnicity (rather than simply 'birthplace'). See Roger Ballard, 'Britain's Visible Minorities: A Demographic Overview', Working Paper (Stalybridge: Centre for Applied South Asian Studies, 1999), p.6.
92. Nussbaum, *Clash Within* (2007), p.317.
93. For Ved Nanda's testimony before Congress, see *Human Rights in India. Hearings before the Subcommittee on International Organizations of the Committee on International Relations, House of Representatives, Ninety-Fourth Congress, Second Session (23, 28, 29 June, 16, 23 September 1976)* (Washington DC: US Government Printing Office, 1976), pp.39–47. For his academic writings, see Ved P. Nanda, 'From Gandhi to Gandhi—International Legal Responses to the Destruction of Human Rights and Fundamental Freedoms in India', *Denver Journal of International Law and Policy*, vol.6, no.1 (1976), pp.19–42. For journalistic writings, see Ved P. Nanda, 'Can the World Remain Silent?' reprinted in Desai (ed.), *The Smugglers of Truth* (1978), pp.67–70.
94. Nussbaum, *Clash Within* (2007), p.317. For Nanda's 'defence' of the HSS, see Ved P. Nanda, 'The Hindu Diaspora in the United States', in Wendy Doniger and Martha C. Nussbaum (eds.), *Pluralism and Democracy in India: Debating the Hindu Right* (New York: Oxford University Press, 2015), pp.346–66.
95. Hasmukh Velji Shah, 'April 1976 Conference', http://fisi.org.uk/?page_id=745. Accessed on 5 November 2016.
96. Prem N. Chopra, *India at the Crossroads* (New Delhi: Sterling Publishers, 2004), pp.153–4.
97. Modi, *Apatkal main Gujarat* (2001), p.159. Sahasrabuddhe and Vajpayee report that he contributed 'one lakh rupees'; *The People versus Emergency* (1991), p.517.
98. Chopra, *India at the Crossroads* (2004), p.155.
99. Chopra, *India at the Crossroads* (2004), p.155; Suman Guha Mozumder, 'Mukund Mody, Founder of OFBJP, dies', *India Abroad* (New York), 21 June 2013, p.43.
100. 'OF-BJP founder Mukund Mody passes away in US', *Business Standard*, 5 June 2013: http://www.business-standard.com/article/pti-stories/of-bjp-founder-mukund-mody-passes-away-in-us-113060501142_1.html. Accessed on 27 May 2016; Aprajita Sikri, 'Why Many Have Harked Back to Revive Affiliations with RSS', *India Abroad* (New York), 5 May 1989, p.14.
101. Chopra, *India at the Crossroads* (2004), p.154; Vanya Mehta, 'Foreign Returns', *The Caravan*, 1 April 2014: http://www.caravanmagazine.in/reportage/foreign-returns. Accessed on 27 May 2016.

102. 'Ramesh Bhutada: Seeking Higher Goals Through Business Skills', *Indo American News*, 6 September 2018: http://www.indoamerican-news.com/ramesh-bhutada-seeking-higher-goals-through-business-skills/. Accessed on 5 July 2023.
103. Azad Essa, *Hostile Homelands: The New Alliance Between India and Israel* (London: Pluto, 2023), pp.107–8; Seshadri Kumar, 'Ramesh Bhutada: Pioneer Places Philanthropy Over Bottom Line': https://india-herald.com/ramesh-bhutada-pioneer-places-philanthropy-over-bottom-line-p1992-1.htm. Accessed on 16 November 2017.
104. Latha Varadarajan, 'Mother India and Her Children Abroad: The Role of the Diaspora in India's Foreign Policy', in David M. Malone, C. Raja Mohan and Srinath Raghavan (eds.), *The Oxford Handbook of Indian Foreign Policy* (Oxford: Oxford University Press, 2015), pp.285–6, 291.
105. Mario Rutten and Pravin Patel, 'Contested Family Relations and Government Policy: Links between Patel Migrants in Britain and India', in Gijsbert Oonk (ed.), *Global Indian Diasporas: Exploring Trajectories of Migration and Theory* (Amsterdam: International Institute of Asian Studies/Amsterdam University Press, 2007), p.180.
106. See, for instance: Harald Fischer-Tiné, 'Indian Nationalism and the "World Forces": Transnational and Diasporic Dimensions of the Indian Freedom Movement on the Eve of the First World War', *Journal of Global History*, vol.2, no.3 (2007), pp.325–44; Sunil Amrith, *Crossing the Bay of Bengal: The Furies of Nature and the Fortunes of Migrants* (Cambridge, MA; Harvard University Press, 2013); Seema Sohi, *Echoes of Mutiny: Race, Surveillance and Indian Anticolonialism in North America* (New York: Oxford University Press, 2015).
107. Kapur, *Diaspora, Development and Democracy: The Domestic Impact of International Migration* (2010); Rina Agarwala, 'Tapping the Indian Diaspora for Indian Development', in Alejandro Portes and Patricia Fernández-Kelly (eds.), *The State and the Grassroots: Immigrant Transnational Organizations in Four Continents* (Oxford: Berghahn Books, 2015), pp.84–110.
108. M.C. Lall, *India's Missed Opportunity: India's Relationship with Non-Resident Indians* (Aldershot: Ashgate, 2001).
109. Rutten and Patel, 'Contested Family Relations and Government Policy' (2007), p.183; Asaf Hussain, 'The Indian Diaspora in Britain: Political Interventionism and Diaspora Activism', *Asian Affairs*, vol.32, no.3 (2005), pp.189–208; Chandrashekhar Bhat, 'India and the Indian Diaspora: Interlinkages and Expectations', in Ajay Dubey (ed.), *Indian Diaspora: Global Identity* (Delhi: Kalinga, 2003), pp.11–34; A. Didar Singh and S. Irudaya Rajan, *Politics of Migration: Indian Emigration in a Globalized World* (New Delhi: Routledge India, 2015).
110. Jonathan Fox, 'Unpacking "Transnational Citizenship"', *Annual Review of Political Science*, vol.8 (2005), pp.171–201; Rainer Baubök, 'Expansive

Citizenship: Voting Beyond Territory and Membership', *PS: Political Science and Politics*, vol.38, no.4 (2005), pp.683–87.
111. Niraja Gopal Jayal, *Citizenship and its Discontents: An Indian History* (Ranikhet: Permanent Black, 2013), p.100.
112. Sanjoy Chakravorty, Devesh Kapur, and Nirvikar Singh, *The Other One Percent: Indians in America* (New York: Oxford University Press, 2017), p.276.
113. Letter from J. N. Bhat, Consul (Public Relations), Consulate General of India, New York, to A.N.D. Haksar, Joint Secretary (XP), MEA (17 February 1976), NAI, MEA, AMS Division, WII/307/1/76.
114. Letter, T.N. Kaul, Indian Ambassador to USA, to Indira Gandhi (22 February 1976), NMML, T.N. Kaul Papers, Subject File S.No.4 Part I.
115. Information Service of India, New York, report on seminar on 'Emergency in India' held on 10 April 1976 at Vassar College, Poughkeepsie, New York, signed by J.N. Bhat, Consul (Public Relations), Consulate General of India, New York (14 April 1976), NAI, MEA, AMS Division, WII/307/1/76.
116. Letter from S.R. Sen, Executive Director of the International Bank for Reconstruction and Development to T.N. Kaul, Ambassador of India to the United States (14 April 1976), NAI, MEA, AMS Division, WII/307/1/76.
117. 'Report of Committee appointed to investigate the conduct and activities of Shri Subramanian Swamy, Member of the Rajya Sabha' (12 November 1976), NMML, Jayaprakash Narayan Papers, 3rd Instalment, Subject File 318A.
118. 'Report of Committee appointed to investigate the conduct and activities of Shri Subramanian Swamy, Member of the Rajya Sabha' (12 November 1976), NMML, Jayaprakash Narayan Papers, 3rd Instalment, Subject File 318A.
119. Telex message, Embassy of India, Washington DC, to Ministry of External Affairs (8 August 1975), in NAI, Ministry of Home Affairs papers, Desk IV Section, II/14011/21/75-S&P(D.IV).
120. Memorandum, C.V. Narasimhan, JS(IS), to A.N.D. Haksar, JS(XP), Ministry of External Affairs (22 August 1975), to be sent to the Embassy of India in Washington, in NAI, Ministry of Home Affairs papers, Desk IV Section, II/14011/21/75-S&P(D.IV).
121. Memorandum, C.V. Narasimhan, JS(IS), to A.N.D. Haksar, JS(XP), Ministry of External Affairs (22 August 1975), to be sent to the Embassy of India in Washington, in NAI, Ministry of Home Affairs papers, Desk IV Section, II/14011/21/75-S&P(D.IV).
122. Memoranda, J.S. Teja, Joint Secretary (AMS), MEA (5 and 12 February 1976), NAI, MEA, WII/307/1/76.
123. 'Impounding of passports' table, attached to memorandum, J. Abraham, Minister (Consular) to High Commissioner B.K. Nehru (21 June 1977), NMML, B.K. Nehru Papers, S.No. 40. Sood, Bharati, and another FISI member in Britain who had his passport impounded, Ramanbhai Khatri,

were among those 'felicitated' at a public FISI meeting in Bombay in July 1977, 'Anti-emergency fighters felicitated in city', *Times of India*, 9 July 1977, p.4.
124. Note, H.A. Barari, Deputy Director, Intelligence Bureau, Ministry of Home Affairs, to J.S. Teja, Ministry of External Affairs; B.N. Tandon, Secretary, Prime Minister's Secretariat; C.V. Narasimhan, Ministry of Home Affairs (31 January 1976) in NAI, MEA, AMS, WII/102/11/76 Volume I. The story, which originated with the Press Trust of India news agency, appeared in several newspapers, including the *Patriot* and the *Hindustan Times*; 'Extract from the *Patriot* dated 29.1.76: Confidential CIA papers seized', in NAI, MEA, AMS, WII/102/11/76 Volume I; 'CIA documents seized', *Hindustan Times*, 29 January 1976, NAI, MEA, AMS, WII/102/11/76 Volume II.
125. Subrahmanyam, 'Overseas Indians' (1977), pp.60–5.
126. Tandon, *PMO Diary II—The Emergency* (2006), pp.347, 362, 370. See also 'Don't get alarmed, U.K. Asians told', *Times of India*, 25 June 1976, p. 9; 'Hitendra hopes UK trip was fruitful', *Times of India*, 29 June 1976, p.15. Jaisukhlal Hathi, a former minister from Gujarat, had wide connections in the UK through his work for the Bharatiya Vidya Bhavan; Jaisukhlal Hathi, *As It Happened! An Autobiography* (Mumbai: Bharatiya Vidya Bhavan, 2002), pp.313–23.
127. Amrit Wilson, 'Winning friends for Mrs Gandhi', *The Guardian*, 11 March 1976, p.13; 'Indian stand irks West: PM', *Times of India*, 16 September 1975, p.1.
128. Handwritten minute on memorandum, P.C. Kapoor, Under Secretary, External Publicity Division, Ministry of External Affairs, XM-304/6(10)/75 (October 1975), NAI, MEA, AMS Division, WII/102/31/75 Vol. II.
129. Summary of Indira Gandhi's letter in 'A background note on attitude of publicity media in USA/UK/FRG/France to India and our efforts to project the correct picture in these countries' (n.d., probably December 1975) in NAI, MEA, AMS Division, WII/102/31/75 Volume III.
130. Direct quotation of Indira Gandhi's letter in 'A background note on attitude of publicity media…' (n.d., probably December 1975) in NAI, MEA, AMS Division, WII/102/31/75 Volume III.
131. Letter, T.N. Kaul, Indian Ambassador to USA, to Indira Gandhi (23 March 1976), NMML, T.N. Kaul Papers, Subject File S.No. 4 Part I.
132. Letter, T.N. Kaul, Indian Ambassador to USA, to Indira Gandhi (23 March 1976), NMML, T.N. Kaul Papers, Subject File S.No. 4 Part I.
133. Memorandum, Nirmala Prasad, Deputy Secretary (Policy Planning Division), MEA (13 December 1977), No. F.(I)/234(6)/77, NAI, MEA, WII/234/1/77; 'Report on Seminar on people of Indian Origin Abroad—12th to 14th Nov., 1977—India International Centre', NAI, MEA, WII/234/1/77.

134. L.M. Singhvi et al., 'Foreword', *Report of the High Level Committee on Indian Diaspora* (New Delhi: Government of India, Ministry of External Affairs, Non Resident Indians and Persons of Indian Origin Division, 2001): http://indiandiaspora.nic.in/diasporapdf/part1-for.pdf. Accessed on 25 August 2015. It should be noted that the Jana Sangh's desire to engage the diaspora predates the Emergency; from at least the mid-1960s, the party pressurised the Congress government not to 'disown' and ignore Indians overseas. See Mohammed Ali Kishore, *Jana Sangh and India's Foreign Policy* (New Delhi: Associated Publishing House, 1969), pp.111–24.
135. Shastri, *Memoirs of a Global Hindu* (2008), pp.47, 118.
136. Chopra, *India at the Crossroads* (2004), p.155.
137. 'Indians abroad plead for voting rights', *Times of India*, 30 December 1987, p.7.
138. Rutten and Patel, 'Contested Family Relations and Government Policy' (2007), p.184. This was the latest in a series of government attempts to encourage investment by overseas Indians that began at least as early as the 1960s with the foundation of the India Investment Centre. During the Emergency, attracting 'foreign capital of Indian origin' was made a priority as part of the fourteenth point of the twenty-point programme: 'Liberalisation of investment procedures'. Naujoks, *Migration* (2013), p.55; A.K. Ghosh, Additional Secretary, 'Note for the Cabinet Committee on Economic Policy and Co-ordination', No.12(139)/LP/75 (8 September 1975), NAI, Prime Minister's Office Papers, 37/633/14/75 PMS.
139. World Bank Group, 'Remittances Brave Global Headwinds', *Migration and Development Brief 37*, November 2022.
140. Government of India, Pravasi Bharatiya Divas website: https://pbdindia.gov.in/. Accessed on 3 June 2023.
141. Singhvi et al., 'Foreword', *Report of the High Level Committee on Indian Diaspora* (2001).
142. Naujoks, *Migration* (2013), pp.52–3; *Report of the High Level Committee* (2001), pp.411–12, http://indiandiaspora.nic.in/diasporapdf/chapter 28.pdf. Accessed on 29 May 2016.
143. *Reason for Emergency: Saving Nation from Lawlessness* (New Delhi: Directorate of Advertising and Publicity, 1975), p.2.
144. Mary Tyler, *My Years in an Indian Prison* (London: V. Gollancz, 1977). The Indian High Commission reported the Alliance Against Fascist Dictatorship in India's activities to the Ministry of External Affairs; D.C. Manners, Counsellor (Political and Education), High Commission of India, London, 'Political Report for the Month of January, 1976' (23 February 1976), No. LON/POL/101/1/76, in NAI, MEA, Historical Division, HI/1012(56)/76.
145. 'Tug-of-war for hosting Indira's UK visit', *Times of India*, 16 October 1978, p.9; 'Indian groups in UK active', *Times of India*, 21 October 1978, p.9. The main contesters were the Southall-based Overseas Congress led

by Harbans Singh Ruprah and Tarsem Singh Toor, and the Birmingham-based Overseas Congress led by Piara Singh Uppal.
146. Arun Gandhi, *The Morarji Papers: Fall of the Janata Government* (New Delhi: Vision Books, 1983), pp.69–70.
147. Lindsay Mackie and John Andrews, 'Gandhi gets rough ride at meeting', *The Guardian*, 15 November 1978, p.1.
148. Pranab Mukherjee, *The Dramatic Decade: The Indira Gandhi Years* (New Delhi: Rupa, 2015), pp.205–6.
149. 'Sikh assassin is gaoled for 30 years', *The Guardian*, 31 October 1987, p.5; Josephides, *Indian Workers' Association* (1991), p.14.
150. Mehta, 'Foreign Returns' (2014).
151. Arvind Rajagopal, 'The Emergency as Prehistory of the New Indian Middle Class', *Modern Asian Studies*, vol.45, no.5 (2011), p.1014.
152. In a recent article, Jaffrelot argues that 'the Emergency played the role of a catalyst—no more, no less'—Christophe Jaffrelot, 'Who Mainstreamed BJP?', *Indian Express*, 21 July 2015: http://indianexpress.com/article/opinion/columns/who-mainstreamed-bjp/. Accessed on 22 July 2015.
153. Jaffrelot, *The Hindu Nationalist Movement* (1996), p.269.
154. No author, *RSS Resolves: 1950–2007* (New Delhi: Suruchi Prakashan, 2007), p.78. The Akhil Bharatiya Karyakari Mandal is the RSS's highest executive decision-making body.
155. Benedict Anderson, 'Exodus', *Critical Enquiry*, vol.20, no.2 (1994), pp.314–27. This point builds on the argument made by Jaffrelot and Therwath in 'The Sangh Parivar and the Hindu Diaspora in the West: What Kind of "Long-Distance Nationalism"?' (2007), p.278.

4. FROM MILTON KEYNES TO AYODHYA

1. 'Saffron wave' refers to the dramatic rise of Hindu nationalism as a political force at the end of the twentieth century, and references the colour associated with—amongst other things—this movement. The phrase is taken from the title of Thomas Blom-Hansen's influential book, *The Saffron Wave: Democracy and Hindu Nationalism in Modern India* (Princeton, NJ: Princeton University Press, 1999).
2. Christophe Jaffrelot, *Religion, Caste, and Politics in India* (New York: Columbia University Press, 2011), pp.33–4.
3. Christophe Jaffrelot and Ingrid Therwath, 'Hindu Nationalism in the United Kingdom and North America', in Deana Heath and Chandana Mathur (eds.), *Communalism and Globalization in South Asia and its Diaspora* (Abingdon: Routledge, 2011), p.44.
4. Jaffrelot and Therwath, 'The Sangh Parivar and the Hindu Diaspora in the West' (2007), p.278. See also Peter van der Veer, 'Hindu Nationalism and the Discourse of Modernity: The Vishva Hindu Parishad', in Martin E. Marty and R. Scott Appleby (eds.), *Accounting for Fundamentalisms: The*

Dynamic Character of Movements (Chicago: Chicago University Press, 1994), pp.653–68.
5. Christophe Jaffrelot (ed.), *Hindu Nationalism: A Reader* (Delhi: Permanent Black, 2007), p.20.
6. Manjari Katju, *Vishwa Hindu Parishad and Indian Politics* (Hyderabad: Orient Longman, 2010), p.2.
7. Katju, *Vishwa Hindu Parishad* (2010), pp.6–7.
8. T. Basu, P. Datta, S. Sarkar, T. Sarkar, and S. Sen, *Khaki Shorts and Saffron Flags* (New Delhi: Orient Longman, 1993), Chapter 4.
9. Amartya Sen, *The Argumentative Indian* (London: Penguin, 2005), p.xiv.
10. Majari Katju, *Hinduising Democracy: The Vishva Hindu Parishad in Contemporary India* (New Delhi: New Text, 2017), pp.12–13.
11. Chetan Bhatt, *Liberation and Purity: Race, Religious Movements and the Ethics of Postmodernity* (London: University College London Press, 1997), p.181.
12. Peter van der Veer, *Religious Nationalism: Hindus and Muslims in India* (London: University of California Press, 1994), p.141.
13. Vasudha Dalmia and Heinrich Stietencron, 'Introduction', in Vasudha Dalmia and Heinrich Stietencron (eds.), *Representing Hinduism: The Construction of Religious Traditions and National Identity* (London: Sage, 1995), p.29.
14. Veer, *Religious Nationalism* (1994), p.133. See also Benedict Anderson, *Imagined Communities: Reflections on the Origin and Spread of Nationalism* (London: Verso, 2006), p.5.
15. Liz Mathew, 'Leftists Refuse to Believe Ram was Born in Ayodhya: ICHR chief', *Indian Express*, 26 July 2015: http://indianexpress.com/article/india/india-others/leftists-refuse-to-believe-ram-was-born-in-ayodhya-ichr-chief/. Accessed on 25 August 2015.
16. Veer, *Religious Nationalism* (1994), p.142
17. Zoya Hasan, 'Majoritarianism and the Future of India's Democracy', *Social Scientist*, vol.48, no.1/2 (2020, p.10; '"History Was Accelerated in the Wake of BJP's 2019 Victory": The Wire Interviews Christophe Jaffrelot', *The Wire*, 24 January 2020: https://thewire.in/politics/christophe-jaffrelot-bjp-india-caa-part-one. Accessed on 9 May 2023.
18. Vera Lazzaretti, 'Ayodhya 2.0 in Banaras? Judicial discourses and rituals of place in the making of Hindu majoritarianism', *Contemporary South Asia* (2023), DOI: 10.1080/09584935.2023.2188173.
19. Gyanendra Pandey, 'The Civilized and the Barbarian: The "New" Politics of Late Twentieth Century India and the World', in Gyanendra Pandey (ed.), *Hindus and Others: The Question of Identity Today* (New Delhi: Viking, 1993), p.10.
20. Sugata Bose, *The Nation as Mother and Other Visions of Nationhood* (Gurgaon: Penguin, 2017).
21. There is a very extensive literature on Hindutva and gender. It is too voluminous to list here (although some is cited in Chapter 1), but

scholars who have made particularly important contributions include Tanika Sarkar, Sikata Banerjee, Amrita Basu, Kalyani Devaki Menon, and Paola Bacchetta.

22. Paola Bacchetta, 'Sacred Space in Conflict in India: The Babri Masjid Affair', *Growth and Change*, vol.31, no.2 (2000), p.278.
23. Bishnupriya Ghosh, 'Queering Hindutva: Unruly Bodies and Pleasures in Sadhvi Rithambara's Performances', in Paola Bacchetta and Margaret Power (eds.), *Rightwing Women: From Conservatives to Extremists Around the World* (London: Routledge, 2002), p.268.
24. Patricia Jeffrey and Roger Jeffrey, *Confronting Saffron Demography: Religion, Fertility, and Women's Status in India* (New Delhi: Three Essays Collective, 2006).
25. Thomas Blom Hansen, *The Saffron Wave: Democracy and Hindu Nationalism in Modern India* (Chichester; Princeton University Press, 1999), p.174. See also Richard Davis, 'The Iconography of Rama's Chariot', in David Ludden (ed.), *Contesting the Nation: Religion, Community, and the Politics of Democracy in India* (Philadelphia, PA: University of Pennsylvania Press, 1996), pp.27–54
26. Anuradha Kapur, 'Deity to Crusader: The Changing Iconography of Ram', in Pandey (ed.), *Hindus and Others* (1993), pp.79–109.
27. Romila Thapar, 'The Ramayana Syndrome', *Seminar*, no.353 (1988), pp.73–5.
28. Mani Shankar Aiyar, *Confessions of a Secular Fundamentalist* (New Delhi: Penguin, 2004), p.25.
29. 'Sri Rama Janma Bhumi Movement at a Glance', n.d: http://shreeramjanmabhoomi.org/about/sri-rama-janma-bhumi-at-a-glance/. Accessed on 24 August 2015. See also Eric Hobsbawm and Terence Ranger (eds.), *The Invention of Tradition* (Cambridge: Cambridge University Press, 1983).
30. 'Sri Rama Janma Bhumi Movement at a Glance', n.d. Figures for the RSP vary wildly; another set of VHP figures, cited by Hansen, claim 350,000 bricks (Hansen, 1999, p.176), and Manjari Katju cites a more specific number of 297,705 places where *shila* ceremonies took place, with 110 million participants (Katju, 2010, p.57). These inconsistencies indicate high overestimations of the actual figures, but also the importance to the VHP to stress extremely high levels of participation.
31. Pawan Dixit, 'Ram temple in Ayodhya: Bricks donated in 1980s likely to be preserved, displayed', *Hindustan Times*, 27 September 2021: https://www.hindustantimes.com/cities/lucknow-news/ram-temple-in-ayodhya-bricks-donated-in-1980s-likely-to-be-preserved-displayed-101632682480559.html. Accessed on 4 May 2023.
32. VHP, *Facts and Our Duty* (Bombay, n.d.); cited in Hansen, *The Saffron Wave* (1999), p.176
33. Hansen, *The Saffron Wave* (1999), p.161.

34. *Times of India*, 10 October 1989; cited in K.N. Panikkar, 'Religious Symbols and Political Mobilisation: Agitation for a Mandir at Ayodhya', *Social Scientist*, vol.21, no.7/8 (1993), p.67.
35. Katju, *Vishwa Hindu Parishad* (2010), p.55.
36. Jan Platvoet, 'Rituals of Confrontation: The Ayodhya Conflict', in Jan Platvoet and Karel van der Toorn (eds.), *Pluralism and Identity: Studies in Ritual Behaviour* (Leiden, Netherlands; EJ Brill, 1995), p.208.
37. Veer, *Religious Nationalism* (1994), p.664. See also Neera Chandhoke, 'The Tragedy of Ayodhya', *Frontline*, vol.17, no.13 (2000).
38. Hari Babu Kansal, 'Vishwa Hindu Parishad Abroad', *Hindu Vishwa*, Silver jubilee issue, English edition (1989–1990), p.94. Online: https://groups.yahoo.com/neo/groups/quranohadees/conversations/topics/72.
39. Arvind Rajagopal, 'Expatriate Nationalism: Disjunctive Discourses', in R. Ghose (ed.), *In Quest of a Secular Symbol: Ayodhya and After* (Perth, Australia: Indian Ocean Centre & South Asian Research Unit, Curtin University of Technology Press, 1996), p.113.
40. Parita Mukta, 'The Public Face of Hindu Nationalism', *Ethnic and Racial Studies*, vol.23, no.3 (2000), pp.452–3.
41. Jaffrelot and Therwath, 'The Sangh Parivar and the Hindu Diaspora in the West' (2007), p.283.
42. Jaffrelot and Therwath, 'The Sangh Parivar and the Hindu Diaspora in the West' (2007), p.287.
43. Rashmee Ahmed, 'Overseas Booty, Inland Discord', *Times of India*, 31 March 2002. Note, it is unclear from the article the year when these donations were meant to have happened.
44. AWAAZ—South Asia Watch Limited, 'In Bad Faith? British Charity and Hindu Extremism' (London: AWAAZ—South Asia Watch Limited, 2004), p.53.
45. Christophe Jaffrelot, 'The Parivar in America', *Indian Express*, 14 August 2013: http://archive.indianexpress.com/news/the-parivar-in-america/1155541/. Accessed on 25 August 2015.
46. Vishwa Bandhu Gupta, speaking in Anand Patwardhan's film, *Ram ke Naam* (1992).
47. Puja Guha, 'Measuring International Remittances In India Concepts And Empirics', ProGlo Working Paper No.1, National Institute of Advanced Studies, Bangalore, and Amsterdam Institute for Social Science Research (2011), pp.10–15. See also Devesh Kapur, Ajay S. Mehta, and R. Moon Dutt, 'Indian Diaspora Philanthropy', in Paula D. Johnson, Lincoln C. Chen, and Peter F. Geithner (eds.), *Diaspora Philanthropy and Equitable Development in China and India* (Cambridge, MA: Global Equity Initiative and Harvard University Press, 2004), pp.172–213.
48. '"Can't Send It Officially": A First-Hand Encounter with the VHP's International Conduit', *Outlook*, 22 March 1999: http://www.outlookindia.com/article/cant-send-it-officially/207158. Accessed on 24 August 2015.

49. Om Prakash Tiwari, 'Where is the Missing File of VHP?', *Rastriya Sahara*, 6 February 1999.
50. A.G. Noorani, 'Taxing Hindutva', *Frontline*, 9 April 1999, p.106.
51. Kishore Ruparelia, quoted in 'Can't Send It Officially', *Outlook* (1999).
52. Devesh Kapur, *Diaspora, Development, and Democracy: The Domestic Impact of International Migration from India* (Princeton University Press, 2010), p.246.
53. Stacey Burlet, 'Re-awakenings? Hindu Nationalism Goes Global', in Roy Starrs (ed.), *Asian Nationalism in an Age of Globalisation* (Richmond: Curzon Press, 2001), p.10.
54. Douglas Haynes, 'From Tribute to Philanthropy: The Politics of Gift Giving in a Western Indian City', *The Journal of Asian Studies*, vol.46, no.2 (1987), pp.339–60; Natascha Dekkers and Mario Rutten, 'Diaspora Philanthropy from a Homeland Perspective: Reciprocity and Contestation over Donations in Central Gujarat, India', ProGlo Working Paper No.2, National Institute of Advanced Studies, Bangalore, and Amsterdam Institute for Social Science Research (2011); Verne Dusenbery and Darsham Tatla, *Sikh Diaspora Philanthropy in Punjab: Global Giving for Local Good* (Oxford: Oxford University Press, 1999).
55. For a detailed report on campaign in 2016–17, see: Association for Democratic Reforms, *Analysis of Contribution Report of Electoral Trusts* (January 2018): https://adrindia.org/content/analysis-contribution-report-electoral-trusts---fy-2016-17. Accessed on 23 April 2019. See also: Association for Democratic Reforms, 'The Foreign Hand in Political Funding' (October 2016): https://adrindia.org/content/foreign-hand-political-funding. Accessed on 29 April 2019.
56. Dhiraj D. Shah, in Yajur Shah, 'Virat Hindu Sammelan', 21 January 2013: https://vimeo.com/57850294. Accessed on 24 August 2014.
57. 'Swayamsevak', 'A History of the Hindu Swayamsevak Sangh' (n.d.).
58. Stacey Burlet, 'Re-awakenings? Hindu Nationalism Goes Global', in Roy Starrs (ed.), *Asian Nationalism in an Age of Globalisation* (Richmond: Curzon Press, 2001), pp.1–18; Chetan Bhatt, '*Dharmo Rakshati Rakshitah*: Hindutva Movements in the UK', *Ethnic and Racial Studies*, vol.23, no.3 (2000), pp.569–93; Mukta, 'The Public Face of Hindu Nationalism' (2000), pp.452–3; John Zavos, 'Situating Hindu Nationalism in the UK: Vishwa Hindu Parishad and the Development of British Hindu Identity', *Commonwealth and Comparative Politics*, vol.48, no.1 (2010), pp.2–22.
59. Hasmukh Shah, 'Hindu Sangam 1984', in *Sangh Sandesh*, 'HSS 50th Anniversary Special Edition' (2016), pp.56–7.
60. Hasmukh Shah, in Yajur Shah, 'Hindu Sangam', 14 January 2013: http://vimeo.com/57388215. Accessed on 24 August 2014.
61. Hasmukh Shah, 'Hindu Sangam 1984', in *Sangh Sandesh*, 'HSS 50th Anniversary Special Edition' (2016), pp.56–7.
62. Hasmukh Shah, in Shah, 'Hindu Sangam'.

63. Hasmukh Shah, in Shah, 'Hindu Sangam'. See also H.V. Seshadri, *Hindus Abroad: Dilemma: Dollar or Dharma?* (New Delhi: Suruchi Prakashan, 1990), pp.65–6.
64. Dhiraj D. Shah, in Shah, 'Virat Hindu Samelan', 21 January 2013.
65. 'England Hosts Largest Ever Hindu Gathering Outside India', *Hinduism Today Magazine*, November 1989: http://www.hinduismtoday.com/modules/smartsection/item.php?itemid=1150. Accessed on 26 August 2015.
66. Mukta, 'The Public Face of Hindu Nationalism' (2000), p.457.
67. *Virat Hindu Sammelan Souvenir* (1989), p.247.
68. Raymond Brady Williams, *An Introduction to Swaminarayan Hinduism* (Cambridge: Cambridge University Press, 2001), p.60.
69. Martha Nussbaum, *The Clash Within: Democracy, Religious Violence, and India's Future* (London; Harvard University Press, 2007), pp. 322-27; Parita Mukta, 'The Public face of Hindu Nationalism', *Ethnic and Racial Studies*, vol.23, no.3 (2000), pp. 442-66.
70. Manjari Katju, *Vishwa Hindu Parishad and Indian Politics* (Hyderabad; Orient Longman, 2010), p. 157.
71. Shankar Tattwawadi (ed.), Sarsanghchalak Goes Abroad (New Delhi; Suruchi Prakashan, 1995); Sangh Sandesh, September–October 2000, vol. XI, no. 5, p. 10, Cited in AWAAZ - South Asia Watch, 'In Bad Faith?' (2004), pp. 47-8; 'Four day meet of RSS pracharaks begins today in Vadodara, Mohan Bhagwat to attend', *The Indian Express*, 17 December 2016: https://indianexpress.com/article/india/four-day-meet-of-rss-pracharaks-begins-today-in-vadodara-mohan-bhagwat-to-attend-4431261. Accessed on 12 September 2023.
72. Mukta, 'The Public Face of Hindu Nationalism' (2000). BAPS is also discussed in Chapter 6.
73. Pramukh Swami, in *Virat Hindu Sammelan Souvenir* (1989), p.16. Translated from Gujarati original and cited by Mukta, 'The Public Face of Hindu Nationalism' (2000), p.454.
74. Madhukar Dattatraya Deoras, in *Virat Hindu Sammelan Souvenir* (1989), pp.17–18.
75. Shankar Tatwawadi, 'Margaret Thatcher at HSS: A historic event', *News Bharati*, 12 April 2013: http://www.newsbharati.com/Encyc/2013/4/12/MargaretThatcheratHSSAhistoricevent/. Accessed on 10 January 2014.
76. YouTube, 'Mrs Thatcher's visit to Finchley Pratap Shakha': https://youtu.be/pkbfDSIRBC4. Accessed on 7 June 2023.
77. 'England Hosts Largest Ever Hindu Gathering Outside India', *Hinduism Today Magazine* (1989). See also: D. Shah in Yajur Shah, 'Virat Hindu Samelan'.
78. Mukta, 'The Public Face of Hindu Nationalism' (2000), p.454.
79. Gita Sahgal, 'Secular Spaces: The Experience of Asian Women Organizing', in Gita Sahgal (ed.), *Refusing Holy Orders: Women and Fundamentalism in Britain* (London: Virago Press, 1992), p.172.

80. Mukta, 'The Public Face of Hindu Nationalism' (2000), p.453.
81. D. Shah in Yajur Shah, 'Virat Hindu Samelan', 2013; 'England Hosts Largest Ever Hindu Gathering Outside India', *Hinduism Today Magazine* (1989).
82. 'England Hosts Largest Ever Hindu Gathering Outside India', *Hinduism Today Magazine* (1989).
83. K.S. Lal, 'Shri Ram Janmabhumi Temple at Ayodhya', in *Virat Hindu Sammelan Souvenir* (1989), p.134.
84. Bhatt, '*Dharmo Rakshati Rakshitah*' (2000), p.585. Emphasis in original.
85. An Early Day Motion tabled by Keith Vaz MP in July 2006 to honour the attendance of Morari Bapu at the Ram Katha festival in Leicester shows another angle to his importance in the diaspora. Keith Vaz MP (primary sponsor), 'Shree Morari Bapu at the Ram Katha Festival in Leicester', House of Commons, Early Day Motion 2634, Session 2005–6, tabled on 24 July 2006.
86. Hansen, *The Saffron Wave* (1999), p.161.
87. Zavos, 'Situating Hindu Nationalism in the UK' (2010), p.8.
88. Rajagopal, 'Expatriate Nationalism', in Ghose (ed.), *In Quest of a Secular Symbol* (1996), p.126.
89. Stacey Burlet and Helen Reid, 'Cooperation and Conflict: The South Asian Diaspora after Ayodhya', *Journal of Ethnic and Migration Studies/New Community*, vol.21, no.4 (1995), p.589.
90. Burlet and Reid, 'Cooperation and Conflict', *Journal of Ethnic and Migration Studies/New Community* (1995), p.593.
91. 'England Hosts Largest Ever Hindu Gathering Outside India', *Hinduism Today Magazine* (1989).
92. 'England Hosts Largest Ever Hindu Gathering Outside India', *Hinduism Today Magazine* (1989).
93. Zavos, 'Situating Hindu Nationalism in the UK' (2010), pp.2–22.
94. Steven Vertovec, *The Hindu Diaspora: Comparative Patterns* (London: Routledge, 2000), p.36.
95. 'Morari Bapu Profile', *Total Bhakti*, n.d.: http://www.totalbhakti.com/guru-profiles/morari-bapu-profile.php. Accessed on 28 September 2015.
96. 'Cruise Katha Organized by Param Shakti Peeth of America', *Desh Videsh*, n.d.: http://www.deshvidesh.com/Desh-Videsh-advertisers-2010/PARAM-SHAKTI-PEETH-OF-AMERICA.html. Accessed on 28 September 2015; 'A Journey to the Caribbeans (sic) with Didi Maa Sadhvi Ritambara', *India Herald*, 2 November 2016: http://india-herald.com/a-journey-to-the-caribbeans-with-didi-maa-sadhvi-ritambara-p5319-1.htm. Accessed on 20 November 2018.
97. See, for instance, the special issue on 'Women and Religious Nationalism in India', *Bulletin of Concerned Asian Scholars*, vol.25, no.4 (1993); Nira Yuval-Davis, *Gender and Nation* (London: Sage, 1997).
98. Report of witness statement given to the Central Bureau of Investigation. 'Court to Watch Video Footage of Demolition', *Times of India*, 19 July

2003: http://articles.timesofindia.indiatimes.com/2003-07-19/india/27190226_1_ayodhya-demolition-case-cbi-counsel-rai-bareli. Accessed on 24 August 2015.
99. Council of Indian Muslims (UK), Press Release: 'Stop Terrorist Leader from Entering Britain: British Indian Muslims Demand', 27 July 2010: http://www.coimuk.org/content/stop-terrorist-leader-entering-britain-british-indian-muslims-demand. Accessed on 4 September 2010.
100. Bob Blackman, 15 September 2015: https://twitter.com/bobblackmanmp/status/643583633169739776. Accessed on 28 September 2015.
101. Areeb Ullah, 'Calls to ban "divisive" Hindu activist Sadhvi Rithambara from UK speaking tour', *Middle East Eye*, 16 September 2022: https://www.middleeasteye.net/news/india-uk-modi-ally-sadhvi-rithambara-tour-ban-calls. Accessed on 21 April 2023.
102. Katju, *Vishwa Hindu Parishad* (2010), p.55.
103. Jaffrelot, *The Hindu Nationalist Movement and Indian Politics* (1996), p.396.
104. Bhatt, *Liberation and Purity* (1997), pp.245–6.
105. Bhatt, *Liberation and Purity* (1997), pp.245–6.
106. Arvind Rajagopal and Paromita Vohra, 'On the Aesthetics and Ideology of the Indian Documentary Film: A Conversation', *BioScope: South Asian Screen Studies*, vol.3, no.7 (2012), p.12. See also T. Basu, P. Datta, S. Sarkar, T. Sarkar, and S. Sen, *Khaki Shorts and Saffron Flags* (New Delhi: Orient Longman, 1993), pp.82–3.
107. Ram Puniyani, 'Abode of Ram or House of Allah-Babri Masjid: Ram Janambhumi dispute', in *Ayodhya: Masjid-Mandir Dispute Towards Peaceful Solution* (Mumbai: Center for Study of Society and Secularism & Institute for Peace Studies and Conflict Resolution, 2010), p.21.
108. Bhatt, *Liberation and Purity* (1997), p.247.
109. Bhatt, *Liberation and Purity* (1997), p.246.
110. Bhatt, *Liberation and Purity* (1997), pp.248–9.
111. Arvind Rajagopal, *Politics after Television: Hindu Nationalism and the Reshaping of the Public in India* (Cambridge: Cambridge University Press, 2001), p.1.
112. 'England Hosts Largest Ever Hindu Gathering Outside India', *Hinduism Today Magazine* (1989).
113. Prem Sagar, quoted in 'England Hosts Largest Ever Hindu Gathering Outside India' (1989).
114. Richman, 'Ravana, Divali and Spiritual Unity', in King and Brockington (eds.), *The Intimate Other* (2005), pp.78–128.
115. Vasudha Damlia and Heinrich Stietencron (eds.), *Representing Hinduism: The Construction of Religious Traditions and National Identity* (London: Sage, 1995), pp.18–19. See also Christiane Brosius, *Empowering Visions: The Politics of Representation in Hindu Nationalism* (London: Anthem Press, 2005).
116. Mariam Pirbhai, *Mythologies of Migration, Vocabularies of Indenture: Novels of the South Asian Diaspora in Africa, the Caribbean, and Asia-Pacific* (Toronto:

University of Toronto Press, 2009), p.130. See also Vijay Mishra, *The Literature of the Indian Diaspora: Theorizing the Diasporic Imaginary* (London: Routledge, 2007); and Bhiku Parekh, 'The Ramayana Syndrome: The Tale of the Struggling Exile', *Asian Age*, 30 March 1994.

117. Bhikhu Parekh, 'Some Reflections on the Hindu Diaspora', *New Community*, vol.20, no.4 (1994), p.613. The global resonance of the Ramayana is the topic of a book sold in the RSS bookshop in Delhi: Ravi Kumar, *Ramayana: Around the World—A Living Legend* (Mumbai: Shri Vinayak G Kale, 2008).

118. Guha, *India after Gandhi* (2007), p.641; Jaffrelot, *Religion, Caste, and Politics in India* (2011), p.364.

119. In Bombay alone, property losses, along with lost production, sales, and tax revenues, cost the city an estimated US$3.6 billion. Steven Wilkinson, *Votes and Violence: Electoral Competition and Ethnic Riots in India* (Cambridge: Cambridge University Press, 2004), p.14.

120. 'Pakistanis attack 30 Hindu temples', *New York Times*, 8 December 1992; Shekhar Gupta, 'India in the Dock: Babri Masjid Demolition 1992: How the World Reacted', *India Today*, 5 December 2011: http://indiatoday.intoday.in/story/babri-masjid-demolition-1992-ayodhya-pakistan-international-community/1/162901.html. Accessed on 26 August 2015.

121. Papiya Ghosh, *Partition and the South Asian Diaspora: Extending the Subcontinent* (Abingdon: Routledge, 2007), p.135.

122. Steven Vertovec, 'Three Meanings of "Diaspora", Exemplified Among South Asian Religions', *Diaspora*, vol.7, no.2 (1999), p.7.

123. *The Independent*, 11 December 1992, cited in Bhatt, Chetan, *Liberation and Purity* (1997), p.251.

124. N. Watt, 'Muslim Leaders Blame Nazis for Violence', *The Times*, 10 December 1992; D. Hinds, 'Hindu Premises Targeted in Third Night of Arson', *The Independent*, 10 December 1992; both cited in Apurba Kundu, 'The Ayodhya Aftermath: Hindu versus Muslim Violence in Britain', *Immigrants and Minorities*, vol.13, no.1 (1994), pp.30–1.

125. N. Watt and R. Gledhill, 'Tension Lingers after Hindu Temple Fire', *The Times*, 9 December 1992; cited in Kundu, 'The Ayodhya Aftermath' (1994), p.29; Gita Sahgal, 'Diaspora Politics in Britain: Hindu Identity in the Making', in Ghose (ed.), *In Quest of a Secular Symbol* (1996), p.149.

126. Kundu, 'The Ayodhya Aftermath' (1994), p.28; Burlet and Reid, 'Cooperation and Conflict' (1995), p.589.

127. Letter from VHP-UK/Hasmukh Velji Shah to Michael Lyons, Chairman of the BBC Trust, 'RE: BBC 1, Spook's Programme Series 7 Episode 8, screened on 16th December 2009 Maligning British Hindus, VHP (UK)—World Council of Hindus', 20 December 2009.

128. N. Watt, 'Asian Racial Violence Increases', *The Times*, 12 December 1992. Cited in Kundu, 'The Ayodhya Aftermath' (1994), p.31.

129. Pragna Patel, 'Rama or Rambo?', in Rahila Gupta (ed.), *From Homebreakers to Jailbreakers: Southall Black Sisters* (London: Zed Books, 2003), p.220.

130. Rashmee Ahmed, 'Overseas Booty, Inland Discord', *Times of India* (2002).
131. Quoted in Burlet and Reid, Helen, 'Cooperation and Conflict' (1995), p.594.
132. Patel, 'Rama or Rambo?', in Gupta (ed.), *From Homebreakers to Jailbreakers* (2003), p.231.
133. Vrinda Gopinath, 'Five Reasons Why the BJP Loves the Emergency', *Scroll.in*, 25 June 2015: http://scroll.in/article/736574/five-reasons-why-the-bjp-loves-the-emergency. Accessed on 26 June 2015.
134. Narendra Modi, *Apatkal main Gujarat* (Delhi: Narula Prints, 2001), Chapter 20.
135. Martin Wainwright and Alan Travis, 'Leaders of all religions condemn burnings', *The Guardian*, 9 December 1992.
136. Shastri, *Memoirs of a Global Hindu* (2008), p.116.
137. Dhiraj D. Shah, in Shah, 'Virat Hindu Samelan', 21 January 2013.
138. Ghosh, *Partition and the South Asian Diaspora* (2007), pp.211–12.
139. Anand Arya, *Sangh Sandesh*, October–December 2010, p.18.
140. Arya, *Sangh Sandesh*, 2010, pp.18–19.
141. *ITV Exposure*, 'Charities Behaving Badly', ITV, first aired on Wednesday 18 February 2015.
142. Snigdha Poonam, 'The 3 Most Polarizing Words in India', *Foreign Policy*, 13 February 2020: https://foreignpolicy.com/2020/02/13/jai-shri-ram-india-hindi/. Accessed on 15 May 2023.
143. Letter from L. Galarza, Information Access Team, Home Office, to Edward Anderson, 5 November 2014.
144. Trustees of the Vishwa Hindu Parishad-UK, 'Constitution and Trust Deed', p.2.
145. Katju, *Vishwa Hindu Parishad* (2010), p.154.
146. Trustees of the Vishwa Hindu Parishad-UK, 'Statements of Financial Activities' (2007–20).
147. Trustees of the Vishwa Hindu Parishad-UK, 'Statement of Financial Activities' (2020).
148. South Asia Citizen Web, *Hindu Nationalism in the United States: A Report on Nonprofit Groups* (July 2014).
149. Author's interview with Anil Vartak (New Delhi, 3 May 2014). Therwath, '"Far and Wide": The Sangh Parivar's Global Network', in Jaffrelot (ed.), *The Sangh Parivar: A Reader* (New Delhi: Oxford University Press, 2005), p.417.
150. Bidisha Biswas, 'Nationalism by Proxy: A Comparison of Social Movements Among Diaspora Sikhs and Hindus', *Nationalism and Ethnic Politics*, vol.10, no.2 (2004), p.280.
151. Quoted in Raymond Brady Williams, *Religions of Immigrants from India and Pakistan: New Threads in the American Tapestry* (Cambridge: Cambridge University Press, 1988), p.53.

152. Vishwa Hindu Parishad UK, 'Issues concerning British Hindus', n.d: http://vhp.org.uk/vhpuk/information/issues-concerning-british-hindus/. Accessed on 24 August 2015.
153. Hari Babu Kansal, 'Vishwa Hindu Parishad Abroad', *Hindu Vishwa*, silver jubilee issue 1989–90, English edition, p.94.
154. Patricia Jeffrey and Roger Jeffrey, *Confronting Saffron Demography: Religion, Fertility, and Women's Status in India* (New Delhi: Three Essays Collective, 2006).
155. Vishwa Hindu Parishad, 'World Hindu Conference 1966': http://vhp.org/conferences/world-hindu-conference/world-hindu-conference-1-whc-i/. Accessed on 15 August 2018.
156. World Hindu Congress, 'AboutWHC': http://www.worldhinducongress.org/#. Accessed on 15 August 2018.
157. François Gautier, 'Conference: New Delhi's World Hindu Congress', *Hinduism Today*, April/May/June 2015: https://www.hinduismtoday.com/modules/smartsection/item.php?itemid=5586. Accessed on 15 August 2018.
158. N.K. Singh, 'Even after Imposing Ban, Govt Fails to Neutralise VHP', *India Today*, 15 July 1995.
159. Rajagopal, *Politics after Television* (2001), p.238; Katju, *Vishwa Hindu Parishad* (2010), p.158.
160. Rajagopal, *Politics after Television* (2001), p.238.
161. The Campaign to Stop Funding Hate, 'Unmistakably Sangh: The National HSC and its Hindutva Agenda' (South Asia Citizens Web, 2008), p.7.
162. Shashi Tharoor, 'Growing up Extreme: On the Peculiarly Vicious Fanaticism of Indian Expatriates', *Washington Post*, 15 July 1993.
163. Kansal, 'Vishwa Hindu Parishad Abroad' (1989–1990), p.94; Letter from VHP-UK/ Hasmukh Velji Shah to Michael Lyons, Chairman of the BBC Trust, 'RE: BBC 1, Spook's Programme Series 7 Episode 8, screened on 16th December 2009 Maligning British Hindus, VHP (UK)—World Council of Hindus', 20 December 2009.
164. Author's interview with anonymous civil servant official in the Faith and Participation Team, Department for Communities and Local Government (London, 21 February 2014).
165. Vishwa Hindu Parishad (UK), *Explaining Hindu Dharma: A Guide for Teachers* (Norwich: Chansitor Religious and Moral Education Press, 1996).
166. From an article in the religious education journal, *Resource*, quoted in Ursula Sharma, 'Review of Explaining Hindu Dharma: A Guide for Teachers', *Ethnic and Racial Studies*, vol.23, no.3 (2000), p.619.
167. Vishwa Hindu Parishad (UK), *Explaining Hindu Dharma: A Guide for Teachers* (Norwich: Chansitor Religious and Moral Education Press, 1996), p.72.
168. Ernest Renan, 'Qu'est-ce qu'une nation?', *Bulletin de l'Association Scientifique de France* (1882).

169. Kamala Visweswaran, Michael Witzel, Nandini Manjrenkar, Dipta Bhog, and Uma Chakravarti, 'The Hindutva View of History: Rewriting Textbooks in India and the United States', *Georgetown Journal of International Affairs*, vol.10, no.1 (2009), pp.101–12.
170. Purnima Bose, 'Hindutva Abroad: The California Textbook Controversy', *The Global South*, vol.2, no.1 (2008), pp.11–34.
171. Purnima Bose, 'Hindutva Abroad: The California Textbook Controversy', *The Global South*, vol.2, no.1 (2008), p.13.
172. Deepa Reddy, 'Hindu Trans-nationalisms: Organisations, Ideologies, Network', in Zavos et al (eds.), *Public Hinduisms* (New Delhi: Sage, 2012), p.313.
173. Malory Nye, *Multiculturalism and Minority Religions in Britain* (Richmond: Curzon Press, 2001); John Zavos, 'Stamp It Out: Disciplining the Image of Hinduism in a Multicultural Milieu', *Contemporary South Asia*, vol.16, no.3 (2008) pp.328–9.
174. Maya Warrier, 'The Temple Bull Controversy at Skanda Vale and the Construction of Hindu Identity in Britain', *International Journal of Hindu Studies*, vol.13, no.3 (2010), pp.261–78.
175. Letter from VHP-UK/Hasmukh Velji Shah to Michael Lyons, Chairman of the BBC Trust, 'RE: BBC 1, Spook's Programme Series 7 Episode 8, screened on 16th December 2009 Maligning British Hindus, VHP (UK)— World Council of Hindus', 20 December 2009.
176. Kishan Bhatt, NHSF Public Relations Officer, 'BBC Complaint Letter on Spooks', n.d.: https://www.nhsf.org.uk/2009/12/bbc-complaint-letter-on-spooks/. Accessed on 21 August 2018.
177. Christophe Jaffrelot, 'Hindu Nationalism and the (Not So Easy) Art of Being Outraged: The Ram Setu Controversy', *South Asia Multidisciplinary Academic Journal*, no.2 (2008); Reddy, Deepa, 'Hindu Transnationalisms: Organisations, Ideologies, Network', in John Zavos, Pralay Kanungo, Deepa Reddy, Maya Warrier, and Raymond Brady Williams (eds.), *Public Hinduisms* (New Delhi: Sage, 2012), pp.309–23.
178. Julia Day, 'Spooks Sparks Deluge of Complaints', *The Guardian*, 10 June 2003: https://www.theguardian.com/media/2003/jun/10/broadcasting.race1. Accessed on 1 May 2018.
179. Veena Das, *Critical Events: An Anthropological Perspective on Contemporary India* (New Delhi: Oxford University Press, 1995).
180. Aminah Mohammad-Arif, 'The Paradox of Religion: The (re)Construction of Hindu and Muslim Identities amongst South Asian Diasporas in the United States', *South Asia Multidisciplinary Academic Journal*, vol.1 (2007): http://samaj.revues.org/55.
181. Romila Thapar, 'Imagined Religious Communities? Ancient History and the Modern Search for a Hindu Identity' *Modern Asian Studies*, vol.23, no.2 (1989); Hansen, *The Saffron Wave* (1999), p.66.

182. Prema Kurien, 'Multiculturalism, Immigrant Religion, and Diasporic Nationalism: The Development of an American Hinduism', *Social Problems*, vol.51, no.3 (2004), p.365.
183. Avtar Brah, *Cartographies of Diaspora: Contesting Identities* (London: Routledge, 1996), p.208.

5. CHARITY, SEWA (SERVICE), AND THE 'MODEL MINORITY'

1. Trustees of the Hindu Swayamsevak Sangh, 'Hindu Swayamsevak Sangh (UK) Trust Deed', Amendment 7(d), 20 November 1984, p.6.
2. Christophe Jaffrelot and Ingrid Therwath, 'The Sangh Parivar and the Hindu Diaspora in the West: What Kind of "Long Distance Nationalism"?', *International Political Sociology*, vol.1 (2007), pp.282, 287.
3. Arvind Rajagopal, 'Transnational Networks and Hindu Nationalism', *Bulletin of Concerned Asian Scholars*, vol.29, no.3 (1997), p.58; Jaffrelot and Therwath, 'The Sangh Parivar and the Hindu Diaspora in the West' (2007), p.289.
4. Ingrid Therwath, '"Far and Wide": The Sangh Parivar's Global Network', in Christophe Jaffrelot (ed.), *The Sangh Parivar: A Reader* (New Delhi: Oxford University Press, 2005), p.419.
5. AWAAZ—South Asia Watch Limited, 'In Bad Faith? British Charity and Hindu Extremism' (London: AWAAZ—South Asia Watch Limited, 2004); Sabrang Communications and South Asia Citizens Web, 'The Foreign Exchange of Hate—IDRF and the American Funding of Hindutva' (2002); South Asian Citizens Web, 'Hindu Nationalism in the United States: A Report on Nonprofit Groups' (2014): http://www.sacw.net/article9057.html.
6. Devesh Kapur, *Diaspora, Development, and Democracy: The Domestic Impact of International Migration from India* (Princeton, NJ: Princeton University Press, 2010); Devesh Kapur, 'Firm Opinions, Infirm facts', *Seminar*, no.538 (2004); Devesh Kapur, Ajay S. Mehta, and R. Moon Dutt, 'Indian Diaspora Philanthropy', in P. Geithner, P. Johnson, and L. Chen (eds.), *Diaspora Philanthropy and Equitable Development in China and India* (Cambridge, MA: Global Equity Initiative, Asia Center, Harvard University, 2004), pp.172–213.
7. L.M. Singhvi et al., *Report of the High Level Committee on the Indian Diaspora* (Ministry of External Affairs, Government of India, 2001), pp.481–501.
8. Figures based on tax returns reported in Jasa Macher, *Hindu Nationalist Influence in the United States, 2014–21* (2022), p.21: http://www.sacw.net/article14915.html. Accessed on 12 June 2023.
9. Walter Andersen and Shridhar Damle, *The RSS: A View to the Inside* (Gurgaon: Viking, 2018), p.46.
10. 'Sewa Projects', n.d: http://eshakha.pbworks.com/w/page/7794043/Sewa%20Projects. Accessed on 22 September 2015; 'About Us', n.d.

http://www.rashtriyasewa.org//encyc/2014/1/1/about-us.aspx. Accessed on 22 September 2015.
11. Alok Gupta, 'The great Gujarat earthquake 2001: lessons learnt', *Paper presented at the 22nd Asian Conference on Remote Sensing*, 2001. Available from: https://crisp.nus.edu.sg/~acrs2001/pdf/138gupta.pdf.
12. Edward Luce and Demetri Sevastapulo, 'Blood and Money', *Financial Times*, 20 February 2003.
13. Sabrang Communications and the South Asia Citizens Web, 'The Foreign Exchange of Hate (2002). A rebuttal to the SACW exposé was published by Romesh Rao et al. in 2003: *IDRF: Let the Facts Speak* (Kearney, NE: Morris Publishing, 2003).
14. 'Unsung Heroes: Overcoming Adversity During a Crisis', *Sangh Sandesh*, September 2020: https://hssuk.org/wp-content/uploads/2021/05/SSJuly20_3.3.Coping-with-crisis_FINAL.pdf. Accessed on 9 June 2023.
15. 'Unsung Heroes: Overcoming Adversity During a Crisis', *Sangh Sandesh*, September 2020.
16. AWAAZ—South Asia Watch Limited, 'In Bad Faith? British Charity and Hindu Extremism' (London: AWAAZ—South Asia Watch Limited, 2004).
17. Danish A. Khan, 'British Charity for RSS Used to Fuel Religious Extremism', *The Milli Gazette*, 16–31 March 2004: https://www.milligazette.com/Archives/2004/16-31Mar04-Print-Edition/1603200419.htm. Accessed on 9 June 2023. The four peers were Navnit Dholakia, Baron Dholakia; Bhikhu Chotalal Parekh, Baron Parekh; Adam Patel, Baron Patel of Blackburn; Raj Kumar Bagri, Baron Bagri.
18. Sam Jones, 'India Refuses Visas to Charity Investigators', *The Guardian*, 27 February 2004: http://www.guardian.co.uk/society/2004/feb/27/charities.charitymanagement1.
19. Charity Commission for England and Wales, Inquiry Report into the Hindu Swayamsevak Sangh (published 3 February 2005).
20. Letter from Charity Commission to 'a member of the public', 17 January 2006 (released under the Freedom of Information Act).
21. Charity Commission for England and Wales, Inquiry Report into the Hindu Swayamsevak Sangh (published 3 February 2005); Letter from Charity Commission to 'a member of the public', 17 January 2006 (released under Freedom of Information). Interestingly, the Commission reapplied for visas after the change in government (from BJP to Congress), but visas were still not granted.
22. 'UK Inquiry Clears Sewa International', *India Herald*, 17 February 2005; 'Hindu Charity Exonerated', *Red Hot Curry*, 9 February 2005: http://www.redhotcurry.com/news/2005/hss_charity_commission.htm. Accessed on 9 May 2015.
23. Sewa International (UK) and Hindu Swayamsevak Sangh (UK), 'Charity Commission's Inquiry—Conclusion': http://web.archive.org/web/20050306172547/http://www.sewainternational.com/

download/CC_Report_SEWA_INT_UK_PRESS_RELEASE.pdf. Accessed on 22 September 2015.
24. Sunny Hundal, 'The Campaigns Trying to Turn British Indians Against One Another', *openDemocracy*, 10 December 2019: https://www.opendemocracy.net/en/opendemocracyuk/campaigns-trying-turn-british-indians-against-each-other/. Accessed on 8 June 2023.
25. John Zavos, 'Diaspora Consciousness, Nationalism, and "Religion": The Case of Hindu Nationalism', in Allon Gal, Athena Leoussi, and Anthony Smith, *The Call of the Homeland: Diaspora Nationalisms, Past and Present* (Leiden: Brill, 2010), p.331.
26. Judith Brown, *Global South Asians: Introducing the Modern Diaspora* (Cambridge: Cambridge University Press, 2006), p.175. Emphasis added.
27. Brown, *Global South Asians* (2006), p.175.
28. 'RSS Criticises Report on Misuse of Donations', *Times of India*, 28 February 2004.
29. Martha Nussbaum, *The Clash Within: Democracy, Religious Violence, and India's Future* (London: Harvard University Press, 2007), p.314.
30. Trustees of Sewa Day, 'Summary of the Objects of the Charity set out in its Governing Document', in 'Sewa Day Trustees Annual Report 2012–13' (2013), p.2. Since launching, Sewa Day has increased its frequency to four separate days spread across the year.
31. A notable exception is the work of John Zavos, whose publications and numerous personal interactions on the subject have been extremely enlightening, but have also been developed and departed from in certain ways throughout this chapter. Zavos, 'Small Acts' (2015), pp.243–58; John Zavos, 'Digital Media and Networks of Hindu Activism', *Culture and Religion*, vol.16, no.1 (2015), pp.17–34.
32. Trustees of Hindu Swayamsevak Sangh (UK), 'Hindu Swayamsevak Sangh (UK) Financial Statements 2011' (2011), p.14.
33. Zavos reported that Sewa Day 'developed from a few individuals being involved together in Sewa Week', an earlier NHSF initiative that, unlike Sewa Day's focus on social *action*, raised funds for Sewa International. Zavos, 'Digital media' (2015), pp.12–13.
34. Alessandra Barrow, 'Beyond India: Sangh International and Vernacular Hindutva Politics in the UK', Unpublished Master's thesis, Leiden University (2022), p.24.
35. Trustees of Sewa International (UK), 'Annual Report 2011' (2011), p.5; Trustees of Sewa Day, 'Sewa Day Trust Deed' (2012); Trustees of Sewa International (UK), 'Annual Report 2013' (2013), p.5. In 2012, Sewa UK reported that it donated £10,000 to Sewa Day.
36. 'About Sewa Day', n.d: http://www.sewaday.org/about-sewa-day/. Accessed on 12 June 2023.
37. The Sewa Pioneers Awards publications from 2013 and 2014 do not mention the HSS once. References to the HSS are also almost entirely absent from

Sewa Day's website. This contrasts to the first year; the 2010 report gives a full list of projects and the groups responsible for organising them. The Sangh features most prominently, with seven Hindu Sevika Samiti events, twelve Hindu Swayamsevak Sangh event, and one HSS Bala Gokulum project.

38. Peter North, 'Geographies and Utopias of Cameron's Big Society', *Social & Cultural Geography*, vol.12, no.8 (2011), pp.817–27.
39. 'Resources', n.d: http://www.sewaday.org/resources/. Accessed on 29 August 2015.
40. Arup Ganguly, 'Sunday, 7th October 2012 is Sewa Day', n.d: http://us4.campaign-archive2.com/?u=72fadff38146a83e33687b83e&id=76c387ce1e. Accessed on 29 August 2015.
41. Author's interview with Ram Vaidya (London, 19 October 2012).
42. Prime Minister's Office, 'PM's Message for National Sewa Day', 21 November 2010: https://www.gov.uk/government/news/pms-message-for-national-sewa-day. Accessed on 29 August 2015.
43. David Cameron, 'Big Society Speech', 19 July 2010: https://www.gov.uk/government/speeches/big-society-speech. Accessed on 22 September 2015; John Zavos, 'Small Acts, Big Society: Sewa and Hindu (Nationalist) Identity in Britain', *Ethnic and Racial Studies*, vol.38, no.2 (2015), pp.243–58. Marit Rosol, 'Community Volunteering as Neoliberal Strategy? Green Space Production in Berlin', *Antipode*, vol.44, no.1 (2012), pp.239–57.
44. Trustees of Sewa Day, 'Sewa Day Annual Report 2012' (2012), p.10. It is interesting to note that the Economic Policy Group that produced this report is the same consultancy responsible for the Hindu Forum of Britain's *Social Impact Analysis Report* (see Chapter 6).
45. Trustees of Sewa Day, 'Sewa Day Annual Report 2012' (2012), p.10.
46. Sayeed Warsi, 'The Importance of Faith to Life in Britain', September 2010: http://www.conservatives.com/News/Speeches/2010/09/Sayeeda_Warsi_The_importance_of_faith_to_life_in_Britain.aspx. Accessed on 22 September 2015; cited in Zavos, 'Small Acts' (2015), p.249.
47. Zavos, 'Small Acts' (2015), p.249.
48. Trustees of Sewa Day, 'Sewa Day Annual Report 2011' (2011), p.2.
49. A full list of activities for 2010 is published in the 2011 Sewa Day Annual Report.
50. EPG Economic and Strategy Consulting, 'Social Impact Analysis for Sewa Day on 7 October 2012' (2013), p.15. The 2013 report, however, indicated that 'diversity has significantly increased', with a higher proportion of 'non-Hindu affiliated organisations'.
51. 'NHSF (UK) Does Sewa Day', 15 April 2019: https://www.nhsf.org.uk/2019/04/__trashed/. Accessed on 13 June 2023.
52. Zavos, 'Small Acts' (2015), p.247.
53. EPG Economic and Strategy Consulting, 'Social Impact Analysis for Sewa Day on 6 October 2013' (2014), p.13.

54. Sewa Day 2012, 'Project Finder': http://www.sewaday.org/projects/project-finder-results/. Accessed on 27 February 2013.
55. Trustees of Sewa Day, 'Sewa Day Annuual Report 2013' (2013), p.16.
56. 'Sewa Day 2012', n.d: http://www.stphilipscentre.co.uk/wp-content/uploads/2013/04/Sewa-Day-Final-Small-File.pdf. Accessed on 29 August 2015.
57. 'About Sewa Day', n.d: http://www.sewaday.org/about-sewa-day/. Accessed on 4 April 2018.
58. Barry Gardiner MP (primary sponsor), 'National Sewa Day', House of Commons, Early Day Motion 987, Session 2010–12, tabled on 10 November 2010. The EDM stated: 'That this House congratulates all participants involved in organising the first National Sewa Day on 21 November 2010 as a cross-community, multi-faith initiative for social action to tackle hardship and conserve the environment; and pays tribute to Britain's Hindu, Sikh, Buddhist and Jain communities for leading by the power of their example in a practical way to benefit their fellow citizens'. It was signed by nineteen MPs.
59. V.D. Savarkar, *Hindutva: Who is a Hindu?* (Mumbai: Swatantrayaveer Savarkar Rashtriya Smarak, 1999). This inclusive, paternalist approach is reified by India's Hindu family laws, which defines a Hindu as anyone who is not Muslim, Christian, Parsi, or Jewish—something challenged by many of those appropriated by the Hindu fold.
60. Dhooleka Sarhadi Raj, '"Who the hell do you think you are?" Promoting Religious Identity Among Young Hindus in Britain', *Ethnic and Racial Studies*, vol.23, no.3 (2000), p.548.
61. *ITV Exposure*, 'Charities Behaving Badly', ITV, first aired Wednesday 18 February 2015.
62. Beckerlegge, 'Tradition of Selfless Service', in Zavos, Wyatt, and Hewitt (eds), *The Politics of Cultural Mobilization in India* (2004), p.120.
63. M.S. Golwalkar, *Nityaprerana* (Pune: Bharatiya Vichar Sadhana Pune Prakahshan, 2011).
64. M.S. Golwalkar, *Bunch of Thoughts* (Bangalore: Sahitya Sindhu Prakashana, 1996), p.350.
65. Chris Shilling and Philip Mellor, 'Durkheim, Morality and Modernity: Collective Effervescence, Homo Duplex and the Sources of Moral Action', *The British Journal of Sociology*, vol.49, no.2 (1998), pp.193–209.
66. Zavos, 'Small Acts' (2015), p.247.
67. In their 'Area of Benefit', as described in governing documents submitted to the Charity Commission, Sewa Day list thirteen separate countries: Australia, Finland, India, Indonesia, Kenya, Nepal, Netherlands, New Zealand, Nigeria, Pakistan, South Africa, the United Kingdom, and the United States. 'Sewa Day—Charity Overview', n.d.
68. Trustees of Sewa Day, 'Sewa Day Trustees Annual Report 2013' (2013), p.8.

69. EPG Economic and Strategy Consulting, 'Social Impact Analysis for Sewa Day on 6 October 2013' (2014), p.10.
70. Zavos, John, 'Digital media' (2015), p.27.
71. Zavos, 'Small Acts' (2015), p.246.
72. Gwilym Beckerlegge has best elucidated the Sangh's relationship with *sewa*. Gwilym Beckerlegge, 'Saffron and Seva: The Rashtriya Swayamsevak Sangh's appropriation of Swami Vivekananda', in Antony Copley (ed.), *Hinduism in Public and Private: Reform, Hindutva, Gender, and Sampraday* (New Delhi: Oxford University Press, 2003), pp.31–65; Beckerlegge, 'Tradition of Selfless Service', in Zavos, Wyatt and Hewitt (eds), *The Politics of Cultural Mobilization in India* (2004), pp.105–35.
73. Beckerlegge, 'Tradition of Selfless Service', Zavos, Wyatt and Hewitt (eds), *The Politics of Cultural Mobilization in India* (2004), p.111; Seshadri, *RSS: A Vision in Action* (2001), p.12.
74. Golwalkar, *Bunch of Thoughts* (1996); M.A. Venkata Rao, 'Introduction', in Golwalkar, *Bunch of Thoughts* (1996), p.xix.
75. Rashtriya Swayamsevak Sangh, *RSS Widening Horizons* (New Delhi: Suruchi Prakashan, 1992), n.p. See also M.G. Chitkara, *Rashtriya Swayamsevak Sangh: National Upsurge* (New Delhi: S.B. Nangia, 2004), p.287.
76. 'History', n.d: http://www.vhpsewa.org/inner.php?pid=3#. Accessed on 22 September 2015.
77. Soundarya Chidambaram, 'The "Right" Kind of Welfare in South India's Urban Slums: Seva vs Patronage and the Success of Hindu Nationalist Organizations', *Asian Survey*, vol.52, no.2 (2012), pp.298–9.
78. Soundarya Chidambaram, 'The "Right" Kind of Welfare' (2012), pp.298–320.
79. K.N. Panikkar, 'Ways of Hindutva', *Frontline*, 28 March, 2009.
80. Chidambaram, 'The "Right" Kind of Welfare' (2012), pp.304–5.
81. Rashtriya Swayamsevak Sangh, *RSS Widening Horizons* (1992), n.p.
82. M. Shah, 'Indian, British or Both?', in *Bradford Centenary Hindu Marathon* (Bradford: Hindu Marathon National Committee) pp.103–4; cited in Stacey Burlet, 'Re-awakenings? Hindu Nationalism Goes Global', in Roy Starrs (ed.), *Asian Nationalism in an Age of Globalisation* (Richmond: Curzon Press, 2001), pp.1–18.
83. Shah, 'Indian, British or Both?', in *Bradford Centenary Hindu Marathon* (Bradford: Hindu Marathon National Committee) p.103, cited in Burlet, 'Re-awakenings?', in Starrs (ed.), *Asian Nationalism* (2001), pp.13–14.
84. Burlet, 'Re-awakenings?', in Starrs (ed.), *Asian Nationalism* (2001), p.14.
85. Speech given by the National Hindu Students Forum, in 1994/5, quoted in Raj, 'Who the hell do you think you are?' (2000), p.546.
86. Zavos, 'Small Acts' (2015), p.247.
87. Golwalkar, *Bunch of Thoughts* (1996), pp.347–8.
88. Author's interview with Anil Vartak (New Delhi, 3 May 2014).
89. Golwalkar, *Bunch of Thoughts* (1996), pp.347–8.

90. Balasaheb Deoras, 'Message to the Virat Hindu Sammelan at Milton Keynes, UK', cited in H.V. Seshadri, *Hindus Abroad: Dilemma: Dollar or Dharma?* (New Delhi: Suruchi Prakashan, 1990), p.13.
91. Hari Babu Kansal, 'Vishwa Hindu Parishad Abroad', *Hindu Vishwa*, Silver jubilee issue, English edition (1989–90), p.94.
92. Shankar Tattwawadi (ed.), *Sarsanghchalak Goes Abroad: A Collection of Lectures Delivered by Prof. Rajendra Singh on Foreign Land* (New Delhi: Suruchi Prakashan, 1995), p.9.
93. Singh's lecture was titled 'Role of the Cultural Ambassador'. Tattwawadi (ed.), *Sarsanghchalak Goes Abroad* (1995), pp.19–20.
94. Jagdish Chandra Sharda Shastri, compiled and edited by Ratan Sharda, *Memoirs of a Global Hindu* (Mumbai: Vishwa Adhyayan Kendra, 2008), p.40.
95. Shastri, *Memoirs of a Global Hindu* (2008), pp.52–4; Ved Nanda, 'The Hindu Diaspora in the United States', in Wendy Doniger and Martha Nussbaum (eds.), *Pluralism and Democracy in India: Debating the Hindu Right* (New York: Oxford University Press, 2015), pp.354–5.
96. K. Suryanarayana Rao (All-India Head of Service, RSS), *Seva Disha—Building an Integrated and Self-Reliant Society*, Chennai, 1997: http://www.hssworld.org/seva/sevadisha. Accessed on 22 September 2015; cited in AWAAZ—South Asia Watch Limited, 'In Bad Faith? British Charity and Hindu Extremism' (2004), p.11.
97. 'RSS Karnataka Greets veteran Pracharak K Suryanarayana Rao (Suruji) on his 90th Birthday', *Samvada*, 5 November 2014: http://samvada.org/2014/news/suruji-90/. Accessed on 30 August 2015.
98. Sanjiv Oza, 'Vishwa Dharma Ki Jai!', in *Sangh Sandesh*, 'HSS 50th Anniversary Special Edition' (2016), p.88.
99. Arun Kunkani, 'Leading Through Innovation in UK Sangh Work', in *Sangh Sandesh*, 'HSS 50th Anniversary Special Edition' (2016), p.96.
100. Rajni Parmar, 'Hindu Marathon Manchester 1994', 1 October 2014: https://www.youtube.com/watch?v=WgIVwFovVZ0. Accessed on 22 September 2015.
101. Vikash Mistry comment (29 January 2013) on Yajur Shah, 'The Hindu Marathon', 10 January 2013: http://vimeo.com/57159524. Accessed on 22 September 2015.
102. AWAAZ—South Asia Watch Limited, 'In Bad Faith? British Charity and Hindu Extremism' (2004), p.54.
103. Shah, 'The Hindu Marathon', 2013. Parmar is also a core member of the HSS's Kendriya Karyakari Mandal (Central Executive Committee), and from 2009 has been Vistaar Pramukh (Director of Development and Expansion). See HSS annual reports and financial statement (2009–14).
104. Shah, 'The Hindu Marathon', 2013.
105. Arjun Lal Sharma in Parmar, 'Hindu Marathon Manchester 1994', 2014.
106. Rajnini Parmar, 'Hindu Marathon 1993', video uploaded to the Hindu Marathon Facebook page, 17 August 2014: https://www.facebook.

com/rajni.parmar.733/videos/10154549052775061/. Accessed on 22 September 2015.
107. Shah, 'The Hindu Marathon', 2013.
108. Parmar, 'Hindu Marathon 1993', video uploaded by to Hindu Marathon Facebook page, 2014.
109. Parmar, 'Hindu Marathon Manchester 1994', 2014.
110. S. Charnjiv Singh, 'Gurus are the real representatives', *Organiser*, 13 July 1997.
111. Shah, 'The Hindu Marathon', 2013.
112. Sewa International Annual Report 2011, p.2. 'Sangh to focus on culture, character development', *Asian Lite*, 26 September 2014: http://asianlite.com/news/uk-news/sangh-to-focus-on-culture-character-development/. Accessed on 22 September 2015.
113. Dhiraj M. Shah has been HSS Nidhi Pramukh (Treasurer), Saha Karyvaha (Joint Secretary) since 2006, and Karyavaha (Secretary) since 2009. Trustees of the Hindu Swayamsevak Sangh, 'Hindu Swayamsevak Sangh Annual Reports'—2006 to 2011.
114. Register of Charities, 'Kalyan Ashram Trust', n.d: http://apps.charitycommission.gov.uk/Showcharity/RegisterOfCharities/ContactAndTrustees.aspx?RegisteredCharityNumber=1146848&SubsidiaryNumber=0. Accessed on 22 September 2015.
115. *Sangh Sandesh*, January–March 2008, p.7.
116. An article reporting on a talk, given by hardline French Hindutva activist François Gautier, organised by the NHSF, notes Ladwa's role as the organisation's founder. The article notes that Ladwa 'thanked him [Gautier] for putting the spine back into Hindus'. 'National Hindu Students Forum, 'Hindus Form Your Own Identity', 5 December 2001: https://web.archive.org/web/20031204194334/http://www.nhsf.org.uk:80/media/index.htm. Accessed on 23 July 2018.
117. 'About Our Founder': https://indiaincgroup.com/our-founder/. Accessed on 13 June 2023.
118. Manoj Ladwa, 'Modi Has United India Like No Prime Minister in Decades', *Time*, 28 May 2019: https://time.com/5595467/narendra-modi-india-unite-prime-minister/; 'Who is Manoj Ladwa and Why Modi Loves Him', *NewsClick*: https://www.newsclick.in/Manoj-Ladwa-Modi-Loves. Both accessed on 14 June 2023.
119. 'Labour Party "hijacked" by coalition of hard left extremists, Jihadi sympathisers: Manoj Ladwa', *ANI*, 25 September 2019: https://www.aninews.in/news/world/europe/labour-party-hijacked-by-coalition-of-hard-left-extremists-jihadi-sympathisers-manoj-ladwa20190925235927/. Accessed on 14 June 2023.
120. Jaffrelot and Therwath, 'The Sangh Parivar and the Hindu Diaspora in the West' (2007), p.282.

121. Gautam Appa and Anish Vanaik (eds.), *Narendra Modi Exposed: Challenging the Myths Surrounding the BJP's Prime Ministerial Candidate* (London: AWAAZ Network/The Monitoring Group, 2014), pp.60–1.
122. 'About Us', *NHSF*: https://web.archive.org/web/20041012032333/https://www.nhsf.org.uk/aboutus.htm. Accessed on 23 July 2018.
123. Alessandra Barrow, 'Beyond India: Sangh International and Vernacular Hindutva Politics in the UK', unpublished Master's thesis, Leiden University (2022), p.24.
124. Chirag Patel, 'Caste Within the Single Equality Bill 2010': https://www.nhsf.org.uk/2010/01/caste-within-the-single-equality-bill-2010/. Accessed on 10 April 2018.
125. Kishan Bhatt, 'BBC Complaint Letter on Spooks', December 2009, http://www.nhsf.org.uk/2009/12/bbccomplaintletteronspooks/. Accessed on 23 July 2018; 'Indian Prime Minister Modi to Receive "Olympics Style" Welcome at Wembley Stadium', *NHSF*: https://www.nhsf.org.uk/2015/08/primeministermodiwelcome/. Accessed on 23 July 2018.
126. Sanjiv Oza, 'Vishwa Dharma Ki Jai!', *Sangh Sandesh* (2016), p.88.
127. Parmar, 'Hindu Marathon Manchester 1994', 2014.
128. Parmar, 'Hindu Marathon Manchester 1994', 2014.
129. Department for Work and Pensions, 'Family Resources Survey: Financial Year 2020 to 2021', 31 March 2022.
130. Ministry of Housing, Communities and Local Government, 'English indices of deprivation 2019', 26 September 2019.
131. Department for Environment, Food and Rural Affairs, 'United Kingdom Food Security Report 2021: Theme 4: Food Security at Household Level', 22 December 2021.
132. Ministry of Housing, Communities and Local Government, 'English Housing Survey 2017 to 2018: home ownership', 17 July 2019.
133. UK Government, 'English Language Skills', 30 September 2020: https://www.ethnicity-facts-figures.service.gov.uk/uk-population-by-ethnicity/demographics/english-language-skills/latest#. Accessed on 20 June 2023.
134. Rishi Sunak and Saratha Rajeswaran, *A Portrait of Modern Britain* (Policy Exchange, 2014), p.63; *Youth Cohort Study & Longitudinal Study of Young People in England: The Activities and Experiences of 16 Year Olds: England 2007* (Statistical Bulletin: Department for Children, Schools, and Families/National Statistics, 2008), p.18.
135. 'Ethnic group differences in health, employment, education and housing shown in England and Wales' Census 2021': https://www.ons.gov.uk/peoplepopulationandcommunity/culturalidentity/ethnicity/articles/ethnicgroupdifferencesinhealthemploymenteducationandhousingshowninenglandandwalescensus2021/2023-03-15. Accessed on 20 June 2023.
136. Department for Work and Pensions, 'Households below average income: for financial years ending 1995 to 2022', 23 March 2023.

137. Laia Bécares, 'Which Ethnic Groups have the Poorest Health? Ethnic Health Inequalities 1991 to 2011', in *Dynamics of Diversity: Evidence from the 2011 Census* (ESRC Centre on Dynamics of Ethnicity, 2013), pp.1–4.
138. Andrew Bryson, 'Britain's Richest Asians', 19 April 2006: http://www.telegraph.co.uk/finance/2936997/Britains-richest-Asians.html. Accessed on 22 September 2015.
139. 'India's diaspora is bigger and more influential than any in history', *The Economist*, 12 June 2023.
140. Ingrid Therwath, 'Working for India or Against Islam? Islamophobia in Indian American Lobbies', *South Asia Multidisciplinary Academic Journal* (2007), p.3. See also: Daniel Sabbagh, 'Le Statut des 'Asiatiques' aux Etats-Unis: L'Identité Américaine dans un Miroir', *Critique Internationale*, vol.20 (2003), pp.69–92, and Christopher Dumm and Nisha Jain, *A Portrait of the Indian American Community: An In-Depth Report based on the U.S. Census* (NewYork: The Indian American Center for Political Awareness, 2004); Vijay Prashad, *The Karma of Brown Folk* (Minneapolis, MN: University of Minnesota Press, 2001), p.170.
141. Zavos, 'Small Acts' (2015), p.250.
142. Rajni Parmar, 'HM97', 16 October 2014: https://www.youtube.com/watch?v=8wSF-XWuFCk. Accessed on 22 September 2015. Parsi aphorism originally from the *Qissa-i Sanjan* (an account of early Zoroastrian migrants to India).
143. Bhikhu Parekh, *Rethinking Multiculturalism: Culture Diversity and Political Theory* (Basingstoke: Palgrave, 2000), p.196.
144. Parekh, *Rethinking Multiculturalism* (2000), p.196; Rajagopalan Radhakrishnan, *Diasporic Mediations: Between Home and Location* (Minneapolis, MN: University of Minnesota Press, 1996), p.211.
145. BBC Three, *Free Speech*, aired on 12 June 2013: http://www.bbc.co.uk/programmes/b02x90jj. Accessed on 22 September 2015.
146. Anthony Wells, 'Where the Public Stands on Immigration', Results of YouGov Survey from 24–5 April 2018: https://yougov.co.uk/news/2018/04/27/where-public-stands-immigration/. Accessed on 23 July 2018.
147. Stephen Jivraj, 'Who Feels British? The Relationship Between Ethnicity, Religion and National Identity in England' (Dynamics of Diversity: Evidence from the 2011 Census, ESRC Centre on Dynamics of Ethnicity, 2013), pp.1–4.
148. Ceri Peach, 'Demographics of BrAsian settlement', in Ali, Kalra and Sayyid (eds.), *A Postcolonial People* (2008), pp.177–81.
149. Ludi Simpson, 'More Segregation or More Mixing?' (Dynamics of Diversity: Evidence from the 2011 Census, ESRC Centre on Dynamics of Ethnicity, 2013), pp.1–4. The study suggests that Indians and Bangladeshis have become more evenly spread between 1991 and 2011, but Pakistanis remain at a similar level.

150. G. Catney et al, 'Ethnic diversification and neighbourhood mixing: A rapid response analysis of the 2021 Census of England and Wales', *The Geographical Journal*, vol.189 (2023), pp.63–77.
151. Richard Cracknell et al., 'Census 2011 Constituency results: England and Wales', House of Commons Library, Research Paper 13/20, 18 March 2013.
152. Pew Research Center, *The Rise of Asian Americans* (2013): http://www.pewsocialtrends.org/2012/06/19/the-rise-of-asian-americans/. Accessed on 4 January 2022.
153. Jacob L. Vigdor, 'Measuring Immigrant Assimilation in the United States', Civic Report no.53 (Manhattan Institute for Policy Research, 2008).
154. Prema Kurien, 'Multiculturalism, Immigrant Religion, and Diasporic Nationalism: The Development of an American Hinduism', *Social Problems*, vol.51, no.3 (2004), p.372.
155. Banyan, 'Why Brahmins Lead Western Firms but Rarely Indian Ones', *The Economist*, 1 January 2022: https://www.economist.com/asia/2022/01/01/why-brahmins-lead-western-firms-but-rarely-indian-ones. Accessed on 4 January 2022.
156. 'Has the Bhagavad Gita replaced The Art of War as the hip new ancient Eastern management text?', asked a 2005 *Bloomberg* article on 'Karma Capitalism': https://www.bloomberg.com/news/articles/2006-10-29/karma-capitalism. Accessed on 4 January 2022.
157. Pavan Varma, *Being Indian* (New Delhi: Penguin, 2004); Danial Lak, *Indian Express: The Future of a New Superpower* (New Delhi: Penguin, 2008). Both cited in Meera Nanda, *The God Market* (New Delhi: Random House, 2009), pp.154–5.
158. Oliver Moody, 'The Silk Road to Silicon Valley—5,000 Years of Indian Innovation', *The Times*, 3 October 2017.
159. Arvind Rajagopal, 'Expatriate Nationalism: Disjunctive Discourses', in R. Ghose (ed.), *In Quest of a Secular Symbol: Ayodhya and After* (Perth, Australia: Indian Ocean Centre & South Asian Research Unit, Curtin University of Technology Press, 1996), p.121.
160. Virag Pachpore, 'Vishwa Sangh Shibir 2010: An exposure to global; confident Hindutva', 17 January, 2011: http://samvada.org/2011/news/vishwa-sangh-shibir-2010-an-exposure-to-global-confident-hindutva/. Accessed on 8 April 2015.
161. Maya Parmar, 'Reading the Double Diaspora: Cultural Representations of Gujarati East Africans in Britain' (unpublished PhD thesis, University of Leeds, 2013), p.26.
162. 'East African Asians Finding British Success', *Lakeland Ledger* (31 August 1972), p.5.
163. House of Lords debate on 'Ugandan Asians', 6 December 2012: http://www.publications.parliament.uk/pa/ld201213/ldhansrd/text/121206-0002.htm. Accessed on 22 September 2015.

164. 'King celebrates Ugandan Asians who fled Idi Amin's regime to safety in the UK decades ago', ITV News: https://www.itv.com/news/2022-11-02/king-celebrates-ugandan-asians-who-fled-to-safety-in-the-uk-decades-ago. Accessed on 12 June 2023.
165. Runnymede Trust, *Connecting British Hindus: An Enquiry into the Identity and Public Engagement of Hindus in Britain* (London: Runnymede Trust/Hindu Forum of Britain, 2006), pp. 52, 58.
166. Parmar, 'Reading the Double Diaspora' (2013), pp. 26–7.
167. Bernd Debusmann Jr, 'US immigration: Why Indians are fleeing halfway around the world', 10 October 2022: https://www.bbc.co.uk/news/world-us-canada-62893926; 'Over 22k Indians seek asylum in US since 2014: Official data', *Economic Times*: https://economictimes.indiatimes.com/nri/visa-and-immigration/over-22k-indians-seek-asylum-in-us-since-2014-official-data/articleshow/71818354.cms?from=mdr. Both accessed on 13 June 2023.
168. Seshadri, *Dollar or Dharma?* (1990), p. 66.
169. Sara Danius, Stefan Jonsson and Gayatri Chakravorty Spivak, 'An Interview with Gayatri Chakravorty Spivak', *boundary 2*, vol. 20, no. 2 (1993), pp. 24–50.
170. Greg Noble, Scott Poynting, and Paul Tabar, 'Youth, Ethnicity and the Mapping of Identities: Strategic Essentialism and Strategic Hybridity among Male Arabic-speaking Youth in South-western Sydney', *Communal/Plural*, vol. 7, no. 1 (1999), pp. 29–44.
171. A wide range of Asian Youth Movements and activist groups self-identified as Black, for instance: the Southall Black Sisters, United Black Youth League, and the Black Consciousness Group. The Channel 4 current affairs programme, *The Bandung File* (1984–9), produced by Tariq Ali, Darcus Howe, and others, also promoted a view of shared Black perspectives and struggles for recognition. While no longer widespread, a unified Black political identity still resonates for some Asian activists, and the language of 'person of colour' also reflects a degree of inclusivity and shared experience (although essentialising tendencies are still problematic and frequently rejected). For more on the South Asian diaspora and Blackness, see Tariq Modood, 'Political Blackness and British Asians', *Sociology*, vol. 28, no. 4 (1994), pp. 859–76; Anandi Ramamurthy, *Black Star: Britain's Asian Youth Movements* (London: Pluto Press, 2013).
172. Seshadri, *Dollar or Dharma?* (1990), p. 60.
173. Seshadri, *Dollar or Dharma?* (1990), p. 66.
174. Vijay Prashad, *Uncle Swami: South Asians in America Today* (Noida: Harper Collins, 2013), p. 64.
175. Ramamurthy, *Black Star* (2013) pp. 8, 193–209.
176. Prashad, *The Karma of Brown Folk* (2001); Prashad, *Uncle Swami* (2013); Monisha Das Gupta, *Unruly Immigrants* (Durham: Duke University Press, 2005); Sunil Bhatia, *American Karma: Race, Culture, and Identity*

in the Indian Diaspora (New York: New York University Press, 2007); Therwath, 'Working for India or Against Islam?' (2007); Vinay Lal, *The Other Indians: A Political and Cultural History of South Asians in America* (Los Angeles: University of California, Asian American Studies Center Press, 2008); Vani Kannan, '"Model Minority" or Potential Terrorist? Affective Economies, Rhetorics of Silence and the Murder of Sunando Sen', *Studies on Asia*, series IV, vol.4, no.1 (2014), pp.7–43.

177. Prashad, *Uncle Swami* (2013), p.98.
178. Therwath, 'Working for India or Against Islam?' (2007).
179. Sangay K. Mishra, *Desis Divided: The Political Lives of South Asian Americans* (Minneapolis, MN: University of Minnesota Press, 2016), pp.65–6.
180. Hundal, 'The War on Terror' in Bingham (ed.), *Having Faith* (2007), p.86.
181. Burlet, 'Re-awakenings?', in Starrs (ed.), *Asian Nationalism* (2001), p.13.
182. Burlet, 'Re-awakenings?', in Starrs (ed.), *Asian Nationalism* (2001), p.13.
183. ITV, 'Exposure: Charities Behaving Badly', 2015.
184. Unlike North America, where 'Asian' refers usually to East Asians, in Britain the term 'Asian' is usually shorthand for South Asian only.
185. Efforts to emphasise the growing importance of 'Hindu' identity can be seen in the Hindu Forum of Britain's report, *Connecting British Hindus*. The development of different types of identity for Hindu Indians is closely examined by Dhooleka Raj, who notes that 'stressing either religion or ethnicity for ethnic minorities ignores the important ways in which nationalist identity is being reconceived'; Raj, 'Who the hell do you think you are?' (2000), p.537.
186. Philip Lewis, 'Arenas of Ethnic Negotiation: Cooperation and Conflict in Bradford', in Tariq Modood and Pnina Werbner (eds.), *The Politics of Multiculturalism in Europe: Racism, Identity and Community* (London: Zed, 1997), p.130.
187. The Hindu Forum of Britain's *Connecting British Hindus* report stated that: 'Many chose to describe themselves as Indian in order to express their ties with India', but 'Overall 75% of the respondents to the online survey noted that they described themselves as a Hindu, rather than by their ethnicity', p.30.
188. Raj, 'Who the hell do you think you are?' (2000), p.543.
189. 'Complaints Over Use of "Asian" Label in Grooming Cases', BBC News, 16 May 2012: http://www.bbc.co.uk/news/uk-18092605. Accessed on 22 September 2015; 'Hey, don't call me Asian!', *Times of India*, 11 January 2005: http://timesofindia.indiatimes.com/world/rest-of-world/Hey-dont-call-me-an-Asian/articleshow/987415.cms. Accessed on 22 September 2015; Sarfraz Mansoor, 'Don't Call Me Asian', BBC Radio 4, 11 January 2005.
190. In 2013, an article in *The Times* noted that 'the Hindu Council UK, the Network of Sikh Organisations, the Sikh Media Monitoring Group and

the Sikh Awareness Society—have sponsored an online petition calling on politicians and the media to stop using vague terms that "besmirch" their communities'. Ruth Gledhill, 'Sex Gangs' Asian Label Insults us, say Hindus and Sikhs', *The Times*, 31 December 2013; Shivani Nagarajah, 'Mistaken Identity', *The Guardian*, 5 September 2005. For a wider context to the Sikh-Muslims dynamic outside India, see Christine Moliner, '*Frères ennemis*? Relations between Panjabi Sikhs and Muslims in the Diaspora', *South Asia Multidisciplinary Academic Journal*, vol.1 (2007) n.p.; Katy Sian, 'Don't freak I'm a Sikh', in Salman Sayyid and AbdoolKarim Vakil (eds.), *Thinking Through Islamophobia: Global Perspectives* (London: Hurst, 2011), pp.251–4.

191. Roger Ballard quoted in Nagarajah, 'Mistaken Identity', *The Guardian*, 5 September 2005.
192. Arun Kundnani, 'An Unholy Alliance? Racism, Religion and Communalism', 30 July 2002: http://www.irr.org.uk/news/an-unholy-alliance-racism-religion-and-communalism/. Accessed on 23 September 2015.
193. Nick Britten, 'Ethnic Radio Station to Ban 'Asian' Description', *The Telegraph*, 23 January 2002.
194. Raju, '"Asians" and Hindus': http://www.nhsf.info/index.php?option=com_content&view=article&id=346:qasiansq-and-hindus&catid=239:misconceptions&Itemid=233. Accessed on 23 September 2015.
195. J. Ambedkar, 'Vibrant Hindu Youth', in *Bradford Centenary Hindu Marathon* (Bradford: Hindu Marathon National Committee, 1997), pp.51–2; cited in Burlet, 'Re-awakenings' (2001), p.7.
196. Raj, 'Who the hell do you think you are?' (2000), pp.535–58.
197. Raj, 'Who the hell do you think you are?' (2000), pp.544–5.
198. The 2009–11 data on reported hate crimes showed that 1.8% of South Asian adults were victims of racially motivated crime, compared to 1.1% for Chinese people, 0.9% for Black people, and 0.1% for white people. Crime Survey for England and Wales, *Hate crime and crimes against older people report 2011–2012* (London: Crown Prosecution Service, 2012); Institute of Race Relations, 'Racial Violence', n.d: http://www.irr.org.uk/research/statistics/racial-violence/#_edn1. See also Vani Kannan, '"Model Minority" or Potential Terrorist? Affective Economies, Rhetorics of Silence and the Murder of Sunando Sen', *Studies on Asia*, series IV, vol.4, no.1 (2014), pp.7–43.
199. House of Commons, Home Affairs Select Committee, 'Counter-terrorism and Community Relations in the Aftermath of the London bombings', Oral and Written, Tuesday 13 September 2005.
200. House of Commons, Home Affairs Select Committee, 'Counter-terrorism and Community Relations in the Aftermath of the London bombings', Oral and Written, Tuesday 13 September 2005.

201. Jonathan Githens-Mazer and Robert Lambert, *Islamophobia and Anti-Muslim Hate Crime: A London Case Study* (University of Exeter: European Muslim Research Centre, 2010), p.5.
202. Grahame Allen and Yago Zayed, *Hate Crime Statistics*, House of Commons Library Research Briefing, 2 November 2022.
203. Shankar Tatwawadi, 'Margaret Thatcher at HSS: A Historic Event', 12 April 2013: http://en.newsbharati.com/Encyc/2013/4/12/Margaret-Thatcher-at-HSS-A-historic-event.aspx. Accessed on 23 September 2015.
204. 'Bob Blackman MP Praises HSS Activities', *VSK Kerala*, n.d: http://vskkerala.com/bob-blackman-mp-praises-hss-activities/nggallery/page/1. Accessed on 23 September 2015.
205. Ken Livingstone, House of Commons, Home Affairs Committee, Terrorism and Community Relations, Sixth Report of Session 2004–5, Volume III: Oral and Written Evidence.
206. Priti Patel, 'Message from Priti Patel MP, the Prime Minister's UK Indian Diaspora Champion, for the event "RSS: A Vision in Action—a new dawn" hosted by the Hindu Swayamsevak Sangh UK', Letter to Hindu Swayamsevak Sangh (UK), 21 September, 2014: http://hssuk.org/priti-patel-congratulates-hss-uk/. Accessed on 23 September 2015.
207. Hindu Forum of Britain, 'Hindu Forum of Britain (HFB) Gives a Fitting Reply to CNN', 15 February 2014: http://www.hfb.org.uk/index.php?option=com_k2&view=item&id=96:hfb-challenged-the-author-foran-open-debate-on-the-book-the-hindus&Itemid=60. Accessed on 27 September 2015. The Wendy Doniger case is discussed in more depth in Chapter 6.
208. Peter van der Veer, *Religious Nationalism: Hindus and Muslims in India* (Berkeley, CA: University of California Press, 1994), pp.66–7.
209. Dhooleka Sarhadi Raj, *Where are you from? Middle Class Migrants in the Modern World* (Berkeley, CA: University of California Press, 2003), pp.49–52.
210. Madhav Kendra (Centre) is named after RSS ideologue and leader Madhav Sadashiv Golwalkar. Response to Freedom of Information request to the NHS Information Centre for Health and Social Care, 12 July 2010: https://www.whatdotheyknow.com/request/grant_funded_services_collection#incoming-99478. Accessed on 27 September 2014.
211. Sewa Day, 'Unaudited Financial Statements', 31 March 2021; Sewa Day, 'Unaudited Financial Statements', 31 March 2023.
212. House of Commons, 'The Register of Members' Financial Interests, as at 16 May 2016'.
213. House of Commons Debate, 14 April 2016, vol.608, col.520.
214. Alessandra Barrow, 'Beyond India' (2022), p.56.
215. EPG Economic and Strategy Consulting, 'Social Impact Analysis for Sewa Day 2012', p.40.

216. Seshadri, *Dollar or Dharma?* (1990), p.66.
217. Golwalkar, *Bunch of Thoughts* (1996), p.350.

6.'NEO-HINDUTVA'

1. Much of the material in this chapter is adapted from an article published in *Contemporary South Asia*: Edward Anderson, '"Neo-Hindutva": the Asia House M.F. Husain campaign and the mainstreaming of Hindu nationalist rhetoric in Britain', *Contemporary South Asia*, vol.23, no.1 (2015), pp.45–66.
2. 'Temple Vandal Let Off "Lightly"', Hindus Hurt', *Hindustan Times*, 29 December 2003: http://www.hindustantimes.com/news-feed/nm2/temple-vandal-let-off-lightly-hindus-hurt/article1-9714.aspx. Accessed on 14 November 2014. In evidence to the Home Affairs Select Committee on Terrorism and Community Relations (Sixth Report of Session 2004–5, 25 January 2005), Ken Macdonald QC, Director of Public Prosecutions, referred to the perpetrators as 'two fundamentalist Christians'. The culprits, Toby Champney and Benjamin Lloyd Jones, received two months imprisonment for racially aggravated criminal damage and a fine of £400 for racially aggravated threatening behaviour, respectively.
3. Prasun Sonwalkar, 'Hindu Forum of Britain Launched', *Organiser*, 11 April 2004.
4. 'UK Hindus Meet to Discuss Attacks', BBC News, 14 December 2003: http://news.bbc.co.uk/1/hi/uk/3317169.stm. Accessed on 22 August 2015.
5. House of Commons, Home Affairs Select Committee, Sixth Report, Session 2004–5, Examination of Witnesses, 14 December 2004.
6. Hindu Forum of Britain, 'Press Release': http://www.hinduforum.org.uk/Default.aspx?sID=760&cID=14&ctID=43&lID=0. Accessed on 14 November 2013. See also: London-wise Race Hate Crime Forum, *Annual Report 2004–5* (London: Metropolitan Police Authority, 2005), p.14; Metropolitan Police Authority, Report 11 of the 8 March 2007 meeting of the Equal Opportunities & Diversity Board: http://policeauthority.org/metropolitan/committees/x-eodb/2007/070308/11/index.html. Accessed on 22 August 2015.
7. House of Commons, Home Affairs Select Committee, Sixth Report, Session 2004–5, Examination of Witnesses, 14 December 2004.
8. Neeti Nair, *Hurt Sentiments: Secularism and Belonging in South Asia* (Cambridge, MA: Harvard University Press, 2023).
9. Deepa Reddy, 'Hindutva as Praxis', *Religion Compass*, vol.5, no.8 (2011), p.421.
10. Christophe Jaffrelot, 'Hindu Nationalism and the (Not So Easy) Art of Being Outraged: The Ram Setu Controversy', *South Asia Multidisciplinary Academic Journal*, no.2 (2008), p.2; Deborah Sutton, '"So called caste":

S.N. Balagangadhara, the Ghent School and the Politics of Grievance', *Contemporary South Asia*, vol.26, no.3 (2018), p.336–49.
11. Excerpts of this introduction have been previously published in the Introduction of Edward Anderson and Arkotong Longkumer (eds.), *'Neo-Hindutva': Evolving Forms, Spaces, and Expressions of Hindu Nationalism* (London: Routledge, 2019).
12. The 1971 to 2001 figures from Ceri Peach and Richard Gale, 'Muslims, Hindus and Sikhs in the New Religious Landscape of England', *Geographical Review*, vol.93, no.4 (2003), p.479. The 2011 figures combine England and Wales, and Scotland, census data, with a contemporaneous list provided on the National Council of Hindu Temples UK website. The 2021 numbers combine the 2021 England and Wales census data with the number of Hindu temples listed in Emma Tomalin and Jasjit Singh, *A Survey of Hindu Buildings in England* (Historic England/ University of Leeds, June 2018).
13. Peter van der Veer, 'Transnational Religion: Hindu and Muslim Movements', *Global Networks*, vol.2, no.2 (2002), pp.95–109; Steven Vertovec, *The Hindu Diaspora: Comparative Patterns* (London: Routledge, 2000).
14. Talal Asad, 'Multiculturalism and British Identity in the Wake of the Rushdie Affair', *Politics & Society*, vol.18, no.4 (1990), p.457.
15. Khadijah Elshayyal, *Muslim Identity Politics: Islam, Activism and Equality in Britain* (London: I.B. Tauris, 2018), pp.77–9.
16. Neeti Nair, *Hurt Sentiments* (2023), p.10.
17. Pragna Patel, 'The Impact of Hindu Fundamentalism in Britain', n.d: http://www.sacw.net/aii/Hfund.html. Accessed on 22 August 2015.
18. A. Sivanandan, 'RAT and the Degradation of Black Struggle', *Race & Class*, vol.26, no.4 (1985), p.13.
19. Danièle Joly and Khursheed Wadia, *Muslim Women and Power: Political and Civil Engagement in West European Societies* (London: Palgrave Macmillan, 2017), p.56.
20. Stacey Burlet and Helen Reid, 'Cooperation and Conflict: The South Asian Diaspora after Ayodhya', *Journal of Ethnic and Migration Studies/ New Community*, vol.21, no.4 (1995), p.594.
21. John Zavos, 'Diaspora Consciousness, Nationalism, and "Religion": The Case of Hindu Nationalism', in Allon Gal, Athena Leoussi, and Anthony Smith (eds.), *The Call of the Homeland: Diaspora Nationalisms, Past and Present* (Leiden: Brill, 2010), p.330.
22. Runnymede Trust, *Connecting British Hindus: An Inquiry into the Identity and Public Engagement of Hindus in Britain* (commissioned by the Hindu Forum of Britain; sponsored by the Cohesion and Faiths Unit of the Department for Communities and Local Government, 2006), p.4.
23. 'Government to work closely with Hindu Forum of Britain: Tony Blair', *AsianVoice*, 5 June 2004, p.13; cited in John Zavos, 'Stamp it out: Disciplining the Image of Hinduism in a Multicultural Milieu', *Contemporary South Asia*, vol.16, no.3 (2008), p.337.

24. Stuart Hall, 'Old and New Identities, Old and New Ethnicities', in A.D. King (ed.), *Culture, Globalisation and the World System* (London: Macmillan, 1991), p.54.
25. John Zavos, 'Hindu Organisation and the Negotiation of Public Space in Contemporary Britain', in John Zavos, Pralay Kanungo, Deepa Reddy, Maya Warrier, and Raymond Brady Williams (eds.), *Public Hinduisms* (New Delhi: Sage, 2012), p.79.
26. Jenny Taylor, 'After Secularism: Inner-city Governance and New Religious Discourse', *Whitefield Institute Briefing*, vol.7, no.5 (December 2002), n.p.
27. John Austin, Roy Taylor, and Kate Dixon, *Review of the Inner Cities Religious Council* (London: Ministry for Local Government and Housing, 1998), p.20; cited in Zavos, 'Hindu Organisation…' (2012), p.80.
28. R. Furbey and M. Macey, 'Religion and Urban Regeneration: A Place for Faith?', *Policy and Politics*, vol.33, no.1 (2005), p.97.
29. John Zavos, 'Stamp it out' (2008), pp.323–37.
30. Deepa Reddy, 'Hindutva as Praxis', *Religion Compass*, vol.5, no.8 (2011), p.42.
31. Zavos, 'Stamp it out' (2008), p.332; Thomas Blom Hansen, 'Politics as Permanent Performance: The Production of Political Authority in the Locality', in J. Zavos, A. Wyatt, and V. Hewitt (eds.), *Politics of Cultural Mobilisation in India* (New Delhi: Oxford University Press, 2004), p.4.
32. Zavos, 'Diaspora Consciousness…', in Gal, Leoussi and Smith (eds.), *The Call of the Homeland* (2010), p.331.
33. Zavos, 'Diaspora Consciousness', in Gal, Leoussi and Smith (eds.), *The Call of the Homeland* (2010), p.331; Zavos, 'Stamp it out' (2008), p.333.
34. Zavos, 'Stamp it out' (2008), p.334.
35. *HFB Annual Report 2005*, p.3; cited in Zavos, 'Stamp it out' (2008), pp.334–5.
36. Runnymede Trust, *Connecting British Hindus: An Inquiry into the Identity and Public Engagement of Hindus in Britain* (London: Hindu Forum of Britain, 2006).
37. Zavos, 'Hindu Organisation', in Zavos, Kanungo, Reddy, Warrier, and Williams (eds.), *Public Hinduisms* (2012), p.85; 'Ramesh Kallidai profile', *The Guardian*, n.d, http://commentisfree.theguardian.com/ramesh_kallidai/profile.html. Accessed on 14 November 2013.
38. Hindu Forum of Britain, 'State Funeral Queen Elizabeth II at Westminster Abbey': https://www.hfb.org.uk/news/state-funeral-queen-elizabeth-ii-at-westminster-abbey-on-monday-19th-september/. Accessed on 22 June 2023; Westminster Abbey, 'Order of Service: The State Funeral of Her Majesty Queen Elizabeth II', 19 September 2022.
39. Kim Knott, 'Becoming a "Faith Community": British Hindus, Identity, and the Politics of Representation', *Journal of Religion in Europe*, vol.5, no.2 (2009), pp.85–114.

40. Author's interview with an anonymous DCLG official (London, 21 February 2014).
41. Author's interview with Ian Bradshaw (London, 28 January 2014).
42. Zavos, 'Stamp it out' (2008), pp.327, 334.
43. Hindu Forum of Britain, 'Social Impact Analysis for Activities in 2011' (Hindu Forum of Britain, 2013), n.p.
44. AWAAZ—South Asia Watch, *In Bad Faith? British Charity and Hindu Extremism* (2004).
45. Author's interview with Swaminathan Vaidyanathan (London, 15 November 2013).
46. Sonwalkar, 'Hindu Forum of Britain Launched', *Organiser*, 2004.
47. Author's interview with Swaminathan Vaidyanathan (London, 15 November 2013).
48. Hindu Forum of Britain homepage: http://www.hfb.org.uk/. Accessed on 27 July 2019 and 19 June 2023.
49. HFB Homepage: http://www.hfb.org.uk/. Accessed on 25 November 2013; 'HFB Members' page, *HFB*, n.d.: http://www.hfb.org.uk/Default.aspx?sID=6. Accessed on 25 November 2013; Runnymede Trust, *Connecting British Hindus* (2006), p.70. Hindu Forum of Britain, 'Social Impact Analysis for Activities in 2011' (2013), p.4; Hindu Forum of Britain, *Diwali at Westminster 2013* (Hindu Forum of Britain, 2013), pp.24–5.
50. Amartya Sen, *The Argumentative India:Writings on Indian Culture, History and Identity* (London: Penguin, 2005), pp.69–72.
51 Arjun Appadurai, *Fear of Small Numbers: An Essay on the Geography of Small Numbers* (London: Duke University Press, 2006).
52. Nikita Sud, *Liberalization, Hindu Nationalism and the State: A Biography of Gujarat* (Oxford: Oxford University Press, 2012), p.117.
53. Author's interview with Swaminathan Vaidyanathan (London, 15 November 2013).
54. Smira Shackle, 'The NS Interview: Bharti Tailor', *New Statesman*, 20 April 2011: http://www.newstatesman.com/religion/2011/04/interview-hinduism-british. Accessed on 23 August 2015.
55. Vijay Prashad, *Uncle Swami: South Asians in America Today* (Noida: Harper Collins, 2013), p.89.
56. Sunny Hundal, 'Ramesh Kallidai, Hindu Fanatic', 13 June 2007: http://www.pickledpolitics.com/archives/1194; Sunny Hundal, 'Touchier than thou', *The Guardian*, 25 May 2006: http://www.theguardian.com/commentisfree/2006/may/25/competingtobevictims. Both accessed on 3 January 2014.
57. Sunder Katwala, Sunny Hundal, Priyamvada Gopal, et al., 'Race and Faith: A New Agenda. New Generation Network', 20 November 2006: http://www.theguardian.com/commentisfree/2006/nov/20/whyweneedanewdiscourseon. Accessed on 14 November 2013.

58. British Muslims for Secular Democracy, cited in Charlie Pottins, 'A Bad Day for Kelly, it's Kallidai', 12 June 2007: http://randompottins.blogspot.co.uk/2007/06/bad-day-for-kelly-its-kallidai.html.
59. Andrew Gilligan, 'Revealed: The Rise and Rise of the Fundamentalist Father', *Evening Standard*, 11 June 2007.
60. Gilligan, 'Revealed', *Evening Standard* (2007).
61. Gilligan, 'Revealed', *Evening Standard* (2007).
62. Kalpana Wilson, *Race, Racism and Development: Interrogating History, Discourse and Practice* (London: Zed Books, 2012), pp.234–5; Dhaliwal, 'Religion, Moral Hegemony and Local Cartographies of Power' (unpublished PhD thesis, 2011), pp.60–1.
63. Darra Singh, Chair of the Commission on Integration and Cohesion, in Commission on Integration and Cohesion, 'Our Shared Future', June 2007, p.3: http://resources.cohesioninstitute.org.uk/Publications/Documents/Document/DownloadDocumentsFile.aspx?recordId=18&file=PDFversion. Accessed on 27 September 2015.
64. Wilson, *Race, Racism and Development* (2012), p.234.
65. Anandi Ramamurthy, *Black Star: Britain's Asian Youth Movements* (London: Pluto Press, 2013), p.202.
66. Ted Cantle, *Community Cohesion: A Report of the Independent Review Team chaired by Ted Cantle* (London: the Home Office, 2001).
67. 'First Hindu grant for increasing awareness of global poverty in Britain', *Organiser*, 13 August 2006; Gilligan, 'Revealed', *Evening Standard* (2007). Hindu Aid (Company No. 04699256), launched in 2006, was dissolved in 2013. It is distinct from Hindu Aid UK (Charity No. 1195722), which was launched in 2020.
68. 'First Hindu Grant for Increasing Awareness of Global Poverty in Britain', *Organiser*, 13 August 2006. The year preceding the DFID grant, Companies House data shows that the charity's income was just £2,500; cited in Gilligan, 'Revealed', *Evening Standard* (2007).
69. Ravi, 'The Rise and Rise of Ramesh Kallidai', *Sangh Samachar* blog, June 19, 2007: http://sanghsamachar.wordpress.com/2007/06/19/the-rise-and-rise-of-ramesh-kallidai/. Accessed on 22 August 2015.
70. 'Shri Guruji Birth Centenary Celebrations in UK: Sangh Meet Turns Out a Grand Hindu Sangam', *Organiser*, 13 May 2007. The *Organiser* also notes that 'Leaders of Shri Kutch Satsang, Swaminarayan Mandir, National Council of Hindu Temples, Hindu Forum of Britain, ISKCON-Bhaktivedanta Manor, Hindu Council of UK, Vishwa Hindu Parishad (UK), Singh Sabha Gurudwara-Southall, National Congress of Gujarati Organisations (UK) and Hindu Swayamsevak Sangh (UK)' were all present.
71. Hindu Forum of Britain press statement, quoted in 'Hindu Forum Condemns Attack on Ramesh Kallidai', 12 June 2007: http://www.redhotcurry.com/archive/news/2007/hfb_ramesh-kallidai.htm. Accessed on 3 May 2015.

72. House of Commons, Home Affairs Select Committee, Sixth Report, Session 2004–5, Examination of Witnesses, 16 November 2004.
73. House of Commons, Home Affairs Select Committee, Sixth Report, Session 2004–5, Written Evidence, Joint memorandum submitted by Tony McNulty MP, Joan Ryan MP, Peter Luff MP, Stephen Pound MP, Keith Vaz MP, Laura Moffatt MP, Karen Buck MP, and Barry Gardiner MP, 13 December 2004.
74. Andrew Dismore MP (primary sponsor), 'Terrorism and Community Relations', House of Commons, Early Day Motion 212, Session 2004–5, tabled on 29 November 2004.
75. House of Commons, Home Affairs Select Committee, Sixth Report, Session 2004–5, Written Evidence, Supplementary memorandum submitted by the Home Office, 11 January 2005.
76. House of Commons, Home Affairs Select Committee, Sixth Report, Session 2004–5, Written Evidence, Memorandum submitted by the Swaminarayan Hindu Mission, 6 December 2004.
77. House of Commons, Home Affairs Select Committee, Sixth Report, Session 2004–5, Examination of Witnesses, 14 December 2004.
78. House of Commons, Home Affairs Select Committee, Sixth Report, Session 2004–5, Examination of Witnesses, 14 December 2004.
79. House of Commons, Home Affairs Select Committee, Sixth Report, Session 2004–5, Examination of Witnesses, 14 December 2004.
80. Parita Mukta, 'The Public Face of Hindu Nationalism', *Ethnic and Racial Studies*, vol.23, no.3 (2000), p.462; Jaffrelot and Therwath, 'The Sangh Parivar and the Hindu Diaspora in the West: What Kind of "Long-Distance Nationalism"?', *International Political Sociology*, vol.1 (2007), p.285.
81. Edward Simpson, 'Is Anthropology Legal? Earthquakes, Blitzkrieg, and Ethical Futures', *Focaal*, vol.74, no.1 (2016), pp.113–28; Hannah Kim, 'Public Engagement and Personal Desires: BAPS Swaminarayan Temples and Their Contribution to the Discourses on Religion', *International Journal of Hindu Studies*, vol.13, no.3 (2009), pp.357–90.
82. Trustees of the Hindu Swayamsevak Sangh, 'Hindu Swayamsevak Sangh Trustees Annual Report 2009' (2009), p.3.
83. *Sangh Sandesh*, October–December, 2010, p.1.
84. *Sangh Sandesh*, October–December, 2010, p.12.
85. 'The Changing Dimensions of Hindus Globally', *Asian Voice*, 23 December 2017, p.13.
86. Author's interview with Swaminathan Vaidyanathan (London, 15 November 2013).
87. Hussain Kesvani, 'A Hindu Temple Has Put A Stop To An Event Featuring A Former EDL Leader', *BuzzFeed News*, 29 January 2016: https://www.buzzfeed.com/husseinkesvani/a-hindu-temple-has-cancelled-an-event-that-featured. Accessed on 10 March 2019.

88. 'Constituency data: Ethnic groups, 2021 Census': https://commonslibrary.parliament.uk/constituency-statistics-ethnicity/. Accessed on 21 June 2023.
89. Blackman and Gardiner are the only serving British Members of Parliament to be given Indian civilian honours. Just four other British politicians have ever been awarded Padma awards: MPs Fenner Brockway and Julius Silverman were awarded Padma Bhushans for campaigning for Indian self-rule, and Labour Peers Meghnad Desai and Bhikhu Parekh both received the same honour as Members of the House of Lords.
90. Michael Safi and Jessica Elgot, 'Tories Disown Firebrand Hindu Activist After Commons Visit', *The Guardian*, 26 October 2017: https://www.theguardian.com/politics/2017/oct/26/tories-disown-firebrand-hindu-activist-after-commons-visit. Accessed on 7 September 2019.
91. Aisha Gani, 'This Far-Right Anti-Muslim Extremist was in Parliament at an Event Addressed by Amber Rudd', *BuzzFeed News*, 25 October 2017: https://www.buzzfeed.com/aishagani/amber-rudd-spoke-at-an-event-in-parliament-attended-by-an. Accessed on 7 September 2019.
92. 'Hindu Girls Targeted by Extremists', *Metro*, 22 February 2007: http://metro.co.uk/2007/02/22/hindu-girls-targeted-by-extremists-108990/. Accessed on 22 May 2015.
93. Charlie Pottins, 'Is the Met Assisting Hate Propaganda?', 4 March 2007: http://randompottins.blogspot.co.uk/2007/03/is-met-assisting-hate-propaganda.html. Accessed on 14 November 2014.
94. Registration was available through either NHSF or HFB websites, or through an HFB email address or telephone number.
95. National Hindu Students Forum, 'Hindu Security Conference a Success', 22 February 2007: http://www.nhsf.org.uk/2007/02/hindu-security-conference-a-success/. Accessed on 14 November 2013.
96. 'Hindu Girls Targeted by Extremists', *Metro*, 2007. In a later statement, the Forum denied Kallidai had given figures for the numbers converted.
97. 'Hindu Girls Risking Muslim Honey Trap Claim Forum', *Manchester Evening News*, 30 March 2007: http://www.manchestereveningnews.co.uk/news/local-news/hindu-girls-risking-muslim-honey-987486. Accessed on 22 August 2015.
98. Charlie Pottins, 'Is the Met Assisting Hate Propaganda?', 4 March 2007.
99. Yassir Suleiman, 'Narratives of Conversion to Islam: Female Perspectives' (Cambridge: Prince Alwaleed Bin Talal Centre of Islamic Studies, University of Cambridge, 2013), p.86. Report available online: http://www.cis.cam.ac.uk/reports/post/203-narratives-of-conversion-to-islam-in-britain-female-perspectives. Accessed on 22 August 2015.
100. Nathan Lean, *The Islamophobia Industry: How the Right Manufactures Fears of Muslims* (London: Pluto Press, 2012).
101. Katy P. Sian, '"Forced" conversions in the British Sikh diaspora', *South Asian Popular Culture*, vol.9, no.2 (2011), pp.115–30; Katy P. Sian,

'Understanding Inter-Brasian Conflict, *Sikh Formations*, vol.7, no.2 (2011), pp.111–30.
102. Shankar Tattwawadi (ed.), *Sarsanghchalak Goes Abroad: A Collection of Lectures Delivered by Prof. Rajendra Singh on Foreign Land* (New Delhi: Suruchi Prakashan, 1995), p.73.
103. Dhooleka Sarhadi Raj, 'Who the hell do you think you are?' Promoting Religious Identity Among Young Hindus in Britain', *Ethnic and Racial Studies*, vol.23, no.3 (2000), p.555.
104. Demographers broadly dismiss the very notion of 'Muslim fertility'; whilst the Muslim population of India might be growing, various socio-economic factors are deemed relevant, rather than anything related to religion. Jeffrey and Jeffrey, *Confronting Saffron Demography* (2006), p.33.
105. Jeffrey and Jeffrey, *Confronting Saffron Demography* (2006), p.32.
106. Whilst many publications have perpetuated this fear, of prominence is the 2003 book *Religious Demography of India* by A.P. Joshi et al., the foreword to which was written by L.K. Advani; Jeffrey and Jeffrey, *Confronting Saffron Demography* (2006), pp.2–3.
107. Renaud Camus, *Le Grand Remplacement* (Paris: David Reinharc, 2011).
108. K.V. Paliwal, *India Heading Towards an Islamic State: A Warning!* (New Delhi: Hindu Writers' Forum, n.d.), p.9.
109. G. Ananthakrishnan, '"Love Jihad" Racket: VHP, Christian Groups Find Common Cause', *Times of India*, 13 October 2009: http://timesofindia.indiatimes.com/india/Love-Jihad-racket-VHP-Christian-groups-find-common-cause/articleshow/5117548.cms. Accessed on 22 August 2015.
110. Insight UK, 'Open Letter to the Prime Minister of the UK', 14 October 2022: https://insightuk.org/open-letter-to-the-prime-minister-of-the-uk. Accessed on 21 June 2023.
111. Insight UK, 'A Report on the State of Hinduism in Religious Education in UK Schools', 14 January 2021: https://insightuk.org/wp-content/uploads/2021/01/Hinduism-in-RE_Project-report.pdf. Accessed on 21 June 2023.
112. Insight UK, 'Open Letter to the Prime Minister of the UK', 14 October 2022.
113. This section draws upon and expands: Edward Anderson, '"Neo-Hindutva": the Asia House M.F. Husain Campaign and the Mainstreaming of Hindu Nationalist Rhetoric in Britain', *Contemporary South Asia*, vol.23, no.1 (2015), pp.45–66.
114. Amit Roy, 'Vandals Close Exhibition', *Daily Telegraph*, 29 May 2006.
115. Tapati Guha-Takurta explains the subtext of the title of Om Nagpal's article, published in *Vichar Mimansa* based in Madhya Pradesh: '*Yeh Chitrakar hai ya Kasai?*' (Is this an artist or a butcher). Qassab (plural of Qassai/Kasai) is a Muslim caste involved in butchery, a profession with contentious associations with cow slaughter. Tapati Guha-Takurta, *Monuments, Objects,*

Histories: Institutions of Art in Colonial and Post-Colonial India (New York: Columbia University Press, 2004), p.356, n.23.

116. Smita Narula, 'Politics by Other Means: Attacks Against Christians in India', *Human Rights Watch*, vol.11, no.6 (1999): http://www.hrw.org/reports/1999/indiachr/. Accessed on 22 August 2015.
117. Guha-Takurta, *Monuments, Objects, Histories* (2004), p.247.
118. Hindu Janajagruti Samiti's name is a call-to-arms in itself. 'Communicative strategies and connectivity with audiences often revolved around the metaphor of "awakening" (as a verb, *jangruti* or *janajagruti;* as a command *jago!* or *uthao!*) was a resounding refrain in the early incidents of mass mobilisation against perceived colonial, and occasionally communal of class/caste-oriented, iniquities', Raminder Kaur, *Performative Politics and the Cultures of Hinduism: Public Uses of Religion in Western India* (London: Anthem Press, 2005), p.11.
119. Sumathi Ramaswamy (ed.) *Barefoot Across the Nation: M.F. Husain and the Idea of India* (London: Routledge, 2011).
120. Maqbool Fida Husain vs Raj Kumar Pandey, CLR Revision Petition No. 114/2007, http://indiankanoon.org/doc/1191397/. See also: Salil Tripathi, *Offence: The Hindu Case* (London: Seagull Books, 2009), pp.26–7.
121. Randeep Ramesh, 'Artist Cleared of Insulting Hindu Faith', *The Guardian*, 9 September, 2008.
122. Ramaswamy, *The Goddess and the Nation* (2010), p.6.
123. 'Qatar Nationality for Husain Win for Hindutva: Bajrang Dal', *Indian Express*, 2010: http://indianexpress.com/article/india/latest-news/qatar-nationality-for-husain-win-for-hindutva-bajrang-dal/. Accessed on 23 August 2015.
124. Hindu Forum of Britain, 'Hindu Forum asks Asia House to withdraw M.F. Husain Exhibition', 2006.
125. National Hindu Students Forum (UK), 'Mobilising a Protest and Getting Our Voice Heard—Be Active, Be NHSF!', 19 May 2006: http://www.nhsf.org.uk/index.php?option=com_content&task=view&id=413&Itemid=134. Accessed on 23 September 2015.
126. Letter from Amrita Jhaveri and Mallika Advani to Claire Hsu, 4 July 2006, Asia Art Archive (MON.HUM).
127. Rashmee Roshan Lall, 'UK Hindus Slam India as "Pseudo-Secular"', *The Times of India*, 25 May 2006.
128. 'Protest at Asia House Gallery's Exhibition of MF Husain's Offensive Paintings', *Organiser*, 28 May 2006: http://organiser.org/archives/historic/dynamic/modulesa7a0.html?name=Content&pa=showpage&pid=132&page=41. Accessed on 22 August 2015.
129. Hindu Human Rights, 'HHR Bio', n.d.: http://www.hinduhumanrights.info/hhr-bio/. Accessed on 22 November 2014.
130. Dhooleka Raj, 'Hindu Protest in London-stan: Lord Ram's Modern Transnational Epic Journey', paper presented at the Hindu Trans-

Nationalism: Organization, Ideologies, Networks Conference, Rice University, Houston, TX, 20–1 November 2009.
131. Hindu Human Rights, 'Rise of the Alternative Hindu Activist', 11 January 2014: http://www.youtube.com/watch?v=lepRG0kSXHg. Accessed on 22 November 2014.
132. Zavos, 'Stamp it out' (2008), pp.332–3.
133. Pragna Patel, 'Faith in the State? Asian Women's Struggles for Human Rights in the UK', *Feminist Legal Studies*, vol.16 (2008), p.16.
134. 'Husain's Painting Exhibition Cancelled in UK', *Times of India*, 25 May 2006: http://articles.timesofindia.indiatimes.com/2006-05-25/rest-of-world/27819171_1_painting-exhibition-m-f-Husain-second-highest-price. Accessed on 22 August 2015; Lord Meghnad Desai, 'Closure Threat to Artistic Freedom', *The Guardian*, 26 May 2006.
135. Zavos, 'Stamp it out' (2008), p.334.
136. Sunny Hundal, 'The War on Terror—Not Just an Issue for Muslims', in Alex Bigham (ed.), *Having Faith in Foreign Policy* (London: The Foreign Policy Centre, 2007), p.86.
137. Sangay Mishra, *Desis Divided: The Political Lives of South Asian Americans* (Minneapolis, MN: University of Minnesota Press, 2016), p.132.
138. Prema Kurien, 'Multiculturalism and "American" Religion: The Case of Hindu Indian Americans', *Social Forces,* vol.85, no.2 (2006), p.730.
139. Prema Kurien, *A Place at the Multicultural Table: The Development of an American Hinduism* (New Bunswick, NJ: Rutgers University Press, 2007), p.186.
140. Sanjoy Chakravorty, Devesh Kapur and Nirvikar Singh, *The Other One Percent: Indians in America* (Oxford: Oxford University Press, 2016), p.155.
141. Arthur J. Pais, '*Bhai* Ackerman Hails Growing India-Israel Ties', *Rediff*, 20 September 1999: https://www.rediff.com/news/1999/sep/20us.htm. Accessed on 22 June 2023.
142. Prema Kurien, 'What is American about American Hinduism? Hindu Umbrella Organisations in the United States in Comparative Perspective', in Zavos, Kanungo, Reddy, Warrier, and Williams (eds.), *Public Hinduisms* (2012), p.105; Prema Kurien, *A Place at the Multicultural Table: The Development of an American Hinduism* (New Bunswick, NJ: Rutgers University Press, 2007), p.148.
143. Azad Essa, *Hostile Homelands: The New Alliance Between India and Israel* (London: Pluto, 2023), p.120.
144. Azad Essa, *Hostile Homelands* (2023), pp.116–19.
145. House of Commons, Home Affairs Select Committee, Sixth Report, Session 2004–5, Written Evidence, Memorandum submitted by the Hindu Forum of Britain, 14 December 2004.
146. Eviane Cheng Leidig, 'Immigrant, Nationalist and Proud: A Twitter Analysis of Indian Diaspora Supporters for Brexit and Trump', *Media and Communication*, vol.7, no.1 (2019), pp.77–89.

147. Namit Hans, 'Happy Birthday Donald Trump—Hindu Sena cuts cake for 'messiah against Islamic terror', *Indian Express*, 15 June 2016: http://indianexpress.com/article/india/india-news-india/happy-birthday-donald-trump-hindu-sena-cuts-cake-for-messiah-against-islamic-terror-2852167/. Accessed on 20 February 2017.
148. Dean Murphy, 'Two Unlikely Allies Come Together in Fight Against Muslims', *New York Times*, 2 June 2001.
149. Quoted in Azad Essa, *Hostile Homelands* (2023), p.110.
150. Swamijyoti, 'All About the Hindu-Jewish Dialogue', 2008: http://www.scribd.com/doc/7347993/All-About-the-HinduJewish-Dialogue. Accessed on 22 August 2015.
151. Azad Essa, *Hostile Homelands: The New Alliance Between India and Israel* (London: Pluto, 2023), p. 112.
152. Prashad, *Uncle Swami* (2013), pp.64–8.
153. Chetan Bhatt, *Hindu Nationalism: Origins, Ideologies and Modern Myths* (Oxford: Berg, 2001), p.103.
154. Akanksha Mehta, 'Right-Wing Sisterhood: Everyday Politics of Hindu Nationalist Women in India and Zionist Settler Women in Israel-Palestine' (unpublished PhD thesis, SOAS University of London, 2017).
155. Edward Anderson and Christophe Jaffrelot, 'Hindu Nationalism and the "Saffronisation of the Public Sphere": an Interview with Christophe Jaffrelot', *Contemporary South Asia*, vol.26, no.4 (2018), p.287. For more on the concept of 'ethnic democracy', see Sammy Smooha, 'The Model of Ethnic Democracy: Israel as a Jewish and Democratic State', *Nations and Nationalism*, vol.8, no.4 (2002), pp.475–503.
156. M.S. Golwalkar, *We, Our Nationhood Defined* (1939), e-book edition: https://www.scribd.com/doc/95053816/We-or-Our-Nationhood-Defined-Shri-M-S-Golwalkar-Guruji-1. Accessed on 21 June 2023.
157. Raj, 'Who the hell do you think you are?' (2000), p.555.
158. Charlie Pottins, 'Is the Met Assisting Hate Propaganda?', 4 March 2007.
159. Prashad, *Uncle Swami* (2013), pp.61–99.
160. 'UK Hindus Meet to Discuss Attacks', BBC News, 14 December 2003: http://news.bbc.co.uk/1/hi/uk/3317169.stm. Accessed on 22 August 2015.
161. Kurien, 'Multiculturalism and "American" Religion', *Social Forces* (2006), p.736; Charles Taylor, 'The Politics of Recognition', in Amy Gutmann (ed.), *Multiculturalism and the Politics of Recognition* (Princeton, NJ: Princeton University Press, 1992), pp.25–73; Nancy Fraser, *Justice Interruptus: Critical Reflections of the 'Postsocialist' Condition* (London: Routledge, 1997).
162. Prema Kurien, *A Place at the Multicultural Table: The Development of an American Hinduism* (New Bunswick, NJ: Rutgers University Press, 2007), p.241.
163. Deepa Reddy, 'Hindu Transnationalisms: Organisations, Ideologies, Network', in Zavos, Kanungo, Reddy, Warrier, and Williams (eds.), *Public Hinduisms* (2012), p.313.

164. Kurien, 'Multiculturalism and "American" Religion' (2006), pp.725–6
165. Amélie Blom and Nicolas Jaoul, 'Introduction. The Moral and Affectual Dimension of Collective Action in South Asia', *South Asia Multidisciplinary Academic Journal*, vol.2 (2008): http://samaj.revues.org/1912. Accessed on 22 August 2015.
166. 'Media Watch: It's Minority, Handle with Care', *Organiser*, 11 June 2006.
167. Pragna Patel and Hannana Siddiqui, 'Shrinking Secular Space: Asian Women at the Intersect of Race, Religion and Gender', in Ravi Thiara and Aisha Gill (eds.), *Violence Against Women in South Asian Communities: Issues for Policy and Practice* (London: Jessica Kingsley, 2010), pp.114–15.
168. Ramesh Kallidai, 'Screaming Hot Bhaijiyas, the Ramesh Kallidai column', *Asian Voice*, 17 July 2004.
169. Kajri Jain, *Gods in the Bazaar: The Economies of Indian Calendar Art* (London: Duke University Press, 2007), p.296.
170. Billstickers, comment on Sunny Hundal, 'Touchier Than Thou', *The Guardian*, 25 May 2006 (comment on 28 May): http://discussion.theguardian.com/comment-permalink/165679. Accessed on 22 August 2015.
171. Ajay Prakash, 'London Art Gallery Closes M.F. Husain Exhibition After Paintings Vandalised', *World Socialist Web Site*, 3 July 2006: http://www.wsws.org/en/articles/2006/07/husa-j03.html. Accessed on 23 September 2015; 'Hindu Law Board Offers Rs 51 cr for Killing Hussain', *Outlook*, 22 February 2006: http://news.outlookindia.com/items.aspx?artid=357292. Accessed on 22 August 2015.
172. Falgun Paurnima, 'HJS Protest against Christie's Auction of Husain's Paintings', *Hindu Janajagruti Samiti*, 21 March 2008: http://www.hindujagruti.org/news/4064.html. Accessed on 23 September 2015.
173. 'Hindu Groups Protest Screening of "Sita Sings the Blues"', *Times of India*, 18 August 2011: http://timesofindia.indiatimes.com/nri/cinema/Hindu-groups-protest-screening-of-Sita-Sings-the-Blues/articleshow/9648895.cms. Accessed on 22 August 2015.
174. Author's communication with anonymous curator at Boston Museum of Fine Arts, March 2014.
175. 'Media Watch: It's Minority, Handle with Care', *Organiser*, 11 June 2006.
176. Salil Tripathi, 'Equal Opportunity Fundamentalism', *Tehelka*, 17 February 2007.
177. 'The Protest over Ram Setu', *Hindustan Times*, 23 September 2007: http://www.hindustantimes.com/StoryPage/Print/249325.aspx?s=p. Accessed on 22 August 2015.
178. Jaffrelot, 'Hindu Nationalism and the (Not So Easy) Art of Being Outraged' (2008), p.2
179. Daniel Cefaï, *Pourquoi se Mobilise-t-on? Les Théories de l'Action Collective* (Paris: La Découverte-MAUSS, 2007), p.163, quoted in Amélie Blom and Nicolas Jaoul, 'Introduction. The Moral and Affectual Dimension

of Collective Action in South Asia', *South Asia Multidisciplinary Academic Journal*, vol.2 (2008), p.2.
180. Emile Durkheim, *The Elementary Forms of the Religious Life*, trans. Joseph Ward Swain (London: Allen and Unwin, 1976).
181. Arun Chaudhuri, 'American Hindu Activism and the Politics of Anxiety', in Zavos, Kanungo, Reddy, Warrier, and Williams (eds.), *Public Hinduisms* (2012), p.332.
182. Richard Seymour, *The Twittering Machine* (London: The Indigo Press, 2019), pp.32–3.
183. Ved P. Nanda, 'The Hindu Diaspora in the United States', in Wendy Doniger and Martha Nussbuam (eds.), *Pluralism and Democracy in India: Debating the Hindu Right* (Oxford: Oxford University Press, 2015), p.359.
184. Note that whilst neither cow protection nor dissatisfaction with the Asian marker are the sole preserves of the Hindu nationalist movement, they still indicate a strong 'family resemblance' with the rhetoric of the Sangh (and at times organisational collaboration).
185. 'The Man Behind the Thought Revolution': https://www.rajivmalhotra.com/. Accessed on 23 June 2023.
186. Rajiv Malhotra, 'Does South Asian Studies Undermine India?', *Rediff*, 4 December 2003: https://www.rediff.com/news/2003/dec/08rajiv.htm. Accessed on 23 June 2023; Rajiv Malhotra and Aravindan Neelakandan, *Breaking India: Western Interventions in Dravidian and Dalit Faultlines* (Amaryllis, 2011).
187. Rajiv Malhotra, 'Wendy's Child Syndrome', 2002: http://creative.sulekha.com/risa-lila-1-wendy-s-child-syndrome_103338_blog. Accessed on 22 August 2015.
188. Wendy Doniger, 'In Full: Author Wendy Doniger's Statement on Withdrawal of "The Hindus"', *The Wall Street Journal India*, 12 February 2014: http://blogs.wsj.com/indiarealtime/2014/02/12/in-full-author-wendy-donigers-statement-on-withdrawal-of-the-hindus/. Accessed on 22 August 2015.
189. Hartosh Singh Bal, 'Publishers Failed to Stand Up to Dinanath Batra in Ways That Matter. What Will this Mean for the Future of Debate in India', *The Caravan*, 1 December 2014.
190. Shougat Dasgupta, 'Dinanath Batra: Here Comes the Book Police', *Live Mint*, 12 February 2014: http://www.livemint.com/Specials/ZL8MkEyTobNWPEQm05jYDL/Dinanath-Batra-Here-comes-the-book-police.html. Accessed on 22 August 2015.
191. Shougat Dasgupta, 'Dinanath Batra: Here Comes the Book Police', *Live Mint*, 12 February 2014.
192. 'Hindu Forum of Britain (HFB) Gives a Fitting Reply to CNN', *HFB*, 15 February 2014: http://www.hfb.org.uk/index.php?option=com_k2&view=item&id=96:hfb-challenged-the-author-for-an-open-debate-on-the-book-the-hindus&Itemid=60. Accessed on 22 August 2015.

193. Madhava Turumella, HFB Vice President, CNN News, 14 February 2014.
194. 'Desecration of Hindu Sentiments in Parliament', *HFB*, 28 February 2014: http://www.hfb.org.uk/index.php?option=com_k2&view=item&id=97:desecration-of-hindu-sentiments-in-parliament&Itemid=60. Accessed on 22 August 2015.
195. Hilary Metcalf and Heather Rolfe, *Caste Discrimination and Harassment in Great Britain* (National Institute of Economic and Social Research, 2010); Meena Dhanda et al., 'Caste in Britain: Socio-legal Review', Equality and Human Rights Commission Research Report 91 (2014).
196. Hindu Forum of Britain, *Caste in the UK: A Summary of the Consultation with the Hindu Community in Britain* (Hindu Forum of Britain, 2008), p.6.
197. 'Minutes to Anti-Legislation Caste [sic] Lobby Group Meeting', House of Commons, 15 March 2011. Released under the Freedom of Information Act: https://www.whatdotheyknow.com/request/niesr_report_caste#incoming-398922.
198. Annapurna Waughray, 'Caste in Britain: Public Consultation on Caste and Equality Law', *Economic and Political Weekly*, vol.53, no.10 (10 March 2019).
199. Sutton, '"So called caste"' (2018), pp.336–49.
200. This argument is at the heart of Hindutva rhetoric on caste and has also been made both by 'mainstream' organisations, such as the HFB and NCHT, as well as activist-writers including Rajiv Malhotra and Prakash Shah. See Prakash Shah, *Against Caste in British Law: A Critical Perspective of the Caste Discrimination Provision in the Equality Act 2010* (Basingstoke: Palgrave Macmillan, 2015); Rajiv Malhotra and Aravindan Neelakandan, *Breaking India: Western Interventions in Dravidian and Dalit Faultlines* (New Delhi: Amaryllis, 2011).
201. Annapurna Waughray, 'Caste in Britain: Public Consultation on Caste and Equality Law', *Economic and Political Weekly*, vol.53, no.10 (10 March 2019); Meena Dhanda, Annapurna Waughray, David Keane et al., 'Caste in Britain: Socio-Legal Review', *Equality and Human Rights Commission Research Report no.91* (Manchester: Equality and Human Rights Commission, 2014).
202. Satish Sharma, Introduction in *Caste, Conversion and a "Thoroughly Colonial Conspiracy"*, National Council of Hindu Temples UK, 2017, p.9. Archived online: https://archive.org/details/MergedFile/page/n1. Accessed on 7 September 2019.
203. Trupti Patel letter to *Asian Voice*, 5 May 2015: https://www.asian-voice.com/Opinion/Editorial/Letters/Your-Voice162. Accessed on 7 September 2019.
204. Reena Kumar, 'Hindu Temple Charity Faces Probe Over Tory Party Endorsement', *Eastern Eye*, 6 May 2015.
205. Satish Sharma, *Shubh Sandesh*, 5 June 2017: http://www.nchtuk.org/index.php?option=com_acymailing&ctrl=archive&task=view&mailid=

150&key=uiAg81eT&subid=6315-7294e321ef71b428472226ad5554f3%E2%80%A6. Accessed on 23 July 2019.
206. Kirsty Weakley, 'Regulator Contacts Charities Over Election Activity', *Civil Society*, 9 June 2017: https://www.civilsociety.co.uk/news/regulator-contacts-charities-over-election-activity.html. Accessed on 7 September 2019.
207. Nicole Martin and Omar Khan, *Ethnic Minorities at the 2017 British General Election* (Runnymede Trust, February 2019): https://www.runnymedetrust.org/uploads/2017%20Election%20Briefing.pdf. Accessed on 7 September 2019.
208. British Future, 'New Research Shows Ethnic Minority Votes Increasingly Up For Grabs', 25 May 2015: http://www.britishfuture.org/articles/ethnic-minority-votes-up-for-grabs/. Accessed on 7 September 2019.
209. Ash Sarkar, 'Brace Yourself for a "Hinduphobia" Moral Panic', *Novara Media*, 18 November 2022: https://novaramedia.com/2022/11/18/brace-yourselves-for-a-hinduphobia-moral-panic/. Accessed on 6 July 2023.
210. Matthew Francis, 'Mrs Thatcher's Peacock Blue Sari: Ethnic Minorities, Electoral Politics and the Conservative Party, c.1974–86', *Contemporary British History*, vol.31, no.2 (2017), pp.274–93.
211. Shankar Tatwawadi, 'Margaret Thatcher at HSS: A historic event', *News Bharati*, 12 April 2013: http://www.newsbharati.com/Encyc/2013/4/12/MargaretThatcheratHSSAhistoricevent/. Accessed on 10 January 2014.
212. Margaret Thatcher in television interview for Granada *World in Action*, 30 January 1978 (https://www.margaretthatcher.org/document/103485).
213. Muhammad Anwar, 'The Politics of the BrAsian Electorate', in N. Ali, V.S. Kalra, and S. Sayyid, *A Postcolonial People: South Asians in Britain* (London: Hurst, 2006), p.195.
214. Nicole Martin, Maria Sobolewska and Neema Begum, 'Left Out of the Left Behind: Ethnic Minority Support for Brexit' (January 2019): https://papers.ssrn.com/sol3/papers.cfm?abstract_id=3320418. Accessed on 10 February 2019.
215. Early Day Motion 944 ('Riots in India'), Tabled 6 March 2002, 2001–2 Session: https://edm.parliament.uk/early-day-motion/21213/riots-in-india.
216. Early Day Motion 479 ('Narendra Modi'), Tabled 4 September 2013, 2013–14 Session: https://edm.parliament.uk/early-day-motion/45964.
217. Jeremy Corbyn (@jeremycorbyn), 'The situation in Kashmir is deeply disturbing. Human rights abuses taking place are unacceptable. The rights of the Kashmiri people must be respected and UN resolutions implemented', 11 August 2019: https://twitter.com/jeremycorbyn/status/1160480451066306560; The Labour Party, 'Conference

Arrangements Committee: Report 5 to Conference 2019', 25 September 2019.
218. Sima Kotecha, 'General election 2019: Labour seeks to calm Hindu voters' anger', BBC News, 12 November 2019: https://www.bbc.co.uk/news/election-2019-50382791; Dipesh Gadher, 'Labour Party "institutionally biased against India and Indians"', *The Times*, 6 October 2019.
219. Open letter from Trupti Patel/HFB and Saish Sharma/NCHTUK to Jeremy Corbyn, 10 October 2019.
220. Sunny Hundal, 'Concerns over 'foreign interference' as India-linked Hindu nationalist group targets Labour candidates', *Open Democracy*, 6 November 2019: https://www.opendemocracy.net/en/opendemocracyuk/concerns-over-foreign-interference-as-india-linked-hindu-nationalist-group-targets-labour-candidates/.
221. Office for National Statistics, 'Population of the UK by Country of Birth and Nationality', January to December 2019: https://www.ons.gov.uk/peoplepopulationandcommunity/populationandmigration/internationalmigration/datasets/populationoftheunitedkingdombycountryofbirthandnationality. Accessed on 27 May 2020.
222. Ashley Cowburn, 'Zac Goldsmith squirms after being asked to name favourite Bollywood film in cringeworthy interview', *The Independent*, 1 May 2016: https://www.independent.co.uk/news/uk/politics/zac-goldsmith-bollywood-favourite-film-actor-awards-cringeworthy-interview-watch-video-a7008896.html. Accessed on 31 July 2023.
223. Aisha Gani, 'Zac Goldsmith Criticised Over Leaflet Aimed at British Indians', *The Guardian*, 16 March 2016: https://www.theguardian.com/politics/2016/mar/16/zac-goldsmith-leaflet-british-indians-heirlooms. Accessed on 7 September 2019.
224. Author's correspondence with Joe Twyman, co-founder of Deltapoll, who conducted aggregate level analysis on the 2019 General Election.
225. Sunder Katwala, 'The Conservatives, Ethnic Minority Voters, and the Election. Next to No Progress', *Conservative Home*, 22 December 2019: https://www.conservativehome.com/platform/2019/12/sunder-katwala-the-conservatives-ethnic-minority-voters-and-the-election-next-to-no-progress.html. Accessed on 5 May 2020; Omar Khan, 'The BJP Supporters' Targeting of British Indian Voters is Divisive—and it won't work', *The Guardian*, 14 November 2019: https://amp.theguardian.com/commentisfree/2019/nov/14/friends-of-bjp-indian-voters-tories?. Accessed on 29 May 2020; Omar Khan (@omaromalleykhan), 'Ofc there's more to it & it is v likely there was a swing amg Indian voters from Labour to Conservative But pls be serious, dont just repeat BJP propaganda designed to divide communities There's more to British ethnic minority voting than "id politics"', 16 December 2019: https://twitter.com/omaromalleykhan/status/1206701990912430083.

226. Jim Moher, *Stepping on White Corns* (London: JGM Books, 2007).
227. Ken Livingstone, *You Can't Say That* (London: Faber and Faber, 2011), p.93.
228. 'Draft submission by Brent South CLP officers to the NEC Inquiry', cited in Moher, *Stepping on White Corns* (2007), p.194.
229. Ladwa left the Labour Party under Jeremy Corbyn's leadership, blaming an 'institutional bias' against Indians, and claiming that the party had been 'hijacked' by 'hard-left extremists and jihadi sympathisers'. Dipesh Gadher, 'Labour Party "institutionally biased against India and Indians"', *The Times*, 6 October 2019.
230. Kounteya Sinha, 'Narendra Modi to Address British Parliament', 13 August 2013: https://timesofindia.indiatimes.com/india/Narendra-Modi-to-address-British-parliament/articleshow/21811288.cms. Accessed on 19 September 2019.
231. Pieter Friedrich, 'All in the Family: The American Sangh's Affair with Tusli Gabbard', *Caravan*, 1 August 2019: https://caravanmagazine.in/politics/american-sangh-affair-tulsi-gabbard.
232. Pieter Friedrich, 'All in the Family: The American Sangh's Affair with Tusli Gabbard', *Caravan*, 1 August 2019.
233. Pieter Friedrich, 'Money Trail: Diaspora Diplomacy's Financial Whitewashing of Hindutva', 27 September 2020, *The Polis Project*: https://www.thepolisproject.com/read/money-trail-diaspora-diplomacys-financial-whitewashing-of-hindutva/. Accessed on 5 July 2023.
234. Jasa Macher, *Hindu Nationalist Influence in the United States, 2014–21* (2022): http://www.sacw.net/article14915.html. Accessed on 12 June 2023.
235. Jasa Macher, *Hindu Nationalist Influence in the United States, 2014–21* (2022); H.Res.417—113th Congress (2013–14).
236. Véronique Bénéï, '*Nations, Diaspora and Area Studies: South Asia, from Great Britain to the United States*, in Jackie Assayag and Véronique Bénéï (eds.), *Remapping Knowledge: The Making of South Asian Studies in India, Europe and America (19th–20th Centuries)* (New Delhi: Three Essays Collective, 2005), p.78.
237. Andrew J. Nicholson, 'Is Yoga Hindu? On the Fuzziness of Religious Boundaries', *Common Knowledge*, vol.19, no.3 (2013), pp.490–505.
238. Hindu American Foundation, 'The Coalition Against Genocide: A Nexus of Islamophobia Unveiled', 7 March 2013.
239. Smita Narula, 'Overlooked Danger: The Security and Rights Implications of Hindu Nationalism in India', *Harvard Human Rights Journal*, vol.16 (2003), p.46.
240. Deepa Reddy, 'Hindu Transnationalisms', in *Public Hinduisms* (2012), p.319.

CONCLUSION

1. Australian Bureau of Statistics. 'Australia's Population by Country of Birth', *ABS* (2021): https://www.abs.gov.au/statistics/people/population/australias-population-country-birth/latest-release.
2. 'Narendra Modi receives rock-star reception in Sydney as Anthony Albanese hails "rich friendship"', *The Guardian*, 23 May 2023: https://www.theguardian.com/australia-news/2023/may/23/narendra-modi-receives-rock-star-reception-in-sydney-as-anthony-albanese-hails-rich-friendship. Accessed on 4 July 2023.
3. Rhea Mogul, '"Modi is the boss": Australian leader gives India's prime minister a rock star welcome', CNN, 23 May 2023: https://edition.cnn.com/2023/05/24/india/india-narendra-modi-australia-visit-intl-hnk/index.html. Accessed on 1 July 2023.
4. 'IADF Welcome Partners', *Indian Australian Diaspora Foundation*: https://iadf.org.au/partners. Accessed on 1 July 2023.
5. 'Sheena Sood—The Far-Right's Weaponization of Spirituality Toward Ethnonationalism': https://www.soas.ac.uk/about/event/sheena-sood-far-rights-weaponization-spirituality-toward-ethnonationalism. Accessed on 29 June 2023.
6. David Curry, United States Commission on International Religious Freedom Commissioner, 'USCIRF Urges President Biden to Raise Religious Freedom Concerns During India State Visit', 20 June 2023: https://www.uscirf.gov/news-room/releases-statements/uscirf-urges-president-biden-raise-religious-freedom-concerns-during. Accessed on 30 June 2023.
7. Statement by David C. Mulford, US Ambassador to India, New Delhi, 'Issue of Gujarat Chief Minister Narendra Modi's Visa Status', US Department of State, 21 March 2005: https://2001-2009.state.gov/p/sca/rls/rm/2005/43701.htm. Accessed on 20 July 2023.
8. 'Remarks by President Biden and Prime Minister Modi of the Republic of India at Arrival Ceremony', 22 June 2023: https://www.whitehouse.gov/briefing-room/speeches-remarks/2023/06/22/remarks-by-president-biden-and-prime-minister-modi-of-the-republic-of-india-at-arrival-ceremony/. Accessed on 30 June 2023.
9. 'Remarks by President Biden and Prime Minister Modi', 22 June 2023.
10. 'India got freedom after 1,000 years of foreign rule, Narendra Modi tells US Congress', 23 June 2023: https://scroll.in/latest/1051436/india-got-freedom-after-1000-years-of-foreign-rule-says-narendra-modi-at-us-congress. Accessed on 4 July 2023.
11. 'Hindu society has been at war for over 1000 years', *Organiser*, 10 January 2023: https://organiser.org/2023/01/10/104033/rss-news/hindu-society-has-been-at-war-for-over-1000-years-it-is-natural-for-people-those-at-war-to-be-aggressive/. Accessed on 30 June 2022.

12. Amy Wang, 'White House defends WSJ reporter facing harassment over Modi question', *Washington Post*, 28 June 2023: https://www.washingtonpost.com/politics/2023/06/28/white-house-modi-reporter-wall-street-journal/. Accessed on 1 July 2023.
13. Amy Wang, 'White House defends WSJ reporter facing harassment over Modi question', 28 June 2023.
14. Sophie Landrin, 'Supporters of Indian PM harass and cyberstalk American journalist', *Le Monde*, 30 June 2023: https://www.lemonde.fr/en/international/article/2023/06/30/supporters-of-indian-pm-harrass-and-cyberstalk-american-journalist-sabrina-siddiqui-after-question-on-religious-minorities_6039865_4.html. Accessed on 20 June 2023.
15. Amy Wang, 'White House defends WSJ reporter facing harassment over Modi question', 28 June 2023.
16. Christophe Jaffrelot, *Modi's India: Hindu Nationalism and the Rise of Ethnic Democracy* (Princeton, NJ: Princeton University Press, 2021), p.99.
17. Ingrid Therwath, 'Cyber-Hindutva: Hindu nationalism, the diaspora and the Web', *e-Diasporas Atlas*, April 2012.
18. 'India secretly works to preserve reputation after 'flawed democracy' rating', *The Guardian*, 22 June 2023: https://www.theguardian.com/world/2023/jun/22/india-democracy-index-flawed-preserve-reputation-narendra-modi. Accessed on 2 July 2023.
19. Adapa Prasad, vice-president of OFBJP-US, cited in Neha Thirani Bagri, 'How the BJP turned a small band of non-resident Indians into a global PR machine', *Quartz*, 28 September 2016: https://qz.com/india/790858/from-babri-to-balochistan-the-rise-of-the-overseas-friends-of-the-bjp-as-narendra-modis-global-megaphone. Accessed on 2 July 2023.
20. 'India's diaspora is bigger and more influential than any in history', *The Economist*, 12 June 2023.
21. Alexander Ulmer, 'From U.S. suburbs, "friends of Modi" set to blitz India with calls in re-election drive', *Reuters*, 24 December 2018: https://www.reuters.com/article/us-india-election-usa-insight-idUSKCN1ON03H. Accessed on 4 July 2023.
22. 'After campaign from 12K km away, BJP overseas group in US celebrates win', *Business Standard*, 23 May 2019: https://www.business-standard.com/article/news-ians/after-campaign-from-12k-km-away-bjp-overseas-group-in-us-celebrates-win-119052301940_1.html. Accessed on 30 June 2023.
23. Prasun Sonwalkar, 'BJP taps NRIs in UK to campaign for Narendra Modi', *Hindustan Times*, 7 March 2019: https://www.hindustantimes.com/india-news/bjp-taps-nris-in-uk-to-campaign-for-narendra-modi/story-iOiU4dh0kHWQmUp6EfV9sM.html. Accessed on 1 July 2023.
24. Aaron Schrank, 'How people in LA are helping elect a Prime Minister in India', *LAist*, 24 April 2019: https://laist.com/news/modi-india-election-diaspora-support-los-angeles-bjp. Accessed on 2 July 2023.

25. Jasa Macher, *Hindu Nationalist Influence in the United States, 2014–21* (2022), p.28: http://www.sacw.net/article14915.html. Accessed on 12 June 2023.
26. Azad Essa, *Hostile Homelands: The New Alliance Between India and Israel* (London: Pluto, 2023).
27. Raju Rajugopal, '"Hinduphobia" in America? Two Competing Narratives Coming From Two Very Different Motivations', *American Kahani*, 15 May 2021: https://americankahani.com/perspectives/hinduphobia-in-america-two-competing-narratives-coming-from-two-very-different-motivations/. Accessed on 4 July 2023.
28. Amrit Wilson, 'The New Strategies of Hindu Supremacists in Britain', *Byline Times*, 9 December 2021: https://bylinetimes.com/2021/12/09/the-new-strategies-of-hindu-supremacists-in-britain/. Accessed on 4 July 2023.

BIBLIOGRAPHY

Note: This is a selected, focused bibliography—full citations of all sources used throughout the book can be found in the footnotes. The bibliography's secondary sources section concentrates mainly on books and certain key journal articles. Where edited volumes contain several relevant chapters, only the volume as a whole has been included in the bibliography. Numerous individual pieces published in newspapers, magazines, and on websites, remain in the footnotes rather than this bibliography. Instead, simple lists of periodicals and websites are included below.

PRIMARY SOURCES

Official Records

United Kingdom

Charity Commission
Crown Prosecution Service
Department for Work and Pensions
Department for Environment, Food and Rural Affairs
Department of Housing, Communities and Local Government
Hansard Parliamentary records
Home Office
House of Commons, Home Affairs Committee
House of Commons, Early Day Motions
Metropolitan Police Authority
Office for National Statistics
Prime Minister's Office

BIBLIOGRAPHY

India

Consulate General of India, New York
Delhi High Court
Directorate of Advertising and Publicity
Election Commission of India
Embassy of India, Washington DC
Government of India Press
High Commission of India, London
High Commission of India, Nairobi
National Archives of India
Nehru Memorial Museum and Library
Ministry of External Affairs
Ministry of Home Affairs
Prime Minister's Office

Other

Asia Art Archive
Embassy of the United States, New Delhi
United States Commission on International Religious Freedom Commissioner
United States Department of State
United States House of Representatives, Subcommittee on International Organizations of the Committee on International Relations
White House Briefing Room
World Bank Group

Other published primary sources

Aadeesh, Aanand (ed.), *Shree Gurujee and his RSS*, New Delhi: M.D. Publications, 2007.
Advani, L.K., *A Prisoner's Scrapbook*, New Delhi: Arnold-Heinemann, 1978.
———, *The People Betrayed*, New Delhi: Vision Books, 1979.
———, *My Country My Life*, New Delhi: Rupa, 2008.
Ambedkar, J., 'Vibrant Hindu Youth', in *Bradford Centenary Hindu Marathon*, Bradford: Hindu Marathon National Committee, 1997, pp. 51–2.
Bajpai, Suresh Chandra, *RSS at a Glance*, New Delhi: Suruchi Prakashan, 2011.

BIBLIOGRAPHY

Bhishikar, C.P., *Shri Guruji: Pioneer of a New Era*, Bangalore: Sahitya Sindhu Prakashana, 1999.

Chitkara, M.G., *Rashtriya Swayamsevak Sangh: National Upsurge*, New Delhi: S.B. Nangia, 2004.

Constitution of the Rashtriya Swayamsevak Sangh. Translated and reproduced in D.R. Goyal, *Rashtriya Swayamsevak Sangh*, New Delhi: Radakrishna Prakashan, 2000, pp.256–68.

Desai, Makarand, 'Introduction', in Makarand Desai (ed.), *Smugglers of Truth*, Vadodara: Friends of Society India Society International, 1978, n.p.

Deshpande, B.V. and S.R. Ramaswamy, *Dr Hedgewar the Epoch-Maker*, Bangalore: Sahitya Sindhu, 1981.

Deoras, Balasaheb, 'Message to the Virat Hindu Sammelan at Milton Keynes, UK', in H.V. Seshadri, *Hindus Abroad: Dilemma – Dollar or Dharma?*, New Delhi: Suruchi Prakshan, 1990, p.13.

Dhooria, Ram Lall, *I Was a Swayamsevak (An Inside View of the RSS)*, New Delhi: Sampradayikta Virodhi Committee, 1969.

Elenjimittam, Anthony, *Philosophy and Action of the RSS for the Hind Swaraj*, Bombay: Laxmi Publications, 1951.

EPG Economic and Strategy Consulting and the Hindu Forum of Britain, *Social Impact Analysis for Sewa Day on 7 October 2012*, EPG Economic and Strategy Consulting, 2013.

———, *Social Impact Analysis for Sewa Day on 6 October 2013*, EPG Economic and Strategy Consulting, 2014.

Godbole, Vasudev, 'Indian Institute for Research into True History Newsletter', no.11, 16 October 1983.

Hindu Forum of Britain, 'Annual Report', 2005.

———, *Diwali at Westminster 2011*, Hindu Forum of Britain, 2011.

———, *Diwali at Westminster 2013*, Hindu Forum of Britain, 2013.

———, *Social Impact Analysis for Activities in 2011*, Hindu Forum of Britain, 2013.

———, *Caste in the UK: A summary of the consultation with the Hindu community in Britain*, Hindu Forum of Britain, 2008.

Kansal, Hari Babu, 'Vishwa Hindu Parishad Abroad', *Hindu Vishwa*, silver jubilee issue 1989–90, p.94, English edition. Online: https://groups.yahoo.com/neo/groups/quranohadees/conversations/topics/72. Accessed on 27 September 2015.

Kumar, Ravi, *Ramayana: Around the World – A Living Legend*, Mumbai: Shri Vinayak G. Kale, 2008.

Kumar, Vijay, *Aao Khelen Khel*, Lucknow: Lokhit Prakashan, 2010.

BIBLIOGRAPHY

Kunte, Sharad (ed.), *Vishwa Sangh Shibir 2010 Souvenir*, Pune: Vishwa Adhyayan Kendra, 2010.

Kunte, Sharad, 'Vishwa Sangha Shibir: An Overview', in Sharad Kunte (ed.), *Vishwa Sangh Shibir 2010 Souvenir*, Pune: Vishwa Adhyayan Kendra, 2010, pp.5–9.

Golwalkar, M.S., *We, Our Nationhood Defined*, Nagpur: Bharat Prakashan, 1947.

———, *Bunch of Thoughts*, Bangalore: Sahitya Sindhu Prakashana, 1996.

———, *Samadhan (Press Meets and Statements of Shri Guruji)*, New Delhi: Suruchi Prakashan, 2000.

———, *Nityaprerana*, Pune: Bharatiya Vichar Sadhana Pune Prakahshan, 2011.

Hindu Swayamsevak Sangh UK, 'Guidelines for Vistaraks' (Vistarak Yojna), n.d.

Hindu Swayamsevak Sangh Canada, 'Hindu Swayamsevak Sangh: A Journey. Global Presence, Growth and Origins': www.hsscanada.org/downloads/presentations/rss_history_short.ppt. Accessed on 26 February 2015.

Malkani, K.R., *The RSS Story*, New Delhi: Impex India, 1980.

Modi, Narendra, *Apatkal Mein Gujarat*, Delhi: Narula Prints, 2001.

Nanda, Ved, 'Overview of HSS Work in 2011', 18 October 2011: https://xa.yimg.com/kq/groups/20147388/1173079528/name/GD. Accessed on 24 September 2015.

Nardev Vedalankar, Pandit and Manohar Somera, *Arya Samaj and Indians Abroad*, New Delhi: Sarvadeshik Arya Pratinidhi Sabha, 1975.

No author, *The Pen in Revolt: Underground Literature Published During the Emergency*, New Delhi: Press Institute of India, 1978.

No author, *RSS: Spearheading National Renaissance*, Bangalore: Prakashan Vibhag, 1985.

No author, 'Vishwa Sangh Shibir 1995 at Kayavarohan, Vadodara, Gujarat, Press Release', posted on 'soc.culture.indian.marathi' website by Gaurang Desai of the Hindu Swayamevak Sangh (USA) on 17 January, 1996: https://groups.google.com/forum/#!topic/soc.culture.indian.marathi/xLAqc6rX0nU. Accessed on 14 September 2015.

No author, *National Movements and the RSS*, New Delhi: Suruchi Prakashan, 2000.

No author, *Vishwa Sangh Shibir 2005 Souvenir*, Karnavati: Antar Rashtriya Sahayog Pratishthan, 2005.

No author, *RSS Resolves: 1950–2007*, New Delhi: Suruchi Prakashan, 2007.

No author, *Khel Book*, Hindu Swayamsevak Sangh (UK), n.d.
Organiser (various issues).
Paliwal, K.V., *India Heading Towards an Islamic State: A Warning!*, New Delhi: Hindu Writers' Forum, n.d.
Parmanand, Bhai, *The Story of My Life*, Delhi: S. Chand, 1982.
Rashtriya Swayamsevak Sangh, *Keshav Baliram Hedgewar: The Master Man-Maker*, 1986.
―――, *Vishwa Sangh Shibir-'90 Souvenir*, Antara Rashtriya Sahayoga Parishad, Bangalore Chapter, 1991.
―――, *Widening Horizons*, New Delhi: Suruchi Prakashan, 1992.
―――, 'Annual Report submitted by RSS General Secretary Bhaiyyaji Joshi at ABPS-2012', 16 March 2012.
Rashtriya Sewa Samvardhan Samiti, *Sewa Darpan: Sewa Samarchar*, no.8, April–July 2010.
Rawat, Atul, 'A Rainbow Across the Horizon', in Aadeesh, Aanand (ed.), *Shree Gurujee and his RSS*, New Delhi: M.D. Publications, 2007.
Runnymede Trust, *Connecting British Hindus: An Inquiry into the Identity and Public Engagement of Hindus in Britain*, Commissioned by the Hindu Forum of Britain; sponsored by the Cohesion and Faiths Unit of the Department for Communities and Local Government, 2006.
Sangh Sandesh (various issues).
Sahasrabuddhe, P.G. and Vajpayee, Manik Chandra, *The People versus Emergency: A Saga of Struggle*, trans. Sudhakar Raje, New Delhi: Suruchi Prakashan, 1991.
Savarkar, V.D., *Hindutva: Who is a Hindu?*, Mumbai: Swatantrayaveer Savarkar Rashtriya Smarak, 1999.
Sharad Kunte, 'Shri Laxmanrao Bhide – Architect of International Sangh work', in Sharad Kunte (ed.) *Vishwa Sangh Shibir 2010 Souvenir*, Pune: Vishwa Adhyayan Kendra, 2010, p.198.
Shankarrao Tatwadi, 'Vishwa Vibhag – A leap beyond the shores', in Sharad Kunte (ed.), *Vishwa Sangh Shibir 2010 Souvenir*, Pune: Vishwa Adhyayan Kendra, 2010, pp.201–3.
Swami Tilak, 'Future Trends in the Lives of Hindus Around the World', in H.V. Seshadri, *Hindus Abroad: Dilemma – Dollar or Dharma?*, New Delhi: Suruchi Prakshan, 1990, pp.15–16.
Sudarshan, K.S., *Hindutva in Modern Perspective*, Nagpur: Shri Bharati Prakashan, 2007.
Shah, M., 'Indian, British or Both?', in *Bradford Centenary Hindu Marathon*, Bradford: Hindu Marathon National Committee, 1997, p.103.

Shastri, Jagdish Chandra Sharda, (compiled and edited by Ratan Sharda), *Memoirs of a Global Hindu*, Mumbai: Vishwa Adhyayan Kendra, 2008.
Seshadri, H.V., *Hindu Renaissance Under Way*, Bangalore: Jagarana Prakashana, 1984.
———, *Hindus Abroad: Dilemma: Dollar or Dharma?*, New Delhi: Suruchi Prakashan, 1990.
———, *RSS – A Vision in Action*, Bangalore: Sahitya Sindhu Prakashana, 2001.
———, *Shri Guruji*, New Delhi: Suruchi Prakashan, 2006.
Sinha, Rakesh, 'A Tribute to Ma. Chamanlaji: State-Centric Life and Nation-Builders', in Sharad Kunte (ed.) *Vishwa Sangh Shibir 2010 Souvenir*, Pune: Vishwa Adhyayan Kendra, 2010, pp.199–200.
Subrahmanyam, M.C., 'Overseas Indians' Fight for Restoration of Democracy', *The Indian Review*, vol.73, no.3, 1977, pp.60–5.
Swamy, Subramanian, *Hindus Under Siege – The Way Out*, New Delhi: Har-Anand Publications, 2006.
Tattwawadi, Shankar (ed.), *Sarsanghchalak Goes Abroad: A Collection of Lectures Delivered by Prof. Rajendra Singh on Foreign Land*, New Delhi: Suruchi Prakashan, 1995.
Venkata Rao, M.A., 'Introduction', in M.S. Golwalkar, *Bunch of Thoughts*, Bangalore: Sahitya Sindhu Prakashan, 1996, pp.x–xix.
Vishwa Hindu Parishad, *Facts and Our Duty*, Bombay, n.d.
Vishwa Hindu Parishad (UK), *Explaining Hindu Dharma: A Guide for Teachers*, Norwich: Chansitor Religious and Moral Education Press, 1996.

Documents submitted to the Charity Commission

Annual Reports, Financial Statements, and Trust Deeds (2000–14) of:
Hindu Swayamsevak Sangh
Kalyan Ashram Trust
Sewa Day UK
Sewa International UK
Vishwa Hindu Parishad UK

Websites (selected)

Archivesofrss.org
Cityhindusnetwork.org.uk
Eshakha.pbworks.com
Hcb.org.uk
Hfb.org.uk

Hinduexistence.org
Hinduhumanrights.info
HinduismToday.com
Hindujagruti.org
Hindunet.org
hssmru.org
Hssstories.wordpress.com
HssUK.org
Hssuk-sip.blogspot.com
HssUS.org
Hvk.org
Nhsf.org.uk
Rashtriyasewa.org
Rss.org
Sabrang.com
Sacw.net
Samvada.org
Sewaday.org
VakMumbai.org
Vhp.org.uk

SECONDARY SOURCES

Newspapers, magazines, and other news services

Asian Age
Asian Voice
BBC News
Business Standard
Byline Times
The Caravan
The Conversation
Daily Pioneer
The Economist
Evening Standard
Financial Express
Financial Times
Foreign Policy
Frontline
The Guardian

The Hindu
Hinduism Today
Hindustan Times
India Herald
India Today
Indian Express
The Independent
Indo-American News
Lakeland Ledger
Leicester Mercury
Live Mint
MailOnline
Manchester Evening News
Metro
New Statesman
New York Times
Outlook
Reuters
Seminar
Sunday Mercury
Tehelka
The Telegraph
Time
The Times
Times of India
Wall Street Journal
Washington Post
Vice

Published books and articles

Ali, N., V.S. Kalra, and S. Sayyid (eds.), *A Postcolonial People: South Asians in Britain*, New York: Columbia University Press, 2008.

Amrith, Sunil, *Migration and Diaspora in Modern Asia*, Cambridge: Cambridge University Press, 2011.

Anand, Dibyesh, *Hindu Nationalism in India and the Politics of Fear*, New York: Palgrave Macmillan, 2011.

Andersen, Walter and Shridhar Damle, *The Brotherhood in Saffron: The Rashtriya Swayamsevak Sangh and Hindu Revivalism*, New Delhi: Vistaar, 1987.

BIBLIOGRAPHY

———, 'RSS Ideology, Organization, and Training', in Christophe Jaffrelot (ed.), *The Sangh Parivar: A Reader*, New Delhi: Oxford University Press, 2005, pp. 23–55.

———, *The RSS: A View to the Inside,* Gurgaon: Penguin Random House, 2018.

Anderson, Benedict, 'Exodus', *Critical Enquiry*, vol. 20, no. 2, (1994), pp. 314–27.

———, *Imagined Communities: Reflections on the Origin and Spread of Nationalism*, London: Verso, 2006.

Anderson, Edward, '"Neo-Hindutva": the Asia House M. F. Husain campaign and the mainstreaming of Hindu nationalist rhetoric in Britain', *Contemporary South Asia*, vol. 23, no. 1 (2015), pp. 45–66.

Anderson, Edward and Arkotong Longkumer (eds.) *Neo-Hindutva: Evolving Forms, Spaces, and Expressions of Hindu Nationalism*, Abingdon: Routledge, 2020.

Anderson, Edward and Christophe Jaffrelot, 'Hindu Nationalism and the "Saffronisation of the Public Sphere": an Interview with Christophe Jaffrelot', *Contemporary South Asia*, vol. 26, no. 4 (2018), pp. 468–82.

Anderson, Edward and Patrick Clibbens, '"Smugglers of Truth": the Indian diaspora, Hindu nationalism, and the Emergency (1975–77)', *Modern Asian Studies*, vol. 52, no. 1 (2018), pp. 1729–73.

Appa, Gautam and Anish Vanaik (eds.), *Narendra Modi Exposed: Challenging the Myths Surrounding the BJP's Prime Ministerial Candidate*, London: AWAAZ Network/The Monitoring Group, 2014.

Appadurai, Arjun, 'Global Ethnoscapes: Notes and Queries for a Transnational Anthropology', in Richard Fox (ed.), *Recapturing Anthropology* (Santa Fe, NM: School of American Research Press, 1991), pp. 191–210.

———, *Modernity at Large: Cultural Dimensions of Globalization*, London: University of Minnesota Press, 1996.

———, *Fear of Small Numbers: An Essay on the Geography of Small Numbers*, London: Duke University Press, 2006.

AWAAZ – South Asia Watch Limited, 'In Bad Faith? British Charity and Hindu Extremism', London: AWAAZ – South Asia Watch Limited, 2004.

Bacchetta, Paola and Margaret Power (eds.), *Right Wing Women: From Conservatives to Extremists Around the World*, London: Routledge, 2002.

Ballard, Roger (ed.), *Desh Pardesh: The South Asian Presence in Britain*, London: Hurst, 1994.

BIBLIOGRAPHY

Basch, Linda, Nina Glick Schiller, and Christina Szanton Blanc, *Nations Unbound: Transnational Projects, Postcolonial Predicaments and Deterritorialized Nation-States*, Basel, Switzerland: Gordon and Breach, 2002.

Basu, Tapan, Pradip Datta, Sumit Sarkar, Tanika Sarkar, and Sambuddha Sen, *Khaki Shorts and Saffron Flags*, New Delhi: Orient Longman, 1993.

Beckerlegge, Gwilym (ed.), *From Sacred Text to Internet*, Aldershot: Ashgate, 2001,

Bhabha, Homi, *The Location of Culture*, London: Routledge, 1994.

Bharati, Agehananda, 'Ritualistic Tolerance and Ideological Rigour: The Paradigm of the Expatriate Hindus in East Africa', *Contributions to Indian Sociology*, vol.10, no.2 (1976), pp.317–39.

Bhatia, Sunil, *American Karma: Race, Culture, and Identity in the Indian Diaspora*, New York: New York University Press, 2007.

Bhatt, Chetan, *Liberation and Purity: Race, New Religious Movements and the Ethics of Postmodernity*, London: University College London Press, 1997

———, '*Dharmo Rakshati Rakshitah*: Hindutva Movements in the UK', *Ethnic and Racial Studies*, vol.23, no.3 (2000), pp.569–93.

———, *Hindu Nationalism: Origins, Ideologies and Modern Myths*, Oxford: Berg, 2001.

Bhatt, Chetan and Parita Mukta, 'Hindutva in the West: Mapping the Antinomies of Diaspora Nationalism', *Ethnic and Racial Studies*, vol.23, no.3 (2000), pp.407–41.

Blom, Amélie and Nicolas Jaoul, 'Introduction. The Moral and Affectual Dimension of Collective Action in South Asia', *South Asia Multidisciplinary Academic Journal*, vol.2 (2008).

Bose, Sugata, *The Nation as Mother and Other Visions of Nationhood*, Gurgaon: Penguin, 2017.

Brah, Avtar, *Cartographies of Diaspora: Contesting Identities*, London: Routledge, 1996.

Brosius, Christiane, *Empowering Visions: The Politics of Representation in Hindu Nationalism*, London: Anthem Press, 2005.

Burlet, Stacey, 'Re-awakenings? Hindu Nationalism Goes Global', in Roy Starrs (ed.), *Asian Nationalism in an Age of Globalisation*, Richmond: Curzon Press, 2001, pp.1–18.

Burlet, Stacey and Helen Reid, 'Cooperation and Conflict: The South Asian Diaspora after Ayodhya', *Journal of Ethnic and Migration Studies/ New Community*, vol.21, no.4 (1995), pp.587–9.

BIBLIOGRAPHY

Casolari, Marzia, 'Hindutva's Foreign Tie-Up in the 1930s: Archival Evidence', *Economic and Political Weekly*, vol.35, no.4 (2000), pp.218–28.

Chakravorty, Sanjoy, Devesh Kapur, and Nirvikar Singh, *The Other One Percent: Indians in America*, New York: Oxford University Press, 2017.

Chandra, Bipan, *Communalism in Modern India: A Historiographical Overview*, New Delhi: Vikas, 1984.

Chatterjee, Partha, 'History and the Nationalization of Hinduism', *Social Research*, vol.59, no.1 (1992), pp.111–49.

Chatterji, Joya, 'Dispositions and Destinations: Refugee Agency and "Mobility Capital" in the Bengal Diaspora, 1947–2007', *Comparative Studies in Society and History*, vol.55, no.2 (2013), pp.273–304.

Chatterji, Joya and David Washbrook (eds.), *Routledge Handbook of the South Asian Diaspora*, Abingdon: Routledge, 2013.

Chaudhuri, Rudra, 'Re-reading the Indian Emergency: Britain, the United States and India's Constitutional Autocracy, 1975–1977', *Diplomacy & Statecraft*, vol.29, no.3 (2018), pp.477–98.

Chopra, Rohit, *Technology and Nationalism in India: Cultural Negotiations from Colonialism to Cyberspace*, Amherst, NY: Cambria Press, 2008.

———, *The Virtual Hindu Rashtra: Saffron Nationalism and New Media*, Noida: Harper Collins, 2019.

Christou, Anastasia and Elizabeth Mavroudi (eds.), *Dismantling Diasporas: Rethinking the Geographies of Diasporic Identity, Connection and Development*, Abingdon: Routledge, 2016.

Clarke, Colin, Ceri Peach, and Steven Vertovec (eds.), *South Asians Overseas*, Cambridge: Cambridge University Press, 1990.

Copeman, Jacob and Aya Ikegame (eds.), *The Guru in South Asia: New Interdisciplinary Perspectives*, London: Routledge, 2012.

Copley, Antony (ed.), *Hinduism in Public and Private: Reform, Hindutva, Gender and Sampraday*, New Delhi: Oxford University Press, 2003.

Coward, H.J. Hinnells and R.B. Williams (eds.), *The South Asian Religious Diaspora in Britain, Canada, and the United States*, Albany, NY: State University of New York Press, 2000.

Das, Veena, *Critical Events: An Anthropological Perspective on Contemporary India*, New Delhi: Oxford University Press, 1995.

Doniger, Wendy and Martha Nussbaum (eds.), *Pluralism and Democracy in India: Debating the Hindu Right*, New York: Oxford University Press, 2014.

Essa, Azad, *Hostile Homelands: The New Alliance Between India and Israel*, London: Pluto, 2023.

Falcone, Jessica Marie, '"I spy...": The (Im)possibilities of Ethical Participant Observation with Antagonists, Religious Extremists, and Other Tough Nuts', *Michigan Discussions in Anthropology*, vol.18 (2010), pp.243–82.

———, 'Putting the "Fun" in Fundamentalism: Religious Nationalism and the Split Self at Hindutva Summer Camps in the United States', *ETHOS – Journal for the Society for Psychological Anthropology*, vol.40, no.2, (2012), pp.164–95.

Foucault, Michel, 'Des Espaces Autres. Hétérotopies', *Architecture, Mouvement, Continuité*, vol.5 (1984), pp.46–9.

Freitag, Sandria B., 'Sacred Symbol as Mobilizing Ideology: The North Indian Search for a "Hindu" community', *Comparative Studies in Society and History*, vol.22, no.4 (1980), pp.597–625.

Froerer, Peggy, 'Disciplining the Saffron Way: Moral Education and the Hindu Rashtra', *Modern Asian Studies*, vol.41, no.5 (2007), pp.1033–71.

Fuller, Christopher, *The Camphor Flame: Popular Hinduism and Society in India*, Princeton, NJ: Princeton University Press, 2004.

Ghose, Rajeshwari (ed.), *In Quest of a Secular Symbol: Ayodhya and After*, Perth, Australia: Indian Ocean Centre & South Asian Research Unit, Curtin University of Technology Press, 1996.

Ghosh, Anindita, *Power in Print: Popular Publishing and the Politics of Language and Culture in a Colonial Society*, New Delhi: Oxford University Press, 2006.

Ghosh, Papiya, *Partition and the South Asian Diaspora: Extending the Subcontinent*, Abingdon: Routledge, 2007.

Gittinger, Juli L., *Hinduism and Hindu Nationalism Online*, Abingdon: Routledge, 2018.

Gould, William, *Hindu Nationalism and the Language of Politics in Late Colonial India*, Cambridge: Cambridge University Press, 2004.

Goyal, D.R., *Rashtriya Swayamsevak Sangh*, New Delhi: Radhakrishna Prakasan, 2000.

Graham, Bruce, *Hindu Nationalism and Indian Politics: The Origins and Development of the Bharatiya Jana Sangh*, Cambridge: Cambridge University Press, 1990.

Guha, Ramachandra, *India after Gandhi: The History of the World's Largest Democracy*, New Delhi: Picador, 2007.

Gupta, Monisha Das, *Unruly Immigrants*, Durham, NC: Duke University Press, 2005.

BIBLIOGRAPHY

Hall, Stuart, 'Cultural Identity and Diaspora', in Jonathan Rutherford (ed.), *Identity, Community, Culture, Difference*, London: Lawrence and Wishart, 1990, pp. 222–37.

Hansen, Thomas Blom, *The Saffron Wave: Democracy and Hindu Nationalism in Modern India*, Chichester: Princeton University Press, 1999.

Harper, Tim, and Sunil Amrith (eds.), *Sites of Asian Interaction: Ideas, Networks and Mobility*, Cambridge: Cambridge University Press, 2014.

Hobsbawm, Eric and Terence Ranger (eds.), *The Invention of Tradition*, Cambridge: Cambridge University Press, 1983, pp. 1–14.

Jaffrelot, Christophe, 'Hindu Nationalism: Strategic Syncretism in Ideology Building', *Economic and Political Weekly*, vol. 28, no. 12/13 (1993), pp. 517–24.

———, *The Hindu Nationalist Movement and Indian Politics*, London: Hurst, 1996.

———, 'Hindu Nationalism and the (Not So Easy) Art of Being Outraged: The Ram Setu Controversy', *South Asia Multidisciplinary Academic Journal*, vol. 2 (2008).

———, 'The Hindu nationalist reinterpretation of pilgrimage in India: the limits of *Yatra* politics', *Nations and Nationalism*, vol. 15, no. 1 (2009), pp. 1–19.

———, *Modi's India: Hindu Nationalism and the Rise of Ethnic Democracy*, Princeton, NJ: Princeton University Press, 2021.

———, *Religion, Caste, and Politics in India*, New Delhi: Primus Books, 2010.

Jaffrelot, Christophe (ed.), *The Sangh Parivar: A Reader*, Princeton, NJ: Princeton University Press, 2007.

—, *Hindu Nationalism: A Reader*, Delhi: Permanent Black, 2007.

Jaffrelot, Christophe and Ingrid Therwath, 'Hindu Nationalism in the United Kingdom and North America', in, Deana Heath, and Chandana Mathur (eds.), *Communalism and Globalization in South Asia and its Diaspora*, Abingdon: Routledge, 2011, pp. 44–57.

———, 'The Sangh Parivar and the Hindu Diaspora in the West: What Kind of "Long Distance Nationalism"?', *International Political Sociology*, vol. 1, (2007), pp. 278–95.

———, 'The Global Sangh Parivar: A Study of Contemporary International Hinduism', in Abigail Green and Vincent Viaene (eds.), *Religious Internationals in the Modern World*, London: Palgrave Macmillan, 2012, pp. 343–64.

Jaffrelot, Christophe and Pratinav Anil, *India's First Dictatorship: The Emergency, 1975–77*, London: Hurst, 2020.

Jeffrey, Patricia and Roger Jeffrey, *Confronting Saffron Demography: Religion, Fertility, and Women's Status in India*, New Delhi: Three Essays Collective, 2006.

Kalra, Virinder, Raminder Kaur, and John Hutnyk, *Diaspora and Hybridity*, London: Sage, 2006.

Kanungo, Pralay, *RSS's Tryst with Politics. From Hedgewar to Sudarshan*, Delhi: Manohar, 2003.

Kapur, Devesh, *Diaspora, Development, and Democracy: The Domestic Impact of International Migration from India*, Princeton, NJ: Princeton University Press, 2010.

Katju, Manjari, *Vishwa Hindu Parishad and Indian Politics*, Hyderabad: Orient Longman, 2010.

———, *Hinduising Democracy: The Vishva Hindu Parishad in Contemporary India*, New Delhi: New Text, 2017.

Kaul, Nitasha and Annapurna Menon, 'Hindutva in Western Societies: Entanglements and Paradoxes', in Ruben Gowricharn (ed.), *New Perspectives on the Indian Diaspora*, Abingdon: Routledge, 2022, pp. 160–84.

Kaur, Raminder, *Performative Politics and the Cultures of Hinduism: Public Uses of Religion in Western India*, London: Anthem Press, 2005.

Kelkar, Sanjeev, *Lost Years of the RSS*, New Delhi: Sage, 2011.

Kinnvall, Catarina, *Globalization and Religious Nationalism in India*, London: Routledge, 2006.

Kundu, Apurba, 'The Ayodhya Aftermath: Hindu versus Muslim Violence in Britain', *Immigrants and Minorities*, vol. 13, no. 1 (1994), pp. 26–47.

Kurien, Prema, 'Multiculturalism, Immigrant Religion, and Diasporic Nationalism: The Development of an American Hinduism', *Social Problems*, vol. 51, no. 3 (2004), pp. 362–85.

———, *A Place at the Multicultural Table: The Development of an American Hinduism*, New Brunswick, NJ: Rutgers University Press, 2007.

———, 'Who Speaks for Indian Americans? Religion, Ethnicity, and Political Formation', *American Quarterly*, vol. 59, no. 3 (2007), pp. 759–83.

Lal, Vinay, 'The Politics of History on the Internet: Cyber-Diasporic Hinduism and the North American Hindu Diaspora', *Diaspora*, vol. 8 (1999), pp. 137–72.

———, *The Other Indians: A Political and Cultural History of South Asians in America*, Los Angeles: University of California, Asian American Studies Center Press, 2008.

BIBLIOGRAPHY

Leidig, Eviane, 'Immigrant, Nationalist and Proud: A Twitter Analysis of Indian Diaspora Supporters for Brexit and Trump', *Media and Communication*, vol.7, no.1 (2019), pp.77–89.

———, 'Hindutva as a Variant of Right-Wing Extremism', *Patterns of Prejudice*, vol.54, no.3 (2020), pp.215–37.

Levitt, Peggy, *The Transnational Villagers*, London: University of California Press, 2001.

———, 'Religion as a Path to Civic Engagement', *Ethnic and Racial Studies*, vol.31, no.4 (2008), pp.766–91.

Levitt, Peggy and Mary Waters (eds.), *The Changing Face of Home: The Transnational Lives of the Second Generation*, New York: Russell Sage Foundation, 2002.

Ludden, David (ed.), *Contesting the Nation: Religion, Community and the Politics of Democracy in India*, Philadelphia, PA: University of Pennsylvania Press, 1996.

Macher, Jasa, *Hindu Nationalist Influence in the United States, 2014–2021* (released via sacw.net, 2022).

Mathew, Biju and Vijay Prashad, 'The Protean Forms of Yankee Hindutva', *Ethnic and Racial Studies*, vol.23, no.3 (2000), pp.516–34.

Mathur, Shubh, *The Everyday Life of Hindu Nationalism: An Ethnographic Account*, New Delhi: Three Essays Collective, 2008.

McGuire, J., P. Reeves and H. Brasted (eds.), *Politics of Violence: from Ayodhya to Behrampada*, New Delhi: Sage, 1996.

McKean, Lise, *Divine Enterprise: Gurus and the Hindu Nationalist Movement*, London: University of Chicago Press, 1996.

Menon, Kalyani Devaki, *Everyday Nationalism: Women of the Hindu Right in India*, Philadelphia, PA: University of Pennsylvania Press, 2009.

Mishra, Sangay K., *Desis Divided: The Political Lives of South Asian Americans*, Minneapolis, MN: University of Minnesota Press, 2016.

———, 'Hindu nationalism and Indian American diasporic mobilizations', in Ruben Gowricharn (ed.), *New Perspectives on the Indian Diaspora*, Abingdon: Routledge, 2022.

Modood, Tariq, 'Political Blackness and British Asians', *Sociology*, vol.28, no.4 (1994), pp.859–76.

Modood, Tariq and Pnina Werbner (eds.), *The Politics of Multiculturalism in Europe: Racism, Identity and Community*, London: Zed, 1997.

Mukherjee, Sumita, *Nationalism, Education and Migrant Identities: The England Returned*, Abingdon: Routledge, 2009.

Mukta, Parita, 'The Public Face of Hindu Nationalism', *Ethnic and Racial Studies*, vol.23, no.3, (2000), pp.442–66.

Nair, Neeti, *Hurt Sentiments: Secularism and Belonging in South Asia*, Cambridge, MA: Harvard University Press, 2023.

Nanda, Meera, *Prophets Facing Backward: Postmodern Critiques of Science and the Hindu Nationalism in India*, New Brunswick, NJ: Rutgers University Press, 2004.

———, *The God Market*, New Delhi: Random House, 2009.

Noorani, A.G., *The RSS: A Menace to India*, New Delhi: LeftWord Books, 2019.

Nussbaum, Martha, *The Clash Within: Democracy, Religious Violence, and India's Future*, London: Harvard University Press, 2007.

Oonk, Gijsbert, *Settled Strangers: Asian Business Elites in East Africa (1800–2000)*, New Delhi: Sage, 2013.

Oonk, Gijsbert (ed.), *Global Indian Diasporas: Exploring Trajectories of Migration and Theory*, Amsterdam: International Institute of Asian Studies/Amsterdam University Press, 2007.

Pandey, Gyanendra (ed.), *Hindus and Others: The Question of Identity Today*, New Delhi: Viking, 1993.

Panikkar, K.N., *Communalism in India: History, Politics, and Culture*, New Delhi: Manohar, 1991.

———, 'Religious Symbols and Political Mobilisation: Agitation for a Mandir at Ayodhya', *Social Scientist*, vol.21, no.7/8 (1993), pp.63–78.

Parekh, Bhikhu, 'Some Reflections on the Hindu Diaspora', *New Community*, vol.20, no.4, (1994), pp. 603–20.

Parekh, Bhikhu, Gurharpal Singh, and Steven Vertovec (eds.), *Culture and Economy in the Indian Diaspora*, London: Routledge, 2002.

Patel, Ian Sanjay, *We're Here Because You Were There: Immigration and the End of Empire*, London: Verso, 2021.

Patel, Pragna, 'Rama or Rambo? The Rise of Hindu Fundamentalism', in Rahila Gupta (ed.), *From Homebreakers to Jailbreakers: Southall Black Sisters*, London: Zed Books, 2003, pp.212–33.

Prashad, Vijay, *The Karma of Brown Folk*, Minneapolis, MN: University of Minnesota Press, 2001.

———, *Uncle Swami: South Asians in America Today*, Noida: Harper Collins, 2013.

Raj, Dhooleka Sarhadi, 'Who the hell do you think you are?' Promoting Religious Identity among Young Hindus in Britain', *Ethnic and Racial Studies*, vol.23, no.3 (2000), pp.535–58.

———, *Where are you from? Middle Class Migrants in the Modern World*, Berkeley, CA: University of California Press, 2003.

Rajagopal, Arvind, 'Transnational Networks and Hindu Nationalism', *Bulletin of Concerned Asian Scholars*, vol.29, no.3 (1997), pp.45–58.

———, 'Hindu Nationalism in the US: Changing Configurations of Political Practice', *Ethnic and Racial Studies*, vol.23 (2000), pp.463–70.

———, *Politics After Television: Hindu Nationalism and the Reshaping of the Public in India*, Cambridge: Cambridge University Press, 2001.

Ramamurthy, Anandi, *Black Star: Britain's Asian Youth Movements*, London: Pluto Press, 2013.

Ramaswamy, Sumathi (ed.), *Barefoot Across the Nation: M.F. Husain and the Idea of India*, London: Routledge, 2011.

Rayaprol, A., *Negotiating Identities: Women in the Indian Diaspora*, Delhi: Oxford University Press, 1997.

Reddy, Deepa, 'Hindutva as Praxis', *Religion Compass*, vol.5, no.8 (2011), pp.412–26.

Reddy, Deepa and John Zavos, 'Temple Publics: Religious Institutions and the Construction of Contemporary Hindu Communities', *International Journal of Hindu Studies*, vol.13, no.3 (2009), pp.241–60.

Sabrang Communications and the South Asia Citizens Web, 'The Foreign Exchange of Hate – IDRF and the American Funding of Hindutva', 2002.

Safran, William, 'Diasporas in Modern Societies: Myths of Homeland and Return', *Diaspora: A Journal of Transnational Studies*, vol.1, no.1 (1991), pp.83–99.

Sahgal, Gita and Nira Yuval-Davis (eds.), *Refusing Holy Orders: Women and Fundamentalism in Britain*, London: Virago Press, 1992.

Sarkar, Tanika and Amrita Basu (eds.) *Women, Gender and Religious Nationalism*, Cambridge: Cambridge University Press, 2022.

Sarkar, Tanika and Urvashi Butalia (eds.), *Women and the Hindu Right: a collection of essays*, Delhi: Kali for Women, 1995.

Sen, Amartya, *The Argumentative India: Writings on Indian Culture, History and Identity*, London: Penguin, 2005.

Sen, Atreyee, *Shiv Sena Women: Violence and Communalism in a Bombay Slum*, New Delhi: Zubaan, 2008.

Shani, Ornit, *Communalism, Caste and Hindu Nationalism: The Violence in Gujarat*, Cambridge: Cambridge University Press, 2007.

Sharma, Jyotirmaya, *Hindutva: Exploring the Idea of Hindu Nationalism*, New Delhi: Penguin-Viking, 2003.

Simpson, Edward, *The Political Biography of an Earthquake: Aftermath and Amnesia in Gujarat, India*, London: Hurst, 2013.

BIBLIOGRAPHY

Sivanandan, A., 'RAT and the Degradation of Black Struggle', *Race & Class*, vol.26, no.4 (1985), pp.1–33.

Sud, Nikita, *Liberalization, Hindu Nationalism and the State: A Biography of Gujarat*, Oxford: Oxford University Press, 2012.

Sutton, Deborah, '"So called caste": S.N. Balagangadhara, the Ghent School and the Politics of Grievance', *Contemporary South Asia*, vol.26, no.3 (2018), pp.336–49.

Taylor, Charles, 'The Politics of Recognition', in Amy Gutmann (ed.), *Multiculturalism and the Politics of Recognition*, Princeton, NJ: Princeton University Press, 1992, pp.25–73.

Thapar, Romila, 'Imagined Religious Communities? Ancient History and the Modern Search for a Hindu Identity', *Modern Asian Studies*, vol.23, no.2 (1989), pp.209–31.

———, 'On Historical Scholarship and the Uses of the Past (interview with Parita Mukta)', *Ethnic and Racial Studies*, vol.23, no.3 (2000), pp.594–616.

———, *The Past as Present: Forging Contemporary Identities Through History*, New Delhi: Aleph, 2014.

The Campaign to Stop Funding Hate, 'Unmistakably Sangh: The National HSC and its Hindutva Agenda', South Asia Citizens Web (www.sacw.net), 2008.

Therwath, Ingrid, '"Far and Wide": The Sangh Parivar's Global Network', in Christophe Jaffrelot (ed.), *The Sangh Parivar: A Reader*, New Delhi: Oxford University Press, 2005, pp.411–28.

———, 'Cyber-Hindutva: Hindu Nationalism, the Diaspora and the Web', *e-Diasporas Atlas*, Fondation Maison des Sciences de l'Homme (2012).

———, 'Working for India or Against Islam? Islamophobia in Indian American Lobbies', *South Asia Multidisciplinary Academic Journal*, vol.1 (2007).

Tripathi, Salil, *Offence: The Hindu Case*, London: Seagull Books, 2009.

Vanaik, Achin, *The Furies of Indian Communalism: Religion, Modernity and Secularization*, London: Verso, 1997.

Veer, Peter van der, *Nation and Migration*, Philadelphia, PA: University of Pennsylvania Press, 1995.

———, *Religious Nationalism: Hindus and Muslims in India*, Berkeley, CA: University of California Press, 1994.

Vertovec, Steven, *The Hindu Diaspora: Comparative Patterns*, London: Routledge, 2000.

———, *Transnationalism*, London: Routledge, 2009.

Warrier, Maya, 'The Temple Bull Controversy at Skanda Vale and the Construction of Hindu Identity in Britain', *International Journal of Hindu Studies*, vol.13, no.3 (2010), pp.261–78.

Waughray, Annapurna, 'Caste in Britain: Public Consultation on Caste and Equality Law', *Economic and Political Weekly*, vol.53, no.10 (10 March 2019).

Werbner, Pnina and Tariq Modood (eds.), *Debating Cultural Hybridity*, London: Zed Books, 1997.

Williams, Raymond Brady, *An Introduction to Swaminarayan Hinduism*, Cambridge: Cambridge University Press, 2001.

Wilson, Amrit, *Dreams, Questions, Struggles: South Asian Women in Britain*, London: Pluto Press, 2006.

Wilson, Kalpana, *Race, Racism and Development: Interrogating History, Discourse and Practice*, London: Zed Books, 2012.

Zavos, John, *The Emergence of Hindu Nationalism in India*, Delhi: Oxford University Press, 2000.

———, 'Diaspora Consciousness, Nationalism, and 'Religion': The Case of Hindu Nationalism', in Allon Gal, Athena Leoussi and Anthony Smith (eds.), *The Call of the Homeland: Diaspora Nationalisms, Past and Present*, Leiden: Brill, 2010, pp.323–43.

———, 'Digital Media and Networks of Hindu Activism', *Culture and Religion*, vol.16, no.1 (2015), pp.17–34.

———, 'Negotiating Multiculturalism: Religion and the Organisation of Hindu Identity in Contemporary Britain', *Journal of Ethnic and Migration Studies*, vol.35, no.6 (2009), pp.881–900.

———, 'Situating Hindu Nationalism in the UK: Vishwa Hindu Parishad and the Development of British Hindu Identity', *Commonwealth and Comparative Politics*, vol.48, no.1 (2010), pp.2–22.

———, 'Small acts, Big Society: Sewa and Hindu (Nationalist) Identity in Britain', *Ethnic and Racial Studies*, vol.38, no.2 (2015), pp.243–58.

———, 'Stamp It Out: Disciplining the Image of Hinduism in a Multicultural Milieu', *Contemporary South Asia*, vol.16, no.3 (2008), pp.323–37.

Zavos, John, Andrew Wyatt, and Vernon Hewitt (eds.), *The Politics of Cultural Mobilization in India*, New Delhi: Oxford University Press, 2004.

Zavos, John, Pralay Kanungo, Deepa Reddy, Maya Warrier, and Raymond Brady Williams (eds.), *Public Hinduisms*, New Delhi: Sage, 2012.

INDEX

Note: Page numbers followed by '*n*' refer to notes, '*t*' refer to tables.

7/7 terrorist attacks (London), 249, 288
post-7/7 landscape, 69, 253, 255, 278, 297

adivasis, 166
Advani, L.K., 160, 181, 330
    Ayodhya mobilisations, 168
    on Chamanlal, 31
    on the Emergency, 129, 142
    incarceration during the Emergency, 126
    Ram Rath Yatra, 169, 171, 172, 174
Akali Dal, 159
Akhil Bharatiya Karyakari Mandal, 161
Akhil Bharatiya Vidyarthi Parishad (ABVP), 144, 239
Albanese, Anthony, 325–6
Alexandra Palace conference (London, 24–5 Apr 1976), 136–7, 146
Alliance Against Communalism and for Democracy in South Asia, 193
Alliance Against Fascist Dictatorship in India, 158
Amar Deep (newspaper), 142
American Hindus Against Defamation (AHAD), 297
American Israel Public Affairs Committee (AIPAC), 297
American Jewish Committee, 298
Amin, Idi, 38, 361*n*71
Anderson, Benedict, 17, 75–6
    'long-distance nationalism', 17, 22, 26, 75–6, 111, 131, 161, 165, 211
Andhra Pradesh cyclone (1977), 212, 228
Anglo Asian Conservative Society, 315
'anti-Romeo' squads, 171, 290
anti-Semitism, 264
    See also Zionist-Hindutva dynamic
Apatkaleen Sangharsh Bulletin, 142
Arya Samaj, 28, 36, 83, 234
Asia House exhibition. *See* M.F. Husain Asia House affair

INDEX

Asian marker, disassociation of, 198, 252–5, 307
Asian Voice (newspaper), 303, 313
Asian Youth Movements, 11, 147, 252, 334, 419n171
Australia, 325–6
AWAAZ, 18, 51, 193, 214, 215, 288, 296, 334
Ayodhya mobilisations. See *Ramjanmabhoomi* movement

Babri Masjid demolition, 21, 70, 163, 164, 169, 170, 172, 190
    post-demolition tensions, 172, 190–5
    See also Ramjanmabhoomi movement
Babur, emperor, 163, 194
Bajrang Dal, 292, 299
Bangladeshis, 243, 245, 246, 253
Bapu, Morari, 180, 184, 185, 186
Batra, Dinanath, 309
BBC's *Spooks* controversy, 205–6, 240
Bhaarat Welfare Trust, 187, 213
Bhagwat, Mohan, 29–30, 63, 72, 88, 111, 377–8n62
    Britain tour (2016), 46, 48
    as guest in Hindu Marathon, 236
    on VSS, 98
Bharat Mata (Mother India), 170
    defamation of, 293
Bharat Mata temple (Haridwar), 180
Bharatiya Jana Sangh (later the BJP), 127, 129, 133, 156
Bharatiya Janata Party (BJP), 15, 18, 52, 167, 207, 274, 292, 320, 326, 330
    campaigns using digital tools, 331
    diasporic support, 30–1, 107
    digital activism, 328–9
    election victory (2014), 1, 2
    election victory (2019), 331
    global ranks, 331
    India-Israel relations (during BJP-led government), 300
    leaders as *pracharaks*, 49
    'love jihad', response to, 290
    NRI investment, 156
    online donations, 332
    'PM CARES Fund', 229
    protest against the BJP government, 333–4
    Ram Rajya, promised to make, 168
    Ram Rath Yatra, 169, 171, 172, 174
    Ram temple dispute, verdict on, 169
    'Swachh Bharat' (Clean India), 229
    young activists during the Emergency, 126, 144–6, 147, 161
    See also Advani, L.K.; Modi, Narendra; Rashtriya Swaymasevak Sangh (RSS)
Bharatiya Janata Yuva Morcha, 56
Bharatiya Swayamsevak Sangh (BSS), 26–39, 63–4, 75
    Bhide's contribution to, 33–4
    Chamanlal's contribution to, 29, 31, 32–3
    communications system, 34
    first official *shakha*, 29
    'missionary' tours, 29, 33–4

INDEX

networks of connectivity, 31–2, 35
popularity, measuring, 37
See also Shastri, Jagdish Chandra Sharda
Bharatiya Yuvak Sangh, 41
Bhide, Laxmanrao, 29, 31, 32–3, 45, 134, 357*n*33
Bhutada, Ramesh, 149–50
'Big Society', 219, 221, 221, 222
BJP. *See* Bharatiya Janata Party (BJP)
Blackman, Bob, 69, 92–3, 188, 237, 256, 260
    Padma Shri award, 285, 429*n*89
Blair, Tony, 239, 269, 270
'blasphemy', 266, 267, 270
    Danish cartoon controversy, 303, 304
    Doniger Affair, 257, 303, 305, 307, 308–10
    image-based, 295, 303 265, 291–7, 303, 304–5, 306, 307, 322
    M.F. Husain Asia House affair, 265, 291–7, 303, 304–5, 306, 307, 322
    Rushdie Affair (1988–9), 191, 249, 251, 253, 268–9, 297, 302, 303
Bochasanwasi Shree Akshar Purushottam Swaminarayan Sanstha (BAPS), 181, 225, 271, 279–80, 281–2
Bradford, 42, 179, 185
    Hindu Marathon in, 234–5, 244
Britain
    Afro-Caribbean population, 250

Blackness and identity separation desire, 250–5
crime against Hindus and Sikhs, 255
donations for Ram Janmabhoomi movement, 175
Hindu communities, consolidation of, 9
Hindu population and temples, 267
literature on Hindu nationalism, 18–19
minority status of Hindus, 69–70
post-Babri Masjid demolition violence, 190–1, 193, 194–5
post-war period of migration, 9–10
registered Hindu temple, 39
significance of religion to government, 269–70
Sikh and Muslim groups, charity and public service, 232
South Asians arrival, 8–9
wariness of British Hindutva, 273–4
See also individual organisations and activities by their names
British Muslims for Secular Democracy, 277
British Nationalist Party, 283–4
British Nationality Act (1948), 9, 38
British Sangh Parivar. *See* Hindu Marathon; Hindu Swayamsevak Sangh (HSS); HSS training camps; 'model

INDEX

minority' narrative; Sewa Day; Sewa International UK; *shakhas* (in Britain)
Brooker, Cory, 6–7
BSS. *See* Bharatiya Swayamsevak Sangh (BSS)
Buddhism, 202, 224
Bunch of Thoughts (Golwalkar), 68, 227, 230–1

California textbook controversy, 203–4, 205
Cameron, David, 3, 219, 221, 221, 317
Campbell, Alastair, 269
Canada, 174, 233, 335
    anti-Emergency activism, 134, 155
caste discrimination, 311–10, 323–4
caste legislation, 310–19, 323–4
"Channel 4", 214–15
charity and public service, 22–3, 67, 209–61, 337
    central to Hindu nationalism, 22, 209
    diasporic vernacularisation, 229–30, 260, 337
    four-fold dividends, 257–8
    Gujarat earthquake fundraising controversy (2001), 22, 131, 210, 213–17
    HSS Trust Deed, 25–6, 58, 80, 209
    natural disasters and fundraising, 212
    organisations, 213
    overseas financing, regulations, 212
    public relations' platform, 231–3
    Ram Navami celebrations (Nagpur), 227
    rise of charity initiatives in India, 228–9
    Sangh's prescription for social work, 227–34
    types of philanthropic donations, 211–12
    See also Hindu Marathon; 'model minority' narrative; Sewa Day; Sewa International UK
Charity Commission, 80, 87, 97, 175, 214, 226, 259, 314, 337
Charles, Prince, 140
Chitkara, M.G., 119, 120, 130
Citizenship (Amendment) Act (2019), 157
Clarke, Charles, 280
Coalition Against Genocide, 321, 334
coeducation, 66, 67, 68, 94
Commission on Integration and Cohesion (CIC), 277
Commonwealth Immigrants Act (1962, 1968), 38, 148
Commonwealth Immigration Act (1971), 38, 148
communalism, 6, 11, 317–18
    rejecting, 332–6
Congress Party, 126, 152, 159, 160
    See also the Emergency (1975–7)
Connecting British Hindus: An Inquiry into the Identity and Public Engagement of Hindus in Britain, 271

INDEX

Conservative Party, 3, 13, 96, 216, 221, 311, 312
   and Hindu nationalism, 4
   Hindu voters' shift, 266, 313–19
conversion. *See* 'Hindu Security Conference'
Corbyn, Jeremy, 239, 314, 316–17, 437n217, 439n229
Crown Prosecution Service, 264
'cyber-Hindutva', 329

Dalit Solidarity Network, 316, 333
Dalits, 204
   caste legislation, 310–19, 323–4
   organisations, 311, 333
dana (giving), 113, 114, 211
Danish cartoon controversy, 303, 304
Dar-es-Salaam, 38
Davdra, Bhavin, 102
defamation, 297–301, 302–7
   Doniger Affair, 257, 303, 305, 307, 308–10
   M.F. Husain Asia House affair, 265, 291–7, 303, 304–5, 306, 307, 322
   Rushdie Affair (1988–9), 191, 249, 251, 253, 268–9, 297, 302, 303
   Spooks controversy, 205–6, 240
Defence and Internal Security of India Rules (DISIR), 129
Democratic Party, 12
demographic anxieties, 289–90
Deoras, Madhukar Dattatraya, 129, 182, 232, 364–5n131

Department for Communities and Local Government (DCLG), 271, 273, 278
Desai, Hitendra, 154–5
Desai, Lord Meghnad, 296
Desai, Makarand, 134–5, 137, 145–6, 147
Deshmukh, Nanaji, 134
Dhesi, Tanmanjeet Singh, 317
Dhooria, Ram Lall, 115, 117
digital misinformation, 4–6
Doniger, campaign against, 257, 303, 305, 307, 308–10
Doordarshan, 189

Ealing temple attack (West London), 263
East Africa
   Africanisation policies, 10, 36–8
   anti-Emergency activism, 134
   Golwalkar on failure of Hindus in, 231–2
   Hindutva activity hub in, 34–5
   sewa-related projects in, 233
   See also Kenya
East Africa: Sangh Parivar in, 28–32
   Bhide and senior Sangh leaders role, 29, 32–5
   connectivity to India, 34–5
   Sewa Day, 230–1
   shakhas in, 65–6
   See also Bharatiya Swayamsevak Sangh (BSS)
East African Asians
   anti-Emergency activism, 146, 148
   'colonial sandwich', 36
   emigration to, 38, 39

exodus of, 10, 26, 35–6, 37–8, 147, 255–6
experiences in HSS (Britain), 44
India's diaspora policy and, 151
kinship networks, 40
maintenance of traditional Indian values, 40
model minority narrative, 248
religious and cultural organisations establishment, 39–40
in RSS Officer Training Camp, 97
UK citizenship, 38, 40
See also 'model minority' narrative
East India Company, 8
Economic Policy Group, 221
ecumenical conferences
   'Global Vision 2000', 200, 237
   World Hindu Congress (2014), 199–200
   See also Virat Hindu Sammelan (VHS)
ecumenism, 36–7, 197, 224–6
   evolution of Hinduism towards, 268
   HFB's conservative ecumenism, 264, 324, 337
   Sangh's prescription for social work, 227–34
   Sewa Day, 218, 219, 222, 224–6
   VHP as an ecumenical body, 165–6, 197–8, 201, 207, 228
   VHP-UK's ecumenical role, 180, 182

See also Hindu Marathon; Sewa International UK
Ekal Vidyalaya, 213, 309
Ekamata Yatra, 171–2
Elst, Koenraad, 295
the Emergency (1975–7), 21, 125–62, 340, 385n9
   Alexandra Palace conference (London, 24–5 Apr 1976), 136–7, 146
   arrests and incarceration, 126, 129–30, 132, 385n9
   circulation of underground literature, 131, 142
   coercive programmes, 126
   diplomatic relations under pressure, 139–41
   and Gujarati diaspora, 146
   and Hindu nationalist activism overseas, 131–9
   Hindu nationalist politics, 144–50
   imposition of, 126
   legacy, 160
   March elections announcement, 139, 160
   negative foreign press coverage, 138, 139, 141
   non-Hindu nationalist campaigns, 133
   postponed elections, 126
   press censorship, 126, 141–4, 154
   socialists campaign (1976), 133
   state–diaspora relations, 127, 128–9, 150–9
   Subramanian Swamy's role during, 31, 134, 135–7, 138, 139, 144, 152, 153

INDEX

and the Sangh Parivar in India, 129–31
'transnational citizenship', 128–9, 150–9
See also Friends of India Society International (FISI)
Empire Windrush, HMT, 9
English Defence League (EDL), 284, 299, 307
Equality Act (2010), 311
e-shakha, 62, 105, 213
Essentials of Hindutva (Savarkar), 13–14
Evening Standard article 'scandal', 277–8, 283
Explaining Hindu Dharma—A Guide for Teachers, 202–3

Facebook, 86, 90, 95, 109, 253, 295, 323
Faith Communities Consultative Council, 201
fascism, 18, 58, 160, 319
through the lens of Hindutva, 52
See also the Emergency (1975–7)
Federation of Hindu Associations in Southern California, 321
Fernandes, George, 133, 138–9, 141, 158
Fiji, 7–8, 35, 155
Foot, Michael, 140
Ford, Gerald, 139
Foreign and Commonwealth Office (FCO), 139–40
Foreign Contribution (Regulation) Act, 175, 212
Freedom of Information Act, 195

Friends of India Society International (FISI), 134, 135, 138, 148, 149, 154, 156, 157, 159, 192, 336
Alexandra Palace conference (London, 24–5 Apr 1976), 136–7, 146
fundamentalism, 52, 268, 296, 302, 305

Gabbard, Tulsi, 319–20
Gandhi, Indira, 21, 131, 132, 146
diaspora Congress supporters' organisations, use of, 159
Kaul's letter to, 152, 155
March elections announcement, 139, 160
reinstated as prime minister, 160
response to anti-Emergency activism, 154–5, 157–8, 159
State of Emergency imposition, 126
See also the Emergency (1975–7)
Gandhi, Rahul, 159
Gandhi, Sonia, 159
Gardiner, Barry, 224, 239, 285, 310, 319, 429n89
Ghar Wapsi (returning home) programmes, 225
Ghosh, Tapan, 273–4, 285
Giri, Swami Satyamitranand, 34, 180–2, 186, 236
Global Hindu Electronic Network, 16
Goldsmith, Zac, 317–18
Golwalkar, M.S., 52, 66, 68, 83, 113

469

INDEX

'Hindu' term, use of, 260–1
  on failure of Hindus in East
    Africa, 231–2
  on Indian *shibirs*, 82, 84
  on *kabaddi* (game), 58
  on literature for Hindus
    abroad, 16
  on public social action, 230–1
  orders for inclusive charitable
    efforts, 225
'Great Replacement' theory, 289
Grover, Chamanlal, 29, 31, 32–3,
  42, 105
  anti-Emergency role, 134,
    135
Guardian, The, 138, 296, 325
Gujarat earthquake fundraising
  controversy (2001), 22, 131,
  210, 213–17
Gujarat Samachar (newspaper),
  142
Gujarat violence (2002), 131,
  191, 210, 252, 258, 273, 316
Gujarati diaspora, 146, 181, 185
  Gujarat earthquake
    fundraising (2001), 210
Gujaratis, 37, 39, 117, 145, 146
Gupta, Vishwa Bandhu, 175–6
guru dakshina, 211

Hathi, Jaisukhlal, 154–5
hawala transactions, 176
Hedgewar, K.B., 43, 52, 82, 83,
  84, 91, 182
  anniversary of, 177–8
  on donations, 211
  prescription for social work,
    227
Hindu 'cosmopolitanism', 268
Hindu Aid, 278–9

Hindu American Foundation
  (HAF), 320, 321
Hindu Council of Kenya, 36
Hindu Council UK, 263, 272
Hindu Education Foundation, 203
Hindu Forum of Britain (HFB),
  255, 257, 271–5, 323, 337–8
  advisory role, 271–2
  alignment with the Sangh
    Parivar, 279–86
  alliance with HHR, 296
  ambitions, 274
  annual Diwali event (Oct
    2017), 285
  campaign against Doniger,
    309–10
  Caste in the UK report (2008),
    311
  caste legislation, opposing,
    310–13
  challenges to, 276–8
  conservative ecumenism of,
    264, 324, 337
  definition of Hinduism, 275
  establishment, 264
  Evening Standard article
    'scandal', 277–8, 283
  Jagdeesh Singh's accusation
    against VHP, 279–81, 282
  relationship with the Jewish
    community, 298
  resonance with Hindutva and
    the Sangh Parivar, 264–5
  RSS foundation day
    celebration (2010), 282–3
  status, rise of, 272
  strategy, 273
  VHP-UK and HSS, 307
  weaponisation of hurt
    religious sentiments, 265

INDEX

website, 274–5
See also 'Hindu Security Conference'; M.F. Husain Asia House affair
Hindu Human Rights (HHR), 294, 295–6, 295, 323
Hindu Janajagruti Samiti (HJS), 292–3, 296, 304, 309, 323
Hindu Marathon, 210, 230, 234–42
   achievement, 234
   aims of, 234–5
   chief guests, 236–7
   ecumenical aspect, 241
   Hindutva and, 236, 240
   multiculturalist rhetoric, 234–5
   organisations launch, helping, 239–40
   organisers skills development, 237–8
   participants, 235–6
   for relationships development, 237
   Sangh lineage representation, 236, 237
   and Sewa Day differences, 241–2
   sponsorship, 236, 241
   videos of, 235
   See also 'model minority' narrative
Hindu nationalism
   charity central to Hindu nationalism, 22, 209
   defined, 1
   fundraising as a key process, 216
   intervention in the identities, 28
   literature on, 15–16, 18–19, 27, 211
   Modi's international trips and growth of, 325–7
   spheres of influence, 14
   See also individual organisations and activities by their names
Hindu nationalist movement: and the Emergency
   anti-Emergency activities, 127–8
   comparisons with Gandhian *satyagraha*, 130, 131
   incarceration of members and leaders, 126, 129–30
   legacy, 148
   meeting outside Indian Embassy (Washington DC), 132
   Narendra Modi and other protagonists, 144–50
   political fortunes, 127
   rise of, in the post-Emergency period, 171
   See also the Emergency (1975–7)
Hindu *rashtra*, 104, 174, 189, 225
   RSS as the 'Hindu Rashtra in miniature', 84
   women role, 171
Hindu Sahitya Kendra (HSK), 16, 188
Hindu Sangam, 179–80, 234
'Hindu Security Conference', 263, 240, 286–91, 301, 307
   demographic issues, 289–90
   'love jihad' rhetoric, 171, 240, 286, 287–90
   media coverage, 287–8
   poster, 286–7

representatives, 263, 287
Hindu Students Council, 200, 239
Hindu Swayamsevak Sangh (HSS), 1, 19, 21, 26, 39–75, 326, 336, 360–1*n*75
  activities in London and the Midlands, 45
  adaptation of, 63–7
  Advait Cultural Centre event (Wembley), 279
  annual income, 59
  British Hindus population, 39
  Charity Commission inquiry, 210, 214, 215–16
  culture, values, and the pedagogy of, 70–5
  'Dharma Bee' contest, 75
  drop-out rates, 59–61, 60*t*
  establishment of, 39, 41
  first *shakha* in, 41–2
  Guidelines for Vistaraks, 54–6
  heterosociality of, 66, 67
  India and England organisers relationship, 53
  Keshav Pratishthan, 50–1
  martial training of, 68–9
  Milton Keynes gathering, 178
  participation as responses to minority status, 76–7
  pracharaks role, 33, 48–51, 52–3
  prescription for social work, 227–34
  as a registered charity, 45
  RSS leaders overseas tours, 45–8
  shakhas as core of modus operandi, 58, 62
  space for *shakhas*, 42
  submission of the ego, 71–2
  support and encouragement, 42–3
  Swaminathan on, 284
  synchronicity and divergence of RSS and HSS, 61–3
  universality references, 25–6
  views on Buddhism, 224
  vistaraks role, 54–6
  women role, 43, 66, 67
  working patterns, 30
  See also Hindu Marathon; HSS training camps; 'model minority' narrative; Sewa Day; Sewa International UK; *shakhas* (in Britain)
Hindu Vivek Kendra (HVK), 15–16
Hindu(tva) representation, 23–4, 265, 266
  American politics and, 319–21
  'The British Hindu Manifesto', 313–14
  campaigns against Corbyn, 316–17
  caste legislation and the politics of, 310–19, 323–4
  communalism into British politics, 317–18
  HFB as representatives of Hindus, 271, 274
  Labour to Conservative shift, 313–19
  struggles for recognition, 265, 301–7
  See also Hindu Forum of Britain (HFB); 'neo-Hindutva'; National Council of Hindu Temples (NCHT)

INDEX

'Hinduphobia', 308–9, 312, 335
Hindus Abroad: Dilemma: Dollar or Dharma? (Seshadri), 43–4, 81, 249, 250
Hindus, The (Doniger), 257, 303, 305, 307, 308–10
Hinduism
  aggressive, 70
  HFP's definition of, 275
  evolution of, 267–71
  'misunderstood' aspects of, 74
  VHP as the representative of, 201–6, 207–8
  See also 'blasphemy'; ecumenism; Hindutva/diasporic Hindutva; 'neo-Hindutva'
Hindutva/diasporic Hindutva
  academic attention, lack of, 17
  activity hub in East Africa, 34–5
  boom of, 228
  dominance, 13
  fascism and, 52
  global and universalist rhetoric, 13–14
  Gujarat earthquake fundraising to promote, 214–15
  internal dynamics (in UK), 53–4
  lens of 'brokerage', 197–8
  literature on, 15–16, 18–19, 27
  manliness, promotion of, 68–9
  online spaces, 18
  'popularity' of, 107
  position of the British state towards, 270
  reconceptualisation of, 266
  rejection of, 332–6
  the Sammelan linked to, 184
  Seshadri on, 43–4, 100
  of Sevika Samiti, 66–7
  social media campaigns, 3
  'vernacularisation' of, 14, 229–30, 260, 266, 337
  See also 'neo-Hindutva' *and individual organisations and activities by their names*
Home Office, 74, 195, 354, 270, 273, 278
Hosabale, Dattatreya, 48, 256, 283
Hostile Homelands (Essa), 298
House of Commons Home Affairs Select Committee, 147, 279–81, 282, 285–6
House of Lords, 215, 248, 313
HSS *shakhas*. *See* shakhas (in Britain)
HSS training camps, 70
  age bracket, 87
  attendance at, 88
  central role in the HSS's operations, 80
  chief guests at, 90–3, 91–2*t*
  contributions of, 106
  discipline and spirit of, 87
  divergence and idiosyncrasy, 80
  fiftieth anniversary *Maha Shibir*, 90
  first camp, 85
  focus on youth, 100–1
  Gujaratis domination, 117
  leadership at, 87, 88–9
  members views, 86
  organisers, 79, 86, 88, 96, 100, 105

473

INDEX

participants' family, inviting, 86, 106
participation in Indian camps, 123–4, 96–101
pilgrimage aspects, 110–14
'projects', 95
public events, 107–10
public functions, 81, 85
'return' to sacred Mother India, 110–14
'Roles and Responsibilities of Karyakartas', 89
RSS- HSS co-ordination, 26–7, 41–5, 50–1
Sangh Internship Programme (SIP), 79–80, 94–6
sewa activities, 95
visits by Sangh leaders, 88–9
See also shakhas (in Britain)
HSS Trust Deed, 25–6, 58, 80
Birmingham meeting (1983), 209
HSS. *See* Hindu Swayamsevak Sangh (HSS)
Husain, Maqbool Fida. *See* M.F. Husain Asia House affair

In Quest of a Secular Symbol, 18–19
India Abroad (newspaper), 152
India Development and Relief Fund, 217
India Global Forum, 239
India Heading Towards an Islamic State: A Warning!, 290
India's negative human rights reputation, 330
Indian American Centre for Political Action, 297–8
Indian Americans, 4, 194, 204, 297, 304, 320–21, 330
    Ayodhya temple construction and, 4
    donations for *Ram Janmabhoomi* movement, 175
    'Global Vision 2000', 200
    population growth, 6
    post-9/11 'terror factor', 250–1
    support for Trump, 6
    Supreme Court's 2019 verdict and, 194
    See also 'model minority' narrative
Indian Australian Diaspora Foundation, 326
Indian Business Association, 7
Indian Development and Relief Fund, 213
Indian diaspora
    anti-Emergency mobilisation, 127, 130, 131–9
    anti-immigrant rhetoric, 10–11
    deprivation of, 10–11
    identity, 8
    literature for, 15–16
    patterns of mobility, 7–8
    political identities, 11–12
    spread of, 7
    Tharoor on, 200
    'transplanted culture', 19–20
Indian Emergency. *See* the Emergency (1975–7)
Indian General Election (2014), 1, 15, 83, 131, 238, 310, 329, 331
Indian High Commission, 5, 35, 36, 132, 142, 333
Indian Ministry of External Affairs, 36

INDEX

Indian Muslim Federation, 175, 190
Indian Overseas Congress groups, 159
Indian Penal Code, 303
Indian Science Congress (2015), 247
Indian-American Intellectuals Forum, 304
Infinity Foundation, 308
Inner Cities Religious Council (ICRC), 269–70
Insight UK, 290–1
Instagram, 218, 240
Inter Faith Network, 201, 202, 280
International Dalit Solidarity Network, 11
International Development and Relief Fund, 214
ISKCON (International Society for Krishna Consciousness), 205, 225, 234, 271
Islamophobia, 12, 70, 85, 245, 335
    anti-Muslim stereotype, 250–5
    'love jihad' rhetoric, 171, 240, 286, 287–90
ITV Exposure, 86–7

Jaffrelot, Christophe, 17, 52, 61, 116, 131, 165, 169, 175, 239, 282, 305
'Jai Shri Ram' (slogan), 5, 174, 189, 194
Jainism, 202, 224
Jana Sangh. *See* Bharatiya Jana Sangh (later the BJP)
Janata Party, 156, 160

Jewish–Hindu connections, 297–301
Johnson, Boris, 4, 317
Joshi, Murli Manohar, 200

kabaddi (game), 58, 63
Kallidai, Ramesh, 264, 272, 276, 277, 278–9, 294, 302, 305
    on blasphemy, 303
    on Golwalkar, 279
    Jagdeesh Singh's accusation against VHP, 279–81, 282
    'love jihad' rhetoric, 286, 287–8, 290
Kalyan Ashram Trust UK, 95, 213, 215, 237
Kankani, Arun, 53, 64, 89
Kansal, Hari Babu, 199, 232
Kapoor, Coomi, 147
'karma capitalism', 247
Karmabhoomi, 22, 70, 123, 230
karsevaks (volunteers), 163, 172
karyakartas (active workers/organisers), 29, 32, 53, 54, 63, 83
    role in training camps, 79, 86, 88, 96, 100, 105
Kashmir, 239, 318
    Article 370, abrogation of, 316
Kaul, T.N., 152, 155
Kendriya Karyakari Mandal, 88
Kenya, 10, 26
    Arya Samaj in, 28, 36
    BSS establishment, 29
    'Deendayal Bhavan' (Nairobi), 34–5
    East African Asians, exodus of, 37–8
    separate schools in, 36
    stereotypes of tripartite, 36

INDEX

'keyboard warriors', 4
Khalistan movement, 333
Khan, Omar, 318
Khan, Sadiq, 317, 318
Khomeini, Ayatollah, 251, 303
Kunte, Sharad, 30, 98, 111

Labour Party, 3, 12, 311, 314, 315–16, 317
   as 'anti-Hindu', 3, 312, 216
   ethnic minority backgrounds politicians in, 12
   India's Kashmir policy, criticism of, 239, 316, 318
   Indian activists in, 319
   Ladwa's criticism, 239
   South Asian diaspora's support, 12
Ladwa, Manoj, 238–9
Leicester: communal tension and violence (Sep 2022), 5–6, 53–4, 194, 290
Livingstone, Ken, 319
London mayoral elections (2016), 317–18
'long-distance nationalism', 17, 22, 26, 75–6, 111, 131, 161, 165, 211

M.F. Husain Asia House affair, 265, 291–7, 303, 304–5, 306, 307, 322
Maa Charity Trust, 187, 213
Maintenance of Internal Security Act (MISA), 129
Malhotra Committee, 156
Malhotra, Rajiv, 308–9, 313
Malkani, K.R., 61–2
Manchester, 109
Mangeshkar, Lata, 185

marginalisation, 27, 36, 69–70, 72, 75, 77
Matrubhoomi, 22, 70–1, 230
Mauritius, 33
May, Theresa, 270, 314
Menendez, Bob, 6–7
Milton Keynes gathering (Aug 1989). *See* Virat Hindu Sammelan (VHS)
Ministry of External Affairs (MEA), 140, 154, 155, 157, 212
'mobility capital', 40–1
'model minority' narrative, 2, 10, 11, 211, 220–1, 242–6, 296
   Blackness, 250–5, 419n171
   Hindu success and Hindu culture connection, 246–50
   Indian origin as CEOs, 243–4, 247
   'karma capitalism', 247
   multiculturalism, 244–5
   promotion of, as response to racism, 249
   reification of, 255–7
   'self-defence', 69, 257
   stereotypes of integration, 245–6
   'strategic essentialism', 249
   'strategic hybridity', 249–50
   welfare benefits, 243
Modi, Narendra, 1, 214, 247, 310, 321
   address to US Congress, 327–8
   Australia visit, 325–6
   Ayodhya temple project, 3–4
   Cameron's government and, 317

Corbyn's criticism, 316, 318
election campaign (2014),
    2, 238, 331
India-Israel relations, 300
international trips and Hindu
    nationalism growth, 325–7
letters exchange between
    Makarand Desai and, 145,
    146, 147
Madison Square Garden event
    (Sep 2014), 2, 320
on the Emergency, 129–30,
    149
role during the Emergency,
    126, 144–6, 147, 161
UK House of Commons visit
    (2013), 319
United States visit (2023),
    326–8
US media's press conference
    with, 328–9
Wembley Stadium event
    (London, 2015), 3, 317
See also Bharatiya Janata Party
    (BJP)
Mody, Mukund, 149, 156
Motherland, The (periodical), 142
Mukherjee, Pranab, 159
multiculturalism, 5, 9, 19, 23,
    93, 183, 201-208, 218, 220,
    224–5, 234–5, 244–5, 302–3,
    337–8
    evolution of, 267–71
Muslim Council of Britain, 205,
    206, 269

Nagpur, 28, 51, 91, 97, 119, 227
Nanda, Ved Prakash, 73–4, 106,
    148, 217, 306–7
Naoroji, Dadabhai, 12

Narayan, Jayaprakash ('JP'), 132,
    138, 141, 158, 160
National Council for Education
    and Research Training, 203
National Council of Hindu
    Temples (NCHT), 216, 265,
    284, 285, 317,
    323, 338
    caste legislation, opposing,
        312–14 'Dharma Rising'
        (2015), 313
National Democratic Alliance,
    160
National Hindu Students Forum
    (NHSF), 56, 205, 218, 222,
    224, 225–6, 239–40, 287
    campaigns, 240
    fears of Hindu female
        conversion, 289
    growth of, 241–2
    M.F. Husain protests, support
        for, 294
    report on Hindu identity
        issue, 253, 254
    and Union of Jewish Students,
        298, 301
    website, 240
National Hindu Welfare Support,
    289
Nehru, Jawaharlal, 151, 230
'neo-Hindutva', 23, 93, 210,
    263–324, 338–9
    diaspora Hinduism and
        multiculturalism,
        evolution of, 267–71
    Doniger, campaign against,
        257, 303, 305, 307,
        308–10
    'hard' neo-Hindutva, 23, 266,
        296, 322, 338

477

Hindu–Jewish connections, 297–301
legitimacy, 323
Modi-era, 285
multiculturalism, 265, 302–3, 337–8
organisations, 203, 206, 264, 265, 271, 338
as a product of the digital revolution, 322, 323
public expressions of, 302
'soft' neo-Hindutva, 23, 266, 296, 322, 338
struggles for recognition, 265, 301–7
term, 266
See also Hindu Forum of Britain (HFB); 'Hindu Security Conference'; Hindu(tva) representation
neo-Vedantist universalism, 167
Netanyahu, Benjamin, 300
the Netherlands, 174, 233
New Delhi, 28, 29, 127, 131, 137, 139, 152, 154, 155, 299, 339
New Generation Network, 276–7
New Jersey, 299
Independence Day parade, India's seventy-fifth (Aug 2022), 6–7
New York Times, 138, 154
NHSF. *See* National Hindu Students Forum (NHSF)
Non-Resident Indians (NRIs), 7, 48, 56, 59, 106, 109, 111, 117, 122, 123, 151, 156, 162, 198, 331
Non-Resident Indians for Secularism and Democracy, 193

Nyerere, Julius, 38

Organiser (newspaper), 15, 35, 102–3, 106, 237, 250, 263, 279, 305, 328
Orientalist, 168, 247, 257, 312
outrage, 301, 302–7
See also 'blasphemy'
Overseas Bharatiya Jana Sangh, 41
Overseas Friends of the BJP (OFBJP), 3, 34–5, 149, 157, 238, 317, 326, 330, 331, 332
Oza, Rameshbhai, 180, 185
Oza, Sanjiv, 240–1

Pakistanis, 243, 245, 246, 253
Param Shakti Peeth, 187, 213
Parmar, Rajnikant, 235
Passport Act, 153
Patel, C.B., 263–4, 283, 301
Patel, Priti, 4, 48, 243, 256–7, 285
Patel, Trupti, 272, 313, 316–17
Pathak, Yashwant, 97–8
The People versus Emergency: A Saga of Struggle, 132
'Person of Indian Origin' card scheme (1999), 157
philanthropy. *See* charity and public service
pilgrimage, 110–14
as 'communitas', 114–17
'PM CARES Fund', 229
postcolonialism, 335
Powell, Enoch, 38, 147
pracharaks (full-time workers), 29, 63
role of, 33, 48–51, 52–3, 363n113

INDEX

Pramukh Swami, 181, 182
Prashad, Vijay, 73, 250, 251, 276, 300, 301
Pravasi Bharatiya Divas, 123, 157
public service. *See* charity and public service

Race Relations Act (1976), 148
racism, 2, 11, 36–8, 75, 249, 284, 312, 335, 336
    Blackness and identity separation desire, 250–5
Raj, Dhooleka, 19–20, 27, 109, 254, 289, 301
Rajugopal, Raju, 335
Ram ke Naam (documentary), 175
Ram Rath Yatra, 169, 171, 172, 174
Ram Sethu campaigns, 305–6
Ram Shila Puja (RSP), 171, 173–5, 178, 192
    diasporic donations, 175–7
Ram temple mobilisations. See *Ramjanmabhoomi* movement
Ramayana (television series), 189–90
Ramjanmabhoomi movement, 3–4, 125, 131, 161, 163–208
    Allahabad High Court verdict (2010), 168
    Ayodhya as a metaphor of Hindu identity, 169–70, 174
    Babri Masjid demolition, 21, 70, 164, 169, 170, 172, 190
    Ekamata Yatra, 171–2
    existential threat to Hindu India, 171
    gendered angle to, 170
    new Ram temple construction, first brick to, 164
    political struggle, 167–8
    post-Babri Masjid demolition violence, 172, 190–5
    Ram as a metaphor, 171, 173
    Ram Janmabhoomi, term, 163
    Ram Rath Yatra, 169, 171, 172, 174
    Ram Shila Pujas and diasporic donations, 173–7, 192
    roles for women, 170–1
    root cause for, 163–4
    Supreme Court of India's verdict (2019), 169, 194
    video distribution, 188–90
    See also VHP (Vishwa Hindu Parishad); Virat Hindu Sammelan (VHS)
Rao, K. Suryanarayana, 233–4
Rao, Y. Sudershan, 168
Rashtriya Swaymasevak Sangh (RSS), 17, 22, 23, 76, 292
    anti-Emergency activism, 129–31, 132, 144
    banning of, 129, 132
    in Britain, 26, 27, 39–45, 56–75
    communications system, 34
    condemning anti-Sangh 'propaganda', 217
    and diasporic *vistaraks* differences, 56
    in East Africa, 26, 27, 28–35
    foundation day celebration (2010), 282–3
    guru dakshina, 211
    incarceration of members and leaders, 129–30, 385n9
    institutional structures, 48–56

479

INDEX

new technologies, adopters of, 16
as 'paramilitary', 13
physical fitness, interpretation of, 68
pracharaks role, 33, 48–51, 52–3
RSS leaders overseas tours, 34, 45–8
Sarsanghchalak Goes Abroad (pamphlet), 14
selfless service, prescription for, 228
vistaraks role, 54–6
welfare projects, 229
See also Bharatiya Swayamsevak Sangh (BSS); the Emergency (1975–7); Hindu Swayamsevak Sangh (HSS); training camps (Indian-based)
Red Crescent Society, 223
're-masculinization', 68–9
remittances, 22, 177, 211–12
See also charity and public service
representation. *See* Hindu(tva) representation
Reserve Bank of India (RBI), 175–6
Rithambara, Sadhvi, 168, 186–8
Robinson, Tommy, 245, 284, 285
RSS training camps. *See* training camps (Indian-based)
RSS. *See* Rashtriya Swaymasevak Sangh (RSS)
Rushdie Affair (1988–9), 191, 249, 251, 253, 268–9, 297, 302, 303

Sagar, Ramanand, 189
Samanvaya Parivar, 213
Sangh camps. *See* training camps; training camps (Indian-based)
Sangh Internship Programme (SIP), 79–80, 94–6
Sangh Parivar
anti-Emergency mobilisation as legacy, 148
assertive 'manliness', promotion of, 68–70
banning of, 129
Britain, 39–45, 56–63, 165
cadres role during the Emergency, 127–8
'capture of civil society space', 229
diasporic funding, 22
East Africa, 28–35
focus on Ram's birthplace, 171
initial development, 20
interconnected nature of, 56
modus operandi, 20
networks top-down management, 29–30
social work, prescription for, 227–34
Swaminarayan temples, 181, 256, 279–80
See also the wings of Sangh by their names
Sangh Sandesh, 47, 89, 95, 102, 110, 142, 193, 240, 282–3
Sangh Shiksha Varg, 83, 85–6
Sangharsh ma Gujarat (Modi), 145
Saraswati, Chinmayananda, 167
Satanic Verses, The (Rushdie), 251, 268, 269, 302. *See* Rushdie Affair (1988–9)

480

INDEX

Satya Samachar, 142
Satyanarayana, M.C., 43
Satyavani (journal), 135, 143, 158
Savarkar, V.D., 13–14, 112
Scout Movement, 82, 83
secularism, 1, 4, 13, 268, 332
Seshadri, H.V., 27, 43–4, 70, 71, 161, 249, 250
Sevika Samiti, 43, 46, 54, 60, 66–7, 87, 369n199
Sewa Bharati, 228, 279
Sewa Day, 22–3, 210–11, 217–24, 229, 230, 258, 259–61
   critical approach, 220–1
   during the Covid-19 pandemic, 259
   events in secular spaces, 223, 225
   events, 219–20, 226
   Golwalkar on public social action, 230–1
   government funding, 259–60
   government's relationship with, 221–2
   high degree of ecumenism, 218, 219, 222, 224–6
   and Hindu Marathon differences, 241–2
   ideological consonance with the Sangh, 219, 224–7
   inclusion of non-Hindus, 223–4, 225
   inter-faith activity, 219, 222–3, 224
   international outreach, 226–7
   linked to Hindu nationalism, 218
   organisational strategy, 219, 220
   organisers, 218, 219
   public image of, 221
   for relationships development, 237
   Sangh's prescription for social work, 227–34
   scope of, 217–18
   as secular and non-denominational, 219, 222
   sewa as 'a universal concept', 219
   'Sewa Pioneers Awards', 225–6
   'Social Impact Analysis' report (2012), 222, 223, 260
   Social Return on Investment (SROI), 221
   See also 'model minority' narrative
Sewa International UK (SIUK), 18, 212, 214–17, 218, 223, 233, 238, 239, 260
Sewa UK. *See* Sewa Day
sewa. *See* charity and public service
Shah, Dhiraj D., 37, 44, 71, 85, 180, 191
   director of Sewa UK, 218
   on the Emergency, 142
   on the Sammelan, 184
   as a trustee, 238
Shah, Hasmukh, 148–9, 179, 180, 191, 235
Shah, Yajur, 235, 240
shakhas, 20, 336
   circulation of literature, 63
   coeducational elements, 66–7
   as a daily activity, 57
   games, 63, 66
   Hindu identity pride, 252
   in India, 57–8, 65

INDEX

language differences, 65
meaning, 26, 57
overseas activities of, 29–30
pracharaks role, 33, 48–51, 52–3, 363n113
programme of, 57–8, 61–2, 63
uniform, 65
vistaraks role, 54–6
shakhas (in Britain), 27, 56–61
adaptation of, 63–7
attendance of, 59, 62
bauddhik (discussion), 53, 58, 67, 74
'cyber-shakha' and 'e-shakha', 62, 105, 213
drop-out rates, 59–61, 60t
emphasis on comradeship and community, 72
enculturation, 73–5
flag ceremony, 53, 58, 65, 67, 72
government funding, 259
pedagogy, 72–5
physical training and self-defence, 68–9, 75
prayer, 29, 58, 112
programmes, 58–9
rules for, 85
space for cultural instruction, 73
synchronicity and divergence from RSS, 61–3
uniform, 65
Sharma, Satish, 313, 314, 317
Shastri, Jagdish Chandra Sharda, 37, 63–4, 65, 103, 104, 112, 233
connection with *swayamsevaks*, 32

letter to Chamanlal, 29
Memoirs of a Global Hindu, 28
'missionary' tours, 29, 33
sail from Bombay to Mombasa, 28–9
shibirs. *See* training camps; training camps (Indian-based)
Shiv Sena, 292
Sikhs, 12, 36, 41, 237, 288–9, 302
Asian marker, disassociation of, 253–4
Sikhism, 222, 224, 245
Singh, Jagdeesh, 279–81, 282
Singh, Rajendra, 50–1, 161, 289
address to British *sevikas* (1995), 81
overseas tour, 34, 45–7, 46–7t, 88
sewa, promoting, 232–3
on *shakha* system, 64
Singhal, Ashok, 97, 168, 172, 200
Smugglers of Truth, 143
Socialist International, 133, 138–9, 158
Sood, Jagdish Mitra, 45, 134, 154
South Asia Solidarity Group, 11
South Asian diaspora
Blackness, 250–5, 419n171
centre-left parties and, 12
during the Emergency, 147–8
term, 8
voting patterns, 314–19
Southall Black Sisters, 11
Spooks (BBC spy drama), 205–6, 240
'The Story of Ramjanmabhoomi—Past, Present and Future' (film), 188–9
Sudarshan, K.S., 47, 180

482

INDEX

Sunak, Rishi, 12, 243
Sunni Waqf Board, 169
Sunrise Radio, 253–4
Suruchi Prakashan, 15
'Swachh Bharat' (Clean India), 229
Swaminarayan temple (Neasden), 181, 256, 279–80
Swaminathan Vaidyanathan, 274, 275, 283–4
Swamy, Subramanian, 31, 134, 135–7, 138, 139, 144, 152, 153, 286, 313, 387n41
swayamsevaks (volunteer members), 20, 29
   at Hindu Sangam, 179
   imprisonment, 129
   initiative and dynamism, 30–2
   overseas activity, before the first *shakha*, 31
   role of, 52–3, 130
   in *shakha*, 57
   strength and unity, displays and symbolism of, 107–10
   training camps, 79, 82, 83, 86, 87, 90, 96
   uniform, 65
   Vartak on duty of, 231
   views on *sewa*, 229–30
   See also training camps; training camps (Indian-based)

Tailor, Bharti, 282–3
Tanzania, 10, 38
Thackeray, Bal, 292
Tharoor, Shashi, 200
Thatcher, Margaret, 182–3, 256, 315
Therwath, Ingrid, 61, 165, 175, 212, 239, 282

Time (magazine), 238
Times of India, 106, 294, 302, 319
Times, The, 138
tourism, 110–11
training camps, 21–2, 79–124
   Ayodhya conflict verdict related 'press statement', 193–4
   background to, 83–5
   bauddhiks, 105
   character-based training, 81, 83
   'Charities Behaving Badly' episode, 86–7
   communitas and the equalising effects, 114–17
   as core of the RSS's functioning, 83
   development of, 85–93
   discourse of voluntarism, 122–3
   form of, 82–3, 85–6
   games at, 115
   glossy souvenir volume, 110
   heterotopia of, 84, 117–23
   and Hindu Sangam similarities, 179
   for *karyakartas*, 79, 86, 88, 96, 100, 105
   kinds of training, 81
   marching of *swayamsevaks*, 85
   martial arts displays, 84, 106, 108
   mukhya shikshaks (chief instructors), 83
   multi-directional and polycentric influence, 104–7
   outside India, 89–90
   performance, 84–5, 111

pilgrimage aspects, 110–14
practical skills and knowledge, 81, 82
proselytical priority, 109
a pseudo-utopian society, 84
public displays of marching, 84, 107–8
re-enculturation of Sangh activities, 107
samarop (public function), 81, 85
and *shakhas*, 81, 124
significance of, 124
and social media, 86, 108–9
socialising and building networks, 101–4
solidarity and inclusivity sense, promoting, 84
strength and unity, displays and symbolism of, 107–10
touristic elements, 110–11
transnationalism of, 89
See also Vishwa Sangh Shibir (VSS)
training camps (Indian-based), 96–101
attendance of diaspora *swayamsevaks*, 97
Britain organisers in, 80, 96
focus on youth, 100–1
'NRI' Instructor Training Camp (Bangalore, 2001), 117–18
See also Vishwa Sangh Shibir (VSS)
'transnational citizenship', 128–9, 150–9
transnational Hindutva networks development of, 125–6, 127–8, 131

See also the Emergency (1975–7); Hindu nationalist movement: and the Emergency; Sangh Parivar
Trump, Donald
election campaign (2016), 299
Hindu nationalist support for, 2–3, 6, 299, 319–20
'Howdy Modi' rally (2019), 2–3, 150
Turumella, Madhava, 257, 309–10

Uganda Argus (newspaper), 38
Ugandan Asian exodus, 10, 38, 39, 248
UK-India Awards initiative, 239
Union of Jewish Students (UJS), 298, 301
United States (US)
anti-Emergency activism, 134
on the Emergency, 139, 140
Hindu–Jewish connections, 297–9, 301
HSS summer camps, 68
India as a crucial ally of, 326–7
pedagogy of the HSS, 74–5
Ram Shila Pujas, 174
Sewa Day in, 226
shakhas in, 59
'unauthorised' migrants, 249
See also Indian Americans; 'model minority' narrative; Trump, Donald
United States Commission on International Religious Freedom, 326–7
Upadhyaya, Deendayal, 34
US India Political Action Committee, 297

INDEX

Uttar Pradesh, 21, 163, 190. *See Ramjanmabhoomi* movement

Vaidya, Ram, 51, 52, 224
Vajpayee, Atal Behari, 126, 161
   engagement with the diaspora, 156
   first *shakha* in London, 41–2
   Kenya visit, 34, 156
   Mukund Mody's relationship with, 149
   prime ministership, 157, 160
Varktak, Anil, 31, 73, 100–1, 110, 196, 231
Vaz, Keith, 264
Vedic Foundation, 203
VHP (Vishwa Hindu Parishad), 15, 74, 165–72, 253, 292, 326
   activities abroad, 195–206, 207, 208
   aim of, 166, 198–9, 200
   Allahabad conference, 166
   branches, 167
   campaign against Doniger, 309
   campaigns, 166, 167
   camps of, 199
   circulation of videos, 174–5
   demographic propaganda, 289
   as an ecumenical body, 165–6, 197–8, 201, 207, 228
   ethno-religious activism engagement, 165–6
   foreign funds under investigation, 175–6
   'Global Vision 2000', 200, 237
   'Help Line' to deal with 'love jihad', 290
   international perspective, 166–7
   Jagdeesh Singh's allegations, 279–81, 282
   leadership of VHP branches, 196
   leadership, 165
   lens of 'brokerage', 197–8
   networking and co-ordinating activities, 197
   Ram Shila Puja co-ordination, 173, 174
   Ramjanmabhoomi muktiyagna samita (action committees), 174
   relationship with the RSS and BJP, 165
   representation of Hinduism as success, 201–6, 207–8
   school curricula, efforts to impact, 203–4, 205
   Spooks controversy, 205–6, 240
   transnational funding, 175–7
   World Hindu Congress (2014), 199–200
   See also VHP-A; VHP-UK
VHP-A, 195, 197, 198
   annual income, 196
   California textbook controversy, 203–4, 205
   'Global Vision 2000', 200, 201
VHP-UK
   aims of, 198–9
   annual income, 196
   Britain government's attitudes towards, 201–2
   ecumenical role of, 180, 182
   as Inter Faith Network member, 201, 202
   matrimonial service, 199

485

Milton Keynes gathering, 178
networking and co-ordinating activities, 197
on post-Babri Masjid demolition violence, 191
Ram Janmabhoomi movement funds, 175, 176
Ram Janmabhoomi movement role, 195–6
representation of Hinduism as success, 201–6, 207–8
Spooks controversy, 205–6, 240
support to ISKCON's campaign, 205
Swaminathan on, 284
VHS. *See* Virat Hindu Sammelan (VHS)
Virat Hindu Sammelan (VHS), 177–90
attendees' experiences, 185–6
brochure, 182–3
ecumenical raison d'être of the VHP, 180
ideological elements to, 184
'inspiration and guidance', 180–1
messages of support, 182–4
as 'mini-Kumbha Mela', 178
participation of women, 187–8
precursor of, 179–80
and *Ram Janmabhoomi* movement, 179, 184, 185
Ram *shila* ceremony, 178
representatives, 182
sermons and hosting, 186–7
souvenir publication, 178, 182, 184
Swaminarayan involvement in, 181–2

Vishwa Adhyayan Kendra (VAK), 29–30, 106
Vishwa Sangh Shibir (VSS), 80, 97–101, 248
'calm and green environment' of, 120
equalising aspect, 115
focus on youth, 100–1
heterotopian dimension, 117–23
interactions with senior leaders, 102–4
intra-diaspora inspiration, 101–2
locations and participants, 98–9, 99*t*
multi-directional and polycentric influence, 104–7
pilgrimage aspects, 110–14
registration process, 118–19
Vishwa Vibhag of RSS (Global Division), 30–1
before the first *shakha*, 31
Bhagwat's Britain tour (2016), 46, 48
in Delhi, 76
headquarters transfer to Leicester, 45
networks of connectivity, 31–2
Rajendra Singh's overseas tour, 34, 45–6, 46–7*t*, 88
See also Hindu Swayamsevak Sangh (HSS); Sangh Parivar; *shakhas*; *shakhas* (in Britain)
vistaraks (temporary workers)
deployment to NHSF, 240
role of, 54–6

INDEX

Vivekananda, Swami, 166, 199–200, 237
VSS. *See* Vishwa Sangh Shibir (VSS)
Vyasmaan, Rohit, 299

'War on Terror', 69, 90, 251–2
Warsi, Sayeeda, 221
Washington DC, 30, 131, 132, 200, 237

Wendy Doniger. *See* Doniger, campaign against
Westernisation, 71–2
Widening Horizons, 74, 228
World War, Second, 9, 41

'Yankee Hindutva', 17, 73
YouTube, 63, 90, 109

Zionist-Hindutva dynamic, 297–301